Lecture Notes in Computer Science 14167

Founding Editors

Gerhard Goos
Juris Hartmanis

Editorial Board Members

The series Lecture Notes in Computer Science (LNCS), including its subseries Lecture Notes in Artificial Intelligence (LNAI) and Lecture Notes in Bioinformatics (LNBI), has established itself as a medium for the publication of new developments in computer science and information technology research, teaching, and education.

LNCS enjoys close cooperation with the computer science R & D community, the series counts many renowned academics among its volume editors and paper authors, and collaborates with prestigious societies. Its mission is to serve this international community by providing an invaluable service, mainly focused on the publication of conference and workshop proceedings and postproceedings. LNCS commenced publication in 1973.

Jie Fu · Tomas Kroupa ·
Yezekael Hayel
Editors

Decision and Game Theory for Security

14th International Conference, GameSec 2023
Avignon, France, October 18–20, 2023
Proceedings

 Springer

Editors
Jie Fu 🔟
University of Florida
Gainesville, FL, USA

Tomas Kroupa 🔟
Czech Technical University in Prague
Prague, Czech Republic

Yezekael Hayel 🔟
University of Avignon
Avignon, France

ISSN 0302-9743   ISSN 1611-3349 (electronic)
Lecture Notes in Computer Science
ISBN 978-3-031-50669-7   ISBN 978-3-031-50670-3 (eBook)
https://doi.org/10.1007/978-3-031-50670-3

This Springer imprint is published by the registered company Springer Nature Switzerland AG
The registered company address is: Gewerbestrasse 11, 6330 Cham, Switzerland

Paper in this product is recyclable.

Preface

With the rapid development of information, automation, and communication technology, the security of these emerging systems is more important now than ever. This special issue addresses the pressing need for secure cyber-physical systems in the face of technological advancements. In particular, it focuses on developing theories and methods for protecting heterogeneous, large-scale, and dynamic cyber-physical systems and managing security risks that critical infrastructures face. The guest editors invited novel, high-quality theoretical and empirical contributions which leverage decision theory and game theory to address security problems and related problems such as privacy, trust, or bias in emerging systems. The goal of this special issue is to enhance research efforts in order to identify major challenges and recent results that explore the interdisciplinary connections between game theory, control, distributed optimization, adversarial reasoning, machine learning, mechanism design, behavioral analysis, risk assessments, and security, reputation, trust and privacy problems.

GameSec 2023, the 14th Conference on Decision and Game Theory for Security, tried to encourage and attract contributions to game theory for security. GameSec 2023 received 33 submissions. The reviewing process was single-blind. Each paper received 3 reviews. Each PC member reviewed 1 to 4 papers, with an average review load of 3 papers. After extensive discussions among the Technical Program Committee (TPC) chairs and the general chair, 19 papers were accepted as full articles. 10 papers with borderline scores were proposed to participate in a rebuttal phase. Among them, 4 articles were accepted as short papers (2 pages long) and to present a poster at the conference. GameSec 2023 featured 3 papers on "Mechanism design and imperfect information", 3 papers on "Security games", 3 papers on "Learning in security games", 3 papers on "Cyber deception", 3 papers on "Economics of security" and 4 papers on "Information and privacy". This volume contains all the 19 full papers accepted to GameSec 2023, and the 4 short papers accepted as posters. We hope that readers will find this volume a useful resource for their security and game theory research.

GameSec 2023 was held in Avignon, France, during October 18–20, 2023. The conference was held in person, but due to the long-tailed impact of COVID-19, some attendees participated remotely. We are particularly grateful to Avignon University for its support of the conference.

The GameSec conference series was inaugurated in 2010 in Berlin,Germany. Over 14 editions, GameSec has become an important venue for interdisciplinary security research.

The previous conferences were held in College Park (USA, 2011), Budapest (Hungary, 2012), Fort Worth (USA, 2013), Los Angeles (USA, 2014), London (UK, 2015), New York (USA, 2016), Vienna (Austria, 2017), Seattle (USA, 2018),

Stockholm (Sweden 2019), College Park (USA/virtual conference, 2020), Prague (Czech Republic/virtual conference, 2021) and Pittsburgh (USA, 2022).

October 2023

Yezekael Hayel
Jie Fu
Tomas Kroupa

Organization

General Chair

Yezekael Hayel   Avignon University, France

Technical Program Committee Chairs

Jie Fu   University of Florida, USA
Tomas Kroupa   Czech Technical University, Czech Republic

Publicity Co-chairs

Francesco De Pellegrini   Avignon University, France
Charles Kamhoua   US Army Research Laboratory, USA
Luyao Zhang   Duke Kunshan University, China

Web Chair

Tania Jimenez   Avignon University, France

Steering Board

Tansu Alpcan   University of Melbourne, Australia
John S. Baras   University of Maryland, USA
Tamer Basar   University of Illinois at Urbana-Champaign, USA
Anthony Ephremides   University of Maryland, USA
Radha Poovendran   University of Washington, USA
Milind Tambe   Harvard University, USA

Advisory Committee

Fei Fang   Carnegie Mellon University, USA
Tiffany Bao   Arizona State University, USA
Branislav Bosansky   Czech Technical University, Czech Republic
Stefan Rass   Johannes Kepler University Linz, Austria
Manos Panaousis   University of Greenwich, UK
Quanyan Zhu   New York University, USA

Program Committee

Jens Grossklags   Technical University of Munich, Germany
Henger Li   Tulane University, USA

Christian Lebiere	Carnegie Mellon University, USA
Ahmed H. Anwar Hemida	Army Research Lab, USA
Konstantin Avrachenkov	Inria, France
Edward Cranford	Carnegie Mellon University, USA
Ashish Ranjan Hota	Indian Institute of Technology Kharagpur, India
Francesco De Pellegrini	Avignon University, France
Alexandre Reiffers	IMT, France
Andrew Clark	WPI, USA
Palvi Aggarwal	Carnegie Mellon University, USA
Bo An	Nanyang Technological University, Singapore
Svetlana Boudko	Norwegian Computing Center, Norway
Carlos Barreto	KTH, Sweden
Andrey Garnaev	Rutgers University, USA
Quanyan Zhu	New York University, USA
Spiros Mancoridis	Drexel University, USA
Jun Zhuang	SUNY Buffalo, USA
Yevgeniy Vorobeychik	Washington University in St. Louis, USA
Robert Gutzwiller	Arizona State University, USA
Christopher Kiekintveld	University of Texas at El Paso, USA
Yee Wei Law	University of South Australia, Australia
Katerina Mitrokotsa	Chalmers University of Technology, USA
Murat Kantarcioglu	University of Texas at Dallas, USA
Shana Moothedath	Iowa State University, USA
Abdellatif Kobbane	ENSIAS, Mohammed V University, Morocco
Jayneel Vora	University of California Davis, USA
Palash Sarkar	Indian Statistical Institute, India
Siddhant Bhambri	Arizona State University, USA
Stefan Rass	Johannes Kepler University Linz, Austria
Sanjay Bhattacherjee	University of Kent, UK
Shaunak Bopardikar	Michigan State University, USA
Habtamu Abie	Norwegian Computing Centre, Norway
Parinaz Naghizadeh	Ohio State University, USA
Zizhan Zheng	Tulane University, USA
Tomáš Votroubek	Czech Technical University, Czech Republic
Karel Horák	Czech Technical University, Czech Republic
Abderrahim Benslimane	Avignon University, France
Andrew Cullen	University of Melbourne, Australia

Sponsors

Avignon University
Springer

Short Papers

Incentive-Based Software Security: Fair Micro-Payments for Writing Secure Code (Extended Abstract)[1]

Stefan Rass[1,2] and Martin Pinzger[3]

[1] Johannes Kepler University, LIT Secure and Correct Systems Lab,
Altenbergerstraße 69, 4040, Linz, Austria
stefan.rass@jku.at

[2] Institute for Artificial Intelligence and Cybersecurity, Alpen-Adria-University
Klagenfurt, Universitätsstrasse 65-67, 9020, Klagenfurt, Austria

[3] Department of Informatics Systems, Alpen-Adria-University Klagenfurt,
Klagenfurt, Austria

Abstract. We describe a mechanism to create fair and explainable incentives for software developers to reward contributions to security of a product. We use cooperative game theory to model the actions of the developer team inside a risk management workflow, considering the team to actively work against known threats, and thereby receive micro-payments based on their performance, and calculated using the Shapley-value. We corroborate our model with a worked example based on real-life data.

Keywords: Incentive based security · Shapley-value · Cooperative game · Software Security

1 Introduction

Security has the unfortunate fate of not generating revenue by itself, but rather preventing damage at additional cost. As such, it does not necessarily "add"to the functionality of a system, but only protects it from malfunctions. Consequently, people may take considerably less satisfaction from implementing a security mechanism, since the system is working before and after, with no visible improvement other than increased robustness and security. Prior game theoretic models have discovered reasons as to why investments into more security are not necessarily made [1].

In some cases, such investments are, however, obligatory due to independent auditing, legal or (security) standard compliance. If dedicated budgets are available, why not use parts of them for an incentive mechanism for developers of software products to not only aim at correct functionality, but also for security? We propose one such mechanism here: let a standard risk management process (e.g., ISO27000) have

---

[1] This work was supported by the Karl Popper Kolleg "Responsible Safe and Secure Robotic Systems Engineering (SEEROSE)" at Universität Klagenfurt

delivered a set of threats, with corresponding countermeasures, culminating in security design goals for a software product. We quantify security via its implied reduction of the risk level, based on the expected loss $B = \text{impact} \times \text{likelihood}$, where developer's actions can reduce both, the impact and/or the likelihood. Parts of the, due to the developer's work, *no-longer expected* losses B can then be paid back to the team as incentive for security. The Shapley-value can provide a fair mechanism to this end, leveraging features of software repositories like `git`, such as *cherry picking* or *audited pull requests*.

2   Method: Team Rewards from Risk Reductions

Specifically, let the threat list be $T_1, \ldots, T_n$, with T_i associated with $k_i \geq 1$ countermeasures $C_{i,1}, \ldots, C_{i,k_i}$, where each $C_{i,j}$ is verifiable by a number $m_{i,j}$ of unit tests $U_{i,j,1}, \ldots, U_{i,j,m_{i,j}}$. After the team S has made a commit to the repository, we can evaluate the newly implemented countermeasures (e.g., along an audited pull request): If $n(S)$ unit tests pass among the (constant) total of m tests to cover all threats and countermeasures, then the accomplishment of the team S is definable as $0 \leq v(S) := n(S)/m \leq 1$. Therein, the contribution without the i-th person is $v(S \setminus \{i\})$, from which we can compute the *Shapley-value* to quantify the security contribution of the i-th team member.

The resulting mechanism inherits desirable properties from the Shapley-value: (i) a developer not having added to the product's security receives no reward (null-player), (ii) the entire added value of security is paid back to the team (efficiency), (iii) equal contributions imply equal rewards (symmetry), and (iv) contributions with multiple benefits imply a cumulative reward (linearity).

3   A Worked Example

The full version of this work [2] contains a detailed example, based on a real-life software product with known (but already fixed) vulnerabilities. Our example considers (for simplicity) only one threat "loss of customer data", possibly manifesting via three known vulnerabilities with concrete Common Vulnerability Enumeration (CVE) numbers. These directly imply countermeasures, and test-cases based on the CVE description. We then (hypothetically) assume three developers to have addressed the issues collaboratively. The incentive payments are then taken proportional (based on the Shapley-value) the *loss B that has been avoided* thanks to the developer's work. A full numeric example based on publicly available risk data is given in [2], together with conclusions.

References

1. Daughety, A.F., Reinganum, J.F.: Product safety: Liability, R&D, and signaling. Am. Econ. Rev. **85**(5), 1187–1206 (1995). https://ideas.repec.org/a/aea/aecrev/v85y1995i5p1187-1206.html
2. Rass, S., Pinzger, M.: Incentive-based software security: fair micro-payments for writing secure code. https://arxiv.org/abs/2309.05338 (2023)

Using Game Theory Approach for COVID-19 Risk Analysis and Medical Resource Allocation

Cheng Kuang Wu(iD)

School of Computer Science, Guangdong University of Science and Technology,
Guangdong,523083, China
shapleyvalue@hotmail.com

The outbreak of COVID-19 has not only increased global mortality rates but has also had a tremendous socio-economic impact, that is not limited to countries directly affected by the disease. The outbreak has reduced the consumption of goods and services, led to a collapse on the tourism industry in many areas, increased enterprise operating costs, and accelerated the flight of foreign capital, generating huge economic costs worldwide [3]. Experts from the World Health Organization discovered that China's large-scale urban and regional blockades and electronic surveillance measures imposed by compulsory public power had been used to monitor hundreds of thousands of Chinese people without the COVID-19 infection. This method of joint defense has a high degree of coverage and effectiveness and provides unique insights into China's efforts to prevent the virus from spreading to other areas of the country and even globally [2]. However, the current government agency lacks specific measures for rational decision-making and does not apply mathematical models to capture the interactions between the attackers (coronaviruses) and the defender (response commander). The administrator of the organization should have a tool to measure the strength of the COVID-19 and the resistance capability of the responding medical resources.

The proposed model is applied to evaluate the risk value for affected districts (or states) and for the deployment of medical resources for emergency response to the COVID-19 disease outbreak. A simplified workflow chart summarizing the principles of fair medical resource allocation is shown in Fig. 1. Two game-theoretic models are constructed, representing the two stages needed for the economical deployment of the available resources. In the first step, the interactions of four factors (i.e., infection rate, treatment rate, recovery rate, and death rate) for a group of coronaviruses and the response commander for the district are modeled as a zero-sum and non-cooperative game. Then a mixed strategy Nash equilibrium method is used to derive the risk value (RV) for each district based on the COVID-19 disease outbreak data for the USA, April 12, 2020 [1]. In the second step, the interactions of all response commanders of the affected districts within the whole administrative region are likened to the playing of a cooperative game. All risk values for the affected districts are utilized to compute a Shapley-Shubik power index for each district. The number of responses and deployment of medical resources in the affected districts is computed from the Shapley-Shubik power indexes for all districts. Finally, the emergency operations center (EOC) launches a coordinated emergency response for the deployment of existing medical

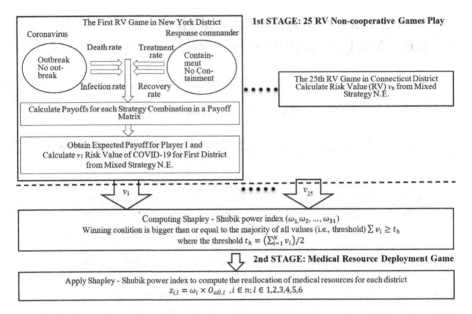

Fig. 1. A workflow for 25 afflicted districts to deploy medical resources

resources in all affected districts in an attempt to increase the survival ratio of COVID-19 patients.

The experiment only considers affected districts (states) with 3000 or more confirmed cases [1], as of 12 April 2020. Given the limited number of resources, the administrator can choose to reallocate resources from lower RV response districts (e.g., South Carolina, Wisconsin, Arizona, Alabama, North Carolina, Virginia, Tennessee, and Ohio) to support the ten higher RV response districts, namely New York, New Jersey, Massachusetts, Michigan, Illinois, Louisiana, Washington, Connecticut, Indiana, and Colorado. Resources from the lower RV districts are redistributed to the nearest high RV districts (or states). The proposed Shapley-Shubik index (SSI) division is better than a proportional (RV) division because it allows a player (i.e., a response commander of the affected district) to be part of more than one coalition (i.e., multiple players) in a cooperative game (i.e., the medical resource deployment game).

References

1. Dong, E., Du, H., Gardner, L.: An interactive web-based dashboard to track COVID-19 in real time. Lancet. Inf. Dis. **20** (5), 533–534 (2020). https://doi.org/10.1016/S1473-3099(20)30120-1
2. Kai, K., Jon, C.: China's aggressive measures have slowed the coronavirus. they may not work in other countries. Sci. **2** (03). Accessed 2 Mar 2020. https://www.sciencemag.org/news/2020/03/china-s-aggressive-measures-have-slowed-coronavirus-

they-may-not-work-other-countries?fbclid=IwAR3mzUvArfzqNsqPmMlynuGF5Mh 32xN3RIi-ctAB_qrWJC2t6STVZqzKLzc.
3. WebMD. What Are Epidemics, Pandemics, and Outbreaks. Accessed 24 Feb 2021. https://www.webmd.com/cold-and-flu/what-are-epidemics-pandemics-outbreaks

Shapley Value to Rank Vulnerabilities on Attack Graphs: Applications to Cyberdeception[1]

Martin Waffo Kemgne[1] (ID), Olivier Tsemogne[2] (ID)
and Charles Kamhoua[3] (ID)

[1] AIMS Rwanda, Kigali, Rwanda
martin.kemgne@aims.ac.rw
[2] IMT Atlantique, Brest, France
olivier.tsemogne@gmail.com
[3] DEVCOM Army Research Laboratory, Adelphi, USA
charles.a.kamhoua.civ@army.mil

Abstract. Attack graphs are pivotal in cybersecurity, providing insights into potential attack paths. Effective cybersecurity and cyberdeception necessitate the prioritization of vulnerabilities for resource allocation and proactive defense. However, current methods fall short in capturing vulnerability interactions and addressing multi-target scenarios. In response, we introduce a cooperative game framework utilizing the Shapley value for vulnerability ranking, enhancing fairness and realism. Simulations demonstrate the Shapley value's superiority in honeypot allocation and vulnerability prioritization. Our study contributes a novel centrality measure with practical applications in network security and cyberdeception.

Keywords: Attack graphs · Shapley value · Honeypots · Cyberdeception · Network security · Vulnerability

1 Introduction

Cybersecurity faces escalating threats [1, 10]. Traditional defense measures struggle with evolving threats, emphasizing the need for vulnerability understanding and prioritization. Attack graphs, revealing potential attack paths [5, 8], are valuable for this purpose. However, current methods have limitations, often neglecting vulnerability interactions and multi-target scenarios.

We propose using the Shapley value, a comprehensive approach, to rank vulnerabilities. Unlike traditional centrality measures, it considers vulnerability interactions and diverse target costs, enhancing fair resource allocation and risk mitigation in cybersecurity.

---

[1] Distribution Statement A: Approved for public release. Distribution is unlimited.

Our research demonstrates the Shapley value's effectiveness through simulations, particularly in honeypot deployment and vulnerability prioritization. In summary, we introduce a novel centrality measure based on cooperative game theory, showcasing its practical applications in network security and cyberdeception.

2   System Model

Our network attack graph comprises nodes representing various devices (e.g., phones, computers, IP cameras). Entry points for attackers are denoted as S_0, while S_s represents the attacker's target nodes. Vulnerabilities are depicted as edges in the graph. Specifically, an edge from node A to B signifies that nodes A and B are in communication range, and node A has a vulnerability that node B exposes, creating a potential pathway for the attacker. To prioritize network defense, we assign costs to target nodes, indicating their importance. Higher values denote more critical assets, often housing valuable information attractive to attackers. Additionally, each vulnerability associated with a node carries a weight reflecting its significance, contributing to different attack scenarios or overall network security. This model assumes that attackers possess knowledge about target node values, enabling them to strategize their actions.

3   Game Model

Let $G = \{S, \tau, S_0, S_s\}$ represent our network attack graph. Each node in the graph represents a tool, and each edge represents a vulnerability for moving between tools.

We have e entry points ($S_s = \{E_1, E_2, ..., E_e\}$) and t targets ($S_s = \{T_1, T_2, ..., T_t\}$). The attacker starts at an entry point $E \in \mathscr{E} = \{E_1, E_2, ..., E_e\}$ and aims to reach a target $T \in \mathscr{T} = \{T_1, T_2, ..., T_t\}$. The various scenarios for this movement are represented by paths from E to T. In our game, we define $\mathscr{C}_{T_i}$ as the set of paths from E to T_i, identified by their edges. With n vulnerabilities, we use $N = \{1, 2, ..., n\}$ to represent them. Each target T_i is associated with a cost m_i. The function v representing the game is defined as follows:

$$v(S) = \begin{cases} m_i & \text{if } \exists\, T \in \mathscr{C}_{T_{i_j}} \text{ such that } T \subseteq S, i = 1, 2, ..., n \\ \max(m_{i_1}, m_{i_2}, ..., m_{i_r}) & \text{if } \exists\, T \in \cap_{j=1}^{r} \mathscr{C}_{T_{i_j}} \text{ such that } T \subseteq S \\ 0 & \text{otherwise} \end{cases}$$

4   Simulations

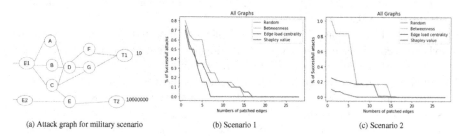

(a) Attack graph for military scenario   (b) Scenario 1   (c) Scenario 2

Fig. 1. Attack graph and Comparative plot for military scenario

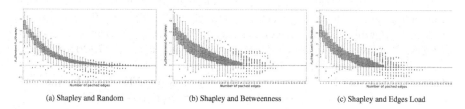

(a) Shapley and Random   (b) Shapley and Betweenness   (c) Shapley and Edges Load

Fig. 2. Graph of comparison different probability and cost

5   Conclusion

Our study introduces the Shapley value, a cooperative game theory concept, for ranking vulnerabilities within attack graphs. We establish a cooperative game framework over attack graphs, calculate the Shapley value for ranking, and validate our approach through extensive simulations. Comparative analyses confirm the Shapley value's superiority over other centrality measures, optimizing honeypot allocation. The Shapley value excels by considering vulnerability interactions and fairly distributing importance. Simulations demonstrate its cost-effective honeypot deployment while factoring each vulnerability's contribution to overall attack risk and target-specific costs. Our findings highlight the Shapley value's potential in enhancing network security and cyberdeception, particularly in optimizing honeypot allocation. Future research avenues include integrating the Shapley value with other methods and applying it to complex attack graph scenarios with repeated vulnerabilities.

References

1. Almeshekah, M.H., Spafford, E.H.: Cyber security deception. Cyber Deception: Building the Scientific Foundation pp. 23–50, Springer Cham (2016). https://doi.org/10.1007/978-3-319-32699-3

2. Anwar, A.H., Kamhoua, C.: Game theory on attack graph for cyber deception. In: Zhu, Q., Baras, J.S., Poovendran, R., Chen, J. (eds) Decision and Game Theory for Security. GameSec 2020. LNCS, vol 12513. Springer, Cham (2020). https://doi.org/10.1007/978-3-030-64793-3_24

3. Anwar, A.H., Kamhoua, C., Leslie, N.: Honeypot allocation over attack graphs in cyber deception games. In: 2020 International Conference on Computing, Networking and Communications (ICNC), pp. 502–506. IEEE (2020)

4. Cadini, F., Zio, E., Petrescu, C.A.: Using centrality measures to rank the importance of the components of a complex network infrastructure. In: Setola, R., Geretshuber, S. (eds) Critical Information Infrastructure Security. CRITIS 2008. LNCS, vol 5508. Springer, Berlin, Heidelberg (2009). https://doi.org/10.1007/978-3-642-03552-4_14

5. Dantu, R., Loper, K., Kolan, P.: Risk management using behavior based attack graphs. In: International Conference on Information Technology: Coding and Computing, 2004. Proceedings. ITCC 2004. vol. 1, pp. 445–449. IEEE (2004)

6. Faigle, U., Grabisch, M., Jiménez-Losada, A., Ordóñez, M.: Games on concept lattices: Shapley value and core. Discret. Appl. Math. 198, 29–47 (2016). https://doi.org/10.1016/j.dam.2015.08.004

7. Gallon, L., Bascou, J.J.: Using cvss in attack graphs. In: 2011 Sixth International Conference on Availability, Reliability and Security. pp. 59–66. IEEE (2011)

8. Hong, J.B., Kim, D.S., Haqiq, A.: What vulnerability do we need to patch first? In: 2014 44th Annual IEEE/IFIP International Conference on Dependable Systems and Networks. pp. 684–689. IEEE (2014)

9. Ignatov, D.I., Kwuida, L.: Interpretable concept-based xlassification with shapley values. In: Alam, M., Braun, T., Yun, B. (eds) Ontologies and Concepts in Mind and Machine. ICCS 2020. LNCS, vol 12277. Springer, Cham (2020). https://doi.org/10.1007/978-3-030-57855-8_7

10. Rolando, M., Rossi, M., Sanarico, N., Mandrioli, D.: A formal approach to sensor placement and configuration in a network intrusion detection system. In: Proceedings of the 2006 International Workshop on Software Engineering for Secure Systems. pp. 65–71 (2006)

11. Shapley, L.S.: A value for n-person games. In: Contributions to the Theory of Games, Vol. 2. Princeton University Press, NJ, USA (1953)

Solving Security Models with Perfect Observability

Paolo Zappala[1,2], Amal Benhamiche[1], Matthieu Chardy[1],
Francesco De Pellegrini[2] and Rosa Figueiredo[2]

[1] Orange Innovation, Orange, 44 Avenue de la République, Châtillon, 92320,
France
{name.surname}@orange.com

[2] LIA, Avignon Université, 301 Rue Baruch de Spinoza, Avignon, 84140, France
{name.surname}@univ-avignon.fr

Extended Abstract

Sequential models with perfect observability represent situations in which communication is public and observable by all the agents. Such models are applied within different domains of security, such as intrusion detection [1], blockchain protocols [4] and wiretap channels [2]. The extensive-form game with perfect information is the representation used to identify the solution of these models. To date, the literature provides methods to identify specific solutions for small-size extensive-form games. We provide the first method to identify all solutions that is also scalable with the size of the games.

We consider a game in extensive form with perfect information.

Definition 1 (extensive-form game). *An extensive-form game is a tuple* $\Gamma = \langle \mathcal{I}, \mathcal{A}, H', H, P, u \rangle$, *where:*

- $\mathcal{I} = \{1, \dots, N\}$ *is the set of players;*
- H' *is the set of histories with* $\emptyset \in H'$;
- $\mathcal{A} : h' \in H' \to A$ *is a function that provides for every history a set of actions A, i.e., for all* $a \in A$, *we have* $h' + (a) \in H'$;
- $H = \{h \in H' | \mathcal{A}(h) = \emptyset\} \subset H'$ *is the set of outcomes;*
- $P : H' \setminus H \to \mathcal{I}$ *is a function that indicates which player* $P(h') \in \mathcal{I}$ *acts after observing the history* $h' \in H' \setminus H$;
- $u = (u_i)_{i \in \mathcal{I}}$, *with* $u_i : H \to \mathbb{R}$ *the utility function of player* $i \in \mathcal{I}$.

Every player picks a strategy, i.e., she chooses an action for every history observed. Formally, a *strategy* s_i of a player $i \in \mathcal{I}$ is a function $s_i \in S_i = \{s_i : h \in H_i \mapsto a \in \mathcal{A}(h)\}$ that gives for every history $h \in H_i = \{h \in H : P(h) = i\}$ an available action $a \in \mathcal{A}(h)$. A strategy profile $\bar{s} \in S := \times_i S_i$ is a *Nash equilibrium* if no player can increase her utility by changing unilaterally her strategy, i.e, if for every $i \in \mathcal{I}$ and for all $s_i \in S_i$ it holds $u_i(\bar{s}_i, \bar{s}_{-i}) \geq u_i(s_i, \bar{s}_{-i})$. A specific equilibrium can be computed efficiently with the backward induction algorithm (cf., e.g., [3]). The absence of methods to compute all the other Nash equilibria limits the insights for security models [3, 4]. Hereafter, we provide a method to enumerate all the Nash equilibria of an extensive-form game.

We define $I : H \times H \to \mathcal{I}$, where $I(h, h') = P(h \cap h')$, the function that maps the pair of outcomes $h, h' \in H$ with $h \neq h'$ to the player $I(h, h')$ that separates their paths from the root of the game tree. This relation between outcomes and strategies allows us to define a graph-based method to identify all the outcomes of Nash equilibria. We consider the following problem from graph theory.

Problem (MC). *Existence of a maximal clique excluding a set of vertices*
Input. $\langle H, E, X \rangle$ *defining a graph* $\langle H, E \rangle$ *and a subset of vertices* $X \subset H$.
Output. Is *there a vertex set* $C \subset H \setminus X$ *that induces a maximal clique?*

We introduce the following algorithm to determine whether a target outcome is a Nash equilibrium. The iteration of the algorithm over all outcomes permits the enumeration of the equilibria.

ALGORITHM: NASH

Input: A game Γ, the set of its outcomes H, the function $I : H \times H \to \mathcal{I}$ and an outcome $h \in H$.
Output: Is h a realisation of a Nash equilibrium?
$boolean = True$;
for $i \in \mathcal{I}$ **do**
  $H_i \leftarrow \{h' \in H \setminus \{h\} | I(h, h') = i\}$;
  $X_i \leftarrow \{h' \in H_i | u_i(h) < u_i(h')\}$;
  $E|_{H_i} = \{(h, h') \in H_i | I(h, h') = i\}$;
  if *Output of Problem (MC) with input* $\langle H_i, X_i, E|_{H_i} \rangle$ *is negative* **then**
    $boolean = False$;
  end
end

The algorithm has an efficient representation, i.e., it does not require to enumerate the strategies of the game. Furthermore, it relies on a graph theoretical problem whose instances are often easy to compute, as verified for the vast majority of outcomes we have tested. Finally, this algorithm is parallelizable, a condition that is key in order to scale the solution method for larger games.

References

1. Kantzavelou, I., Katsikas, S.: A generic intrusion detection game godel in IT security. In: Furnell, S., Katsikas, S.K., Lioy, A. (eds) Trust, Privacy and Security in Digital Business. TrustBus 2008. LNCS, vol 5185. Springer, Berlin, Heidelberg (2008). https://doi.org/10.1007/978-3-540-85735-8_15
2. Mukherjee, A., Swindlehurst, A. L.: Jamming games in the mimo wiretap channel with an active eavesdropper. IEEE Trans. Signal Process **61** (1), 82–91 (2012)

3. Raya, M., Manshaei, M.H., Félegyházi, M., Hubaux, J.P.: Revocation games in ephemeral networks. In: Proceedings of the 15th ACM conference on Computer and communications security. pp. 199–210 (2008)
4. Zappalà, P., Belotti, M., Potop-Butucaru, M., Secci, S.: Game theoretical framework for analyzing blockchains robustness. In: 35th International Symposium on Distributed Computing. p. 25 (2021)

Contents

Cyber Deception

Economics of Security

Information and Privacy

Mechanism Design and Imperfect Information

Observable Perfect Equilibrium

Sam Ganzfried[(✉)]

Ganzfried Research, Miami Beach, USA
sam.ganzfried@gmail.com
https://www.ganzfriedresearch.com/

Abstract. While Nash equilibrium has emerged as the central game-theoretic solution concept, many important games contain several Nash equilibria and we must determine how to select between them in order to create real strategic agents. Several Nash equilibrium refinement concepts have been proposed and studied for sequential imperfect-information games, the most prominent being trembling-hand perfect equilibrium, quasi-perfect equilibrium, and recently one-sided quasi-perfect equilibrium. These concepts are robust to certain arbitrarily small mistakes, and are guaranteed to always exist; however, we argue that neither of these is the correct concept for developing strong agents in sequential games of imperfect information. We define a new equilibrium refinement concept for extensive-form games called observable perfect equilibrium in which the solution is robust over trembles in publicly-observable action probabilities (not necessarily over all action probabilities that may not be observable by opposing players). Observable perfect equilibrium correctly captures the assumption that the opponent is playing as rationally as possible given mistakes that have been observed (while previous solution concepts do not). We prove that observable perfect equilibrium is always guaranteed to exist, and demonstrate that it leads to a different solution than the prior extensive-form refinements in no-limit poker. We expect observable perfect equilibrium to be a useful equilibrium refinement concept for modeling many important imperfect-information games of interest in artificial intelligence.

Keywords: Nash equilibrium refinement · imperfect information

1 Introduction

When developing a strategy for a human or computer agent to play in a game, the starting point is typically a Nash equilibrium. Even if additional information is available about the opponents, e.g., from historical data or observations of play, we would often still opt to start playing a Nash equilibrium strategy until we are confident in our ability to successfully exploit opponents by deviating [13,16]. It is well known that several conceptual and computational limitations exist for Nash equilibrium. For multiplayer and two-player non-zero-sum games, it is PPAD-hard to compute or approximate one Nash equilibrium [6,7,10,27],

J. Fu et al. (Eds.): GameSec 2023, LNCS 14167, pp. 3–22, 2023.
https://doi.org/10.1007/978-3-031-50670-3_1

different Nash equilibria may give different values to the players, and following a Nash equilibrium strategy provides no performance guarantee. Even for two-player zero-sum games, in which these issues do not arise, there can still exist multiple Nash equilibria that we must select from. Therefore several solution concepts that refine Nash equilibrium in various ways have been proposed to help select one that is more preferable in some way. Most of the common equilibrium refinements are based on the idea of ensuring robustness against certain arbitrarily small "trembles" in players' execution of a given strategy. Variants of these Nash equilibrium refinements have been devised for simultaneous strategic-form games as well as sequential games of perfect and imperfect information. In this paper we will be primarily interested in sequential games of imperfect information, which are more complex than the other games classes and have received significant interest recently in artificial intelligence due to their ability to model many important scenarios. To simplify analysis we will primarily be studying a subclass of these games in which there are two players, only one player has private information, and both players take a single action; however, our results apply broadly to extensive-form imperfect-information games. We will also be primarily focused on two-player zero-sum games, though some analysis also applies to two-player non-zero-sum and multiplayer games. We will show that existing Nash equilibrium refinement concepts have limitations in sequential imperfect-information games, and propose the new concept of observable perfect equilibrium that addresses these limitations.

A *strategic-form game* (aka *normal-form game*) consists of a finite set of players $N = \{1, \ldots, n\}$, a finite set of pure strategies S_i for each player $i \in N$, and a real-valued utility for each player for each strategy vector (aka *strategy profile*), $u_i : \times_i S_i \to \mathbb{R}$. A *mixed strategy* σ_i for player i is a probability distribution over pure strategies, where $\sigma_i(s_{i'})$ is the probability that player i plays pure strategy $s_{i'} \in S_i$ under σ_i. Let Σ_i denote the full set of mixed strategies for player i. A strategy profile $\sigma^* = (\sigma_1^*, \ldots, \sigma_n^*)$ is a *Nash equilibrium* if $u_i(\sigma_i^*, \sigma_{-i}^*) \geq u_i(\sigma_i, \sigma_{-i}^*)$ for all $\sigma_i \in \Sigma_i$ for all $i \in N$, where $\sigma_{-i}^* \in \Sigma_{-i}$ denotes the vector of the components of strategy σ^* for all players excluding player i. Here u_i denotes the expected utility for player i, and Σ_{-i} denotes the set of strategy profiles for all players excluding player i.

Nash equilibrium has emerged as the central solution concept in game theory, and is guaranteed to exist in all finite strategic-form games [25, 26]. However, games may contain multiple Nash equilibria and it is not clear which one should be played. A popular refinement of Nash equilibrium is *trembling hand perfect equilibrium* [28]. Given a strategic-form game G, define G' to be a *perturbed game* which is identical to G except only totally mixed strategies (i.e., strategies that play all pure strategies with non-zero probability) can be played. A strategy profile σ^* in G is a trembling-hand perfect equilibrium (THPE) if there is a sequence of perturbed games that converges to G in which there is a sequence of Nash equilibria of the perturbed games that converges to σ^*. It has been shown that every finite strategic-form game has at least one THPE [28]. The following result provides an alternative equivalent characterization of THPE [9]:

Theorem 1. *Let σ^* be a strategy profile of an n-player strategic-form game G. Then σ^* is a trembling-hand perfect equilibrium if and only if σ^* is a limit point of a sequence $\{\sigma(\epsilon)\}_{\epsilon \to 0}$ of totally mixed strategy profiles with the property that σ^* is a best response for all players against every element $\sigma(\epsilon)$ in this sequence.*

While the strategic form can be used to model simultaneous actions, settings with sequential moves are typically modelled using the *extensive form* representation. The extensive form can also model simultaneous actions, as well as chance events and imperfect information (i.e., situations where some information is available to only some of the agents and not to others). Extensive-form games consist primarily of a game tree; each non-terminal node has an associated player (possibly *chance*) that makes the decision at that node, and each terminal node has associated utilities for the players. Additionally, game states are partitioned into *information sets*, where the player whose turn it is to move cannot distinguish among the states in the same information set. Therefore, in any given information set, a player must choose actions with the same distribution at each state contained in the information set. If no player forgets information that he previously knew, we say that the game has *perfect recall*. A (behavioral) *strategy* for player i, $\sigma_i \in \Sigma_i$, is a function that assigns a probability distribution over all actions at each information set belonging to i. Similarly to strategic-form games, it can be shown that all extensive-form games with perfect recall contain at least one Nash equilibrium in mixed strategies. The concept of *extensive-form trembling hand perfect equilibrium* (EFTHPE) is defined analogously to THPE by requiring that every action at every information set for each player is taken with non-zero probability in perturbed games. EFTHPE are then limits of equilibria of such perturbed games as the tremble probabilities go to zero. It has been proven that an EFTHPE exists in every extensive-form game [9].

2   Observable Perfect Equilibrium

In order to simplify our analysis we define a subset of extensive-form information games called *two-player one-step extensive-form imperfect-information games* (OSEFGs):

- There are two players, P1 and P2.
- Player 1 is dealt private information τ_1 from a finite set T_1 uniformly at random.[1]
- Player 1 can then choose action a_1 from finite set A_1.
- Player 2 observes the action a_1 but not τ_1.
- Player 2 then chooses action a_2 from finite set A_2.
- Both players are then given payoff $u_i(\tau_1, a_1, a_2)$.

For mixed strategy σ_1 for player 1, $\sigma_1(\tau_1, a_1)$ denotes the probability that player 1 takes action $a_1 \in A_1$ with private information $\tau_1 \in T_1$. Similarly for

---

[1] Note that all of our analysis will still hold if we assume that τ_1 is selected from an arbitrary probability distribution.

mixed strategy σ_2 for player 2, $\sigma_2(a_1, a_2)$ denotes the probability that player 2 takes action $a_2 \in A_2$ following observed action $a_1 \in A_1$ of player 1.

Suppose we are in the position of player 2 responding to the observed action $a_1 \in A_1$. If both players are following a Nash equilibrium strategy, then we know that we are best responding to player 1's strategy. However, suppose that we are following our component from Nash equilibrium strategy profile σ^* in which $\sigma_1^*(\tau_1, a_1) = 0$ for all $\tau_1 \in T_1$. Our observation is clearly inconsistent with player 1 following σ^*, since they would never choose action a_1. Since our strategy is part of a Nash equilibrium, it ensures that player 1 cannot profitably deviate from σ_1^* with any $\tau_1 \in T_1$ and take a_1; however, there may be many such strategies, and we would like to choose the best one given that we have actually observed player 1 irrationally playing a_1. In this situation, playing an EFTHPE strategy may ensure that we play a stronger strategy against this opponent, who has selected an action that they should not rationally play, since EFTHPE explicitly ensures robustness against the possibility of "trembling" and playing such an action with small probability.

Extensive-form trembling-hand perfect equilibrium assumes that all players take all actions at all information sets with non-zero probability. In the situation described above, we know that player 1 is taking a_1 at some information set with non-zero probability; however, we really have no further information beyond that. It is very possible that they are playing a strategy that takes $a_1' \in A_1$ with zero probability with all $\tau_1 \in T_1$. The core assumption of game theory is that, in the absence of any information the contrary, we assume that all players are behaving rationally. Now clearly that assumption is violated in this case when we observe player 1 irrationally playing a_1. However, it seems a bit extreme to now assume that all players are playing all actions with nonzero probability. If we assume that the opponent is playing *as rationally as possible given our observations*, then we would only consider trembles that are consistent with our observations of their play. Such trembles must satisfy $\sigma_1(\tau_1, a_1) > 0$ for at least one $\tau_1 \in T_1$, or alternatively, $\sum_{\tau_1 \in T_1} \sigma_1(\tau_1, a_1) > 0$. The concept of *observable perfect equilibrium* (OPE) captures this assumption that all players are playing as rationally as possible subject to the constraint that their play is consistent with our observations.

Definition 1. *Let G be a two-player one-step extensive-form game of imperfect information, and suppose that player 2 has observed public action a_1 from player 1. Then σ^* is an observable perfect equilibrium if there is a sequence of perturbed games, in which player 1 is required to play a_1 with non-zero probability for at least one $\tau_1 \in T_1$, that converges to G, in which there is a sequence of Nash equilibria of the perturbed games that converges to σ^*.*

Proposition 1. *Every observable perfect equilibrium is a Nash equilibrium.*

Proof. Let σ^* be an observable perfect equilibrium of G, where a_1 is the observed public action of player 1. Then there exists a sequence of games $\{G_\epsilon\}$ converging to G in which player 1 is forced to play a_1 with non-zero probability for at least one $\tau_1 \in T_1$, and a sequence of Nash equilibria $\{(\sigma_1^\epsilon, \sigma_2^\epsilon)\}$ that converges to σ^*.

Suppose that σ^* is not a Nash equilibrium of the original game G. Suppose that player 2 can profitably deviate to σ_2. Then we have

$$u_2(\sigma_1^*, \sigma_2) > u_2(\sigma_1^*, \sigma_2^*)$$

$$u_2\left(\lim_{\epsilon \to 0} \sigma_1^\epsilon, \sigma_2\right) > u_2\left(\lim_{\epsilon \to 0} \sigma_1^\epsilon, \lim_{\epsilon \to 0} \sigma_2^\epsilon\right)$$

By continuity of expected utility,

$$\lim_{\epsilon \to 0}\left[u_2\left(\sigma_1^\epsilon, \sigma_2\right) - u_2\left(\sigma_1^\epsilon, \sigma_2^\epsilon\right)\right] > 0$$

So there exists some $\epsilon > 0$ for which

$$u_2\left(\sigma_1^\epsilon, \sigma_2\right) > u_2\left(\sigma_1^\epsilon, \sigma_2^\epsilon\right)$$

This contradicts the fact that σ^ϵ is a Nash equilibrium of G_ϵ.

Now suppose player 1 can profitably deviate to σ_1. By similar reasoning as above, there exists some $\epsilon' > 0$ such that

$$u_1\left(\sigma_1, \sigma_2^\epsilon\right) > u_1\left(\sigma_1^\epsilon, \sigma_2^\epsilon\right)$$

for all $\epsilon \in (0, \epsilon']$. If $\sum_{\tau_1 \in T_1} \sigma_1(\tau_1, a_1) \geq \epsilon'$ then we are done, since σ_1 is a valid strategy in $G_{\epsilon'}$. Otherwise, let $\epsilon^* = \sum_{\tau_1 \in T_1} \sigma_1(\tau_1, a_1) < \epsilon'$. Then σ_1 is a valid strategy in G_{ϵ^*}. So player 1 can profitably deviate from $\sigma_1^{\epsilon^*}$ in G_{ϵ^*}. This contradicts the fact that σ^{ϵ^*} is a Nash equilibrium of G_{ϵ^*}.

So we have shown that neither player can profitably deviate from σ^*, and therefore σ^* is a Nash equilibrium.

We can extend Definition 1 to general n-player extensive-form imperfect-information games by adding analogous constraints for all observed actions (i.e., by requiring that the sum of the probabilities of strategy sequences taken consistent with our observations is nonzero). This is useful because we are no longer required to reason about trembles that are incompatible with the current path of play, which are irrelevant at this point. For general extensive-form games, there is a further consideration about what trembles should be considered for future moves beyond the current path of play. Extensive-form trembling hand perfect equilibrium assumes that all players may tremble in future actions, while an alternative concept called *quasi-perfect equilibrium* (QPE) assumes that only the opposing players tremble for future actions (even if we have trembled previously ourselves) [8]. The related concept of *one-sided quasi-perfect equilibrium* (OSQPE) assumes that only the opposing players can tremble at all and we cannot [11]. OSQPE is the most computationally efficient and is also the most similar to observable perfect equilibrium.

In two-player one-step extensive-form imperfect-information games quasi-perfect equilibrium and extensive-form trembling-hand perfect equilibrium are identical, since both players only take a single action along the path of play. They both require that both player 1 and player 2 put non-zero probability trembles on all actions. Both of these potentially differ from one-sided quasi-perfect equilibrium, which from the perspective of player 2 requires that player 1 puts non-zero probability trembles on all possible actions, while player 2 does not have this requirement. Note that all three of these concepts potentially differ from observable perfect equilibrium (from the perspective of player 2), which requires only that player 1 makes a non-zero probability tremble at some information set consistent with taking the observed action a_1 and no requirement on player 2.

Observable perfect equilibrium is fundamentally different from other equilibrium refinements in that it is dependent on the action taken by the other player. For each observed action a_1 we compute a potentially different strategy for ourselves, conditionally on having observed a_1. In contrast, all other equilibrium refinement concepts compute a full strategy profile for all players in advance of game play. If play contains longer sequences of actions than just a single move for each player, we can recompute our OPE strategy after each new observation (again by assuming positive probability trembles for all actions consistent with the path of play). Note that in aggregate over all information sets an OPE still defines a full strategy; we just do not need to compute it in entirety to implement it.

We can view the relation between OPE and other solution concepts analogously to the relation between endgame solving [15] and standard offline game solving in large imperfect-information games. Previously the standard approach for approximating Nash equilibrium strategies in large imperfect-information games was to first apply an abstraction algorithm to create a significantly smaller game that is strategically similar to the full game [3, 17–19, 22, 29, 30], then solve the abstract game using an equilibrium-finding algorithm such as counterfactual regret minimization (CFR) [31] or a generalization of Nesterov's excessive gap technique [20]. With endgame solving [15], the portion of the game tree that we have reached is solved in real time to a finer degree of granularity than in the offline abstract equilibrium computation. This focused computation led to superhuman play in two-player [4, 24] and six-player no-limit Texas hold 'em [5]. OPE similarly achieves computational advantages over other equilibrium refinement concepts such as TFPE, QPE, and OSQPE, by focusing computation in real time only on the portion of the game tree we have reached (and observed an opponent's "tremble"). However, unlike endgame solving, OPE still guarantees that the computed strategy remains a Nash equilibrium, while it has been shown that endgame solving may produce strategies that are not Nash equilibria of the full game (even if the trunk strategy were an exact Nash equilibrium) [15].

In order to show existence of observable perfect equilibrium and an algorithm for its computation, we first review results for the related concept of one-sided quasi-perfect equilibrium. One-sided quasi-perfect equilibrium assumes that the game is two-player zero-sum and that we play the role of the "machine player" while the opponent is the "human player." A key subroutine in the computation of one-sided quasi-perfect equilibrium in two-player zero-sum games is the solution to an optimization formulation for an ϵ-quasi-perfect equilibrium strategy profile (where the trembles for the human player are lower bounded by $\ell_h(\epsilon)$). The vector $\ell_h(\epsilon)$ has entries $\ell_h(\epsilon)[\sigma] = \epsilon^{|\sigma|}$, where $|\sigma|$ denotes the number of actions for player h in the sequence σ. In the OSEFG setting there is just a single action per player per sequence, so we have $l_h(\epsilon) = \epsilon$. It has been shown that the optimization formulation (1) corresponds to a one-sided quasi-perfect equilibrium [11]. In (1), x_m is the vector of the machine player's strategy sequences, x_h is the vector of the human player's strategy sequences, and A_m is the payoff matrix from the machine player's perspective. The vector f_h and matrix F_h are constants that encode the sequence-form representation of the information set structure for the human player, and f_m, F_m are analogous for the machine player [23].

$$\max_{\mathbf{x_m}} \min_{\mathbf{x_h}} \ \mathbf{x}_m^T \mathbf{A}_m \mathbf{x}_h$$
$$\text{s.t. } \mathbf{F}_m \mathbf{x}_m = \mathbf{f}_m$$
$$\mathbf{x}_m \geq \mathbf{0} \tag{1}$$
$$\mathbf{F}_h \mathbf{x}_h = \mathbf{f}_h$$
$$\mathbf{x}_h \geq \ell_h(\epsilon)$$

The following result has been proven from this formulation [11].

Lemma 1. *Consider the bilinear saddle point problem (1). Then, for any $\epsilon > 0$ for which the domain of the minimization problem is nonempty, any solution to (1) is a one-sided ϵ-quasi-perfect strategy profile.*

From Lemma 1 they are able to prove the existence of one-sided quasi-perfect equilibrium as a corollary [11].

Corollary 1. *Every two-player zero-sum extensive-form game with perfect recall has at least one-sided quasi-perfect equilibrium.*

We can obtain analogous results for observable perfect equilibrium using similar reasoning. We refer to the players as we did originally, where player 2 corresponds to ourselves (i.e., the "machine player"), and player 1 corresponds to the opponent (i.e., the "human player"). Note that the optimization formulation (2) differs from (1) only in the constraints for player 1's strategy vector. The inequality $\mathbf{c}^T \mathbf{x}_1 \geq \epsilon$ encodes the constraint that the sum of the probabilities that player 1 takes strategy sequences that are consistent with our observations of play so far is at least ϵ, where $\mathbf{c}$ is a constant vector.

$$\max_{\mathbf{x_2}} \min_{\mathbf{x_1}} \ \mathbf{x}_2^T \mathbf{A}_2 \mathbf{x}_1$$
$$\text{s.t. } \mathbf{F}_2 \mathbf{x}_2 = \mathbf{f}_2$$
$$\mathbf{x}_2 \geq \mathbf{0} \tag{2}$$
$$\mathbf{F}_1 \mathbf{x}_1 = \mathbf{f}_1$$
$$\mathbf{c}^T \mathbf{x}_1 \geq \epsilon$$

Lemma 2. *Consider the bilinear saddle point problem (2). Then, for any $\epsilon > 0$ for which the domain of the minimization problem is nonempty, any solution to (2) is an ϵ-observable-perfect strategy profile.*

Corollary 2. *Every two-player zero-sum extensive-form game with perfect recall has at least one observable perfect equilibrium.*

For one-sided quasi-perfect equilibrium, it has been shown that formulation (1) implies the following linear programming formulation (3) for an ϵ-quasi-perfect equilibrium strategy for the machine player [11]. In (3), $\mathbf{v}$ is a new vector of free variables, while all other quantities are the same as in (1).

$$\begin{aligned} \arg\max_{\mathbf{x_m},\mathbf{v}} \; & (A_m \ell_h(\epsilon))^T x_m + (f_h - F_h \ell_h(\epsilon))^T v \\ \text{s.t. } & \mathbf{A}_m^T \mathbf{x}_m - \mathbf{F}_h \mathbf{v} \geq 0 \\ & \mathbf{F}_m \mathbf{x}_m = \mathbf{f}_m \\ & \mathbf{x_m} \geq \mathbf{0} \\ & \mathbf{v} \text{ free} \end{aligned} \qquad (3)$$

Proposition 2. *Any limit point of solutions to the trembling linear program (3) as the trembling magnitude $\epsilon \to 0^+$ is a one-sided quasi-perfect equilibrium strategy for the machine player.*

This linear programming formulation leads to a polynomial-time algorithm for computation of one-sided quasi-perfect equilibrium by solving the problem for consecutively smaller values of ϵ until a termination criterion is met [11]. It is argued that this computation is more efficient than analogous algorithms for extensive-form trembling-hand perfect equilibrium and quasi-perfect equilibrium, because the OSQPE formulation only depends on ϵ through the objective, while EFTHPE depends on ϵ through the left-hand-side of constraints, and QPE depends on ϵ in both the right-hand-side of constraints and the objective. We now provide a linear program formulation for ϵ-observable perfect equilibrium that is analogous to (3), which also implies a polynomial-time algorithm for computation of observable-perfect equilibrium with the same computational advantages as for OSQPE. Note that in our new LP formulation (4) ϵ occurs only in the objective, as it did in (3). Note also that our objective has only about half as many terms as the corresponding OSQPE objective, suggesting that OPE can be computed faster than OSQPE. This agrees with the intuition described above, since OPE only considers trembles for the opponent consistent with our observations of the path of play, while OSQPE considers all possible (past and future) trembles for the opponent.

$$\begin{aligned} \arg\max_{\mathbf{x_2},w,\mathbf{v}} \; & \mathbf{f}_1^T \mathbf{v} + \epsilon w \\ \text{s.t. } & \mathbf{F}_1^T \mathbf{v} + w\mathbf{c} = \mathbf{A}_2^T \mathbf{x}_2 \\ & \mathbf{F}_2 \mathbf{x}_2 = \mathbf{f}_2 \\ & \mathbf{x_2} \geq \mathbf{0} \\ & w \geq 0 \\ & \mathbf{v} \text{ free} \end{aligned} \qquad (4)$$

Proposition 3. *Any limit point of solutions to the trembling linear program (4) as the trembling magnitude $\epsilon \to 0^+$ is an observable perfect equilibrium strategy for player 2.*

Proof. First we create the dual of the minimization problem inside of (2):

$$\min_{\mathbf{x_1}:\mathbf{F}_1\mathbf{x}_1=\mathbf{f}_1,\mathbf{c}^T\mathbf{x}_1\geq\epsilon} = \begin{array}{c} \max_{w,\mathbf{v}} \ \mathbf{f}_1^T\mathbf{v} + \epsilon w \\ \text{s.t. } \mathbf{F}_1^T\mathbf{v} + w\mathbf{c} = \mathbf{A}_2^T\mathbf{x}_2 \\ w \geq 0 \\ \mathbf{v} \text{ free} \end{array} \qquad (5)$$

Next we substitute this new dual formulation back into the outer maximization problem to create a single maximization problem for player 2's strategy:

$$\begin{array}{c} \arg\max_{\mathbf{x_2},w,\mathbf{v}} \ \mathbf{f}_1^T\mathbf{v} + \epsilon w \\ \text{s.t. } \mathbf{F}_1^T\mathbf{v} + w\mathbf{c} = \mathbf{A}_2^T\mathbf{x}_2 \\ \mathbf{F}_2\mathbf{x}_2 = \mathbf{f}_2 \\ \mathbf{x_2} \geq \mathbf{0} \\ w \geq 0 \\ \mathbf{v} \text{ free} \end{array} \qquad (6)$$

3   No-Limit Poker

In this section we illustrate how observable perfect equilibrium leads to a different strategy profile than the other equilibrium refinement concepts in no-limit poker. Poker has been a major AI challenge problem in recent years, with no-limit Texas hold 'em in particular being the most popular variant for humans. No-limit Texas hold 'em is a large sequential game of imperfect information, and just recently computers have achieved superhuman performance, first in the two-player variant [4, 24] and subsequently for six players [5]. These agents attempt to compute approximations of Nash equilibrium strategies by first running an *abstraction algorithm* to create a smaller strategically-similar game, and then solving the abstract game using an equilibrium-finding algorithm such as counterfactual regret minimization. Counterfactual regret minimization (CFR) is an iterative self-play procedure that has been proven to converge to Nash equilibrium in two-player zero-sum [31], though it has been demonstrated to not converge to Nash equilibrium in a simplified three-player poker game [1]. The key insight that led to superhuman play was to combine these abstraction and equilibrium-finding approaches with endgame solving [15], in which the portion of the game we have reached during a hand is resolved in a finer granularity in real time. It is somewhat remarkable that these approaches have achieved such strong performance despite numerous theoretical limitations: the abstraction algorithms have no performance guarantee, endgame solving has no performance guarantee, CFR does not guarantee convergence to Nash equilibrium for more than two players, and furthermore even if CFR did converge for more than two players there can be multiple Nash equilibria and following one has no performance guarantee. It turns out that even ignoring all of these theoretical limitations, there is an additional challenge present. Even if we are in the two-player zero-sum setting and are able to compute an exact Nash equilibrium, the game may contain many Nash equilibria, and we would like to choose the "best" one. As we will see, even the simplest two-player no-limit poker game contains infinitely many Nash equilibria.

In the *no-limit clairvoyance game* [2], player 1 is dealt a *winning hand* (W) and a *losing hand* (L) each with probability $\frac{1}{2}$. (While player 2 is not explicitly dealt a "hand," we can view player 2 as always being dealt a medium-strength hand that wins against a losing hand and loses to a winning hand.) Both players have initial chip stacks of size n, and they both ante \$0.50 (creating an initial pot of \$1). P1 is allowed to bet any integral amount $x \in [0, n]$ (a bet of 0 is called a *check*).[2] Then P2 is allowed to call or fold (but not raise). This game clearly falls into the class of one-step extensive-form imperfect-information games. The game is small enough that its solution can be computed analytically (even for the continuous version) [2].

- P1 bets n with prob. 1 with a winning hand.
- P1 bets n with prob. $\frac{n}{1+n}$ with a losing hand (and checks otherwise).
- For all $x \in (0, n]$, P2 calls a bet of size x with prob. $\frac{1}{1+x}$.

It was shown by Ankenman and Chen [2] that this strategy profile constitutes a Nash equilibrium. (They also show that these frequencies are optimal in many other poker variants.) Here is a sketch of that argument.

Proposition 4. *The strategy profile presented above is a Nash equilibrium of the no-limit clairvoyance game.*

Proof. Player 2 must call a bet of size x with probability $\frac{1}{1+x}$ in order to make player 1 indifferent between betting x and checking with a losing hand. For a given x, player 1 must bluff $\frac{x}{1+x}$ as often as he value bets for player 2 to be indifferent between calling and folding. Given these values, the expected payoff to player 1 of betting size x is $v(x) = \frac{x}{2(1+x)}$. This function is monotonically increasing, and therefore player 1 will maximize his payoff with $x = n$.

Despite the simplicity of this game, the solution has been used in order to interpret bet sizes for the opponent that fall outside an abstracted game model by many strong agents for full no-limit Texas hold 'em [12,14,21]. Thus, its solution still captures important aspects of realistic forms of poker played competitively.

It turns out that player 2 does not need to call a bet of size $x \neq n$ with exact probability $\frac{1}{1+x}$: he need only not call with such an extreme probability that player 1 has an incentive to change his bet size to x (with either a winning or losing hand). In particular, it can be shown that player 2 need only call a bet of size x with any probability (which can be different for different values of x) in the interval $\left[\frac{1}{1+x}, \min\left\{\frac{n}{x(1+n)}, 1\right\}\right]$ in order to remain in equilibrium.[3]

---

[2] In the original formulation of the no-limit clairvoyance game [2] player 1 is allowed to bet any real value in $[0, n]$, making the game a continuous game, since player 1's pure strategy space is infinite. For simplicity we consider the discrete game where player 1 is restricted to only betting integer values, though much of our equilibrium analysis will still apply for the continuous version as well.

[3] Note that if x is required to be integral then we always have $x \geq \frac{n}{1+n}$, and $\min\left\{\frac{n}{x(1+n)}, 1\right\} = \frac{n}{x(1+n)}$. However, our solution also holds for the continuous game.

Proposition 5. *A strategy profile* σ^* *in the no-limit clairvoyance game is a Nash equilibrium if and only if under* σ^* *player 1 bets n with probability 1 with a winning hand and bets n with probability* $\frac{n}{1+n}$ *with a losing hand, and for all* $x \in (0, n]$ *player 2 calls vs. a bet of size x with probability in the interval* $\left[\frac{1}{1+x}, \min\left\{ \frac{n}{x(1+n)}, 1 \right\} \right]$.

Proof. We have already argued that the Nash equilibrium strategy for player 1 is unique. Note that for $x \in (0, n)$, player 1 will never actually bet x in equilibrium, and player 2 must call with probability that ensures that player 1 will not want to deviate and bet x. Suppose player 2 calls with probability $p' < \frac{1}{1+x}$, for some $x \in (0, n)$. If player 1 bets x with a losing hand, expected payoff is

$$p'(-0.5 - x) + (1 - p')(0.5)$$
$$= p'(-1 - x) + 0.5$$
$$> \frac{-1 - x}{1 + x} + 0.5$$
$$= -0.5$$

If instead player 1 checks with a losing hand, the expected payoff is -0.5. So player 1 will strictly prefer to bet x than to check, and will have incentive to deviate from his equilibrium strategy.

Now suppose player 2 calls with probability $p' > \min\left\{ \frac{n}{x(1+n)}, 1 \right\}$, for some $x \in (0, n)$. First suppose that $\frac{n}{x(1+n)} \leq 1$. If player 2 bets x with a winning hand, his expected payoff is

$$p'(0.5 + x) + (1 - p')(0.5)$$
$$= 0.5p' + p'x + 0.5 - 0.5p'$$
$$> \frac{xn}{x(1 + n)} + 0.5$$
$$= \frac{1.5n + 0.5}{1 + n}$$

If instead player 1 bets n, the expected payoff is

$$\frac{1}{1 + n}(0.5 + n) + \left(1 - \frac{1}{1 + n}\right)(0.5)$$
$$= \frac{1.5n + 0.5}{1 + n}$$

So player 1 will strictly prefer to bet x than to bet n, and will have incentive to deviate from his equilibrium strategy.

Our analysis so far has shown that for $\frac{n}{x(1+n)} \leq 1$, the strategy profile is a Nash equilibrium if and only if player 2 calls a bet of size x with probability in the interval $\left[\frac{1}{1+x}, \frac{n}{x(1+n)} \right]$ for all $x \in (0, n]$.

Now suppose that $\frac{n}{x(1+n)} > 1$. Suppose that player 2 calls a bet of x with probability 1. If player 1 bets x, his expected payoff is

$$1(0.5 + x) + 0(0.5)$$
$$= x + 0.5$$
$$< \frac{n}{1+n} + 0.5$$
$$= \frac{1.5n + 0.5}{1+n}$$

If instead player 1 bets n, the expected payoff as shown above is $\frac{1.5n+0.5}{1+n}$. So player 1 will not have incentive to deviate and bet x instead of n.

So we have shown that player 2 has infinitely many Nash equilibrium strategies that differ in their frequencies of calling vs. "suboptimal" bet sizes of player 1. Which of these strategies should we play when we encounter an opponent who bets a suboptimal size? One argument for calling with probability at the lower bound of the interval—$\frac{1}{1+x}$—is as follows (note that the previously-computed equilibrium strategy uses this value [2]). If the opponent bets x as opposed to the optimal size of n that he should bet in equilibrium, then a reasonable deduction is that he isn't even aware that n would have been the optimal size, and believes that x is optimal. Therefore, it would make sense to play a strategy that is an equilibrium in the game where the opponent is restricted to only betting x (or to betting 0, i.e., checking). Doing so would correspond to calling a bet of x with probability $\frac{1}{1+x}$. The other equilibria pay more heed to the concern that the opponent could exploit us by deviating to bet x instead of n; but we need not be as concerned about this possibility, since a rational opponent who knew to bet n would not bet x.

One could use a similar argument to defend calling with probability at the upper bound of the interval—$\min\left\{\frac{n}{x(1+n)}, 1\right\}$. If the opponent somehow knew that betting n was part of an optimal strategy but did not know that checking was, then perhaps we should follow an equilibrium of the game where the opponent is restricted to only betting x or n, in which case our calling frequency should focus on dissuading the opponent from betting x with a winning hand instead of n.

The first argument seems much more natural than the second, as it seems much more reasonable that a human is aware they should check sometimes with weak hands, but may have trouble computing that n is the optimal size and guess that it is x. However, both arguments could be appropriate depending on assumptions about the reasoning process of the opponent. The entire point of Nash equilibrium as a prescriptive solution concept is that we do not have any additional information about the players' reasoning process, so will opt to assume that all players are fully rational. If any additional information is available— such as historical data (either from our specific opponents' play or from a larger population of players), observations of play from the current match, a prior distribution, or any other model of the reasoning mechanism of the opponents—then we should clearly utilize this information and not simply follow a Nash equilibrium. Without any such additional information, it does not seem clear whether we should call with the lower bound probability, upper bound probability, or a value in the middle of the interval. The point of the equilibrium refinements we have considered is exactly to help us select between equilibria in a theoretically principled way in the absence of any additional information that could be used to model the specific opponents.

For the remainder of our analysis we will restrict our attention to the no-limit clairvoyance game with $n = 2$, with extensive-form game tree given by Fig. 1.

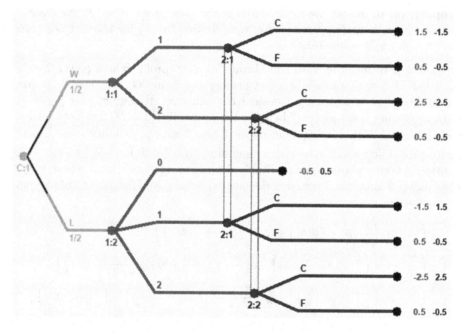

Fig. 1. No-limit clairvoyance game with $n = 2$.

According to our above analysis, the unique Nash equilibrium strategy for player 1 is to bet 2 with probability 1 with a winning hand, to bet 2 with probability $\frac{2}{3}$ with a losing hand, and to check with probability $\frac{1}{3}$ with a losing hand. The Nash equilibrium strategies for player 2 are to call a bet of 2 with probability $\frac{1}{3}$, and to call a bet of 1 with probability in the interval $\left[\frac{1}{2}, \frac{2}{3}\right]$. As it turns out, the unique trembling-hand perfect equilibrium strategy for player 2 is to call vs. a bet of 1 with probability $\frac{2}{3}$.[4] Since this is a one-step extensive-form imperfect-information game, this is also the unique quasi-perfect equilibrium. And since player 2's strategy is fully mixed, this is also the unique one-sided quasi-perfect equilibrium. However, the unique observable perfect equilibrium strategy for player 2 is to call with probability $\frac{5}{9}$. Interestingly, the OPE corresponds to a different strategy for this game than all the other refinements we have considered, and none of them correspond to the "natural" argument for calling with probability $\frac{1}{2}$ based on an assumption about the typical reasoning of human opponents. The OPE value of $\frac{5}{9}$ corresponds to the solution assuming only that player 1 has bet 1 but that otherwise all players are playing as rationally as possible. Note also that the OPE does not simply correspond to the average of the two interval boundaries, which would be $\frac{7}{12}$.

Proposition 6. *In the no-limit clairvoyance game with $n = 2$, the unique extensive-form trembling-hand perfect equilibrium strategy for player 2 is to call vs. a bet of 1 with probability $\frac{2}{3}$.*

Proof. Let μ denote the Nash equilibrium strategy profile where player 2 calls vs. a bet of 1 with probability $\frac{2}{3}$. Consider the game G_ϵ where each action probability must be at least ϵ. Consider the following strategy $\sigma_{\epsilon,1}^*$ for player 1. With a winning hand player 1 bets 2 with probability $1 - 2\epsilon$, and bets 1 with probability 2ϵ. With a losing hand player 1 bets 2 with probability $\frac{2(1-2\epsilon)}{3}$, bets 1 with probability ϵ and bets 0 with remaining probability $1 - \frac{2(1-2\epsilon)}{3} - \epsilon = \frac{1+\epsilon}{3}$. Consider whether player 1 can profitably deviate to strategy ϕ from this strategy when player 2 follows μ. First, we calculate expected payoff for player 1 of playing $\sigma_{\epsilon,1}^*$ against μ:

$$\frac{1}{2}\left((1-2\epsilon)\left(\frac{1}{3}(2.5) + \frac{2}{3}(0.5)\right) + (2\epsilon)\left(\frac{2}{3}(1.5) + \frac{1}{3}(0.5)\right)\right)$$

$$+ \frac{1}{2}\left(\frac{2(1-2\epsilon)}{3}\left(\frac{1}{3}(-2.5) + \frac{2}{3}(0.5)\right) + \epsilon\left(\frac{2}{3}(-1.5) + \frac{1}{3}(0.5)\right) + \left(\frac{1+\epsilon}{3}(-0.5)\right)\right)$$

$$= \frac{1}{2}\left((1-2\epsilon)\left(\frac{7}{6}\right) + (2\epsilon)\left(\frac{7}{6}\right)\right) + \frac{1}{2}\left(\frac{2(1-2\epsilon)}{3}(-0.5) + \epsilon\left(-\frac{5}{6}\right) + \left(\frac{1+\epsilon}{3}(-0.5)\right)\right)$$

$$= \frac{7}{12} + \frac{1}{2}\left(-\frac{1}{3} + \frac{2\epsilon}{3} - \frac{5\epsilon}{6} - \frac{1}{6} - \frac{\epsilon}{6}\right)$$

$$= \frac{1}{3} - \frac{\epsilon}{6}$$

---

[4] Observe that this game explicitly shows that Theorem 1 does not hold in general for extensive-form games, since all of the Nash equilibria in this game satisfy the alternative formulation of trembling-hand perfect equilibrium. To see this, consider the sequence of strategies for player 1 that bet 1 with probability ϵ with a winning hand and with probability $\frac{\epsilon}{2}$ with a losing hand. This sequence will converge to the unique Nash equilibrium strategy for player 1 as $\epsilon \to 0$, and furthermore player 2 is indifferent between calling and folding vs. a bet of 1 against all of these strategies, so all of player 2's Nash equilibrium strategies are best responses. So the equivalent formulation of trembling-hand perfect equilibrium is only valid for simultaneous strategic-form games and does not apply to extensive-form games.

If instead player 1 plays ϕ, expected payoff is

$$\frac{1}{2}\left((1-\phi(W,1))\left(\frac{7}{6}\right)+\phi(W,1)\left(\frac{7}{6}\right)\right)$$

$$+\frac{1}{2}\left(\phi(L,2)(-0.5)+\phi(L,1)\left(-\frac{5}{6}\right)+(1-\phi(L,2)-\phi(L,1))(-0.5)\right)$$

$$=\frac{7}{12}+\frac{1}{2}\left(-\frac{\phi(L,1)}{3}-0.5\right)$$

$$=\frac{1}{3}-\frac{\phi(L,1)}{6}$$

Since $\phi(L,1)\geq\epsilon$, this quantity is maximized with $\phi(L,1)=\epsilon$, producing expected payoff $\frac{1}{3}-\frac{\epsilon}{6}$. Since this is the same expected payoff as playing $\sigma^*_{\epsilon,1}$, player 1 cannot profitably deviate from $\sigma^*_{\epsilon,1}$. So the strategy profile where player 1 follows $\sigma^*_{\epsilon,1}$ and player 2 follows μ is a Nash equilibrium of G_ϵ. By taking the limit as $\epsilon\to 0$ it follows that μ is a trembling-hand perfect equilibrium of the original game G.

Now let μ_α denote the Nash equilibrium strategy profile where player 2 calls vs. a bet of 1 with probability α, where $\frac{1}{2}\leq\alpha<\frac{2}{3}$. Suppose that player 1 plays strategy ϕ against this strategy in G_ϵ. Then player 1's expected payoff is:

$$\frac{1}{2}\left((1-\phi(W,1))\left(\frac{1}{3}(2.5)+\frac{2}{3}(0.5)\right)+\phi(W,1)(\alpha(1.5)+(1-\alpha)(0.5))\right)$$

$$+\frac{1}{2}\left(\phi(L,2)\left(\frac{1}{3}(-2.5)+\frac{2}{3}(0.5)\right)+\phi(L,1)(\alpha(-1.5)+(1-\alpha)(0.5))\right)$$

$$+\frac{1}{2}((1-\phi(L,2)-\phi(L,1))(-0.5))$$

$$=\frac{1}{2}\left((1-\phi(W,1))\left(\frac{7}{6}\right)+\phi(W,1)(\alpha+0.5)\right)$$

$$+\frac{1}{2}(\phi(L,2)(-0.5)+\phi(L,1)(-2\alpha+0.5)+(1-\phi(L,2)-\phi(L,1))(-0.5))$$

$$=\frac{1}{2}\left(\phi(W,1)\left(\alpha-\frac{2}{3}\right)+\frac{7}{6}+\phi(L,1)(-2\alpha+1)-0.5\right)$$

$$=\frac{1}{2}\left(\phi(W,1)\left(\alpha-\frac{2}{3}\right)+\phi(L,1)(-2\alpha+1)+\frac{2}{3}\right)$$

For $\alpha\in\left(\frac{1}{2},\frac{2}{3}\right)$, this is maximized in G_ϵ with $\phi(W,1)=\epsilon$, $\phi(L,1)=\epsilon$. However, if $\phi(W,1)=\phi(L,1)=\epsilon$, then player 2's expected payoff of calling vs. a bet of 1 will be $\epsilon(-1.5)+\epsilon(1.5)=0$, while the expected payoff of folding vs. a bet of 1 is -0.5. So player 2 will strictly prefer to call vs. a bet of 1, and can profitably deviate from μ_α. So there is no Nash equilibrium of G_ϵ in which player

2 plays μ_α, and therefore there cannot be a sequence of equilibria converging to μ_α in G as $\epsilon \to 0$. So μ_α is not trembling-hand perfect.

Now suppose that $\alpha = \frac{1}{2}$. Then the expected payoff is maximized in G_ϵ with $\phi(W, 1) = \epsilon$, while $\phi(L, 2)$ can be any value at least ϵ, since the coefficient is $-2\alpha + 1 = 0$. Against this strategy, player 2's expected payoff of calling vs. a bet of 1 is

$$\epsilon(-1.5) + \phi(L, 2)(1.5) \geq \epsilon(-1.5) + \epsilon(1.5) = 0.$$

And as before the expected payoff of folding vs a bet of 1 is -0.5. So again player 2 will strictly prefer to call vs. a bet of 1, and μ_α is not trembling-hand perfect.

Corollary 3. *In the no-limit clairvoyance game with $n = 2$, the unique quasi-perfect equilibrium strategy for player 2 is to call vs. a bet of 1 with probability $\frac{2}{3}$. This is also the unique one-sided quasi-perfect equilibrium strategy.*

Proposition 7. *In the no-limit clairvoyance game with $n = 2$, the unique observable perfect equilibrium strategy for player 2 is to call vs. a bet of 1 with probability $\frac{5}{9}$.*

Proof. Let μ denote the Nash equilibrium strategy profile where player 2 calls vs. a bet of 1 with probability $\frac{5}{9}$. Consider the game G_ϵ where the sum of the probability that player 1 bets 1 with a winning hand and with a losing hand is at least ϵ. Consider the following strategy $\sigma_{\epsilon,1}^*$ for player 1. With a winning hand they 2 with probability $1 - \frac{2\epsilon}{3}$ and bet 1 with probability $\frac{2\epsilon}{3}$. With a losing hand they bet 2 with probability $\frac{2(3-2\epsilon)}{9}$, bet 1 with probability $\frac{\epsilon}{3}$, and bet 0 with remaining probability $1 - \frac{2(3-2\epsilon)}{9} - \frac{\epsilon}{3} = \frac{3+\epsilon}{9}$. Consider whether player 1 can profitably deviate to strategy ϕ from this strategy when player 2 follows μ. First, we calculate expected payoff for player 1 of playing $\sigma_{\epsilon,1}^*$ against μ:

$$\frac{1}{2}\left(\left(1 - \frac{2\epsilon}{3}\right)\left(\frac{1}{3}(2.5) + \frac{2}{3}(0.5)\right) + \left(\frac{2\epsilon}{3}\right)\left(\frac{5}{9}(1.5) + \frac{4}{9}(0.5)\right)\right)$$

$$+ \frac{1}{2}\left(\frac{2(3-2\epsilon)}{9}\left(\frac{1}{3}(-2.5) + \frac{2}{3}(0.5)\right) + \frac{\epsilon}{3}\left(\frac{5}{9}(-1.5) + \frac{4}{9}(0.5)\right) + \frac{3+\epsilon}{9}(-0.5)\right)$$

$$= \frac{1}{2}\left(\left(1 - \frac{2\epsilon}{3}\right)\left(\frac{7}{6}\right) + \left(\frac{2\epsilon}{3}\right)\left(\frac{19}{18}\right)\right) + \frac{1}{2}\left(\frac{2(3-2\epsilon)}{9}(-0.5) + \frac{\epsilon}{3}\left(-\frac{11}{18}\right) + \left(\frac{3+\epsilon}{9}(-0.5)\right)\right)$$

$$= \frac{1}{2}\left(-\frac{2\epsilon}{27} + \frac{7}{6}\right) + \frac{1}{2}\left(-\frac{1}{3} + \frac{2\epsilon}{9} - \frac{11\epsilon}{54} - \frac{1}{6} - \frac{\epsilon}{18}\right)$$

$$= \frac{1}{3} - \frac{\epsilon}{18}$$

If instead player 1 plays ϕ, expected payoff is

$$\frac{1}{2}\left((1-\phi(W,1))\left(\frac{7}{6}\right)+\phi(W,1)\left(\frac{19}{18}\right)\right)$$

$$+\frac{1}{2}\left(\phi(L,2)(-0.5)+\phi(L,1)\left(-\frac{11}{18}\right)+(1-\phi(L,2)-\phi(L,1))(-0.5)\right)$$

$$=\frac{1}{2}\left(\frac{7}{6}-\frac{\phi(W,1)}{9}\right)+\frac{1}{2}\left(-0.5-\frac{\phi(L,1)}{9}\right)$$

$$=\frac{1}{3}-\frac{\phi(W,1)}{18}-\frac{\phi(L,1)}{18}$$

Given the constraint that $\phi(W,1)+\phi(L,1)\geq\epsilon$, this is maximized at $\phi(W,1)+\phi(L,1)=\epsilon$, producing expected payoff $\frac{1}{3}-\frac{\epsilon}{18}$. Since this is the same expected payoff as playing $\sigma^*_{\epsilon,1}$, player 1 cannot profitably deviate from $\sigma^*_{\epsilon,1}$. So the strategy profile where player 1 follows $\sigma^*_{\epsilon,1}$ and player 2 follows μ is a Nash equilibrium of G_ϵ. By taking the limit as $\epsilon\to 0$ it follows that μ is an observable perfect equilibrium of the original game G.

Now let μ_α denote the Nash equilibrium strategy profile where player 2 calls vs. a bet of 1 with probability α, where $\frac{1}{2}\leq\alpha\leq\frac{2}{3}$. Suppose that player 1 plays strategy ϕ against this strategy in G_ϵ. Then player 1's expected payoff is:

$$\frac{1}{2}\left((1-\phi(W,1))\left(\frac{1}{3}(2.5)+\frac{2}{3}(0.5)\right)+\phi(W,1)\left(\alpha(1.5)+(1-\alpha)(0.5)\right)\right)$$

$$+\frac{1}{2}\left(\phi(L,2)\left(\frac{1}{3}(-2.5)+\frac{2}{3}(0.5)\right)+\phi(L,1)\left(\alpha(-1.5)+(1-\alpha)(0.5)\right)\right)$$

$$+\frac{1}{2}\left((1-\phi(L,2)-\phi(L,1))(-0.5)\right)$$

$$=\frac{1}{2}\left((1-\phi(W,1))\left(\frac{7}{6}\right)+\phi(W,1)\left(\alpha+0.5\right)\right)$$

$$+\frac{1}{2}\left(\phi(L,2)(-0.5)+\phi(L,1)(-2\alpha+0.5)+(1-\phi(L,2)-\phi(L,1))(-0.5)\right)$$

$$=\frac{1}{2}\left(\phi(W,1)\left(\alpha-\frac{2}{3}\right)+\frac{7}{6}+\phi(L,1)(-2\alpha+1)-0.5\right)$$

$$=\frac{1}{2}\left(\phi(W,1)\left(\alpha-\frac{2}{3}\right)+\phi(L,1)(-2\alpha+1)+\frac{2}{3}\right)$$

We want to maximize this subject to $\phi(W,1)+\phi(L,1)\geq\epsilon$. For $\frac{1}{2}<\alpha<\frac{5}{9}$, it is maximized by $\phi(W,1)=0$, $\phi(L,q)=\epsilon$. Against this strategy, player 2's expected payoff of calling vs. a bet of 1 is strictly larger than folding, so player

2 can profitably deviate from μ_α. So there is no Nash equilibrium of G_ϵ in which player 2 plays μ_α, and therefore there cannot be a sequence of equilibria converging to μ_α in G as $\epsilon \to 0$. So μ_α is not observable perfect.

For $\frac{5}{9} < \alpha < \frac{2}{3}$, the expression is maximized by $\phi(W, 1) = \epsilon$, $\phi(L, q) = 0$. Against this strategy, player 2 strictly prefers to fold vs. a bet 1 of than to call. So μ_α is not observable perfect.

For $\alpha = \frac{1}{2}$, the expression is maximized by $\phi(W, 1) = 0$ and $\phi(L, q) \geq \epsilon$. Against this strategy, player 2 strictly prefers to call vs. a bet 1 of than to fold. So μ_α is not observable perfect.

For $\alpha = \frac{2}{3}$, the expression is maximized by $\phi(W, 1) \geq \epsilon$ and $\phi(L, q) = 0$. Against this strategy, player 2 strictly prefers to fold vs. a bet 1 of than to call. So μ_α is not observable perfect.

4   Conclusion

We presented a new solution concept for sequential imperfect-information games called observable perfect equilibrium that captures the assumption that all players are playing as rationally as possible given the fact that some players have taken observable suboptimal actions. We believe that this is more compelling than other solution concepts that assume that one or all players make certain types of mistakes for all other actions including those that have not been observed. We showed that every observable perfect equilibrium is a Nash equilibrium, which implies that observable perfect equilibrium is a refinement of Nash equilibrium. We also showed that observable perfect equilibrium is always guaranteed to exist. We showed that an OPE can be computed in polynomial time in two-player zero-sum games based on repeatedly solving a linear program formulation. We also argued that computation of OPE is more efficient than computation of the related concept of one-sided quasi-perfect equilibrium, which in turn has been shown to be more efficient than computation of quasi-perfect equilibrium and extensive-form trembling-hand perfect equilibrium.

We demonstrated that observable perfect equilibrium leads to a different solution in no-limit poker than EFTHPE, QPE, and OSQPE. While we only considered a simplified game called the no-limit clairvoyance game, this game encodes several elements of the complexity of full no-limit Texas hold 'em, and in fact conclusions from this game have been incorporated into some of the strongest agents for no-limit Texas hold 'em. So we expect our analysis to extend to significantly more complex settings than the example considered. We think that observable perfect equilibrium captures the theoretically-correct solution concept for sequential imperfect-information games, and furthermore is more practical to compute than other solutions.

Future work should explore the scalability of the algorithm we have presented. While algorithms based on solving linear programs run in polynomial time, they often run into memory and speed issues that prevent them from being competitive with algorithms such as counterfactual regret minimization and fictitious play on extremely large games. Perhaps these algorithms can be modified in such a way that they are guaranteed to converge to an observable perfect equilibrium in two-player zero-sum games (currently they are just guaranteed to converge to Nash equilibrium and not to any specific refinement).

While the focus of this paper has been on two-player games, and two-player zero-sum games specifically, the concept of observable perfect equilibrium is generally applicable to multiplayer games and non-zero-sum games as well. It has been argued that one-sided quasi-perfect equilibrium is inappropriate for non-zero-sum (and multi-player) games and should not be used [11]. By contrast, we see no reason why observable perfect equilibrium cannot be applied to these games with the same theoretical and computational advantages as for the two-player zero-sum setting. In the future we would like to study applicability of observable perfect equilibrium to these settings and develop new algorithms for its computation.

References

1. Abou Risk, N., Szafron, D.: Using counterfactual regret minimization to create competitive multiplayer poker agents. In: Proceedings of the International Conference on Autonomous Agents and Multi-Agent Systems (AAMAS), pp. 159–166 (2010)
2. Ankenman, J., Chen, B.: The Mathematics of Poker. ConJelCo LLC, Pittsburgh (2006)
3. Billings, D., et al.: Approximating game-theoretic optimal strategies for full-scale poker. In: Proceedings of the 18th International Joint Conference on Artificial Intelligence (IJCAI) (2003)
4. Brown, N., Sandholm, T.: Superhuman AI for heads-up no-limit poker: libratus beats top professionals. Science **359**, 418–424 (2017)
5. Brown, N., Sandholm, T.: Superhuman AI for multiplayer poker. Science **365**, 885–890 (2019)
6. Chen, X., Deng, X.: 3-Nash is PPAD-complete. Electronic Colloquium on Computational Complexity Report No. 134, pp. 1–12 (2005)
7. Chen, X., Deng, X.: Settling the complexity of 2-player Nash equilibrium. In: Proceedings of the Annual Symposium on Foundations of Computer Science (FOCS) (2006)
8. van Damme, E.: A relation between perfect equilibria in extensive form games and proper equilibria in normal form games. Internat. J. Game Theory **13**, 1–13 (1984)
9. van Damme, E.: Stability and Perfection of Nash Equilibrium. Springer, New York (1987)
10. Daskalakis, C., Goldberg, P., Papadimitriou, C.: The complexity of computing a Nash equilibrium. SIAM J. Comput. **1**(39), 195–259 (2009)
11. Farina, G., Sandholm, T.: Equilibrium refinement for the age of machines: the one-sided quasi-perfect equilibrium. In: Conference on Neural Information Processing Systems (NeurIPS) (2021)
12. Ganzfried, S.: Reflections on the first man vs. machine no-limit Texas hold 'em competition. AI Mag. **38**(2), 77–85 (2017)
13. Ganzfried, S., Sandholm, T.: Game theory-based opponent modeling in large imperfect-information games. In: Proceedings of the International Conference on Autonomous Agents and Multi-Agent Systems (AAMAS) (2011)

14. Ganzfried, S., Sandholm, T.: Action translation in extensive-form games with large action spaces: axioms, paradoxes, and the pseudo-harmonic mapping. In: Proceedings of the International Joint Conference on Artificial Intelligence (IJCAI) (2013)

15. Ganzfried, S., Sandholm, T.: Endgame solving in large imperfect-information games. In: Proceedings of the International Conference on Autonomous Agents and Multi-Agent Systems (AAMAS) (2015)

16. Ganzfried, S., Sandholm, T.: Safe opponent exploitation. ACM Trans. Econ. Comput. (TEAC) **3**(8), 1–28 (2015)

17. Gilpin, A., Sandholm, T.: A competitive Texas Hold'em poker player via automated abstraction and real-time equilibrium computation. In: Proceedings of the National Conference on Artificial Intelligence (AAAI) (2006)

18. Gilpin, A., Sandholm, T.: Better automated abstraction techniques for imperfect information games, with application to Texas Hold'em poker. In: Proceedings of the International Conference on Autonomous Agents and Multi-Agent Systems (AAMAS) (2007)

19. Gilpin, A., Sandholm, T., Sørensen, T.B.: A heads-up no-limit Texas Hold'em poker player: discretized betting models and automatically generated equilibrium-finding programs. In: Proceedings of the International Conference on Autonomous Agents and Multi-Agent Systems (AAMAS) (2008)

20. Hoda, S., Gilpin, A., Peña, J., Sandholm, T.: Smoothing techniques for computing Nash equilibria of sequential games. Math. Oper. Res. **35**(2), 494–512 (2010)

21. Jackson, E.: Slumbot NL: solving large games with counterfactual regret minimization using sampling and distributed processing. In: AAAI Workshop on Computer Poker and Incomplete Information (2013)

22. Johanson, M., Burch, N., Valenzano, R., Bowling, M.: Evaluating state-space abstractions in extensive-form games. In: Proceedings of the International Conference on Autonomous Agents and Multi-Agent Systems (AAMAS) (2013)

23. Koller, D., Megiddo, N., von Stengel, B.: Fast algorithms for finding randomized strategies in game trees. In: Proceedings of the 26th ACM Symposium on Theory of Computing (STOC), pp. 750–760 (1994)

24. Moravčík, M., et al.: Deepstack: expert-level artificial intelligence in heads-up no-limit poker. Science **356**, 508–513 (2017)

25. Nash, J.: Equilibrium points in n-person games. Proc. Natl. Acad. Sci. **36**, 48–49 (1950)

26. Nash, J.: Non-cooperative games. Ann. Math. **54**, 289–295 (1951)

27. Rubinstein, A.: Settling the complexity of computing approximate two-player Nash equilibria. In: Proceedings of the Annual Symposium on Theory of Computing (STOC) (2017)

28. Selten, R.: Reexamination of the perfectness concept for equilibrium points in extensive games. Internat. J. Game Theory **4**, 25–55 (1975)

29. Shi, J., Littman, M.L.: Abstraction methods for game theoretic poker. In: Marsland, T., Frank, I. (eds.) CG 2000. LNCS, vol. 2063, pp. 333–345. Springer, Heidelberg (2001). https://doi.org/10.1007/3-540-45579-5_22

30. Waugh, K., Zinkevich, M., Johanson, M., Kan, M., Schnizlein, D., Bowling, M.: A practical use of imperfect recall. In: Proceedings of the Symposium on Abstraction, Reformulation and Approximation (SARA) (2009)

31. Zinkevich, M., Bowling, M., Johanson, M., Piccione, C.: Regret minimization in games with incomplete information. In: Proceedings of the Annual Conference on Neural Information Processing Systems (NIPS) (2007)

Does Cyber-Insurance Benefit the Insured or the Attacker? – A Game of Cyber-Insurance

Zhen Li[1] and Qi Liao[2](✉)

[1] Department of Economics and Management, Albion College, Albion, USA
zli@albion.edu
[2] Department of Computer Science, Central Michigan University,
Mount Pleasant, USA
liao1q@cmich.edu

Abstract. Cyber-insurance is an insurance policy that protects the insured from a variety of cybersecurity incidents such as cyber-attacks, ransomware, and data breaches. The rapid expansion of cyber-insurance in recent years hints the strong demand for cyber-insurance and its benefits. However, the impacts of cyber-insurance practice on cybersecurity enhancement and cyber-attackers are largely unknown. In this paper we study the optimal cybersecurity investment and cyber-insurance decision-making systematically with special attention paid to the effects of the attacker's strategies. The economic modeling analysis and simulation study suggest that although cyber-insurance may be beneficial for the insured from a financial perspective, cyber-insurance practice may not be optimal from the societal cybersecurity perspective. Purchasing cyber-insurance decreases organizations' optimal cybersecurity investment and increases the attacker's expected payoffs. Therefore, the attacker has a motive to manipulate cyber-insurance by selective cyber-attacks on organizations up to a critical point, beyond which we discovered that imposing further threat will force organizations to invest more in cybersecurity. The attacker is capable of "playing god" by controlling the probabilities of initiating cyber-attacks and acts strategically to influence organizations' incentives to whether to purchase cyber-insurance to harvest benefits. This study of cyber-insurance' effects on attackers and their strategic manipulation of cyber-insurance provides insights for the future of the cyber-insurance market.

Keywords: cyber-insurance · cybersecurity investment · attacker manipulation · economic modeling and analysis · pricing · game theory

J. Fu et al. (Eds.): GameSec 2023, LNCS 14167, pp. 23–42, 2023.
https://doi.org/10.1007/978-3-031-50670-3_2

1   Introduction

Organizations in nearly every industry deal with cyber risk on a daily basis, and the financial devastation of cyber-attacks is only growing. The cybersecurity risks and incidents confronting organizations provide incentives for organizations to invest in cybersecurity. Since cyber-insurance became an option over a decade ago, the number of organizations purchasing cyber-insurance has been rising.

Cyber-insurance is an insurance policy that provides the insured with a combination of coverage options to protect the insured from losses due to a variety of cyber incidents such as data breaches, ransomware, denial-of-service attacks, etc. Coverage may include the liability of lost data, the damage to technology assets, the cost of business disruptions, informing affected clients, paying ransoms, and expenses and costs associated with legal issues. Like any insurance product, cyber-insurance pools the risks of cyber-attacks among policyholders. While cyber-insurance does not fundamentally change the overall destruction that a cybersecurity incident can cause, it reduces the organization's out-of-pocket payment ("private loss") in case of such an incident. In other words, cyber-insurance is to mitigate the organization's financial risk exposure in the aftermath.

Cyber-insurance is still in its early stage and its effects on cybersecurity remain an open question. Unlike the established insurances (e.g., home, auto, health, etc.) where the odds of incidents are more of "act of god" (e.g., a lightening hitting a house), in the new cyber-insurance, the odds of cyber-incidents are more controllable by the attacker. In some senses, the attacker's action is like the "hand of god" that controls the chance of cyber incidents. Therefore, this research focuses on the attacker's perspective and asks questions such as "Is cyber-insurance really good for cybersecurity?", "Can attackers benefit from the practice of cyber-insurance?", etc. By modelling a game between the attacker and the organization, we study the optimal strategies of both parties. Using a cybersecurity portfolio that consists of both cybersecurity investment (infrastructures, technologies, etc.) and cyber-insurance, we formulate an optimization problem to derive the optimal choice for the organization to choose between additional cybersecurity investment and purchasing cyber-insurance or not.

The novelty of this research is that it aims to study the possibility of the attacker's manipulation of cyber-insurance in their own favors by measuring the optimal cybersecurity investment level of the organization with and without cyber-insurance. A key determinant is the cyber threat imposed on the organization by the attacker. The attacker's action affects the organization's incentives to purchase cyber-insurance. Depending on how cyber-insurance may affect the attacker's benefits, the attacker strategically chooses attack probability imposed on the organization.

The modeling analysis and simulation study suggest a decrease in the organization's optimal cybersecurity investment with cyber-insurance, and there is a significant increase in the attacker's expected payoffs as the organization shifts from no cyber-insurance to cyber-insurance. Beyond that point of switch, imposing further threat on the organization will force the organization to invest more in cybersecurity. In this scenario, the best response of the attacker is to impose just the right amount of cyber threat to "induce" the organization to purchase cyber-insurance. One of our important contributions is the finding of the critical point of attack probability for the organization switching to cyber-insurance therefore significantly increase attack payoff. To the best of our knowledge, this is the first study of the implications of cyber-insurance on the benefits of the attacker per se and the attacker's potential to manipulate the mechanism to serve their own best interests.

The rest of the paper is organized as follows. Section 2 reviews literatures on cyber-insurance. Section 3 conducts economic analysis on the organization's optimal cybersecurity investment with and without purchasing cyber-insurance, the organization's optimal cyber-insurance option, the effects of the organization's actions on the attacker, and the attacker's optimal strategy of launching attacks. Section 4 illustrates results from simulation study. Finally, Sect. 5 concludes our work and discusses future research.

2   Related Work

Compared to established lines of insurance services, cyber-insurance is at its early stage of development. Cyber-insurance is subject to not only general problems prevailing insurance markets like adverse selection and moral hazard [7], it is much more complicated and challenging than other lines of insurance. The cyber-insurance market is particularly complex as it has to tackle with challenges and obstacles prevailing in the insurance market such as the diversity of insurance coverage generating uncertainty and the moral hazard problem [22,32]. Without considering catastrophic scenarios, the vast majority of cyber risks are insurable and cyber-insurance can be profitable [12,19,21]. The insurers may offer not only cyber-insurance contracts but also risk management services [25]. Post-incident covering by cyber-insurance contracts is commonly seen [28]. It is generally agreed that cyber-insurance is effective at post-incident responses [18,25].

While cyber-insurance appears to be a viable method for cyber risk transfer, numerous problems with the insurability of cyber risks impede the development of the cyber-insurance market. Surveys and literature reviews classified researches on cyber-insurance into various areas, identified and categorized practical research problems and cyber-insurance challenges, provided the landscape and trends of the research and proposed possible solutions [1,6,28]. There are concerns about the insurance coverage, lack of information, and the complexity of the cyber-related claims [2]. Problems such as information asymmetries due to lack of data hinder cyber risk management via cyber-insurance [3,15]. A three-player game [27] implies attacks motivate the organizations to consider cyber-insurance option for transferring the risks. With malicious users present, equilibrium cyber-insurance contract that specifies user security fails to exist, and thus cyber-insurers fail to underwrite contracts conditioning the premiums on security in a general setting [8]. Recent empirical evidence suggests today's cyber-insurance market is not effectively exercising predicted governance functions on cybersecurity [33].

The effects of cyber-insurance on cybersecurity investment is an open question. Cyber-insurance could result in higher cybersecurity investment depending on the insurers' ability to deal with potential adverse selection, moral hazard, and other problems in the cyber-insurance market [12]. An insurance contract incentivizing the insured to adopt preventative measures and implement best practices can improve cybersecurity provided by premium discrimination and the design of customized policies [11,13,30]. Security interdependence affects the incentive of users to invest in self-protection with and without cyber-insurance [29]. The key to improving overall network security lies in incentivizing users to invest in sufficient self-defense investments despite of the possible free-riding on others' investing in the network. Under conditions of no information asymmetry between the insurer and the insured, cyber-insurance incentivizes users to invest in self-defense [5,16].

Nevertheless, in a model where a user's probability to incur cyber damage depends on both private security and network security, competitive cyber-insurers may fail to improve network security [24]. Modeling the reactivity of the attacker to cybersecurity investment as an endogenous risk generating mechanism, it was shown that cyber-insurance may have negative effects on security investment [17]. Without contract discrimination, the cyber-insurance market equilibrium is inefficient and does not increase cybersecurity [13,14,20]. There is little empirical evidence that cyber-insurance gives motives for the insured to invest in cybersecurity [26,31]. A big challenge is the insurers' missing solid methodologies, standards, and tools to carry out their measurements [23]. A unifying framework was introduced considering interdependent security, correlated risk, and information asymmetries of cyber-insurance to understand the discrepancies [4]. A more recent study questions to what extent cyber-insurance companies influence global diffusion of cybersecurity protection and increase cybersecurity mechanisms [32]. To date, the cybersecurity implication of cyber-insurance remains a field of ambiguity.

Our research is related to existing literature on the incentive mechanisms of cyber-insurance but focuses on a novel angle. Based on the observation of cyber risk not being random and is largely in the control of the attacker, we have a particular interest in the attacker's attitude towards cyber-insurance, i.e., would the attacker welcome cyber-insurance? Since the attacker's likelihood of attack is a key determining factor of the organization's decision, the attacker can intentionally manipulate the whole system by adjusting their attack strategies in terms of attack probabilities to influence organizations' decision of purchasing cyber-insurance, thus benefit the most from the practice of cyber-insurance.

Shifting risks to the insurer or shifting liability on the insured to invest more is not enough for a successful cyber-insurance market. This paper considers a cybersecurity portfolio that consists of both optimal cybersecurity infrastructure investment and cyber-insurance purchase. By extending the Gordon-Loeb model [9,10], economic cost-benefit analysis determines the optimal amount of cybersecurity investment by taking into account the vulnerability of the organization to a security breach and its potential loss. Our model predicts the critical point (threshold) for the organization to shift from no insurance to insurance. Such a shift can benefit the attacker thus the attacker has the motive to push the organization to become insured. To generalize, no matter whether cyber-insurance has a positive or adverse overall effects on cybersecurity, the attacker can induce the organization to act in a way that is to the benefit of the attacker.

3   Game of Cyber-Insurance

There are two components of financial investment in cybersecurity portfolio: investment in fundamental cybersecurity infrastructure ("cybersecurity investment") and investment in cyber-insurance policy ("cyber-insurance"). The key difference between cybersecurity investment and cyber-insurance is that the former is preventive affecting the organization's fundamental vulnerability to cyber-attacks and the latter is aftermath coverage and clean-up, which by itself, does not affect the inherent vulnerability of the organization.

How much should the organization invest in cybersecurity? All in all, the organization is driven by the desire to earn profit, and its decisions are largely the result of cost-benefit analysis. We apply and extend economic production theory to the problem of assessing the impacts of cybersecurity investment and cyber-insurance. The production theory framework is based on the analysis of the relationship between cybersecurity inputs and output, or equivalently, costs and benefits. Table 1 lists the variables used in the model and their brief meanings.

Table 1. Symbols and Definitions

Symbol/Variable	Definition
C_s	cost of additional cybersecurity investment
C_i	cost of cyber-insurance (premium on cyber-insurance policy)
L_0	cyber incident loss without cyber-insurance
L_1	cyber incident loss with cyber-insurance (e.g., deductible)
t	attack probability
r	attack success rate at existing cybersecurity investment
$R(C_s, r)$	attack success rate with additional cybersecurity investment
P^a	attacker's payoff from a successful attack
C^a	attacker's cost of launching an attack

3.1 Inputs and Output of Cybersecurity Investment and Cyber-Insurance

We consider a one-period model of an organization contemplating a cybersecurity portfolio made up of cybersecurity investment and cyber-insurance. The organization is risk-neutral meaning that it is indifferent to amounts of investments or forms of investments as long as they have the same expected net value, regardless of various levels of risk and uncertainty.

Cybersecurity inputs include cybersecurity investment used to strengthen cybersecurity systems such as intrusion detection/prevention systems, firewalls, malware detection, antivirus and improved software, one time password tokens, two-factor authentications, encryptions, internal control systems, user education/training programs, etc. The organization's additional spending on cybersecurity investment is represented by C_s. In the context of cyber-insurance, cybersecurity inputs also include cyber-insurance policy premium, represented by C_i, had the organization chosen to purchase cyber-insurance.

Cybersecurity output is gauged by the reduced attack success rate generated by cybersecurity investment and the reduced incident loss private to the organization under the coverage of cyber-insurance. Following the Gordon-Loeb model [9], we measure the potential loss of cyber incident using triple variables $\{t, r, L_0\}$ where $t \in [0, 1]$ is the attack probability that the attacker may launch an attack on the organization, $r \in [0, 1]$ is the attack success rate at existing cybersecurity investment, and L_0 is the incident loss of a successful attack.

Specifically, the parameter r is used to denote the attack success rate at existing cybersecurity investment, the probability that without additional cybersecurity investment, a cyber attack will result in the organization's being victim of the attack and the loss L_0 occurring. Typically, the attack probability on the organization and the attack success rate would lie in the interior of $0 < t < 1$ and $0 < r < 1$. $t \times r \times L_0$ is the organization's expected loss conditioned on neither no additional cybersecurity investment nor cyber-insurance coverage. The organization's cybersecurity investment decision is on incremental investment spending, based on the implicit assumption that the organization already has some cybersecurity infrastructure in place, resulting in existing current attack success rate. Therefore, there are no incremental fixed costs associated with additional cybersecurity investment, only variable costs.

The expenditure of C_s is to reduce attack success rate r. Let $R(C_s, r)$ be the attack success rate on the organization that has additional investment amount of C_s. $R(C_s, r)$ is continuously twice differentiable. The nature of cyber vulnerability leads to the following features of the R function:

- $R(C_s, 0) = 0$ for all C_s. That is, if the organization is perfectly secure, then it will remain perfectly secure regardless of additional cybersecurity investment.
- $R(0, r) = r$ for all r. That is, if there is no additional cybersecurity investment, attack success rate remains unchanged.
- $R'(C_s, r) < 0$ and $R''(C_s, r) > 0$ for all $r \in (0, 1)$ where R' and R'' denote the first-order and second-order partial derivatives of the R function with

respect to C_s, respectively. That is, cybersecurity is increasing in cybersecurity investment at a decreasing rate.

The third feature of the R function implies that no finite cybersecurity investment can make the organization perfectly secure.

Cyber-insurance is specifically designed to address cyber-incident-related losses. Being insured does not reduce incident loss, but it may significantly decrease the organization's private loss in case of incident. The organization has to pay a premium to be insured. Due to moral hazard concerns, insurance policies normally come with deductibles. The premium and the deductible are the inputs of cyber-insurance.

Purchasing cyber-insurance does not change the incident loss L_0. Acquiring cyber-insurance does not increase or decrease the attack success rate, either. That is, r (and hence $R(C_s, r)$) is independent of C_i. The expenditure of C_i is to reduce the organization's private loss of incident. Suppose cyber-insurance reduces the organization's private loss from L_0 to L_1. L_1 includes the deductible and the part of incident loss not covered by cyber-insurance. It can also be extended to include the net present value of expected future increase in premiums.

The organization can affect the attack success rate via cybersecurity investment and expected private loss via cybersecurity investment and cyber-insurance, but the organization cannot invest to reduce attack probability. Hence attack probability t is exogenous to the organization, which is the control variable of the attacker. The organization decides on cybersecurity investment and cyber-insurance to reduce the expected net loss private to the organization.

3.2   Organization's Strategy

To determine the amount to invest in cybersecurity and cyber-insurance, the organization compares the expected benefits and expected costs of the two.

Choose Optimal Cybersecurity Investment Without Cyber-Insurance. For comparison, we begin with the case when cyber-insurance is not an option yet, i.e., $C_i \equiv 0$. The expected benefit of cybersecurity investment is equal to the reduction in the organization's expected loss attributed to additional cybersecurity investment.

$$[r - R(C_s, r)]tL_0 \tag{1}$$

Since C_s is the cost of cybersecurity investment, the expected net benefit of cybersecurity investment is

$$[r - R(C_s, r)]tL_0 - C_s \tag{2}$$

Of variables in (2), t is the control variable of the attacker. r and L_0 are the given parameters specifying the existing status of cybersecurity of the organization. C_s is the only control variable of the organization. The risk-neutral organization's goal is to choose optimal additional cybersecurity investment C_s^* that maximizes (2).

C_s^* is found by solving the first-order condition of the objective function (2) with respect to C_s.

$$- R'(C_s^*, r)tL_0 = 1 \tag{3}$$

where the left-hand-side is the marginal benefit of cybersecurity investment measured by the decrease in attack success rate when increasing cybersecurity investment by one unit. This partial derivative can be interpreted as the marginal productivity of cybersecurity investment. The right-hand-side is the marginal cost of increasing cybersecurity investment by one unit.

Choose Optimal Cybersecurity Investment with Cyber-Insurance. When cyber-insurance is an option, the organization makes rational choice to determine if it needs cyber-insurance based on its own risk exposure. The insurer offers various combinations of premium and deductible to the organization, corresponding to the coverage and the attack success rate. In the one-period model, we assume the price of purchasing cyber-insurance depends on existing cybersecurity investment but not on the additional cybersecurity investment the organization will choose after purchasing cyber-insurance (which will affect future premium). Hence the organization's choice of cybersecurity investment (after being insured) does not affect the current premium, similar to a driver's current driving habits (after being insured) does not affect the current premium on the auto insurance policy.

The premium and the deductible are inversely related. The inverse relationship may apply to the following scenarios:

- The organization chooses a cyber-insurance policy that has a high deductible to reduce the premium, or a high premium to reduce the deductible.
- The organization pays a high premium on a cyber-insurance policy with broad coverage that reduces the organization's private loss in case of incident.

Cyber-insurance reduces the organization's private loss from L_0 to L_1. L_1 captures the deductible. Taking as given its chosen cyber-insurance package of $\{L_1, C_i\}$, the organization's expected benefit of additional cybersecurity investment with cyber-insurance is

$$[r - R(C_s, r)]tL_1 \tag{4}$$

The expected net benefit of additional cybersecurity investment with cyber-insurance is

$$[r - R(C_s, r)]tL_1 - C_s \tag{5}$$

The organization chooses optimal additional cybersecurity investment, C_s^{**}, to maximize (5):

$$- R'(C_s^{**}, r)tL_1 = 1 \tag{6}$$

Effects of Cyber-Insurance on Cybersecurity Investment. The optimal additional cybersecurity investment increases in attack probability as well as the organization's private loss.

From (3),

$$- R'(C_s^*, r) = \frac{1}{tL_0} \tag{7}$$

From (6),

$$- R'(C_s^{**}, r) = \frac{1}{tL_1} \tag{8}$$

If the organization were perfectly secure ($r = 0$), then no cybersecurity investment would be necessary ($C_s^* = C_s^{**} = 0$). At some sufficiently large attack success rate, it would be optimal to make positive additional cybersecurity investment.

Since R' is increasing in C_s and $L_0 > L_1$, optimal additional cybersecurity investment decreases when the organization has cyber-insurance coverage, i.e., $C_s^{**} < C_s^*$.

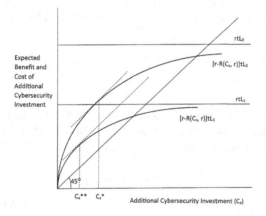

Fig. 1. Optimal additional cybersecurity investment with and without cyber-insurance.

Figure 1 illustrates the relative amounts of optimal additional cybersecurity investment. The horizontal axis is various levels of additional cybersecurity investment. The vertical axis measures expected benefits and costs of cybersecurity investment with and without cyber-insurance. The concave curves are for (1) and (4), respectively, of which, the lower curve is for (4). Both curves of expected benefits start from the origin at $R(0, r) = r$. They increase at a decreasing rate and converge to rtL_0 and rtL_1, respectively, as $C_s \to \infty$. The 45° line is the cost curve of cybersecurity investment. The vertical distance between the concave benefit curve and the linear cost curve is the expected net benefit, as in (2) and (5), and the corresponding level of cybersecurity investment is the optimal. Note the intersection of the expected benefit curve and the cost curve corresponds to the largest feasible additional cybersecurity investment. As long as cybersecurity investment stays below this amount, the organization's expected net benefit is positive. That is, it would receive a net benefit from additional cybersecurity investment. Nevertheless, the net benefit is maximized at an amount lower than the feasible upper-bound. As shown, the organization holding a cyber-insurance policy decreases additional cybersecurity investment.

The first-order conditions represented by (7) and (8) are applicable when the organization's optimal additional cybersecurity investment has an interior solution. In general, the organization chooses nonzero additional cybersecurity investment if and only if (2) or (5) is nonnegative. It is possible that the organization's optimal additional cybersecurity investment is zero in the following two scenarios.

- The organization is perfectly secure thus $R(C_s, 0) = 0$ for any C_s. Optimal additional cybersecurity investment is hence zero, the origin in Fig. 1.
- The organization's expected net benefit of additional cybersecurity investment is negative for any C_s, i.e., if the concave curve in Fig. 1 falls entirely below the $45°$ cost line. This could be the case if the organization has little expected private loss (i.e., attack probability is small and private loss is small) and/or cybersecurity investment is ineffective at reducing attack success rate (i.e., $R(C_s, r)$ is high).

Since $L_1 < L_0$, the latter scenario is more likely to occur with cyber-insurance.

Choose Optimal Cyber-Insurance. The cost of cyber-insurance is C_i and the expected benefit of being insured is $R(C_s^{**}, r)t(L_0 - L_1)$. The organization decides on cyber-insurance purchase to maximize expected net benefit of cyber-insurance.

$$R(C_s^{**}, r)t(L_0 - L_1(C_i)) - C_i \tag{9}$$

Recall C_i and L_1 are inversely related and C_s^{**} depends on L_1. If L_1 is continuously differentiable in C_i and the optimal cyber-insurance has an interior solution, the optimal cyber-insurance premium C_i^* solves the first-order condition of (9). If L_1 is not continuously differentiable in C_i, which is more likely to be the case, the organization would choose the optimal insurance package $\{L_1^*, C_i^*\}$ from available discrete cyber-insurance packages that generates the largest expected net benefit, i.e., $R(C_s^{**}(L_1^*), r)t(L_0 - L_1^*) - C_i^* \geq R(C_s^{**}(L_1), r)t(L_0 - L_1) - C_i$ for all $\{L_1, C_i\}$.

It is possible that the organization's optimal cyber-insurance does not have an interior solution. In general, the organization would not purchase cyber-insurance if the expected net benefit of cyber-insurance (9) is not positive. The organization's optimal cyber-insurance is zero in the following two scenarios.

- The organization is perfectly secure thus $R(C_s^{**}(L_1), 0) = 0$ for any L_1.
- The organization's expected net benefit of cyber-insurance is negative for any $\{L_1, C_i\}$. This could be the case if the organization has little expected

incident loss (i.e., attack probability is small and incident loss is small) and/or the cyber-insurance policy offered is unfavorable.

3.3   Attacker's Strategy

The attacker launches cyber-attacks to maximize expected net payoff:

$$\max_t R(C_s(t), r)tP^a - tC^a \tag{10}$$

where P^a is the attacker's payoff received from a successful attack and C^a is the cost of attack. For simplicity, assume the game between the organization and the attacker is zero sum, i.e., $L_0 = P^a$. Given t, the attacker's highest possible expected net payoff is $R(0, r)tL_0 - C^a = rtL_0 - C^a$. This is the default benchmark of zero additional cybersecurity investment with and without cyber-insurance. As C_s increases, the attacker's expected net payoff decreases since $R(C_s, r)$ is decreasing in C_s.

Attacking the organization is profitable as long as $R(C_s(t), r)L_0 > C^a$. The parameters characterizing the organization's attractiveness to the attacker are $R(C_s, r)$ and L_0. Whether the organization buys cyber-insurance does not affect L_0 that is either paid by the organization, the insurer, or both. $R(C_s, r)$ increases as C_s decreases. The organization's purchasing cyber-insurance is beneficial to the attacker if the organization reduces additional cybersecurity investment when insured. Such potential gain for the attacker can only be realized if the organization chooses to buy cyber-insurance.

From (9), the organization chooses to buy cyber-insurance if it faces a high attack probability and there exists a cyber-insurance bundle that satisfies

$$t \geq \frac{C_i}{R(C_s^{**}, r)(L_0 - L_1)} \tag{11}$$

where the right-hand side is the lowest attack probability making the organization willingness to buy cyber-insurance, which is decreasing in L_0. It implies that compared to small and medium-sized organizations, large organizations with high incident loss are more likely to buy cyber-insurance.

Buying cyber-insurance is beneficial for the organization when (11) holds true. Since t is a control variable of the attacker, the attacker can affect the organization's decision to buy cyber-insurance. When t increases, the organization is more likely to buy cyber-insurance, other things constant.

Nevertheless, other things are not constant. Although r and L_0 are exogenous and $\{L_1, C_i\}$ are predetermined, C_s increases with t, and hence R is decreasing in t. The attacker faces a tradeoff when raising the attack probability on the insured organization: an increase in t increases optimal additional cybersecurity investment, decreasing attack success rate and hence expected payoff while the increased t itself increases the expected payoff. The attacker has to control t strategically to generate a positive net gain.

With and without cyber-insurance, the attacker chooses t to solve (10). The first-order condition is

$$R'(C_s, r)\frac{dC_s}{dt}tL_0 + R(C_s, r)L_0 = C^a \tag{12}$$

Combined with (7) and (8), the attacker's optimal attack probability solves $\frac{dC_s^*}{dt} = R(C_s^*, r)L_0 - C^a$ without cyber-insurance, and $\frac{dC_s^{**}}{dt} = \frac{L_1}{L_0}(R(C_s^{**}, r)L_0 - C^a)$ with cyber-insurance.

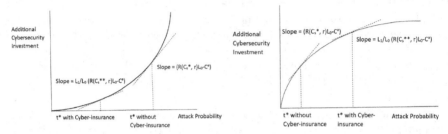

(a) Case I: Additional cybersecurity invest-ment is increasing in attack probability at an increasing rate

(b) Case II: Additional cybersecurity invest-ment is increasing in attack probability at a decreasing rate

Fig. 2. The attacker's optimal attack probability with and without cyber-insurance, depending on the organization's choice of additional cybersecurity investment in response to attacker's attack probability.

$L_1 < L_0$, $C_s^* > C_s^{**}$ and $R(C_s^*, r) < R(C_s^{**}, r)$. The relative size of $\frac{dC_s^*}{dt}$ and $\frac{dC_s^{**}}{dt}$ depends. Facing the tradeoff, how cyber-insurance affects the attacker's optimal attack probability depends on how cybersecurity investment responds to attack probability. Suppose $(R(C_s^*, r)L_0 - R(C_s^{**}, r)L_1) > C^a(1 - \frac{L_1}{L_0})$, thus $\frac{dC_s^*}{dt} > \frac{dC_s^{**}}{dt}$. If cybersecurity investment is increasing in attack probability at an increasing rate (Fig. 2a), the attacker shall decrease the attack probability on the insured organization. If cybersecurity investment is increasing in attack probability at a decreasing rate (Fig. 2b), the attacker shall increase the attack probability on the insured organization. $\frac{dC_s}{dt}$ measures the slope of the cybersecurity investment curve. It would be the opposite if $\frac{dC_s^*}{dt} < \frac{dC_s^{**}}{dt}$.

In summary, if the attacker holds constant attack probability, the introduction of cyber-insurance benefits the attacker by decreasing the organization's additional cybersecurity investment. The attacker may increase attack probability to "induce" the organization to become insured. If the organization is already insured, the attacker needs to choose the optimal attack probability strategically to maximize the attack payoff. In practice, the attacker often lacks the knowledge of which organization is insured. Thus, Case II in Fig. 2 is in favor of the attacker as it justifies the consistent strategy of increasing the attack probability regardless of whether the organization is insured or not. As counteracts, the organization shall consider the appropriate mechanism to adjust cybersecurity investment in response to the attacker's attack probability. It is also necessary to keep the purchase of cyber-insurance private information unreleased to the attacker.

4   Simulation Study

In this section, we conduct simulations to study the attacker's strategies and their impact on the organization's strategy of cybersecurity portfolio in terms of cybersecurity investment and cyber-insurance. In particular, we study the effects of attack probability on the organization's additional cybersecurity investment and on the attacker's expected payoffs with and without cyber-insurance.

The following function of attack success rate is used in simulations:

$$R(C_s, r) = \frac{r}{(\alpha C_s + 1)^\beta} \tag{13}$$

where $\alpha > 0$ and $\beta \geq 1$. $R(C_s, r)$ is decreasing in both α and β. Such a R function has a relatively simple functional form and satisfies all the three features the function shall have, as specified in Sect. 3.1. For illustration purpose and without loss of generality, we set the parameter values at $\alpha = 0.5$ and $\beta = 1.2$. The simulation results hold for all values of $\alpha > 0$ and $\beta \geq 1$.

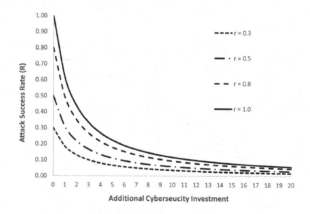

Fig. 3. Organization benefits from additional cybersecurity investment with decreasing attack success rate at a diminishing effect.

4.1   Attack Success Rate vs. Optimal Cybersecurity Investment with Cyber-Insurance

Figure 3 illustrates, given attack success rate at existing cybersecurity investment, how attack success rate changes with additional cybersecurity investment.

As shown, while attack success rate decreases with additional cybersecurity investment, additional cybersecurity investment cannot reduce attack success rate to zero. Recall r is the attack success rate at $C_s = 0$ and $R(0, r) = r$. Let additional cybersecurity investment ranges between 0 and 20, $R(C_s, r)$ decreases when C_s increases, calculated using (13). Unless the organization is perfectly secure that does not require additional cybersecurity investment ($r = 0$), the organization that is vulnerable to cyber-threat benefits from additional cybersecurity investment. However, the organization cannot be 100% secure with additional cybersecurity investment.

The marginal effect of cybersecurity investment can be found by solving for the partial derivative of (13) with respect to C_s,

$$R'(C_s, r) = -\beta\alpha r(\alpha C_s + 1)^{-1-\beta} \tag{14}$$

Combining (7) and (8) with (14), we find optimal additional cybersecurity investment without and with cyber-insurance.

$$C_s^* = \frac{(\alpha\beta rtL_0)^{\frac{1}{1+\beta}} - 1}{\alpha} \tag{15}$$

$$C_s^{**} = \frac{(\alpha\beta rtL_1)^{\frac{1}{1+\beta}} - 1}{\alpha} \tag{16}$$

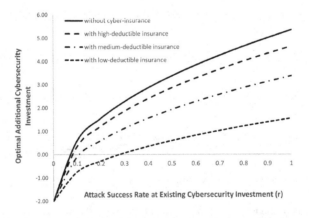

Fig. 4. While optimal additional cybersecurity investment (insured or not) increases when attack success rate (at existing cybersecurity investment) rises, cyber-insurance actually reduces optimal cybersecurity investment and increases the critical point (threshold) of cybersecurity investment. Organizations will not invest in additional cybersecurity below the critical point.

Figure 4 illustrates the organization's optimal additional cybersecurity investment given attack success rate at existing cybersecurity investment. Set $t = 0.3$

and $L_0 = 100$, three scenarios of private loss with cyber-insurance ($L_1 = 80$, $L_1 = 50$, and $L_1 = 20$) are considered. The horizontal axis measures attack success rate at existing cybersecurity investment. The vertical axis is the organization's optimal additional cybersecurity investment. The intersection of any curve and the horizontal axis is the *critical point* or *threshold* of attack success rate at existing cybersecurity investment that the organization would choose to invest more in cybersecurity.

The organization will not choose additional cybersecurity investment ($C_s = 0$) if the attack success rate is below the critical point. From (15) and (16), the optimal additional cybersecurity investment equals zero until $r = \frac{1}{\alpha\beta t L_0}$ without cyber-insurance and $r = \frac{1}{\alpha\beta t L_1}$ with cyber-insurance. At the specified parameters, the former is 0.056 and the latter is 0.07, 0.11 and 0.28, at $L_1 = 80$, $L_1 = 50$, and $L_1 = 20$, respectively. As private loss decreases, the organization's willingness to invest in cybersecurity decreases.

Key observations from Fig. 4 include: 1) As attack success rate increases, optimal additional cybersecurity investment increases, insured or not; 2) Being insured decreases optimal additional cybersecurity investment. The decrease is increasing in the coverage of cyber-insurance; 3) Being insured increases the critical point (threshold) of additional cybersecurity investment. The threshold is increasing in the coverage of cyber-insurance.

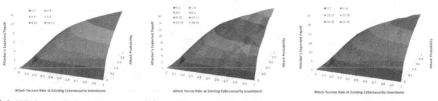

(a) Without Cyber-Insurance   (b) With High-deductible Cyber-insurance   (c) With Low-Deductible Cyber-insurance

Fig. 5. The attacker's expected payoff grows from having no cyber-insurance (a) to having cyber-insurance (b and c)

4.2. Attacker's Expected Net Payoff

To study the effects of cyber-insurance on the attacker's expected payoff, we adopt a simplified "high deductible + low premium" + "low deductible + high premium" pricing model: Policy A with a bundle of $\{L_1 = 50, C_i = 3\}$ and Policy B with a bundle of $\{L_1 = 20, C_i = 7\}$. Figure 5 compares the attacker's expected payoff in three scenarios: without cyber-insurance, with cyber-insurance of high deductible (Policy A) and with cyber-insurance of low deductible (Policy B). The attacker's cost function is largely composed of fixed or sunk cost in acquiring knowledge and malware to launch attacks. The additional cost occurred on attacking one more target is small. Moreover, the fixed cost of attack is the same with and without cyber-insurance. It is canceled out for comparison purpose. As shown in the figure, the peak payoff increases from range 10–12 (5a) to range 14–16 (5b), then to range 25–30 (5c). The results suggest that the attacker benefits from the organization's purchasing cyber-insurance and benefits further if the organization chooses cyber-insurance with low deductible.

4.3   Attack Strategy

For cyber-insurance, the organization chooses to purchase a policy bundle $\{L_1, C_i\}$ if

$$R(C_s^{**}, r)t(L_0 - L_1) \geq C_i \tag{17}$$

From (13),

$$R(C_s^{**}, r) = \frac{r}{(\alpha C_s^{**} + 1)^\beta} \tag{18}$$

Combined with (16),

$$R(C_s^{**}, r) = \frac{r}{(\alpha \beta r t L_1)^{\frac{\beta}{1+\beta}}} \tag{19}$$

Combined with (17), we can find that an insurance policy $\{L_1, C_i\}$ is beneficial to the organization facing attack probability

$$t \geq \{\frac{C_i(\alpha \beta r L_1)^{\frac{\beta}{1+\beta}}}{r(L_0 - L_1)}\}^{1+\beta} \tag{20}$$

where the right-hand side is the critical point (threshold) that the attacker may choose to trigger the organization to buy cyber-insurance.

Note (20) also provides insights on the role of parameters' configuration on organization's choice of cyber insurance and the attacker's best response. The condition would fail when the right-hand term is larger than one that could occur at $C_i(\alpha \beta r L_1)^{\frac{\beta}{1+\beta}} > r(L_0 - L_1)$, in which case, the organization would not choose cyber insurance regardless of the attacker's strategy. The cyber-insurance-policy specifications $\{L_1, C_i\}$ are among the key variables determining the value of the right-hand term. In a way, the attacker and the insurer may have aligned interests to make the organization choose cyber insurance, hence the efforts of insurance companies to promote cyber insurance can serve the purposes of cyber attackers.

Figure 6 shows the critical point (threshold) of attack probability at various attack success rate at existing cybersecurity investment and various available cyber-insurance policy options. The organization will not buy cyber-insurance if the attack probability is below the threshold. The threshold attack probability decreases if the organization is more vulnerable to cyber attacks (higher attack success rate). In the case the calculated threshold attack probability is above 1, the organization does not buy cyber-insurance regardless.

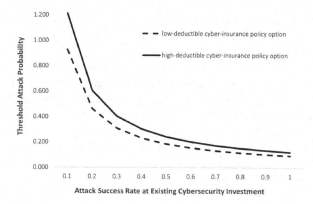

Fig. 6. If the attack probability is below the critical point (threshold), the organization will not buy cyber-insurance. The attacker may strategically choose an attack probability that will trigger the organization to buy cyber-insurance that benefits the attacker.

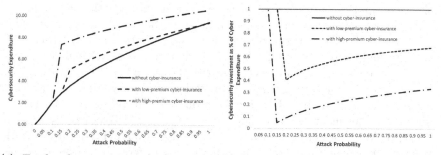

(a) Total cybersecurity expenditure rises sharply at the critical point

(b) Share of cybersecurity investment drops sharply at the critical point

Fig. 7. Manipulating attack probabilities may significantly increase organization's total cybersecurity expenditure through purchasing cyber-insurance at the critical point. The share of cybersecurity investment may also be decreased significantly at the critical point of attack probability due to purchasing cyber-insurance and bounces back gradually after being insured.

4.4   Cybersecurity Portfolio

Lastly, we simulate how the organization's cybersecurity portfolio in terms of total expenditure on both cybersecurity investment and cyber-insurance is affected by the attacker's actions. Without cyber-insurance, the organization's spending on cybersecurity investment is C_s^* as in (15). When the organization buys cyber-insurance, its total expenditure is $C_s^{**} + C_i^*$.

Figure 7a illustrates how the organization's total cybersecurity expenditure changes with attack probability. Total cybersecurity expenditure increases regardless, indicating an increased spending on cybersecurity when the organization faces increased attack probability. At the parameters used in the simulations, especially the significant premium compared to optimal additional cybersecurity investment, total cybersecurity expenditure increases sharply at the critical point after buying cyber-insurance.

Figure 7b is cybersecurity investment as a fraction of the total expenditure. The share of cybersecurity investment falls sharply at the critical point when the organization buys cyber-insurance and the share bounces back as the organization increases cybersecurity investment at increasing attack probability. Empowered with the critical point (threshold), the attacker may manipulate attack probability to trigger the organization to buy cyber-insurance thus significantly increase the attacker's expected payoffs.

5   Conclusion

While more and more organizations adopt cyber-insurance, the effects of cyber-insurance on cybersecurity remains unclear. This research study focuses on a novel angle and sheds light on the overlooked issue of the effects of cyber-insurance from the attacker's perspective, and studies whether the attacker may manipulate and ultimately benefit from the cyber-insurance practice. Our research models a game between the attacker, whose strategy is to control attack probability, and the organization, whose strategy is to choose optimal cybersecurity portfolio consisting of both cybersecurity investment and cyber-insurance. The economic modeling analysis and simulation study suggest that although cyber-insurance may be beneficial for the insured organization from a financial perspective, cyber-insurance may not always be the best from the cybersecurity perspective. Especially, the attacker may benefit from cyber-insurance with higher expected payoff from increased attack success rate resulting from the organization's reduced optimal security investment. This paper contributes further by identifying the critical point (threshold) of such attack probability for organizations to switch to cyber-insurance practice, therefore significantly increase the cyber attack payoffs. In the future we plan to focus on the extension and the application of the model. For example, the details of cyber insurance policies will be explored by relating the premiums and deductibles to the risks. Self insurance may be included as an alternative in addition to prevention/mitigation and market insurance. Our future work will also study how the development of the cyber-insurance market shall take into account the implications of the market to the attacker and the counteracts to prevent the possible manipulation of the market by the attacker.

References

1. Aziz, B.: A systematic literature review of cyber insurance challenges. In: Proceedings of International Conference on Information Technology Systems and Innovation (ICITSI), Bandung, Indonesia, pp. 357–363 (2020)
2. Bandyopadhyay, T., Mookerjee, V.: A model to analyze the challenge of using cyber insurance. Inf. Syst. Front. **21**, 301–325 (2019)

3. Bandyopadhyay, T., Mookerjee, V.S., Rao, R.C.: Why IT managers don't go for cyber-insurance products. Commun. ACM **52**(11), 68–73 (2009)
4. Böhme, R., Schwartz, G.: Modeling cyber-insurance: towards a unifying framework. In: Proceedings of the 9th Workshop on the Economics of Information Security (WEIS), Cambridge, MA (2010)
5. Bolot, J.C., Lelarge, M.: Cyber insurance as an incentive for internet security. In: Proceedings of Workshop on the Economics of Information Security (WEIS), Hanover, NH, pp. 269–290 (2008)
6. Dambra, S., Bilge, L., Balzarotti, D.: SoK: cyber insurance - technical challenges and a system security roadmap. In: Proceedings of IEEE Symposium on Security and Privacy (SP), San Francisco, CA, pp. 1367–1383 (2020)
7. Ehrlich, I., Becker, G.S.: Market insurance, self-insurance, and self-protection. J. Polit. Econ. **80**(4), 623–648 (1972)
8. Schwartz, G., Shetty, N., Walrand, J.: Why cyber-insurance contracts fail to reflect cyber-risks. In: Proceedings of 51st Annual Allerton Conference on Communication, Control, and Computing (Allerton), Monticello, IL, pp. 781–787 (2013)
9. Gordon, L.A., Loeb, M.P.: The economics of information security investment. ACM Trans. Inf. Syst. Secur. **5**(4), 438–457 (2002)
10. Gordon, L.A., Loeb, M.P., Lucyshyn, W., Zhou, L.: Increasing cybersecurity investments in private sector firms. J. Cybersecur. **1**(1), 3–17 (2015)
11. Hayel, Y., Zhu, Q.: Attack-aware cyber insurance for risk sharing in computer networks. In: Proceedings of the sixth International Conference on Decision and Game Theory for Security (GameSec), London, UK, pp. 22–34 (2015)
12. Kesan, J.P., Majuca, R.P., Yurcik, W.: Cyber-insurance as a market-based solution to the problem of cybersecurity. In: Proceedings of the 4th Workshop on the Economics of Information Security (WEIS), Cambridge, MA (2005)
13. Khalili, M.M., Naghizadeh, P., Liu, M.: Designing cyber insurance policies: the role of pre-screening and security interdependence. IEEE Trans. Inf. Forensics Secur. **13**(9), 2226–2239 (2018)
14. Khalili, M.M., Zhang, X., Liu, M.: Effective premium discrimination for designing cyber insurance policies with rare losses. In: Proceedings of the 10th International Conference on Decision and Game Theory for Security (GameSec), Stockholm, Sweden, pp. 259–275 (2019)
15. Laszka, A., Panaousis, E., Grossklags, J.: Cyber-insurance as a signaling game: self-reporting and external security audits. In: Proceedings of the 9th Conference on Decision and Game Theory for Security (GameSec), Seattle, WA, pp. 508–520 (2018)
16. Lelarge, M., Bolot, J.C.: Economic incentives to increase security in the internet: the case for insurance. In: Proceedings of IEEE International Conference on Computer Communications (INFOCOM), Rio de Janeiro, Brazil, pp. 1494–1502 (2009)
17. Massaccia, F., Swierzbinskic, J., Williams, J.: Cyberinsurance and public policy: self-protection and insurance with endogenous adversaries. In: Proceedings of 16th Annual Workshop on the Economics of Information Security (WEIS), La Jolla, CA, pp. 1–38 (2017)
18. Nurse, J.R., Axon, L., Erola, A., Agrafiotis, I., Goldsmith, M., Creese, S.: The data that drives cyber insurance: a study into the underwriting and claims processes. In: Proceedings of 2020 International Conference on Cyber Situational Awareness, Data Analytics and Assessment (CyberSA), Dublin, Ireland, pp. 1–8. (2020)
19. Pal, R., Golubchik, L., Psounis, K.: Aegis - a novel cyber-insurance model. In: Proceedings of Conference on Decision and Game Theory for Security (GameSec), College Park, Maryland, pp. 131–150 (2011)

20. Pal, R., Golubchik, L., Psounis, K., Hui, P.: Will cyber-insurance improve network security? A market analysis. In: Proceedings of IEEE Conference on Computer Communications (INFOCOM), Toronto, Canada, pp. 235–243 (2014)
21. Pal, R., Golubchik, L., Psounis, K., Hui, P.: The technologization of insurance: an empirical analysis of big data and artificial intelligence's impact on cybersecurity and privacy. ACM SIGMETRICS Perform. Eval. Rev. **45**(4), 7–15 (2018)
22. Panda, S., Woods, D.W., Laszka, A., Fielder, A., Panaousis, E.: Post-incident audits on cyber insurance discounts. Comput. Secur. **87**, 101593 (2019)
23. Romanosky, S., Ablon, L., Kuehn, A., Jones, T.: Content analysis of cyber insurance policies: how do carriers price cyber risk? J. Cybersecur. **5**(1), 1–19 (2019)
24. Shetty, N., Schwartz, G., Walrand, J.: Can competitive insurers improve network security? In: Proceedings of the Third International Conference on Trust and Trustworthy Computing (TRUST), Berlin, Germany, pp. 308–322 (2010)
25. Talesh, S.A.: Data breach, privacy, and cyber insurance: how insurance companies act as "compliance managers" for businesses. Law Soc. Inquiry **43**(2), 417–440 (2018)
26. Talesh, S.A., Cunningham, B.: The technologization of insurance: an empirical analysis of big data and artificial intelligence's impact on cybersecurity and privacy. Utah Law Rev. **2021**(5), 967–1027 (2021)
27. Tosh, D.K., et al.: Three layer game theoretic decision framework for cyber-investment and cyber-insurance. In: Proceedings of the 8th International Conference on Decision and Game Theory for Security (GameSec), Vienna, Austria, pp. 519–532 (2017)
28. Tsohou, A., Diamantopoulou, V., Gritzalis, S., Lambrinoudakis, C.: Cyber insurance: state of the art, trends and future directions. Int. J. Inf. Secur. 1–12 (2023)
29. Uuganbayar, G., Yautsiukhin, A., Martinelli, F.: Cyber insurance and security interdependence: friends or foes? In: Proceedings of 2018 International Conference on Cyber Situational Awareness, Data Analytics and Assessment (Cyber SA), Glasgow, UK, pp. 1–4 (2018)
30. Uuganbayar, G., Yautsiukhin, A., Martinelli, F., Massacci, F.: Optimisation of cyber insurance coverage with selection of cost effective security controls. Comput. Secur. **101**(102121), 1–21 (2021)
31. Wolff, J.: Cyberinsurance Policy: Rethinking Risk in an Age of Ransomware, Computer Fraud, Data Breaches, and Cyberattacks. The MIT Press, Cambridge (2022)
32. Woods, D.W., Böhme, R.: How cyber insurance shapes incident response: a mixed methods study. In: Proceedings of the 20th Annual Workshop on the Economics of Information Security (WEIS), pp. 1–35 (2021)
33. Woods, D.W., Moore, T.: Does insurance have a future in governing cybersecurity? IEEE Secur. Priv. **18**(1), 21–27 (2020)

Rule Enforcing Through Ordering

David Sychrovsky[1]([⊠])[iD], Sameer Desai[2][iD], and Martin Loebl[1][iD]

[1] Charles University, Prague, Czechia
{sychrovsky,loebl}@kam.mff.cuni.cz
[2] University of Passau, Passau, Germany

Abstract. In many real world situations, like minor traffic offenses in big cities, a central authority is tasked with periodic administering punishments to a large number of individuals. Common practice is to give each individual a chance to suffer a smaller *fine* and be guaranteed to avoid the legal process with probable considerably larger punishment. However, thanks to the large number of offenders and a limited capacity of the central authority, the individual risk is typically small and a rational individual will *not* choose to pay the fine. Here we show that if the central authority processes the offenders in a publicly known order, it properly incentives the offenders to pay the fine. We show analytically and on realistic experiments that our mechanism promotes non-cooperation and incentives individuals to pay. Moreover, the same holds for an arbitrary coalition. We quantify the expected total payment the central authority receives, and show it increases considerably.

Keywords: rule enforcing · mechanism design · non-cooperation

1 Introduction

In this work, we study a special case of a classic dilemma, how to effectively enforce a rule in a large population with only a very small number of enforcing agents. This task is impossible if the large population cooperates and thus a critical aspect of any suggested mechanism is the promotion of non-cooperation. A well-known count Dracula way is to make the punishment for breaking the rule extremely severe. We suggest an alternative mechanism, for a special case of the dilemma motivated by collecting fines for traffic violations.

In many large cities, there is a huge number of traffic offences, highly exceeding the capacity of state employees assigned to manage them. The assigned state employees should primarily concentrate on serious and repetitive offenders. However, a large number of minor offences are still to be settled which makes the former considerably harder. A common practise is that a smaller *fine* is assigned

This work has been supported by the CoSP, project n. 823748 H202-MSCA-RISE-2018. Computational resources were supplied by the project e-Infrastruktura CZ (e-INFRA CZ LM2018140) supported by the Ministry of Education, Youth and Sports of the Czech Republic.

J. Fu et al. (Eds.): GameSec 2023, LNCS 14167, pp. 43–62, 2023.
https://doi.org/10.1007/978-3-031-50670-3_3

in an almost automated way and if an offender settles this fine then the legal process does not start. Otherwise, the legal process should start with considerably larger cost for the offender. The offence is also forgotten after a certain *judiciary period*.

However, thanks to the limited capacity of state employees, legal processes for non-repetitive minor traffic offenses are typically enforced in a small number of cases[1]. The individual risk is thus small and a large fraction of the offenders *choose* to ignore the fine. In this paper, we propose a simple mechanism which properly incentives the offenders to pay the fine even under these conditions.

1.1   Main Contribution

In our proposed mechanism, the central authority processes the offenders in a given order. Each offender is aware of his position in this 'queue of offenders' and has the option of publicly donating money to a fund of traffic infrastructure or a charity predetermined by the central authority. If their total donations amount to at least the fine, it is used to settle the offence. After the judiciary period expires, or if the legal process is started, the fund retains the individual donation. The central authority periodically sorts offenders in ascending order of their average donation, and starts the legal process with those who paid the least on average.

Compared to processing the offenders in random order, this mechanism increases the individual risk of some offenders. This incentives them to pay the fine, which in turn puts others in danger. We show both analytically and on realistic experiments that under the proposed mechanism, the strategic behaviour of the offenders is to engage with the mechanism, and quantify the expected revenue of the charity. Moreover, we show it is not beneficial for any group of offenders to ignore the mechanism and share the cost of those who enter the legal process. Finally, we study how the central authority can most efficiently use its limited capacity to maximize the revenue of the charity.

This paper is a continuation of [1], where the authors introduced the model studied here. We extend their work by providing a complete solution to w-Fines, see Sect. 3, as well as producing more thorough numerical experiments.

1.2   Related Work

To our best knowledge, the field of non-cooperative mechanism design has not been studied extensively yet. Our approach is somewhat similar to that of [2], where the authors consider a variation of the elimination game which includes bids. Our model can also be viewed as a generalization of the stopping games [3], where participants choose a time to stop bidding and trade off their gain from outlasting other players for the cost accumulated over time in the game. In our case, the "prize" won by the lowest paying participant is cost of entering the

---

[1] For instance, in the city of Prague considerably more than 100 000 such offenses are dismissed every year because the judiciary period expires.

legal process. However, both approaches did not consider the ranking of players, which is at the core of our mechanism.

2 Problem Definition

Informally, we model the interaction of agents as a game we call *Queue*. Queue consists of a finite sequence of *Round*, in which each agent can choose to pay, however with some probability they forget and pay nothing. Those who paid at least the fine in total, or spent enough time in Queue are removed. The rest is ordered according to the amount they paid on average. A fixed number of those at the start are then forced to pay a large penalty, and leave Queue. Let us now define the interaction formally, starting with how Round is realized.

2.1 Round: One Step in Queue

Round is a parametric game $\mathbb{O}\,(\mathcal{N}) = \mathbb{O}(\mathcal{N}, F, Q, T, k, p)$, where $\mathcal{N}$ is an ordered subset of agents[2], $F \in \mathbb{N}$ is the fine, $Q > F$ is the cost associated with entering the legal process, $T \in \mathbb{N}$ is the judiciary period, i.e., the number of Round instances after which agents are removed, $k \in \mathbb{N}$ is the number of agents forced to pay Q in each Round, $p \in [0, 1]$ is the probability of ignorance.

Each $a \in \mathcal{N}$ is characterized by a triplet (n_a, t_a, m_a) and his strategy π_a. The triplet corresponds to his *observations*—his position n_a in $\mathcal{N}$, the number t_a of past Round games he participated in[3], and his total individual payment m_a in the past Round games.

Round proceeds in three phases

1. Each agent $a \in \mathcal{N}$, based on his observation, declares his strategy for this Round $\pi_a \in \Delta^{F+1}$, where Δ is the probability simplex. His payment μ_a is then sampled from[4]

$$\mu_a \sim p\sigma^0 + (1 - p)\pi_a(n_a, t_a, m_a), \tag{1}$$

where σ^ν is the pure strategy of paying ν.
2. Each agent's total payment and time is updated

$$m_a \leftarrow m_a + \mu_a, \tag{2}$$
$$t_a \leftarrow t_a + 1, \tag{3}$$

and $\mathcal{N}$ is sorted[5] according to the ratio of current total payment and time m_a/t_a.

---

[2] The agents are ordered according to their average payment in ascending order, i.e. those who paid the least on average are sorted to the front of $\mathcal{N}$.

[3] This includes the current Round, i.e. $t_a \geq 1$.

[4] This simulates that with probability p, the agent forgot to act in this Round.

[5] We use stable sort, i.e. whenever there is a tie, the original order is preserved.

3. Some agents are removed from $\mathcal{N}$, which is done in three sub-phases. We call such agents *terminal* and denote the set of terminal agents in this Round as $\mathcal{T}$.
   (a) All agents $a \in \mathcal{N}$ with $m_a \geq F$ are removed.
   (b) First k agents in $\mathcal{N}$ have their m_a increased by Q and are removed.
   (c) All agents $a \in \mathcal{N}$ with $t_a \geq T$ are removed.

The result of each Round is the ordered set of agents $\mathcal{N} \setminus \mathcal{T}$, and the set of terminal agents $\mathcal{T}$. Only the terminal agents are assigned their final utility.

Definition 1 (Utility). *The utility of each agent $a \in \mathcal{T}$ is the negative amount he paid*

$$u_a = -m_a. \tag{4}$$

2.2   Queue: A Game on Updating Sequences

Formally, Queue is $\mathbb{G} = \mathbb{G}(F, Q, T, k, p, x, x_0, w)$, where F, Q, T, k and p have the same meaning as in Sect. 2.1, x is the number of entering agents after each Round, x_0 is the initial size of $\mathcal{N}$ and w is the horizon, i.e. the number of repetitions of Round.

Queue aggregates Round in the following two simple phases. Starting with $\mathcal{N}^1$ s.t. $|\mathcal{N}^1| = x_0$, and $m_a, t_a = 1$ for each $a \in \mathcal{N}^1$. We repeat them w-times.

1. The agents in $\mathcal{N}^t$ play Round and non-terminal agents proceed to the next iteration.

$$\mathcal{N}^{t+1}, \mathcal{T}^{t+1} \leftarrow \mathbb{O}(\mathcal{N}^t). \tag{5}$$

2. x new agents enter the game

$$\mathcal{N}^{t+1} \leftarrow \mathcal{N}^t \cup X, \tag{6}$$

where X is a set of agents with $m_a, t_a = 0$, and $|X| = x$. These new agents are sorted to the end of $\mathcal{N}^{t+1}$.

In the last Round, all agents terminate, $\mathcal{T}^w \leftarrow \mathcal{T}^w \cup \mathcal{N}^w$.

The new agents come from universum U. The strategy of all agents is then given as $\pi = \times_{a \in U} \pi_a$. We denote space of all such strategies as Π.

Each agents wants to choose strategy π_a, which maximizes their utility in $\mathbb{G}$ given strategies of other agents π_{-a}. A strategy profile $\pi \in \Pi$ is an equilibrium, if no agent can increase his utility. Formally,

Definition 2 (ϵ-Equilibrium). $\pi \in \Pi$ *is an ϵ-equilibrium of $\mathbb{G}$ if $\forall \bar{\pi} \in \Pi$, $\forall t \in \{1, \ldots w\}$ and $\forall a \in \mathcal{T}^t$,*

$$\mathbb{E}_\pi [u_a(\pi)] \geq \mathbb{E}_{(\bar{\pi}_a \pi_{-a})} [u_a(\bar{\pi}_a, \pi_{-a})] - \epsilon. \tag{7}$$

We note that the equilibrium always exists which can be shown by a standard transformation to a normal form game.

2.3   Avalanche Effect

Intuitively, every agent wants to pay as little as possible, while avoiding paying Q. This translate to paying more than the others. However, if all agents adapt this reasoning, the only option to avoid paying Q is to pay F. We formally show this in Sect. 3.1.

Crucially, not all other agents can use this reasoning thanks to the probability of ignorance. But as that vanishes, the agents should be incentivised to pay more. Similarly, if the number of entering agents increases, so should the total payment. We formally capture this in the *avalanche effect*.

Definition 3 (Avalanche effect). *We say that Queue exhibits the* avalanche effect *if at least one of the following holds in equilibrium when changing p, or x.*

1. *The expected terminal payment of all agents is increasing with $p \to 0^+$*

$$\lim_{p \to 0^+} \frac{\mathrm{d}}{\mathrm{d}p} \sum_{a \in T} m_a < 0. \tag{8}$$

2. *The expected terminal payment of all agents decreases slower than $1/x$*

$$\frac{\mathrm{d}}{\mathrm{d}x} \sum_{a \in T} m_a > 0, \quad \forall x > 0. \tag{9}$$

2.4   Division Problem

In our model, the judiciary period is split into T equal time intervals and sorted at the start of each interval. The central authority can process kT offenders over the judiciary period, and xT will enter the system.

The central authority can influence the system in two ways.

1. it can choose how often the sorting takes place, and
2. it can virtually split the entering offenders into g groups of size x/g, and process k/g offenders in each.

The *Division problem* is how to set T and g to maximize the expected revenue the central authority receives. We refer to the two cases as *Time-Division problem* and *Group-Division problem* respectively.

3   Analytic Solution

As described in Sect. 1, the individual risk when the central authority processes the agents in random order is typically small, i.e. $kQ/|\mathcal{N}| \ll F$. Each agent is also guaranteed to pay $kQ/|\mathcal{N}|$ if everyone cooperates and shares the costs of those entering the legal process. Let us begin by showing that this is not the case in our proposed system. That is, there is no coalition can benefit from choosing to pay nothing and share the cost of those forced to pay Q. In our setting, this is analogous to coalition proofness.

Proposition 1. *Let $\mathcal{A}$ be a set of agents using strategy $\pi_a = \sigma^0 \; \forall a \in \mathcal{A}$, and sharing the cost, i.e. their utility becomes*

$$\tilde{u}_a = -\frac{1}{|\mathcal{A}|} \sum_{i=1}^{w} \sum_{a \in \mathcal{A} \cap \mathcal{T}^i} m_a, \forall a \in \mathcal{A}.$$

If $\tilde{u}_a < 0$, then $\exists a' \in \mathcal{A}$ s.t. a' can deviate and increase his utility.

Proof. We split the proof into two parts according to how much an individual needs to contribute.

1. $0 > \tilde{u}_a > Q$: In this situation, not all agents of $\mathcal{A}$ were forced to pay Q. Consider the agent $a' \in \mathcal{N}$ who terminated last. Then, since a' paid zero, his original utility is zero and $\tilde{u}_a < u_a$. Therefore, a' would benefit from leaving the coalition $\mathcal{A}$.
2. $\tilde{u}_a = -Q$: In this case, all agents were forced to enter the legal process. Any $a \in \mathcal{A}$ would therefore benefit from paying the fine, since then his utility is $u_a = -F > -Q = \tilde{u}_a$.

While existence of an analytic solution of Queue remains an open question, we can find it in certain special cases.

3.1   Active Participants

Let us first focus on a situation when no agent forgets to participate in Round, i.e. $p = 0$. Then it is easy to see that $\pi_a = \sigma^F$ is unique equilibrium. Consider the first agent $a \in \mathcal{N}$ in the first Round, who chose to pay $\mu_a < F$. Then he is forced to pay Q, resulting to utility $u_a = -Q - \mu_a < -F$. Therefore, switching to paying F is beneficial and the strategy of paying $\mu_a < F$ is not an equilibrium. This means all agents will pay F in the first Round, and the situation thus repeat in the following Round.

3.2 w-Fines: Special Case of Queue

Let us focus on the system without the introduction of the option to donate a portion of the fine. Thus after scaling currency we can let $F = 1$, and there are only two pure strategies σ^0, σ^F the agents can take. If now $T = w$ and no agents are added after each Round $x = 0$, we call the game w-*Fines*.

Definition 4 (w- Fines). *We refer to reduced Queue*

$$\mathbb{F}(w, F, Q, k, p, x_0) = \mathbb{G}(F, Q, w, k, p, 0, x_0, w)$$

as w-Fines.

We begin by showing a crucial property of w-Fines.

Lemma 1. *In the w-Fines, the expected payment of $\forall a \in \mathcal{N}$ depends only on the actions of agents in front of a.*

Proof. If a pays zero, he remains in the Queue and is sorted in front of agents who were behind him. He is potentially forced to pay Q, depending on the actions of agents in front of him. If he pays $F = 1$, he is removed. In either case, the actions of agents behind a have no impact on his payment. $\qquad \square$

In each Round, $a \in \mathcal{N}$ has $n_a - 1$ agents in front of him. Due to the probability of ignorance, even if all the agents decide to pay, a can estimate the probability that at most $k - 1$ will forget. If that happens, a will be forced to pay Q in this Round. Formally,

Definition 5. *Let n be a positive integer. We denote by $\alpha(p, n, k)$ the probability that in $n - 1$ independent coin tosses with the head probability p, the number of heads is less than k.*

Since α will be important in the following discussion, we briefly mention some of its properties.

Lemma 2. *Let $k < np$, then $\alpha(p, n + 1, k) \leq e^{-\frac{(np-k)^2}{2np}}$.*

Proof. Let ξ_i denote the random variable such that

$$\xi_i = \begin{cases} 1 & \text{w.p. } p, \\ 0 & \text{otherwise,} \end{cases}$$

and $\xi^n = \sum_{i=1}^{n} \xi_i$. Thus, $\mathbb{E}[\xi_i] = p$ and $\mathbb{E}[\xi^n] = np$. As per the Chernoff bounds, $\mathbb{P}[\xi^n \leq (1 - \delta)np] \leq e^{\frac{-\delta^2 np}{2}}$, for all $0 < \delta < 1$. Thus $\alpha(p, n + 1, k) = \mathbb{P}[\xi^n \leq k] \leq e^{-\left(1-\frac{k}{np}\right)^2 np/2} = e^{-\frac{(np-k)^2}{2np}}$.

Proposition 2. *If $\alpha(p, n, k) \leq F/Q \leq \frac{1}{4}$ then $np > k$. Moreover for each positive integer w and large enough n, $\alpha(p, n, k) \geq \alpha(p, wn, wk)$.*

Proof. For $\gamma \sim B(n, p)$ if $p < 1 - \frac{1}{n}$, then $\frac{1}{4} < \Pr(\gamma \leq np)$ [4]. Therefore, when $\frac{1}{4} \geq \frac{F}{Q}$, then $k < np$. Further, we note that Lemma 2 is tight for large enough np. Hence, it suffices to prove the proposition for the upper bound $e^{-\frac{(np-k)^2}{2np}}$ for which the statement clearly holds.

Finally, we report a result that strengthens the second part of Proposition 2 for $w = 2$.

Theorem 1. $\alpha(p, n, k) \geq \alpha(p, 2n, 2k)$ for $1 \leq k < np - p$.

The proof can be found in Appendix A.

Single Sorting Instance. We start by analysing the 1-Fines game, which is equivalent to one Round. In this case, when an agent is sufficiently far from the start of $\mathcal{N}$, it is beneficial to pay nothing, while near the start it is beneficial to pay and avoid paying Q. The boundary between the two will prove important.

Definition 6 (Critical strategy). *Let $r > 0$ be the smallest integer such that $\alpha(p, r, k)Q \leq F$. Then r is called* critical position.

The critical strategy is

$$\pi_a^{\text{crit}}(n_a, t_a, m_a) = \begin{cases} \sigma^F & \text{if } \alpha(p, n_a, k)Q > F, \\ \sigma^0 & \text{otherwise.} \end{cases} \tag{10}$$

We note that $t_a = 1$ and $m_a = 0 \ \forall a \in \mathcal{N}$ for 1-Fines. We will show that π_a^{crit} is the only equilibrium of the 1-Fines. First, we define α^{crit} as the probability with which an agent is forced to pay Q when all agents follow π_a^{crit}.

Proposition 3. *Let r be the critical position. Then if all agents but a follow π_b^{crit}, and a uses σ^0, then a is forced to pay Q w.p.*

$$\alpha^{\text{crit}}(p, r, n_a, k) = \begin{cases} \alpha(p, n_a, k) & \text{if } n_a < r, \\ \alpha(p, r, k - (n_a - r)) & \text{otherwise.} \end{cases} \tag{11}$$

Proof. Fix $a \in \mathcal{N}$. When $\alpha(p, n_a, k) > F/Q$ (i.e. $n_a < r$), then agents in front of a pay F and thus a will not pay Q only if enough of them forget. If $n_a \geq r$, then $n_a - r$ agents choose not to pay. Therefore, a only needs $k - (n_a - r)$ of the r agents to forget. □

Observe that $\alpha^{\text{crit}} \leq \alpha$, since some agents may choose to pay zero. Also, by Definition 5, $\alpha^{\text{crit}} = 0$ for $n_a > r + k$.

Proposition 4. *Let r be the critical position and let all agents follow π_a^{crit}, except for $a \in \mathcal{N}$, whose strategy is $\pi_a = (q, 1 - q)$. Then the expected payment of a is*

$$(1 - p - q)F + (p + q)\alpha^{\text{crit}}(p, r, n_a, k)Q. \tag{12}$$

Proof. By definition of π_a, a pays F w.p. $1 - p - q$ and he does not forget. If he does, or pays zero w.p. q, he is forced to pay Q w.p. $\alpha^{\text{crit}}(p, r, n_a, k)$. □

Corollary 1. *Let r be the critical position and let all agents follow π_a^{crit}. Then the expected payment of $a \in \mathcal{N}$ is*

$$G_a^1(p, n_a, k) = \begin{cases} (1 - p)F + p\alpha^{\text{crit}}(p, r, n_a, k)Q, & \text{if } n_a < r, \\ \alpha^{\text{crit}}(p, r, n_a, k)Q, & \text{otherwise.} \end{cases} \tag{13}$$

Theorem 2. *The strategy π_a^{crit} is unique equilibrium of 1-Fines.*

Proof. Consider $a \in \mathcal{N}$ in the sorted order. We will show by induction π_a^{crit} is a unique best-response to strategies of agents in front of a given agent. For the first agent, π_a^{crit} clearly maximizes the utility $-G_a$ of a. In the induction step we assume a' in front of a follow π_a^{crit}. Following Lemma 1, the actions of the others can be arbitrary. Observe the π_a^{crit} minimizes the expected payment (12). Thus a wants to follow π_a^{crit}. □

More Sorting Instances. In this section we present analytic solution of the general w-Fines game, $w \geq 1$. We start by defining extension of π_a^{crit}, and showing no agent can benefit by deviating from it. Later, we discuss some properties of this analytic solution.

In w-Fines, no agents are added after sorting. After the first Round the game is thus identical to $(w - 1)$-Fines. This recursive relation motivates us to introduce the analogues of the variables used in the previous section recursively. We use upper index to denote the game length w and number of Round, i.e. in the previous section we would use $r^{1,1}$ for the critical position r.

We extend Definition 6 of critical strategy to pay F if a's position is in front of some critical position $r^{w,t}$, defined below. Note that since the second Round corresponds to $(w - 1)$-Fines, $r^{w,l} = r^{w-1,l-1}$ for $l > 1$ and in particular $r^{w,w} = \cdots = r^{2,2} = r^{1,1} = r$.

Definition 7 (w-Critical strategy). *The w-critical strategy is*

$$\pi_a^{\text{crit},w}(n_a, t_a, m_a) = \begin{cases} \sigma^F & \text{if } n_a < r^{w,t_a}, \\ \sigma^0 & \text{otherwise.} \end{cases} \tag{14}$$

Let all agents follow $\pi_a^{\text{crit},w}$. Then if $w > 1$ and $a \in \mathcal{N}^1$ does not terminate in the first Round, his expected payment in the remaining $w - 1$ rounds is

$$\mathcal{G}_a^w(p, n_a, k) = \mathbb{E}_{\gamma \sim B(\min(n_a, r^{w,1})-1, 1-p)}[G_a^{w-1}(p, n_a - \gamma - k, k)], \tag{15}$$

where G_a^{w-1} is the recursive extension of the expected payment G_a^1 (see Corollary 1). A formula for G_a^w is given in Proposition 5 below.

In words, since all agents positioned in front of $\min(n_a, r^{w,1})$ want to pay F, a's position decreases by $\gamma + k, \gamma \sim B(\min(n_a, r^{2,1}) - 1, 1 - p)$. At the new position, a is expected to pay G_a^{w-1}.

Proposition 5. *Let all agents follow $\pi_a^{\text{crit},w}$, and $w > 1$. Then the expected payment of an agent $a \in \mathcal{N}$ is*

$$G_a^w(p, n_a, k) = \begin{cases} (1-p)F + pX^w(p, r^{w,1}, n_a, k), & \text{if } n_a < r^{w,1}, \\ X^w(p, r^{w,1}, n_a, k), & \text{otherwise,} \end{cases} \tag{16}$$

where

$$X^w(p, r^{w,1}, n_a, k) =$$
$$\alpha^{\text{crit}}(p, r^{w,1}, n_a, k)Q + (1 - \alpha^{\text{crit}}(p, r^{w,1}, n_a, k))\mathcal{G}_a^w(p, n_a, k)$$

is a's expected payment if he does not pay F in the first Round.

It remains to determine critical positions $r^{w,l}$. Recursively, $r^{w,l} = r^{w-1,l-1}$ for $l > 1$. Hence it remains to define $r^{w,1}$. Similarly to Definition 6, we define the critical position in the first Round as the smallest $r^{w,1} \in \mathbb{N}$ such that $\alpha(p, r^{w,1}, k)Q + (1 - \alpha(p, r^{w,1}, k))\mathcal{G}_a^w(p, r^{w,1}, k) \leq F$.

In words, assume all agents in front of a want to pay F. In the first Round, if a pays zero he risks paying Q w.p. α and the expected payment in the remaining rounds w.p. $1 - \alpha$. The critical position $r^{w,1}$ is the smallest position n_a at which, assuming all agents in front of it try to pay F, it is beneficial to pay zero.

Lemma 3. *Let $w > 1$. Then $r^{w,1} \geq r^{w-1,1} + k$.*

Proof. By definition, $r^{w,1}$ is the smallest integer such that $\alpha(p, r^{w,1}, k)Q + (1 - \alpha(p, r^{w,1}, k))\mathcal{G}_a^w(p, r^{w,1}, k) \leq F$. For a contradiction we assume that $r^{w,1} < r^{w-1,1} + k$. It suffices to show that $\mathcal{G}_a^w(p, r^{w,1}, k) > F$ since this inequality along with $Q > F$ violates the defining property of $r^{w,1}$.

If $r^{w,1} - k < r^{w-1,1}$ then for each $\gamma \geq 0$,

$$G_a^{w-1}(p, r^{w,1} - \gamma - k, k) = (1 - p)F + pX^{w-1}(p, r^{w-1,1}, r^{w,1} - \gamma - k, k),$$

see Proposition 5. Moreover, by the defining property of $r^{w-1,1}$

$$X^{w-1}(p, r^{w-1,1}, r^{w,1} - \gamma - k, k) > F.$$

Hence for each $\gamma \geq 0$,

$$G_a^{w-1}(p, r^{w,1} - \gamma - k, k) > F$$

and thus $\mathcal{G}_a^w(p, r^{w,1}, k) > F$. □

We are now ready to show the main result of this section.

Theorem 3 (Equilibrium of w-Fines). *$\pi_a^{\mathrm{crit},w}$ is unique equilibrium of w-Fines.*

Proof We proceed by induction on w. For $w = 1$ we use Theorem 2. After the first Round, the game corresponds to $(w - 1)$-Fines and there is a unique equilibrium by the induction assumption. In the first Round, we can use a modification of proof of Theorem 2: consider agents of $\mathcal{N}^1$ in the sorted order and use induction over agents. For an agent $a \in \mathcal{N}^1$ let his strategy be $\pi_a = (q, 1 - q)$ in the first Round, he follows $\pi_a^{\mathrm{crit},w}$ from the second Round, and let all agents in front of him follow $\pi_a^{\mathrm{crit},w}$. Then his expected payment is

$$(1 - p - q)F + (p + q)X^w(p, r^{w,1}, n_a, k), \tag{17}$$

This is because w.p. $1 - p - q$ he pays F and leaves. Otherwise, since all agents in front of him follow $\pi_a^{\mathrm{crit},w}$, and he also follows $\pi_a^{\mathrm{crit},w}$ from the second Round, his expected payment is $X^w(p, r^{w,1}, n_a, k)$.

Strategy $\pi_a^{\mathrm{crit},w}$ is chosen to minimize a's expected payment (17). Therefore, a will follow it even in the first Round. □

Proposition 6. *Let $w > 0$ be an integer and let all players follow $\pi_a^{\mathrm{crit},w}$. Then the total expected payment of w-Fines is*

$$wkQ + F(1 - p)\sum_{t=1}^{w}(r^{t,1} - 1). \tag{18}$$

Proof. In the first Round, $(1 - p)(r^{w,1} - 1)$ agents are expected to pay F, and k are forced to pay Q. In the remaining rounds, the situation is analogous. □

Theorem 4. *Equilibrium strategies of all w-Fines exhibit the avalanche effect.*

Proof. Since $\lim_{p \to 0^+} \alpha(p, n, k) = 1$ and $Q > F$, the critical position in the last Round $r^{w,w} \to \infty$. Using Lemma 3, the equilibrium strategies of all w-Fines satisfy $\pi_a^{\mathrm{crit},w} \to \sigma^F \; \forall w \geq 1$. Thus, $\pi_a^{\mathrm{crit},w}$ satisfies Definition 3. $\qquad\square$

In this simplified model, decreasing the probability of ignorance virtually increases the number of state employees assigned to processing the fines. This allows the central authority to increase the total payment through advertising, rather than hiring additional employees, which may be much cheaper. We show in Sect. 4 that these results translate well to a more general case where non-zero number of agents enter the system in each Round.

Division Problem. To give a partial answer to the Division problem in this setting, we will compare the total expected payment of w-Fines with k, and 1-Fines with wk.

Theorem 5. *Let $Q \gg F$. Then the equilibrium strategy of $\mathbb{F}(w, F, Q, k, p, x_0)$ achieves a higher total payment than the equilibrium of $\mathbb{F}(1, F, Q, wk, p, x_0)$ in expectation by at least $F(1-p)w[k(w-1)-1]$.*

Proof. By Proposition 6 and Lemma 3, the expectation of the total payment of $\mathbb{F}(w, F, Q, k, p, x_0)$ is at least

$$wkQ + F(1-p) \sum_{t=1}^{w} (r^{1,1}(k) - 1) + (t-1)k,$$

while the expectation of the total payment of $\mathbb{F}(1, F, Q, wk, p, x_0)$ is

$$wkQ + F(1-p)(r^{1,1}(wk) - 1).$$

To finish the proof, we note that by Proposition 2, if $Q \gg F$ then $wr^{1,1}(k) \geq r^{1,1}(wk)$. $\qquad\square$

4   Experiments

We investigate two approaches based on how the agents choose their payments. In Sect. 4.1, we define a simple strategy based on how the agent's position changes over the course of the Queue. In Sect. 4.2, we use reinforcement learning to obtain a strategy which approximates equilibrium. In both cases we simplify the model by assuming the function π_a is the same for all agents. The code is available at GitHub.

4.1   Basic Rational Strategy

To model behaviour of real decision makers, we introduce *basic rational strategy* (BRS). Informally, each agent keeps track of a quantity he is willing to pay in each Round. If, based on his shift in Queue since last Round, he determines he will reach the beginning before T steps, his willingness to pay increases. Formally,

Definition 8 (basic rational strategy). *Let $a \in \mathcal{N}$, (n'_a, t'_a, m'_a) be the observation of a in previous Round, and (n_a, t_a, m_a) his current observation. We call ω_a the willingness to pay of a. In the first Round a participates in, i.e. when $t_a = 0$, his willingness to pay is $\omega_a = 0$. In subsequent Round games, the willingness to pay is updated before declaring π_a according to*

$$\omega_a \leftarrow \begin{cases} \min(F - m_a, \omega_a + 1), & n_a < (n_a - n'_a)(T - t_a), \\ \max(0, \omega_a - 1), & \text{otherwise.} \end{cases} \tag{19}$$

The strategy of a is to pay ω_a, i.e. $\pi_a = \sigma^{\omega_a}$.

Note that this is a generalization of the approach introduced in Sect. 2.1, as π_a is not a function of only the observation in the current Round, but also depends on history. This makes this strategy non-Markovian. As such, the Definition 2 does not apply. However, in our experiments we simply assess the effect of agents using BRS, and make no claims regarding its optimality.

4.2   Reinforcement Learning

In order to approximate an equilibrium of Queue, we employ an iterative algorithm. In each iteration, the algorithm approximates $\overline{\pi}_a$ such that

$$\overline{\pi}_a \in \arg\max \mathbb{E}_{(\overline{\pi}_a, \pi_{-a})} [u_a(\overline{\pi}_a, \pi_{-a})]. \tag{20}$$

In words, we find $\overline{\pi}_a$ such that it maximizes utility of a, assuming $\mathcal{N} \setminus \{a\}$ follow π. We denote as τ the iteration of the learning algorithm and π^τ the strategy the algorithm approximates the best-response against in iteration τ.

We use Proximal policy optimization (PPO) [5] to find $\overline{\pi}$, utilizing trajectories of all terminal agents for the update. For details on our implementation, see Appendix B. This approach is not guaranteed to converge in general but if it does converge, the resulting strategy is an equilibrium [6]. Similar approach was successfully used before [7].

NashConv. In order to quantify the quality of the learned solution, we adapt the notion of NashConv [8]. NashConv measures the negative difference in utility agents are expected to receive under π^τ and the approximate best-response $\pi^{\tau+1}$. We approximate the latter by having a fraction of agents ρ follow $\pi^{\tau+1}$ while the rest follows π^τ. Formally,

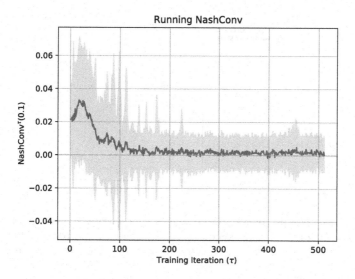

Fig. 1. Evolution of NashConv during training, averaged over one hundred random seeds. The colored ares show standard error. (Color figure online)

Definition 9 (NashConv). *Let each agent added to Queue follow $\pi^{\tau+1}$ w.p. ρ and π^{τ} otherwise. Let $\overline{\mathcal{N}}$ be the set of agents following $\pi^{\tau+1}$ and their expected utility*

$$\mathcal{BRU}(\rho, \pi^{\tau+1}, \pi^{\tau}) = \mathbb{E}_{\left(\pi^{\tau+1}_{\overline{\mathcal{N}}}, \pi^{\tau}_{-\overline{\mathcal{N}}}\right)} \left[u_a(\pi^{\tau+1}_a, \pi^{\tau}_{-a}) | a \in \overline{\mathcal{N}} \right].$$

Then

$$\text{NashConv}^{\tau}(\rho) = \mathcal{BRU}(\rho, \pi^{\tau+1}, \pi^{\tau}) - \mathbb{E}_{\pi^{\tau}} \left[u_a(\pi^{\tau}) \right]. \tag{21}$$

NashConv and ϵ-equilibrium are closely connected – if ρ is small enough such that $|\overline{\mathcal{N}}| \ll |\mathcal{N}|$, then NashConv $\approx \epsilon$. In Fig. 1 we present a representative example of the evolution of NashConv during training. We averaged the results over one hundred random seeds, and also show the standard error. The results suggest that, although there is a considerable amount of noise, the algorithm was able to reach a sufficiently close approximation of the equilibrium. Moreover, we verified this trend translates to other experiments presented below.

4.3   Results

In this section, we numerically demonstrate the Avalanche effect and the Division problem. Specifically, we show the total expected revenue, which is given as $\mathbb{E}_{\pi} \left[\sum_{a \in \mathcal{T}} m_a \right]$. Unless stated otherwise, we use $F = T = 4$, $Q = 6$, $x = x_0 = 32$, $k = 2$ and $p = 1/2$ in all our experiments. Note that with these parameters if the ordering is not introduced[6], the individual risk in the first Round is $kQ/x =$

---

[6] That is if the agents in $\mathcal{N}^t$ which are forced to pay Q are selected at random.

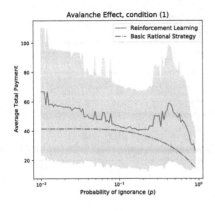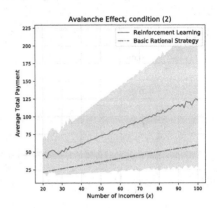

Fig. 2. Expected total payment of terminal agents for varying probability of ignorance p (left) and number of incoming offenders x (right) averaged over ten random seeds and showing also the standard error. The figures demonstrate the Avalanche effect defined in Sect. 2.3.

$0.375 \ll F$. Thus it is not rational to pay F and the revenue of the central authority would be $kQ = 12$.

Note that the standard error is considerably high in all figures presented below. This is partly due to the noise introduced by the learning algorithm, which (if convergent) find a course correlated equilibrium. As these may vary significantly in e.g. social welfare, similar variance can be expected in our case.

Avalanche Effect. In Fig. 2 we show the total expected payment as a function of the probability of ignorance p, and the number of entering agents x. The results suggest that the Queue exhibits the Avalanche effect in a general setting. In fact, it exhibits both properties of Definition 3. Interestingly, the learned solution achieves a considerably higher total payment compared to BRS.

Division Problem. In this section, we numerically study the Division problem introduced in Sect. 2.4. Results for both the Time- and Group-Division problem are presented in Fig. 3.

For the Time-Division problem, BRS seems to drastically overpay the learned strategy if the sorting is frequent, i.e. T is large. On the other hand, when T is small the willingness to pay doesn't increase. This leads to paying only $kQ = 48$ for $T = 1$, while the learned strategy prefers to pay more. When the game is sorted more often, the learned strategy seems to favor lower total payments.

In the Group-Division scenario, both BRS and the learned strategy pay less in larger system. Splitting the game into several smaller thus increases the total payment of the offenders. This is in agreement with the analytic solution presented in Sect. 3.2, suggesting the incoming agents don't impact Queue much.

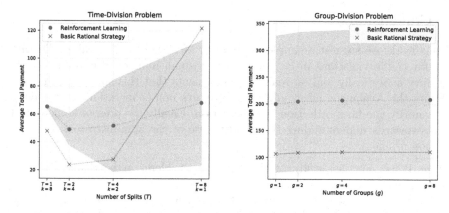

Fig. 3. Expected total payment of terminal agents for varying number of sortings T (left) and number of splits g (right). The results are averaged over ten random seeds and the colored areas show standard error. The figures investigate the Division problem defined in Sect. 2.4. (Color figure online)

Exploitability of Basic Rational Strategy. The BRS is a heuristic designed to capture realistic behaviour of humans. However, it is not guaranteed to make optimal decisions. In this section, we investigate exploitability of BRS. Specifically, we let 90% of the agents follow BRS, with the rest refining their strategy using PPO. We compare the expected payment of agents following each of the strategies after convergence. We present our results in Fig. 4 for varying probability of ignorance p and number of entering agents x. In all cases the learning algorithm is able to find strategy which achieves vastly lower expected payment, suggesting the BRS is quite exploitable.

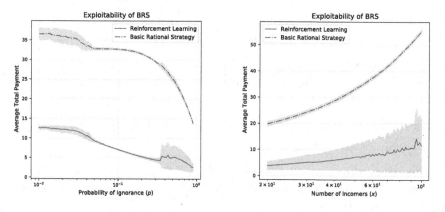

Fig. 4. Expected total payment of terminal agents for varying probability of ignorance p (left) and number of incoming offenders x (right) averaged over ten random seeds and showing also the standard error. The training was done with 90% of agents following BRS., i.e. approximating best-response to BRS.

5   Conclusion

In this work, we suggest a simple mechanism for rule enforcing, like collecting fines for traffic violations in large cities, by a small number of administrators. We show analytically and on realistic experiments that this simple mechanism exhibits the Avalanche effect and thus supports non-cooperation of offenders. We quantify the fines collection in expectation. Finally, we present some initial results towards understanding the effective use of the administrators, i.e., the Division problem.

Future Work: Further study of the Division problem, in particular possible strengthening of Lemma 3 is our work in progress.

We see a limitation of our numerical approach in that we limit ourselves to scenarios where all agents share the same strategy π_a. We would like to improve on our results by having each agent follow one of a few leaders, similar to how we investigated exploitability of BRS.

A   Proof of Theorem 1

Theorem 1 $\alpha(p, n, k) \geq \alpha(p, 2n, 2k)$ *for* $1 \leq k < np - p$.

We will prove the theorem in a sequence of lemmas. Note that $\alpha(p, n, k) = \mathbb{P}[X \leq k]$ for $X \sim B(n - 1, p)$.

Lemma 4. *For random variables* $X \sim B(n, p)$ *and* $Y \sim B(2n, p)$ *and* $1 < k < np$, *we have* $\mathbb{P}[X \leq k] \geq \mathbb{P}[Y \leq 2k]$.

Proof. We make use of the Camp-Paulson approximation [4,9] to the normal distribution for a binomial distribution which states that for $X \sim B(n, p)$

$$\left| \mathbb{P}[X \leq k] - \Phi\left(\frac{c - m}{\theta} \right) \right| \leq \frac{0.007}{\sqrt{np(1 - p)}},$$

where $c = (1 - b)r^{\frac{1}{3}}, m = 1 - a, \theta = \sqrt{br^{\frac{2}{3}} + a}, b = \frac{1}{9(k+1)}, a = \frac{1}{9(n-k)}, r = \frac{(k+1)(1-p)}{p(n-k)}$, and $\Phi(x) = \frac{1}{\sqrt{2\pi}} \int_{-\infty}^{x} e^{-\frac{t^2}{2}} dt$.

Since Φ is an increasing function it suffices to show the inequality between the arguments of Φ for $k < np$. We define $r(n, x) = \frac{(x+1)(1-p)}{p(n-x)}, c(n, x) = \left(1 - \frac{1}{9(x+1)}\right) r(n, x)^{\frac{1}{3}} = \frac{9x+8}{9(x+1)} r(n, x)^{\frac{1}{3}}, m(n, x) = 1 - \frac{1}{9(n-x)}$ and $\theta(n, x) = \sqrt{\frac{1}{9(x+1)} r(n, x)^{2/3} + \frac{1}{9(n-x)}}$.

Thus we need to show that $\frac{c(n,x) - m(n,x)}{\theta(n,x)} > \frac{c(2n,2x) - m(2n,2x)}{\theta(2n,2x)}$ for $k < np$. We prove this in two parts. Our first claim will show that there is a $K_n < np$, where $c(n, x) - m(n, x)$ is zero.   □

Claim. $c(n, x) - m(n, x)$ *is an increasing function of* x *for* $0 < x < n$ *and there exists* $K_n < np$ *such that* $c(n, x) < m(n, x)$ *for all* $x < K$ *and* $c(n, x) > m(n, x)$ *for all* $x > K$.

Proof. It is easy to see that for $0 < x < n$, $r(x)$ and $c(x)$ are increasing functions and $m(n,x)$ is a decreasing function. Thus for $0 < x < np$ we have $1 > m(n,x) \geq 1 - \frac{1}{9(n-np)}$ and $(1 - \frac{1}{9(x+1)}) \leq (1 - \frac{1}{9(np+1)})$. We first find the condition for $x > 0$ such that $r(n,x) < \left(\frac{y-1}{y}\right)^3$ for some $y > 0$. Note here that we can assume that such an x exists as we are assuming $p > \frac{1}{n}$. The inequality holds for all $x < \frac{np(y-1)^3 - y^3(1-p)}{y^3(1-p)+p(y-1)^3}$. Since $y > 0$, we have that the inequality holds for all $x < np\left(\frac{y-1}{y}\right)^3 - 1 + p$. Thus for $y = 9(n - np)$ we have, $c(n,x) = \frac{9x+8}{9(x+1)}\left(1 - \frac{1}{9(n-np)}\right) < m(n,x)$.

$$
\begin{aligned}
c(n,np) &= \frac{9np+8}{9(np+1)}\left(\frac{(np+1)(1-p)}{p(n-np)}\right)^{1/3} = \frac{9np+8}{9(np+1)}\left(\frac{np+1}{np}\right)^{1/3} \\
&\geq \frac{9np+8}{9(np+1)}\left(\frac{np+1}{np}\right)^{1/3} = \frac{9np+8}{9np}\left(\frac{np}{np+1}\right)^{2/3} \\
&= \left(1 + \frac{8}{9np}\right)\left(\frac{np}{np+1}\right)^{2/3}
\end{aligned}
$$

It is easy to see that $\left(1 + \frac{8}{9x}\right)\left(\frac{x}{x+1}\right)^{2/3} > 1$ for all $x > 0$. Thus $c(n,np) > 1 > m(n,np)$. This proves the claim. $\square$

Notice that K_n is very close to np but nevertheless lower than np. We are now ready to partly prove Theorem 1.

Lemma 5. *For $0 < x < \frac{K_{2n}}{2}$, $\frac{c(n,x)-m(n,x)}{\theta(n,x)} > \frac{c(2n,2x)-m(2n,2x)}{\theta(2n,2x)}$.*

Proof. To do this we see some properties of $\frac{c(n,x)-m(n,x)}{\theta(n,x)}$. Individually the functions compare as follows for $1 \leq x < n$.

$$
\begin{aligned}
\left(\frac{\theta(2n,2x)}{\theta(n,x)}\right)^2 &= \frac{1}{2}\left(\frac{x+1}{2x+1}\right)^{1/3}\frac{(2n-2x)^{1/3}(1-p)^{2/3} + (2x+1)^{1/3}p^{2/3}}{(n-x)^{1/3}(1-p)^{2/3} + (x+1)^{1/3}p^{2/3}} \\
&\leq \frac{1}{2}\left(\frac{x+1}{2x+1}\right)^{1/3}\frac{(2n-2x)^{1/3}(1-p)^{2/3} + (2x+2)^{1/3}p^{2/3}}{(n-x)^{1/3}(1-p)^{2/3} + (x+1)^{1/3}p^{2/3}} \\
&\leq \frac{1}{2^{2/3}}\left(\frac{x+1}{2x+1}\right)^{1/3} < 1
\end{aligned}
$$

Also $\frac{c(n,x)}{c(2n,2x)} = 2^{1/3}\left(\frac{9x+8}{18x+8}\right)\left(\frac{2x+1}{x+1}\right)^{2/3} > 1$ as this is a decreasing function for $x > 0$ with its limit at 1, and $m(n,x) - m(2n,2x) = \frac{1}{9(2n-2x)} - \frac{1}{9(n-x)} = -\frac{1}{9(2n-2x)} < 0$.

Thus we have $c(2n, 2x) - m(2n, 2x) < c(n, x) - m(n, x)$. It follows that $K_n \leq \frac{K_{2n}}{2}$. Thus for $x \leq K_n$ we have $\frac{\theta(2n,2x)}{\theta(n,x)} \frac{c(n,x)-m(n,x)}{c(2n,2x)-m(2n,2x)} < 1$ i.e., $\left| \frac{c(2n,2x)-m(2n,2x)}{\theta(2n,2x)} \right| \geq \left| \frac{c(n,x)-m(n,x)}{\theta(n,x)} \right|$ but both quantities are negative and so $\frac{c(2n,2x)-m(2n,2x)}{\theta(2n,2x)} \leq \frac{c(n,x)-m(n,x)}{\theta(n,x)}$. For $K_n < x < \frac{K_{2n}}{2}$ we have $\frac{c(2n,2x)-m(2n,2x)}{\theta(2n,2x)} \leq 0 \leq \frac{c(n,x)-m(n,x)}{\theta(n,x)}$. $\qquad\square$

Lemma 5 allows us to state a weaker result.

Corollary 2. *For random variables $X \sim B(n, p)$ and $Y \sim B(n + \lceil n/p \rceil, p)$ and $k < \max\{\frac{n}{2}, np\}$, we have $\mathbb{P}[X \leq k] \geq \mathbb{P}[Y \leq 2k]$.*

Proof. The proof follows from the fact that $n + \frac{n}{p} > 2n$ and $2x < (np + n)\left(\frac{9\frac{n}{p}-9np-1}{9\frac{n}{p}-9np}\right) - 1 + p < K_{n+\frac{n}{p}}$. $\qquad\square$

Now we can complete the proof of Theorem 1.

Proof (of Theorem 1). Notice that $c - m$ and θ are monotonically increasing in x. The difference between using n and $2n$ is just the rate of increase. We have shown for $x < K_{2n}$, $(c - m)(n, x)\theta^2(2n, 2x) > (c - m)(2n, 2x)\theta^2(n, x)$. Now we show the inequality holds for $x = np$, i.e., the two functions haven't crossed each other.

Define $r_1 = \frac{np+1}{np}, r_2 = \frac{2np+1}{2np}, b_1 = \frac{1}{9(np+1)}, b_2 = \frac{1}{9(2np+1)}, a = \frac{1}{18(n-np)}$, $\theta_1 = b_1 r_1^{2/3} + 2a$ and $\theta_2 = b_2 r_2^{2/3} + 2a$. Thus we have

$$1 \leq \frac{r_1}{r_2} = 2\left(\frac{np+1}{2np+1}\right) = \frac{2b_2}{b_1} \leq 2 \qquad (22)$$

$(c - m)(n, np)\theta^2(2n, 2np) - (c - m)(2n, 2np)\theta^2(n, np)$

$= ((1 - b_1)r_1^{1/3} - 1 + 2a)\theta_2 - ((1 - b_2)r_2^{1/3} - 1 + a)\theta_1$

$= \dfrac{2^{1/3}(2np + 1)^{1/3}(9np + 8)(n - np) - 2^{2/3}(np + 1)^{1/3}(18np + 8)(n - np)}{81[(np + 1)(2np + 1)]^{2/3}2np(n - np)}$

$+ \dfrac{2[2np(np + 1)]^{2/3} - 2[np(2np + 1)]^{2/3} + 18(np + 1)2^{1/3}[np(2np + 1)]^{2/3}]^{2/3}}{81[(2np + 1)(np + 1)]^{2/3}(2np)(n - np)2}$

$- \dfrac{18(2np + 1)[2np(np + 1)]^{2/3}}{81[(2np + 1)(np + 1)]^{2/3}(2np)(n - np)2}$

$+ \dfrac{18(n - np)[np(np + 1)]^{1/3}(2np + 1)^{2/3} - 9(n - np)[2np(2np + 1)]^{1/3}(np + 1)^{2/3}}{81(n - np)[(np + 1)(2np + 1)]^{2/3}(2np)}$

$+ \dfrac{9[(np + 1)(2np + 1)]^{2/3}(2np) + 2(np + 1)^{2/3}(2np + 1)^{1/3}(2np)^{1/3}}{81(n - np)[(np + 1)(2np + 1)]^{2/3}(2np)2}$

$- \dfrac{2(np + 1)^{1/3}(2np + 1)^{2/3}(np)^{1/3}}{81(n - np)[(np + 1)(2np + 1)]^{2/3}(2np)2}$

Using $p^3 - q^3 = (p-q)(p^2 + pq + q^2)$ we have,

$$2^{1/3}(2x+1)^{1/3}(9x+8) - 9[2x(2x+1)]^{1/3}(x+1)^{2/3}$$
$$= 2^{1/3}(2x+1)^{1/3}[8 + 9x^{1/3}(x^{2/3} - (x+1)^{2/3})]$$
$$= 2^{1/3}(2x+1)^{1/3}\left[8 + \left(\frac{-9x^{1/3}(2x+1)}{x^{4/3} + x^{2/3}(x+1)^{2/3} + (x+1)^{4/3}}\right)\right] \quad (23)$$

and,

$$18[x(x+1)]^{1/3}(2x+1)^{2/3} - 2^{2/3}(x+1)^{1/3}(18x+8)$$
$$= (x+1)^{1/3}[8 + 18x^{1/3}((2x+1)^{2/3} - (2x)^{2/3})]$$
$$= (x+1)^{1/3}\left[8 + \left(\frac{18x^{1/3}(4x+1)}{(2x+1)^{4/3} + (2x(2x+1))^{2/3} + (2x)^{4/3}}\right)\right] \quad (24)$$

Note that the sum of (23) and (24) is positive for $x \geq 1$. Thus all the terms with $n - np$ in the numerator add up to a positive quantity. The only other negative component is $\frac{18(np+1)2^{1/3}[np(2np+1)]^{2/3} - 18(2np+1)[2np(np+1)]^{2/3}}{81[(2np+1)(np+1)]^{2/3}(2np)(n-np)2}$, which is dominated by $\frac{9[(np+1)(2np+1)]^{2/3}(2np)}{81(n-np)[(np+1)(2np+1)]^{2/3}(2np)2}$.

Thus $\frac{c(n,np)-m(n,np)}{\theta(n,np)} \Big/ \frac{c(2n,2np)-m(2n,2np)}{\theta(2n,2np)} \geq \frac{\theta(n,np)}{\theta(2n,2np)} \geq 1$.   □

B   Learning Algorithm

The shared strategy π_a is represented by a neural network and trained from trajectories of all terminal agents. When selecting the strategy for a Round, we mask all actions which would lead to $m_a + \mu_a > F$. This makes the agents unable to overpay the fine F. We use fully-connected networks for both the actor and the critic. Both take as input the observation[7] of a in Round, i.e. (n_a, t_a, m_a). The actor network has two hidden layers with four hidden units, and the critic has three hidden layers with 32 units each, all using the ReLU activation function. The rest of the hyperparameters are given in Table 1.

---

[7] We normalize the observation to $[0,1]^3$.

Table 1. Hyperparameters of the learning algorithm.

Parameter	Value	Description
ε	0.05	Policy update clipping
γ	1	Reward discounting
λ	0.95	Advantage decay factor
N_{train}	32	Number of training updates per cycle
N_{epochs}	512	Number of training epochs
N_{train}	$2 \cdot 10^4$	Train buffer size
α_{actor}	$3 \cdot 10^{-4}$	Actor learning rate
α_{critic}	10^{-3}	Critic learning rate
c_{H}	10^{-3}	Entropy regularization weight
$\bar{c}$	0.1	Gradient norm clipping

References

1. Loebl, M., Sychrovsky, D., Desai, S.: Promoting non-cooperation through ordering. In: The 14th Workshop on Optimization and Learning in Multiagent Systems. OptLearnMAS (2023)
2. Lee, A., Chiam, C., Li, J.: The Bidding Elimination Game (2020)
3. de Campagnolle, M.R., Kobylanski, M., Quenez, M.: Dynkin games in a general framework (2013)
4. Greenberg, S., Mohri, M.: Tight lower bound on the probability of a binomial exceeding its expectation. Stat. Probab. Lett. **86**, 91–98 (2014)
5. Schulman, J., Wolski, F., Dhariwal, P., Radford, A., Klimov, O.: Proximal policy optimization algorithms. CoRR, abs/1707.06347 (2017)
6. Ghosh, D., Machado, M.C., Le Roux, N.: An operator view of policy gradient methods. In: Proceedings of the 34th International Conference on Neural Information Processing Systems, NIPS 2020. Curran Associates Inc., Red Hook (2020)
7. Baker, B., et al.: Emergent tool use from multi-agent autocurricula. In: International Conference on Learning Representations (2020)
8. Lanctot, M., et al.: A unified game-theoretic approach to multiagent reinforcement learning. In: Guyon, I., et al. (eds.) Advances in Neural Information Processing Systems, vol. 30. Curran Associates Inc. (2017)
9. Lesch, S.M., Jeske, D.R.: Some suggestions for teaching about normal approximations to poisson and binomial distribution functions. Am. Stat. **63**(3), 274–277 (2009)

Security Games

Multi-defender Security Games
with Schedules

Zimeng Song[1], Chun Kai Ling[2(✉)], and Fei Fang[2]

[1] Tsinghua University, Beijing, China
zmsongzm@gmail.com
[2] Carnegie Mellon University, Pittsburgh, USA
{chunkail,feif}@cs.cmu.edu

Abstract. Stackelberg Security Games are often used to model strategic interactions in high-stakes security settings. The majority of existing models focus on single-defender settings where a single entity assumes command of all security assets. However, many realistic scenarios feature *multiple heterogeneous defenders* with their own interests and priorities embedded in a more complex system. Furthermore, defenders rarely choose targets to protect. Instead, they have a multitude of defensive resources or *schedules* at its disposal, each with different protective capabilities. In this paper, we study security games featuring multiple defenders and schedules simultaneously. We show that unlike prior work on multi-defender security games, the introduction of schedules can cause non-existence of equilibrium even under rather restricted environments. We prove that under the mild restriction that any subset of a schedule is also a schedule, non-existence of equilibrium is not only avoided, but can be computed in polynomial time in games with two defenders. Under additional assumptions, our algorithm can be extended to games with more than two defenders and its computation scaled up in special classes of games with compactly represented schedules such as those used in patrolling applications. Experimental results suggest that our methods scale gracefully with game size, making our algorithms amongst the few that can tackle multiple heterogeneous defenders.

Keywords: Security Games · Stackelberg Equilibrium · Game Theory

1 Introduction

The past decades have seen a wave of interest in Stackelberg Security Games (SSG), with applications to infrastructure [23], wildlife poaching [5–7] and cybersecurity [2,21,29]. SSGs are played between a single defender allocating defensive resources over a finite set of targets and an attacker who, after observing this allocation, best responds by attacking the target least defended [25].

Numerous variants of SSGs better reflecting the real world have been proposed. Amongst the most well-researched extension are settings with *scheduling*

Z. Song—Independent Researcher.
Equal contribution between authors Song and Ling.

J. Fu et al. (Eds.): GameSec 2023, LNCS 14167, pp. 65–85, 2023.
https://doi.org/10.1007/978-3-031-50670-3_4

constraints. Instead of guarding a single target, the defender chooses a *set* of targets instead, making it possible to model real world problems such as planning patrols for anti-poaching [3,5,7,28] and the US coast guard [22,24], infrastructure protection [12], and optimal placement of police checkpoints [11]. Another less explored extension is the *multi-defender setting*, where multiple defenders (e.g., city, state and federal law enforcement), each utilize distinct resources in tandem, potentially resulting in miscoordination [13]. Recent work in [8,9] solved the challenging problem of finding equilibrium when defenders are heterogeneous, both in the coordinated and uncoordinated case.

Unfortunately, there is almost no literature on settings exhibiting both scheduling *and* multiple defenders. Our work fills this non-trivial gap. In contrast to the positive results of [8,9], we show that equilibrium may not exist with the inclusion of scheduling constraints, even under extremely stringent constraints on other aspects of the problem. We then guarantee existence of equilibrium in two defender settings when restricted to schedules satisfying the *subset-of-a-schedule-is-also-a-schedule* structure [16], on top of other mild restrictions. We construct polynomial time algorithms for computing equilibrium in such restricted settings and propose two extensions. The first utilizes an additional assumption of Monotone Schedules to handle the general multi-defender setting. The second scales to scenarios with a large (possibly exponential) number of schedules in structured domains such as patrolling. Empirically, our algorithms scale gracefully, making them viable for use in the real world.

2   Background and Related Work

Our work is motivated by the security application played on the layered network in Fig. 1a, where vertices represent neighborhoods and edges represent connecting roads. Distinct law enforcement agencies (e.g., local and federal police) patrol along a path starting from vertex a to vertex e. Patrols provide defence, or *coverage* to the neighborhoods they pass (Fig. 1a). By randomizing or splitting their patrols, agencies can broaden coverage at the expense of thinning them (Fig. 1b). Coverage at each neighborhood is accumulated over patrols (Fig. 1c). An attacker chooses a single neighborhood to attack based on this coverage, giving negative reward to law enforcement agencies. Neighborhoods and law enforcement are non-homogeneous: neighborhoods differ in density and demographics, local police value local businesses and inhabitants, while federal agencies focus on federal government assets. Given these competing objectives, how should law enforcement agencies plan their patrols?

The closest pieces of work to us are by Lou et al. [20] and Gan et al. [8,9]. The work by Gan et. al. [8] focuses on the case with multiple heterogeneous defenders without schedules, showing that an equilibrium always exists and can be computed in polynomial time in both the coordinated and uncoordinated case by extending the classic water-filling algorithm [15]. However, their model is limited by the lack of schedules. This is not merely an issue of computation: our work shows that the inclusion of schedules can trigger non-existence of equilibrium.

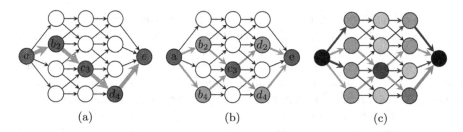

Fig. 1. Multi-defender Patrolling on Layered Networks. Vertices are targets and black edges are roads connecting targets. (a) The green path shows a patrol route by a single defender, passing through b_2, c_3 and d_4. Protected nodes are shaded, with the darkness indicating degree of protection. (b) A coverage obtained by splitting/randomizing patrols. Thinner arrows indicate smaller patrols. Compared to Fig. (a), more targets are covered, but with lower intensity. (c) A joint patrol with two defenders; the first employs the route in Fig. (b) and the second follows the blue paths. The orange edge is used by both defenders. (Color figure online)

The work by Lou et al. [20] consider multiple defenders and scheduling, analyzing equilibrium in terms of the Price of Anarchy between defenders and giving conditions for their existence.[1] However, the bulk of their work concerns homogeneous defenders; their results for heterogeneous defenders limited (e.g., having every target completely covered). Here, they acknowledge possible non-existence of equilibrium, proposing approximate solvers based on Mixed-Integer Program with quadratic constraints. In contrast, our work makes additional assumptions but guarantees existence and polynomial time solutions.

SSGs as a whole have a long and illustrious history. First introduced by von Stackelberg [26] to model competitive firms and the first mover's advantage, it saw a resurgence beginning with [27] alongside a wave of applications primarily in the domain of security which modeled defenders as first movers or leaders [1,25]. Since then, an enormous amount of literature has surfaced, e.g., computing equilibrium in sequential settings [4,17,19], handling bounded rationality of defenders [14], and various other structural assumptions such games on networks [18], each catering to different variants of security applications.

3   Nash-Stackelberg Equilibrium with Scheduling

Our setting involves n heterogeneous defenders, T heterogeneous targets and a single attacker. Each defender allocates defensive resources which induce *coverage* over targets, a quantitative measure of the degree to which each target is protected. For example, coverage can refer to the average number of police officers patrolling at a particular neighborhood (Fig. 1). As is customary in security games, we employ *Stackelberg leadership* models. Each defender first independently *commits* to its coverage. The attacker then chooses to attack a target $t \in [T]$ with the lowest total coverage under this commitment.

---

[1] We point out [20] and [8] use different tie-breaking models for the attacker.

Formally, each defender i has an *attainable set* of coverage $V^i \subset \mathbb{R}_+^T$ (which we define concretely later), from which it chooses a *coverage vector* $v^i \in V^i$, where defender i contributes $v^i(j)$ coverage to target j. A *coverage profile* $\mathbf{v} = (v^1, v^2, \cdots, v^n) \in V^1 \times V^2 \cdots \times V^n$ is an ordered tuple of coverages from each defender. We assume that coverage accumulates across defenders additively, such that for a given coverage profile $\mathbf{v}$, the *total coverage* of all defenders is $v^{total} = \sum_{i \in [n]} v^i$. The total coverage on target j is $v^{total}(j) = \sum_{i \in [n]} v^i(j) \geq 0$.

We assume *coverage independent payoffs*: each defender's payoff is based on the attacked target, but *not* on the coverage itself. In practical terms, this means that an attack would "always succeed", and the purpose of coverage is to redirect the attacker elsewhere. For example, security officers may not be able to prevent a determined terrorist attack, but having more officers in crowded areas may make the cost of attack prohibitively high such that the attack occurs at a less populated area. This assumption means there is no need to work explicitly with numerical values for defender payoffs. Instead, each defender i has a fixed order of preference over targets given by the total order $\succ_i$. We write $j \succ_i k$ (resp. $j \prec_i k$) if defender i prefers target j over k to be attacked (resp. not attacked). We assume that there are no ties in defender preferences, hence $j =_i k$ if and only if $j = k$. We write $j \succeq_i k$ if and only if $j \succ_i k$ or $j =_i k$, with $j \preceq_i k$ being defined analogously. Preference orders differ between defenders, hence $j \succ_i k$ does not imply $j \succ_{i'} k$ for $i \neq i'$. For any target $t \in [T]$, we define the set $\mathcal{T}_t^{\succ i} = \{k \in [T] | k \succ_i t\}$, i.e., the set of targets which defender i strictly prefers to be attacked over target t. $\mathcal{T}_t^{\prec i}$, $\mathcal{T}_t^{\succeq i}$, and $\mathcal{T}_t^{\preceq i}$ are defined analogously.

We now define formally define the Nash-Stackelberg equilibrium (NSE) given V^i and $\succ_i$ for each defender. We call a tuple $(v^1, \ldots, v^n, t) \in V^1 \times \cdots \times V^n \times [T]$ a strategy profile, abbreviated by $(\mathbf{v}, t)$. Strategy profiles are an NSE when (i) the attacker is attacking a least covered target and (ii) neither defender i is willing to unilaterally deviate their coverage from v^i to $\widehat{v^i} \in V^i$ (written as $v^i \to \widehat{v^i}$), assuming that the attacker could react to this deviation by possibly adjusting its target from t to $\hat{t}$. The NSE is named as such because the attacker best responds to the total coverage as if it was a Stackelberg follower, while defenders interact amongst themselves as if it were Nash. The former condition is formalized easily.

Definition 1 (Attacker's Best Response Set). Given a total coverage $v^{total} \in \mathbb{R}_+^T$, its attacker best response set is[2]

$$B(v^{total}) = \operatorname*{Argmin}_{t \in [T]} v^{total}(t) = \left\{ t \in [T] \middle| v^{total}(t) = \min_{t' \in [T]} v^{total}(t') \right\} \quad (1)$$

Definition 2 (Attacker Incentive Compatibility (AIC)). A strategy profile $(\mathbf{v}, t)$ is *attacker incentive compatible* if and only if $t \in B(v^{total})$.

---

[2] In this paper, we use superscripts $(\cdot)^i$ to specify a defender's index, and brackets $()$ for elements in a vector. We capitalize Argmax to denote the subset of maximal elements, and lower case argmax when referring to an arbitrary one.

Essentially, a tuple $(\mathbf{v}, t)$ is AIC when the attacker does not strictly prefer some target $\hat{t} \neq t$ over t. Naturally, we desire profiles which are AIC.

As noted by [9], condition (ii) contains an important nuance: if defender i deviates via $v^i \to \hat{v}^i$ such that $\hat{v}^{total}$ does not have a unique minimum coverage (i.e., $|B(\hat{v}^{total})| > 1$), how should the attacker break ties? In single-defender scenarios, one typically breaks ties in favor of the defender, also called the *Strong* Stackelberg equilibrium. With multiple defenders, this is ambiguous since defenders are heterogeneous. This is a non-trivial discussion, since the way the attacker breaks ties significantly affects the space of equilibrium. There are two natural choices for breaking ties: either punish or prioritize the deviating defender. These choices mirror the concepts of weak and strong Stackelberg equilibrium in single-defender settings. As [9] argue, the second convention of benefiting the deviating defender can lead to spurious deviations from defenders. For example, a defender may make a trivial "identity" deviation from $v^i \to v^i$, yet demand a nontrivial change in attacked target. As such we adopt the former concept. This means that deviating players are pessimistic towards any change in attacked target after their deviation (this pessimism exists only for deviations).

Definition 3 (Defender i-Weakly Attacker Incentive Compatibility (i-WAIC)). A strategy profile $(\mathbf{v}, t)$ is i-WAIC if and only if (i) $t \in B(v^{total})$ and (ii) $\hat{t} \in B(v^{total}) \implies \hat{t} \succeq_i t$.

Definition 4 (Defender i-Incentive Compatibility (i-IC)). A strategy profile $(\mathbf{v}, t)$ is i-IC if and only if there does not exist $\hat{v}^i \in V^i$ and $\hat{t} \succ_i t$ such that $(v^1, v^2, \cdots, v^{i-1}, \hat{v}^i, v^{i+1}, \cdots, v^n, \hat{t})$ is i-WAIC.

Definition 5 (Nash-Stackelberg Equilibrium (NSE)). A strategy profile $(\mathbf{v}, t)$ is an NSE if and only if it is AIC and i-IC for all $i \in [n]$.

Put simply, $(\mathbf{v}, t)$ is i-WAIC if it is AIC and the choice of t is made such as to break ties *against* defender i (clearly, this is a strictly stronger condition than AIC). Consequently, $(\mathbf{v}, t)$ is i-IC if there is no deviation $v^i \to \hat{v}^i$ such that defender i benefits strictly when the attacker changes it's best-response $t \to \hat{t}$ while breaking ties against defender i. Thus, any candidate NSE $(\mathbf{v}, t)$ is only required be AIC, allowing us to freely choose how the attacker tiebreaks, as though t was the "agreed upon norm" target for the attacker. However, if defender i deviates, we use the stronger notion of WAIC for post-deviation tiebreaking.

Remark 1. Our model does not completely generalize [9] due to coverage independent payoffs and additive coverage. However, these assumptions are related to their cases of correlated defenders and non-overlapping payoffs respectively.

4 Analysis and Algorithms

Clearly, the existence and computation of NSE depends on the set V^i. The simplest specification of V^i is obtained by explicitly specifying schedules and requiring *clearance constraints*. Suppose each defender $i \in [n]$ has 1 unit of divisible defensive resource to allocate across a set of $S^i > 0$ *schedules* $\mathcal{S}^i = \{s_1^i, s_2^i, \cdots s_{S^i}^i\}$. Each $s_z^i \in \mathbb{R}_+^T$ is the non-negative coverage over all T targets when defender i allocates its entire defensive resource to the z-th schedule. $s_z^i(j), j \in [T]$ is the coverage specific to target j. Each defender d_i's *strategy* is a distribution $x^i \in \mathbb{R}_+^{S^i}$ over its set of schedules, where $\sum_{s_z^i \in \mathcal{S}^i} x^i(s_z^i) = 1$.

Assumption 1 (Clearance). *Given schedules $\mathcal{S}^i$, the coverage vector v^i is said to satisfy clearance if all defensive resources are fully utilized, i.e.,*

$$V^i = \left\{ v \in \mathbb{R}_+^T \middle| \exists x^i \text{ such that } \forall j \in [T] \ v(j) = \sum_{s_z^i \in \mathcal{S}^i} x^i(s_z^i) \cdot s_z^i(j) \right\}.$$

The clearance constraint on V^i essentially requires defenders to expend as much as they can, preventing them from "slacking off". When each schedule attacks a distinct target, i.e., $\mathcal{S}^i = \{e_1, e_2, \ldots, e_T\}$, clearance constraints reduce to the setting of [9] and equilibria will exist. However, our focus is on the scheduled setting. Indeed, we now demonstrate an instance where NSE do not exist.[3]

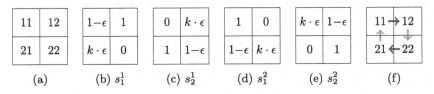

Fig. 2. Illustration of Example 1. (a) Target labels. Defender 1 prefers diagonal (green) targets attacked; defender 2 prefers off diagonal (blue) targets. (b–e) Defender schedules s_1^1, s_2^1, s_1^2 and s_2^2. (f) Cyclic behavior. Green/blue arrows indicate changes in targets induced by defender 1/2 deviating. (Color figure online)

Example 1. The game in Fig. 2 has $n = 2$ defenders and $T = 4$ targets. Targets $11, 12, 21, 22$ are organized in a 2×2 matrix. Defender 1 has preferences $22 \succ_1 11 \succ_1 12 \succ_1 21$ (i.e., prefers diagonal targets attacked) while defender 2 has them in reverse, $21 \succ_2 12 \succ_2 11 \succ_2 22$ (i.e., prefers off diagonal targets attacked). Each has 2 schedules, $s_1^1 = (1-\epsilon, 1, k\epsilon, 0)$, $s_2^1 = (0, k\epsilon, 1, 1-\epsilon)$ and $s_1^2 = (1, 0, 1-\epsilon, k\epsilon)$, $s_2^2 = (k\epsilon, 1-\epsilon, 0, 1)$, where $k \geq 1$, $0 \leq \epsilon \ll 1$ and $k\epsilon < 1$.

Suppose (for now) that $\epsilon = 0$ in Example 1. Then, defender 1 decides how to split its coverage across rows, while defender 2 the columns. Suppose $(\mathbf{v}, t)$ is a NSE. If $t = 11$, defender 2 is incentivized to deviate to $\widehat{v}^2 = s_1^2$ regardless of v^1, since this always causes 12 to have the "lowest" coverage and $12 \succ_2 11$. The same may be said for $t = 22$, $t = 12$ and $t = 21$, where the latter two have defender 1 deviating. This "cyclic" behavior (Fig. 2f) implies that no equilibrium exists.

---

[3] An earlier version of this paper included an incorrect example.

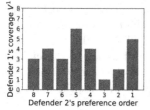 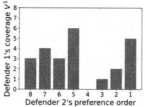 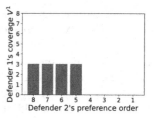

Fig. 3. Left to right: reductions to obtain t-standard coverage for defender 1

The above argument is only partially correct. When $\epsilon = 0$, Example 1 has a NSE $(\mathbf{v}, 11)$ where $v^1 = v^2 = (0.5, 0.5, 0.5, 0.5)$. If defender 2 deviates to $\widehat{v}^2 = s_1^2$, the attacker tiebreaks, choosing target 22 over target 12, which hurts defender 2. It may be verified that this is indeed a NSE. Introducing $\epsilon = 10^{-3}$ and $k = 100$ fixes this, ensuring target 12 possesses the *strictly* lowest coverage after deviation regardless of v^1. The full derivation is deferred to the extended version.

The non-existence is caused by the rigid enforcement of schedules. For example, even though defender 1 prefers 11 to be attacked over 12, defending 11 through schedule s_1^1 forces it to simultaneously defend 12, which it rather not defend. Our fix expands the attainable coverage V^i: instead of clearance, defenders may provide *less coverage* than what they could have. This assumption was used by [16] and is quite reasonable. For example, a patroller may deliberately let down their guard at areas of lower priority, *encouraging* attacks there.

Assumption 2 (Subset-of-a-Schedule-is-Also-a-Schedule (SSAS))

$$V^i = \left\{ v \in \mathbb{R}_+^T \,\middle|\, \exists x^i \text{ such that } \forall j \in [T] \; v(j) \le \sum_{s_z^i \in \mathcal{S}^i} x^i(s_z^i) \cdot s_z^i(j) \right\}.$$

Assumption 2 is obtained from Assumption 1 by replacing the equality constraint by an inequality. Checking if $v^i \in V^i$ is done efficiently using linear programs. Clearly, V^i under SSAS is a superset of that under clearance. Under SSAS, Example 1 with $\epsilon = 0$ has a NSE $(v^1, v^2, 11)$, where $v^1 = (0, 0.5, 0.5, 0)$, $v_2 = (0, 0, 0, 1.0)$. Details, alongside the $\epsilon > 0$ case are in the extended version.

4.1   Existence and Computation of NSE Assuming SSAS

For now, we restrict ourselves to 2 defenders. Under SSAS, any NSE can be converted into a simpler canonical form, which we exploit to guarantee existence for all $\mathcal{S}^i$, together with a polynomial time algorithm. We present these results via a series of reductions. **All proofs are deferred to the appendix.**

Lemma 1. *If (v^1, v^2, t) is an NSE, then there exists another NSE $(\widetilde{v}^1, v^2, t)$ such that (i) $\widetilde{v}^1(t) = 0$ and (ii) $\widetilde{v}^1(j) = v^1(j)$ for all targets $j \ne t \in [T]$.*

Applying Lemma 1 to each defender guarantees that each NSE $(\mathbf{v}, t)$ must correspond to an NSE with zero coverage on t. If we knew the attacked target

t, we can reduce our search to coverage profiles with zero coverage on t. Now, for some NSE $(\mathbf{v}, t)$ consider defender 1's coverage profile v^1 based on defender 2's preference ordering. For illustration, assume WLOG that the targets are ordered in *decreasing* order of defender 2's preference of attacked target. An example is shown in Fig. 3(a), where $t = 4$ and $T = 8$, and the height of each bar corresponds to $v^1(j)$ for each target j. Lemma 1 simply says that the coverage profile in Fig. 3(b) would also constitute an NSE.

Suppose defender 1's goal is to discourage defender 2 from deviating. Since target 4 is attacked, defender 2 benefits from deviating if and only if it can induce some target in $\mathcal{T}_4^{\succ 2}$ to be the new attack target. It does so by increasing coverage over targets in $\mathcal{T}_4^{\prec 2}$ (potentially reducing v^2 elsewhere). Conversely, defender 1 prevents this deviation by ensuring that its minimum coverage v^1 over $\mathcal{T}_4^{\succ 2}$ is as high as possible. Since v^1 shown in in Fig. 3 is part of an NSE, defender 2 does not have a coverage $\widehat{v}^2$ such that $\widehat{v}^2(j) > 3$ for all $\mathcal{T}_4^{\prec 2}$. If such a $\widehat{v}^2$ existed, defender 2 could simply deviate to that (placing no coverage on targets in $\mathcal{T}_4^{\succ 2}$), This induces either target $6 \succ_2 4$ to be attacked. Hence, for defender 1 to discourage deviations from defender 2, it should reduce v^1 in all targets belonging to $\mathcal{T}_4^{\succ 2}$ to be 3, and similarly for all $\mathcal{T}_4^{\prec 2}$, as shown in Fig. 3(c). This new coverage remains a NSE. Lemma 2 formalizes the above argument.

Lemma 2. *Suppose (v^1, v^2, t) is an NSE with $v^1(t) = v^2(t) = 0$. Then there exists another coverage $\widetilde{v}^1$ where (i) $\widetilde{v}^1(t) = 0$, (ii) $\widetilde{v}^1(j) = 0$ for all $j \prec_2 t$, and (iii) $\widetilde{v}^1(j) = \min_{k \succ_2 t} v^1(k)$ for all $j \succ_2 t$, such that $(\widetilde{v}^1, v^2, t)$ is an NSE.*

Lemma 2 allows us to transform any NSE (v^1, v^2, t) into a new NSE by adjusting v^1 appropriately. Clearly, a similar process can be done for defender 2 and v^2. Applying Lemma 2 for both player yields coverages with simpler structures.

Definition 6 (t-standard Coverage). For fixed $t \in [T]$, $v^1 \in V^1$ is a t-standard coverage for defender 1 if (i) there exists $h^1 \geq 0$ and $v^1(j) = h^1$ for all $j \succ_2 t$, and (ii) $v^1(j) = 0$ for all $j \preceq_2 t$. The same holds for defender 2.

Reducing a coverage in an NSE (v^1, v^2, t) into one containing t-standard coverage is done by first applying Lemma 1 to each player, followed by Lemma 2 to each player. Figure 3 illustrates how v^1 evolves according to this reduction as per the prior discussions. Let $\mathcal{H}$ be the (possibly empty) set of NSE (v^1, v^2, t) such that both v^1 and v^2 are t-standard coverage. For a fixed $t \in [T]$, we define $\mathcal{H}_t$ to be all NSE (v^1, v^2, t) in $\mathcal{H}$ where t is attacked. By definition, we have (i) $\mathcal{H}_t$ and $\mathcal{H}_{t'}$ are disjoint when $t \neq t'$, and (ii) $\mathcal{H} = \bigcup_{t \in [T]} \mathcal{H}_t$. The existence of NSE is equivalent to saying that $\mathcal{H}$ is non-empty.

Our algorithm for computing an NSE under Assumption 2 is straightforward: iterate over all targets $t \in [T]$ and search for some element in $\mathcal{H}_t$. Finding some element (if it exists) of $\mathcal{H}_t$ for any t is done in polynomial time by solving 4 linear programs with size polynomial in S^i, n and T, as shown in Algorithm 1. MAXIMINCOV$(\mathcal{T}, V^i)$ is an oracle finding the coverage $v^i \in V^i$ which maximizes the minimum coverage over a given set of targets $\mathcal{T}$. MAXIMINCOV returns $+\infty$ when $\mathcal{T} = \emptyset$. When V^i is defined by a finite set of schedules $\mathcal{S}^i$ and SSAS, MAXIMINCOV can be implemented via linear programming (Algorithm 2).

Algorithm 1 NSE for 2 defenders	**Algorithm 2** MAXIMINCOV
Input: n, T, V^1, V^2	
Output: an NSE $(\mathbf{v}, t)$	**Input:** schedules $\mathcal{S}^i, \mathcal{T} \subseteq [T]$
for $t = 1$ **to** T **do**	**Output:** i's Maximin coverage over $\mathcal{T}$
$\quad h^1 \leftarrow$ MAXIMINCOV$(\mathcal{T}_t^{\succ 2}, V^1)$	**Solve:** max $\quad h$
$\quad g^1 \leftarrow$ MAXIMINCOV$(\mathcal{T}_t^{\preceq 2}, V^2)$	$\quad$ s.t. $v^i(t) \leq \sum\limits_{s_z^i \in \mathcal{S}^i} x^i(z) \cdot s_z^i(t) \quad \forall t \in [T]$
$\quad h^2 \leftarrow$ MAXIMINCOV$(\mathcal{T}_t^{\succ 1}, V^2)$	
$\quad g^2 \leftarrow$ MAXIMINCOV$(\mathcal{T}_t^{\preceq 1}, V^1)$	$\quad v^i(j) \geq h \quad \forall j \in \mathcal{T}$
$\quad$ **if** $h^1 \geq g^1$ and $h^2 \geq g^2$ **then**	
$\quad\quad$ **for** $j = 1$ **to** T **do**	$\quad \sum\limits_{z \in [S^i]} x^i(z) = 1, \quad x^i \in \mathbb{R}_+^{\mathcal{S}^i}$
$\quad\quad\quad v^1(j) \leftarrow h^1$ if $j \in \mathcal{T}_t^{\succ 2}$ else 0	
$\quad\quad\quad v^2(j) \leftarrow h^2$ if $j \in \mathcal{T}_t^{\succ 1}$ else 0	
$\quad\quad$ **return** (v^1, v^2, t)	

Fig. 4. Left: Solving NSE in 2 defender games. Right: A linear program finding the Maximin coverage for defender i when V^i is given by schedules $\mathcal{S}^i$ and SSAS.

Theorem 1. *Under the SSAS assumption (Assumption 2), $\mathcal{H} \neq \emptyset$, i.e., an NSE always exists. Consequently, Algorithm 1 is guaranteed to return an NSE.*

4.2 Efficiency of NSE

Blindly applying Algorithm 1 can lead to a pathology where the attacked target is undesirable for both players, i.e., a NSE $(\mathbf{v}, t)$ can have $v^1(\widetilde{t}) \geq 0$ and $v^2(\widetilde{t}) \geq 0$ when $\widetilde{t} \succ_1 t$ and $\widetilde{t} \succ_2 t$. For example, suppose $1 \succ_1 2 \succ_1 3$ and $1 \succ_2 2 \succ_2 3$ where defenders possess identity schedules, i.e., $\mathcal{S}^i = \{(1, 0, 0), (0, 1, 0), (0, 0, 1)\}$. Setting $\widetilde{v}^1 = \widetilde{v}^2 = (1, 0, 0)$, we find that $(\widetilde{\mathbf{v}}, 2)$ is an NSE as it is AIC and neither defender can give target 1 a coverage strictly greater than 1 by deviating. However, both defenders prefer target 1 to be attacked. Indeed, a trivial NSE is $(\mathbf{v}, 1)$ where $v^1 = v^2 = (0, 0, 0)$, i.e., the profile $(\mathbf{v}, 1)$ "Pareto dominates" $(\widetilde{\mathbf{v}}, 2)$.

Definition 7 (Inefficiency). An NSE $(v^1, v^2, t) \in \mathcal{H}_t$ is inefficient (resp. efficient) if and only if there exists j where $j \succ_1 t$ and $j \succ_2 t$. Targets constituting inefficient (resp. efficient) NSE are called inefficient (resp. efficient) targets.

Targets where $\mathcal{H}_t = \emptyset$ are neither efficient nor inefficient. There may exist multiple efficient NSE. However, we show that efficient NSE exists under SSAS.

Lemma 3. *Let $j, t \in [T]$ such that $\mathcal{H}_t \neq \emptyset$, $j \succ_1 t$ and $j \succ_2 t$. Then, $\mathcal{H}_j \neq \emptyset$.*

4.3 Exploiting Additional Structure in V^i

We now move towards characterizing and solving for equilibrium in two classes of games which contain even more structure in V^i.

Finding NSE Under Monotone Schedules. The first is the case of *Monotone Schedules*, where each defender's schedule places less coverage on targets preferred to be attacked. This allows us to efficiently solve for NSE when $n \geq 2$.

Assumption 3 (Monotone schedules (MS)). *A schedule $s_z^i \in S^i$ is Monotone if $j \succ_i t \implies s_z^i(j) \leq s_z^i(t)$. The game possesses Monotone Schedules (MS) if all defender schedules are monotone.*

Theorem 2. *Under both MS and SSAS, a NSE exists for $n \geq 2$. It can be computed in polynomial time in the number of schedules, n, and T.*

Proof. Define $\pi_i(t) \in [T]$ such that target t is the $\pi_i(t)$-th preferred target of defender i. Define a matrix $\mathcal{M} \in \mathbb{R}^{n \times T}$, where $\mathcal{M}_{i,\pi_i(j)} =$ MAXIMINCOV$(\mathcal{T}_j^{\preceq i}, V^i)$ for each defender i and target j.[4] $\mathcal{M}$ is non-decreasing from left to right. Let $F(t) = \max_i \mathcal{M}_{i,\pi_i(t)}$. For convenience, we assume $F(t) \neq F(t')$ for $t \neq t'$ such that $\text{Argmin}_t F(t) = \{k^*\}$. We construct a NSE $(\mathbf{v}, k^*)$ where:

1. for all defenders i, $v^i(k^*) = 0$ such that $v^{total}(k^*) = 0$, and
2. for every $t \neq k^*$, we find a defender i where $\mathcal{M}_{i,\pi_i(t)} = F(t)$. We set coverage $v^i(t) = F(k^*)$ and $v^{i'}(t) = 0$ for all $i' \in [n] \backslash \{i\}$.

Clearly, the above algorithm runs polynomial time. In Step 2, we have by definition at least one defender i satisfying $\mathcal{M}_{i,\pi_i(t)} = F(t)$. We first show that $\mathbf{v}$ is achievable, i.e., $v^i \in V^i$ for all defenders i. Fix $i \in [n]$. Let $\mathcal{T}$ be the set of targets covered by it, each with coverage $F(k^*)$. By Step 1, $k^* \notin \mathcal{T}$. Furthermore, $\mathcal{T} \subseteq \mathcal{T}_{k^*}^{\preceq i}$. If target $j \in \mathcal{T}$ and $j \succ_i k^*$, then $\mathcal{M}_{i,\pi_i(j)} \leq \mathcal{M}_{i,\pi_i(k^*)}$ since $\mathcal{M}$ is non-decreasing. This contradicts $\mathcal{M}_{i,\pi_i(j)} = F(j) > F(k^*) \geq \mathcal{M}_{i,\pi_i(k^*)}$ from the definition of F and k^*. Now, let j^* be defender i's most preferred target in $\mathcal{T}$. Consider a coverage $\widetilde{v}^i$ with $\widetilde{v}^i(j) = F(j^*)$ for $j \preceq_i j^*$ and $\widetilde{v}^i(j) = 0$ otherwise. In Step 2, $v^i(j^*) > 0$ implies $F(j^*) = \mathcal{M}_{i,\pi_i(j^*)}$, because only targets j such that $F(j) = \mathcal{M}_{i,\pi_i(j)}$ are covered by i. Hence, $F(j^*) = \mathcal{M}_{i,\pi_i(j^*)} =$ MAXIMINCOV$(\mathcal{T}_{j^*}^{\preceq i}, V^i)$ and $\widetilde{v}^i \in V^i$. Since $F(j^*) \geq F(k^*)$, $\widetilde{v}^i(j) \geq v^i(j)$ for $j \in [T]$, i.e., coverage of $\widetilde{v}^i$ is no less than v^i. Because $\widetilde{v}^i \in V^i$, $v^i \in V^i$ by SSAS.

Lastly, we show that $(\mathbf{v}, k^*)$ is indeed an NSE. It is AIC since $v^{total}(k^*) = 0$. Next, we prove that for any defender i, any $\widehat{v}^i \in V^i$ and any target $t \succ_i k^*$, $(v^1, \cdots, \widehat{v}^i, \cdots, v^n, t)$ is not i-WAIC. First, we show that $\widehat{v}^{total}(t) \geq F(k^*)$. We have $\widehat{v}^{total}(t) = \widehat{v}^i(t) + \sum_{i' \neq i} v^{i'}(t) \geq \sum_{i' \neq i} v^{i'}(t)$. Since v^i has no coverage on $\mathcal{T}_{k^*}^{\succ i}$, $v^i(t) = 0$. Therefore, $\sum_{i' \neq i} v^{i'}(t) = v^{total}(t) = F(k^*)$. We have

---

[4] i.e., for each defender, reorder targets from most to least preferred (Fig. 3) and compute the maximin coverage for targets comprising t and everything less preferred.

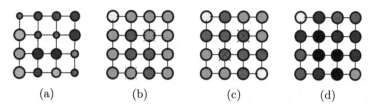

Fig. 5. Public Security Game with $m = 4$, $r = 2$, using the L1-distance. (a) Preference profiles for defenders. Size of nodes represent relative values of targets for each defender. (b) Coverage by the defender 1, v^1 by evenly distributing resource between buildings marked by in green. Darker targets enjoy a higher coverage. Note that overlapping regions get double the coverage. (c) Same as (b), but for defender 2. (d) Total coverage v^{total} accrued over both entities. (Color figure online)

$\widehat{v}^{total}(t) \geq \sum_{i' \neq i} v^{i'}(t) = F(k^*)$. Second, $\widehat{v}^{total}(k^*) \leq F(k^*)$. $\widehat{v}^{total}(k^*) = \widehat{v}^i(k^*)$ since $v^{i'}(k^*) = 0$ for any $i' \neq i$. We claim that $\widehat{v}^i(k^*) \leq F(k^*)$. If $\widehat{v}^i(k^*) > F(k^*)$, defender i can cover all targets in $T_{k^*}^{\preceq i}$ with $\widehat{v}^i(k^*) > F(k^*)$ by MS. Therefore, $\mathcal{M}_{i,\pi_i(k^*)} > F(k^*)$, which conflicts with $F(k^*) = \max_{i'} \mathcal{M}_{i',\pi_{i'}(k^*)}$. We have $\widehat{v}^{total}(k^*) = \widehat{v}^i(k^*) \leq F(k^*)$. In conclusion, $\widehat{v}^{total}(t) \geq \widehat{v}^{total}(k^*)$. If $t \in B(\widehat{v}^{total})$, $k^* \in B(\widehat{v}^{total})$ holds, so $(v^1, \cdots, \widehat{v}^i, \cdots, v^n, t)$ is not i-WAIC. $(\mathbf{v}, k^*)$ is i-IC. ∎

Efficient Solvers when V^i is Compactly Represented. In Algorithm 1, we were required to optimize over t-standard coverage for each defender. This involves solving linear programs. Unfortunately, the number of schedules can be prohibitively large. For example, in patrolling on layered networks, the number of schedules is exponential in its depth and is computationally infeasible for large games. Fortunately, both our proof of existence and algorithm operate in the space of attainable coverage V^i and not directly on x and S^i. In our example, V^i can be expressed as flows in the network (and more generally, any directed acyclic graph with a source and a sink), which in turn is a polyhedron with a polynomial number of constraints (in terms of the number of edges and vertices).

5 Experiments

Our experiments are conducted on an Intel(R) Core(TM) i7-7700K CPU @ 4.20 GHz. We use Gurobi [10] to solve linear programs. We seek to answer the following. (i) Can NSE be practically computed for reasonable environments? How does computational time scale with parameters such as T, S^i, V^i, and n? (ii) How does an NSE look like qualitatively? When $n = 2$, how many NSE are efficient? What proportion of targets are included in *some* NSE? (iii) What is the quality (in terms of the attacked target) in the multiple-defender setting as compared to single defender settings? We explore 3 synthetically generated games, where defender preferences $\succ_i$ are generated uniformly at random.

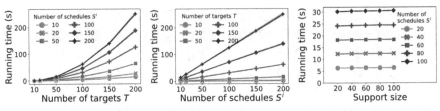

(a) Runtime as T varies   (b) Runtime as S^i varies   (c) Runtime as support size

varies, $T = 100$

Fig. 6. Wallclock time to find one efficient NSE using the algorithm in Fig. 4.

- *Randomly Generated Schedules (RGS).* We generate games with random schedules where each s_j^i is a random integer from $[0, 10]$, and the number of schedules S^i, T are specified. In some cases, we limit each schedule's support size to be smaller than T (with the support again randomly selected).
- *Public Security on Grids (PSG).*
  An event is held in the streets of Manhattan, which we abstract as a $m \times m$ grid (Fig. 5), where each vertex represents a target (building). The security for the event is managed by two entities: the city police and VIP security detail, each with different priorities. Each places checkpoints distributed across buildings in the city, which provide coverage in a radius r. The level of coverage is dependent on the average number of officers allocated to it. An example with $m = 4, r = 2$ is shown in Fig. 5.
- *Patrolling on Layered Networks (PLN).* We follow the motivating example in Sect. 2, varying the width and number of layers. Each patrol can only change its "level" (position on the y-axis) by at most one step between layers. Unlike the public security game, there are now an exponential number of paths, hence computational costs become an important consideration as well.

5.1 Computational Costs of Computing NSE

We first restrict ourselves to 2-defender settings under SASS. We evaluate computational efficiency of the algorithms of Fig. 4, with results for RGS, PSG and PLN summarized in Figs. 6 and 7. For PLN, we utilized the efficient method in Sect. 4.3. We ran 100 trials for each parameter setting and report the mean computation time and their standard errors (which were mostly negligible).

In RGS, we varied T, S^i and the support size of each schedule. As expected, the average running time increases superlinearly with T (Fig. 6a), since the loop in Algorithm 1 is repeated more times, and calls to MAXIMINCOV also incur a higher cost. However, Fig. 6b shows that as S^i increases, the required running time increases linearly. This is unexpected, since S^i is involved in the MAXIMIN-COV subroutine, whose constraint matrix grows linearly with S^i. This suggests that the runtime of MAXIMINCOV grows linearly with S^i, atypical of linear programs. This could be because (i) our problems are small by standards of modern

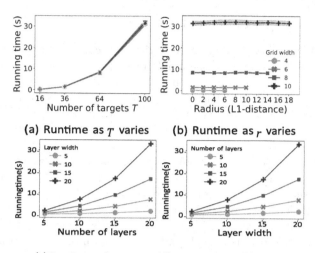

(a) Runtime as T varies (b) Runtime as r varies

(c) Runtime as layers vary (d) Runtime as width varies

Fig. 7. Top: Wallclock time to compute NSE for PSG using the algorithm in Fig. 4. Bottom: Computing NSE for PLN using the method in Sect. 4.3.

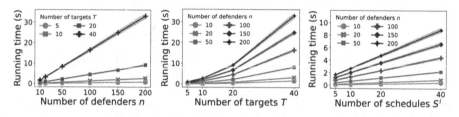

Fig. 8. Top: Running time for RGS under MSS assumptions. Top: Wallclock time as n increases. Bottom: Running time as T and S^i vary.

solvers, or (ii) the solver exploits additional structure under the hood. Lastly, Fig. 6c shows that adjusting support size does not impact running time. This is unsurprising since the solver is not explicitly told to exploit sparsity.

In PSG, we varied T by increasing the grid size m from 4 to 10. As with RGS, Fig. 7aa running time superlinearly with T. We also indirectly adjusted the support size by adjusting r, the radius of security coverage (Fig. 7b). Once again, we did not notice any appreciable difference in running times. Similarly for PLN, we note a superlinear growth in running time as the network enlarges, be it from increasing layers or width of the network (Fig. 7c and 7d).

We now examine multiple defenders in RGS under SSAS and MSS. Again, we ran 100 rounds for each scenario and report the means (standard errors were negligible) in Fig. 8. We observe running times increasing linearly with n and schedules (omitted due to space constraints), but superlinearly with T.

5.2   Quality of NSE Computed

We now investigate the quality of NSE that are computed with 2 defenders, under the SSAS assumption. If there only defender 1 existed (e.g., $V^2 = \{0\})$), then defender 1 simply chooses $v^1 = 0$ and t to be its most desired target to be attacked. The existence of defender 2 makes it such that both defenders must compromise to reach an NSE, with the target to be attacked worsened from defender 1's perspective. In essence, this is the "cost of partnership".

We investigate this degradation in quality of attacked target (in ordinal terms) from the perspective of a single defender. In each run, we compute all the *efficient* NSE and their attacked target's rank in terms of the preference order $\succ_i$. This *rank suboptimality* is a measure of the degradation of policy. Since there are multiple efficient NSE, we consider 3 cases: (i) the optimistic case where we tiebreak to benefit defender 1, (ii) tiebreaking by averaging and (iii) the pessimistic case we tiebreak against defender 1. For each of these settings, we run the experiment 100 times and report the frequency of every rank suboptimality (Fig. 9).

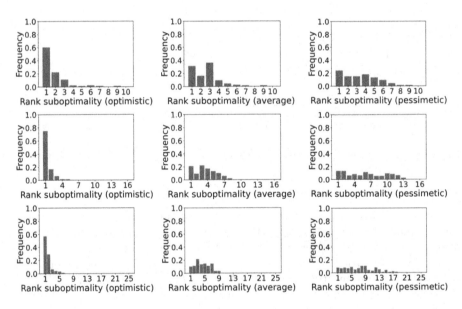

Fig. 9. Rank suboptimality. From top to bottom: RGS with 10 targets, schedules, and full suport, PSG with $m = 4$, $r = 2$, PLN with 5 layers each of width 5.

5.3   Number of Targets Included in NSE

Recall that each of the T targets may be efficient, inefficient or not part of any NSE. We investigate for randomly generated 2 defender games in RGS, PSG

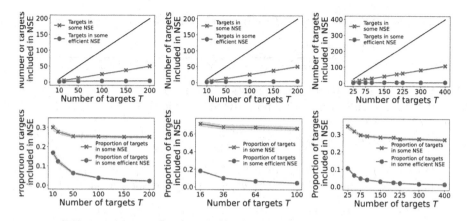

Fig. 10. Top (resp. bottom): #targets (resp. ratio over T) that are efficient NSE as T increases. Left to right: Results for RGS, PSG and PLN respectively.

and PLN the number and proportion of these targets as T varies. For RGS, we fix $S^i = 200$. Our results are reported in Fig. 10. We can see that in all our experiments, the number of efficient targets (or NSE) increase linearly with T, the *proportion* of such targets decreases and tapers off at around 100 targets.

6   Conclusion

In this paper, we explored the problem of multidefender security games in the presence of schedules in the restricted setting of coverage dependant utilities. We show that even in this restricted case, equilibrium may not exist under clearance constraints in contrast to prior work. We show that equilibrium is guaranteed under SSAS and present polynomial time solvers, as well as several extensions. Future work include removing the restriction on coverage dependant utilities as well as extensions to the non-additive or uncoordinated setting.

Acknowledgements. This research was sponsored by the U.S. Army Combat Capabilities Development Command Army Research Laboratory under CRA W911NF-13-2-0045. Co-author Fang is supported in part by NSF grant IIS-2046640 (CAREER) and Sloan Research Fellowship.

A   Appendix

A.1   Proof of Lemma 1

Proof. Since $v^1 \in V^1$ and $\widetilde{v}^1(j) \leq v^1(j)$ for all $j \in [T]$, we have $\widetilde{v}^1 \in V^1$ by Assumption 2. We now show that $(\widetilde{v}^1, v^2, t)$ is AIC, 1-IC, and 2-IC.

1. $(\widetilde{v}^1, v^2, t)$ is AIC. For all $j \in [T]$ and $j \neq t$, we have

$$\widetilde{v}^1(j) + v^2(j) \underbrace{= v^1(j) + v^2(j)}_{\text{definition of } \widetilde{v}^1} \geq \underbrace{v^1(t) + v^2(t)}_{(v^1, v^2, t) \text{ is AIC}} \geq \underbrace{\widetilde{v}^1(t) + v^2(t)}_{\text{by definition of } \widetilde{v}^1} \ .$$

2. $(\widetilde{v}^1, v^2, t)$ is 1-IC. If not, there exists $\widehat{v}^1 \in \mathcal{V}^1, j \succ_1 t$ where $(\widehat{v}^1, v^2, j)$ is 1-WAIC, implying (v^1, v^2, t) is not 1-IC and not an NSE.

3. $(\widetilde{v}^1, v^2, t)$ is 2-IC. Suppose otherwise. Then there exists $\widehat{v}^2 \in \mathcal{V}^2, j \succ_2 t$ where $(\widetilde{v}^1, \widehat{v}^2, j)$ is 2-WAIC, implying that $\widetilde{v}^1(k) + \widehat{v}^2(k) > \widetilde{v}^1(j) + \widehat{v}^2(j)$ for $k \prec_2 j$, and $\widetilde{v}^1(k) + \widehat{v}^2(k) \geq \widetilde{v}^1(j) + \widehat{v}^2(j)$ for $k \succ_2 j$. Then for any $k \succ_2 j(\succ_2 t)$, $\widetilde{v}^1(k) + \widehat{v}^2(k) \geq \widetilde{v}^1(j) + \widehat{v}^2(j)$ indicates that $v^1(k) + \widehat{v}^2(k) \geq v^1(j) + \widehat{v}^2(j)$ by definition of $\widetilde{v}^1$ that $\widetilde{v}^1(k) = v^1(k), \widetilde{v}^1(j) = v^1(j)$. Besides, for any $k \prec_2 j$,

$$\underbrace{v^1(k) + \widehat{v}^2(k) \geq \widetilde{v}^1(k) + \widehat{v}^2(k)}_{\text{by definition of } \widetilde{v}^1} > \underbrace{\widetilde{v}^1(j) + \widehat{v}^2(j)}_{(\widetilde{v}^1, \widehat{v}^2, j) \text{ is 2-WAIC}} = \underbrace{v^1(j) + \widehat{v}^2(j)}_{\text{by definition of } \widetilde{v}^1} \ .$$

Since $(v^1, \widehat{v}^2, j)$ is 2-WAIC, (v^1, v^2, t) is not 2-IC and not an NSE.

A.2 Proof of Lemma 2

Proof. $v^1 \in V^1$ and $\widetilde{v}^1$ has no more coverage than v^1, so $\widetilde{v}^1 \in V^1$ by the SSAS assumption. By the definition of NSE, it is sufficient to show that $(\widetilde{v}^1, v^2, t)$ is AIC, 1-IC, and 2-IC to prove the Lemma.

1. $(\widetilde{v}^1, v^2, t)$ is AIC. $t \in B(\widetilde{v}^1, v^2)$ because $\widetilde{v}^1(t) + v^2(t) = 0$.
2. $(\widetilde{v}^1, v^2, t)$ is 1-IC. If not, then there exists $\widehat{v}^1 \in V^1, j \succ_1 t$ such that $(\widehat{v}^1, v^2, j)$ is 1-WAIC. Therefore, (v^1, v^2, t) is also not 1-IC, contradicting the assumption that (v^1, v^2, t) is an NSE.
3. $(\widetilde{v}^1, v^2, t)$ is 2-IC. We prove this by contradiction. Suppose $(\widetilde{v}^1, v^2, t)$ is not 2-IC, then there exists $\widehat{v}^2 \in V^2, j \succ_2 t$ where $(\widetilde{v}^1, \widehat{v}^2, j)$ is 2-WAIC. By definition of 2-WAIC, we have that $\widetilde{v}^1(k') + \widehat{v}^2(k') > \widetilde{v}^1(j) + \widehat{v}^2(j)$ for any target $k' \prec_2 j$, and $\widetilde{v}^1(k') + \widehat{v}^2(k') \geq \widetilde{v}^1(j) + \widehat{v}^2(j)$ for any target $k' \succ_2 j$. Consider $u^2 \in V^2$ such that $u^2(k') = \widehat{v}^2(k')$ for any target $k' \preceq_2 t$ and $u^2(k') = 0$ for any target $k' \succ_2 t$. Notice that there always exist a unique target $k \in [T]$ such that (v^1, u^2, k) is 2-WAIC. We claim that if k is the target that (v^1, u^2, k) is 2-WAIC, then $k \succ_2 t$. We prove this by excluding other targets $e \preceq_2 t$. Notice that there is a target $m \succ_2 t$ that $v^1(m) = \min_{k' \succ_2 t} v^1(k')$. Consider a target $e \preceq_2 t$, then

$$\underbrace{v^1(e) + u^2(e) \geq \widetilde{v}^1(e) + u^2(e)}_{\text{by definition of } \widetilde{v}^1} \underbrace{= \widetilde{v}^1(e) + \widehat{v}^2(e)}_{\text{by definition of } u^2} > \underbrace{\min_{k' \succ_2 t} \{\widetilde{v}^1(k') + \widehat{v}^2(k')\}}_{(\widetilde{v}^1, \widehat{v}^2, j) \text{ is 2-WAIC}}$$

$$\underbrace{\geq \min_{k' \succ_2 t} \widetilde{v}^1(k')}_{\widehat{v}^2(k') \geq 0} \underbrace{= v^1(m)}_{\text{by definition of } m} \underbrace{= v^1(m) + u^2(m)}_{u^2(m)=0} \ .$$

Thus, e has more coverage than m, so (v^1, u^2, e) is not 2-WAIC. Then $k \preceq_2 t$ does not hold. There exists a target $k \succ_2 t$ such that (v^1, u^2, k) is 2-WAIC, so (v^1, v^2, t) is not 2-IC, which contradicts that (v^1, v^2, t) is an NSE. ∎

A.3   Proof of Theorem 1

To better understand the structure of $\mathcal{H}$, we introduce *partial* sets $\mathcal{H}_t^1 \subset V^1, \mathcal{H}_t^2 \subset V^2$ for $\mathcal{H}_t$ and show how they compose the set $\mathcal{H}_t$.

Definition 8. $\mathcal{H}_t^1$ is the set of $v^1 \in V^1$ such that there exists $h^1 \geq 0, v^1(j) = h^1$ for any target $j \in T_t^{\succ 2}, v^1(j) = 0$ for any target $j \in T_t^{\preceq 2}$,and there does not exist $j \succ_2 t$ and $\widehat{v}^2 \in V^2, (v^1, \widehat{v}^2, j)$ is 2-WAIC. Similar for $\mathcal{H}_t^2$.

Theorem 3. $\mathcal{H}_t = \mathcal{H}_t^1 \times \mathcal{H}_t^2 \times \{t\}$.

Proof. For any $(v^1, v^2, t) \in \mathcal{H}_t$, v^1 and v^2 are t-standard coverage. Since $\mathcal{H}_t$ only contains NSEs, (v^1, v^2, t) is 1-IC and 2-IC. Thus, $v^1 \in \mathcal{H}_t^1, v^2 \in \mathcal{H}_t^2$. We now show that for any coverage $v^1 \in \mathcal{H}_t^1$ and $v^2 \in \mathcal{H}_t^2$, $(v^1, v^2, t) \in \mathcal{H}_t$. First, (v^1, v^2, t) is an NSE. (v^1, v^2, t) is AIC because $v^1(t) = v^2(t) = 0$. Also, (v^1, v^2, t) is 1-IC and 2-IC by definition of $\mathcal{H}_t^1$ and $\mathcal{H}_t^2$. Second, v^1 and v^2 are t-standard coverage. Thus, $(v^1, v^2, t) \in \mathcal{H}_t$.   ∎

Theorem 3 decomposes the space of $\mathcal{H}_t$. Next we consider how to compute $\mathcal{H}_t^1$ and $\mathcal{H}_t^2$, which provides us an NSE in $\mathcal{H}_t$. We first consider the reduction of the set containing deviation strategies.

Lemma 4. For a target t and a coverage $v^1 \in \mathcal{H}_t^1$, if there is a $\widehat{v}^2 \in V^2$ and $j \succ_2 t$ such that $(v^1, \widehat{v}^2, j)$ is 2-WAIC, we construct $u^2 \in V^2$ such that $u^2(k) = 0$ for $k \in T_t^{\succ 2}$ and $u^2(k) = \min_{k' \preceq_2 t} \widehat{v}^2(k')$ for $k \in T_t^{\preceq 2}$, then there exists a target $m \succ_2 t$ such that (v^1, u^2, m) is 2-WAIC.

Proof. In a 2-WAIC strategy profile $(v^1, \widehat{v}^2, j)$ and $j \succ_2 t$, $v^1(k) + \widehat{v}^2(k) > v^1(j) + \widehat{v}^2(j)$ for any target $k \preceq_2 t$. Since $v^1 \in \mathcal{H}_t^1$, $v^1(k) = 0$ for any target $k \preceq_2 t$. So, $\min_{k \preceq_2 t} \widehat{v}^2(k) > v^1(j) + \widehat{v}^2(j)$. We have $u^2(k) > v^1(j) + \widehat{v}^2(j)$ by definition of u, so any target $k \in T_t^{\preceq 2}$ is not the attacked target. There always exists a target m such that (v^1, u^2, m) is 2-WAIC, and here $m \succ_2 t$.   ∎

Lemma 4 reduces the deviation $\widehat{v}^2$ to u^2 with a canonical structure that $u^2(k)$ are equal for targets $k \in T_t^{\preceq 2}$, but $u^2(k) = 0$ elsewhere. The computation of u^2 is related to the oracle MAXIMINCOV. For convenience, we use $M^i(T)$ instead of MAXIMINCOV(T, V^i) when the set of coverage is default to be V^i. Formally, $M^i(T) = \max_{v^i \in V^i} \min_{j \in T} v^i(j)$ for $T \neq \emptyset$, and $M^i(T) = +\infty$ for $T = \emptyset$. With this notation, we give a sufficient and necessary condition for $\mathcal{H}_t^i \neq \emptyset$.

Theorem 4. $\mathcal{H}_t^1 \neq \emptyset$ if and only if $M^1(T_t^{\succ 2}) \geq M^2(T_t^{\preceq 2})$. Similarly, $\mathcal{H}_t^2 \neq \emptyset$ if and only if $M^2(T_t^{\succ 1}) \geq M^1(T_t^{\preceq 1})$.

Proof. We prove the first claim for $\mathcal{H}_t^1 \neq \emptyset$, and it is same for $\mathcal{H}_t^2 \neq \emptyset$.

1. When $M^1(T_t^{\succ 2}) \geq M^2(T_t^{\preceq 2})$, we consider a coverage $v^1 \in V^1$ of defender 1 such that $v^1(k) = M^1(T_t^{\succ 2})$ for target $k \succ_2 t$, and $v^1(k) = 0$ elsewhere. For any coverage $\widehat{v}^2 \in V^2$, there is a target $m \in T_t^{\preceq 2}$ such that $v^1(m) + \widehat{v}^2(m) \leq M^2(T_t^{\preceq 2}) \leq v^1(k)$ for any target $k \in T_t^{\succ 2}$. Any target $k \in T_t^{\succ 2}$ has no less coverage than target m given coverage $(v^1, \widehat{v}^2)$, so there does not exist target $j \succ_2 t$ such that $(v^1, \widehat{v}^2, j)$ is 2-WAIC. Thus, $v^1 \in \mathcal{H}_t^1$ by definition.

2. When $M^1(T_t^{\succ_2}) < M^2(T_t^{\preceq_2})$, we want to show that $\mathcal{H}_t^1 = \emptyset$. $M^1(T_t^{\succ_2}) \neq +\infty$, so for any $v^1 \in V^1$, there exists target $j \succ_2 t$ such that $v^1(j) \leq M^1(T_t^{\succ_2})$. Then consider a coverage $\widehat{v}^2 \in V^2$ of defender 2 such that $\widehat{v}^2(k) = M^2(T_t^{\preceq_2})$ for targets $k \in T_t^{\preceq_2}$ and $\widehat{v}^2(k) = 0$ for other targets. In the coverage profile $(v^1, \widehat{v}^2)$, target $k \in T_t^{\preceq_2}$ has strictly more coverage than target j. Notice that there always exists a target j' such that $(v^1, \widehat{v}^2, j')$ is 2-WAIC. Thus, for any $v^1 \in V^1$, there exists $\widehat{v}^2 \in V^2$, such that there exists $j' \succ_2 t$ and $(v^1, \widehat{v}^2, j')$ is 2-WAIC. Therefore, $\mathcal{H}_t^1 = \emptyset$. ∎

Corollary 1. *For any defender $i \in [2]$, there exists $t \in [T]$ such that $\mathcal{H}_t^i \neq \emptyset$.*

Proof. Let $i' \neq i$ be another defender. There exists a target t such that for any target $j \in [T]$, $t \succeq_{i'} j$. Then $M^i(T_t^{\succ_{i'}}) = M^i(\emptyset) = +\infty$. However, $M^{i'}(T_k^{\preceq_{i'}}) = M^{i'}([T])$ is finite. Therefore, $\mathcal{H}_t^i \neq \emptyset$. ∎

Lemma 5. *For any set of targets $T' \subset T$, $M_i(T') \geq M_i(T)$ holds.*

Proof. Let v^{i*} be the coverage when $M_i(T)$ achieves the maximum. Let $v^i = v^{i*}$, then we have $\min_{t_j \in T'} v^i(j) \geq M_i(T)$. Therefore $M_i(T') \geq M_i(T)$. ∎

Lemma 6. *For two defenders i, i' and targets $t \succ_{i'} j$, if $\mathcal{H}_j^i \neq \emptyset$, then $\mathcal{H}_t^i \neq \emptyset$.*

Proof. Since $t \succ_{i'} j$, we have $T_t^{\succ_{i'}} \subset T_j^{\succ_{i'}}$ and $T_j^{\preceq_{i'}} \subset T_t^{\preceq_{i'}}$. By $\mathcal{H}_j^i \neq \emptyset$, we have $M^i(T_j^{\succ_{i'}}) \geq M^{i'}(T_j^{\preceq_{i'}})$. Then using Lemma 5, we get $M^i(T_t^{\succ_{i'}}) \geq M^i(T_j^{\succ_{i'}}) \geq M^{i'}(T_j^{\preceq_{i'}}) \geq M^{i'}(T_t^{\preceq_{i'}})$. By Theorem 4, $\mathcal{H}_k^i \neq \emptyset$. ∎

Theorem 5. $\mathcal{H} \neq \emptyset$.

Proof. Suppose $T^1 = \{t \in [T] | \mathcal{H}_t^2 \neq \emptyset\}$ and $T^2 = \{t \in [T] | \mathcal{H}_t^1 \neq \emptyset\}$. By Corollary 1, $T^1, T^2 \neq \emptyset$ and $T^2 \neq \emptyset$. There is a unique $j_1 \in T^1$ ($j_2 \in T^2$) such that for any $t \in T^1$, $t \succeq_1 j_1$ (for any $t \in T^2$, $t \succeq_2 j_2$). It is sufficient to show that $T^1 \cap T^2 \neq \emptyset$. If we show this, then there is a target $j \in T^1 \cap T^2$. We have $\mathcal{H}_j^1 \neq \emptyset, \mathcal{H}_j^2 \neq \emptyset$, and thus $\mathcal{H} \neq \emptyset$. Next we prove $T^1 \cap T^2 \neq \emptyset$ by contradiction.

Suppose $T^1 \cap T^2 = \emptyset$. Since $T^1, T^2 \neq \emptyset$ and $T^1 \cap T^2 = \emptyset$, we have $\overline{T^1} = [T] \setminus T^1 \neq \emptyset$, and $\overline{T^2} = [T] \setminus T^2 \neq \emptyset$. There is a unique $k_1 \in \overline{T^1}$ ($k_2 \in \overline{T^2}$) such that for any $t \in \overline{T^1}$, $k_1 \succeq_1 t$ (for any $t \in \overline{T^2}$, $k_2 \succeq_2 t$). By Lemma 6, for any target $t \succ_1 j_1$, $t \in T^1$, and for any target $t \succ_2 j_2$, $t \in T^2$. Therefore, $j_1 \succ_1 k_1$ and $j_2 \succ_2 k_2$. Then we have $T_{k_1}^{\succ_1} = T^1, T_{k_1}^{\preceq_1} = \overline{T^1}$, and $T_{k_2}^{\succ_2} = T^2, T_{k_2}^{\preceq_2} = \overline{T^2}$. By Theorem 4 and $\mathcal{H}_{k_1}^2 = \emptyset, \mathcal{H}_{k_2}^1 = \emptyset$, we have $M^2(T^1) < M^1(\overline{T^1})$ and $M^1(T^2) < M^2(\overline{T^2})$. By $T^1 \cap T^2 = \emptyset$, $T^2 \subset \overline{T^1}$ and $T^1 \subset \overline{T^2}$. By Lemma 5, $M^1(\overline{T^1}) < M^1(T^2)$ and $M^2(\overline{T^2}) < M^2(T^1)$. Combining this with previous inequality, we get $M^2(T^1) < M^1(T^2)$ and $M^1(T^2) < M^2(T^1)$, which are contradictory.

Therefore, $T^1 \cap T^2 \neq \emptyset$. There is a target $j \in T^1 \cap T^2$. By definition of T^1, T^2, we have $\mathcal{H}_j^1, \mathcal{H}_j^2 \neq \emptyset$. Thus, $\mathcal{H}_j \neq \emptyset$ by Theorem 3. $\mathcal{H}_j \subset \mathcal{H}$, so $\mathcal{H} \neq \emptyset$. ∎

A.4   Proof of Lemma 3

Proof. By Theorem 3 in the appendix, $\mathcal{H}_t = \mathcal{H}_t^1 \times \mathcal{H}_t^2 \times \{t\}$. $\mathcal{H}_t \neq \emptyset$, so $\mathcal{H}_t^1, \mathcal{H}_t^2 \neq \emptyset$. Since $j \succ_1 t, j \succ_2 t$, further by Lemma 6 in the appendix, we have $\mathcal{H}_j^1, \mathcal{H}_j^2 \neq \emptyset$. Use Theorem 3 again, $\mathcal{H}_j = \mathcal{H}_j^1 \times \mathcal{H}_j^2 \times \{j\}$. Therefore, $\mathcal{H}_j \neq \emptyset$.   ∎

A.5   Proof of Theorem 2 where $F(t) \neq F(t')$

Proof. Here, $\mathrm{Argmin}_t F(t)$ may not be a singleton, and we handle the edge case of selecting a specific k^* from $\mathrm{Argmin}_t F(t)$. Consider the set $\mathcal{F} = \mathrm{Argmin}_t F(t)$ and let $\underline{F} = \min_{t' \in [T]} F(t')$. For any $t, j \in \mathcal{F}, t \neq j$, we say $t \lhd j$ if for any defender i, $\mathcal{M}_{i,\pi_i(t)} = \underline{F} \implies t \succ_i j$. We show that $\lhd$ is transitive. Suppose $t \lhd j$ and $j \lhd j'$. Hence, $t \succ_i j$ for any defender i where $\mathcal{M}_{i,\pi_i(t)} = \underline{F}$. On one hand, $\mathcal{M}_{i,\pi_i(j)} \geq \mathcal{M}_{i,\pi_i(t)} \geq \underline{F}$ since $t \succ_i j$. On the other hand, $j \in \mathcal{F}$, so $\mathcal{M}_{i,\pi_i(j)} \leq \underline{F}$. Therefore, $\mathcal{M}_{i,\pi_i(j)} = \underline{F}$. Using a similar argument on $j \lhd j'$ gives us $\mathcal{M}_{i,\pi_i(t)} = \mathcal{M}_{i,\pi_i(j')} = \underline{F}$ and $t \succ_i j \succ_i j'$. So, $t \lhd j'$ and $\lhd$ is transitive.

We claim there exists a target $k^* \in \mathcal{F}$ such that $\nexists t \in \mathcal{F}, t \lhd k^*$. If not, then for any $k_q \in \mathcal{F}$, there exists $k_{q+1} \in \mathcal{F}$ where $k_{q+1} \lhd k_q$. Thus, we can construct an infinite sequence $\cdots \lhd k_2 \lhd k_1$. Since $\lhd$ is transitive, each k_q must be distinct, which is not possible with a finite number of targets. Now we select a target k^*.

Once k^* is selected, we set $v^i(k^*) = 0$ for all defenders i. For any $t \neq k^*$, we have $F(t) \geq F(k^*)$. For a fixed t, there are two cases: (i) if $F(t) > F(k^*)$, for any defender i such that $\mathcal{M}_{i,\pi_i(t)} = F(t)$, we have $k^* \succ_i t$, since $\mathcal{M}_{i,\pi_i(t)} > F(k^*) \geq \mathcal{M}_{i,\pi_i(k^*)}$. (ii) If $F(t) = F(k^*)$, there is at least one defender i satisfying $\mathcal{M}_{i,\pi_i(t)} = F(t)$ such that $k^* \succ_i t$, otherwise $t \lhd k^*$, contradicting the choice of k^*. Thus, for any $t \neq k^*$, there always exists a defender i where $\mathcal{M}_{i,\pi_i(t)} = F(t)$ and $k^* \succ_i t$. Our construction sets $v^i(t) = F(k^*)$ and $v^{i'}(t) = 0$ for $i' \neq i$. Showing $\mathbf{v}$ is feasible and $(\mathbf{v}, k^*)$ is an NSE is same with the main proof of Theorem 2.∎

References

1. An, B., Tambe, M., Sinha, A.: Stackelberg security games (SSG) basics and application overview. Improving Homeland Security Decisions, p. 485 (2017)
2. Attiah, A., Chatterjee, M., Zou, C.C.: A game theoretic approach to model cyber attack and defense strategies. In: 2018 IEEE International Conference on Communications (ICC), pp. 1–7. IEEE (2018)
3. Basak, A., Fang, F., Nguyen, T.H., Kiekintveld, C.: Combining graph contraction and strategy generation for green security games. In: Zhu, Q., Alpcan, T., Panaousis, E., Tambe, M., Casey, W. (eds.) GameSec 2016. LNCS, vol. 9996, pp. 251–271. Springer, Cham (2016). https://doi.org/10.1007/978-3-319-47413-7_15
4. Černỳ, J., Bošanskỳ, B., Kiekintveld, C.: Incremental strategy generation for Stackelberg equilibria in extensive-form games. In: Proceedings of the 2018 ACM Conference on Economics and Computation, pp. 151–168. ACM (2018)
5. Fang, F., et al.: Paws-a deployed game-theoretic application to combat poaching. AI Mag. **38**(1), 23 (2017)
6. Fang, F., et al.: Deploying paws: field optimization of the protection assistant for wildlife security (2016)

7. Fang, F., Stone, P., Tambe, M.: When security games go green: designing defender strategies to prevent poaching and illegal fishing. In: IJCAI, pp. 2589–2595 (2015)
8. Gan, J., Elkind, E., Kraus, S., Wooldridge, M.: Defense coordination in security games: equilibrium analysis and mechanism design. Artif. Intell. **313**, 103791 (2022)
9. Gan, J., Elkind, E., Wooldridge, M.: Stackelberg security games with multiple uncoordinated defenders (2018)
10. Gurobi Optimization, L.: Gurobi optimizer reference manual (2021). http://www.gurobi.com
11. Jain, M., An, B., Tambe, M.: Security games applied to real-world: research contributions and challenges. In: Jajodia, S., Ghosh, A., Subrahmanian, V., Swarup, V., Wang, C., Wang, X. (eds.) Moving Target Defense II. Advances in Information Security, vol. 100, pp. 15–39. Springer, New York (2013). https://doi.org/10.1007/978-1-4614-5416-8_2
12. Jain, M., Kardes, E., Kiekintveld, C., Ordónez, F., Tambe, M.: Security games with arbitrary schedules: a branch and price approach. In: Proceedings of the AAAI Conference on Artificial Intelligence, vol. 24, pp. 792–797 (2010)
13. Jiang, A.X., Procaccia, A.D., Qian, Y., Shah, N., Tambe, M.: Defender (mis) coordination in security games. In: Twenty-Third International Joint Conference on Artificial Intelligence (2013)
14. Kar, D., et al.: Trends and applications in Stackelberg security games. In: Handbook of Dynamic Game Theory, pp. 1–47 (2017)
15. Kiekintveld, C., Jain, M., Tsai, J., Pita, J., Ordóñez, F., Tambe, M.: Computing optimal randomized resource allocations for massive security games. In: Proceedings of The 8th International Conference on Autonomous Agents and Multiagent Systems-Volume 1, pp. 689–696. International Foundation for Autonomous Agents and Multiagent Systems (2009)
16. Korzhyk, D., Conitzer, V., Parr, R.: Complexity of computing optimal Stackelberg strategies in security resource allocation games. In: Proceedings of the AAAI Conference on Artificial Intelligence, vol. 24, pp. 805–810 (2010)
17. Letchford, J., Conitzer, V.: Computing optimal strategies to commit to in extensive-form games. In: Proceedings of the 11th ACM Conference on Electronic Commerce, pp. 83–92. ACM (2010)
18. Letchford, J., Vorobeychik, Y.: Computing optimal security strategies for interdependent assets. arXiv preprint arXiv:1210.4873 (2012)
19. Ling, C.K., Brown, N.: Safe search for Stackelberg equilibria in extensive-form games. In: Proceedings of the AAAI Conference on Artificial Intelligence, vol. 35, pp. 5541–5548 (2021)
20. Lou, J., Vorobeychik, Y.: Equilibrium analysis of multi-defender security games. In: Twenty-Fourth International Joint Conference on Artificial Intelligence (2015)
21. Pawlick, J., Colbert, E., Zhu, Q.: A game-theoretic taxonomy and survey of defensive deception for cybersecurity and privacy. ACM Comput. Surv. (CSUR) **52**(4), 1–28 (2019)
22. Pita, J., et al.: Armor security for Los Angeles international airport. In: AAAI, pp. 1884–1885 (2008)
23. Pita, J., et al.: Using game theory for Los Angeles airport security. AI Mag. **30**(1), 43 (2009)
24. Shieh, E., et al.: Protect: a deployed game theoretic system to protect the ports of the united states. In: Proceedings of the 11th International Conference on Autonomous Agents and Multiagent Systems, vol. 1, pp. 13–20 (2012)

25. Tambe, M.: Security and Game Theory: Algorithms, Deployed Systems, Lessons Learned. Cambridge University Press, Cambridge (2011)
26. Von Stackelberg, H.: Marktform und gleichgewicht. Springer, Heidelberg (1934)
27. Von Stengel, B., Zamir, S.: Leadership games with convex strategy sets. Games Econom. Behav. **69**(2), 446–457 (2010)
28. Wang, Y., et al.: Deep reinforcement learning for green security games with real-time information. In: Proceedings of the AAAI Conference on Artificial Intelligence, vol. 33, pp. 1401–1408 (2019)
29. Zarreh, A., Saygin, C., Wan, H., Lee, Y., Bracho, A.: A game theory based cyber-security assessment model for advanced manufacturing systems. Procedia Manufacturing **26**, 1255–1264 (2018)

Asymmetric Centrality Game Against Network Epidemic Propagation

Willie Kouam[1,2]($\boxtimes$) (ID), Yezekael Hayel[2] (ID), Gabriel Deugoué[1] (ID),
Olivier Tsemogne[4] (ID), and Charles Kamhoua[3] (ID)

[1] University of Dschang, Dschang, Cameroon
[2] CERI/LIA, Avignon Université, Avignon, France
willie.kouam@alumni.univ-avignon.fr, yezekael.hayel@univ-avignon.fr
[3] DEVCOM Army Research Laboratory, Adelphi, USA
charles.a.kamhoua.civ@army.mil
[4] IMT Atlantique, Brest, France

Abstract. The Mirai botnet network epidemic discovered in 2016 falls into the category of numerous epidemics propagated by attackers over a network to gain control over multiple devices. This particular epidemic has been employed in some of the most extensive and widespread distributed denial of service (DDoS) attacks [24]. To take control of numerous devices, the attacker's strategy consists of injecting malicious code from an infected device into one or more vulnerable neighboring devices. This initiates a conflict, as the defender attempts to restrict the attacker's influence and control. Intelligent and rational agents (defender and attacker) thus engage in a conflictual interaction, constantly competing for optimal strategies within the network. Their objective is to gain control over the most crucial devices, which are identified using *centrality measures*. Nevertheless, an agent's perception of the significance of devices may vary due to factors such as variations in roles, information accessibility, available resources, and diverse viewpoints on risks, issues, or opportunities [8]. Consequently, the agents involved in the process may hold different views regarding the significance of devices, resulting in the utilization of different centrality measures. The significance of considering these variations in centrality measures, as well as the impact on each agent's objective, is emphasized by our analysis. Hence, we propose a non-zero-sum game model to identify the optimal centrality measure for each agent in the context of controlling an epidemic spread. Our model also provides the NE (Nash Equilibrium) strategy profile for agents at each stage of the game. Numerical experiments show that, by taking into account these differences in centrality measures and using our game model, defenders effectively limit the impact of epidemics caused by malicious attackers.

Keywords: Epidemic network · Cyber deception · Centrality measure · Non-zero-sum game

© The Author(s), under exclusive license to Springer Nature Switzerland AG 2023
J. Fu et al. (Eds.): GameSec 2023, LNCS 14167, pp. 86–109, 2023.
https://doi.org/10.1007/978-3-031-50670-3_5

1   Introduction

Networks have become an essential part of our daily lives, ranging from social networks to transportation networks, and even cyber networks. One of the critical challenges in these networks is controlling epidemics that spread through them [16]. The spread of epidemics in a network is commonly due to an agent attempting to compromise devices in the network through a cyber-attack, which spreads like a virus, infecting other devices in the network. To prevent this, various techniques have been developed, including the use of game theory [9,25,26]. However, motivated by propagation scenarios involving two main agents, one of which aimed to eventually compromise the system, we take into consideration a wide range of games wherein the attacker and the defender's interactions are dynamic, involve uncertainty, and could extend over a long period of time. In recent years, game theory has emerged as a powerful tool to model and analyze the strategic interactions between agents in such networked systems and has been applied in many fields, including cyber security [5].

In the field of game theory for cyber security, the problem of epidemic control has become increasingly important due to the rise of epidemics caused by malicious intelligent and rational agents, who generally have complete information about the state of the network. Due to the attacker's informational advantage, a variety of deception techniques have been developed to safeguard the network. Deception is a cyber defense mechanism that aims to intentionally misguide the cyber attacker by hiding true information or presenting false information to attackers, in order to prevent or at least to reduce damages from cyber attacks [21]. One important cyber deception technique under uncertainty is the use of tools such as honeypots to mislead attackers and detect attacks [1]. Therefore, the authors of [22], employing honeypot placement as a defense technique, recently proposed a one-sided partially observable stochastic game framework for determining an optimal strategy for both the attacker and defender in the context of network epidemic problems. However, the proposed value iteration (VI) algorithm presents a major problem related to scalability (24 nodes in the context of lateral movement problems with lower dimensional states and belief spaces). Meanwhile, the epidemic control problem generally applies to networks with numerous devices and, henceforth, requires more efficient tools. To address this issue, the authors of [23] modeled the epidemic control problem as a game between two players who make decisions based on centrality measures, which are measures of a device's importance or influence in a network. Nonetheless, the study only examines the scenario where both agents use the same centrality measures from the outset of the game. In practice, however, agents may hold varying perspectives and levels of knowledge regarding the significance of devices within a network. Due to the asymmetry of the agents' knowledge, they may have divergent preferences regarding the centrality measures they choose, as these decisions are influenced by the information available to each of them.

Exploring the scenario in which agents use distinct centrality measures holds significant importance for various reasons. Firstly, different centrality measures capture various aspects of a device's significance in a network [15]. Due to agents' lack of awareness of each other's methods, they may have distinct opinions on which nodes are the most important. Secondly, agents may have varying preferences for using different centrality measures due to factors like implementation complexity and impact on the network. For instance, one agent may prefer degree centrality for its simplicity, while another agent may favor betweenness centrality for its consideration of the network's overall structure. Finally, the use of different centrality measures may lead to different decisions and outcomes, affecting the effectiveness of epidemic control strategies. Studying the impact of different centrality measures on agents' decisions and strategies can help us understand how information and objectives influence decision-making and the resilience of epidemic control strategies to errors or inaccuracies in centrality measures.

This article thus presents a new approach to the centrality game on a network using a cyber deception technique. The proposed game is asymmetric, with two players making decisions based on their respective centrality measures. The game is modeled as a two-player non-zero-sum game on a graph, where the nodes represent devices in the network, and the edges represent attacks using specific vulnerabilities. The attacker sequentially chooses from any infected node, adjacent and susceptible nodes to attack keeping his position secret from the defender. On his side, the defender chooses edges that will act as honeypots, to detect and counteract unauthorized use of information systems; the proposed model considers several factors. First, each player chooses his or her centrality measure at the start of the game, and this choice is common knowledge. Second, the attacker does not observe all the actions of the defender after a given time slot. Third, the detection of transmission means that the defender cures the infected node, the source of the transmission. Moreover, although the nodes lack intelligence and rationality, they have the potential to make decisions based on their current state. During each time slot, a node has the potential to transition from a Susceptible to a Resistant state or from an Infected to a Susceptible state, but the exact probabilities of these changes are only known to the defender. This assumes that a time slot of the game consists of two stages: the stage of *strategic interactions* and the stage of *random transitions*. We thus propose four key contributions for improving the scalability of the proposed solution:

- a two-player non-zero-sum infinite horizon stochastic game is studied in which no player observes the opponent's actions,
- a coupled system in which two players act strategically and a set of nodes react to their individual states,
- an investigation of the impact of different centrality measures on agents' strategies and the game outcome,
- an examination of the effects of network topology and parameter settings on the game outcome.

Our results highlight the importance of taking into account the heterogeneity in agents' perspectives when designing strategies for epidemic control problems in networks.

2   Related Work

A common cause of epidemic spread in networks is the attempt by an agent to compromise the computers in the network through a cyber attack, with various goals such as distributed denial of service (DDoS). Indeed, DDoS follows the furtive preliminary recruitment of devices into a zombie army called a botnet [12]. A report by [11] revealed that during the period between April 2013 and May 2014, DDoS attacks affected 38% of companies that provide financial services or operate online services for the public. The mathematical modeling of epidemics borrows fundamental notions from epidemiology in that the population is divided into compartments and the name of the epidemic is derived from the possible compartments and the possible transitions of an individual between compartments. Thus, several epidemic models can be distinguished, namely SIS, SIR, etc. The concept of Nash equilibrium has been used in several works including various epidemic models to determine a profile of equilibrium strategies between conflicting agents. For example, the NE concept is used in [19] and [20] to stop the spread of SIS epidemics in a decentralized manner and to optimize influence in competitive contexts. To compare the advantages of centralized and decentralized protection of a network against threats, Trajanovski, Hayel, et al. [19] discuss the price of anarchy (PoA) in a single community, bipartite, and multi-community networks. They prove the existence of the Nash equilibrium and outline a reinforcement learning algorithm to find the NE in pure strategies. However, like several other authors, they did not include strategic defense mechanisms as deception schemes, despite their effectiveness in contexts with asymmetric information and an attacker's advantage. Several deception methods exist in the literature related to network security. In [17] numerous deception techniques have been proposed for network security, such as impersonation, delays, fakes, camouflage, false excuses, and social engineering because traditional cybersecurity approaches face a continual cycle of detecting and responding to new threats and vulnerabilities. Therefore, game models are more elaborated and computers can examine the huge number of possible threat scenarios in cyber systems better than humans. However here, no one is guaranteed to have information dominance in terms of intelligence and accessibility. Hence the importance of game theory for cyber security. Because of these observations, the authors of [22] employed a SIR-type game model integrating game theory and cyber deception for epidemics. Indeed, they modeled the problem as a partially observable stochastic game on a graph in which the defender aims to optimize the placement of honeypots to mislead the attacker as much as possible. However, the proposed approach presents problems related to the scalability with the size and complexity of the proposed Heuristic Search Value Iteration (HSVI) algorithm [10].

According to some authors, the globality of the proposed solution in the previous approach may be responsible for these limitations, as it does not consider the topology of the considered graph. Therefore, [23] proposed an approach in which the agents pose their actions taking into account the influence of the nodes in the graph, influence measured through various centrality measures [2]. The authors of [23] demonstrated that their model is a game of centralities thresholds, and provided the necessary conditions for obtaining a Nash equilibrium. However, these results were based on the assumption that the two agents in conflict act according to the same centrality measure, which is not always the case in real-world situations. Indeed, in most cyber security problems, the protagonists do not have identical information and resources. As a result of this asymmetry, there can be an asymmetry in their perceptions of a node's importance within the graph. The selection of the centrality measure is thus influenced, resulting in agents eventually opting for different centrality measures.

3   General Model Description

In this game, there are two sides: the attacker, who controls the malware and wants to infect as many devices in the network as possible, and the defender, who wants to stop or reduce the infection. The devices in the network will make a decision based on their own state. As the game progresses, different stages will occur, and we'll explain each one in more detail. So, in summary, it's a battle between the attacker and defender to control the network, and the network devices will make a probabilistic decision based on their current state.

3.1   Problem Description

The attacker tries to infect a maximum number of devices in the network to reach a minimum threshold that will allow her to launch her attack. She can do this because some devices have weak points that can be easily taken advantage of. For example, many devices use default passwords that don't change for a long time, so they are more likely to be hacked, due to the relatively limited range of default passwords. Knowing the status of each device through frequent probes enables the attacker to infect and compromise the system to spread the malware. To prevent this spread, we suggest the defender deploy a patch for infected devices and use a cyber deception technique. An Intrusion Detection System (IDS) installed on certain network edges can identify code transmissions and nullify them, but this defensive action could reveal the defender's countermeasures to the attacker. To conceal the defensive measure, we propose that the defender allows the code to reach its target, revealing to the attacker that the device is infected, and then disinfects the device before the attacker's subsequent probe. The tool thus used is called an *intrusion-proof system (IPS)* in the following. It can detect malicious connectivity attempts and automatically install patches on infected devices that are sources of the malware propagation attempt. Additionally, users of infected or vulnerable devices can choose to accept the patch or customize their password, and the defender is informed of their decision. The probabilities of infected devices accepting patches and vulnerable devices customizing passwords are known only to the defender and are not reported to the attacker.

3.2   System Model

This section provides a detailed description of the interactions between the attacker and the defender in the context of an epidemic spread. The model takes into consideration three main factors: the conflicting interests of the two parties, the dynamic spread of the virus through the network, and the response of each device depending on its current state. To distinguish between the strategic interactions of the players and the internal state transitions of the devices, the model assumes that the game is divided into time slots, with each time slot comprising two stages: the strategic stage (the first stage) and the reactive stage (the second stage).

3.2.1   Time Slot Description

A time slot in this framework involves two distinct stages: firstly, the strategic actions of the attacker and defender, and secondly, the probabilistic moves/reactions of the devices, which depend on their current state, i.e., internal state transitions of the devices.

Strategic stage: The two players (attacker and defender) make their actions, which result in an intermediate state $a(z)_i$ for each device i of the network.

- *Attacker:* Assuming perfect information about the state of each device in the network at every time slot, the attacker is the strategic and rational agent who spreads malware through the network by silently propagating it from each infected device to adjacent susceptible devices. However, the attacker may not want to transmit the malware to all susceptible neighbors of each infected device, as doing so could expose the infected devices and raise the defender's suspicions.
- *Defender:* In order to limit the spread of the malware, the defender acts strategically by using IPSs to monitor a limited number of edges at each time slot. Whenever a malware transmission is detected on edge, the defender cures the two devices involved in the transmission (i.e., the source device and the target device). The defender's choice of IPS locations is not revealed to the attacker; these IPSs are only available for a single time slot, and the interaction between the attacker and defender is repeated at each time interval.
- It should be noted that each player's actions are influenced by the centrality measure he/she has chosen to evaluate the influence of the network devices. After establishing the action profile, the system enters an intermediate state $a(z)$, indicating the beginning of the second stage within the current time slot.

Reactive Stage: During the second stage of a time slot, each device has the ability to take an action that can result in a change of its internal state. The transition depends on the device's current state and the specific self-restoration process used. An infected device can perform tasks such as updating software or running a malware scan to eliminate the threat with probability α, and then transition to the susceptible state. Alternatively, a susceptible device can choose with probability ρ, to install an immunization mechanism to become resistant. Regardless of the action taken, each device i will transition from the intermediate state $a(z)_i$ to a final state z_i', as depicted in Fig. 1. Not being informed of these transition probabilities, the attacker cannot infer the defender's actions, since an infected device may become susceptible due to either an IPS or its own decision.

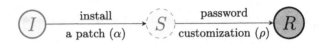

Fig. 1. Possible state transitions of a node depending on the decision taken.

Illustration of a Time Slot Sequence: We present a hypothetical situation for our game with two different scenarios. In the first one (a), both agents use degree centrality, while in the second scenario (b), the defender uses betweenness centrality and the attacker uses degree centrality. In each scenario, the attacker selects from any infected node the susceptible neighbor with the highest centrality value. Meanwhile, the defender chooses two nodes with the highest centrality values to protect.

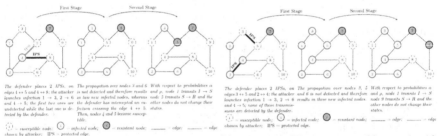

(a) A time slot of the game: a possible scenario with 10 devices when both defender and attacker use *degree centrality*.

(b) A time slot of the game: a possible scenario with 10 devices when the defender uses *betweenness centrality* and the attacker uses *degree centrality*.

After explaining the sequence of events within a given time slot, the following section focuses on describing the *asymmetric game* model. This model is used to determine the optimal strategies of the attacker and defender at each time slot. It should be noted that, in our context, a player's optimal strategy comprises two key components. The first one is the selection of the centrality measure, and the second one is the computation of the optimal probability distribution associated with it. In the following, we refer to the centrality measure used by the defender as c^d and the centrality measure used by the attacker as c^a. Furthermore, we assume that the centrality measure used by each player is common knowledge information.

3.3 Definition of the Asymmetric Centrality Game

Without loss of generality, we focus on the defender's goal of minimizing and the attacker's goal of maximizing the number of infected devices at each time slot. Considering the fact that only the attacker knows the state of the system at each time slot, which is private information for her, the *asymmetric centrality game* is the *non-zero sum Bayesian game* defined by the tuple $\mathcal{G} = (G, N, Z, A = A_1 \times A_2, \alpha, \rho, \mathcal{O}, \mathcal{R}_d, \mathcal{R}_a, b^0)$, where:

- $G = (V, E)$ is a non-directed graph representing the network where $V = \{1, 2, 3, ..., |V|\}$ is the set of nodes and $E \subseteq \{e \in 2^{|V|}, |e| = 2\}$ is the set of edges,
- N is the set of players: the defender (player 1) and the attacker (player 2),
- The network at time t is the sub-graph of the network at time $t - 1$, consisting of non-resistant nodes, i.e. at time t, $V = V \setminus R^{t-1}$ (where M^{t-1} represents the set of nodes of type M at the end of time slot $t - 1$),
- Z is the set of possible states of the network and each state z is defined by, $z = (z_i)_{i=1}^{|V|}$; where
  $$z_i = \begin{cases} S & \text{if node } i \text{ is susceptible} \\ I & \text{if node } i \text{ is infected} \end{cases} ; \text{ for all } i \in V. \text{ The attacker knows the state}$$
  of the network while the defender has to update his belief at each time slot t,
- The set A_1 refers to the actions available to the defender, which involve selecting up to h edges to deploy IPSs. The defender lacks knowledge about the state of the network at each time t, so all edges in the set $\mathbb{S} = E \cap (V \times V)$ are potentially usable by the attacker. However, since $\mathbb{S}$ may be quite large, the defender should limit his field of action by playing over the set $\mathbb{S}_b$ at each time t, referred to as the **defender's critical zone**. This set is defined by $\mathbb{S}_b = \bigcup_{z \in \mathrm{supp}(b)} \mathbb{S}_z$ where $\mathbb{S}_z = \{(i, j) \in I^t \times S^t : \{i, j\} \in E\}$ and $\mathrm{supp}(b) = \{z \in Z \mid b(z) \neq 0\}$ is the support of the belief b over the network state. Then, the defender's actions space is accordingly, $A_1 = \begin{cases} \mathcal{P}_h(\mathbb{S}_b) & \text{if } |\mathbb{S}_b| > h \\ \{2^{\mathbb{S}_b}\} & \text{otherwise} \end{cases}$,
- The set of actions available to the attacker is denoted as A_2. To perform an action, the attacker selects a set T_i of adjacent susceptible nodes from any infected node i, as the targets for propagating the malware. The attacker strategically avoids targeting the same susceptible node from different infected sources to minimize the likelihood of detection, as doing so would not yield any additional benefit. Thus, an action a_2 for the attacker at time t can be represented as a tuple $T = (T_i)_{i \in I^t} \equiv \bigcup_{i \in I^t} T_i'$, with $T_i' = \{\{i, j\}, j \in T_i\}$ that
  satisfy the properties: $\begin{cases} \forall i \in I^t, & T_i \subseteq S^t \\ \forall i \in I^t, \forall j \in T_i, & (i, j) \in \mathbb{S}_z \\ \forall k, l \in I^t, & k \neq l \implies T_k \cap T_l = \emptyset \end{cases}$,
- $\mathcal{O}$ represents the set of observations made by the defender, which depends on the state of each node at the end of each time slot. The defender observes a node if its state changes from I to S or from S to R. When there is no

observation for the defender, then $o_i = \mathfrak{X}$. A defender's observation profile can thus be defined as a tuple $o(z, a, z') = (o_i)_{i \in V}$, with $o_i \in \{z'_i, \mathfrak{X}\}$, $\forall i \in V$,
- $\mathcal{R}_d$ is the defender's reward and $\mathcal{R}_a$ the attacker's one at each time slot, b^0 is the defender's initial belief.

4 Asymmetric Centrality Game Solution

Every agent aims to hold the most crucial positions within the graph. To achieve this, each agent focuses on nodes with high centrality values from their individual perspective (c^a for the attacker and c^d for the defender). The model's outcome thus depends on the centrality of each node, which rewards the defender if a node transits from an infected to a susceptible or resistant state, while the attacker benefits from infecting a node.

4.1 Players' Rewards Associated with an Action Profile

When an action profile $(W, T) \in A_1 \times A_2$ is implemented, the centrality value of any node is rewarded to the defender, if the node transits from infected to susceptible or resistant, or to the attacker, if the node transits from susceptible to infected. Table 1 displays the expected partial reward for both players, which includes the centrality value of node i according to both the defender's and attacker's centrality measures, denoted as c_i^d and c_i^a respectively.

Table 1. The players expected reward resulting from a joint action (W, T) on one edge $\{i, j\}$.

		ATTACKER: Propagate $i \to j$?	
		Propagate ($\{i,j\} \in T$)	No propagate ($\{i,j\} \notin T$)
DEFENDER:	Watch ($\{i,j\} \in W$)	$c_i^d, -c_i^a$	0
Watch $\{i,j\}$?	No watch ($\{i,j\} \notin W$)	$-(1-\alpha)\,c_j^d, (1-\alpha)\,c_j^a$	0

At a given state z, the rewards associated to an action profile $(W, T) \in A_1 \times A_2$ are assigned to the defender and attacker as follows:

$$\mathcal{R}_d(W, T) = \sum_{\substack{\{i,j\} \in \mathbb{S}_z \\ \{i,j\} \in W \\ j \in T_i}} c_i^d - \sum_{\substack{\{i,j\} \in \mathbb{S}_z \\ \{i,j\} \notin W \\ j \in T_i}} (1-\alpha)\,c_j^d = \sum_{\substack{\{i,j\} \in \mathbb{S} \\ \{i,j\} \in W \\ j \in T_i}} c_i^d - \sum_{\substack{\{i,j\} \in \mathbb{S} \\ \{i,j\} \notin W \\ j \in T_i}} (1-\alpha)\,c_j^d,$$

$$\mathcal{R}_a\left(W,T\right) = \sum_{\substack{\{i,j\}\in\mathbb{S}_z \\ \{i,j\}\notin W \\ j\in T_i}} \left(1-\alpha\right)c_j^a - \sum_{\substack{\{i,j\}\in\mathbb{S}_z \\ \{i,j\}\in W \\ j\in T_i}} c_i^a = \sum_{\substack{\{i,j\}\in\mathbb{S} \\ \{i,j\}\notin W \\ j\in T_i}} \left(1-\alpha\right)c_j^a - \sum_{\substack{\{i,j\}\in\mathbb{S} \\ \{i,j\}\in W \\ j\in T_i}} c_i^a.$$

Indeed, for all $\{i,j\}\in\mathbb{S}\setminus\mathbb{S}_z$, we never get $j\in T_i$.

4.2 Players' Rewards Associated with a Strategy Profile

Denote by Π_i the strategy space for player i. Let's consider mixed strategies $\pi_1 \in \Pi_1$ for the defender and $\pi_2 : Z \longrightarrow \Delta\left(A_2\right) \in \Pi_2$ for the attacker.

- *Defender's reward:* The expected reward of the defender with belief $b\in\Delta\left(Z\right)$ associated to the strategy profile $\pi = \left(\pi_1,\pi_2\right)$ is $\mathcal{R}_d\left(\pi|b\right) = \sum_{z\in Z} b\left(z\right)\mathcal{R}_d\left(\pi|z\right)$,

where

$$\mathcal{R}_d\left(\pi|z\right) = \sum_{\left(W,T\right)\in A_1\times A_2} \pi_1\left(W\right)\pi_2\left(T|z\right)\mathcal{R}_d\left(W,T\right),$$

$$= \sum_{\substack{\{i,j\}\in\mathbb{S} \\ \left(W,T\right)\in A_1\times A_2 \\ \{i,j\}\in W \\ j\in T_i}} \pi_1\left(W\right)\pi_2\left(T|z\right)c_i^d + \sum_{\substack{\{i,j\}\in\mathbb{S} \\ \left(W,T\right)\in A_1\times A_2 \\ \{i,j\}\notin W \\ j\in T_i}} \pi_1\left(W\right)\pi_2\left(T|z\right)\left(\alpha-1\right)c_j^d,$$

$$= \sum_{\{i,j\}\in\mathbb{S}} \pi_1\left(i,j\right)\pi_2\left(i,j|z\right)\left(c_i^d + \left(1-\alpha\right)c_j^d\right) - \sum_{\{i,j\}\in\mathbb{S}} \left(1-\alpha\right)\pi_2\left(i,j|z\right)c_j^d,$$

$$\pi_1\left(i,j\right) = \sum_{\substack{W\in A_1 \\ \{i,j\}\in W}} \pi_1\left(W\right) \text{ and } \pi_2\left(i,j|z\right) = \sum_{\substack{T\in A_2 \\ j\in T_i}} \pi_2\left(T|z\right) \text{ being respectively}$$

the probabilities that the defender watches edge $\{i,j\}$ and the attacker targets node j from node i at state z. Therefore,

$$\mathcal{R}_d\left(\pi|b\right) = \sum_{z\in Z} b(z)\left(\sum_{\{i,j\}\in\mathbb{S}} \pi_1\left(i,j\right)\pi_2\left(i,j|z\right)\left(c_i^d + \left(1-\alpha\right)c_j^d\right) - \sum_{\{i,j\}\in\mathbb{S}} \left(1-\alpha\right)\pi_2\left(i,j|z\right)c_j^d\right)$$

$$= \sum_{\{i,j\}\in\mathbb{S}} \pi_1\left(i,j\right)\varphi_d\left(i,j|b,\pi_2\right) - \sum_{\{i,j\}\in\mathbb{S}} \psi_d\left(i,j|b,\pi_2\right)$$

where, $\varphi_d\left(i,j|b,\pi_2\right) = \pi_2\left(i,j|b\right)\left(c_i^d + \left(1-\alpha\right)c_j^d\right)$ is the defender's expected profit in case of detected virus transmission from i to j, $\psi_d\left(i,j|b,\pi_2\right) = \left(1-\alpha\right)\pi_2\left(i,j|b\right)c_j^d$ is the marginal loss of the defender in case of malware transmission from nodes i to j, and $\pi_2\left(i,j|b\right) = \sum_{z\in Z}\pi_2\left(i,j|z\right)b\left(z\right)$ is the marginal probability that the attacker spreads the virus from i to j knowing b.

- *Attacker's reward:* The expected reward of the attacker associated with the strategy profile $\pi = (\pi_1, \pi_2)$, when the defender's belief is $b \in \Delta(Z)$, is given by $\mathcal{R}_a(\pi|b) = \sum_{z \in Z} b(z) \mathcal{R}_a(\pi|z)$.

$$
\mathcal{R}_a(\pi|z) = \sum_{(W,T) \in A_1 \times A_2} \pi_1(W) \pi_2(T|z) \mathcal{R}_a(W,T)
$$

$$
= \sum_{\substack{\{i,j\} \in S \\ (W,T) \in A_1 \times A_2 \\ \{i,j\} \notin W \\ j \in T_i}} \pi_1(W) \pi_2(T|z)(1-\alpha) c_j^a - \sum_{\substack{\{i,j\} \in S \\ (W,T) \in A_1 \times A_2 \\ \{i,j\} \in W \\ j \in T_i}} \pi_1(W) \pi_2(T|z) c_i^a,
$$

$$
= \sum_{\{i,j\} \in S} \pi_2(i,j|z) \left((1-\alpha) c_j^a - \pi_1(i,j) \left((1-\alpha) c_j^a + c_i^a \right) \right),
$$

Therefore,

$$
\mathcal{R}_a(\pi|b) = \sum_{z \in Z} b(z) \sum_{\{i,j\} \in S} \pi_2(i,j|z) \left((1-\alpha) c_j^a - \pi_1(i,j) \left((1-\alpha) c_j^a + c_i^a \right) \right),
$$

$$
= \sum_{\{i,j\} \in S} \pi_2(i,j|b) \varphi_a(i,j|\pi_1),
$$

where $\varphi_a(i,j|\pi_1) = (1-\alpha) c_j^a - \pi_1(i,j) \left((1-\alpha) c_j^a + c_i^a \right) = \left(1 - \pi_1(i,j) \right) (1-\alpha) c_j^a - \pi_1(i,j) c_i^a$ is the expected reward of the attacker in case she targets the node j from i and $\pi_2(i,j|b) = \sum_{\{i,j\} \in S} \pi_2(i,j|z) b(z)$ has the same interpretation as above.

Furthermore, at each time slot, the main goal for every player is to optimize his payoff by considering the strategy his opponent has chosen. This means that each player aims to play the strategy that best responds to his opponent's strategy.

4.3   Players Solution Approach

- **Defender solution approach:** Suppose the attacker has a strategy denoted as $\pi_2 \in \Pi_2$. A strategy $\pi_1 \in \Pi_1$ employed by the defender is considered as the optimal response to π_2 if it maximizes the reward $\mathcal{R}_d(\pi|b) = \sum_{\{i,j\} \in S} \pi_1(i,j) \varphi_d(i,j|b,\pi_2) - \sum_{\{i,j\} \in S} \psi_d(i,j|b,\pi_2)$.

In addition, knowing the strategy π_2 allows us to determine the coefficients $\varphi_d(i,j|b,\pi_2)$ and $\psi_d(i,j|b,\pi_2)$ for all $\{i,j\} \in S$. Once these coefficients are fixed, the maximum payoff for the defender can be obtained by maximizing $\sum_{\{i,j\}\in\mathbb{S}} \pi_1(i,j)\,\varphi_d(i,j|b,\pi_2)$. To achieve this maximum payoff, the defender should focus on the top h edges of $\mathbb{S}_b$ according to their rank value $r(i,j|b,\pi_2) = 1 + |\{\{x,y\}\in\mathbb{S}_b : \varphi_d(x,y|b,\pi_2) > \varphi_d(i,j|b,\pi_2)\}|$, and set $\pi_1(i,j) = 0$ for the remaining edges. In other words, π_1 best responds to π_2 if $\pi_1(i,j) = 0$ whenever $r(i,j|b,\pi_2) > h$, i.e., if $\pi_1(i,j) = 0$ for all $\{i,j\}$ not in the set $\mathrm{SL}_d(\pi_2) = \{\{x,y\}\in\mathbb{S}_b : r(x,y|b,\pi_2) \leqslant h\}$ of the h top-ranked edges of $\mathbb{S}_b$ according to $\varphi_d(\cdot|b,\pi_2)$. $\mathrm{SL}_d(\pi_2)$ is called *short list* of the defender, best responding to the attacker's strategy π_2. It is important for the defender to choose a pseudo probability distribution π_1 over $\mathbb{S}_b$ that is consistent with some probability distribution over A_1.

- **Attacker solution approach:** In the same way, an attacker's strategy $\pi_2 \in \Pi_2$ is considered as the best response to a defender's strategy $\pi_1 \in \Pi_1$ when the reward $\mathcal{R}_a(\pi|b) = \sum_{\{i,j\}\in\mathbb{S}} \pi_2(i,j|b)\,\varphi_a(i,j|\pi_1)$ is maximized. The maximum reward for a fixed defender's strategy π_1 and thus, fixed coefficients $\varphi_a(i,j|\pi_1)$ and $b(z)$ is achieved when $\pi_2(i,j|z) = 0$ in any possible state z (i.e., $b(z) \neq 0$) where $\varphi_a(i,j|\pi_1)$ is not maximal. In other words, for all possible states $z \in Z$, $\pi_2(i,j|z) = 0$ if $\{i,j\} \notin \mathrm{SL}_a(\pi_1) = \{\{x,y\}\in\mathbb{S} : \forall\{u,v\}\in\mathbb{S}, \varphi_a(x,y|\pi_1) \geqslant \varphi_a(u,v|\pi_1)\}$, which is referred to as the *short list* of the attacker best responding to the defender's strategy π_1. This implies that at state z, the attacker may only transmit the virus from each infected node i to a susceptible neighbor j if $\varphi_a(i,j|\pi_1)$ is equal to the maximum possible value.

4.4 Nash Equilibria Properties

A strategy profile $\pi^* = (\pi_1^*, \pi_2^*)$ is a Nash equilibrium if and only if each player best responds to his/her opponent's strategy and no player can unilaterally change his strategy. The short lists of players associated with their best responses as defined above satisfy the following proposition:

Proposition 1. *Suppose that* $\mathrm{SL}_d(\pi_2^*) \neq \mathbb{S}$ *then, the shortlist of the defender is a subset of the short list of the attacker, i.e.,* $\mathrm{SL}_d(\pi_2^*) \subseteq \mathrm{SL}_a(\pi_1^*)$.

This means that the defender does not need to worry about the attacker's insignificant target in advance unless he wants to monitor all edges of the graph.

Proof. Suppose that $\mathrm{SL}_d(\pi_2^*) \neq \mathbb{S}$ and take any $\{i,j\} \notin \mathrm{SL}_a(\pi_1^*)$. Then, for all $z \in Z$, $\pi_2^*(i,j|z) = 0$ and $\varphi_d(i,j|b,\pi_2^*) = \sum_{z\in Z} b(z)\,\pi_2^*(i,j|z)\left(c_i^d + (1-\alpha)\,c_j^d\right) = 0$. In this case, $\{i,j\}$ is minimally ranked according to $\varphi_d(\cdot|b,\pi_2^*)$ because $\varphi_d(u,v|b,\pi_2^*) \geqslant 0$, $\forall\{u,v\} \in \mathbb{S}$. Since $\mathrm{SL}_d(\pi_2^*) \neq \mathbb{S}$, at least one edge $\{x,y\} \in \mathbb{S}$ is not h top-ranked according to $\varphi_d(\cdot|b,\pi_2^*)$.

As $\varphi_d(x,y|b,\pi_2^*) \geqslant 0 = \varphi_d(i,j|b,\pi_2^*)$, we conclude that $\{i,j\}$ is not h top-ranked according to φ_d i.e., $\{i,j\} \notin \mathrm{SL}_d(\pi_2^*)$. ∎

The previous inclusion relation between the short lists (Proposition 1) leads us to the following proposition, which shows that our game is actually a game of thresholds.

Proposition 2. *1. For all $\{k,l\} \in SL_a(\pi_1^*) \setminus SL_d(\pi_2^*)$, $\{i,j\} \in SL_d(\pi_2^*)$, and $\{u,v\} \in \mathbb{S} \setminus SL_a(\pi_1^*)$, it holds:* $\begin{cases} c_j^a \geqslant c_l^a > c_v^a \\ c_j^a > c_l^a \iff \pi_1^*\{i,j\} > 0 \end{cases}$.
2. For all couples $\{k,l\}, \{k',l'\} \in SL_a(\pi_1^*) \setminus SL_d(\pi_2^*)$, it holds: $c_l^a = c_{l'}^a$.

This implies that, at Nash equilibrium,

- The objective of the defender is to safeguard nodes with centrality values that exceed a specific threshold θ_1. Similarly, the attacker's goal is to target nodes with centrality values not lower than another threshold θ_2. Moreover, the specific values of *these thresholds are determined based on the centrality measure employed by the attacker.*
- From the attacker's perspective, all the nodes that the defender should leave unprotected have the same centrality values.
  However, note that this proposition does not state that $SL_2(\pi_1^*) \setminus SL_1(\pi_2^*)$ is a non-empty set.

Proof. From $\{k,l\} \notin SL_d(\pi_2^*)$, it comes $\pi_1^*(k,l) = 0$. From $\{k,l\} \in SL_a(\pi_1^*)$, it comes that $\varphi_a(k,l|\pi_1^*) = (1-\alpha)c_l^a$ is maximal. This point leads to the second statement of the Proposition 2 because, taking $\{k',l'\} \in SL_a(\pi_1^*) \setminus SL_d(\pi_2^*)$, implies $\varphi_a(k',l'|\pi_1^*) = (1-\alpha)c_{l'}^a$ is maximal too, and then, $(1-\alpha)c_l^a = (1-\alpha)c_{l'}^a$, i.e., $c_l^a = c_{l'}^a$.

Note that $\{u,v\} \notin SL_a(\pi_1^*)$, and from Proposition 1, $\{u,v\} \notin SL_d(\pi_2^*)$ so, $\pi_1^*(u,v) = 0$. In this case, $\varphi_a(u,v|\pi_1^*) = (1-\alpha)c_v^a$ and, since $\varphi_a(k,l|\pi_1^*) = (1-\alpha)c_l^a$ is maximal, it comes $(1-\alpha)c_l^a > (1-\alpha)c_v^a$ and, consequently, $c_l^a > c_v^a$.

In addition, the maximality of $\varphi_a(k,l|\pi_1^*)$ also applies to $\{i,j\}$ and, therefore

$$(1-\alpha)c_j^a - \pi_1^*(i,j)\left(c_i^a + (1-\alpha)c_j^a\right) = (1-\alpha)c_l^a. \text{ Then, } \pi_1^*(i,j)\left(c_i^a + (1-\alpha)c_j^a\right) = (1-\alpha)\left(c_j^a - c_l^a\right).$$ The positivity of $c_j^a - c_l^a$ relies on that of $c_i^a + (1-\alpha)c_j^a$, thus $c_j^a \geqslant c_l^a$. ∎

Since we have demonstrated that players act in accordance with centrality thresholds, it is evident that these thresholds have a direct impact on players' optimal responses. The Proposition 3 provides a more specific characterization of shortlists $SL_d(\pi_2^*)$ and $SL_a(\pi_1^*)$ by taking into account these centrality thresholds.

Proposition 3. *For some centrality values θ_1 and θ_2, it holds:*

1. $SL_d(\pi_2^*) = \{\{i,j\} \in \mathbb{S}_b : c_j^a \geqslant \theta_1\}$; $SL_a(\pi_1^*) = \{\{i,j\} \in \mathbb{S} : c_j^a \geqslant \theta_2\}$;

2. $\begin{cases} \text{For some } \{i,j\} \in SL_d(\pi_2^*), \text{ it holds } c_j^a = \theta_1 \text{ and } \pi_1^*(i,j) \neq 0, \\ \text{For some } \{k,l\} \in SL_a(\pi_1^*), \text{ it holds } c_l^a = \theta_2 \text{ and } \pi_2^*(k,l|b) \neq 0; \end{cases}$

3. $\theta_2 \leqslant \theta_1$. In particular, if $\theta_2 < \theta_1$, then no centrality value can lie in the space $]\theta_2, \theta_1[$.

Proof. Consider $\theta_k = \displaystyle\min_{\{\text{source},\text{target}\} \in \mathrm{SL}_p(\pi^*_{-k})} c^a_{\text{target}}$, for $(k, p) \in \{(1, d), (2, a)\}$.

By this definition, $c^a_j \geqslant \theta_k$ for any $\{i, j\} \in \mathrm{SL}_p(\pi^*_{-k})$. Conversely, on the one hand, take any $\{k, l\} \in \mathbb{S}$ such that $c^a_l \geqslant \theta_2$. The minimum value θ_2 is attained for some $\{k', l'\} \in \mathrm{SL}_a(\pi^*_1)$. Then, from the inequality $c^a_l \geqslant c^a_{l'}$ and proposition 2.1, it comes $\{k, l\} \in \mathrm{SL}_a(\pi^*_1)$ (indeed, suppose $\{k, l\} \in \mathbb{S} \setminus \mathrm{SL}_a(\pi^*_1)$, we have, $c^a_l < c^a_{l'}$). Similarly, take any $\{i, j\} \in \mathbb{S}$ such that $c^a_j \geqslant \theta_1$. With the same reasoning, we get $\{i, j\} \in \mathrm{SL}_d(\pi^*_2)$. Point 1 is proven.

For the proof of point 2, since $\theta_k = \displaystyle\min_{\{\text{source},\text{target}\} \in \mathrm{SL}_p(\pi^*_{-k})} c^a_{\text{target}}$, for $(k, p) \in \{(1, d), (2, a)\}$, they are attained for some $\{i, j\} \in \mathrm{SL}_d(\pi^*_2)$ and $\{k, l\} \in \mathrm{SL}_a(\pi^*_1)$ respectively.

Since $\mathrm{SL}_d(\pi^*_2) \subseteq \mathrm{SL}_a(\pi^*_1)$ and the definition of θ_k, $k = 1, 2$, we have $\theta_2 \leqslant \theta_1$ (and more specifically $\theta_2 < \theta_1$ iff $\mathrm{SL}_d(\pi^*_2) \subset \mathrm{SL}_a(\pi^*_1)$). Moreover, let's assume that there is $\{u, v\} \in \mathrm{SL}_a(\pi^*_1)$ and $\{i, j\} \in \mathbb{S}$ such that $\theta_2 = c^a_v$ and $c^a_j \in]\theta_2, \theta_1[$. In this case, $\{i, j\}, \{u, v\} \in \mathrm{SL}_a(\pi^*_1) \setminus \mathrm{SL}_d(\pi^*_2)$; by Proposition 2.2 $c^a_j = \theta_2$, which is absurd. Point 3 is proven. ∎

Once a factual definition of short lists of players is provided, it becomes apparent that they are determined by *centrality thresholds that are established based solely on the centrality measure of the attacker*. The following section aims to elucidate the mathematical properties that determine these thresholds and emphasize the associated optimal strategy for each player.

5   Nash Equilibria Analysis

It is assumed that the players are playing a strategy profile $\pi^* = (\pi^*_1, \pi^*_2)$ that is a Nash equilibrium. Additionally, the defender holds a belief b about the network state. This means that the set of possible strategies that each player can choose from, denoted by $\mathrm{supp}(\pi^*_k)$, are contained within their respective short lists, denoted by $\mathrm{SL}_p(\pi^*_{-k})$, $(k, p) \in \{(1, d), (2, a)\}$, which are determined by their individual thresholds θ_k. In this section, based on the definition of the attacker's shortlist $\mathrm{SL}_a(\pi^*_1)$, we denote by s the maximum value of φ_a under the Nash equilibrium, i.e., $s = \displaystyle\max_{\{i,j\} \in \mathbb{S}} \varphi_a(i, j | \pi^*_1)$.

Proposition 4. *1. The probability of the defender placing an IPS on any edge $\{i, j\} \in \mathbb{S}_b$ is expressed as:*

$$
\begin{cases}
\{i, j\} \in \mathrm{SL}_a(\pi^*_1) \iff \varphi_a(i, j | \pi^*_1) = s \text{ and } \pi^*_1(i, j) = \dfrac{(1 - \alpha) c^a_j - s}{c^a_i + (1 - \alpha) c^a_j}. \\
\{i, j\} \notin \mathrm{SL}_a(\pi^*_1) \implies \varphi_a(i, j | \pi^*_1) < s \text{ and } \pi^*_1(i, j) = 0
\end{cases}
$$

2. Mathematically speaking, the total probability of protection for every edge in $\mathbb{S}_b$ is equal to the number of IPSs that the defender has. This is represented by the equation: $\displaystyle\sum_{\substack{\{i,j\} \in \mathbb{S}_b \\ c^a_j \geqslant \theta_1}} \pi^*_1(i, j) = h.$

3. *The highest value s that the attacker tries to achieve when making her decision*

is expressed as: $s = (1 - \alpha) \dfrac{\left(\displaystyle\sum_{\substack{\{i,j\}\in \mathbb{S}_b \\ c_j^a \geqslant \theta_1}} \dfrac{c_j^a}{c_i^a + (1-\alpha)\, c_j^a} \right) - \dfrac{h}{1 - \alpha}}{\displaystyle\sum_{\substack{\{i,j\}\in \mathbb{S}_b \\ c_j^a \geqslant \theta_1}} \dfrac{1}{c_i^a + (1-\alpha)\, c_j^a}}.$

Proof. 1. The comparison of $\varphi_a\left(i,j|\pi_1^*\right)$ and s is according to the definition of the attacker's shortlist $\mathrm{SL}_a(\pi_1^*)$. On the one hand, if $\{i,j\} \in \mathrm{SL}_a\left(\pi_1^*\right)$ then,

$s = (1-\alpha)\, c_j^a - \pi_1^*\left(i,j\right)\left(c_i^a + (1-\alpha)\, c_j^a\right) \iff \pi_1^*\left(i,j\right) = \frac{(1-\alpha)c_j^a - s}{c_i^a + (1-\alpha)c_j^a}.$

On the other hand, if $\{i,j\} \notin \mathrm{SL}_a\left(\pi_1^*\right)$ then, $\{i,j\} \notin \mathrm{SL}_d\left(\pi_2^*\right)$; the assertion 1 is proven.

2. A defender's action is to select h edges to protect from his short list $\mathrm{SL}_d\left(\pi_2^*\right)$. It is important to remember that for every edge $\{i,j\}$ in the selected list, the value of $\pi_1^*(i,j)$ is equal to the sum of the values of $\pi^*(W)$ for all $W \in A_1$ such that $\{i,j\}$ belongs to W, i.e. $\pi_1^*\left(i,j\right) = \displaystyle\sum_{\substack{W\in A_1 \\ \{i,j\}\in W}} \pi_1^*(W)$. Then,

$$\sum_{\substack{\{i,j\}\in \mathbb{S}_b \\ c_j^a \geqslant \theta_1}} \pi_1^*(i,j) = \sum_{\substack{\{i,j\}\in \mathbb{S}_b \\ c_j^a \geqslant \theta_1}} \sum_{\substack{W\in A_1 \\ \{i,j\}\in W}} \pi_1^*(W) = h\sum_{W\in A_1} \pi_1^*(W) = h.$$

In fact, since an action consists of h elements, it will be repeated h times in the sum. This leads us to the conclusion shown in assertion 2, which is based on the fact that π_1^* represents a probability distribution over the defender's actions set A_1.

3. The assertion 3 comes from assertion 2 and the first point of assertion 1.

∎

Based on Proposition 3, the recommended course of action for the defender in response to the attacker's strategy involves the prior construction of the defender's short list. This process entails the careful selection of the suitable centrality measure to assess the impact of the network nodes. As a result, the defender's optimal strategy can be summarized in two key stages: the selection of the centrality measure and the subsequent computation of the corresponding π_1^* optimal strategy.

Proposition 5. *At Nash equilibrium, the defender must use the attacker's centrality measure to assess the significance of nodes in the graph. This implies that the defender's decisions are based on the same centrality measure as that of the attacker.*

Proof. The defender's best response, represented by the set $\mathrm{SL}_d(\pi_2^*)$ is determined by a centrality threshold based on the attacker's centrality measure (first point of proposition (3)). Moreover, the defender's optimal strategy π_1^*

on $\mathrm{SL}_d(\pi_2^*)$ is still influenced by the attacker's centrality measure (first assertion of proposition (1)). To put it simply, if the defender wants to play optimally, he needs to take into account the attacker's centrality measure when making decisions. ∎

The following proposition allows us to determine at each time t, if a given (θ_1, θ_2) is a Nash equilibrium:

Proposition 6. *1. a) At Nash equilibrium, we have*
$$\sum_{\substack{\{i,j\}\in\mathbb{S}_b \\ c_j^a \geqslant \theta_1}} \frac{c_j^a - \theta_1}{c_i^a + (1-\alpha)\,c_j^a} \leqslant \frac{h}{1-\alpha}.$$

b) If in particular $\theta_1 > \theta_2$, then
$$\sum_{\substack{\{i,j\}\in\mathbb{S}_b \\ c_j^a \geqslant \theta_1}} \frac{c_j^a - \theta_2}{c_i^a + (1-\alpha)\,c_j^a} = \sum_{\substack{\{i,j\}\in\mathbb{S}_b \\ c_j^a \geqslant \theta_2}} \frac{c_j^a - \theta_2}{c_i^a + (1-\alpha)\,c_j^a} = \frac{h}{1-\alpha}.$$

2. Assuming that the set $\mathrm{Last}_h \subseteq \{\{i,j\} \in \mathbb{S}_b : c_j^a \geqslant \theta_1\}$ contains the h last-ranked elements of $\mathbb{S}_b$ based on their $\pi_1^*(i,j)$ values, it follows
$$\sum_{\{i,j\}\in\mathrm{Last}_h} \pi_1^*(i,j) \geqslant \frac{h\,(h-1)}{|\mathbb{S}_b| - 1}.$$

3. a) If $s \leqslant 0$ then $\theta_1 = \min\limits_{\{i,j\}\in\mathbb{S}_b} c_j^a$.

b) If $s > 0$ then the attacker infects a susceptible node j if and only if that is for some infected node i, it holds $\varphi_2(i,j|\pi_1) = s$.

Proof. The positivity of $\pi_1^*(i,j)$ for all $\{i,j\}$ in the defender's shortlist implies $(1-\alpha)\,c_j^a \geqslant s$ then $(1-\alpha)\,\theta_1 \geqslant s$. Moreover,

$$(1-\alpha)\,\theta_1 \geqslant s \iff \theta_1 \geqslant \frac{\left(\displaystyle\sum_{\substack{\{i,j\}\in\mathbb{S}_b \\ c_j^a\geqslant\theta_1}} \frac{c_j^a}{c_i^a + (1-\alpha)\,c_j^a}\right) - \dfrac{h}{1-\alpha}}{\displaystyle\sum_{\substack{\{i,j\}\in\mathbb{S}_b \\ c_j^a\geqslant\theta_1}} \frac{1}{c_i^a + (1-\alpha)\,c_j^a}} \iff \sum_{\substack{\{i,j\}\in\mathbb{S}_b \\ c_j^a\geqslant\theta_1}} \frac{c_j^a - \theta_1}{c_i^a + (1-\alpha)\,c_j^a} \leqslant \frac{h}{1-\alpha}.$$

In case $\theta_1 > \theta_2$, there exist $\{i,j\} \in \mathrm{SL}_a(\pi_1^*) \setminus \mathrm{SL}_d(\pi_2^*)$, such that $c_j^a = \theta_2$ and then,

$$\pi_1^*(i,j) = \frac{(1-\alpha)\,c_j^a - s}{c_i^a + (1-\alpha)\,c_j^a} = \frac{(1-\alpha)\,\theta_2 - s}{c_i^a + (1-\alpha)\,\theta_2} = 0. \text{ So, we get}$$

$$s = (1-\alpha)\,\theta_2 \iff \frac{\left(\displaystyle\sum_{\substack{\{i,j\}\in\mathbb{S}_b \\ c_j^a\geqslant\theta_1}} \frac{c_j^a}{c_i^a + (1-\alpha)\,c_j^a}\right) - \dfrac{h}{1-\alpha}}{\displaystyle\sum_{\substack{\{i,j\}\in\mathbb{S}_b \\ c_j^a\geqslant\theta_1}} \frac{1}{c_i^a + (1-\alpha)\,c_j^a}} = \theta_2 \iff \sum_{\substack{\{i,j\}\in\mathbb{S}_b \\ c_j^a\geqslant\theta_2}} \frac{c_j^a - \theta_2}{c_i^a + (1-\alpha)\,c_j^a} = \frac{h}{1-\alpha}.$$

Thus, $(1 - \alpha) c_j^a \geqslant s$ in the general case, and $s = (1 - \alpha) \theta_2$ in case $\theta_1 > \theta_2$. The assertion 1 is thus proven.

Assertion 2 is a condition that comes from [27], where the authors give the condition to pass from the probability on elements to the probability on the associated sets of size h.

For the proof of 3, suppose $s \leqslant 0$. That is, for any $\{i, j\} \in \mathbb{S}_b$, we get successively:

$$\varphi_a (i, j | \pi_1) \leqslant 0, \iff (1 - \alpha) c_j^a - \pi_1^*(i, j)(c_i^a + (1 - \alpha) c_j^a) \leqslant 0,$$

$$\iff \pi_1^* (i, j) \geqslant \frac{(1 - \alpha) c_j^a}{c_i^a + (1 - \alpha) c_j^a} > 0, \forall \{i, j\} \in \mathbb{S}_b,$$

$$\iff c_j^a \geqslant \theta_1 \ for \ all \ \{i, j\} \in \mathbb{S}_b \iff \theta_1 = \min_{\{i, j\} \in \mathbb{S}_b} c_j^a.$$

Suppose on the other hand that $s > 0$. From the definition of the attacker's shortlist, it comes: $\mathcal{R} (\pi^* | b) = \sum_{\substack{\{i,j\} \in \mathbb{S} \\ \varphi_a(i,j|\pi_1^*) \ \text{is maximal}}} \pi_2^* (i, j | b) \varphi_a (i, j | \pi_1^*) =$

$s \sum_{\substack{\{i,j\} \in \mathbb{S} \\ \varphi_a(i,j|\pi_1^*) = s}} \pi_2^* (i, j | b)$. The maximization of this result imposes the maximiza-

tion of the $\pi_2^* (i, j | b)$'s value whenever $\varphi_a (i, j | \pi_1^*)$ is maximal.　■

6　Numerical Illustrations

Communication and information exchange are integral to modern society and, as such, networks have become essential infrastructure. Therefore, protecting these networks against the spread of malicious software is of utmost importance. As we have previously demonstrated, one effective strategy for epidemic propagation in networks is to target the most central devices above a certain centrality threshold. In this section, we present a simulation of the impact of our centrality game on epidemic dynamics, focusing on the scenario of complete information, where the defender has perfect knowledge about the network state. In our experiments, we employ some popular centrality measures described in [3]: degree centrality (**D**), betweenness centrality (**B**), eigenvector centrality (**E**), clustering coeffi-cient centrality (**Clus**), and closeness centrality (**Clo**). However, our model is flexible enough to incorporate alternative centrality measures if desired. The simulation has several realizations and a realization ends once all the nodes in the graph have become resistant. Some parameters employed for these simu-lations are as follows: $\alpha = 0.1$, $\varrho = 0.2$, and 10 IPSs for the defender. The program presents the results of the subsequent metrics upon completion of each realization:

- The epidemic peak (EP), the maximum number of infected nodes reached in the network during a given period;
- The time this peak is attained (TP), i.e., the number of periods it took to reach this peak;
- The time for the control of the epidemic (TC), i.e., the first period at which the number of edges in the stake is not greater than the number of IPSs. From that period onward, the defender prevents any infection;
- The time for the virus extinction (TE), i.e., the period after which there are no more infected nodes in the network.

The objectives of this section can be summarized into two main goals. The first goal is to show how different centrality measures affect the optimal strategies of the players, as previously defined, and identify the most effective centrality measure for the attacker. The second objective consists of the evaluation of the defender's loss if he does not adopt the recommended optimal strategy. To closely mimic real-world scenarios, we conducted our experiments on two prominent network types that have experienced epidemic spread in recent years. The mathematical graph model chosen for the mathematical modeling of each of them was selected on the basis of the main characteristics of the networks developed in [14].

- *Power network (Ukraine power grid hack, December 2015)*: From a physical concept, it is reasonable to conceptualize the power system as a *small-world network* (East China Power Grid [4]). From the perspective of the system comprising networks of varying voltage levels, the power supply and distribution networks at the middle and low voltage levels within cities are strongly interconnected, whereas the transmission networks at higher voltage levels are sparsely connected. From the point of view of the transmission network of the same voltage stage, the network of each region is closely connected, while the network of different regions is sparsely connected. This observation suggests that the power system exhibits the characteristics of a small-world network, characterized by significant local clustering and limited global interconnection [6].
- *Social network (the spread of false information regarding COVID-19 vaccines on social media platforms [18])*: An example is the social network *Twitter*. We have used the *Barabási-Albert* model for its mathematical representation, because of its ability to capture some key features of the latter. The Barabási-Albert model is a preferential growth model that is based on two fundamental principles: continuous network growth (which reflects the fact that social networks are constantly expanding) and preferential attachment (which refers to the fact that new vertices tend to connect to existing vertices that already have many links).

6.1   Optimal Strategic Defense (*OSD*) Against Optimal Strategic Attack (*OSA*): Best Centrality Measure for the Attacker

We assume that players adopt their optimal strategies as defined above. Since there are several ways to measure the centrality value of a node, the question that arises is therefore as follows: which centrality measure should the attacker use to maximize her payoff (i.e., to maximize the number of infected nodes of the graph)? We therefore study the effectiveness of various centrality measures in identifying critical nodes to attack in the context of epidemic spread. To accomplish this task, we generated:

- a Watts-Strogatz graph with the following characteristics: number of nodes = 1000; degree of each node in the initial graph = 20; probability of modifying each edge = 0.1. Obtaining a graph containing 10000 edges;
- a Barabási-Albert graph with the following characteristics: number of nodes = 1000; number of connection for each node = 15. This results in a graph containing 14775 edges.

Considering that each graph contains 7 infected nodes at the beginning of the game, we performed for each one a simulation containing 100 realizations for every centrality measure mentioned above. We then obtained the following results:

- *Watts-Strogatz graph:* According to the table (2a) given our Watts-Strogatz graph model, *closeness centrality* appears as the best centrality measure for the attacker to infect a maximum number of nodes. Indeed, nodes with high closeness centrality are geographically close to many other nodes in terms of the shortest path length. In the given Watts-Strogatz graph model, the graph structure combines local clustering and short average path lengths. This is achieved through the initial ring structure and the subsequent random rewiring process [14]. As a result, many nodes in the network are relatively close to each other, both in terms of clustering and path lengths. Nodes with higher closeness centrality are likely to be positioned in densely connected areas of the graph, making them potential hubs for spreading the infection.

Watts-Strogatz graph			
Metrics/ Measures	EP	TP	TC	TE
D	675.59	6	1154	1359
Clus	676.23	6	995	1249
B	533.65	9	358	468
E	675.35	5	1041	1392
Clo	678.5	8	1354	1682

Barabási-Albert graph			
Metrics/ Measures	EP	TP	TC	TE
D	180.04	2	145	266
Clus	693.93	5	542	692
B	62.86	3	92	171
E	196.15	2	185	242
Clo	561.68	9	750	1067

(a) Average results for optimal strategic defense against optimal strategic attack (both players use the same centrality measure). *closeness centrality proves ideal for the attacker. The proximity of the epidemic peak for some centrality measures can be attributed to the regular distribution of nodes and the low probability of edge modification, resulting in nodes with almost similar structural properties. Betweenness and closeness differ by 14.48% increase at peak.*

(b) Average results for optimal strategic defense against optimal strategic attack (both players use the same centrality measure). *Since the attacker aims to maximize the number of infected nodes, she will select the* **clustering coefficient centrality** *as the metric. The impact of the centrality measure on the expected result is also visible. For example, between closeness centrality and clustering coefficient centrality, there is an increase of 13, 2% at the epidemic peak.*

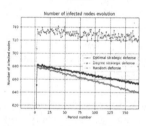

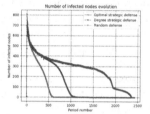

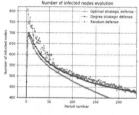

(c) Infected nodes variation for the *Watts-Strogatz* graph (with a zoomed-in view highlighting the peaks during the epidemic propagation). *The results show that when the defender deviates from the recommended optimal strategy, the attacker achieves a higher success rate in infecting nodes and a longer time of extinction. Specifically, when the defender employs the DSD strategy, the peak rises to 682.65, signifying a noticeable increase of 0.4%. Despite the small difference in peak values, this strategy progressively becomes more dangerous for the defender over time. It leads to a greater number of infected nodes and prolongs the time until extinction, taking approximately 2048 periods compared to 1682 for OSD. For example, at period 1500, there is a significant 28% surge in infected nodes. In contrast, opting for the RD strategy results in a 7% rise at the epidemic peak.*

(d) Infected nodes variation for the *Barabási-Albert* graph (with a zoomed-in view highlighting the peaks during the epidemic). *As announced in the theoretical demonstrations, when the defender does not follow the recommended optimal strategy, the epidemic peak becomes higher. Specifically, when the defender employs the DSD strategy, the peak rises to 700.5, representing a small increase of 0.6%. Although the difference between these peaks is small, this strategy becomes increasingly perilous for the defender over time. It results in a higher number of infected nodes and a longer time for the epidemic extinction, taking around 1216 periods compared to 692 for OSD. For instance, at period number 500, there is a significant 30% surge in infected nodes. On the other hand, if the RD strategy is chosen, there is a notable 11% increase observed at the time of the epidemic's peak.*

- *Barabási-Albert graph:* The *clustering coefficient centrality* is identified as the most effective centrality measure for propagating malware, as shown in table (2b). The Barabási-Albert graph model is a preferential attachment model, where new nodes are more likely to connect to already well-connected nodes. As a result, this model tends to create a scale-free network structure with a few highly connected hub nodes and many low-degree nodes. In a scale-free network, the clustering coefficient tends to be relatively low for most nodes but significantly higher for a few hub nodes. These hub nodes act as highly interconnected clusters, forming the backbone of the network. By targeting nodes with high clustering coefficient centrality, an attacker can exploit these densely connected clusters to infect a maximum number of nodes efficiently.

6.2 Sub-optimal Defense Against Optimal Strategic Attack

We have demonstrated that the defender's optimal strategy requires the adoption of the same centrality measure as the attacker (in our previous simulations, *closeness centrality* for the Watts-Strogatz model and *clustering coefficient centrality* for the Barabási-Albert model). However, in some cases, implementing this strategy in practice can incur high costs (e.g., the time complexity of implementing the attacker's centrality measure). Additionally, the defender may face limitations in terms of resources or sophistication. Therefore, we employed two main strategies as alternatives to the recommended optimal approach:

- The first strategy (*Degree Strategic Defense "DSD"*) involves the defender using the degree centrality (chosen for its computational simplicity) to assess the significance of the graph's nodes. Subsequently, we determined the defender's optimal probability distribution associated with this centrality measure (assuming that the attacker also employs degree centrality).
- The second strategy (*Random Defense "RD"*) is a purely random approach, wherein the defender selects nodes to protect based on a uniform probability distribution. This strategy does not consider any centrality measure.

In order to evaluate the correlation in terms of the *maximum number of infected nodes* between these strategies and the optimal one, we have compared each of the defender's strategies with the attacker's optimal strategy. It is worth mentioning that these experiments were conducted on the same graphs used earlier. Unsurprisingly, the results depicted in Figs. 2c and 2d clearly demonstrate that regardless of whether it is a *Watts-Strogatz* or *Barabási-Albert* graph, following the recommended *optimal strategy* benefits the defender. Moreover, in our context where the attacker aims to maximize the number of infected nodes, employing the *random defense* strategy is strongly discouraged. However, the following observation applies to both the Watts-Strogatz and Barabási-Albert models:

- The defender's *optimal strategy* (OSD), based on clustering coefficient centrality for the *Barabási-Albert* graph and closeness centrality for the *Watts-Strogatz* graph, is initially close to the *degree strategic defense* strategy. Indeed, at the beginning of the game, nodes with a high degree tend to have a high clustering coefficient and high closeness centrality, which aligns with the optimal strategy. However, as time progresses, the DSD strategy primarily focuses on nodes with a high degree which may have a lower clustering coefficient on the one hand and a lower closeness centrality on the other hand. As a result, the two strategies diverge as the infection progresses.

Additionally, in our *Barabási-Albert* graph, it is important to highlight that the betweenness centrality measure is not suitable for the attacker, who obtains *eleven times as many infected nodes* by using the clustering coefficient. This observation can be explained by the fact that:

- Betweenness centrality measures the frequency with which a node lies on the shortest path between two other nodes in a graph. However, in a *Barabási-Albert* graph characterized by preferential connections and high clustering, this measure fails to capture a node's capacity to propagate an epidemic effectively. Nodes possessing high betweenness centrality may not exhibit extensive connectivity or reside within dense clusters, thus limiting their potential for spreading malware.

7 Conclusion

The notorious *WannaCry Ransomware attack* that occurred in 2017 was one of the worst attacks that ever had before. WannaCry Ransomware is a type of malicious software that blocks user access to files or systems, holding files or entire devices hostage using encryption until the victim pays a ransom in exchange for a decryption key, which allows the user to access the files or systems encrypted by the program [13]. Like the latter, many attacks with the same objectives are perpetrated daily. Using their intelligence and rationality, and due to limited resources, many attackers choose the devices to infect based on their influence in the network, which they determine through various centrality measures. [23] addressed and found a solution to the problem when the defender and the attacker use identical centrality measures. This paper generalized the problem by addressing situations where players opt for different centrality measures. We have demonstrated that in a two-player asymmetric network centrality game, where each player takes action according to its centrality measure, the defender, to play optimally, must use the attacker's centrality measure. Based on the simulations conducted in this study, it has been observed that the appropriate centrality measure for the attacker to infect the maximum number of nodes depends on the type of graph. In particular, we have shown that in certain types of graphs, the clustering coefficient centrality is the most effective for the attacker, while in others, the closeness centrality is more appropriate. Our findings have important implications for the epidemic control problem, as they suggest that the choice of centrality measure can significantly impact the effectiveness of control measures. In particular, our results can inform the development of targeted intervention strategies aimed at reducing the spread of infectious diseases. The objective for us is to use these notions of centrality game to solve problems of the *lateral movement* type [7].

Acknowledgments. The research was sponsored by the U.S. Army Research Office and was accomplished under Cooperative Agreement Numbers W911NF-19-2-0150, W911NF-22-2-0175, and Grant Number W911NF-21-1-0326. The views and conclusions contained in this document are those of the authors and should not be interpreted as representing the official policies, either expressed or implied, of the U.S.

References

1. Anwar, A.H., Kamhoua, C.A., Leslie, N.O., Kiekintveld, C.: Honeypot allocation for cyber deception under uncertainty. IEEE Trans. Netw. Serv. Manage. **19**(3), 3438–3452 (2022)
2. Das, K., Samanta, S., Pal, M.: Study on centrality measures in social networks: a survey. Soc. Netw. Anal. Min. **8**, 1–11 (2018)
3. Dey, P., Bhattacharya, S., Roy, S.: A survey on the role of centrality as seed nodes for information propagation in large scale network. ACM/IMS Trans. Data Sci. **2**(3), 1–25 (2021)
4. Ding, M., Han, P.: Reliability assessment to large-scale power grid based on small-world topological model. In: 2006 International Conference on Power System Technology, pp. 1–5. IEEE (2006)
5. Do, C.T., et al.: Game theory for cyber security and privacy. ACM Comput. Surv. (CSUR) **50**(2), 1–37 (2017)
6. Dong, C., Xiong, X., Xue, Q., Zhang, Z., Niu, K., Zhang, P.: A survey on the network models applied in the industrial network optimization. arXiv preprint arXiv:2209.08294 (2022)
7. Fang, Y., Wang, C., Fang, Z., Huang, C.: LMTracker: lateral movement path detection based on heterogeneous graph embedding. Neurocomputing **474**, 37–47 (2022)
8. Funk, S., Salathé, M., Jansen, V.A.: Modelling the influence of human behaviour on the spread of infectious diseases: a review. J. R. Soc. Interface **7**(50), 1247–1256 (2010)
9. Hayel, Y., Trajanovski, S., Altman, E., Wang, H., Van Mieghem, P.: Complete game-theoretic characterization of sis epidemics protection strategies. In: 53rd IEEE Conference on Decision and Control, pp. 1179–1184. IEEE (2014)
10. Horák, K., Bošanský, B., Pěchouček, M.: Heuristic search value iteration for one-sided partially observable stochastic games. In: Proceedings of the AAAI Conference on Artificial Intelligence, vol. 31 (2017)
11. Hough, P.: Understanding Global Security. Routledge (2013)
12. Kolias, C., Kambourakis, G., Stavrou, A., Voas, J.: DDoS in the IoT: Mirai and other botnets. Computer **50**(7), 80–84 (2017)
13. Mohurle, S., Patil, M.: A brief study of wannacry threat: ransomware attack 2017. Int. J. Adv. Res. Comput. Sci. **8**(5), 1938–1940 (2017)
14. Newman, M.E.: The structure and function of complex networks. SIAM Rev. **45**(2), 167–256 (2003)
15. Oldham, S., Fulcher, B., Parkes, L., Arnatkeviciūtė, A., Suo, C., Fornito, A.: Consistency and differences between centrality measures across distinct classes of networks. PLoS ONE **14**(7), e0220061 (2019)
16. Poghosyan, M., Baronchelli, A.: Epidemic spreading on complex networks. Ph.D. thesis (2017)
17. Rowe, N.C., Rrushi, J., et al.: Introduction to Cyberdeception. Springer, Heidelberg (2016). https://doi.org/10.1007/978-3-319-41187-3
18. Skafle, I., Nordahl-Hansen, A., Quintana, D.S., Wynn, R., Gabarron, E.: Misinformation about COVID-19 vaccines on social media: rapid review. J. Med. Internet Res. **24**(8), e37367 (2022)

19. Trajanovski, S., Hayel, Y., Altman, E., Wang, H., Van Mieghem, P.: Decentralized protection strategies against sis epidemics in networks. IEEE Trans. Control Netw. Syst. **2**(4), 406–419 (2015)
20. Trajanovski, S., Kuipers, F.A., Hayel, Y., Altman, E., Van Mieghem, P.: Designing virus-resistant, high-performance networks: a game-formation approach. IEEE Trans. Control Netw. Syst. **5**(4), 1682–1692 (2017)
21. Tsemogne, O., Hayel, Y., Kamhoua, C., Deugoué, G.: Game theoretic modeling of cyber deception against epidemic botnets in internet of things. IEEE Internet Things J. **9**, 2678–2687 (2021)
22. Tsemogne, O., Hayel, Y., Kamhoua, C., Deugoue, G.: Partially observable stochastic games for cyber deception against network epidemic. In: GameSec 2020. LNCS, vol. 12513, pp. 312–325. Springer, Cham (2020). https://doi.org/10.1007/978-3-030-64793-3_17
23. Tsemogne, O., Kouam, W., Anwar, A.H., Hayel, Y., Kamhoua, C., Deugoué, G.: A network centrality game for epidemic control. In: Fang, F., Xu, H., Hayel, Y. (eds.) GameSec 2022. LNCS, vol. 13727, pp. 255–273. Springer, Cham (2022). https://doi.org/10.1007/978-3-031-26369-9_13
24. Tushir, B., Sehgal, H., Nair, R., Dezfouli, B., Liu, Y.: The impact of dos attacks on resource-constrained IoT devices: a study on the Mirai attack. arXiv preprint arXiv:2104.09041 (2021)
25. Xiao, K., Zhu, C., Xie, J., Zhou, Y., Zhu, X., Zhang, W.: Dynamic defense against stealth malware propagation in cyber-physical systems: a game-theoretical framework. Entropy **22**(8), 894 (2020)
26. Yu, S., Gu, G., Barnawi, A., Guo, S., Stojmenovic, I.: Malware propagation in large-scale networks. IEEE Trans. Knowl. Data Eng. **27**(1), 170–179 (2014)
27. Zaman, A., Marsaglia, G.: Random selection of subsets with specified element probabilities. Commun. Stat.-Theory Methods **19**(11), 4419–4434 (1990)

Shades of Grey: Strategic Bimatrix Stopping Games for Modelling (Un)Ethical Hacking Roles

Eckhard Pflügel[✉]

Faculty of Engineering, Computing and the Environment, Kingston University, Kingston upon Thames KT1 2EE, UK
e.pfluegel@kingston.ac.uk

Abstract. Grey-hat hackers possess specialist skills and knowledge to identify and close vulnerabilities in computer systems but might be tempted to switch from an ethical to an unethical hacking role to disclose or exploit the vulnerabilities for malicious benefit. This paper focuses on the emerging topic of game-theoretical modelling of the phenomenon of grey-hat hackers. A two-player complete information bimatrix game is designed to capture the strategic dilemmas involved in an organisation's interaction with a grey-hat hacker. An equilibrium analysis of the game illustrates these dilemmas from a game-theoretical point. This game is then extended to a class of stochastic bimatrix games called "Shades of Grey". Several game instances are presented, showing how an instance with a full-rank stopping matrix can resolve these dilemmas. This yields a more sophisticated and versatile framework for game-theoretic modelling of (un)ethical hacking roles than previously known in the literature. The paper also incorporates the concept of regular matrix pencils and their spectral analysis to analyse Nash equilibrium solutions for the special class of bimatrix games with rational payoff functions. We believe these linear algebra techniques will be useful to other game-theoretic applications beyond the Shades of Grey games.

Keywords: Strategic security games · Stochastic games · Grey-hat hackers · Equilibrium dilemmas

1 Introduction

Black-hat hackers are computer criminals who maliciously attack systems and exploit vulnerabilities, motivated by rewards such as financial gain. On the other hand, ethical (white-hat) hackers are tasked with improving the security of computer systems by identifying open vulnerabilities and using their expertise to close them. Grey-hat hackers are skilled actors in cyberspace whose behaviour is dictated by contrasting motivations: having discovered an open vulnerability they may cooperate with the system's owner to receive a bounty, or they might choose to attack it, given sufficient incentives. Organisations need to understand

© The Author(s), under exclusive license to Springer Nature Switzerland AG 2023
J. Fu et al. (Eds.): GameSec 2023, LNCS 14167, pp. 110–129, 2023.
https://doi.org/10.1007/978-3-031-50670-3_6

the phenomenon of grey-hat hackers: they need to weigh the advantages and disadvantages of cooperating with them to minimise risks to their assets and maximise benefits resulting from their technical expertise.

While game theory has been successfully applied to model typical scenarios between organisations and black-hat cyber actors using a wide range of different techniques and models [1,11,13,17,20], surprisingly little appears to be known specifically about the interaction with a grey-hat hacker. To the author's knowledge, the only paper explicitly addressing a scenario involving a grey-hat hacker is [3], proposing and analysing a stochastic game based on an inspection game. The nature of a stochastic game in terms of its transition rules helps shape the model's capabilities of considering evolving players. The grey-hat hacker game in [3] continues while the organisation and the hacker are cooperating and stops otherwise. This reflects the wish of the organisation to detect betrayal, upon which the attacker is punished and removed from the game. However, this may not accurately capture the nuanced dynamics of grey-hat hacking scenarios. Such scenarios involve ethical dilemmas, where hackers may have mixed intentions in patching, disclosing or exploiting vulnerabilities. A grey-hat hacker may have their own agenda favouring the white-hat ethical hacking role or, indeed, the black-hat role. Likewise, organisations might have policies and preferences that influence their decision-making. Modelling these aspects through game theory requires a sophisticated game approach, both in terms of the design of the stage game and the stochastic stopping rules. This can be taken into account by the features of the game framework presented in this paper.

The contributions of this paper are as follows. As a first step towards the stochastic bimatrix game proposed in this paper, we propose a two-player coordination game to model the interaction between a grey-hat hacker and an organisation. This complete information bimatrix game possesses a rich Nash equilibrium structure, making it a natural choice for characterising the various decision-making processes and strategic dilemmas involved in this scenario. The paper's main contribution to security games is extending the one-stage game to a stochastic bimatrix stopping game, the Shades of Grey game. Repeating the complete information game and using several stopping strategies shows that the stochastic game can resolve dilemmas under certain conditions, making it more flexible and suitable for real scenarios. As part of our framework to analyse the Shades of Grey game, we consider the linear algebra concept of matrix pencils and their spectral analysis using generalised eigensystems. We establish results expressing Nash equilibrium solutions of bimatrix games with rational payoff functions as generalised nonnegative eigenvectors corresponding to real eigenvalues. While these results are primarily used to analyse the Shades of Grey game, they may also be useful for other game-theoretic applications.

The following notations relating to game theory and generalised eigensystems of linear matrix pencils are used throughout this paper. Uppercase symbols $A, B, C, \ldots$ denote real matrices, assumed to be square and of size $n \geq 2$. Let E (e, respectively) be the square matrix (column vector, respectively) with all entries set to one, e_i the ith unit vector and O the zero matrix, with the size of these being clear from the context. A bimatrix game is a two-person non-zero-sum finite game $\mathcal{G}(A, B)$ where the first (row) player plays a row action and the second (column) player plays a column action. We write x and y for a pure or mixed strategy of the first and second players in the game. A strategy profile $s = ({}^t x, y)$ groups the strategies of each player together. We write $s^* = ({}^t x^*, y^*)$ for a Nash equilibrium, which is a strategy profile satisfying $v_A = {}^t x^* A y^* \geq x A y^* \quad \forall x$ and $v_B = {}^t x^* B y^* \geq x^* B y \quad \forall y$. Nash equilibria may be pure or mixed, and the corresponding Nash equilibrium is called pure or mixed accordingly. Given a Nash equilibrium with the notations above, we refer to $v = (v_A, v_B)$ as the corresponding game value profile. In contrast to the value of a matrix game, bimatrix game value profiles need not be unique. Matrix pencils are expressions of the form $A - \lambda B$ where λ is indeterminate, generalising the concept of a straight line to matrix functions. A matrix pencil $A - \lambda B$ is called a regular matrix pencil if the matrices A and B are square and the characteristic polynomial $f(\lambda) = \det(A - \lambda B)$ does not vanish identically, i.e. $f(\lambda) \not\equiv 0$. The concept of eigenvalues and eigenvectors of a matrix can be generalised to regular matrix pencils as follows: left (right respectively) generalised eigenvectors for the finite eigenvalue μ are nonzero solutions of the equation ${}^t x(A - \mu B) = 0$ (the equation $(A - \mu B)y = 0$ respectively), where μ is a root of the characteristic polynomial f. If $\text{rank}(B) = r \leq n$ we have $\deg(f) \leq r$, the pencil has at the most d finite eigenvalues. If $B = I$, we can see that the finite eigenvalues coincide with the eigenvalues of A in the usual sense. In this paper, for ease of reading, we shall occasionally employ the term "hacker" as a synonym for "grey-hat hacker" and refer to generalised eigenvectors simply as eigenvectors if no confusion arises.

The remainder of the paper is organised as follows. Related work is outlined in Sect. 2, Sect. 3 presents the grey-hat hacker stage game. Section 4 studies a linear algebra approach for solving bimatrix stochastic games. This is used in Sect. 5, where the Shades of Grey game is introduced and analysed. Section 6 is the paper's conclusion.

2 Related Work

This paper relates to several research strands: the area of strategic security games, stochastic games, and the application of linear algebra techniques to game theory. Furthermore, some non-game theory background research into the classification, motivation and impact of grey-hat hacking is indirectly related to this paper. We refer to the review in the [3] for an overview of these issues.

Strategic two-player two-action bimatrix security games have been proposed for many security application scenarios in the literature, for example, the intrusion detection game of [1], or the two-target attack-defence (AD) game in [17]. Using the concept of strategic equivalence, Moulin and Vial [18] have given a complete analysis of two-action bimatrix games based on proving the existence of three classes of such games, each class with its own Nash equilibrium structure. According to these authors, if trivial games are excluded, a two-action bimatrix game has either no pure and one mixed (Type 1), one pure (Type 2) or two pure and one mixed (Type 3) Nash equilibrium solutions. Strategic security games typically are of Type 1. In contrast, the bimatrix game proposed as part of a stochastic game in this paper is of Type 3, which we argue makes it interesting and innovative.

Stochastic games have been introduced in a pioneering paper by Shapley [21]. As explained in [1], stochastic security games have enjoyed popularity for modelling security scenarios due to the increased sophistication of this game model compared to static games. To our knowledge, the stochastic game proposed in the recent paper by Cohen et al. [3] is the first security game specifically modelling the strategic interaction with a grey-hat hacker. The game is a stochastic bimatrix game, and the authors apply the theoretical results of [4] on the Nash equilibrium structure of a class of repeating inspection games to the grey-hat hacker scenario. Various types of inspection games have been investigated extensively in the literature [2,7,9] and lend themselves well for applications due to recent results on the structure of general Nash equilibrium solutions for bimatrix stochastic inspection games [5,6]. In the two-player stochastic inspection game used for this grey-hat hacker game, the inspector and the hacker interact strategically, both with limited resources, playing repeatedly. An interesting feature of this game is the idea of parameterising the stage game, leading to an evolving number of states which are dynamically managed based on a decreasing budget spent by the organisation in each game round. In each round, the players have to decide whether they cooperate or not ("separate" in [3]). In the case of cooperation, the grey-hat hacker helps the organisation to close the vulnerability. In the case of the grey-hat hacker refraining from cooperation, they become a black-hat hacker and exploit the vulnerability. If the organisation inspects in this case, it detects the attack and can punish the attacker. The game terminates in this situation. The actions available to the players are similar to those in our grey-hat hacker stage game introduced in the next section, but there are a number of key differences between the game and the Shades of Grey game introduced in this paper: the stage game is more sophisticated, based on a Type 3 bimatrix game with a rich Nash equilibrium structure rather than an inspection game. The stochastic state model of the Shades of Grey game is simpler. However, flexibility is achieved due to the generic structure of the state transition rules (the stopping matrix), allowing for the creation and analysis of various game profiles that can model the players' preferences more precisely.

Previous work on the relationship between linear algebra and game theory is relevant to Sect. 4 and Sect. 5. The articles [10,12] are classical results on optimal solutions of matrix games, based on studying linear algebra properties of the game matrix. Extensions to bimatrix games are proposed in [15,16]. The idea to use spectral analysis of matrices and matrix pencils for analysing matrix games was first given in [23,24]. The theoretic model underlying the framework for finding stationary solutions of stochastic stopping games is introduced in [19] and generalised in [22]. A modern survey of linear algebra properties of the von Neumann model is [14]. A good introduction to the mathematical concept of linear matrix pencils and their spectral analysis based on generalised eigenvalues and eigenvectors is given in Gantmacher's book [8].

3   The Grey-Hat Hacker Stage Game

In this section, the bimatrix grey-hat hacker stage game is introduced. We describe the game model and justify its suitability for a grey-hat hacker scenario, analyse the structure of its Nash equilibria, and discuss the presence of dilemmas and their impact on the usefulness of the game. This leads to a more general discussion of the model's limitations and how they might be addressed.

3.1   Game Description

In the two-player bimatrix grey-hat hacker game, a hacker $\mathcal{H}$ and an organisation $\mathcal{O}$ interact to decide whether to cooperate or not. Depending on the specific actions, the outcome is for a vulnerability in the organisation's system to be patched or exploited. In what follows, assumptions on the motivation and actions of a grey-hat hacker are made, consistent with characteristics reported in the literature, cf. [3] and the references therein.

A grey-hat hacker does not wish to act maliciously if they are taken seriously by the organisation they contacted about a vulnerability found in their system. This means that a hacker is willing to perform white-hat (ethical) hacking roles if they feel trusted by the organisation. In the case of both players cooperating, $\mathcal{H}$ helps the organisation to close its vulnerability. Both players are rewarded: the hacker receives remuneration as a fee b_f paid by the organisation. It is assumed that white-hat hacking is beneficial to the organisation as it benefits from increased security, compensating for having to pay the fee, expressed as a positive benefit-cost difference $b_p - c_f$. On the other hand, a grey-hat hacker will feel compelled to turn into a black-hat hacker (cyber criminal), if the organisation refuses to cooperate. An organisation might ignore the grey-hat hacker's request to acknowledge the vulnerability's existence and assist with patching it. This is ultimately rooted in the organisation not trusting the hacker. For example, it might not believe the reported existence of the vulnerability or prefer to fix it using in-house resources.

In a situation of mutual betrayal, the grey-hat hacker turned black-hat hacker will exploit the vulnerability, usually with the help of other malicious cyber actors, by disclosing it to them. Consequently, the black-hat hacker earns an attack reward b_a, incentivising their malicious actions. In this case, the defender experiences a loss c_l. The organisation needs to weigh up the impact of their actions, depending on whether they deem the grey-hat hacker trustworthy. No costs or benefits arise to any of the players if the organisation rejects a grey-hat hacker willing to cooperate. It is hence in the organisation's interest to cooperate and benefit from the resulting increased security, specified in the game model as $b_p - c_f > 0$. If the grey-hat hacker betrays the trusting organisation, the organisation incurs the loss c_l due to the vulnerability exploit and additionally the fee c_f paid to the hacker. The grey-hat hacker earns $b_f + b_a$, reduced by the remorse cost of c_r. This situation is disadvantageous to the organisation; it would prefer not to cooperate with the hacker in this case. The resulting game is illustrated in Fig. 1, based on its strategic normal form and the players' actions and utility functions corresponding to the description in the previous paragraph.

$\mathcal{O} \downarrow \mathcal{H} \rightarrow$	not cooperate (betray)	cooperate (not betray)
not cooperate (not employ)	$-c_l$, b_a	0 , 0
cooperate (employ)	$-c_f - c_l$, $b_f + b_a - c_r$	$b_p - c_f$, b_f

Fig. 1. The grey-hat hacker bimatrix game $\mathcal{G}(D, G)$ is where a grey-hat hacker $\mathcal{H}$ and an organisation $\mathcal{O}$ decide whether to cooperate or betray. If both cooperate, the white-hat hacker receives a fee and the organisation benefits from increased security. If both betray, the black-hat hacker exploits the vulnerability, and the defender experiences a loss. A trusting organisation that the grey-hat hacker betrays incurs a loss due to the exploited vulnerability and the fee paid to the grey-hat hacker. The grey-hat hacker benefits from betrayal but experiences a remorse cost. No costs or benefits arise if the organisation rejects the cooperative grey-hat hacker.

The utility functions for the game $\mathcal{G}(D, G)$ for both players can be extracted in usual bimatrix game notation as matrices

$$D = \begin{pmatrix} -c_l & 0 \\ -c_f - c_l & b_p - c_f \end{pmatrix}, \quad G = \begin{pmatrix} b_a & 0 \\ b_f + b_a - c_r & b_f \end{pmatrix}. \tag{1}$$

Figure 2 summarises the different parameters occurring in the utilities, and the assumptions made on them. Note that any change in these assumptions will potentially lead to a new game with a different equilibrium solution structure.

Utilities
c_l – organisation's loss cost due to exploited vulnerability
c_f – organisation's cost of paying a fee for white-hat hacking role
b_p – organisation's benefit of increased security due to patched vulnerability
b_a – black-hat hacker benefit arising from exploiting the vulnerability
c_r – grey-hat hacker's remorse (psychological) cost
b_f – white-hat hacker's remuneration by obtaining fee from the organisation
Assumptions
(A1) All occurring parameters are positive.
(A2) The white-hat hacker is trusted to close the vulnerability: $b_p > c_f$.
(A3) The trusted grey-hat hacker strives to cooperate: $c_r > b_a$.
(A4) A black-hat role is always lucrative: $b_a + b_f - c_r > 0$.

Fig. 2. Parameters and their assumptions in the utility functions for the grey-hat hacker bimatrix game $\mathcal{G}(D, G)$.

3.2 Equilibrium Analysis

As Type 3 bimatrix game, the game has three Nash equilibria. Based on taking into account Assumptions (A)-(A3), one observes payoff changes resulting from unilateral deviation of strategies of the two players in this static game, as illustrated in Fig. 3. This yields the pure equilibrium strategy profiles $s_W^* = ((1,0), \begin{pmatrix} 1 \\ 0 \end{pmatrix})$ and $s_B^* = ((0,1), \begin{pmatrix} 0 \\ 1 \end{pmatrix})$.

$\mathcal{O} \downarrow \mathcal{H} \rightarrow$	not cooperate (betray)	cooperate (not betray)
not cooperate (not employ)	$\cdot, \cdot$	$\downarrow, \leftarrow$
cooperate (employ)	$\uparrow, \rightarrow$	$\cdot, \cdot$

Fig. 3. The pure Nash equilibria in the bimatrix grey-hat hacker stage game are the black-hat (not cooperate, not cooperate) and white-hat hacker (cooperate, cooperate) roles.

The mixed strategy profile is $s^* = ({}^t x^*, y^*)$ where ${}^t x^* = (1 - \frac{b_a}{c_r}, \frac{b_a}{c_r})$ and $y^* = \begin{pmatrix} 1 - \frac{c_f}{b_p} \\ \frac{c_f}{b_p} \end{pmatrix}$. This can be determined using a closed-form expression for 2×2 bimatrix games (cf. [1]), or derived from the linear algebra techniques developed in Sect. 4, see Remark 2. The game value profiles corresponding to the three Nash equilibria are $v_B = (-c_l, b_a)$, $v_W = (b_p - c_f, b_f)$ and $v_G = (\frac{-c_l(b_p - c_f)}{b_p}, \frac{b_a b_f}{c_r})$. Let $\mathcal{V} = \{v_B, v_G, v_W\}$.

To refine the equilibrium analysis of the game, we analyse the Pareto-optimal equilibria. This is useful to identify and understand the outcomes that offer the best possible "global" collective welfare for both players involved. Consider different order functions on $\mathcal{V}$: the total orders $\prec_{\mathcal{O}}$ and $\prec_{\mathcal{H}}$ using componentwise order for players $\mathcal{O}$ and $\mathcal{H}$, and the "product" order $\prec$ defined by $(a_1, a_2) \prec (b_1, b_2)$ if $a_1 < b_1$ and $a_2 < b_2$. The latter is used for a Pareto-optimal ordering of the equilibria.

Based on the assumptions of the model, and the structure of the found Nash equilibrium value profiles, it is clear that

$$v_B \prec_{\mathcal{O}} v_G \prec_{\mathcal{O}} v_W. \tag{2}$$

We will distinguish three cases.

Case $b_a < b_f$: Let us first notice that if $b_a \neq b_f$, since $b_a < c_r$, we have $v_G \prec_{\mathcal{H}} v_W$. Together with (2), we deduce the relation $v_G \prec v_W$. Furthermore, in this case, the fee provided to the white-hat hacker outperforms the gain from attacking. Hence $v_B \prec_{\mathcal{H}} v_W$ and then it holds $v_B \prec v_W$ based on transitivity in (2). No order relationship $\prec_{\mathcal{H}}$ exists between v_B and v_W. As an outcome for this case, we obtain the total ordering $\prec$ as depicted in the Hasse-diagram in Fig. 4(a).

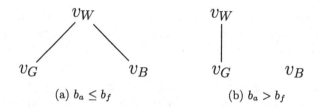

(a) $b_a \leq b_f$ (b) $b_a > b_f$

Fig. 4. The three Nash equilibria in the grey-hat hacker stage game as partially ordered sets with maximal elements for the two scenarios (a) one Pareto-optimal equilibrium (b) two Pareto-optimal equilibria.

Case $b_a > b_f$: In this situation, which is opposite to the white-hat role, one has $v_W \prec_{\mathcal{H}} v_B$ and $v_G \prec_{\mathcal{H}} v_W$. However, (2) shows that $v_W \prec_{\mathcal{O}} v_B$ is not true, so the only relationship that holds is $v_G \prec v_W$. Part (b) in Fig. 4 illustrates $\prec$ in this case.

Case $b_a = b_f$: In this final case, we find $v_G \prec_{\mathcal{H}} v_W$ and hence also $v_G \prec v_W$. Comparing v_B and v_W, due to $b_a = b_f$ we obtain $v_B \prec v_W$, resulting in the same situation as Part (a) in Fig. 4.

In summary, we obtain the following characterisation of the Pareto-optimal Nash equilibria represented as maximal elements of $\mathcal{V}$:

Theorem 1. *Given the generic utility functions and their assumptions (A1)-(A4) in the game $\mathcal{G}(D, G)$ and the order $\prec$, the following statements hold:*

1. *If $b_a > b_f$, the order $\prec$ is partial, it holds $v_G \prec v_W$, and v_W and v_G are maximal elements of $\mathcal{V}$.*
2. *If $b_a \leq b_f$, in addition to the above relation, one has $v_B \prec v_W$. The order $\prec$ is total, and v_W is the only maximal element of $\mathcal{V}$.*

Remark 1. The relation $v_G \prec v_W$ in Theorem 1 for the game $\mathcal{G}(D, G)$ is consistent with a result by Moulin and Vial [18], stating that the mixed Nash equilibrium in any Type 3 bimatrix game can be improved upon.

3.3   Discussion

The game $\mathcal{G}(D, G)$ being Type 3 of the aforementioned typology in [18], appears very appropriate to choose as a suitable type for a grey-hat hacker game. The pure Nash equilibrium solutions directly map to the two extremes of black-hat and white-hat hackers in the "Shades of Grey" scenarios, whilst the interesting additional game-theoretical contribution — the existence of an additional, mixed Nash equilibrium — can be interpreted as representative of the interim motivational state of the grey-hat hacker, caught between the two extreme roles of (un)ethical hacking.

The scenario-specific characteristics must be examined to determine whether a game-theoretical model is suitable for a given scenario in general, not only for the security application domain. These characteristics must be consistent with the model's strategies, utilities and assumptions. Furthermore, upon analysing the game's NE solutions, they should suggest sensible actions and not lead to dilemmas that cannot easily be resolved. The following issues can lead to such a dilemma.

- *Pure versus mixed equilibrium*: A difficult decision for each player to make is whether they should prefer a pure strategy rather than a mixed one. While a pure strategy might appeal to humans from a psychological point of view due to its simple conceptual definition, a mixed strategy might appear more balanced.
- *Multiple Pareto-optimal equilibria*: In this situation, several equilibria exist where a change from one to the other implies that one of the players suffers a reduced payoff. No clear choice is possible in this case.

Dilemmas require resolution; otherwise, the game has no deterministic outcome. Furthermore, mutual knowledge about the dilemma-resolution strategy needs to be available.

Although the present game models the player's utility functions granularly, it still has some shortcomings: both aforementioned types of dilemmas are present. It could be argued that the choice between mixed or pure equilibrium is less problematic if one considers that the mixed equilibrium can always be improved upon. The main issue is the choice of pure equilibrium in the situation $b_a \geq b_f$, where there are two pure Pareto-optimal equilibrium solutions. This aspect will be further addressed in the next section by a more sophisticated game approach capturing players' intentions that cannot be specified by utility functions of a stage game alone but using a stochastic game framework.

4   On Bimatrix Games with Rational Payoff Functions

This section introduces a class of bimatrix games with rational payoff functions. The definition of Nash equilibria for this type of game is stated and a result on sufficient conditions for the existence of these is proven. Furthermore, the special class of rank-1 games is also studied. Sources of inspiration for the techniques used in this section are classical results by Kaplansky [10], Thompson and Weil [22,23] for the game theory and linear algebra aspects, combined with a simple version of a stochastic game that was first formalised and analysed in Shapley's seminal paper [21]. Matrix games with rational payoff functions were considered in [14], where a perturbation theory was developed. The author is unaware of an extension to bimatrix games, as proposed in this section.

4.1   A Sufficient Condition

Denote $\mathcal{B}(A, B, C)$ where $C > 0$ a bimatrix game with rational payoff functions. By this, it is meant a two-player game where the payoffs to Player 1 and Player 2 using the strategy profile $(^t x, y)$ are defined as $u_A(x, y) = \frac{^t x A y}{^t x C y}$ and $u_B(x, y) = \frac{^t x B y}{^t x C y}$ respectively.

A Nash equilibrium concept can be defined as follows:

Definition 1. *A Nash Equilibrium strategy (x^*, y^*) of a bimatrix game with rational payoff functions satisfies $v_A = \frac{^tx^*Ay^*}{^tx^*Cy^*} \geq \frac{^txAy^*}{^txCy^*} \forall x$ and $v_B = \frac{^tx^*By^*}{^tx^*Cy^*} \geq \frac{^tx^*By}{^tx^*Cy} \forall y$. We say that $s^* = (x^*, y^*)$ is a Nash equilibrium and that $v = (v_A, v_B)$ is the corresponding game value profile.*

Define a normalised vector to be one whose components add up to one. The following theorem gives a sufficient condition for the existence of a Nash equilibrium of a bimatrix game with rational payoff functions, using linear algebra concepts.

Theorem 2. *Given the game $\mathcal{B}(A, B, C)$, assume the matrix pencils $A - \lambda C$ and $B - \lambda C$ are both regular. For each pencil, assume is has a real finite eigenvalue μ_A and μ_B, respectively. Furthermore, assume that there exists a normalised nonnegative left eigenvector x_{μ_B} of $B - \lambda C$ to the eigenvalue μ_B and a normalised nonnegative right eigenvector y_{μ_A} of $A - \lambda C$ to the eigenvalue μ_A. Then $(x^*, y^*) = (x_{\mu_B}, y_{\mu_A})$ is a Nash equilibrium of the game and (μ_A, μ_B) is the corresponding game value profile.*

Proof. We have for a normalised nonnegative left eigenvector x_{μ_B} satisfying

$$^tx_{\mu_B}(B - \mu_B C) = 0 \iff {}^tx_{\mu_B}B = \mu_B {}^tx_{\mu_B}C$$

that for any Player 2 strategy y it holds

$$\frac{^tx_{\mu_B}By}{^tx_{\mu_B}Cy} = \mu_B. \tag{3}$$

This trivially implies

$$\frac{^tx_{\mu_B}By_{\mu_A}}{^tx_{\mu_B}Cy_{\mu_A}} \geq \frac{^tx_{\mu_B}By}{^tx_{\mu_B}Cy}.$$

Similarly, we can show for a real nonnegative right eigenvector y_{μ_A} that

$$\frac{^tx_{\mu_B}Ay_{\mu_A}}{^tx_{\mu_B}Cy_{\mu_A}} \geq \frac{^txAy_{\mu_A}}{^txCy_{\mu_A}} \tag{4}$$

for any Player 1 strategy x. Hence, these strategies form, by definition, a Nash equilibrium with payoffs μ_A and μ_B as required. □

Definition 2. *The generalised eigensystem $\mathcal{E}_{A,B,C}$ associated with the pencils $A - \lambda C$ and $B - \lambda C$ is a pair $\mathcal{E}_{A,B,C} = (\mathcal{E}_{A,C}, \mathcal{E}_{B,C})$ where $\mathcal{E}_{A,C}$ is the set of real eigenvalues of $A - \lambda C$ together with their right generalised eigenvectors, and $\mathcal{E}_{B,C}$ the set of real eigenvalues of $B - \lambda C$ together with their left generalised eigenvectors.*

This result generalises existing work on game-theoretic interpretations of specific instances of the matrix pencils $A - \lambda C$ and $B - \lambda C$. If $C = E$, Theorem 2 yields a linear algebra characterisation of sufficient conditions for the existence of a Nash equilibrium for a standard bimatrix game. Weakly completely mixed equilibrium solutions are obtained if eigenvectors are strictly positive. Milchtaich et al. [15,16] investigate weakly completely mixed Nash equilibria of bimatrix games and state a necessary and sufficient condition for their existence, but without using the notion of matrix pencils. For $C = E$ and $B = -A$, Theorem 2 specialises to a result on optimal solutions of matrix games by Thompson and Weil [23]. If $B = -A$, one obtains a special case of the approach by the same authors [22] on the relationship of generalised eigensystems and equilibrium solutions of the von Neumann model [19] for game theory.

Remark 2. The mixed Nash equilibria found for the grey-hat hacker stage game $\mathcal{G}(D, G)$ in Sect. 3.2 can be seen to consist of left and right eigenvectors as in Theorem 2. Hence, the sufficient condition of the theorem can be used to derive this particular Nash equilibrium. Indeed, one verifies, for example, that for the grey-hat hacker mixed equilibrium $s^* = (x^*, y^*)$ with game value profile $v_G = (v_G^{(1)}, v_G^{(2)})$ it holds

$$Ay^* = -\frac{c_l}{b_p} \begin{pmatrix} b_p - c_f \\ b_p - c_f \end{pmatrix} = v_G^{(2)} e = v_G^{(2)} Ey^*$$

and hence $(A - v_G^{(2)} E)y^* = 0$.

A property that will be useful for the equilibrium analysis of the Grey thinking game in Sect. 5.3 is that of interchangeable Nash equilibria. In a two-player game, this is defined as follows: if x_1 and x_2 are any two strategies of the first player and y_1 and y_2 are any two strategies of the second player such that (x_1, y_1) and (x_2, y_2) are two Nash equilibria, then (x_1, y_2) and (x_2, y_1) are also Nash equilibria.

Proposition 1. *The Nash equilibria found by Theorem 2 are interchangeable.*

Proof. Using Eq. (3) we see that x_1 is not only a best response to y_1 but to all Player 2 strategies, which includes y_2. The converse is true for y_2, which is a best response to x_2 but also to x_1. Similarly, we can show that x_2 and y_1 are mutual best responses.   □

4.2   On Rank-1 Bimatrix Games

This section considers the game $\mathcal{B}(A, B, C)$ in the case where $C > 0$, rank$(C) = 1$, and studies the implications on the existence of Nash equilibria. These results will be useful for analysing the Shades of Grey games in Sect. 5.

We commence with a linear algebra result for matrix pencils of the form $A - \lambda C$ and rank$(C) = 1$, which we call rank-1 pencils. We use rank-factorisation to write

$$C = p^t q \tag{5}$$

where $p, q \in \mathbb{R}^n$ are positive column vectors.

The following proposition provides an eigenspace structure result for rank-1 regular matrix pencils.

Proposition 2. *If $^tq\,\mathrm{adj}(A)p = 0$, the rank-1 pencil $A - \lambda p\,^tq$ has no finite eigenvalues. Otherwise, the pencil has the single finite real eigenvalue $c = \frac{\det(A)}{^tq\,\mathrm{adj}(A)p}$. The associated left and right eigenvectors x, y can be determined explicitly using the formulae $^tx = \frac{^tq\,\mathrm{adj}(A)}{^tq\,\mathrm{adj}(A)p}$ and $y = \frac{\mathrm{adj}(A)p}{^tq\,\mathrm{adj}(A)p}$.*

Proof. First, note that the characteristic polynomial $f(\lambda) = \det(A - \lambda p\,^tq)$ is a linear function and one has

$$f(\lambda) = {^tq}\,\mathrm{adj}(A)p\lambda - \det(A).$$

If $^tq\,\mathrm{adj}(A)p = 0$, the pencil has no finite eigenvalues as f is a nonzero constant. Otherwise, based on the definitions of c, x and y as in the proposition, it can be directly verified that $Ay = cp\,^tqy$ and $^txA = c\,^txp\,^tq$. So c is a finite eigenvalue of $A - \lambda p\,^tq$ with left and right eigenvectors x and y. This must be the only such eigenvalue as the degree of f is one. □

The following theorem states sufficient conditions for the existence of a Nash equilibrium solution of the game $\mathcal{B}(A, B, C)$ where $A - \lambda C$ and $B - \lambda C$ are rank-1 pencils, and explicit formulae for their construction.

Theorem 3. *Consider a rank-1 bimatrix game with rational payoff functions $\mathcal{B}(A, B, C)$ where $C = p\,^tq > 0$ and assume $^tq\,\mathrm{adj}(A)p \neq 0$ and $^tq\,\mathrm{adj}(B)p \neq 0$. Define*

$$^tx = \frac{^tq\,\mathrm{adj}(B)}{^tq\,\mathrm{adj}(B)p}, \quad y = \frac{\mathrm{adj}(A)p}{^tq\,\mathrm{adj}(A)p}, \quad \mu_A = \frac{\det(A)}{^tq\,\mathrm{adj}(A)p}, \quad \mu_B = \frac{\det(B)}{^tq\,\mathrm{adj}(B)p}$$

and assume that x and y are nonnegative, satisfying $^txe \neq 0$, $^tey \neq 0$. Define $^tx^* = {^tx}/{^txe}$ and $y^* = y/{^tey}$. Then (x^*, y^*) is a Nash equilibrium of the game and (μ_A, μ_B) is the corresponding game value profile.

4.3   Application to Bimatrix Stochastic Stopping Games

Shapley introduced the notion of stochastic matrix games in [21]. In this paper, he studied how to define the value and optimal solutions of stochastic matrix games and how these relate to the value and optimal solutions of the stage matrix game. The concept of a stationary solution was introduced and used to define the value of the game. Using modern terminology, we say that the game $\mathcal{S}(A, B, S)$ is a two-state undiscounted stochastic bimatrix game, where state transition probabilities depend only on the current state and the chosen strategies. The game has one transient state s_0 "play" and an absorbing state s_1 "stop". The game is described by the payoff matrices A and B specifying a bimatrix stage game repeated in each round, and the stopping matrix S controlling the probabilities of repeating the game jointly for Player 1 and Player 2. Given a strategy profile $(^tx, y)$, the stopping probability is ^txSy and the probability of continuing the game is $1 - {^txSy}$ (see Fig. 5). In the scenario where $A = -B$, the game $\mathcal{S}$ exhibits

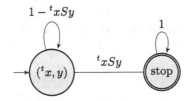

Fig. 5. State transitions in the stochastic stopping game, when playing the strategy profile $(^tx, y)$.

the characteristics of a stochastic matrix game, corresponding to Example 1 in Shapley's paper.

Following Shapley, let us fix a stationary strategy profile $(^tx, y)$ and study the expected utility of the players when using these strategies based on an undiscounted model. The condition

$$0 < {}^txSy \leq 1 \tag{6}$$

will be important in the sequel.

Lemma 1. *Assume the stationary strategy profile $(^tx, y)$ satisfies $0 < {}^txSy \leq 1$. Then the expected number of steps required for the game $\mathcal{S}(A, B, S)$ to stop in state s_1 when the players are using (x, y) in state s_0 is $1/{}^txSy$. The expected resulting payoff profile is $u(x, y) = \left(\frac{{}^txAy}{{}^txSy}, \frac{{}^txBy}{{}^txSy} \right)$.*

Proof. After $k > 0$ iterations, the expected accumulated payoff when playing the same strategy (x, y) in each round of the game is

$$u_{A,k}(x, y) = {}^txAy \sum_{i=1}^{k-1} (1 - {}^txSy)^i \tag{7}$$

and

$$u_{B,k}(x, y) = {}^txBy \sum_{i=0}^{k-1} (1 - {}^txSy)^i \tag{8}$$

since the probability of remaining in state s_0 is $s := 1 - {}^txSy$ where, according to the assumptions of the lemma, $0 \leq s < 1$. The game finishes with probability one. Furthermore, one has $\sum_{i=0}^{\infty} s^i = \frac{1}{1-s}$. The expected game payoff profile u is hence

$$u(x, y) = \lim_{k \to \infty} (u_{A,k}(x, y), u_{B,k}(x, y)) = \left(\frac{{}^txAy}{{}^txSy}, \frac{{}^txBy}{{}^txSy} \right).$$

$\square$

We would like to maximise $u(x, y)$ w.r.t. unilateral changes of strategies of the two players. This immediately leads to the following

Proposition 3. *Let the strategy* (x^*, y^*) *satisfy* $0 < {}^t x^* S y^* \leq 1$ *and assume it is a Nash equilibrium strategy of the bimatrix game with rational payoffs* $\mathcal{B}(A, B, S)$. *Then it is a stationary Nash equilibrium solution of the stochastic stopping game* $\mathcal{S}(A, B, S)$. *The converse statement holds.*

Combining this proposition and Theorem 2, we can state sufficient, constructive conditions for the existence of stationary solutions of $\mathcal{S}(A, B, S)$, based on generalised eigensystems.

Revisiting rank-1 pencils and Theorem 3, we find a formula for constructing a value profile (v_A, v_B) and corresponding Nash equilibrium solutions (x^*, y^*) for a rank-1 bimatrix stochastic game where $S = p^t q$ is a positive matrix. Compute

$$v_A = \frac{\det(A)}{{}^t q \, \mathrm{adj}(A) p}, \quad v_B = \frac{\det(B)}{{}^t q \, \mathrm{adj}(B) p}, \quad {}^t x = \frac{{}^t q \, \mathrm{adj}(B)}{{}^t q \, \mathrm{adj}(B) p}, \quad y = \frac{\mathrm{adj}(A) p}{{}^t q \, \mathrm{adj}(A) p}.$$

The equilibrium solutions (x^*, y^*) are then obtained from (x, y) above by normalisation.

5   The Shades of Grey Stochastic Game

This section introduces Shades of Grey, a generic strategic stochastic bimatrix stopping game. This framework is more flexible than that of [3] regarding the adaptability of the stopping matrix S. We introduce several specific instances of this game, modelling strategic preferences of the two players: the organisation $\mathcal{O}$ and the grey-hat hacker $\mathcal{H}$. For each instance, we then find mixed stationary Nash equilibria. To analyse the Shades of Grey game, we apply the theory of linear matrix pencils, their generalised eigenvalues and eigenvectors, as developed in the previous section.

5.1   Generic Game

The generic Shades of Grey game $\mathcal{G}(D, G, S)$ is, as a stochastic bimatrix stopping game, described by the payoff matrices (7) and (8) for the bimatrix stage game, and a generic stopping matrix which will be denoted by $S = \begin{pmatrix} s_0 & s_1 \\ s_2 & s_3 \end{pmatrix}$ where $0 \leq s_i \leq 1$, not all of the s_i equal to one or to zero: $S \neq E$, $S \neq O$.

As a general, symbolic equilibrium analysis of this game is challenging, we shall consider several specific game instances to express further strategic preferences of the grey-hat hacker and the organisation, inspired by the shortcomings of the stage game model introduced in Sect. 3. We differentiate two classes of such game instances based on the rank of the matrix S.

5.2   Rank-1 Games

The first class is that of Rank-1 Games. We devise specific stopping matrices to express strategic preferences of the two players, based on their personality profile. We identify four games in total.

Tints of White. In this game, a grey-hat hacker strives to be a white-hat hacker. This is modelled by continuing the game with nonzero probability $1 - s_W$ for $0 < s_W < 1$ as long as the white-hat hacking role is played within the stage game, expressed by

$$S_W = \begin{pmatrix} 1 & s_W \\ 1 & s_W \end{pmatrix}.$$

Tints of Black. This game models a grey-hat hacker, favouring the playing of an unethical hacking role. The stopping matrix is formed accordingly as

$$S_B = \begin{pmatrix} s_B & 1 \\ s_B & 1 \end{pmatrix}$$

with $0 < s_B < 1$. This is a preference opposite to that in the previous Tints of Black game.

Innocent Inc. This game assumes the organisation $\mathcal{O}$ to be naïve, believing in ethical hacking and inclined to trust the grey-hat hacker. We have

$$S_I = \begin{pmatrix} 1 & 1 \\ s_I & s_I \end{pmatrix}$$

where $0 < s_I < 1$. When $\mathcal{O}$ chooses not to employ the hacker in one game round, it is disappointed and stops.

Cautious Corp. Here, the idea is to assume that a risk-averse organisation does not easily trust the grey-hat hacker. The stopping matrix is

$$S_C = \begin{pmatrix} s_C & s_C \\ 1 & 1 \end{pmatrix}$$

with $0 < s_C < 1$. If $\mathcal{O}$ employs the ethical hacker, it feels nervous and disengages from the repeated game.

To analyse these games, we focus on the existence of a mixed strategy derived from generalised eigensystems and application of Proposition 3.

Theorem 4. *The rank-1 Shades of Grey games below have a mixed stationary Nash equilibrium solution (x^*, y^*) with corresponding game value profile v as follows:*

(i) Tints of White: $^t x^* = \frac{1}{b_f + s_W(c_r - b_f)}(b_f + s_W(c_r - b_f - b_a), s_W b_a)$,
$y^* = \frac{1}{b_p}(b_p - c_f c_f)$, $v = (\frac{-c_l(b_p - c_f)}{b_p - (1 - s_W)c_f}, \frac{b_a b_f}{b_f + s_W(c_r - b_f)})$,

(ii) Innocent Inc: $^t x^* = \frac{1}{c_r}(c_r - b_a, b_a)$, $y^* = \frac{1}{b_p + (1 - s_I)c_l}\begin{pmatrix} b_p - c_f \\ c_f + (1 - s_I)c_l \end{pmatrix}$, $v = (-\frac{c_l(b_p - c_f)}{b_p + c_l(1 - s_I)}, \frac{b_a b_f}{b_a(s_I - 1) + c_r})$.

For the two remaining games, more assumptions are needed.

Theorem 5. *The rank-1 Shades of Grey games below have a mixed stationary Nash equilibrium solution (x^*, y^*) with corresponding game value profile v as follows:*

(i) *Tints of Black: if* $s_B b_f + c_r - b_f - b_a > 0$, *then* $^t x^* = \frac{1}{s_B b_f + c_r - b_f}(s_B b_f +$

$c_r - b_f - b_a, b_a), y^* = \frac{1}{b_p}\begin{pmatrix} b_p - c_f \\ c_f \end{pmatrix}, v = (\frac{-c_l(b_p - c_f)}{s_B(b_p - c_f) + c_f}, \frac{b_a b_f}{b_f(s_B - 1) + c_r}),$

(ii) *Cautious Corp: if* $(c_l + c_f)s_C - c_l > 0$, *then* $^t x^* = \frac{1}{c_r}(c_r - b_a, b_a),$

$y^* = \frac{1}{s_C(b_p + c_l) - c_l}\begin{pmatrix} s_C(b_p - c_f) \\ s_C(c_f + c_l) - c_l \end{pmatrix}, v = (\frac{-c_l(b_p - c_f)}{s_C(b_p + c_l) - c_l}, \frac{b_a b_f}{s_C(c_r - b_a) + b_a}).$

Proof (of Theorem 4 and 5). The characterisations of the mixed equilibria can be derived from Proposition 3, applied to the following positive rank-factorisations:

$$S_W = \begin{pmatrix} 1 \\ 1 \end{pmatrix}(1 \ s_W), \quad S_I = \begin{pmatrix} 1 \\ s_I \end{pmatrix}(1 \ 1)$$

and

$$S_B = \begin{pmatrix} 1 \\ 1 \end{pmatrix}(s_B \ 1), \quad S_C = \begin{pmatrix} s_C \\ 1 \end{pmatrix}(1 \ 1).$$

$\square$

A more detailed analysis of the complete Nash equilibrium structure of these games shows that the Tints of White and Innocent Inc games both possess two pure equilibria in addition to the mixed equilibrium. For example, in the Tints of White game, the presence of the parameter s_W does not affect the preferred unilateral payoff deviations as illustrated in Fig. 3 as the rational payoff structure is obtained by multiplying the second column of the matrices D and G by the factor $s_W^{-1} > 1$. This means that the pure equilibrium solutions of this game coincide with those of the stage game $\mathcal{G}(D, G)$. Dilemmas remains if mixed equilibrium solutions are present – e.g. if $b_a > b_f/s_W$, the Pareto-dilemma still arises.

5.3   Rank-2 Games

We will study one game instance for the second class, that of Rank-2 Games. The increase in rank will be shown to resolve the dilemmas that were present in the previous rank-1 game models.

Grey Thinking. This game expresses the grey-hat hacker's and the organisation's desire to avoid both the white and black-hat roles, as they lead to dilemmas as presented in Sect. 3. This is modelled by the possibility of an infinite number of repetitions, leading to the nonnegative stopping matrix

$$S = \begin{pmatrix} 1 & 0 \\ 0 & 1 \end{pmatrix}.$$

Due to condition (6), the strategy profiles $((0,1), \begin{pmatrix} 1 \\ 0 \end{pmatrix})$ and $((1,0), \begin{pmatrix} 0 \\ 1 \end{pmatrix})$ are excluded from being considered as stationary equilibrium solutions when using the matrix pencil approach.

Theorem 6. *The Grey Thinking game has one mixed Nash equilibrium* (x^*, y^*) *that cannot be improved upon. Let its associated game value profiles be* (v_D^*, v_G^*). *Then, depending on the comparative relationship between* b_a *and* b_f, *it holds:*

(i) If $b_a < b_f$, the mixed Nash equilibrium is: ${}^t x^* = \frac{1}{2b_f - c_r}(c_r - b_f - b_a, b_a - b_f)$, $y^* = \begin{pmatrix} 0 \\ 1 \end{pmatrix}$ and $v_D^* = b_p - c_f$, $v_G^* = b_f$.

(ii) If $b_a \geq b_f$, the mixed Nash equilibrium is: ${}^t x^* = (1, 0)$, $y^* = \frac{1}{b_p + 2c_l} \begin{pmatrix} c_l - c_f + b_p \\ c_l + c_f \end{pmatrix}$ and $v_D^* = -c_l$, $v_G^* = b_a$.

Proof. The pencils $D - \lambda I$ and $G - \lambda I$ are trivially regular, as the identity matrix has full rank. One finds $\mathcal{E}_D = \left\{ [\mu_D^{(1)}, y_{\mu_D}^{(1)}], [\mu_D^{(2)}, y_{\mu_D}^{(2)}] \right\}$ where

$$\mu_D^{(1)} = -c_l, \quad y_{\mu_D}^{(1)} = \frac{1}{b_p + 2c_l} \begin{pmatrix} c_l + b_p - c_f \\ c_l + c_f \end{pmatrix}, \quad \mu_D^{(2)} = b_p - c_f, \quad y_{\mu_D}^{(2)} = \begin{pmatrix} 0 \\ 1 \end{pmatrix}.$$

For $G - \lambda I$ one obtains $\mathcal{E}_G = \left\{ \left[\mu_G^{(1)}, x_{\mu_G}^{(1)} \right], \left[\mu_G^{(2)}, x_{\mu_G}^{(2)} \right] \right\}$ where

$$\mu_G^{(1)} = b_a, \quad {}^t x_{\mu_G}^{(1)} = (1, 0), \quad \mu_G^{(2)} = b_f, \quad {}^t x_{\mu_G}^{(2)} = \frac{1}{2b_f - c_r}(c_r - b_f - b_a, b_a - b_f).$$

We now distinguish three cases. According to Proposition 1, equilibrium solutions are interchangeable, and hence in each case, we must consider all combinations of left eigenvectors $x_{\mu_G}^{(1)}, x_{\mu_G}^{(2)}$ with right eigenvectors $y_{\mu_D}^{(1)}, y_{\mu_D}^{(2)}$. As $x_{\mu_G}^{(1)} S y_{\mu_D}^{(2)} = 0$, we only need to examine the potential strategy profiles

$$s^{(11)} = (x_{\mu_G}^{(1)}, y_{\mu_D}^{(1)}), \quad s^{(21)} = (x_{\mu_G}^{(2)}, y_{\mu_D}^{(1)}), \quad s^{(22)} = (x_{\mu_G}^{(2)}, y_{\mu_D}^{(2)})$$

with corresponding value profiles

$$v^{(11)} = (-c_l, b_a), \quad v^{(21)} = (-c_l, b_f), \quad v^{(22)} = (b_p - c_f, b_f).$$

If $b_a < b_f$, both $s^{(21)}$ and $s^{(22)}$ have vectors that can be normalised to be nonnegative, but $v^{(21)} \prec v^{(22)}$, so we choose $s^{(22)}$. If $b_a > b_f$, then we find that $s^{(11)}$ is the only choice of eigenvectors that can be normalised to be nonnegative. In the case $b_a = b_f$, the vectors ${}^t x_{\mu_G}^{(1)}$ and ${}^t x_{\mu_G}^{(2)}$ normalise to the same eigenvector $(1, 0)$, which must be combined with $y_{\mu_D}^{(1)}$. Hence, this case is the same as the previous case. Finally, note that none of the pure equilibria improve the mixed equilibria found in the theorem. $\square$

Remark 3. The analysis of this game shows a link between algebraic eigenvalues of a matrix and game theory which was first investigated by Weil [24], but described as "*lacking parsimony*" in his paper. The Grey Thinking game instance shows that specific stochastic stopping games may form such a link that Weil was missing as he restricted his study to static matrix games.

5.4   Note on Discounted Games

So far, our framework based on matrix pencils and their generalised eigensystems assumed an undiscounted stochastic game model. The restriction to strategies x, y with a stopping matrix S verifying the condition $0 < {}^t x S y \leq 1$ ensures convergence of the geometric series in (7) and (8). Due to the non-vanishing denominator, this also leads to a well-defined rational payoff function in the game $\mathcal{B}$. On the other hand, it might rule out the use of specific strategies when dealing with a nonnegative stopping matrix $S \geq 0$ with some entries being zero as in the Black or White Thinking game.

We can extend the matrix pencil framework to discounted stochastic stopping games with limiting average payoffs by considering the complete spectral theory of regular matrix pencils, which includes the concept of the eigenvalue at infinity. Assume $\hat{y}$ is a nonnegative right eigenvector of the pencil $A - \lambda S$ and $\hat{x}$ a left eigenvector of the pencil $B - \lambda S$, both for the eigenvalue at infinity. This means $S\hat{y} = 0$, ${}^t\hat{x}S = 0$ and $A\hat{y} \neq 0$, ${}^t\hat{x}B \neq 0$ ([8]).

Consider the discounted game using the limiting average payoff function ${}^t\hat{x}A y/k$ in round k of the game. Then, reviewing Eqs. (7) and (8), one obtains for Player 1

$$\hat{u}_{A,k}(\hat{x}, \hat{y}) = \frac{{}^t\hat{x}A\hat{y}}{k} \sum_{i=0}^{k-1} 1 = {}^t\hat{x}A\hat{y}.$$

Similarly, for Player 2, one has

$$\hat{u}_{B,k}(\hat{x}, \hat{y}) = {}^t\hat{x}B\hat{y}.$$

In some situations, this yields a correspondence between the eigenvalue at infinity with its associated eigenvectors and stationary solutions of the discounted game model.

The discounted model allows relaxing the condition on the stopping matrix S to be a positive matrix. For example, consider an inspection game akin to the grey-hat hacker game in [3], which stops when the hacker has been caught not cooperating. Assume generic payoff matrices $D = ((d_{ij})) \in \mathbb{R}^{2 \times 2}$ and $G = ((g_{ij})) \in \mathbb{R}^{2 \times 2}$. The stopping matrix is

$$S = \begin{pmatrix} 1 & 0 \\ 0 & 0 \end{pmatrix}.$$

The vectors ${}^t\hat{x} = (0\ 1)$ and $\hat{y} = \begin{pmatrix} 0 \\ 1 \end{pmatrix}$ are left and right eigenvectors to the infinite eigenvalue of the two pencils defining the game. Indeed, they satisfy

$$ {}^t\hat{x}S = (0\ 0), \quad S\hat{y} = \begin{pmatrix} 0 \\ 0 \end{pmatrix}.$$

and for generic matrices D and G the above vectors will not be elements of their left and right nullspaces. When choosing the above strategies $\hat{x}$ and $\hat{y}$, one has

${}^t\hat{x}S\hat{y} = 0$, ${}^t\hat{x}D\hat{y} = d_{22}$ and ${}^t\hat{x}G\hat{y} = g_{22}$. Hence both players never end the game and accumulate payoffs in the undiscounted game. Using the limiting average discount model, they can achieve the utilities $\hat{u}_A = d_{22}$ and $\hat{u}_B = g_{22}$.

Remark 4. Thompson et al. [22] investigated the use of generalised eigensystems for game theory but did not find a meaning for the eigenvalue at infinity. This could be explained by their view of the matrix pencil $A - \lambda B$ originating as an economic production model, see von Neumann's paper [19].

6   Conclusion

In summary, this paper presents several contributions to the field of security games and game theory. Firstly, it introduces a two-player complete information bimatrix game as an initial step. This bimatrix game captures the strategic dilemmas involved in the interaction between a grey-hat hacker and an organisation, modelling an aspect that was not covered in previous security game models in the literature. Furthermore, the paper's main contribution lies in extending the one-stage game to a stochastic framework by introducing the Shades of Grey game. By repeatedly playing the complete information game and employing various stopping strategies, the stochastic game has the ability to address specific player preferences, making it more adaptable and realistic for modelling grey-hat hacking scenarios. Furthermore, a game with a full-rank stopping matrix can resolve dilemmas that were present in the stage game. As another contribution, primarily to analyse the Shades of Grey game, but with potential for broader applications in other game-theoretic contexts, the concept of matrix pencils and their spectral analysis through generalised eigensystems is introduced for finding sufficient conditions for the existence of Nash equilibrium solutions in bimatrix games with rational payoff functions. We argue that combining well-established game-theoretical principles with exploring lesser-known yet intriguing linear algebra concepts to aid in analysing stochastic stopping games is interesting and promising. Future research could build upon this theoretical framework and extend it to other types of stochastic games to obtain a complete classification of two-action strategic stochastic security games.

References

1. Alpcan, T., Başar, T.: Network Security: A Decision and Game-Theoretic Approach. Cambridge University Press, Cambridge, October 2010
2. Avenhaus, R., Canty, M.J.: Playing for time: a sequential inspection game. Eur. J. Oper. Res. **167**(2), 475–492 (2005)
3. Cohen, D., Elalouf, A., Zeev, R.: Collaboration or separation maximizing the partnership between a gray hat hacker and an organization in a two-stage cybersecurity game. Int. J. Inf. Manag. Data Insights **2**(1), 100073 (2022)
4. Deutsch, Y.: A polynomial-time method to compute all Nash equilibria solutions of a general two-person inspection game. Eur. J. Oper. Res. **288**(3), 1036–1052 (2021)

5. Deutsch, Y., Golany, B.: Multiple agents finitely repeated inspection game with dismissals. Ann. Oper. Res. **237**(1–2), 7–26 (2016)
6. Deutsch, Y., Golany, B., Goldberg, N., Rothblum, U.G.: Inspection games with local and global allocation bounds. Nav. Res. Logist. **60**(2), 125–140 (2013)
7. Ferguson, T.S., Melolidakis, C.: On the inspection game. Nav. Res. Logist. **45**(3), 327–334 (1998)
8. Gantmacher, F.R., Brenner, J.L.: Applications of the Theory of Matrices. John Wiley & Sons, Nashville, TN, December 1959
9. Hohzaki, R.: An inspection game with multiple inspectees. Eur. J. Oper. Res. **178**(3), 894–906 (2007)
10. Kaplansky, I.: A contribution to von Neumann's theory of games. Ann. Math. **46**(3), 474–479 (1945)
11. Kar, D., et al.: Trends and applications in Stackelberg security games. Handbook of Dynamic Game Theory, pp. 1–47 (2017)
12. Karlin, S.: Mathematical Methods and Theory in Games, Programming, and Economics, vol. 2. Dover Publications Inc., New York (2003)
13. Korzhyk, D., Yin, Z., Edu, Z., Kiekintveld, C., Conitzer, V., Tambe, M.: Stackelberg vs. nash in security games: an extended investigation of interchangeability, equivalence, and uniqueness. J. Artif. Intell. Res. **41**, 297–327 (2011)
14. Marchi, E., Oviedo, J.A., Cohen, J.E.: Perturbation theory of a nonlinear game of von Neumann. SIAM J. Matrix Anal. Appl. **12**(3), 592–596 (1991)
15. Milchtaich, I.: Computation of completely mixed equilibrium payoffs in bimatrix games. Int. Game Theory Rev. **08**(03), 483–487 (2006)
16. Milchtaich, I., Ostrowski, T.: On some saddle point matrices and applications to completely mixed equilibrium in bimatrix games. Int. J. Math. Game Theory Algebra (IJMGTA) **18**(2), 65–72 (2008)
17. Mohebbi Moghaddam, M., Manshaei, M.H., Zhu, Q.: To trust or not: a security signaling game between service provider and client. In: Khouzani, M.H.R., Panaousis, E., Theodorakopoulos, G. (eds.) GameSec 2015. LNCS, vol. 9406, pp. 322–333. Springer, Cham (2015). https://doi.org/10.1007/978-3-319-25594-1_18
18. Moulin, H., Vial, J.P.: Strategically zero-sum games: the class of games whose completely mixed equilibria cannot be improved upon. Int. J. Game Theory **7**(3), 201–221 (1978)
19. Neumann, J.V.: A model of general economic equilibrium. Rev. Econ. Stud. **13**(1), 1–9 (1945)
20. Panaousis, E., Fielder, A., Malacaria, P., Hankin, C., Smeraldi, F.: Cybersecurity games and investments: a decision support approach. In: Poovendran, R., Saad, W. (eds.) GameSec 2014. LNCS, vol. 8840, pp. 266–286. Springer, Cham (2014). https://doi.org/10.1007/978-3-319-12601-2_15
21. Shapley, L.S.: Stochastic games. Proc. Natl. Acad. Sci. U. S. A. **39**(10), 1095–1100 (1953)
22. Thompson, G.L., Weil, R.L.: Von Neumann model solutions are generalized eigensystems. In: Bruckmann, G., Weber, W. (eds.) Contributions to the Von Neumann Growth Model, pp. 139–154. Springer, Berlin, Heidelberg (1971). https://doi.org/10.1007/978-3-662-24667-2_14
23. Thompson, G.L., Weil, R.L., Jr.: Further relations between game theory and eigensystems. Soc. Ind. Appl. Math. **11**(4), 597–602 (1969)
24. Weil, R.L., Jr.: Game theory and eigensystems. SIAM Rev. Soc. Ind. Appl. Math. **10**(3), 360–367 (1968)

Learning in Security Games

Characterizing and Improving the Robustness of Predict-Then-Optimize Frameworks

Sonja Johnson-Yu[1]([✉]) [iD], Jessie Finocchiaro[1,2] [iD], Kai Wang[3],
Yevgeniy Vorobeychik[5] [iD], Arunesh Sinha[6] [iD], Aparna Taneja[4] [iD],
and Milind Tambe[1,2,4] [iD]

[1] Harvard University, Cambridge, MA, USA
{sjohnsonyu,tambe}@g.harvard.edu, jessie@seas.harvard.edu
[2] Center for Research on Computation and Society, Boston, USA
[3] MIT, Cambridge, USA
kaiwa318@mit.edu
[4] Google Research India, Bangalore, India
[5] Washington University St. Louis, St. Louis, USA
vorobeychik@wustl.edu
[6] Rutgers University, Newark, USA
arunesh.sinha@rutgers.edu

Abstract. Optimization tasks situated in incomplete information settings are often preceded by a prediction problem to estimate the missing information; past work shows the traditional predict-then-optimize (PTO) framework can be improved by training a predictive model with respect to the optimization task through a PTO paradigm called *decision-focused learning*. Little is known, however, about the performance of traditional PTO and decision-focused learning when exposed to *adversarial label drift*. We provide modifications of traditional PTO and decision-focused learning that attempt to improve robustness by anticipating label drift. When the predictive model is perfectly expressive, we cast these learning problems as Stackelberg games. With these games, we provide a necessary condition for when anticipating label drift can improve the performance of a PTO algorithm: if performance can be improved, then the downstream optimization objective must be *asymmetric*. We then bound the loss of decision quality in the presence of adversarial label drift to show there may exist a strict gap between the performance of the two algorithms. We verify our theoretical findings empirically in two asymmetric and two symmetric settings. These experimental results demonstrate that robustified decision-focused learning is generally more robust to adversarial label drift than both robust and traditional PTO.

Keywords: predict-then-optimize · adversarial label drift · decision-focused learning

J. Fu et al. (Eds.): GameSec 2023, LNCS 14167, pp. 133–152, 2023.
https://doi.org/10.1007/978-3-031-50670-3_7

1 Introduction

The *predict-then-optimize* (PTO) framework [4,11,14,24] is a common paradigm for making "smart" decisions with incomplete information. In this framework, one *predicts* information about the state of the world, and then *optimizes* a given reward function based on these predictions, possibly subject to constraints. One example of PTO is the problem of hospital bed demand prediction during the COVID-19 pandemic, when hospitals faced shortages of beds but were able to acquire overflow spaces for patients at an additional cost [17,27]. These hospitals needed to *predict* the true distribution of hospital beds needed and then choose the *optimal* number of overflow beds to purchase [13,20]. For example, one may want to predict the distribution of bed demand, then optimize to order beds such that there are enough beds on 95% of nights. The traditional way of doing this is to train a *two-stage* (TS) model in which one first learns a predictive model to maximize predictive accuracy, and then runs an optimization algorithm maximizing a *decision quality function* over the trained model's predictions. In this paradigm, predictive accuracy is not always aligned with the reward function being optimized [9]. To correct for this, *decision-focused learning* (DFL) [14,33], in contrast to the traditional PTO paradigm of two-stage learning (TS), trains the predictive model to directly optimize the decision quality function and differentiates through the entire prediction and optimization pipeline, making training an end-to-end process. DFL has been shown to outperform TS across a wide variety of domains [9,22,28,32].

While predict-then-optimize frameworks are becoming increasing popular, their *robustness* to label drift at decision time is not well-understood. Understanding robustness enables us to reason about the suitability of the models for various test sets. Differences between labels in train and test sets is common in practice. In hospital bed demand prediction, this difference in labels might arise if the prognosis of different viral variants changes. Our primary method of assessing a model's ability to deal with such differences between training and testing sets is by adding perturbations to the underlying labels at test time and assessing how it impacts the model's downstream performance. Specifically, we study *adversarial* label perturbations, with the intuition that a model that can handle worst-case label drift is robust. This label drift can have a profound effect on the downstream decisions, leading to, for example, a shortage of hospital beds. Before decision-focused learning becomes more widely applied in real-world settings, it is imperative to understand the robustness of predict-then-optimize algorithms to label drift.

Our contributions include the following: First, we propose modifications of both TS and DFL that anticipate label noise in training (Robust TS, Robust DFL, and Algorithm 1). Next, by examining the decision quality function, we give a necessary condition for when a learner can improve performance by anticipating label drift: the decision quality function must be *asymmetric* around the optimal decision (Theorem 1). Moreover, we derive bounds on their relative performance by casting both optimization problems as Stackelberg games (Sect. 4.2) to demonstrate that *Robust DFL is at least as robust as*

Robust TS when the predictive model is perfectly expressive. Finally, we empirically validate these theoretical results by comparing Robust DFL and Robust TS across four domains (Sect. 5) and empirically demonstrate that Robust DFL outperforms Robust TS under adversarial label drift.

1.1 Related Work

Predict-Then-Optimize and Decision-Focused Learning. Predictive models maximizing accuracy on the entire dataset sometimes do so with the consequence of making suboptimal decisions with those predictions in hand (cf. [6,15]). This suboptimal decision-making is partially remedied by decision-focused learning, which integrates the downstream decision-making objective into the learning pipeline. Decision-focused learning has been applied in settings where the optimization task is combinatorial in nature [3,22,33]. Kotary et al. [19] surveys recent efforts to leverage ML to solve constrained optimization problems.

Robustness and Optimization in Machine Learning. Our work falls in the intersection of work on decision-focused learning and the broad literature on adversarial machine learning [12,31]. Much of this literature considers label tampering, which is commonly studied in the context of data poisoning attacks, in which labels in a training dataset are adversarially changed prior to model learning. For example, Butler et al. [8] demonstrate that predict-then-optimize frameworks are susceptible to data poisoning attacks on data features in the training set. In contrast, we are concerned with adversarial drift on labels at test time– after the model has been trained. The literature focusing on adversarial drift at test time [10,16,30] is largely concerned with shifts in features rather than labels, often using robust optimization [21,35] to these shifts in features. A related problem is that of adversarial label contamination, where a small number of labels in the training set are flipped [34]. Also connected is H-infinity control [5], which minimizes the gain in the system states with respect to bounded noise.

2 Background

2.1 Predict-Then-Optimize Problems

In the standard predict-then-optimize framework, one makes a prediction about the state of the world, then optimizes a decision quality function given the prediction. The predictive task is to learn a parameterized (by w) model $m_w : \mathcal{X} \to \mathcal{Y}$ mapping features $x \in \mathcal{X}$ to predict the unknown parameters $m_w(x) = \hat{y} \in \mathcal{Y} \subseteq \mathbb{R}^d$ in the optimization problem. This prediction is used to make decisions based on a *decision quality function* $f : \mathcal{Z} \times \mathcal{Y} \to \mathbb{R}$ mapping decisions $z \in \mathcal{Z} \subseteq \mathbb{R}^\ell$ and true labels $y \in \mathcal{Y}$ to a real-valued reward. Given a prediction $\hat{y}$, the learner computes the optimal decision $z^*(\hat{y})$, where the function $z^* : \mathcal{Y} \to \mathcal{Z}$ is defined

$$z^*(\hat{y}) := \arg\max_{z \in \mathcal{Z}} f(z, \hat{y}) . \tag{1}$$

The decision is then evaluated on the ground truth label y_0 to obtain the decision quality $f(z^*(\hat{y}), y_0)$. The learner is given a dataset $\mathcal{D}_{\text{train}} = \{(x_i, y_i)\}$ to train the predictive model. After the model m_w is trained, a testing dataset $\mathcal{D}_{\text{test}}$ is presented. The trained model then yields predictions of the missing labels and propose the corresponding decisions. The decisions are evaluated on the revealed ground truth labels in the testing set $\frac{1}{|\mathcal{D}_{\text{test}}|} \sum_{(x,y) \in \mathcal{D}_{\text{test}}} f(z^*(m_w(x)), y)$.

Assumptions on f. Throughout, we generally assume that f is L-Lipschitz continuous in both $\mathcal{Y}$ and $\mathcal{Z}$ and its maximum is always attained by some $z \in \mathcal{Z}$ so that $z^*(\cdot)$ is always well-defined. Moreover, we assume that $f(z^*(\cdot), \cdot)$ is quasi-concave-convex, meaning that $f(z^*(\cdot), y)$ is quasiconvex for all $y \in \mathcal{Y}$ and $f(z^*(\hat{y}), \cdot)$ is quasiconcave for all $\hat{y} \in \mathcal{Y}$. This assumption is necessary in order to apply the minimax theorem in Sect. 4.2. If z^* is affine in y, this condition is satisfied by f being quasi-concave-convex.

2.2   Frameworks for Predict-Then-Optimize

We now summarize two existing learning methods with different objectives that the learner uses to train the predictive model m_w. These are visualized in Fig. 1(L). When unclear from context, we refer to TS and DFL as "Standard TS" and "Standard DFL" to disambiguate them from their robust counterparts introduced in Sect. 3.

The two-stage (TS) approach learns a predictive model m_w by minimizing root mean squared error (RMSE):

$$\min_{w} \sum_{(x,y) \in \mathcal{D}_{\text{train}}} \|m_w(x) - y\|^2 \, , \qquad \text{(Standard TS)}$$

where the norm $\| \cdot \|$ denotes the Euclidean norm. We denote the model learned by Standard TS on the training data $\mathcal{D}_{\text{train}}$ by m_T. After the model is learned, given a new input x, the prediction $y_T = m_T(x)$ is then used to optimize the decision quality function $z^*(y_T)$ in Eq. (1).

In contrast, the objective in decision-focused learning is the decision quality function instead of RMSE.

$$\max_{w} \sum_{(x,y) \in \mathcal{D}_{\text{train}}} f(z^*(m_w(x)), y) \qquad \text{(Standard DFL)}$$

Similarly, we call the Standard DFL model m_D learned via training data $\mathcal{D}_{\text{train}}$. The advantage of decision-focused learning is the alignment of the training objective and the testing objective f. To optimize the objective in Standard DFL, it is common to use gradient descent, which requires backpropagating through the optimal decision z^* from Eq. (1). This can be achieved by differentiating through the optimality and KKT conditions (cf. [1,2]).

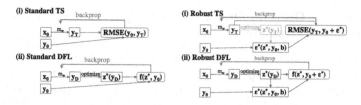

Fig. 1. In TS (left, i), the model optimizes RMSE loss, as opposed to DFL (left, ii), which uses the decision quality function as the loss. Robust analogs (right) are proposed in Sect. 3.

3 Robust Algorithms Anticipating Worst-Case Label Drift

The dependence of optimization on prediction renders Predict-then-Optimize frameworks particularly vulnerable to shifts in the (optimized-upon) labels at test time. *Adversarial training* is often used in the adversarial machine learning literature to mitigate susceptibility to changes in data at test time. It is natural to ask when adversarial training, or some variant thereof, might improve the decision quality of predict-then-optimize frameworks. We consider the case where models m_T and m_D are fully expressive and there is no generalization error, and empirically validate that the intuition from that setting still holds in imperfect generalization settings in Sect. 5.

3.1 Modeling Worst-Case Label Drift

We study the robustness of a model by examining its decision quality under adversarial label drift; intuitively, adversarial drift yields a worst-case decision quality (under some "drift budget") to stress-test a model's robustness.

In understanding the worst case noise, suppose that an "adversary" (*abstraction* for nature generating worst-case label drift) can additively perturb the true parameters y by some small ϵ such that $\|\epsilon\| \le r$ for a fixed budget r at test time. We assume the "adversary" seeks to choose a best response

$$\epsilon \in \epsilon^*(z, y, r) := \underset{\epsilon:\|\epsilon\| \le r}{\arg\min} f(z, y + \epsilon) \tag{2}$$

to minimize the predictive model's decision quality function given the decision z and true parameters y. If $\epsilon^*(z, y, r)$ is not uniquely determined, we slightly abuse notation and take $\epsilon^*(z, y, r)$ to be any choice in the argmin of Eq. (2), and if r is understood from context, we omit it as an argument. We often study $\epsilon_0 \in \epsilon^*(z^*(y_0), y_0, r)$: an optimal response to the optimal decision.

Observe that the "adversary" seeks to minimize the decision quality function even if the predictive model is optimizing root mean squared error, as in two-stage learning. This is because we are concerned with the downstream decisions recommended by the optimization problem, whose quality is measured by f.

3.2 Improving Decision Quality by Anticipating Label Drift: Motivating Examples

We consider two different decision quality functions where either (A) the optimal decision is the same in the presence and absence of noise, or (B) a learner can make a "smarter" decision by anticipating the presence of noise. We leverage insight from (B) to propose incorporate adversarial training into DFL and TS in Sect. 3.3.

Consider a **quadratic decision quality** function pictured in Fig. 2(L), with $\mathcal{Z} = \mathcal{Y} = \mathbb{R}$. In this case, the optimal decision $z^*(\hat{y}) = \hat{y}$. The leader, without anticipating label drift, maximizes their utility by selecting $\hat{y} = y_0$. If they plan for label drift, then the leader can generally choose some $\hat{y} \neq y_0$ or choose $\hat{y} = y_0$. If $\hat{y} \neq y_0$, then $\epsilon^*(\hat{y}, y_0) = \{r\,\text{sign}(y_0 - \hat{y})\}$, resulting in decision quality $1 - (\hat{y} - (y_0 + \epsilon^*))^2$ strictly less than $1 - r^2$. In contrast, if $\hat{y} = y_0$, then $\epsilon^*(y_0, y_0) = \{-r, r\}$, resulting in decision quality $1 - r^2$. Therefore, a learner cannot benefit from anticipating label noise, as their "best" decision in either case (anticipating label noise or not) is to predict $\hat{y} = y_0$.

In contrast, consider the **"asymmetric" decision quality** function in Fig. 2(R), where, again, $\mathcal{Z} = \mathcal{Y} = \mathbb{R}$ and $z^*(\hat{y}) = \hat{y}$ for all $\hat{y} \in \mathcal{Y}$. As above, suppose a learner anticipates adversarial label drift. Broadly, the learner could choose $\hat{y} < y_0$, $\hat{y} = y_0$ (with $\epsilon^*(y_0, y_0) = \{-r\}$), or $\hat{y} > y_0$ (again, with $\epsilon^*(\hat{y}, y_0) = \{-r\}$). Figure 2(R; red) demonstrates that choosing $\hat{y} = y_0$ leads to a poor decision quality once the the adversarial label perturbation is added. Therefore, the best decision for a learner anticipating adversarial label drift is some $\hat{y} < y_0$ such that $\epsilon^*(\hat{y}, y_0) = \{r\}$, which mitigates the adversary's attack (yellow). Therefore the learner is able to leverage the asymmetry of the decision quality function in order to choose a "smarter" decision than simply predicting y_0, as they would do without anticipating noise.

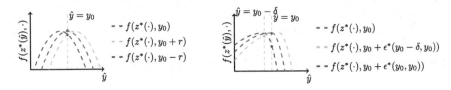

Fig. 2. Two contrasting decision quality functions, both with $z^*(\hat{y}) = \hat{y}$. Different dashed lines represent how the function shifts as y_0 shifts. (L) The optimal decision $z^*(y_0)$ also maximizes the decision quality in the presence of an adversary. Note that $\epsilon^*(y_0, y_0) = \{r, -r\}$, and we demonstrate the decision quality under either adversarially optimal drift (yellow, red lines). (R) The optimal decision in the presence of an adversary is to choose $\hat{y} < y_0$ (yellow dot), as $\epsilon^*(\hat{y}, y_0) = \{r\}$ for such $\hat{y}$. This is in contrast with $\epsilon^*(y_0, y_0) = \{-r\}$. This change in optimal drift leads one to observe that anticipating noise (yellow dot) yields higher decision quality than not anticipating noise (red dot). (Color figure online)

3.3   Robust Model Formulations

Observing that some models can improve their performance by anticipating label noise, we now propose robust formulations of both TS and DFL, when the learner anticipates label drift in the test set for such decision quality functions. The learner commits to a model m_w, and applies the model to every instance in the dataset $(x_0, y_0) \in \mathcal{D}_{\text{train}}$ to produce a prediction $\hat{y} = m_w(x_0)$ and decision $\hat{z} = z^*(\hat{y})$. The "adversary", who knows the true parameters y_0, observes the chosen decision $\hat{z}$ to conduct an attack $\epsilon^*(\hat{z}, y_0, r)$ as defined in Eq. (2).

Definition 1 (Robust two-stage learning). *The learner aims to minimize the root mean squared error between the predictions and the perturbed labels (Fig. 1 (R,i)):*

$$\min_{w} \quad \sum_{(x_0,y_0)\in\mathcal{D}_{train}} \|m_w(x_0) - (y_0 + \epsilon^*_{x_0,y_0})\|^2 \qquad \text{(Robust TS)}$$

$$s.t. \quad \epsilon^*_{x_0,y_0} = \arg\min_{\epsilon:\|\epsilon\|\leq r} f(z^*(m_w(x_0)), y_0 + \epsilon)$$

If the function class given by weights w has high capacity, then we abstract away the model weights and, given any data point (x_0, y_0), we suppose that the model is able to choose $y_{RT} := m_{RT}(x_0)$ that is a solution of the following:

$$\max_{y_{RT}} \quad 1 - \|y_{RT} - (y_0 + \epsilon_{RT})\|^2 \quad s.t. \quad \epsilon_{RT} = \arg\min_{\epsilon:\|\epsilon\|\leq r} f(z^*(y_{RT}), y_0 + \epsilon) \quad (3)$$

Observe that Robust TS is an analogue of standard adversarial training algorithms, where adversarial changes are now made to labels instead of features. While an alternative formulation might use perturbations that attack the RMSE loss instead of the decision quality, this approach disembodies the robust learning problem from the Predict-Then-Optimize context. Because the algorithm is exposed to adversarial label drift at test time, our Robust TS algorithm is best trained with label drift. We find empirical support for Robust TS in Sect. 5.

Definition 2 (Robust decision-focused learning). *The learner aims to maximize the decision quality evaluated on the perturbed labels (Fig. 1 (R, ii)):*

$$\max_{w} \quad \sum_{(x_0,y_0)\in\mathcal{D}_{train}} f(z^*(m_w(x_0)), y_0 + \epsilon^*_{x_0,y_0}) \qquad \text{(Robust DFL)}$$

$$s.t. \quad \epsilon^*_{x_0,y_0} \in \arg\min_{\epsilon:\|\epsilon\|\leq r} f(z^*(m_w(x_0)), y_0 + \epsilon)$$

Similarly to Robust TS, if the model is fully expressive, then the model can find $y_{RD} := m_D(x_0)$ for each (x_0, y_0) pair independently of other data points. This prompts us to solve Robust DFL:

$$\max_{y_{RD}} f(z^*(y_{RD}), y_0 + \epsilon_{RD}) \quad s.t. \quad \epsilon_{RD} = \arg\min_{\epsilon:\|\epsilon\|\leq r} f(z^*(y_{RD}), y_0 + \epsilon) \quad (4)$$

One can understand Eq. (4) as a zero-sum game by observing $\epsilon_{RD} \in$ $\arg\max_{\|\epsilon\| \leq r} -f(z^*(y_{RD}), y_0 + \epsilon)$. Moreover, as ϵ_{RD} is a function of y_{RD}, casting as a Stackelberg game is natural, where the "adversary" adding noise follows observing the model's prediction y_{RD}. Therefore, we can study whether or not the pair (y_{RD}, ϵ_{RD}) is an equilibrium solution. Moreover, if $f(z^*(\cdot), \cdot)$ is quasi-concave-convex, then we can apply the canonical minimax theorem [29] and conclude that (y_{RD}, ϵ_{RD}) is a Nash equilibrium as Eq. (4) is *zero-sum*. Casting this problem as a game is similar to the approach taken by Hardt et al. [18], though their model of noise is anticipating noise on features, rather than labels.

4   Improving Robustness by Anticipating Label Drift

With robust formulations in hand, we now show that if adversarial training can improve the *decision quality regret* of an algorithm when worst-case label drift is added at test time, the optimization objective f must be asymmetric in the parameter space around the optimal decision, demonstrated by studying ϵ^*. Knowing that anticipating label drift can improve decision quality, we discuss how to apply Robust TS and Robust DFL in practice, incorporating max-min optimization into training to be robust to label drift.

4.1   Robustness via Defendability

The examples in Sect. 3.2 develop the intuition that *asymmetry of f around the optimal decision* plays an important role in determining the robustness of the decision quality function when models are perfectly expressive.

Definition 3. *A decision quality function $f : \mathcal{Z} \times \mathcal{Y} \to \mathbb{R}$ is r-defendable at $y_0 \in \mathcal{Y}$ if there exists $\hat{y} \in \mathcal{Y}$ such that $f(z^*(\hat{y}), y_0 + \epsilon^*(z^*(\hat{y}), y_0, r)) > f(z^*(y_0), y_0 + \epsilon^*(z^*(y_0), y_0, r))$.*

Defendability is tightly connected to the pair $(y_0, \epsilon^*(z^*(y_0), y_0))$ not being a Nash equilibrium to the problem in Eq. (4), modulo the ability to apply the minimax theorem. We now show that defendability also implies a certain type of asymmetry in the decision quality function, studied through ϵ^*.

Theorem 1. *Let f be a decision quality function such that $f(z^*(\cdot), \cdot)$ is quasi-concave-convex. If f is r-defendable at y_0, then $\epsilon^*(z^*(y_0), y_0, r) \neq \{\epsilon : \|\epsilon\| = r\}$.*

Proof. For contradiction, suppose $\epsilon^*(z^*(y_0), y_0, r) = \{\epsilon : \|\epsilon\| = r\}$. Since ϵ^* is defined as a best response, we immediately have $f(z^*(\hat{y}), y_0) \geq f(z^*(\hat{y}), y_0 + \epsilon^*(\hat{y}, y_0))$. Moreover, since f is defendable, we have $f(z^*(\hat{y}), y_0 + \epsilon^*(\hat{y}, y_0)) > f(z^*(y_0), y_0 + \epsilon^*(y_0, y_0)) = f(z^*(y_0), y_0 + \epsilon^*(\hat{y}, y_0))$. Finally, as f is quasiconvex in its second argument and all budget-exhausting responses belong in $\epsilon^*(y_0, y_0)$, we have $\max(f(z^*(y_0), y_0 + \epsilon^*(\hat{y}, y_0)), f(z^*(y_0), y_0 - \epsilon^*(\hat{y}, y_0))) = f(z^*(y_0), y_0 + \epsilon^*(\hat{y}, y_0)) \geq f(z^*(y_0), y_0)$. Chaining these together,

$$
\begin{aligned}
f(z^*(\hat{y}), y_0) &\geq f(z^*(\hat{y}), y_0 + \epsilon^*(\hat{y}, y_0)) && \epsilon^* \text{ is best response} \\
&> f(z^*(y_0), y_0 + \epsilon^*(y_0, y_0)) && \text{defendability} \\
&= f(z^*(y_0), y_0 + \epsilon^*(\hat{y}, y_0)) && \text{assumption on } \epsilon^* \\
&\geq f(z^*(y_0), y_0) && \text{quasiconvexity + assumption on } \epsilon^*,
\end{aligned}
$$

which contradicts the optimality of z^*.

Theorem 1 shows that if decision quality can be improved by anticipating label drift, it must be the case that the best response to y_0 must be context-dependent, taking into consideration the shape of f.

In the following section, we will present regret bounds for these robust algorithms. It is important to note, however, that for symmetric decision quality functions, these algorithms yield the same solution pairs as their standard counterparts.

Proposition 1. *Consider decision quality function f and $y_0 \in \mathbb{R}^k$ such that $\epsilon^*(z^*(y_0), y_0, r) = \{\epsilon : \|\epsilon\| = r\}$. Then for any $\epsilon_0 \in \epsilon^*(z^*(y_0), y_0, r)$, the pair (y_0, ϵ_0) is a subgame perfect Nash equilibrium for Standard TS (Eq. (5)), Standard DFL (Eq. (6)), Robust TS (Eq. (3)), and Robust DFL (Eq. (4)).*

Proof. We formally cast standard TS and standard DFL as games when models are perfectly expressive.

$$
\max_{y_T} 1 - \|y_T - y_0\|^2 \quad \text{s.t. } \epsilon^*(y_T, y_0) = \arg\min_{\|\epsilon\| \leq r} f(z^*(y_T), y_0 + \epsilon) \quad (5)
$$

Observe that the leader's payoff is independent of the follower's payoff $-f(z^*(y_T), y_0 + \epsilon)$. Similarly, we cast Standard DFL as a game when models are perfectly expressive.

$$
\max_{y_D} f(z^*(y_D), y_0) \quad \text{s.t. } \epsilon^*(y_D, y_0) = \arg\min_{\|\epsilon\| \leq r} f(z^*(y_D), y_0 + \epsilon) \quad (6)
$$

For standard TS and DFL, since the leader's payoff is independent of the response, choosing y_T or $y_D = y_0$ maximizes the leader's reward, regardless of the adversary's response. Given the decision y_0, the "adversary" playing $\epsilon_0 \in \epsilon^*(z^*(y_0), y_0, r)$ is a best response to optimize their objective.

In Robust TS, there is always a response $\epsilon \in \epsilon^*(z^*(\cdot), y_0)$ such that $\|\epsilon\| = r$ by quasiconvexity of f in its second argument. The objective then becomes $\max_{y_{RT}} 1 - \|y_{RT} - y_0\|^2 + c^2$ for some $c \geq 0$ by quasiconcavity of $f(z^*(\cdot), \cdot)$ in its first objective (which implies that the best response will not improve decision quality). Regardless of the choice of ϵ, then the optimal decision is to report $y_{RT} = y_0$. Thus, (y_0, ϵ_0) is a subgame perfect Nash equilibrium.

Finally in Robust DFL, the assumption implies that f is not r-defendable at y_0 by Theorem 1. Therefore, (y_0, ϵ_0) is a Nash equilibrium, and in turn, a subgame perfect Nash equilibrium since we can apply the minimax theorem.

Proposition 1 suggests that if the adversary's best response to the learner choosing the optimal y_0 can arbitrarily exhaust the noise budget, the standard and robust algorithms have the same solution. Since Robust TS (Eq. (3)) can be understood as a general-sum Stackelberg game, less is known about the convergence to the equilibria than zero-sum Stackelberg games like Robust DFL (c.f., [7]). This may play a larger role in distinguishing the performance of robust and standard algorithms when models have some generalization error, as we demonstrate in Sect. 5. However, for certain asymmetric decision quality functions, we now show that Robust DFL outperforms Robust TS. This yields a simple check to understand whether a decision quality function is robust to label drift.

4.2 Bounding Decision Quality Regret

We now show that Robust DFL yields decision quality no worse than that of Robust TS (Theorem 2). In Proposition 2, we use the piecewise quadratic decision quality function from Sect. 3.2 to demonstrate the performance gap from Robust TS can be *strictly* worse than that of Robust DFL by considering an asymmetric decision quality function, which we show by proving f is defendable implies a strict regret bound.

We start by defining the decision quality regret as the gap in decision quality from of a predictive model to this optimum. Note that while optimizing the decision quality function is a maximization problem for the model, lowering decision quality regret is better as it measures the error induced by poorly responding to label drift.

Definition 4 (Decision quality regret). *Define the decision quality regret of prediction $\hat{y}$ when the ground truth parameter is y_0 with an adversarial perturbation budget r by:*

$$Reg(\hat{y}, y_0; r) = f(z^*(y_0), y_0) - \min_{\epsilon : \|\epsilon\| \leq r} f(z^*(\hat{y}), y_0 + \epsilon)$$

The decision quality regret defined in Definition 4 measures the regret of the (optimal) decision $z^*(\hat{y})$ induced by prediction $\hat{y}$ and the worst-case label deviated up to a perturbation of norm r. We now show that the decision quality regret of the optimal Robust TS prediction y_{RT} as at least as high as that of the optimal Robust DFL prediction y_{RD}.

Theorem 2. *Let $f : \mathcal{Z} \times \mathcal{Y} \to \mathbb{R}$ be a L-Lipschitz decision quality function, and consider some ground truth $y_0 \in \mathcal{Y}$ such that (y_{RD}, ϵ_{RD}) is a solution to Eq. (4) and (y_{RT}, ϵ_{RT}) is a solution to Eq (3). Then*

$$0 \leq Reg(y_{RD}, y_0; r) \leq Reg(y_{RT}, y_0; r) \leq 2L \|y_{RT} - y_0\| + Lr .$$

Proof. The optimality of Robust DFL can be written as a maximization problem with a worst-case objective: $y_D = \arg\max_{\hat{y}} \left(\min_{\epsilon : \|\epsilon\| \leq r} f(z^*(\hat{y}), y_0 + \epsilon) \right)$. In contrast,

---

Algorithm 1. Robust Decision-focused Learning

1: **Input:** training set $\mathcal{D}_{\text{train}}$, learning rate α, model m_w, adversarial learning rate α_{adv}, perturbation budget r
2: **for** epoch $= 1, 2, \cdots$ and $(x_0, y_0) \in \mathcal{D}_{\text{train}}$ **do**
3:    Generate prediction $\hat{y} = m_w(x_0)$
4:    Solve Eq. (1) to get decision $z^* = \arg\max_z f(z, \hat{y})$
5:    Solve Eq. (2) to get perturbation $\hat{\epsilon} = \epsilon^*(z^*, y_0, r)$
6:    Compute decision quality $f(z^*, y_0 + \hat{\epsilon})$
7:    Run approximate gradient ascent $m_w \leftarrow m_w + \alpha \frac{\partial f}{\partial z^*} \frac{\partial z^*}{\partial \hat{y}} \frac{\partial \hat{y}}{\partial w}$
8: **end for**
9: **Return:** predictive model m_w

---

the learner in Robust TS does not maximize the worst-case decision quality, which leads to a prediction y_{TS} with a suboptimal objective. Therefore, we have:

$$\min_{\epsilon: \|\epsilon\| \leq r} f(z^*(y_D), y_0 + \epsilon) \geq \min_{\epsilon: \|\epsilon\| \leq r} f(z^*(y_T), y_0 + \epsilon) . \tag{7}$$

By the definition of the decision quality regret, Eq. 7 directly implies $\text{Reg}(y_D, y_0; r) \leq \text{Reg}(y_T, y_0; r)$. The remaining inequality can be shown by using Lemma 1 (Sect. A), which concludes the proof.

Theorem 2 quantifies the source of decision quality regret in terms of $\|\hat{y} - y_0\|$ and r. While Theorem 2 gives both upper and lower bounds on the decision quality regret incurred by Robust TS, it is unclear at first whether the gap is ever strict. In Proposition 2, we show by counterexample that the decision quality regret of the optimal Robust TS solution can be strictly greater than that of the optimal Robust DFL solution.

Proposition 2. *For all $r \in \mathbb{R}_{++}$, there exists a decision quality $f : \mathcal{Z} \times \mathcal{Y} \to \mathbb{R}$ such that $Reg(y_{RD}, y_0; r) < Reg(y_{RT}, y_0; r)$.*

Proof. In the setting where the model is perfectly expressive, the solution to Robust TS (Eq. 3) yields $y_{RT} = y_0$ as any deviation yields a stronger attack and increased error. We know from Lemma 2 (Sect. A) that a decision quality function f is r-defendable at y_0 if and only if there exists $\hat{y} \in \mathcal{Y}$ such that $\text{Reg}(\hat{y}, y_0; r) < \text{Reg}(y_0, y_0; r) = \text{Reg}(y_{RT}, y_0; r)$, where equality follows as $y_{RT} = y_0$. If $y_{RT} = y_0$, this tells us that f is r-defendable iff $\text{Reg}(\hat{y}, y_0; r) < \text{Reg}(y_{RT}, y_0; r)$, thus the gap is strict if f is r-defendable at y_0. Observe that the decision quality function in Sect. 3.2 is r-defendable, so the definition is feasible.

When models are perfectly expressive, Theorem 2 shows that the gap between the Robust DFL and Robust TS is bounded by Lr. Moreover, Proposition 2 shows that the gap in decision quality regret between Robust DFL and Robust TS is strict for r-defendable decision quality functions. Together, these results highlight the benefits of using decision-focused learning in the presence of label drift for r-defendable decision quality functions.

4.3   Robust Algorithms in Practice

In practice, optimizing the robust algorithms is not simple. In particular, given the pair $(\hat{y}, y_0)$, the computation of the decision quality $f(z^*(\hat{y}), y_0 + \hat{\epsilon})$ requires estimating (i) optimal decision $\hat{z} = z^*(\hat{y})$ by the optimization problem in Eq. (1), and (ii) the optimal adversarial perturbation $\hat{\epsilon} = \epsilon^*(\hat{z}, y_0, r)$ defined in Eq. (2). Both of these values are not generally defined with closed-form solutions. In Algorithm 1, we leverage the idea from DFL to differentiate through optimization problems and apply the concept of adversarial training to solve the problem in Definition 2. We solve for $\hat{\epsilon}$ by running projected gradient descent, which we instantiate multiple times. The time complexities of training the models can be found in Sect. B. While both Robust TS and Robust DFL are slower than their standard counterparts due to the optimization required at each iteration to calculate $\hat{\epsilon}$, both algorithms still run in polynomial time.

5   Experiments

5.1   Experimental Domains

We now compare the non-robust learning methods discussed in Sect. 2.2 and the robust learning methods discussed in Definitions 1 and 2. We evaluate the performance of different learning methods in four different domains that deal with optimizing over uncertain, estimated parameters where model expressivity is limited. Both the linear top-k and demand prediction domains have asymmetric decision quality functions, while portfolio optimization and budget allocation have symmetric decision quality functions. The latter three domains are drawn from Shah et al. [28], which we augment with the first domain in order to have an additional asymmetric domain. For detailed descriptions of each domain, see Sect. C.

- **Demand Prediction** Using features x_0 to predict the bed demand y_0, select number of beds $z^*(\hat{y})$ via an asymmetric decision quality f with a preference to overestimating demand.
- **Linear Top-k** Using a linear model to predict the utilities y_0 of d resources from features x_0, where the relationship between features and labels is cubic, select the k resources with the highest utilities.
- **Portfolio Optimization** Predict the next stock price from historical stock prices and then choose a continuous allocation $z \in Z \subseteq [0,1]^d$ between d stocks [26], maximizing the sum of the immediate net profits and a symmetric quadratic risk penalty term.
- **Budget Allocation** Choose a website on which to run advertisements by predicting the click-through rates on each website for each user and then selecting a set of websites on which to run advertisements to maximize the expected number of users who click on the ad.

The adversarial perturbations added to the labels represents a shift in the bed demand, underlying utilities, stock prices, and click-through rates, respectively. We ran all experiments over 30 different random seeds and present the mean of the performances on the test set. These experiments are run with a predictive model that is not fully expressive; despite this, the results still align with the intuition from our theoretical results.

5.2   Discussion of Empirical Results

In Fig. 3, we plot the effect of the budget for the adversarial perturbations at test-time on the decision quality. The robust algorithms are trained with the same budget as is used at test time, omitting the case where the test budget is 0. For more results on performance when the adversarial budget differs between training and test time, see Sect. C. In Fig. 4, we present the RMSE for each of the algorithms' predictions at test time, varying the adversarial perturbation budget r, in order to show how much generalization error each model incurs. Finally, in Fig. 5, we visualize the test-time predictions from the models in the Demand Prediction domain to show how DFL and Robust DFL have learned to overestimate in order to maximize the reward, which favors overallocation of beds rather than underallocation.

The results presented in Sect. 3 show that Robust DFL will perform better than Robust TS (and TS) in asymmetric domains under perfect expressiveness, and this is verified in our experimental results in Fig. 3. It is notable and surprising that Standard DFL already performs significantly better than both TS and Robust TS in these domains. Therefore in asymmetric domains, it may be useful to spend effort on using even standard DFL for the sake of robustness, rather than on robust version of TS, which ultimately still delivers lower quality.

Robust DFL also offers some improvements over Standard DFL: reducing variance and improving decision quality in high-noise regimes. For example, Robust DFL has a lower variance than DFL, as demonstrated in the Linear Top-k domain of Fig. 3. This difference in variance is statistically significant for most r in Linear Top-k: $p_{r=0.5} < 10^{-5}$, $p_{r=1} < 10^{-5}$, $p_{r=1.5} < 10^{-5}$, $p_{r=2} < 10^{-5}$. Additionally, in the high-noise regimes ($r = 3, 4, 5$) of the Demand Prediction domain, the decision quality yielded by Robust DFL is higher than that of Standard DFL, and this difference is statistically significant ($p_{r=3} < 0.01$, $p_{r=4} < 0.0001$, $p_{r=5} < 10^{-5}$). In the Demand Prediction domain, both Robust DFL and DFL learn to overestimate the bed demand, as seen in Fig. 5, which is incentivized by the decision quality function. We can see, by comparing the left and right sides of Fig. 5, that the addition of label perturbations at train time allow Robust DFL to anticipate and tolerate label drift of a higher magnitude (whereas DFL is non-adaptive because it is not trained with perturbations).

For perfectly expressive models and symmetric decision quality functions, Proposition 1 suggests that all four algorithms will be the same. **Despite the fact that the predictive model is not perfectly expressive, Budget Allocation (bottom right) still exemplifies this phenomenon,** with the qualifi-

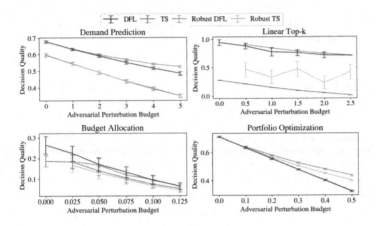

Fig. 3. Effect of adversarial budget on decision quality (30 trials). In the asymmetric Demand Prediction and Linear Top-k domains, DFL and Robust DFL outperform TS and Robust TS.

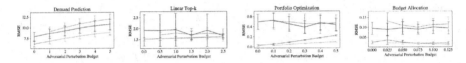

Fig. 4. Effect of adversarial noise budget on RMSE (30 trials). In all domains, DFL/Robust DFL have higher RMSE than TS/Robust TS.

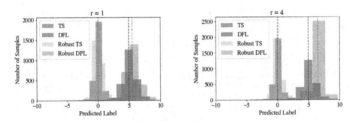

Fig. 5. Predictions from Demand Prediction models, trained on $r = 1$ (L) and $r = 4$ (R) adversarial perturbation budgets.

cation that DFL tends to do slightly better than TS. The Portfolio Optimization domain (bottom left), however, shows an unforeseen result: **the robust algorithms (especially Robust DFL) outperform the standard algorithms.** This demonstrates that, despite the symmetry of the decision quality function implying that TS and DFL are able to learn the optimal solution, the robust algorithms offer a practical improvement in performance when models are not perfectly expressive. Notably, as seen in the third plot of Fig. 4, Robust TS achieves lower RMSE than TS. These results show that robustification can help both symmetric and asymmetric domains.

6 Conclusion

In this work, we study robustness of predict-then-optimize frameworks to characterize when an adversarially trained algorithm might outperform its standard counterpart by anticipating noise in the test set. Leveraging these insights, we propose robust versions of DFL and TS, and we show that Robust DFL outperforms Robust TS when the decision quality function is defendable. Finally, we empirically validate our results with experiments across four domains, finding that Robust DFL does well in asymmetric domains and can even improve performance in symmetric domains.

Acknowledgements. Research was sponsored by the ARO and was accomplished under Grant Number: W911NF-18-1-0208. The views and conclusions contained in this document are those of the authors and should not be interpreted as representing the official policies, either expressed or implied, of ARO or the U.S. Government. The U.S. Government is authorized to reproduce and distribute reprints for Government purposes notwithstanding any copyright notation herein. Additionally, this material is based upon work supported by the National Science Foundation under Award No. 2202898.

A Omitted Proofs

Lemma 1. *Let f be L-Lipschitz and fix $r \in \mathbb{R}_+$. For all $y_0, y \in \mathcal{Y}$,*
$Reg(y, y_0; r) \leq 2L\|y - y_0\| + Lr$

Proof.

$$
\begin{aligned}
\mathrm{Reg}(\hat{y}, y_0; r) &= f(z^*(y_0), y_0) - \min_{\epsilon: \|\epsilon\| \leq r} f(z^*(\hat{y}), y_0 + \epsilon) \\
&= f(z^*(y_0), y_0) - f(z^*(\hat{y}), y_0 + \hat{\epsilon}) \\
&\leq f(z^*(y_0), \hat{y}) + L\|y_0 - \hat{y}\| - f(z^*(\hat{y}), \hat{y}) + L\|y_0 + \hat{\epsilon} - \hat{y}\| \\
&\leq \underbrace{f(z^*(y_0), \hat{y}) - f(z^*(\hat{y}), \hat{y})}_{\leq 0 \text{ by optimality of } z^*} + 2L\|y_0 - \hat{y}\| + Lr \\
&\leq 2L\|y_0 - \hat{y}\| + Lr \ .
\end{aligned}
$$

Lemma 2. *A decision quality function $f : \mathcal{Z} \times \mathcal{Y} \to \mathbb{R}$ is r-defendable at y_0 if and only if there exists $\hat{y} \in \mathcal{Y}$ such that $Reg(\hat{y}, y_0; r) < Reg(y_0, y_0; r)$.*

Proof. f is r-defendable at y_0 if and only if $\exists \hat{y} \in \mathcal{Y}$ such that

$$
\begin{aligned}
& -f(z^*(\hat{y}), y_0 + \hat{\epsilon}) < -f(z^*(y_0), y_0 + \epsilon) \\
\iff & f(z^*(y_0), y_0) - f(z^*(\hat{y}), y_0 + \hat{\epsilon}) < f(z^*(y_0), y_0) - f(z^*(y_0), y_0 + \epsilon) \ ,
\end{aligned}
$$

where $\epsilon := \epsilon^*(z^*(y_0), y_0, r)$ and $\hat{\epsilon} := \epsilon^*(\hat{y}, y_0, r)$.

B   Runtime Analysis

$TS = \Theta(T \cdot N \cdot T_M)$, where T is the number of timesteps of model training, N is the number of instances, and T_M is the time to run the forward and backward passes for the predictive model.

$DFL = \Theta(T \cdot N \cdot (T_M + T_Z + T'_Z + T_{DQ} + T'_{DQ}))$, where T_Z is the time for the forward pass of the optimization and T'_Z is the backward pass for the optimization, and T_{DQ}/T'_{DQ} are the forward and backward passes for calculating the decision quality.

Robust $TS = \Theta(T \cdot N \cdot (T_M + T_Z + I \cdot T_A \cdot (T_{DQ} + T'_{DQ})))$, where T_A is the number of iterations to run projected gradient descent, and I is the number of times the perturbation generation process is instantiated (where more instantiations produce a better $\hat{\epsilon}$).

Robust $DFL = \Theta(T \cdot N \cdot (T_M + T_Z + T'_Z + T_{DQ} + T'_{DQ} + I \cdot T_A \cdot (T_{DQ} + T'_{DQ})))$.

C   Experimental Setup

We now give an overview of the four studied decision quality functions. Note that we do not enforce the concave-convex assumption on the decision quality functions; rather, the associated experiments show the performance in realistic scenarios where the assumption does not always hold.

Demand Prediction Domain. The Demand Prediction task is to predict the number of beds required in a hospital's overflow unit [17,27]. In this setting, one might have a decision quality with a global maximum at the exact demand but also with a strong preference to overestimating bed demand than underestimating, yielding a decision quality like that in Fig. 6, given in Eq. 8.

$$f(z,y) = \frac{1}{1 + e^{-2(z-y+2.73)}} - \frac{1}{0.91(1 + 25e^{-(z-y+2.73)/6})} \qquad (8)$$

– **Predict**: Use feature x_0 to predict the demand y_0.
– **Optimize**: Pick a z^* that maximizes the decision quality f in Eq. 8.

Linear Top-k Domain. The linear model domain requires fitting a linear model to data that express a cubic relationship between features and labels. It is drawn from [28], motivated by the importance of such problems in the AI interpretability literature .

– **Predict**: Use feature $x_0 \in \mathbb{R}^d$ to predict the utility $\hat{y} \in \mathbb{R}^d$, where the true utility of resource n is $y_{0_n} = 10x_{0_n}^3 - 6.5x_{0_n}$.
– **Optimize**: Pick the top $b = 1$ from d resources, $z^*(\hat{y}) = \arg \text{topk}(\hat{y})$.

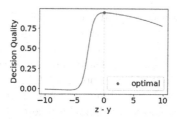

Fig. 6. Decision quality function f for the Demand Prediction domain. The decision quality drops drastically when the demand y is higher than the supply z.

Portfolio Optimization Domain. The Portfolio Optimization domain is a quadratic programming problem [26], where investors choose a continuous allocation $z \in Z \subseteq [0,1]^n$ between n stocks, subject to a budget constraint $Z = \{z \in [0,1]^n : \mathbf{1}^\top z = 1\}$. We implement the Markowitz formulation [23,25].

- **Predict**: Given d historical stock prices for n stocks, $x \in \mathbb{R}^{n \times d}$, predict the next stock prices $y \in \mathbb{R}^n$.
- **Optimize**: Given n predicted stock prices $\hat{y}$, maximize the weighted sum of the immediate net profit minus a risk penalty term, with $f(z,y) = z^\top y - \lambda z^\top Q z$. We let the risk aversion constant $\lambda = 0.1$ and Q be the identity matrix for simplicity.

Budget Allocation Domain. The Budget Allocation domain is a submodular optimization problem adapted from Wilder et al. [33], where the task is to choose a website on which to run advertisements using click-through rates (CTRs) from the Yahoo! Webscope Dataset [36]. This is a particularly difficult problem for Robust DFL due to the combinatorial structure of the optimization problem. The advertisement plan is discrete and it is hard for DFL to differentiate through and learn from discrete decisions.

- **Predict**: Given d features for m websites, $x \in \mathbb{R}^{m \times d}$, predict the CTRs of n users $y \in \mathbb{R}^{m \times n}$.
- **Optimize**: Given the predicted matrix of user/website CTRs $\hat{y}$, select a set of websites (subject to budget constraint r) denoted by $z \in \{0,1\}^m$ on which to run advertisements to maximize the expected number of users who click on the ad at least once. We also incorporate a weight matrix w that represents the number of times that a user will see an ad on a given website.

$$f(z,y) = \sum_{j=0}^{n}(1 - \prod_{i=0}^{m}(1 - z_i \cdot y_{ij})^{w_{ij}})$$

D   Additional Empirical Analysis

Performance of Robust Algorithms with Unknown Noise Budgets. In addition to showing that Robust DFL is robust when the adversarial budget is known at training time, we demonstrate that the generalizability of Robust DFL to different noise budgets. In Fig. 7, each row represents a different training noise budget, while each column represents a testing noise budget. Each cell is combination between training noise and testing noise, containing the difference in decision quality between Robust DFL and Robust TS. We observe that Robust DFL outperforms Robust TS in a higher number of train/test noise combinations. In particular, on and above the diagonal where the train noise is closer to the test noise, the improvement is more significant.

Demand Prediction Robust DFL - Robust TS

train noise budget	test noise budget					
	0.0	1.0	2.0	3.0	4.0	5.0
0.0	0.082	0.090	0.100	0.111	0.123	0.134
1.0	0.077	0.089	0.103	0.118	0.128	0.148
2.0	0.076	0.089	0.106	0.124	0.138	0.159
3.0	0.073	0.090	0.107	0.128	0.147	0.164
4.0	0.068	0.086	0.104	0.123	0.145	0.162
5.0	0.064	0.082	0.105	0.124	0.149	0.174

Demand Prediction Robust DFL - DFL

train noise budget	test noise budget					
	0.0	1.0	2.0	3.0	4.0	5.0
1.0	-0.002	0.001	0.005	0.011	0.009	0.015
2.0	-0.005	0.001	0.006	0.013	0.016	0.025
3.0	-0.007	0.000	0.008	0.018	0.024	0.031
4.0	-0.008	0.000	0.009	0.017	0.026	0.035
5.0	-0.011	-0.001	0.007	0.019	0.028	0.041

Linear Top-k Robust DFL - Robust TS

train noise budget	test noise budget					
	0.0	0.5	1.0	1.5	2.0	2.5
0.0	0.663	0.666	0.625	0.663	0.661	0.693
0.5	0.449	0.443	0.489	0.549	0.511	0.539
1.0	0.364	0.332	0.512	0.435	0.425	0.507
1.5	0.505	0.390	0.266	0.319	0.435	0.387
2.0	0.424	0.460	0.504	0.470	0.512	0.531
2.5	0.539	0.481	0.513	0.462	0.407	0.291

Linear Top-k Robust DFL - DFL

train noise budget	test noise budget					
	0.0	0.5	1.0	1.5	2.0	2.5
0.5	-0.027	0.027	0.036	0.001	0.031	-0.063
1.0	0.030	0.028	0.066	-0.062	0.005	0.000
1.5	0.001	0.026	0.039	0.030	0.030	-0.001
2.0	0.029	0.026	0.066	0.030	0.031	0.001
2.5	0.029	0.002	0.067	0.029	0.031	0.001

Portfolio Optimization Robust DFL - Robust TS

train noise budget	test noise budget					
	0.0	0.1	0.2	0.3	0.4	0.5
0.1	-0.007	0.002	0.012	0.018	0.030	0.038
0.2	-0.010	0.000	0.013	0.025	0.034	0.052
0.3	-0.022	-0.007	0.007	0.021	0.038	0.050
0.4	-0.022	-0.013	0.002	0.016	0.030	0.044
0.5	-0.036	-0.018	-0.005	0.011	0.021	0.035

Portfolio Optimization Robust DFL - DFL

train noise budget	test noise budget					
	0.0	0.1	0.2	0.3	0.4	0.5
0.1	-0.006	0.006	0.019	0.027	0.043	0.054
0.2	-0.012	0.006	0.025	0.042	0.058	0.083
0.3	-0.024	0.000	0.025	0.048	0.075	0.097
0.4	-0.029	-0.005	0.025	0.051	0.080	0.109
0.5	-0.048	-0.011	0.021	0.053	0.083	0.115

Budget Allocation Robust DFL - Robust TS

train noise budget	test noise budget					
	0.0	0.025	0.050	0.075	0.100	0.125
0.000	0.010	0.006	0.004	0.004	0.003	0.001
0.025	0.005	0.002	0.005	0.002	0.003	0.001
0.050	0.007	0.008	0.005	0.002	0.002	0.001
0.075	0.007	0.006	0.005	0.003	0.002	0.001
0.100	0.009	0.007	0.007	0.004	0.004	0.002
0.125	0.009	0.009	0.005	0.004	0.003	0.002

Budget Allocation Robust DFL - DFL

train noise budget	test noise budget					
	0.000	0.025	0.050	0.075	0.100	0.125
0.025	-0.003	-0.005	-0.001	-0.001	0.000	-0.001
0.050	-0.002	-0.002	-0.001	-0.002	-0.001	0.000
0.075	-0.003	-0.002	-0.002	-0.002	-0.001	-0.001
0.100	-0.003	-0.003	0.000	-0.001	0.000	0.000
0.125	-0.037	-0.031	-0.024	-0.019	-0.014	0.000

Fig. 7. The shade of teal depicts the extent to which Robust DFL outperforms Robust TS. The improvement of Robust DFL over DFL highlights the importance of using the decision quality and the importance of considering the adversarial perturbation, respectively. Negative cells are where Robust TS outperforms Robust DFL. Intuitively, these regions are where Robust DFL tries to defend against noise that is simply not present at test time.

References

1. Agrawal, A., Amos, B., Barratt, S., Boyd, S., Diamond, S., Kolter, Z.: Differentiable convex optimization layers. arXiv:1910.12430 (2019). http://arxiv.org/abs/1910.12430, arXiv: 1910.12430
2. Amos, B., Kolter, J.Z.: OptNet: differentiable optimization as a layer in neural networks. In: Proceedings of the 34th International Conference on Machine Learning, pp. 136–145, PMLR (2017). https://proceedings.mlr.press/v70/amos17a.html. ISSN: 2640-3498

3. Amos, B., Koltun, V., Kolter, J.Z.: The limited multi-label projection layer. arXiv preprint arXiv:1906.08707 (2019)
4. Angalakudati, M., et al.: Business analytics for flexible resource allocation under random emergencies. Manage. Sci. **60**(6), 1552–1573 (2014)
5. Başar, T., Bernhard, P.: H-Infinity Optimal Control and Related Minimax Design Problems: A Dynamic Game Approach. Springer Science & Business Media, Cham (2008)
6. Beygelzimer, A., Langford, J.: The offset tree for learning with partial labels. In: Proceedings of the 15th ACM SIGKDD International Conference on Knowledge Discovery and Data Mining, KDD 2009, pp. 129–138. Association for Computing Machinery, New York, NY, USA (2009). https://doi.org/10.1145/1557019.1557040. ISBN 9781605584959
7. Blum, A., Haghtalab, N., Hajiaghayi, M.T., Seddighin, S.: Computing stackelberg equilibria of large general-sum games. In: Fotakis, D., Markakis, E. (eds.) SAGT 2019. LNCS, vol. 11801, pp. 168–182. Springer, Cham (2019). https://doi.org/10. 1007/978-3-030-30473-7_12
8. Butler, R., Tuck, W.W., Sinha, A., Ngyuen, T.: Poisoning attacks on data-based decision making: a preliminary study. In: AASG-22: 3rd Autonomous Agents for Social Good (AASG) held at the 21st International Conference on Autonomous Agents and Multi-Agent Systems (AAMAS) (2022)
9. Cameron, C., Hartford, J., Lundy, T., Leyton-Brown, K.: The perils of learning before optimizing. In: Proceedings of the AAAI Conference on Artificial Intelligence, vol. 36, no. 4, pp. 3708–3715 (2022). https://doi.org/10.1609/aaai.v36i4. 20284, https://ojs.aaai.org/index.php/AAAI/article/view/20284
10. Carlini, N., et al.: On evaluating adversarial robustness (2019). https://arxiv.org/abs/1902.06705
11. Chan, C.W., Farias, V.F., Bambos, N., Escobar, G.J.: Optimizing intensive care unit discharge decisions with patient readmissions. Oper. Res. **60**(6), 1323–1341 (2012)
12. Chen, P.Y., Hsieh, C.J.: Adversarial robustness for machine learning. Imprint (2022)
13. Deschepper, M., Eeckloo, K., Malfait, S., Benoit, D., Callens, S., Vansteelandt, S.: Prediction of hospital bed capacity during the COVID- 19 pandemic. BMC Health Serv. Res. **21**(1), 1–10 (2021)
14. Elmachtoub, A.N., Grigas, P.: Smart "predict, then optimize". Manage. Sci. **68**(1), 9–26 (2022). ISSN 0025-1909, https://doi.org/10.1287/mnsc.2020.3922, https://pubsonline.informs.org/doi/abs/10.1287/mnsc.2020.3922
15. Ford, B., Nguyen, T., Tambe, M., Sintov, N., Fave, F.D.: Beware the soothsayer: from attack prediction accuracy to predictive reliability in security games. In: Khouzani, M.H.R., Panaousis, E., Theodorakopoulos, G. (eds.) GameSec 2015. LNCS, vol. 9406, pp. 35–56. Springer, Cham (2015). https://doi.org/10.1007/978-3-319-25594-1_3
16. Goodfellow, I.J., Shlens, J., Szegedy, C.: Explaining and harnessing adversarial examples (2014). https://doi.org/10.48550/ARXIV.1412.6572, https://arxiv.org/abs/1412.6572
17. Grimm, C.A.: Hospital experiences responding to the COVID-19 pandemic: results of a national pulse survey march 23–27, 2020. US Dept. Health Hum. Serv. Off. Inspector General **41** (2020)
18. Hardt, M., Megiddo, N., Papadimitriou, C., Wootters, M.: Strategic classification. In: Proceedings of the 2016 ACM Conference on Innovations in Theoretical Computer Science, pp. 111–122 (2016)

19. Kotary, J., Fioretto, F., Hentenryck, P.V., Wilder, B.: End-to-end constrained optimization learning: a survey. CoRR abs/2103.16378 (2021). https://arxiv.org/abs/2103.16378
20. Kutafina, E., Bechtold, I., Kabino, K., Jonas, S.M.: Recursive neural networks in hospital bed occupancy forecasting. BMC Med. Inform. Decis. Mak. **19**(1), 1–10 (2019)
21. Madry, A., Makelov, A., Schmidt, L., Tsipras, D., Vladu, A.: Towards deep learning models resistant to adversarial attacks. In: International Conference on Learning Representations (2018)
22. Mandi, J., Demirovi, E., Stuckey, P.J., Guns, T.: Smart predict-and-optimize for hard combinatorial optimization problems. In: Proceedings of the AAAI Conference on Artificial Intelligence **34**(02), 1603–1610 (2020). ISSN 2374–3468, https://doi.org/10.1609/aaai.v34i02.5521, https://ojs.aaai.org/index.php/AAAI/article/view/5521
23. Markowitz, H.M., Todd, G.P.: Mean-Variance Analysis in Portfolio Choice and Capital Markets, vol. 66. John Wiley, Hoboken (2000)
24. Mehrotra, M., Dawande, M., Gavirneni, S., Demirci, M., Tayur, S.: Or practice-production planning with patterns: a problem from processed food manufacturing. Oper. Res. **59**(2), 267–282 (2011)
25. Michaud, R.O.: The Markowitz optimization enigma: is 'optimized' optimal? Financ. Anal. J. **45**(1), 31–42 (1989)
26. Popescu, I.: Robust mean-covariance solutions for stochastic optimization. Oper. Res. **55**(1), 98–112 (2007)
27. Sen-Crowe, B., Sutherland, M., McKenney, M., Elkbuli, A.: A closer look into global hospital beds capacity and resource shortages during the COVID-19 pandemic. J. Surg. Res. **260**, 56–63 (2021)
28. Shah, S., Wilder, B., Perrault, A., Tambe, M.: Learning (local) surrogate loss functions for predict-then-optimize problems. In: Neural Information Processing Systems (2022)
29. Sion, M.: On general minimax theorems (1958)
30. Szegedy, C., et al.: Intriguing properties of neural networks. arXiv preprint arXiv:1312.6199 (2013)
31. Vorobeychik, Y., Kantarcioglu, M.: Adversarial machine learning. In: Synthesis Lectures on Artificial Intelligence and Machine Learning, vol. 12, no. 3, pp. 1–169 (2018)
32. Wang, K., et al.: Decision-focused learning in restless multi-armed bandits with application to maternal and child care domain. arXiv preprint arXiv:2202.00916 (2022)
33. Wilder, B., Dilkina, B., Tambe, M.: Melding the data-decisions pipeline: decision-focused learning for combinatorial optimization. In; Proceedings of the AAAI Conference on Artificial Intelligence, vol. 33, no. 01, pp. 1658–1665 (2019). ISSN 2374–3468, https://doi.org/10.1609/aaai.v33i01.33011658, https://ojs.aaai.org/index.php/AAAI/article/view/3982
34. Xiao, H., Biggio, B., Nelson, B., Xiao, H., Eckert, C., Roli, F.: Support vector machines under adversarial label contamination. Neurocomputing **160**, 53–62 (2015). ISSN 0925–2312. https://doi.org/10.1016/j.neucom.2014.08.081, https://www.sciencedirect.com/science/article/pii/S0925231215001198
35. Xu, H., Caramanis, C., Mannor, S.: Robustness and regularization of support vector machines. J. Mach. Learn. Res. **10**(7) (2009)
36. Yahoo!: Yahoo! webscope dataset (2007). https://webscope.sandbox.yahoo.com/. ydataysm-advertiser-bids-v1.0

Quantisation Effects in Adversarial Cyber-Physical Games

Takuma Adams[1,3]($\boxtimes$) , Andrew C. Cullen[2] , and Tansu Alpcan[1]

[1] Department of Electrical and Electronic Engineering, The University of Melbourne, Parkville, Australia
takuma.adams@unimelb.student.edu.au
[2] School of Computing and Information Systems, The University of Melbourne, Parkville, Australia
[3] Defence Science and Technology Group, Canberra, Australia

Abstract. As the complexity in models of cyber-physical systems increases, conventional game-theoretic tools begin to struggle due to the presence of hard-to-evaluate nonconvex game dynamics. Complex adversarial security games often exhibit nonconvex behaviour such as those admitted by a Kuramoto-Sakaguchi system with Lanchester dynamics. We pose this system as a two-player, zero-sum dynamic security game, where players seek to gain a decision advantage over their opponents. By leveraging multi-agent reinforcement learning, we study the impact action space quantisation has on a player's ability to uncover optimal strategies to achieve a decision advantage in a complex decision-making system. A comparison of solutions on continuous and discrete action spaces reveals good agreement across algorithms indicating convergence to some ϵ-Nash equilibrium. Surprisingly, the higher fidelity offered by continuous action spaces also yields computational advantages compared to discrete spaces in the context of the adversarial decision game.

Keywords: Cyber-Physical Systems · Adversarial Games · Multi-Agent Reinforcement Learning · Dynamical Systems

1 Introduction

The phenomena of collective behaviours in complex systems can be observed in both cooperative and competitive contexts across many different natural [26,27] and cyber-physical [6,17,18] systems. These highly complex systems are frequently represented as networked agents where edges represent the interactions and diffusion of information as permitted by a computing or communication system [4]. Such networked cyber-physical systems are becoming commonplace in our day-to-day lives motivating the need to interrogate security problems. Security problems emerge when agents engage in adversarial activities over the network, like when cyber-security specialists interact with malicious actors through a communication network. Hence, it is imperative that we can model the implications of rational decision-makers intentionally interacting through a network where the synchronicity of their actions would yield a more effective offensive or defensive outcome.

© The Author(s), under exclusive license to Springer Nature Switzerland AG 2023
J. Fu et al. (Eds.): GameSec 2023, LNCS 14167, pp. 153–171, 2023.
https://doi.org/10.1007/978-3-031-50670-3_8

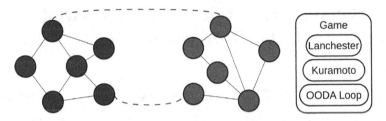

Fig. 1. A conceptual illustration of the NBKL model shows the blue and red nodes, which represent the Blue and Red team agents, respectively, in the two-player zero-sum game played over the NBKL dynamical system. Solid lines represent peer linkages while dashed lines represent the adversarial interactions (surface). (Color figure online)

The notion of synchronous networked agents is aligned with the cyclical nature of human cognition [19,28]. By applying a common decision-theoretic framework to all agents, we can compare decision states and consider the decision-making of multiple interacting agents. This lends itself to the analysis of organisational dynamics in decision-making systems.

We focus on a complex dynamical system that exhibits collective decision behaviour appropriate for the study of adversarial decision-making across the spectrum of cyber-physical systems ranging from human-human, human-machine, and machine-machine teams. This system consists of two teams, each containing multiple agents leveraging collaborative dynamics in an attempt to gain a decision advantage over their opponents in a zero-sum game. We model the cyclic decision state of each agent using a competitive decision framework known as the Obverse, Orient, Decide, and Act (OODA) loop [5]. This framework encodes the oscillating nature of decision states into a four-step process for agents (human and machine) at both the individual and team level [9,10]. The evolution of a team's collective decision state is governed by the nonlinear dynamics of the Kuramoto-Sakaguchi model [20] which models synchronisation between networked oscillators. The Lanchester combat model [12] is a modified Lotka-Volterra model for multiple predator populations engaged in an adversarial manner. Thus, by assigning each agent an initial resource, the decision advantage of a team is quantified by its relative resource attrition according to this combat model [12]. Coupling the decision dynamics with the Lanchester model yields the Networked Boyd Kuramoto Lanchester (NBKL) model [1] illustrated in Fig. 1.

The exploration of strategies employed by rational players to achieve decision superiority is game-theoretic and has shown a promising research direction [7,8]. Since previous work focused on exactly solving static decision games using discrete action spaces, there is scope to explore solutions for dynamic games with continuous action spaces. However, adding additional complexity to an already computationally costly game underscores the need to explore alternate solution methods when exploring higher-resolution spaces. The nonlinear nature of an NBKL-based game makes established solution methods for dynamics games with linear system dynamics or affine nonlinear dynamics (e.g. using linear quadratic regulators [2]) infeasible. Instead, reinforcement learning (RL) methods and their game theoretic interpretations [3] are of interest. Specifically, multi-agent reinforcement learning (MARL) provides a natural solution method in the context of our adversarial system. While the application of MARL to conventional board-style *gridworld* games [13] is well documented, application to complex cyber-physical systems exhibiting cyclic decision dynamics is underexplored.

Hence, we apply well-known MARL algorithms to solve an NBKL-based game with different action spaces to capture the complexities of contemporary cyber-physical and cyber-security systems. Previous work in applying game theory to Kuramoto-based models differs from this work in the choice of state-action space and the application of MARL as a solution method. In this paper we: (1) compare the effectiveness of continuous and discrete action spaces when solving dynamic games on a complex cyber-physical system; (2) apply established MARL methods to solve cyclic decision games; (3) demonstrate the applicability of MARL to approximate optimal solutions to a complex cyber-physical game. Understanding the benefits and drawbacks of different state-action spaces will enable better construction of human-human, human-machine, and machine-machine teams in future complex systems.

The remainder of the paper is arranged as follows. The next section provides an overview of related works before Sect. 3 sets the context of the game-theoretic problem. Section 4 then introduces the models underlying the dynamics of the game followed by the formalisation of the game-theoretic component. Subsequent experimentation is explained in Sect. 6 before concluding with a pathway for future research.

2   Related Work

This section briefly presents background and literature on decision models, especially focusing on cyclic decisions, dynamic games, and multi-agent reinforcement learning.

Decision Frameworks: Establishing robust frameworks to study decision-making allows us to better model and compare the cognitive states of multiple agents as they strive to satisfy objectives. Decision-theoretic frameworks illustrate the cyclical nature of human cognition—notably in the Perception-Action Cycle [19], and Wohl's Stimulus, Hypothesis, Option, and Response model (SHOR) [28]. Another relevant version is OODA [5] which quantises decision-making for humans and machines into four distinct steps. The process has also been shown to capture decision-making for organisations as well as individuals [9,10]. Furthermore, the OODA loop has undergone quantitative treatment by interpreting the decision states of networked individuals through the lens of phase oscillators in the context of Kuramoto-Sakaguchi models [30].

Kuramoto-Sakaguchi: This projection of an oscillator's (agent's) phase onto a cyclic decision space has seen Kuramoto-Sakaguki decision models evolve from pure physics models [11] to mirror complex real-world adversarial decision systems [1,30]. The complexity of these real-world systems makes theoretical results difficult to obtain leaving numerical approximations of static systems the only viable solution. The study of evolving cyber-physical systems has been augmented through a game-theoretic lens [7,8] allowing us to interrogate dynamic games over a finite temporal horizon. We differentiate ourselves from previous game theoretic analyses of cyclic decision games by exploring the impact of continuous action spaces on the ability of players to implement optimal strategies solved for using different solution methods.

Solution Methods: Solution methods utilising linear quadratic regulators [2] require affine nonlinear dynamical systems and hence are not suitable for solving NBKL-based games. Dynamic games on general nonlinear systems without specific assumptions have also been studied in [16] for open-loop and closed-loop information structures. However, that work focuses on the connections between deep neural networks and dynamic games which was also explored earlier in [22]. In the case of a general system such as Kuramoto-Sakaguchi, where obtaining analytical solutions is challenging, most of the literature investigates numerical solutions of games using deep neural networks and deep RL methods. In the context of an adversarial decision-making game, we consider a novel application of MARL to solve a computationally intensive cyber-physical game as opposed to conventional (e.g. board [13] or Atari-style [25]) games with simple updates.

It has been shown that value iteration and related learning methods such as DQN are not very suitable for continuous action spaces due to dependency on the action-value function [29]. Therefore, in continuous action settings, policy gradient methods and actor-critic methods, which build upon both policy iteration and gradients, have been the focal point. The convergence of policy gradient methods to Nash equilibrium in the context of zero-sum Markov games has been recently analysed theoretically [3]. We leverage this finding in our work to explore the applications of gradient methods such as Proximal Policy Optimization (PPO) [21], Policy Gradient (PG) [24] to solve a game over a complex system with different action spaces.

3   Problem Definition

We investigate the impact continuous and discretised action spaces have when solving complex cyber-physical games. The specific cyber-physical system we explore is admitted by the NBKL model (Eqs. 1 and 2). Through game theoretic treatment of the model, we propose an adversarial two-player, zero-sum, dynamic game. We consider a fully observable environment where the decision variable is the frustration—or *intended* decision advantage—between Blue and Red with respect to each other. Each player simultaneously selects a new action at uniform intervals throughout the game's evolution. These actions perform a joint state update, acting on the environment simultaneously.

We solve the system of equations in discrete time where actions, or frustrations, are drawn from discrete and continuous sets bounded between 0 and π. In the context of cyclic decision loops, an action of 0 means that a player wants to be in the same decision state as their opponent, while π indicates an intended advantage of half a decision cycle. The impact of a player's choice of frustration is then realised through attrition of their adversary's resources described by the discrete-time NBKL model introduced in the next section.

4   A Complex, Cyclic Decision-Making Model

The NBKL model is formulated in terms of two teams of agents, denoted $\mathcal{B}$ and $\mathcal{R}$, where each is a set of indices corresponding to agents for the Blue and Red teams respectively. Each agent can only be assigned to one team. The decision dynamics between the teams of the respective rational players are represented in Eq. 1 using a two-network nonlinear Kuramoto-Sakaguchi model [20]. The Kuramoto-Sakaguchi model captures the cyclic behaviour of an agent's internal decision state, $\theta \in [0, 2\pi]$, and provides means for players to have an *intended* decision advantage. The *intended* decision advantage over an adversary is given by our decision variable $\Phi = (\phi, \psi)$, known as a frustration in the physics nomenclature. Frustrations are restricted to an action set $\mathcal{A} \subset [0, \pi]$ such that $\phi \in \mathcal{A}$ and $\psi \in \mathcal{A}$ encode the intended decision advantage of Blue and Red with respect to each other. That is, each player's strategic goal is to have a decision advantage of ϕ or ψ over their adversary's cyclic decision loop.

The decision advantage achieved by a player is quantified through the attrition of their agents' resources, following the framework outlined in Sect. 3. Each agent is assigned a resource quantity $p \in \mathbb{R}^+$, which is updated according to Eq. 2 capturing dynamics similar to predator-prey models in an adversarial context. The resource is tied to a player's utility and measures a single agent's ability to contribute to their respective team's outcome—like hit points in a game. Thus, we assume that only agents with a positive resource contribute to their team as required by many applications and enforce this using Heaviside step functions, $\mathcal{H}$. Combined, $s = [p, \theta]$ encodes the state of the system such that $s \in \mathcal{S}$ where $\mathcal{S}$ is the set of all possible states. The evolution of s is defined in terms of a system of coupled nonlinear differential NBKL equations [1] given by

$$\dot{\theta}_i = \mathcal{H}(p_i) \left(\omega_i - \sum_{j \in \mathcal{B} \cup \mathcal{R}} \mathcal{H}(p_i) \mathcal{K}_{ij} \sigma_{ij} \sin\left(\theta_i - \theta_j - \Phi_{ij}\right) \right) , \tag{1}$$

$$\dot{p}_i = \mathcal{H}(p_i) \left(\sum_{h \in \mathcal{B} \cup \mathcal{R}} \mathcal{H}(p_h) \mathcal{M}_{ih} \frac{\Gamma_{i,h} + \Gamma_{h,i}}{2} \cdot (\delta_h p_h - \delta_i p_i) \frac{\cos\left(\theta_h - \theta_i\right) + 1}{2} \right.$$

$$\left. - \sum_{k \in \mathcal{B} \cup \mathcal{R}} \mathcal{H}(p_k) \epsilon_{ik} \kappa_{ik} p_k d_k \frac{\sin(\theta_k - \theta_i) + 1}{2} O_k \right) , \tag{2}$$

for $i \in \mathcal{B} \cup \mathcal{R}$ where $\dot{\theta}_i$ and $\dot{p}_i$ are the temporal derivatives of the i-th agent's the internal decision state and resource respectively. The coupling strength between

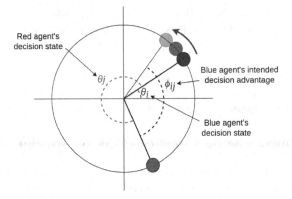

Fig. 2. Illustration of how frustration impacts the decision dynamics of the game. Here, the blue and red dots indicate internal decision-states of two Blue and Red agents with decision-states given by θ_i and θ_j respectively. The Blue agent's intended decision advantage with respect to the Red is given by ϕ_{ij}. (Color figure online)

the i-th and j-th agent is given by σ_{ij}. We also explicitly state the structure of permitted interactions represented as an adjacency matrix between agents denoted $\mathcal{K}_{ij}$—entries are 0 when no interaction occurs and 1 when an edge exists between two agents.

It is clear from Eq. 1 that when $\Phi_{ij} = 0$, the i-th agent will attempt to align its decision state with that of the j-th's. A non-zero frustration then means the i-th agent will align to some decision-state Φ_{ij} ahead of j-th's. The effect of frustration between two connected agents is pictorially shown in Fig. 2, where the non-zero frustration from the Blue agent's perspective, ϕ_{ij}, drives the Blue agent to realise an even greater decision advantage over the Red. By making Φ a decision variable in our game, Blue and Red are required to choose an optimal frustration that most positively impacts their outcomes since the phase difference between two adversarial agents is the realised decision advantage of one and disadvantage of the other.

The networked Lanchester component in Eq. 2 introduces several key terms. Namely, we partition the adjacency matrix $\mathcal{K}$ into two. The inter-team matrix, $\mathcal{M}$, encodes collaboration between peers and resource reallocation through Γ while the intra-team matrix, ϵ, captures linkages at the adversarial surface between the two teams. The decision dynamics influence the attrition of resources through a measure of synchronicity known as the order parameter, O_k. The order parameter is a geometric measure of the alignment of agent decision states (phases), is bounded between 0 (disorder) and 1 (order), and is computed as

$$O_k = \frac{1}{\sum_{j \in \mathcal{B} \cup \mathcal{R}} \mathcal{H}(p_j)} \left\| \sum_{j \in \mathcal{B} \cup \mathcal{R}} \mathcal{H}(p_j) e^{i\theta_j} \right\|_2, \tag{3}$$

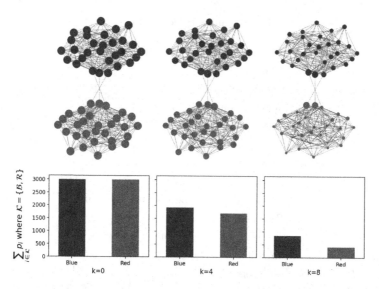

Fig. 3. llustration of the NBKL dynamics and evolution of player resources. Nodes in the top row represent individual agents for the Blue and Red players respectively where the node size indicates the level of resource remaining for the agent in question. The bottom row shows the diminishing total resources available to each player. (Color figure online)

where i in this case is $\sqrt{-1}$ and $||\cdot||_2$ is the L2 norm. Table 1 summarises the remaining components of the coupled system. The evolution of player resources of the NBKL system is shown in Fig. 3. Note the diffusion of resources to the adversarial surface (agents linking Blue and Red) due to Γ while the total quantity of resources for both players decreases.

4.1 Discrete-Time NBKL Model

We define discrete decision points for players at time instances, t_k, by uniformly discretising the finite engagement time horizon $[0, T_f]$. Thus, the NBKL equations are numerically integrated over a series of time intervals $t \in [T_k, T_k + \delta t]$, where δt is long enough to allow for the system dynamics to meaningfully evolve over the decision window. Subsequently, we define $K = T_f/\delta t$ as the number of decisions or turns that each player makes over this finite horizon.

For notational convenience, we define the state, $s(k)$, at time t_k as

$$s(k) := [p_i(t_k)\ \theta_i(t_k)]\ .$$

Thus, the discrete-time counterpart of NBKL dynamics is captured by the following discrete-time nonlinear mapping yielding the Discrete-Time NBKL (DT-NBKL)

$$s(k+1) = f(s(k), \phi(k), \psi(k))\ ,\tag{4}$$

Table 1. Summary of Parameters.

Parameter	Description	Type
θ_i	Phase	$\mathbb{R}^{B+R}$
ω_i	Decision Speed	$\mathbb{R}^{B+R}$
p_i	Agent resource	$\mathbb{R}^{B+R}$
$s = [p, \theta]$	State (phase, resource)	$\mathbb{R}^{2(R+B)}$
$\mathcal{K}_{ij}$	Phase coupling matrix	$\mathbb{R}^{(R+B)^2}$
$\Phi_i = (\phi_i, \psi_i)$	Player frustration	$[0, \pi]^{B+R}$
$\mathcal{M}_{ij}$	Intra-team connectivity	$\{0,1\}^{(R+B)^2}$
ϵ_{ij}	Adversarial coupling matrix	$\{0,1\}^{(R+B)^2}$
Γ_{ij}	Team coupling matrix	$\mathbb{R}^{(R+B)^2}$
δ_i	Inhibitor of internal force transfer	$\mathbb{R}^{B+R}$
d_i	Inhibitor of adversarial outcomes	$\mathbb{R}^{B+R}$
$\mathcal{B}, \mathcal{R}$	Adjacency Matrix	$\mathbb{R}^{(R+B)^2}$
O_i	local order parameter	$\mathbb{R}^{B+R}$
$\mathcal{H}(\cdot)$	Heaviside function	$\{0,1\}$

where $k = 0, 1, \ldots, K$ correspond to $t_0, t_1, \ldots, T_f$ thus allowing us to consider a dynamic NBKL-based game.

5   Game Theoretic Formulation

We formulate the competition between the Blue and Red players within the dynamic environment described by the nonlinear NBKL equations as a two-player, zero-sum, dynamic, non-cooperative game. Here, both Blue and Red control their teams of networked agents $\mathcal{B}$ and $\mathcal{R}$ respectively. Each player can select an action, $(\phi, \psi) \in (\mathcal{A}, \mathcal{A})$, that dictates their strategic goal of either leading or lagging their opponent's decision state given by ϕ and ψ for Blue and Red, respectively. Over the time horizon of this discrete-time game $[0, K]$ (or $[0, T_f]$), the players decide on a series of actions at each time step k yielding the strategy vectors

$$S_B = [\phi_0, \phi_1, \ldots, \phi_K] \quad \text{and} \quad S_R = [\psi_0, \psi_1, \ldots, \psi_K] . \tag{5}$$

At time step K (or time T_f), the game reaches the end of the finite horizon. The resulting end state of the DT-NBKL system is used as a basis to quantify the game outcome for the players. Specifically, let

$$P_B(k) := \sum_{i \in \mathcal{B}} p_i(k) \quad \text{and} \quad P_R(k) := \sum_{i \in \mathcal{R}} p_i(k) , \tag{6}$$

be the team resources of Blue and Red players, respectively at time step k. Moreover, define the incremental changes in these resources as

$$\left.\begin{aligned}
\Delta P_B(k) &:= \sum_{i \in \mathcal{B}} p_i(k) - p_i(k-1) \ , \\
\Delta P_R(k) &:= \sum_{i \in \mathcal{R}} p_i(k) - p_i(k-1) \ .
\end{aligned}\right\} \quad (7)$$

Thus, the utility functions of the players are defined as

$$\left.\begin{aligned}
U_B(S_B, S_R) &= P_B(K, S_B, S_R) - P_R(K, S_B, S_R) \ , \\
U_R(S_B, S_R) &= P_R(K, S_B, S_R) - P_B(K, S_B, S_R) \ ,
\end{aligned}\right\} \quad (8)$$

where P_R and P_B depend on player strategies via the DT-NBKL dynamics in Eq. 4. The zero-sum nature of the game follows from the definitions in Eq. 8, i.e. $U_B + U_R = 0$. These utilities can be considered a measure of the final balance of player resources and can alternatively be in terms of stage costs due to their linear nature

$$\left.\begin{aligned}
U_B(S_B, S_R) &= \sum_{k=0}^{K} Q_B(k) \ , \\
Q_B(k) &:= \Delta P_B(k) - \Delta P_R(k) \ , \\
U_R(S_B, S_R) &= \sum_{k=0}^{K} Q_R(k) \ , \\
Q_R(k) &:= \Delta P_R(k) - \Delta P_B(k) = -Q_B(k) \ .
\end{aligned}\right\} \quad (9)$$

The resulting game is formally defined as follows.

Definition 1 (DT-NBKL Game). *Let the set of two players $\mathcal{P} = \{\mathcal{B}, \mathcal{R}\}$ have the respective continuous strategies (S_B, S_R), defined in Eq. 5 with corresponding utility functions (U_B, U_R) defined in Eq. 8. The DT-NBKL game is defined by the tuple*

$$\mathcal{G}_{NBKL} := \langle \mathcal{P}, (S_B, S_R), (U_B, U_R) \rangle \ .$$

In the given discrete-time game, each player aims to maximise their utility function. Hence, the Blue and Red players solve their respective optimisation problems to determine their best responses to the other player. The well-known Nash equilibrium—along with its relaxed counterpart ϵ-Nash—provide natural solution concepts for the DT-NBKL game as defined in Definitions 2 and 3 respectively.

Definition 2 (Nash Equilibrium). *The strategies (S_B^*, S_R^*) with corresponding utilities (U_B^*, U_R^*) are said to constitute a Nash equilibrium solution of the DT-NBKL game (Definition 1) if*

$$\left.\begin{aligned}
U_B^*(S_B^*, S_R^*) &\geq U_B(S_B, S_R^*) \ , \\
U_R^*(S_B^*, S_R^*) &\geq U_R(S_B^*, S_R) \ ,
\end{aligned}\right\} \quad (10)$$

for all strategies $S_B \neq S_B^*$ and $S_R \neq S_R^*$ [14].

Definition 3 (ϵ-Nash Equilibrium). *The strategies (S_B^*, S_R^*) with corresponding utilities (U_B^*, U_R^*) are said to constitute an ϵ-Nash equilibrium solution of the DT-NBKL game (Definition 1) if*

$$\left.\begin{array}{l} U_B^*(S_B^*, S_R^*) \geq U_B(S_B, S_R^*) - \epsilon \ , \\[4pt] U_R^*(S_B^*, S_R^*) \geq U_R(S_B^*, S_R) - \epsilon \ , \end{array}\right\} \quad (11)$$

for all strategies $S_B \neq S_B^*$ and $S_R \neq S_R^*$ [14].

5.1 Solution Methodologies

Solving a dynamic game over the system defined by Eqs. 1 and 2 is challenging due to complex nonlinear dynamics resulting in a nontrivial state update. Since it is not possible to apply classical solution techniques used for convex two-player zero-sum games such as linear programming, we leverage MARL as outlined in Algorithm 1. In MARL, agents interact with the environment at each time step k to alter the state s_k by taking some action $(\phi_k, \psi)_k \in \mathcal{A} \times \mathcal{A}$ resulting in an updated state and some utility (also called reward in RL) for each player given in Eq. 9. MARL algorithms simultaneously maximise each player's expected cumulative utility at each time step k.

The MARL equivalent of strategy vectors defined in Eq. 5 are the decision-making rules characterised by *policies* mapping a state, s, to an action, a, and is defined as

$$\pi_{\mathcal{B}}(\phi|s) = \mathbb{P}(\phi_k = \phi|s_t = s) \text{ and } \pi_{\mathcal{R}}(\psi|s) = \mathbb{P}(\psi_k = \psi|s_t = s) \ ,$$

for all $(\phi, \psi) \in \mathcal{A} \times \mathcal{A}$, $s \in \mathcal{S}$. As discussed in Sect. 2 value iteration methods may not be suitable for continuous action spaces. In addition, it is a known result that optimal policies, π^*, converge to Nash equilibrium when using multi-agent policy gradient and actor-critic methods [3] making these methods suitable for our game theoretic analysis. Briefly, policy gradient methods are RL schema that learn parameterised policies by optimising π_μ over some differentiable parameter vector $\mu \in \mathbb{R}$ rather than estimating *value* functions which estimate the utility of a player being in a state at a given time step [24]. Actor-critic methods approximate both policy and value functions, V, [23] which can be defined for each player as

$$V_B(n) = \sum_{k=n}^{K} Q_B(k) \text{ and } V_R(n) = \sum_{k=n}^{K} Q_R(k) \ . \quad (12)$$

The optimal value function is one that satisfies Bellman's equations such that

$$\left.\begin{array}{l} V_B^*(k) = \max_{\phi(k)} Q_B(k) + V_B^*(k+1) \ , \\[6pt] V_R^*(k) = \max_{\psi(k)} Q_R(k) + V_R^*(k+1) \ . \end{array}\right\} \quad (13)$$

Algorithm 1 . Generic Multi-agent Reinforcement Learning for DT-NBKL Game

---

Input: Sets of agents $\mathcal{B}$, $\mathcal{R}$ and initial conditions $p_i(0)$, $\theta_i(0)$ $\forall i \in \mathcal{B} \cup \mathcal{R}$
Output: Policies $\pi_B \approx \pi_B^*$ and $\pi_R \approx \pi_R^*$
Initialise: PPO or PG networks G_B and G_R with differentiable policy parameterisations μ_B and μ_R
for each episode **do**
  $s \leftarrow [p_i(0)\ \theta_i(0)] \ \forall i \in \mathcal{B} \cup \mathcal{R}$ ▷*Initialise state*
  $k \leftarrow 0$
  $U_B \leftarrow 0$ and $U_R \leftarrow 0$
  while $P_B > 0.1 P_B(0)$ **and** $P_R > 0.1 P_R(0)$ **and** $k < 8$ **do**
    $k \leftarrow k + 1$
    $a_B \sim G_{\pi_B}(s)$ and $a_R \sim G_{\pi_R}(s)$ ▷*Sample actions*
    $s' \leftarrow f(s, a_B, a_R)$ ▷*Equation 4*
    $Q_B \leftarrow \Delta P_B - \Delta P_R$ and $Q_R \leftarrow \Delta P_R - \Delta P_B$ ▷*Equation 9*
    $U_B \leftarrow U_B + Q_B$ and $U_R \leftarrow U_R + Q_R$
    $s \leftarrow s'$
  end while
  $\mu_B \leftarrow \arg\max_{\mu_B} \mathbb{E}[s, \pi_{\mu_B}(s)]$ and $\mu_R \leftarrow \arg\max_{\mu_R} \mathbb{E}[s, \pi_{\mu_R}(s)]$ ▷*One-step policy ascent to optimise μ_B and μ_R, and update π_B and π_R*
end for

---

6 Results

6.1 Experimental Setup

By leveraging the exact BKL solver introduced by Cullen et al. [7], we create a DT-NBKL MARL environment using PettingZoo's `ParallelEnv` multi-agent API [25], enabling Blue and Red to move simultaneously. This MARL environment enables both Blue and Red to simultaneously learn policies making it possible to draw direct parallels between the policies derived using reinforcement learning methods and the game-theoretic analysis we desire for this complex system. The DT-NBKL system is set up such that each player has a team of 30 agents each with an initial resource of $p_i(0) = 100$ for all $i \in \mathcal{B} \cup \mathcal{R}$. For the majority of results discussed in the next section, both Blue and Red have identical network topologies and are arranged according to an Erdős-Rényi graph as shown in Fig. 3. An additional case with non-identical Blue and Red typologies was explored to investigate the impact of asymmetric networks on DT-NBKL game outcomes.

The exponential nature of the game results in diminishing returns for both players as the game progresses. As such, we introduce a termination criterion terminating the game if either $P_B(k)$ or $P_R(k)$ fell below 10% of its initial quantity. The winning player was rewarded an additional utility equal to $|P_B(k) - P_R(k)|$ while the loser received the negation. Otherwise, the game was truncated after $k = 8$ turns during training as indicated in Algorithm 1 due to the exponential decay associated with the NBKL dynamics. Exponential decay of resources meant both players observed low stage utilities as the number of turns increased resulting in unnecessary computations.

For policy training, RLLib's [15] existing library of policy gradient methods was used. Namely, the well-known PPO [21] and PG [24] algorithms. The discrete and continuous action spaces yielded player actions from $\mathcal{A} = \{0, 1, 2, 3\}$ and the closed set $[0, 1]$ respectively. As such we introduce bijective functions $f_D : \mathcal{A} \rightarrow \{0, \pi/3, 2\pi/3, \pi\}$ and $f_C : \mathcal{A} \rightarrow [0, \pi]$, to map actions back to the decision space. A continuous action space was quantised by uniformly snapping actions to the discrete by applying a surjective mapping $f_Q : \mathcal{A} \rightarrow \{0, \pi/3, 2\pi/3, \pi\}$. Each policy was trained over 196 iterations of 128 episodes each on a 12th Gen Intel Core i7-1255U with 16 GB RAM with no GPU acceleration.

6.2   Analysis of Computed Policies

To determine the relative performance of different action spaces, we analysed the results of the DT-NBKL games in which each player implemented optimal policies trained using different action spaces. We also played different algorithms (PPO and PG) against each other to mitigate the impact of a particular algorithm. Since initial conditions for Blue and Red were symmetrical we could, without loss of generality, study the relative performance from Blue's perspective by playing optimal π_B^* against various π_R^*. 200 DT-NBKL games were played for each combination of policies for a total of 4, 800 games. Test results indicate policies trained using MARL approach an optimal solution in the context of the DT-NBKL game. We also demonstrate that, despite complex dynamics, an optimally chosen frustration is an effective tool that can skew results in a player's favour.

Figure 4 shows that policies trained on continuous action spaces dominate those trained on discrete spaces with continuous π_B^* winning all 800 games played against discrete π_R^* irrespective of the algorithm. Correspondingly, discrete π_B^* loses all 800 games played against continuous π_R^*. Furthermore, we can see that continuous policies performed poorly under quantisation against both naively discrete policy and the original continuous policy. We can see from Figs. 4b and 4d that discrete π_B^* performed even better against quantised π_R^* than discrete π_R^*. This is likely due to variance in the continuous input not accounting for subsequent quantisation. As such, even small deviances from $\pi/2$ significantly impacted the frustration played by the quantised player implying that policies that underwent quantisation were unable to play optimal strategies. While performance was similar across algorithms, one notable outlier was the superior performance of the continuous PPO policy compared to the continuous PG policy.

The optimal strategy for the DT-NBKL game appears to be to play a frustration as close to $\pi/2$ which is equivalent to a quarter of a decision cycle. This is demonstrated in Fig. 5a where, due to the symmetry of the system, we see Blue and Red nearing a stalemate by playing identical strategies. The reason behind the stalemate is discussed further in Sect. 6.3. Despite the dominance of continuous policies, optimal discrete policies exhibit interesting behaviour when

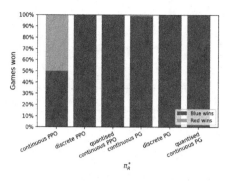

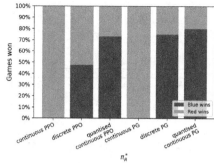

(a) Optimal continuous PPO Blue policy π_B^* against optimal Red policies.

(b) Optimal discrete PPO Blue policy π_B^* against optimal Red policies.

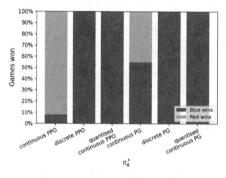

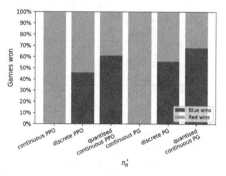

(c) Optimal continuous PG Blue policy π_B^* against optimal Red policies.

(d) Optimal discrete PG Blue policy π_B^* against optimal Red policies.

Fig. 4. Percentage of wins optimal Blue policies observed when played against various optimal Red policies 200 times. The top row is Blue with a PPO algorithm while the bottom row is with a PG. The left column is Blue with a continuous space while the right is with a discrete space. (Color figure online)

playing against continuous policies. Under these conditions, the discrete policy always opts for a greater frustration which is in contrast to when it plays against another optimal discrete policy (Fig. 5b). While the discrete policy still loses, implementing this strategy greatly reduces its losing margin. We can see this by comparing the game outcomes where the strategy induced by optimal discrete π_R^* (Fig. 5c) significantly increases its utility compared to a suboptimal discrete π_R playing against the same π_B^* (Fig. 5d). Similar results were observed for both PPO and PG algorithms.

The consistency of strategies players implemented, along with corresponding utilities is a strong indicator that policies converged to some ϵ-Nash equilibrium as defined in Definition 3. Furthermore, while discrete action spaces did improve in performance as they reached optimality, results showed clear performance benefits for continuous action spaces. From this, we can conclude that an

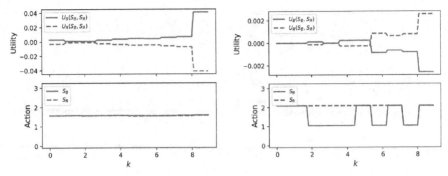

(a) Optimal continuous Blue policy π_B^* vs optimal continuous Red policy π_R^*.

(b) Optimal discrete Blue policy π_B^* vs optimal discrete Red policy π_R^*.

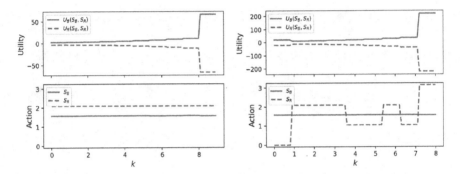

(c) Optimal continuous Blue policy π_B^* vs optimal discrete red policy π_R^*.

(d) Optimal continuous Blue policy π_B^* vs suboptimal discrete Red policy π_R.

Fig. 5. Game outcomes at different game stages (k). Each subplot sees different optimal policies pitted against each other. Note Fig. 5d is an exception where Red implements a suboptimal policy.

optimal strategy realised through a superior choice in frustration can act as a force multiplier to enable one player to dominate another despite identical initial conditions.

6.3 Convergence Analysis

Due to the zero-sum nature of the game, we only need to verify the convergence of the Blue player's policy, π_B, to some optimal value and Red's convergence follows. An indicator of policy convergence is shown in Fig. 6 where Blue's utility, U_B from Eq. 9, converges within the designated training time for all four policies (PPO and PG for both continuous and discrete action spaces). Convergence to a utility of zero is expected due to the zero-sum nature of the DT-NBKL and moving target limitations where both policies are improving simultaneously. Note that the shading in the Figure highlights the 95% confidence interval (CI)

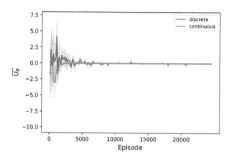 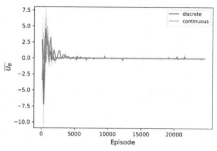

(a) Blue's utility trained with a PPO algorithm.

(b) Blue's utility trained with a PG algorithm.

Fig. 6. Mean utility averaged over a training iteration of 128 episodes for Blue policies trained on various action spaces and algorithms. (Color figure online)

from sample data indicating that discrete policies exhibited higher variance than continuous policies.

An alternative indicator for policy convergence can be obtained by playing an *optimal* policy against previous versions that still be considered *suboptimal*. We assumed a Blue policy with 25,088 episodes (196-th iteration) of training is optimal hence denote it as π_B^*. We then played π_B^* against various π_R trained to degrees of completion (e.g. 7,680 episodes of training). 200 DT-NBKL games were played for each policy match-up. The outcomes of each playoff are shown in Fig. 7 where we can see that in all four cases π_B^* dominates highly suboptimal π_R. The monotonically decreasing performance of π_B^* to 50% as the number of episodes π_R is trained on is a marker of Blue's convergence to an optimal policy. A 50% win rate is expected when two optimal policies play against each other.

An additional worthwhile observation is that policies trained using a continuous action space were marginally computationally faster during training than discrete policies. In particular, the continuous PPO algorithm is noteworthy due to its high performance against all other policies (including continuous PG), while having a faster training time compared to its discrete counterpart as shown in Fig. 8. Further, while training was only sampled five times, the 95% CI was small. The PG algorithm had a greater variance in compute time compared to the PPO algorithm which may be a result of local minimia in the search space. Despite this, continuous PG yielded an overall faster compute time for a fixed number of training episodes. Summary statistics for training time per training iteration of 128 episodes are listed in Table 2. Since training time increases with the number of training episodes, the impact of computation time will become important as more complex decision spaces are explored requiring a longer training duration.

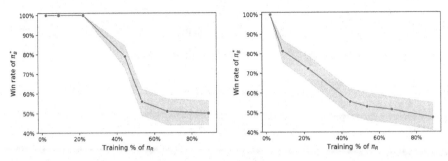

(a) Continuous PPO: Optimal Blue policy π_B^* vs suboptimal Red policy π_R.

(b) Discrete PPO: Optimal Blue policy π_B^* vs suboptimal Red policy π_R.

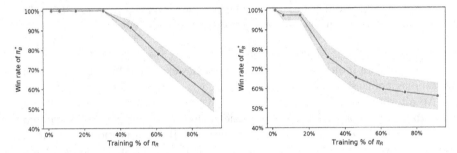

(c) Continuous PG: Optimal Blue policy π_B^* vs suboptimal Red policy π_R.

(d) Discrete PG: Optimal Blue policy π_B^* vs suboptimal Red policy π_R.

Fig. 7. Percentage of DT-NBKL games won by an optimal Blue policy, π_B^*, when played against Red policies, π_R, of varying suboptimality. Each match-up was repeated 200 times. (Color figure online)

7 Conclusion

By combining multiple MARL algorithms with NBKL derived game-theoretic dynamics, we observe that rational players with continuous action spaces perform significantly better than those with discrete action spaces. In other words, choosing an appropriate action space for a player in a heterogeneous scenario

Table 2. Mean training time per training iteration of 128 episodes ($\pm 95\%$ CI).

Algorithm	Action Space	Mean time per iteration
PPO	Continuous	**34.9 ± 2.2**
	Discrete	37.3 ± 2.9
PG	Continuous	**47.2 ± 24.2**
	Discrete	51.3 ± **22.6**

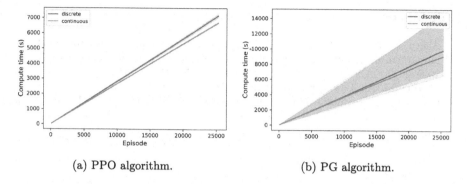

(a) PPO algorithm.   (b) PG algorithm.

Fig. 8. Comparison of training time for different action spaces. Each policy was trained five times.

can effectively guarantee success independent of initial conditions. Furthermore, continuous policies not only performed better but also were computationally more efficient during training. The performance and computational advantages of continuous policies make them an ideal candidate for future research on using MARL to find optimal solutions for dynamic games on cyber-physical systems. This is supported by the agreement between different policies on player strategies (S_B, S_R) and corresponding utilities (U_B, U_R) indicates convergence toward some ϵ-Nash equilibrium. Thus, initial results demonstrate the practical applicability of MARL in the context of dynamic games with complex nonconvex dynamics where traditional approaches may be computationally expensive or infeasible due to continuous action spaces. Contextualising these findings in terms of well-known cyclic decision models provides insight into organisational dynamics, teaming, and the gamut of actions available to players. Therefore, these results have significant implications for the plethora of real-world security systems that exhibit similar adversarial dynamics.

By demonstrating the applicability of this framework, this work has laid the foundation for future work exploring the sensitivity of these game-theoretic scenarios to varied team dynamics. Solving the game for a larger set of decision variables beyond frustration is also of interest. Although initial results are promising, validation against other cyber-physical and security systems such as Multi Particle Environments [25] will strengthen the generalisability of results and application of findings to communication networks, cyber-security, and swarm robotics.

Acknowledgements. This research was supported in part by the Commonwealth of Australia through the Defence Science and Technology Group and the Australian Government Research Training Program Scholarship. We would also like to acknowledge the input and mentorship offered by Dr. Alexander Kalloniatis from Defence Science and Technology Group.

References

1. Ahern, R., Zuparic, M., Hoek, K., Ḳalloniatis, A.: Unifying warfighting functions in mathematical modelling: combat, manoeuvre, and C2. J. Oper. Res. Soc. **73**(9), 2009–2027 (2022). https://doi.org/10.1080/01605682.2021.1956379
2. Al-Tamimi, A., Lewis, F., Abu-Khalaf, M.: Discrete-Time nonlinear HJB solution using approximate dynamic programming: convergence proof. IEEE Trans. Syst. Man Cybern. Part B (Cybernetics) **38**(4), 943–949 (2008). https://doi.org/10.1109/TSMCB.2008.926614
3. Alacaoglu, A., Viano, L., He, N., Volkan, C.: A natural actor-critic framework for zero-sum Markov games. In: Proceedings of Machine Learning Research, pp. 307–366 (2022)
4. Alpcan, T., Başar, T.: Network Security: A Decision and Game-Theoretic Approach. Cambridge University Press, Cambridge, New York (2010)
5. Boyd, J.: Organic Design for Command and Control (1987)
6. Ceron, S., O'Keeffe, K., Petersen, K.: Diverse behaviors in non-uniform chiral and non-chiral swarmalators. Nat. Commun. **14**(1), 940 (2023). https://doi.org/10.1038/s41467-023-36563-4
7. Cullen, A.C., Alpcan, T., Kalloniatis, A.C.: Adversarial decisions on complex dynamical systems using game theory. Phys. A **594**, 126998 (2022). https://doi.org/10.1016/j.physa.2022.126998
8. Demazy, A., Kalloniatis, A., Alpcan, T.: A game-theoretic analysis of the adversarial Boyd-Kuramoto model. In: Bushnell, L., Poovendran, R., Başar, T. (eds.) GameSec 2018. LNCS, vol. 11199, pp. 248–264. Springer, Cham (2018). https://doi.org/10.1007/978-3-030-01554-1_14
9. Grant, T., Kooter, B.: Comparing OODA & other models as operational view C2 architecture. In: 10th International Command and Control Research and Technology Symposium (2005)
10. Johnson, J.: Automating the OODA loop in the age of intelligent machines: reaffirming the role of humans in command-and-control decision-making in the digital age. Def. Stud. **23**(1), 43–67 (2023). https://doi.org/10.1080/14702436.2022.2102486
11. Kalloniatis, A.C., Zuparic, M.L.: Fixed points and stability in the two-network frustrated Kuramoto model. Phys. A **447**, 21–35 (2016). https://doi.org/10.1016/j.physa.2015.11.021
12. Lanchester, F.W.: Aircraft in Warfare the Dawn of the Fourth Arm. Constable limited (1916)
13. Lanctot, M., et al.: A unified game-theoretic approach to multiagent reinforcement learning. In: NeurIPS Proceedings (2017). https://proceedings.neurips.cc/paper/2017/file/3323fe11e9595c09af38fe67567a9394-Paper.pdf
14. Leyton-Brown, K., Shoham, Y.: Essentials of Game Theory: A Concise, Multidisciplinary Introduction. Springer, Cham, Switzerland (2008). oCLC: 231624172, https://doi.org/10.1007/978-3-031-01545-8
15. Liang, E., et al.: RLlib: abstractions for distributed reinforcement learning. In: Proceedings of the 35th International Conference on Machine Learning, vol. 80, pp. 3053–3062 (2018). https://doi.org/10.48550/ARXIV.1712.09381, publisher: arXiv Version Number: 4
16. Liu, G.H., Chen, T., Theodorou, E.: Dynamic game theoretic neural optimizer. In: Proceedings of the 38th International Conference on Machine Learning. Proceedings of Machine Learning Research, vol. 139, pp. 6759–6769. PMLR (2021). https://proceedings.mlr.press/v139/liu21d.html

17. McLennan-Smith, T.A., Roberts, D.O., Sidhu, H.S.: Emergent behavior in an adversarial synchronization and swarming model. Phys. Rev. E **102**(3), 032607 (2020). https://doi.org/10.1103/PhysRevE.102.032607
18. Motter, A.E., Myers, S.A., Anghel, M., Nishikawa, T.: Spontaneous synchrony in power-grid networks. Nat. Phys. **9**(3), 191–197 (2013). https://doi.org/10.1038/nphys2535
19. Neisser, U.: Cognitive Psychology, 1 edn. Psychology Press, London, November 2014. https://doi.org/10.4324/9781315736174
20. Sakaguchi, H., Kuramoto, Y.: A soluble active rotater model showing phase transitions via mutual entertainment. Progress Theor. Phys. **76**(3), 576–581 (1986). https://doi.org/10.1143/PTP.76.576
21. Schulman, J., Wolski, F., Dhariwal, P., Radford, A., Klimov, O.: Proximal Policy Optimization Algorithms (2017). https://doi.org/10.48550/ARXIV.1707. 06347, publisher: arXiv Version Number: 2
22. Schuurmans, D., Zinkevich, M.A.: Deep learning games. In: 30th Conference on Neural Information Processing Systems, vol. 29. Curran Associates, Inc. (2016). https://proceedings.neurips.cc/paper/2016/file/ c4015b7f368e6b4871809f49debe0579-Paper.pdf
23. Sutton, R.S., Barto, A.G.: Reinforcement Learning: An Introduction. Adaptive Computation and Machine Learning Series, second edition edn. The MIT Press, Cambridge, Massachusetts (2018)
24. Sutton, R.S., McAllester, D., Singh, S., Mansour, Y.: Policy gradient methods for reinforcement learning with function approximation. In: Proceedings of the 12th International Conference on Neural Information Processing Systems, pp. 1057–1063. NIPS'99, MIT Press, Cambridge, MA, USA (1999). https://doi.org/10.5555/ 3009657.3009806
25. Terry, J.K., et al.: PettingZoo: gym for multi-agent reinforcement learning (2020). https://doi.org/10.48550/ARXIV.2009.14471, publisher: arXiv Version Number: 7
26. Wiener, N.: Cybernetics or Control and Communication in the Animal and the Machine, 2. edn. MIT Press, Cambridge, MA, USA, reprint edn. (2007)
27. Winfree, A.T.: Biological rhythms and the behavior of populations of coupled oscillators. J. Theor. Biol. **16**(1), 15–42 (1967). https://doi.org/10.1016/0022-5193(67)90051-3
28. Wohl, J.G.: Force management decision requirements for air force tactical command and control. IEEE Trans. Syst. Man Cybern. **11**(9), 618–639 (1981). https:// doi.org/10.1109/TSMC.1981.4308760
29. Zhu, J., Wu, F., Zhao, J.: An overview of the action space for deep reinforcement learning. In: 2021 4th International Conference on Algorithms, Computing and Artificial Intelligence, pp. 1–10. ACM, Sanya, China, December 2021. https://doi. org/10.1145/3508546.3508598
30. Zuparic, M., Angelova, M., Zhu, Y., Kalloniatis, A.: Adversarial decision strategies in multiple network phased oscillators: the blue-green-red Kuramoto-Sakaguchi model. Commun. Nonlinear Sci. Numer. Simul. **95**, 105642 (2021). https://doi. org/10.1016/j.cnsns.2020.105642

Scalable Learning of Intrusion Response Through Recursive Decomposition

Kim Hammar[✉] and Rolf Stadler

Division of Network and Systems Engineering, KTH Royal Institute of Technology,
Stockholm, Sweden
{kimham,stadler}@kth.se

Abstract. We study automated intrusion response for an IT infrastructure and formulate the interaction between an attacker and a defender as a partially observed stochastic game. To solve the game we follow an approach where attack and defense strategies co-evolve through reinforcement learning and self-play toward an equilibrium. Solutions proposed in previous work prove the feasibility of this approach for small infrastructures but do not scale to realistic scenarios due to the exponential growth in computational complexity with the infrastructure size. We address this problem by introducing a method that recursively decomposes the game into subgames with low computational complexity which can be solved in parallel. Applying optimal stopping theory we show that the best response strategies in these subgames exhibit threshold structures, which allows us to compute them efficiently. To solve the decomposed game we introduce an algorithm called Decompositional Fictitious Self-Play (DFSP), which learns Nash equilibria through stochastic approximation. We evaluate the learned strategies in an emulation environment where real intrusions and response actions can be executed. The results show that the learned strategies approximate an equilibrium and that DFSP significantly outperforms a state-of-the-art algorithm for a realistic infrastructure configuration.

Keywords: Cybersecurity · network security · intrusion response · game decomposition · reinforcement learning · game theory · optimal control

1 Introduction

A promising direction of recent research is to automatically find security strategies for an IT infrastructure through reinforcement learning methods, whereby the problem is formulated as a Markov decision problem and strategies are learned through simulation (see survey [18]). While encouraging results have been obtained following this approach (see e.g., [9,12]), key challenges remain. Most of the prior work, for example, follows a decision-theoretic formulation and aims at learning effective defender strategies against a static attacker with a fixed strategy [7–9,12]. Only recently has the problem of learning effective security strategies against dynamic attackers been studied. This approach includes a game-theoretic framing, and the problem becomes one of learning Nash equilibria [1,2,10,19,30,33].

Chief among the remaining challenges is the complexity of the formal model, resulting from the need to describe the target infrastructure with sufficient detail and at a realistic scale. Learning effective strategies with currently known methods is infeasible for most realistic use cases.

In this paper, we address the complexity challenge and present a scalable approach to automatically learn near-optimal defender strategies against dynamic attackers. We apply our approach to an *intrusion response* use case that involves the IT infrastructure of an organization (see Fig. 1). We formalize the use case as a partially observed stochastic game between two players – the operator of the infrastructure, which we call the defender, and an attacker, which seeks to intrude on the infrastructure. To manage the complexity when formalizing the use case, we recursively decompose the game into simpler subgames, which allows detailed

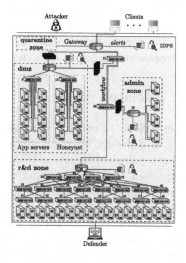

Fig. 1. The target infrastructure and the actors in the intrusion response use case.

modeling of the infrastructure while keeping computational complexity low.

The decomposition involves three steps. First, we partition the infrastructure according to workflows that are isolated from each other. This allows us to decompose the game into *independent subgames* (one per workflow) that can be solved in parallel. Second, the graph structure of a workflow allows us to decompose the workflow games into node subgames. We prove that these subgames have *optimal substructure* [6, Ch. 15], which means that a best response of the original game can be obtained from best responses of the node subgames. Third, we show that the problem of selecting *which* response action to apply on a node can be separated from that of deciding *when* to apply the action, which enables efficient learning of best responses through the application of *optimal stopping* theory [21]. We use this insight to design an efficient reinforcement learning algorithm, called Decompositional Fictitious Self-Play (DFSP), which allows scalable approximation of Nash equilibrium strategies.

Our method for learning the equilibrium strategies and evaluating them is based on a *digital twin* of the target infrastructure, which we use to run attack scenarios and defender responses (see Fig. 2) [9–11]. Such runs produce system measurements and logs, from which we estimate infrastructure statistics. We then use these statistics to instantiate simulations of the infrastructure's dynamics and learn strategies through DFSP.

We summarize the contributions in this paper as follows.

1. We formulate the intrusion response problem as a partially observed stochastic game and prove that, under assumptions often met in practice, the game decomposes into subgames whose best responses can be computed efficiently and in parallel.
2. We design DFSP, an efficient reinforcement learning algorithm for approximating Nash equilibria of the decomposed game.
3. For a realistic use case, we evaluate the learned response strategies against network intrusions on a digital twin.

2 Related Work

Networked systems found in engineering and science often exhibit a modular topological structure that can be exploited for designing control algorithms [24]. System decomposition for the purpose of automatic control was first suggested by Šiljak in 1978 [29] and approaches based on decomposition, such as divide and conquer, layering, and hierarchical structuring are well established in the design of large-scale systems, a notable example being the Internet. Similar decomposition methods are frequently used in robotics and multi-agent systems, as exemplified by the subsumption

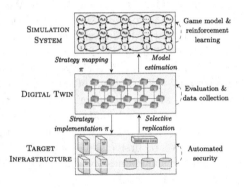

Fig. 2. Our framework for automated intrusion response [9–11].

architecture [4]. Within the fields of decision- and game-theory, decomposition is studied in the context of factored decision processes [27], distributed decision processes [22], factored games [17], and graph-structured games [20].

Decomposition as a means to automate intrusion response has been studied first in [17,25,34,35]. The work in [17] formulates the interaction between a defender and an attacker on a cyber-physical infrastructure as a factored Markov game and introduces a decomposition based on linear programming. Following a similar approach, the work in [35] studies a Markov game formulation and shows that a multi-stage game can be decomposed into a sequence of one-stage games. In a separate line of work, [25] models intrusion response as a minimax control problem and develops a heuristic decomposition based on clustering and influence graphs. This approach resembles the work in [34], which studies a factored decision process and proposes a hierarchical decomposition.

In all of the above works, decomposition is key to obtain effective strategies for large-scale systems. Compared to our work, some of them propose decomposition methods without optimal substructure [25], others do not consider partial observability [17,35], or dynamic attackers [34]. Most importantly, all of the above works evaluate the obtained strategies in a simulation environment. They do not perform evaluation in an emulation environment as we report in this paper, which gives higher confidence that the strategies are effective on the target infrastructure.

For a comprehensive review of prior research on automated intrusion response (beyond work that use decomposition), see [10, §VII].

(a) A workflow.   (b) Attacker actions.   (c) Defender actions.

Fig. 3. Examples of a workflow, attacker actions, and defender actions.

3   The Intrusion Response Use Case

We consider an intrusion response use case that involves the IT infrastructure of an organization. The operator of this infrastructure, which we call the defender, takes measures to protect it against an attacker while providing services to a client population (see Fig. 1). The infrastructure is segmented into *zones* with virtual *nodes* that run network services. Services are realized by *workflows* that are accessed by clients through a gateway, which also is open to the attacker (see Fig. 3a).

The attacker's goal is to intrude on the infrastructure, compromise nodes, and disrupt workflows. It can take three types of actions to achieve this goal: (*i*) reconnaissance; (*ii*) brute-force attacks; and (*iii*) exploits (see Fig. 3b).

The defender continuously monitors the infrastructure through accessing and analyzing intrusion detection alerts and other statistics. It can take four types of defensive actions to respond to possible intrusions: (*i*) migrate nodes between zones; (*ii*) redirect or block network flows; (*iii*) shut down nodes; and (*iv*) revoke access to nodes (see Fig. 3c). When deciding between these actions, the defender must balance two conflicting objectives: maximize workflow utility towards its clients and minimize the cost of intrusion.

4   Formalizing the Intrusion Response Problem

We formalize the above use case as an optimization problem where the goal is to select an optimal sequence of defender actions in response to a sequence of attacker actions. We assume a dynamic attacker, which leads to a game-theoretic formulation of the intrusion response problem. The game is played on the IT infrastructure, which we model as a discrete-time dynamical system whose evolution depends on the actions by the attacker and the defender. Both actors have partial observability of the system state, and their observations depend on the traffic generated by clients requesting service, which we assume can be described by a stationary process.

Notations. Boldface lower case letters (e.g., $\mathbf{x}$) denote row vectors and upper case calligraphic letters (e.g., $\mathcal{V}$) represent sets. The set of probability distributions over $\mathcal{V}$ is written as $\Delta(\mathcal{V})$. A random variable is denoted by upper case (e.g., X) and a random vector is denoted by boldface (e.g., $\mathbf{X} = (X_1, \ldots, X_n)$). $\mathbb{P}$ is the probability measure and the expectation of f with respect to X is expressed as $\mathbb{E}_X[f]$. When f includes many random variables that depend on π we simplify the notation to $\mathbb{E}_\pi[f]$. We use $x \sim f$ to mean that x is sampled from f and sometimes write $\mathbb{P}[x|z,y]$ instead of $\mathbb{P}[X = x|Z = z, Y = y]$ when X, Z, Y are clear from the context. Symbols used throughout the paper are listed in Table 1.

4.1   Modeling the Infrastructure and Services

Following the description in Sect. 3, we consider an IT infrastructure with application servers connected by a communication network that is segmented into zones (see Fig. 1). Overlaid on this physical infrastructure is a virtual infrastructure with tree-structure that includes *nodes*, which collectively offer services to clients.

A service is modeled as a *workflow*, which comprises a set of interdependent nodes. A dependency between two nodes reflects information exchange through service invocations. We assume that each node belongs to exactly one workflow. As an example of a virtual infrastructure, we can think of a microservice architecture where a workflow is defined as a tree of microservices (see Fig. 3a).

Infrastructure. We model the virtual infrastructure as a (finite) directed graph $\mathcal{G} \triangleq \langle \{\text{gw}\} \cup \mathcal{V}, \mathcal{E} \rangle$. The graph has a tree structure and is rooted at the gateway gw. Each node $i \in \mathcal{V}$ has three state variables. $v_{i,t}^{(R)}$ represents the reconnaissance state and realizes the binary random variable $V_{i,t}^{(R)}$. $v_{i,t}^{(R)} = 1$ if the attacker has discovered the node, 0 otherwise. $v_{i,t}^{(I)}$ represents the intrusion state and realizes the binary random variable $V_{i,t}^{(I)}$. $v_{i,t}^{(I)} = 1$ if the attacker has compromised the node, 0 otherwise. Lastly, $v_{i,t}^{(Z)}$ indicates the zone in which the node resides and realizes the random variable $V_{i,t}^{(Z)}$. We call a node $i \in \mathcal{V}$ *active* at time t if it is functional as part of a workflow (denoted $\alpha_{i,t} = 1$). Due to a defender action (e.g., a shut down) a node $i \in \mathcal{V}$ may become inactive (i.e., $\alpha_{i,t} = 0$).

Workflows. We model a workflow $\mathbf{w} \in \mathcal{W}$ as a subtree $\mathcal{G}_\mathbf{w} \triangleq \langle \{\text{gw}\} \cup \mathcal{V}_\mathbf{w}, \mathcal{E}_\mathbf{w} \rangle$ of the infrastructure graph. Workflows do not overlap except for the gateway which belongs to all workflows.

4.2 Modeling Actors

The intrusion response use case involves three types of actors: an attacker, a defender, and clients (see Fig. 1).

Attacker. At each time t, the attacker takes an action $\mathbf{a}_t^{(A)}$, which is defined as the composition of the local actions on all nodes $\mathbf{a}_t^{(A)} \triangleq (a_{1,t}^{(A)}, \ldots, a_{|\mathcal{V}|,t}^{(A)}) \in \mathcal{A}_A$, where $\mathcal{A}_A$ is finite. A local action is either the null action (denoted with $\perp$) or an offensive action (see examples in Fig. 3b). An offensive action on a node i may change the reconnaissance state $v_{i,t}^{(R)}$ or the intrusion state $v_{i,t}^{(I)}$. A node i can only be compromised if it is discovered, i.e., if $v_{i,t}^{(R)} = 1$. We express this constraint as $\mathbf{a}_t^{(A)} \in \mathcal{A}_A(\mathbf{s}_t^{(A)})$.

The attacker state $\mathbf{S}_t^{(A)} \triangleq (V_{i,t}^{(I)}, V_{i,t}^{(R)})_{i \in \mathcal{V}} \in \mathcal{S}_A$ evolves as

$$\mathbf{s}_{t+1}^{(A)} \sim f_A(\cdot \mid \mathbf{S}_t^{(A)} = \mathbf{s}_t^{(A)}, \mathbf{A}_t^{(A)} = \mathbf{a}_t^{(A)}, \mathbf{A}_t^{(D)} = \mathbf{a}_t^{(D)}) \qquad (1)$$

where $\mathbf{S}_t^{(A)}$, $\mathbf{A}_t^{(A)}$, and $\mathbf{A}_t^{(D)}$ are random vectors with realizations $\mathbf{s}_t^{(A)}$, $\mathbf{a}_t^{(A)}$, and $\mathbf{a}_t^{(D)}$. ($\mathbf{A}_t^{(D)}$ represents the defender action at time t.)

Defender. At each time t, the defender takes an action $\mathbf{a}_t^{(D)}$, which is defined as the composition of the local actions on all nodes $\mathbf{a}_t^{(D)} \triangleq (a_{1,t}^{(D)}, \ldots, a_{|\mathcal{V}|,t}^{(D)}) \in \mathcal{A}_D$, where $\mathcal{A}_D$ is finite. A local action is either a defensive action or the null action $\perp$ (see examples in Fig. 3c). Each defensive action $a_{i,t}^{(D)} \neq \perp$ leads to $\mathbf{S}_{i,t+1}^{(A)} = (0,0)$ and may affect $V_{i,t+1}^{(Z)}$.

The defender state $\mathbf{S}_t^{(D)} \triangleq (V_{i,t}^{(Z)})_{i \in \mathcal{V}} \in \mathcal{S}_D$ evolves according to

$$\mathbf{s}_{t+1}^{(D)} \sim f_D(\cdot \mid \mathbf{S}_t^{(D)} = \mathbf{s}_t^{(D)}, \mathbf{A}_t^{(D)} = \mathbf{a}_t^{(D)}) \qquad (2)$$

where $\mathbf{s}_t^{(D)}$ and $\mathbf{a}_t^{(D)}$ realize the random vectors $\mathbf{S}_t^{(D)}$ and $\mathbf{A}_t^{(D)}$.

Clients. Clients consume services of the infrastructure by accessing workflows. We model client behavior through stationary stochastic processes, which affect the observations available to the attacker and the defender.

4.3 Observability and Strategies

At each time t, the defender and the attacker both observe $\mathbf{o}_t \triangleq (o_{1,t}, \ldots, o_{|\mathcal{V}|,t}) \in \mathcal{O}$, where $\mathcal{O}$ is finite. (In our use case $\mathbf{o}_t$ relates to the number of IDPS alerts per node.) $\mathbf{o}_t$ is drawn from the random vector $\mathbf{O}_t \triangleq (\mathbf{O}_{1,t}, \ldots, \mathbf{O}_{|\mathcal{V}|,t})$ whose marginal distributions $Z_{\mathbf{O}_1}, \ldots, Z_{\mathbf{O}_{|\mathcal{V}|}}$ are stationary and conditionally independent given $\mathbf{S}_{i,t}^{(D)}$ and $\mathbf{S}_{i,t}^{(A)}$. (Note that $Z_{\mathbf{O}_i}$ depends on the traffic generated by clients.) As a consequence, the joint conditional distribution Z is given by

$$Z(\mathbf{O}_t = \mathbf{o} \mid \mathbf{s}_t^{(D)}, \mathbf{s}_t^{(A)}) = \prod_{i=1}^{|\mathcal{V}|} Z_{\mathbf{O}_i}(\mathbf{O}_{i,t} = \mathbf{o}_i \mid \mathbf{s}_{i,t}^{(D)}, \mathbf{s}_{i,t}^{(A)}) \qquad \forall \mathbf{o} \in \mathcal{O} \qquad (3)$$

The sequence of observations and states at times $1, \ldots, t$ forms the histories $\mathbf{h}_t^{(D)} \in \mathcal{H}_D$ and $\mathbf{h}_t^{(A)} \in \mathcal{H}_A$. These histories are realizations of the random vectors $\mathbf{H}_t^{(D)} \triangleq (\mathbf{S}_1^{(D)}, \mathbf{A}_1^{(D)}, \mathbf{O}_1, \ldots, \mathbf{A}_{t-1}^{(D)}, \mathbf{S}_t^{(D)}, \mathbf{O}_t)$ and $\mathbf{H}_t^{(A)} \triangleq (\mathbf{S}_1^{(A)}, \mathbf{A}_1^{(A)}, \mathbf{O}_1, \ldots, \mathbf{A}_{t-1}^{(A)}, \mathbf{S}_t^{(A)}, \mathbf{O}_t)$. Based on their respective histories, the defender and the attacker select actions, which define the defender strategy $\pi_D \in \Pi_D : \mathcal{H}_D \to \Delta(\mathcal{A}_D)$ and the attacker strategy $\pi_A \in \Pi_A : \mathcal{H}_A \to \Delta(\mathcal{A}_A)$.

4.4 The Intrusion Response Problem

When selecting the strategy π_D the defender must balance two conflicting objectives: maximize the workflow utility towards its clients and minimize the cost of intrusion. The weight $\eta \geq 0$ controls the trade-off between these two objectives, which results in the bi-objective

$$J \triangleq \sum_{t=1}^{\infty} \gamma^{t-1} \left(\underbrace{\sum_{w \in \mathcal{W}} \sum_{i \in \mathcal{V}_w} \eta u_{i,t}^{(W)}}_{\text{workflows utility}} - \underbrace{c_{i,t}^{(I)}}_{\text{intrusion cost}} \right) \tag{4}$$

where $\gamma \in [0, 1)$ is a discount factor, $c_{i,t}^{(I)}$ is the intrusion cost associated with node i at time t, and $u_{i,t}^{(W)}$ expresses the workflow utility associated with node i at time t. For this paper, we assume that $u_{i,t}^{(W)}$ is proportional to the number of active nodes in the subtree rooted at i and that $c_{i,t}^{(I)} = v_{i,t}^{(I)} + c^{(A)}(\mathbf{a}_{i,t}^{(D)})$, where $c^{(A)}$ is a non-negative function.

Given (4) and an attacker strategy π_A, the intrusion response problem can be stated as

$$\underset{\pi_D \in \Pi_D}{\text{maximize}} \quad \mathbb{E}_{(\pi_D, \pi_A)}[J] \tag{5a}$$

$$\text{subject to} \quad \mathbf{s}_{t+1}^{(D)} \sim f_D\left(\cdot \mid \mathbf{S}_t^{(D)} = \mathbf{s}_t^{(D)}, \mathbf{A}_t^{(D)} = \mathbf{a}_t^{(D)} \right), \quad \mathbf{s}_t^{(D)} \in \mathcal{S}_D \quad \forall t \tag{5b}$$

$$\mathbf{s}_{t+1}^{(A)} \sim f_A\left(\cdot \mid \mathbf{S}_t^{(A)} = \mathbf{s}_t^{(A)}, \mathbf{A}_t = \mathbf{a}_t \right), \quad \mathbf{s}_t^{(A)} \in \mathcal{S}_A \quad \forall t \tag{5c}$$

$$\mathbf{o}_{t+1} \sim Z\left(\cdot \mid \mathbf{S}_{t+1}^{(D)} = \mathbf{s}_{t+1}^{(D)}, \mathbf{S}_{t+1}^{(A)} = \mathbf{s}_{t+1}^{(A)} \right), \quad \mathbf{o}_t \in \mathcal{O} \quad \forall t \tag{5d}$$

$$\mathbf{a}_t^{(A)} \sim \pi_A\left(\cdot \mid \mathbf{H}_t^{(A)} = \mathbf{h}_t^{(A)} \right), \quad \mathbf{a}_t^{(A)} \in \mathcal{A}_A(\mathbf{s}_t^{(A)}) \quad \forall t \tag{5e}$$

$$\mathbf{a}_t^{(D)} \sim \pi_D\left(\cdot \mid \mathbf{H}_t^{(D)} = \mathbf{h}_t^{(D)} \right), \quad \mathbf{a}_t^{(D)} \in \mathcal{A}_D \quad \forall t \tag{5f}$$

$$\mathbf{s}_1^{(A)} \sim \mathbf{b}_1^{(A)}, \quad \mathbf{s}_1^{(D)} \sim \mathbf{b}_1^{(D)} \tag{5g}$$

where $\mathbf{a}_t \triangleq (\mathbf{a}_t^{(D)}, \mathbf{a}_t^{(A)})$, $\mathbb{E}_{(\pi_D, \pi_A)}$ denotes the expectation over the random vectors $(\mathbf{H}_t^{(D)}, \mathbf{H}_t^{(A)})_{t \in \{1, 2, \ldots\}}$ when following the strategy profile (π_D, π_A); (5b)–(5c) are the dynamics constraints; (5d) describes the observations; (5e)–(5f) capture the actions; and (5g) define the initial state distributions. (As a maximizer of (5) exists (see Theorem 1), we write max instead of sup throughout this paper.)

Solving (5) yields an optimal defender strategy against a *static* attacker with a fixed strategy. Note that this defender strategy is generally not optimal against a different attacker strategy. For this reason, we aim to find a defender strategy that maximizes the minimum value of J (4) across all possible attacker strategies. This objective can be formally expressed as a maxmin problem:

$$\underset{\pi_D \in \Pi_D}{\text{maximize}} \; \underset{\pi_A \in \Pi_A}{\text{minimize}} \; \mathbb{E}_{(\pi_D, \pi_A)} [J] \qquad \text{subject to (5b)–(5g)} \qquad (6)$$

Solving (6) corresponds to finding a Nash equilibrium [23, Eq. 1] of a two-player game. Hence the problem of solving (6) can be analyzed through game theory.

5   The Intrusion Response Game

The maxmin problem in (6) defines a stationary, finite, and zero-sum Partially Observed Stochastic Game with Public Observations (a PO-POSG) [16, Def. 1]:

$$\Gamma \triangleq \langle \mathcal{N}, (\mathcal{S}_k)_{k \in \mathcal{N}}, (\mathcal{A}_k)_{k \in \mathcal{N}}, \mathcal{O}, (f_k)_{k \in \mathcal{N}}, Z, u, (\mathbf{b}_1^{(k)})_{k \in \mathcal{N}}, \gamma \rangle \qquad (7)$$

The game Γ has two players $\mathcal{N} = \{D, A\}$ with D being the defender and A being the attacker. $(\mathcal{S}_k)_{k \in \mathcal{N}}$ are the state spaces, $(\mathcal{A}_k)_{k \in \mathcal{N}}$ are the action spaces, and $\mathcal{O}$ is observation space (as defined in Sect. 4). The transition functions $(f_k)_{k \in \mathcal{N}}$ are defined by (5b)–(5c), the observation function Z is defined in (3), and the utility function $u(\mathbf{s}_t, \mathbf{a}_t^{(D)})$ is the expression within brackets in (4). $(\mathbf{b}_1^{(k)})_{k \in \mathcal{N}}$ are the state distributions at $t = 1$ and γ is the discount factor in (4).

Game Play. When the game starts at $t = 1$, $\mathbf{s}_1^{(D)}$ and $\mathbf{s}_1^{(A)}$ are sampled from $\mathbf{b}_1^{(D)}$ and $\mathbf{b}_1^{(A)}$. A play of the game proceeds in time-steps $t = 1, 2, \ldots$. At each time t, the defender observes $\mathbf{h}_t^{(D)}$ and the attacker observes $\mathbf{h}_t^{(A)}$. Based on these histories, both players select actions according to their respective strategies, i.e., $\mathbf{a}_t^{(D)} \sim \pi_D(\cdot \mid \mathbf{h}_t^{(D)})$ and $\mathbf{a}_t^{(A)} \sim \pi_A(\cdot \mid \mathbf{h}_t^{(A)})$. As a result of these actions, five events occur at time $t+1$: (i) $\mathbf{o}_{t+1}$ is sampled from Z; (ii) $\mathbf{s}_{t+1}^{(D)}$

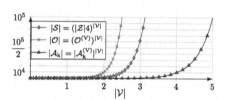

Fig. 4. Growth of $|\mathcal{S}|$, $|\mathcal{O}|$, and $|\mathcal{A}_k|$ in function of $|\mathcal{V}|$, where $k \in \{D, A\}$, $|\mathcal{Z}| = 10$, $|\mathcal{O}^{(V)}| = 100$, and $|\mathcal{A}_D^{(V)}| = |\mathcal{A}_A^{(V)}| = 10$.

is sampled from f_D; (iii) $\mathbf{s}_{t+1}^{(A)}$ is sampled from f_A; (iv) the defender receives the utility $u(\mathbf{s}_t, \mathbf{a}_t^{(D)})$; and ($v$) the attacker receives the utility $-u(\mathbf{s}_t, \mathbf{a}_t^{(D)})$.

Belief States. Based on their histories $\mathbf{h}_t^{(D)}$ and $\mathbf{h}_t^{(A)}$, both players form beliefs about the unobservable components of the state $\mathbf{s}_t$, which are expressed through the belief states $\mathbf{b}_t^{(D)}(\mathbf{s}_t^{(A)}) \triangleq \mathbb{P}[\mathbf{s}_t^{(A)} \mid \mathbf{H}_t^{(D)} = \mathbf{h}_t^{(D)}]$ and $\mathbf{b}_t^{(A)}(\mathbf{s}_t^{(D)}) \triangleq \mathbb{P}[\mathbf{s}_t^{(D)} \mid \mathbf{H}_t^{(A)} = \mathbf{h}_t^{(A)}]$. The belief states are updated at each time $t > 1$ via [16, Eq. 1] and are realizations of $\mathbf{B}_t^{(D)}$ and $\mathbf{B}_t^{(A)}$. The initial beliefs at $t = 1$ are the degenerate distributions $\mathbf{b}_1^{(D)}(\mathbf{0}_{2|\mathcal{V}|}) = 1$ and $\mathbf{b}_1^{(A)}(\mathbf{s}_1^{(D)}) = 1$, where $\mathbf{0}_n$ is the n-dimensional zero-vector and $\mathbf{s}_1^{(D)}$ is given by the infrastructure configuration (see Sect. 4).

Best Response Strategies. A defender strategy $\tilde{\pi}_D \in \Pi_D$ is called a *best response* against $\pi_A \in \Pi_A$ if it *maximizes* J (4). Similarly, an attacker strategy $\tilde{\pi}_A$ is called a best response against π_D if it *minimizes* J (4). Hence, the best response correspondences are

$$B_D(\pi_A) \triangleq \arg\max_{\pi_D \in \Pi_D} \mathbb{E}_{(\pi_D, \pi_A)}[J] \quad \text{and} \quad B_A(\pi_D) \triangleq \arg\min_{\pi_A \in \Pi_A} \mathbb{E}_{(\pi_D, \pi_A)}[J] \quad (8)$$

Optimal Strategies. An optimal defender strategy π_D^* is a best response strategy against any attacker strategy that *minimizes* J. Similarly, an optimal attacker strategy π_A^* is a best response against any defender strategy that *maximizes* J. Hence, when both players follow optimal strategies, they play best response strategies against each other:

$$(\pi_D^*, \pi_A^*) \in B_D(\pi_A^*) \times B_A(\pi_D^*) \quad (9)$$

Since no player has an incentive to change its strategy, (π_D^*, π_A^*) is a Nash equilibrium [23, Eq. 1].

We know from game theory that Γ has a mixed Nash equilibrium [14–16] and we know from Markov decision theory that $B_D(\pi_A)$ and $B_A(\pi_D)$ are non-empty [21]. Based on these standard results, we state the following theorem.

Theorem 1.

(A) Γ (7) with the instantiation described in Sect. 4 has a mixed Nash equilibrium.

(B) The best response correspondences (8) in Γ with the instantiation described in Sect. 4 satisfy $|B_D(\pi_A)| > 0$ and $|B_A(\pi_D)| > 0 \; \forall(\pi_A, \pi_D) \in \Pi_A \times \Pi_D$.

Proof. The statement in (A) follows from the following sufficient conditions: (*i*) Γ is stationary, finite, and zero-sum; (*ii*) Γ has public observations; and (*iii*) $\gamma \in [0, 1)$. Under these conditions, the existence proofs in [14, §3], [15, Thm. 2.3], and [16, Thm. 1] apply, which shows that Γ can be modeled as a finite strategic game for which Nash's theorem applies [23, Thm. 1].

To prove (B), we note that obtaining a pair of best response strategies $(\tilde{\pi}_D, \tilde{\pi}_A) \in B_D(\pi_A) \times B_A(\pi_D)$ for a given strategy pair $(\pi_A, \pi_D) \in \Pi_A \times \Pi_D$ amounts to solving two finite and stationary POMDPs (Partially Observed Markov Decision Processes) with discounted utilities. It then follows from Markov decision theory that a pair of pure best response strategies $(\tilde{\pi}_D, \tilde{\pi}_A)$ exists [21, Thms. 7.6.1–7.6.2]. □

6   Decomposing the Intrusion Response Game

In this section we present the main contribution of the paper. We show how the game Γ (7) with the instantiation described in Sect. 4 can be recursively decomposed into subgames with optimal substructure [6, Ch. 15], which means

Table 1. Notations.

Notation(s)	Description
$\mathcal{G}, \mathcal{G}_{\mathbf{w}}, \mathcal{V}, \mathcal{E}, \mathcal{V}_{\mathbf{w}}, \mathcal{E}_{\mathbf{w}}$	Infrastructure tree, subtree of $\mathbf{w}$, and sets of nodes and edges in $\mathcal{G}$ and $\mathcal{G}_{\mathbf{w}}$
$\mathcal{Z}, \mathcal{W}, \mathcal{A}_D, \mathcal{A}_A(\mathbf{s}_t)$	Network zones, workflows, defender actions, and attacker actions at time t
$\mathcal{A}_D^{(V)}, \mathcal{A}_A^{(V)}(\mathbf{s}_t), \mathcal{O}^{(V)}$	Action and observation spaces per node at time t, $\mathcal{A}_k = (\mathcal{A}_k^{(V)})^{|\mathcal{V}|}$ and $\mathcal{O} = (\mathcal{O}^{(V)})^{|\mathcal{V}|}$
$v_{i,t}^{(I)}, v_{i,t}^{(Z)}, v_{i,t}^{(R)}$	Intrusion state, zone, and reconnaissance state of $i \in \mathcal{V}$ at time t
$V_{i,t}^{(I)}, V_{i,t}^{(Z)}, V_{i,t}^{(R)}$	Random variables with realizations $v_{i,t}^{(I)}, v_{i,t}^{(Z)}, v_{i,t}^{(R)}$
$\Gamma, \mathcal{N}, u, \mathcal{S} = \mathcal{S}_A \times \mathcal{S}_D, \mathcal{O}$	PO-POSG (7), set of players, utility function, state space, and observation space
$\mathbf{s}_t = (\mathbf{s}_t^{(D)}, \mathbf{s}_t^{(A)})$	State at time t
$\mathbf{a}_t = (\mathbf{a}_t^{(D)}, \mathbf{a}_t^{(A)})$	Action at time t
$\mathbf{o}_t, \mathbf{u}_t, \mathbf{a}_t^{(k)}, \mathbf{h}_t^{(k)}$	Observation, utility, action of player k at time t, and history of player k at time t
$\mathcal{B}_k, \mathbf{b}_t^{(k)}, \tilde{\pi}_k, \tilde{\mathbf{a}}^{(k)}$	Belief space, belief state, best response strategy and action of player k
$\mathbf{S}_t, \mathbf{O}_t, \mathbf{A}_t, \mathbf{U}_t, \mathbf{B}_t^{(k)}, \mathbf{H}_t^{(k)}$	Random vectors with realizations $\mathbf{s}_t, \mathbf{o}_t, \mathbf{a}_t, \mathbf{u}_t, \mathbf{b}_t^{(k)}, \mathbf{h}_t^{(k)}$
$\pi_k, Z, u_{i,t}^{(W)}$	Strategy of player k, observation distribution, and workflow utility of node i at time t
$\perp, \mathrm{an}(i), \alpha_{i,t}$	Null action, set of i and its ancestors in $\mathcal{G}$, and active status of node i at time t
$c_{i,t}^{(I)}, c^{(A)}$	Intrusion cost associated with node i at time t and action cost function
f_A, f_D, B_k	Transition functions and best response correspondence of player k

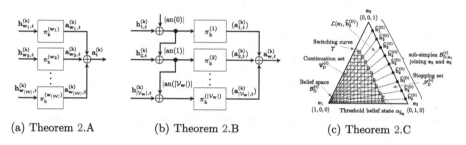

(a) Theorem 2.A   (b) Theorem 2.B   (c) Theorem 2.C

Fig. 5. Illustrations of Theorem 2; arrows indicate inputs and outputs; $\oplus$ denotes vector concatenation; $k \in \{D, A\}$; $\mathbf{h}_{\mathbf{w},t}^{(k)} \triangleq (\mathbf{h}_{j,t}^{(k)})_{j\in\mathcal{V}_{\mathbf{w}}}$; and $\mathbf{a}_{\mathbf{w},t}^{(k)} \triangleq (\mathbf{a}_{j,t}^{(k)})_{j\in\mathcal{V}_{\mathbf{w}}}$.

that a best response (8) of the original game can be obtained from best responses of the subgames. We further show that best responses of the subgames can be computed in parallel and that the space complexity of a subgame is independent of the number of nodes $|\mathcal{V}|$. Note that the space complexity of the original game increases exponentially with $|\mathcal{V}|$ (see Fig. 4).

Theorem 2 (Decomposition theorem).

(A) A game Γ (7) with the instantiation described in Sect. 4 can be decomposed into independent workflow subgames $\Gamma^{(\mathbf{w}_1)}, \ldots, \Gamma^{(\mathbf{w}_{|\mathcal{W}|})}$. Due to their independence, the subgames have optimal substructure.

(B) Each subgame $\Gamma^{(\mathbf{w})}$ can be further decomposed into node subgames $(\Gamma^{(i)})_{i\in\mathcal{V}_{\mathbf{w}}}$ with optimal substructure and space complexities independent of $|\mathcal{V}|$.

(C) *For each subgame $\Gamma^{(i)}$, a best response strategy for the defender can be characterized by switching curves, under the assumption that the observation distributions $Z_{O_1|s^{(A)}}, \ldots, Z_{O_{|V|}|s^{(A)}}$ (3) are totally positive of order 2 (i.e., TP-2 [21, Def. 10.2.1]).*

Statements A and B express that Γ decomposes into independent subgames, which consequently can be solved in parallel (see Fig. 5). This decomposition implies that the largest game that is tractable on a given compute platform scales linearly with the number of processors on the platform. Further, statement C says that a best response strategy for the defender in each subgame can be characterized by switching curves, which can be estimated efficiently.

In the following sections we provide proofs of Theorem 2.A–C. The requisite notations are given in Table 1.

6.1   Proof of Theorem 2.A

Following the instantiation of Γ described in Sect. 4, the state, observation, and action spaces factorize as

$$S = \left(Z \times \{0,1\}^2\right)^{|V|} \quad O = \left(O^{(V)}\right)^{|V|} \quad \mathcal{A}_D = \left(\mathcal{A}_D^{(V)}\right)^{|V|} \quad \mathcal{A}_A = \left(\mathcal{A}_A^{(V)}\right)^{|V|} \quad (10)$$

where $O^{(V)}$, $\mathcal{A}_D^{(V)}$, and $\mathcal{A}_A^{(V)}$ denote the local observation and action spaces for each node.

Since each node belongs to exactly one workflow, (10) implies that Γ can be decomposed into subgames $\Gamma^{(\mathbf{w}_1)}, \ldots, \Gamma^{(\mathbf{w}_{|\mathbf{w}|})}$. To show that the subgames are independent, it suffices to show that they are observation-independent, transition-independent, and utility-independent [27, Defs. 32, 33, 35].

From (3) we have

$$Z\left(O_{i,t+1} = o_{i,t+1} \mid s_{t+1}^{(D)}, s_t^{(A)}\right) = Z\left(O_{i,t+1} = o_{i,t+1} \mid s_{i,t+1}^{(D)}, s_{i,t+1}^{(A)}\right)$$

for all $o_{i,t+1} \in O$, $s_{t+1} \in S$, and $t \geq 1$, which implies observation independence across nodes $i \in V$ and therefore across workflows [27, Def. 33].

From the definitions in Sect. 4 and (1)–(2) we have

$$f_D\left(S_{i,t+1}^{(D)} = s_{i,t+1}^{(D)} \mid s_t^{(D)}, a_t^{(D)}\right) = f_D\left(S_{i,t+1}^{(D)} = s_{i,t+1}^{(D)} \mid s_{i,t}^{(D)}, a_{i,t}^{(D)}\right)$$

$$f_A\left(S_{i,t+1}^{(A)} = s_{i,t+1}^{(A)} \mid s_t^{(A)}, a_t^{(A)}, a_t^{(D)}\right) = f_A\left(S_{i,t+1}^{(A)} = s_{i,t+1}^{(A)} \mid s_{i,t}^{(A)}, a_{i,t}^{(A)}, a_{i,t}^{(D)}\right)$$

for all $s_{i,t} \in S$, $a_{i,t} \in \mathcal{A}$, $i \in V$, and $t \geq 1$, which implies transition independence across nodes $i \in V$ and therefore across workflows [27, Def. 32].

Following (4) and the definition of $u_{i,t}^{(W)}$ (see Sect. 4.4) we can rewrite $u(\cdot)$ as

$$u(\mathbf{s}_t, \mathbf{a}_t^{(D)}) = \underbrace{\sum_{\mathbf{w} \in \mathcal{W}} \sum_{i \in \mathcal{V}_\mathbf{w}} \eta u_{i,t}^{(W)} - c_{i,t}^{(I)}(\mathbf{a}_{i,t}^{(D)}, v_{i,t}^{(I)})}_{\triangleq u_\mathbf{w}} = \sum_{\mathbf{w} \in \mathcal{W}} u_\mathbf{w}\left((\mathbf{s}_{i,t}, \mathbf{a}_{i,t}^{(D)})_{i \in \mathcal{V}_\mathbf{w}}\right)$$

$$(11)$$

The final expression in (11) is a sum of workflow utility functions, each of which depends only on the states and actions of one workflow. Hence, $\Gamma^{(\mathbf{w}_1)}, \dots, \Gamma^{(\mathbf{w}_{|\mathcal{W}|})}$ are utility independent [27, Def. 35]. □

6.2   Proof of Theorem 2.B

Our goal is to show that a workflow subgame $\Gamma^{(\mathbf{w})}$ decomposes into node-level subgames with optimal substructure. That is, we aim to show that a best response in $\Gamma^{(\mathbf{w})}$ can be constructed from best responses of the subgames.

Following the description in Sect. 4, we know that the nodes in a workflow are connected in a tree and that the utility generated by a node i depends on the number of active nodes in the subtree rooted at i. Taking into account this tree structure and the definition of the utility function, we decompose $\Gamma^{(\mathbf{w})}$ into node subgames $(\Gamma^{(i)})_{i \in \mathcal{V}_\mathbf{w}}$ where each subgame depends only on the local state and action of a single node. It follows from (10) that this decomposition is feasible and that the space complexity of a subgame is independent of $|\mathcal{V}|$. Further, we know from Theorem 2.A that the subgames are transition-independent and observation-independent but utility-dependent. To prove optimal substructure it therefore suffices to show that it is possible to redefine the utility functions for the subgames such that at each time t, the best response action in $\Gamma^{(\mathbf{w})}$ for any node i is also a best response in $\Gamma^{(i)}$ and vice versa. For the sake of brevity we give the proof for the defender only. The proof for the attacker is analogous. In this proof, for better readability, we omit the constants γ, η and use the shorthand notations $\mathbf{s}_{\mathbf{w},t}^{(D)} \triangleq (\mathbf{s}_{j,t}^{(D)})_{j \in \mathcal{V}_\mathbf{w}}$, $\mathbf{b}_{\mathbf{w},t}^{(D)} \triangleq (\mathbf{b}_{j,t}^{(D)})_{j \in \mathcal{V}_\mathbf{w}}$, $\mathcal{V} \triangleq \mathcal{V}_{D,\pi_A}^*$, and $\tau \in \arg\min_{k>t} \mathbf{a}_k^{(D)} \neq \bot$, where $\mathcal{V}$ is the value function [21, Thm. 7.4.1]. Further, we use $an(i)$ to denote the set of node i and its ancestors in the infrastructure graph $\mathcal{G}$.

From Bellman's optimality equation [3, Eq. 1], a best response action for node i at time t in $\Gamma^{(\mathbf{w})}$ against an attacker strategy π_A is given by

$$\arg\max_{\mathbf{a}_{i,t}^{(D)} \in \mathcal{A}_D^{(V)}} \left[\mathbb{E}_{\pi_A} \left[\mathbf{U}_t + \mathcal{V}(\mathbf{S}_{t+1}^{(D)}, \mathbf{B}_{t+1}^{(D)}) \mid \mathbf{s}_t^{(D)}, \mathbf{b}_t^{(D)}, \mathbf{a}_{i,t}^{(D)} \right] \right]$$

$$\overset{(a)}{=} \arg\max_{\mathbf{a}_{i,t}^{(D)} \in \mathcal{A}_D^{(V)}} \left[\mathbb{E}_{\pi_A} \left[-c_{i,t}^{(I)} + \mathcal{V}(\mathbf{S}_{t+1}^{(D)}, \mathbf{B}_{t+1}^{(D)}) \mid \mathbf{s}_t^{(D)}, \mathbf{b}_t^{(D)}, \mathbf{a}_{i,t}^{(D)} \right] \right]$$

$$\overset{(b)}{=} \arg\max_{\mathbf{a}_{i,t}^{(D)} \in \mathcal{A}_D^{(V)}} \left[\mathbb{E}_{\pi_A} \left[-c_{i,t}^{(I)} + \sum_{k=t+1}^{\infty} \sum_{j \in \mathcal{V}_\mathbf{w}} \mathbf{U}_{j,k} \mid \mathbf{s}_{\mathbf{w},t}^{(D)}, \mathbf{b}_{\mathbf{w},t}^{(D)}, \mathbf{a}_{i,t}^{(D)} \right] \right]$$

$$\overset{(c)}{=} \underset{\mathbf{a}_{i,t}^{(D)} \in \mathcal{A}_D^{(V)}}{\arg\max} \left[\underset{\pi_A}{\mathbb{E}} \left[-c_{i,t}^{(I)} + \sum_{k=t+1}^{\tau} \sum_{j \in \mathcal{V}_\mathbf{w}} \mathbf{U}_{j,k} \;\middle|\; \mathbf{s}_{\mathbf{w},t}^{(D)}, \mathbf{b}_{\mathbf{w},t}^{(D)}, \mathbf{a}_{i,t}^{(D)} \right] \right]$$

$$\overset{(d)}{=} \underset{\mathbf{a}_{i,t}^{(D)} \in \mathcal{A}_D^{(V)}}{\arg\max} \left[\underset{\pi_A}{\mathbb{E}} \left[-c_{i,t}^{(I)} + \sum_{k=t+1}^{\tau} \sum_{j \in \mathrm{an}(i)} \mathbf{U}_{j,k} \;\middle|\; \mathbf{s}_{\mathbf{w},t}^{(D)}, \mathbf{b}_{\mathbf{w},t}^{(D)}, \mathbf{a}_{i,t}^{(D)} \right] \right]$$

$$\overset{(e)}{=} \underset{\mathbf{a}_{i,t}^{(D)} \in \mathcal{A}_D^{(V)}}{\arg\max} \left[\underset{\pi_A}{\mathbb{E}} \left[-c_{i,t}^{(I)} + \sum_{k=t+1}^{\tau} \sum_{j \in \mathrm{an}(i)} u_{j,k}^{(W)} - c_{j,k}^{(I)} \;\middle|\; \mathbf{s}_{\mathbf{w},t}^{(D)}, \mathbf{b}_{\mathbf{w},t}^{(D)}, \mathbf{a}_{i,t}^{(D)} \right] \right]$$

$$\overset{(f)}{=} \underset{\mathbf{a}_{i,t}^{(D)} \in \mathcal{A}_D^{(V)}}{\arg\max} \left[\underset{\pi_A}{\mathbb{E}} \left[-c_{i,t}^{(I)} + \sum_{k=t+1}^{\tau} |\mathrm{an}(i)| \alpha_{i,t+1} - c_{i,k}^{(I)} \;\middle|\; \mathbf{s}_{i,t}^{(D)}, \mathbf{b}_{i,t}^{(D)}, \mathbf{a}_{i,t}^{(D)} \right] \right] \quad (12)$$

where $\mathbf{U}_t$ denotes the vector of utilities for all nodes at time t. (a) holds because $(\mathbf{U}_{j,t})_{j \in \mathcal{V} \setminus \{i\}}$ and $u_{i,t}^{(W)}$ are independent of $\mathbf{a}_{i,t}^{(D)}$ and therefore does not affect the maximization; (b) follows from the utility independence across workflows (Theorem 2.A) and the definition of the value function $\mathcal{V}$ [21, Thm. 7.4.1]; (c) holds because any $\mathbf{a}_{i,t}^{(D)}$ except $\perp$ leads to $\mathbf{s}_{i,t+1}^{(A)} = (0,0)$, which means that all state variables at time $k > \tau$ are independent of $\mathbf{a}_{i,t}^{(D)}$ and can therefore be moved outside the arg max operator; (d) follows because $(\mathbf{U}_{j,t})_{j \in \mathcal{V} \setminus \mathrm{an}(i)}$ is independent of $\mathbf{a}_{i,t}^{(D)}$; (e) is an expansion of $(\mathbf{U}_{j,k})_{j \in \mathrm{an}(i), k \in \{t+1,\ldots,\tau\}}$ based on (4); and (f) follows because the terms in $(u_{j,k}^{(W)})_{j \in \mathrm{an}(i), k \in \{t+1,\ldots,\tau\}}$ that depend on $\mathbf{a}_{i,t}^{(D)}$ equal $k|\mathrm{an}(i)|\alpha_{t+1,i}$, where k is the constant of proportionality (see Sect. 4). (Recall that $\alpha_{i,t} = 1$ if node i is active at time t and $\alpha_{i,t} = 0$ otherwise.)

The final expression in (12) depends only on local information related to node i. This means that we can use it to define utility functions of the subgames $(\Gamma^{(i)})_{i \in \mathcal{V}_\mathbf{w}}$ such that they become utility-independent. Further, since the maximizer of the final expression in (12) is also a maximizer of the first expression, it follows that a a best response in $\Gamma^{(i)}$ is also a best response for node i in $\Gamma^{(\mathbf{w})}$ and thus in Γ (Theorem 2.A). Hence $(\Gamma^{(i)})_{i \in \mathcal{V}_\mathbf{w}}$ have optimal substructure. $\square$

6.3   Proof of Theorem 2.C

The idea behind this proof is that the problem of selecting *which* defensive action to apply in a subgame $\Gamma^{(i)}$ (Theorem 2.B) against a given attacker strategy can be separated from the problem of deciding *when* to apply it. Through this separation, we can analyze the latter problem using optimal stopping theory. Applying a recent result by Krishnamurthy [21, Thm. 12.3.4], the optimal stopping strategy in $\Gamma^{(i)}$ can be characterized by switching curves.

We perform the above separation by decomposing $\mathbf{a}_{i,t}^{(D)}$ into two subactions: $\mathbf{a}_{i,t}^{(D,1)}$ and $\mathbf{a}_{i,t}^{(D,2)}$ which realize $\mathbf{A}_{i,t}^{(D,1)}$ and $\mathbf{A}_{i,t}^{(D,2)}$. The first subaction $\mathbf{a}_{i,t}^{(D,1)} \neq \perp$ determines the defensive action and the second subaction $\mathbf{a}_{i,t}^{(D,2)} \in \{S,C\}$ determines when to take it. Specifically, if $\mathbf{a}_{i,t}^{(D,2)} = C$, then $\mathbf{a}_{i,t}^{(D)} = \perp$, otherwise $\mathbf{a}_{i,t}^{(D)} = \mathbf{a}_{i,t}^{(D,1)}$. Using this action decomposition, at each time t, a strategy $\pi_D^{(i)}$ in

$\Gamma^{(i)}$ is a joint distribution over $\mathbf{A}_{i,t}^{(D,1)}$ and $\mathbf{A}_{i,t}^{(D,2)}$, which means that it can be represented in an auto-regressive manner as

$$\pi_D^{(i)}(\mathbf{A}_{i,t}^{(D,1)} = \mathbf{a}_{i,t}^{(D,1)}, \mathbf{A}_{i,t}^{(D,2)} = \mathbf{a}_{i,t}^{(D,2)} \mid \mathbf{h}_{i,t}^{(k)}) \tag{13}$$
$$\overset{(a)}{=} \pi_D^{(i)}(\mathbf{A}_{i,t}^{(D,1)} = \mathbf{a}_{i,t}^{(D,1)} \mid \mathbf{h}_{i,t}^{(D)})\pi_D^{(i)}(\mathbf{A}_{i,t}^{(D,2)} = \mathbf{a}_{i,t}^{(D,2)} \mid \mathbf{h}_{i,t}^{(D)}, \mathbf{a}_{i,t}^{(D,1)})$$
$$\overset{(b)}{=} \pi_D^{(i)}(\mathbf{A}_{i,t}^{(D,1)} = \mathbf{a}_{i,t}^{(D,1)} \mid \mathbf{b}_{i,t}^{(D)}, \mathbf{s}_{i,t}^{(D)})\pi_D^{(i)}(\mathbf{A}_{i,t}^{(D,2)} = \mathbf{a}_{i,t}^{(D,2)} \mid \mathbf{b}_{i,t}^{(D)}, \mathbf{s}_{i,t}^{(D)}, \mathbf{a}_{i,t}^{(D,1)})$$
$$\overset{(c)}{=} \pi_D^{(i)}(\mathbf{A}_{i,t}^{(D,1)} = \mathbf{a}_{i,t}^{(D,1)} \mid \mathbf{s}_{i,t}^{(D)})\pi_D^{(i)}(\mathbf{A}_{i,t}^{(D,2)} = \mathbf{a}_{i,t}^{(D,2)} \mid \mathbf{b}_{i,t}^{(D)}, \mathbf{s}_{i,t}^{(D)}, \mathbf{a}_{i,t}^{(D,1)})$$

where (a) follows from the chain rule of probability; (b) holds because $(\mathbf{s}_{i,t}^{(D)}, \mathbf{b}_{i,t}^{(D)})$ is a sufficient statistic for $\mathbf{H}_{i,t}^{(D)}$ [21, Thm 7.2.1]; and (c) follows because any $\mathbf{a}_{i,t}^{(D,1)} \neq \perp$ leads to $\mathbf{S}_{i,t+1}^{(A)} = (0,0)$ and is thus conditionally independent of $\mathbf{B}_{i,t}^{(D)}$ [11, Eq. 16].

The strategy decomposition in (13) means that we can obtain a best response strategy in $\Gamma^{(i)}$ by jointly optimizing two substrategies: $\pi_D^{(i,1)}$ and $\pi_D^{(i,2)}$. The former corresponds to solving an MDP $\mathcal{M}^{(D,1)}$ with state space $\mathbf{s}_i^{(D)} \in \mathcal{Z}$ and the latter corresponds to solving a set of optimal stopping POMDPs $(\mathcal{M}_{i,s^{(D)},a^{(D)}}^{(D,2)})_{s^{(D)} \in \mathcal{Z}, a^{(D)} \in \mathcal{A}_D^{(V)}}$ with state space $\mathbf{s}_i^{(A)} \in \{(0,0), (1,0), (1,1)\}$.

Each stopping problem can be defined with a *single* stop action rather than multiple stop actions [9, §III.C] because

$$\underset{\pi_D \in \Pi_D^{(i,2)}}{\arg\max} \left[\mathbb{E}_{\pi_D} \left[\sum_{t=1}^{\infty} \gamma^{t-1} \mathbf{U}_{i,2,t} \mid \mathbf{B}_{i,1}^{(D)} = \mathbf{e}_1 \right] \right]$$

$$= \underset{\pi_D \in \Pi_D^{(i,2)}}{\arg\max} \left[\mathbb{E}_{\pi_D} \left[\sum_{t=1}^{\tau_1} \gamma^{t-1} \mathbf{U}_{i,2,t} \mid \mathbf{B}_{i,1}^{(D)} = \mathbf{e}_1 \right] + \right.$$

$$\left. \mathbb{E}_{\pi_D} \left[\sum_{t=\tau_1+1}^{\tau_2} \gamma^{t-1} \mathbf{U}_{i,2,t} \mid \mathbf{B}_{i,\tau_1+1}^{(D)} = \mathbf{e}_1 \right] + \dots \right]$$

$$= \underset{\pi_D \in \Pi_D^{(i,2)}}{\arg\max} \left[\mathbb{E}_{\pi_D} \left[\sum_{t=1}^{\tau_1} \gamma^{t-1} \mathbf{U}_{i,2,t} \mid \mathbf{B}_{i,1}^{(D)} = \mathbf{e}_1 \right] \right] \tag{14}$$

where $\Pi_D^{(i,2)}$, $\mathbf{U}_{i,2,t}$, and $\tau_1, \tau_2, \dots$ denote the strategy space, utility, and stopping times in $\mathcal{M}_{i,s^{(D)},a^{(D)}}^{(D,2)}$. Note that the belief space $\mathcal{B}_D^{(i)}$ for each stopping problem is the 2-dimensional unit simplex and that $\mathbf{B}_{i,\tau_j+1}^{(D)} = \mathbf{e}_1 = (1,0,0)$ for each stopping time τ_j since $\mathbf{a}_{i,\tau_j}^{(D,2)} = S \implies \mathbf{s}_{i,\tau_j+1}^{(A)} = (0,0)$.

The transition matrices for each stopping problem are of the form:

$$\begin{bmatrix} 1-p & p & 0 \\ 0 & 1-q & q \\ 0 & 0 & 1 \end{bmatrix} \quad \text{and} \quad \begin{bmatrix} 1 & 0 & 0 \\ 1 & 0 & 0 \\ 1 & 0 & 0 \end{bmatrix} \tag{15}$$

where p is the probability that the attacker performs reconnaissance and q is the probability that the attacker compromises the node. The left matrix in (15) relates to $\mathbf{a}_{i,t}^{(D,2)} = C$ and the right matrix relates to $\mathbf{a}_{i,t}^{(D,2)} = S$. The non-zero second order minors of the matrices are $(1-p)(1-q)$, pq, $1-q$, $1-p$, p, and $(1-p)q$, which implies that the matrices are TP-2 [21, Def. 10.2.1]. Since the distributions $Z_{\mathbf{O}_1|\mathbf{s}^{(A)}}, \ldots, Z_{\mathbf{O}_{|\mathcal{V}|}|\mathbf{s}^{(A)}}$ also are TP-2 by assumption, it follows from [21, Thm. 12.3.4] that there exists a switching curve Υ that partitions $\mathcal{B}_D^{(i)}$ into two individually connected regions: a stopping set $\mathcal{S}_D^{(i)}$ where $\mathbf{a}_{i,t}^{(D,2)} = S$ is a best response and a continuation set $\mathcal{C}_D^{(i)}$ where $\mathbf{a}_{i,t}^{(D,2)} = C$ is a best response (see Fig. 5c).

The argument behind the existence of a switching curve is as follows [21, Thm. 12.3.4]. On any line segment $\mathcal{L}(\mathbf{e}_1, \widehat{\mathbf{b}}^{(D)})$ in $\mathcal{B}_D^{(i)}$ that starts at $\mathbf{e}_1$ and ends at the subsimplex joining $\mathbf{e}_2$ and $\mathbf{e}_3$ (denoted with $\widehat{\mathbf{b}}^{(D)} \in \mathcal{B}_{D,\mathbf{e}_1}^{(i)}$), all belief states are totally ordered with respect to the Monotone Likelihood Ratio (MLR) order [21, Def. 10.1.1]. As a consequence, Topkis's theorem [32, Thm. 6.3] implies that the optimal strategy on $\mathcal{L}(\mathbf{e}_1, \widehat{\mathbf{b}}^{(D)})$ is monotone with respect to the MLR order. Consequently, there exists a threshold belief state $\alpha_{\widehat{\mathbf{b}}^{(D)}}$ on $\mathcal{L}(\mathbf{e}_1, \widehat{\mathbf{b}}^{(D)})$ where the optimal strategy switches from C to S. Since $\mathcal{B}_D^{(i)}$ can be covered by the union of lines $\mathcal{L}(\mathbf{e}_1, \widehat{\mathbf{b}}^{(D)})$, the thresholds $\alpha_{\widehat{\mathbf{b}}_1^{(D)}}, \alpha_{\widehat{\mathbf{b}}_2^{(D)}}, \ldots$ yield a switching curve Υ. $\square$

7   Finding Nash Equilibria of the Decomposed Game

To find a Nash equilibrium of Γ (7) we develop a *fictitious self-play* algorithm called Decompositional Fictitious Self-Play (DFSP), which estimates Nash equilibria based on the decomposition presented above. The pseudocode is listed in Algorithm 1. (In Algorithm 1, $\oplus$ denotes vector concatenation, $-k$ denotes the opponent of player k, and $\mathcal{M}_i^{(k)}$ denotes the best response POMDP of player k in $\Gamma^{(i)}$ (Theorem 2).)

DFSP implements the fictitious play process described in [5] and generates a sequence of strategy profiles (π_D, π_A), (π_D', π_A'), $\ldots$ that converges to a Nash equilibrium (π_D^*, π_A^*) [28, Thms. 7.2.4–7.2.5]. During each step of this process, DFSP learns best responses against the players' current strategies and then updates both players' strategies (lines 8–12 in Algorithm 1). To obtain the best responses, it first finds best responses for the node subgames as constructed in the proof of Theorem 2.B (lines 15–19), and then it combines them through concatenation (lines 20–26).

Finding best responses for node subgames amounts to solving POMDPs. The principal method for solving POMDPs is dynamic programming [21]. Dynamic programming is however intractable in our case, as demonstrated in Fig. 6d. To find the best responses we instead resort to approximation algorithms. More specifically, we use the Proximal Policy Optimization (PPO) algorithm [26, Alg. 1] to find best responses for the attacker, and we use a combination of dynamic programming

---

Algorithm 1: DFSP

```
1  Input:  P-SOLVER: a POMDP solver,
2           δ: convergence criterion, Γ: PO-POSG
3  Output: An approximate Nash equilibrium
4           (π_D, π_A)
5  Algorithm DFSP (P-SOLVER, δ, Γ)
6  │  Initialize π_D, π_A, δ̂
7  │  while δ̂ ≥ δ do
8  │  │  in parallel for k ∈ {D, A} do
9  │  │  │  π_k ←LOCAL-
   │  │  │      BRS(P-SOLVER, Γ, k, π_−k)
10 │  │  │  π̃_k ←COMPOSITE-STRATEGY(Γ, π_k)
11 │  │  │  π_k ←AVERAGE-STRATEGY(π_k, π̃_k)
12 │  │  │  δ̂ ←EXPLOITABILITY(π̃_D, π̃_A) (see (17))
13 │  end
14 │  return (π_D, π_A)
15 Procedure LOCAL-BRS(P-SOLVER, Γ, k, π_−k)
16 │  π_k ← ()
17 │  in parallel for w ∈ W, (i) ∈ V_w do
18 │  │  π_k ← π_k ⊕ P-SOLVER(ℳ_i^(k), π_−k)
19 │  return π_k
20 Procedure COMPOSITE-STRATEGY(Γ, π_k)
21 │  return π_k ←Procedure λ (s_t^(k), b_t^(k))
22 │  │  a_t^(k) ← ()
23 │  │  for w ∈ W, i ∈ V_w do
24 │  │  │  a_t^(k) ← a_t^(k) ⊕ (π_k^(i)(s_{i,t}^(k), b_{i,t}^(k)))
25 │  │  end
26 │  │  return a_t^(k)
```

---

and stochastic approximation to find best responses for the defender. In particular, to find best responses for the defender, we first solve the MDP defined in Sect. 6.3 via the value iteration algorithm [21, Eq. 6.21], which can be done efficiently due to full observability. After solving the MDP, we approximate the optimal switching curves defined in the proof of Theorem 2.C (Sect. 6.3) with the following linear approximation [21, Eq. 12.18].

$$\pi_D(\mathbf{b}^{(D)}) = \begin{cases} S & \text{if } \begin{bmatrix} 0 \ 1 \ \boldsymbol{\theta} \end{bmatrix} \begin{bmatrix} (\mathbf{b}^{(D)})^T \\ -1 \end{bmatrix} > 0 \\ C & \text{otherwise} \end{cases} \qquad \text{s.t } \boldsymbol{\theta} \in \mathbb{R}^2, \theta_2 > 0, \theta_1 \geq 1 \quad (16)$$

The coefficients $\boldsymbol{\theta}$ in (16) are estimated through the stochastic approximation algorithm in [21, Alg. 14] and [9, Alg. 1].

8   Digital Twin and System Identification

The DFSP algorithm described above approximates a Nash equilibrium of Γ (7) by simulating games and updating both players' strategies through reinforcement learning and dynamic programming. We identify the parameters required to instantiate these simulations through system identification based on data from the digital twin in Fig. 2. Details of this process and the configuration of the target infrastructure can be found in [11].

9   Experimental Evaluation

Our approach to find near-optimal defender strategies includes learning Nash equilibrium strategies via the DFSP algorithm and evaluating these strategies on the digital twin (see Fig. 2). This section describes the evaluation results.

Experiment Setup. We evaluate DFSP both on a digital twin of the target infrastructure and in simulations of synthetic infrastructures (see Fig. 1 and Fig. 2). The digital twin is deployed on a server with a 24-core INTEL XEON GOLD 2.10 GHz CPU and 768 GB RAM. Simulations of Γ and executions of DFSP run on a cluster with 2xTESLA P100 GPUS, 4xRTX8000 GPUS, and 3x16-core INTEL XEON 3.50 GHz CPUS. Code and hyperparameters for replicating the experiments is available in [11] and the references therein.

Convergence Metric. To estimate the convergence of the sequence of strategy pairs generated by DFSP, we use the *approximate exploitability* metric $\widehat{\delta}$ [31]:

$$\widehat{\delta} = \mathbb{E}_{\widehat{\pi}_{\mathrm{D}}, \pi_{\mathrm{A}}} [J] - \mathbb{E}_{\pi_{\mathrm{D}}, \widehat{\pi}_{\mathrm{A}}} [J] \tag{17}$$

where J is defined in (4) and $\widehat{\pi}_{\mathrm{k}}$ denotes an approximate best response strategy for player k. The closer $\widehat{\delta}$ becomes to 0, the closer $(\pi_{\mathrm{D}}, \pi_{\mathrm{A}})$ is to a Nash equilibrium.

Baseline Algorithms. We compare the performance of our approach ($\pi^{\mathrm{decomposition}}$) with two baselines: π^{full} and π^{workflow}. Baseline π^{full} solves the full game without decomposition and π^{workflow} decomposes the game on the workflow-level only.

We compare the performance of DFSP with that of Neural Fictitious Self-Play (NFSP) [13, Alg. 1] and PPO [26, Alg. 1], which are the most popular algorithms among related work (see [10, §VII]).

Baseline Strategies. We compare the defender strategies learned through DFSP with three baselines. The first baseline selects actions at random. The second baseline assumes prior knowledge of the opponent's actions and acts optimally based on this information. The last baseline acts according to the following heuristic: shut down a node $i \in \mathcal{V}$ when an IDPS alert occurs, i.e., when $\mathbf{o}_{i,t} > 0$.

9.1   Learning Best Responses Against Static Opponents

We first examine whether our method can discover effective strategies against a *static* opponent strategy, which in game-theoretic terms is the problem of finding best responses (8). The static strategies are defined in [11].

To measure the scalability of $\pi^{\mathrm{decomposition}}$ we compare its performance with π^{workflow} and π^{full} on synthetic infrastructures with varying number of nodes $|\mathcal{V}|$ and workflows $|\mathcal{W}|$. To evaluate the optimal stopping approach described in Sect. 7 we compare its rate of convergence with that of PPO. Figure 6a shows the learning curves. The red, purple, and pink curves represent the results obtained with $\pi^{\mathrm{decomposition}}$; the blue and beige curves represent the results obtained with

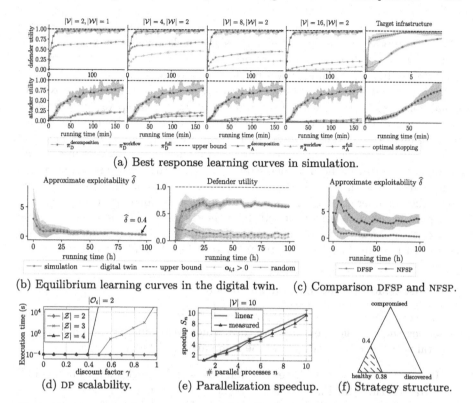

(a) Best response learning curves in simulation.

(b) Equilibrium learning curves in the digital twin.   (c) Comparison DFSP and NFSP.

(d) DP scalability.   (e) Parallelization speedup.   (f) Strategy structure.

Fig. 6. Evaluation results; the curves show the mean and 95% confidence interval for four random seeds; DP is short for dynamic programming; the speedup in (e) is calculated as $S_n = \frac{T_1}{T_n}$ where T_n is the completion time with n processes. (Color figure online)

π^{workflow}; the orange and green curves represent the results obtained with π^{full}; and the dashed black lines relate to the baseline strategy that assumes prior knowledge of the opponent's strategy.

We note in Fig. 6a that all the learning curves of $\pi^{\text{decomposition}}$ converge near the dashed black lines, which suggests that the learned strategies are close to best responses. In contrast, the learning curves of π^{workflow} and π^{full} do not converge near the dashed black lines within the measured time. This is expected as π^{workflow} and π^{full} can not be parallelized like $\pi^{\text{decomposition}}$. (The speedup of parallelization is shown in Fig. 6e.) Lastly, we note in the rightmost plot of Fig. 6a that the optimal stopping approach, which exploits the statement in Theorem 2.C, converges significantly faster than PPO. An example of a learned optimal stopping strategy based on the linear approximation in (16) is shown in Fig. 6f.

9.2   Learning Equilibrium Strategies Through Fictitious Play

Figures 6b–6c show the learning curves of the strategies obtained during the DFSP self-play process and the baselines introduced above. The red curves represent the results from the simulator; the blue curves show the results from the digital twin;

the green curve give the performance of the random baseline; the orange curve relate to the $\mathbf{o}_{i,t} > 0$ baseline; and the dashed black line gives the performance of the baseline strategy that assumes prior knowledge of the attacker actions.

We note that all learning curves in Fig. 6b converge, which suggests that the learned strategies converge as well. Specifically, we observe that the approximate exploitability (17) of the learned strategies converges to small values (left plot), which indicates that the learned strategies approximate a Nash equilibrium both in the simulator and in the digital twin. Further, we see from the middle plot that both baseline strategies show decreasing performance as the attacker updates its strategy. In contrast, the defender strategy learned through DFSP improves its performance over time. This shows the benefit of a game-theoretic approach where the defender strategy is optimized against a dynamic attacker.

Figure 6c compares DFSP with NFSP on the simulator. We observe that DFSP converges significantly faster than NFSP. The fast convergence of DFSP in comparison with NFSP is expected as DFSP is parallelizable while NFSP is not.

9.3   Discussion of the Evaluation Results

In this work, we propose a formal framework based on recursive decomposition for solving the intrusion response use case, which we evaluate experimentally on a digital twin. The key findings can be summarized as follows.

(i)   Our framework approximates optimal defender strategies for a practical IT infrastructure (see Fig. 6b). While we have not evaluated the learned strategies on the target infrastructure due to safety reasons, the fact that they achieve similar performance on the digital twin as on the simulator gives us confidence in the strategies' performance on the target infrastructure.

(ii)   Decomposition provides a scalable approach to automate intrusion response for IT infrastructures (see Fig. 6a and Fig. 6c). The intuition behind this finding is that decomposition allows to design efficient divide-and-conquer algorithms that can be parallelized (see Theorem 2.A–B and Algorithm 1).

(iii)   The theory of optimal stopping provides insight about optimal defender strategies, which enables efficient computation of best responses (see the rightmost plot in Fig. 6a). This property can be explained by the threshold structures of the best response strategies, which drastically reduce the search space of possible strategies (Theorem 2.C).

(iv)   Static defender strategies' performance deteriorate against a dynamic attacker whereas defender strategies learned through DFSP improve over time (see the right plot in Fig. 6b). This finding suggests fundamental limitations of static intrusion response systems, such as the Snort IDPS.

10   Conclusions

We include elements of game theory and reinforcement learning in a framework to address the problem of automated intrusion response for a realistic use case.

We formalize the use case as a partially observed stochastic game. We prove a decomposition theorem stating that the game decomposes recursively into subgames that can be solved efficiently and in parallel, and that the best response defender strategies exhibit threshold structures. This decomposition provides us with a scalable approach to learn near-optimal defender strategies. We develop Decompositional Fictitious Self-Play (DFSP) – a fictitious self-play algorithm for finding Nash equilibria. To assess the learned strategies for a target infrastructure, we evaluate them on a digital twin. The results demonstrate that DFSP converges in reasonable time to near-optimal strategies, both in simulation and on the digital twin, while a state-of-the-art algorithm makes little progress toward an optimal strategy within the same time frame.

References

1. Alpcan, T., Basar, T.: Network Security: A Decision and Game-Theoretic Approach, 1st edn. Cambridge University Press, Cambridge (2010)
2. Altman, E., et al.: Jamming game with incomplete information about the jammer. In: Conference on Performance Evaluation Methodologies and Tools (2009)
3. Bellman, R.: A Markovian decision process. J. Math. Mech. **6**(5), 679–684 (1957)
4. Brooks, R.: A robust layered control system for a mobile robot. IEEE J. Robot. Autom. **2**(1), 14–23 (1986)
5. Brown, G.W.: Iterative solution of games by fictitious play. In: Activity Analysis of Production and Allocation, pp. 374–376 (1951)
6. Cormen, T., et al.: Introduction to Algorithms, 4th edn. The MIT Press, Cambridge (2022)
7. Hammar, K., Stadler, R.: Finding effective security strategies through reinforcement learning and self-play. In: International Conference on Network and Service Management (CNSM 2020), Izmir, Turkey (2020)
8. Hammar, K., Stadler, R.: Learning intrusion prevention policies through optimal stopping. In: International Conference on Network and Service Management (CNSM 2021), Izmir, Turkey (2021). https://arxiv.org/pdf/2106.07160.pdf
9. Hammar, K., Stadler, R.: Intrusion prevention through optimal stopping. IEEE Trans. Netw. Serv. Manag. **19**(3), 2333–2348 (2022)
10. Hammar, K., Stadler, R.: Learning near-optimal intrusion responses against dynamic attackers. IEEE Trans. Netw. Serv. Manag. 1 (2023). https://doi.org/10.1109/TNSM.2023.3293413
11. Hammar, K., Stadler, R.: Scalable learning of intrusion responses through recursive decomposition (2023). https://arxiv.org/abs/2309.03292
12. Han, Y., et al.: Reinforcement learning for autonomous defence in software-defined networking. In: Bushnell, L., Poovendran, R., Başar, T. (eds.) GameSec 2018. LNCS, vol. 11199, pp. 145–165. Springer, Cham (2018). https://doi.org/10.1007/978-3-030-01554-1_9
13. Heinrich, J., Silver, D.: Deep reinforcement learning from self-play in imperfect-information games (2016). https://arxiv.org/abs/1603.01121
14. Hespanha, J., Prandini, M.: Nash equilibria in partial-information games on Markov chains. In: IEEE Conference on Decision and Control (2001)
15. Horák, K.: Scalable algorithms for solving stochastic games with limited partial observability. Ph.D. thesis, Czech Technical University in Prague (2019)

16. Horák, K., Bošanský, B.: Solving partially observable stochastic games with public observations. In: Proceedings of the AAAI Conference on Artificial Intelligence (2019)
17. Huang, L., Chen, J., Zhu, Q.: Factored Markov game theory for secure interdependent infrastructure networks. In: Rass, S., Schauer, S. (eds.) Game Theory for Security and Risk Management. SDGTFA, pp. 99–126. Springer, Cham (2018). https://doi.org/10.1007/978-3-319-75268-6_5
18. Huang, Y., Huang, L., Zhu, Q.: Reinforcement learning for feedback-enabled cyber resilience. Ann. Rev. Control 53, 273–295 (2022)
19. Kamhoua, C., et al.: Game Theory and Machine Learning for Cyber Security. Wiley, Hoboken (2021)
20. Kearns, M., Littman, M., Singh, S.: Graphical models for game theory. In: Seventeenth Conference on Uncertainty in Artificial Intelligence (UAI 2001) (2001)
21. Krishnamurthy, V.: Partially Observed Markov Decision Processes: From Filtering to Controlled Sensing (2016). https://doi.org/10.1017/CBO9781316471104
22. Nair, R., et al.: Networked distributed POMDPs: a synthesis of distributed constraint optimization and POMDPs. In: Conference on Artificial Intelligence and the Innovative Applications of Artificial Intelligence (2005)
23. Nash, J.F.: Non-cooperative games. Ann. Math. 54(2), 286–295 (1951)
24. Ouyang, Y., Tavafoghi, H., Teneketzis, D.: Dynamic games with asymmetric information: common information based perfect Bayesian equilibria and sequential decomposition. IEEE Trans. Autom. Control 62(1), 222–237 (2017)
25. Rasouli, M., Miehling, E., Teneketzis, D.: A scalable decomposition method for the dynamic defense of cyber networks. In: Rass, S., Schauer, S. (eds.) Game Theory for Security and Risk Management. SDGTFA, pp. 75–98. Springer, Cham (2018). https://doi.org/10.1007/978-3-319-75268-6_4
26. Schulman, J., et al.: Proximal policy optimization algorithms (2017). https://arxiv.org/abs/1707.06347
27. Seuken, S., Zilberstein, S.: Formal models and algorithms for decentralized decision making under uncertainty. Auton. Agents Multi-Agent Syst. 17, 190–250 (2008). https://doi.org/10.1007/s10458-007-9026-5
28. Shoham, Y., Leyton-Brown, K.: Multiagent Systems: Algorithmic, Game-Theoretic, and Logical Foundations, Cambridge (2009)
29. Siljak, D.: Large-Scale Dynamic Systems: Stability and Structure. Dover (1978)
30. Tambe, M.: Security and Game Theory: Algorithms, Deployed Systems, Lessons Learned, 1st edn. Cambridge University Press, Cambridge (2011)
31. Timbers, F., et al.: Approximate exploitability: learning a best response in large games (2020). https://arxiv.org/abs/2004.09677
32. Topkis, D.M.: Minimizing a submodular function on a lattice. Oper. Res. 26(2), 305–321 (1978). https://www.jstor.org/stable/169636
33. Tsemogne, O., Hayel, Y., Kamhoua, C., Deugoué, G.: Optimizing intrusion detection systems placement against network virus spreading using a partially observable stochastic minimum-threat path game. In: Fang, F., Xu, H., Hayel, Y. (eds.) GameSec 2022. LNCS, vol. 13727, pp. 274–296. Springer, Cham (2023). https://doi.org/10.1007/978-3-031-26369-9_14
34. Zan, X., et al.: A hierarchical and factored POMDP based automated intrusion response framework. In: Conference on Software Technology and Engineering (2010)
35. Zheng, J., Castañón, D.A.: Decomposition techniques for Markov zero-sum games with nested information. In: 52nd IEEE Conference on Decision and Control (2013)

Cyber Deception

Honeypot Allocation for Cyber Deception in Dynamic Tactical Networks: A Game Theoretic Approach

Md Abu Sayed[1]([envelope]) [ID], Ahmed H. Anwar[2]([envelope]) [ID], Christopher Kiekintveld[1]([envelope]) [ID], and Charles Kamhoua[2]([envelope]) [ID]

[1] University of Texas at El Paso, El Paso, TX 79968, USA
msayed@miners.utep.edu, cdkiekintveld@utep.edu
[2] DEVCOM Army Research Laboratory, Adelphi, MD 20783, USA
a.h.anwar@knights.ucf.edu, charles.a.kamhoua.civ@mail.mil

Abstract. Honeypots play a crucial role in implementing various cyber deception techniques as they possess the capability to divert attackers away from valuable assets. Careful strategic placement of honeypots in networks should consider not only network aspects but also attackers' preferences. The allocation of honeypots in tactical networks under network mobility is of great interest. To achieve this objective, we present a game-theoretic approach that generates optimal honeypot allocation strategies within an attack/defense scenario. Our proposed approach takes into consideration the changes in network connectivity. In particular, we introduce a two-player dynamic game model that explicitly incorporates the future state evolution resulting from changes in network connectivity. The defender's objective is twofold: to maximize the likelihood of the attacker hitting a honeypot and to minimize the cost associated with deception and reconfiguration due to changes in network topology. We present an iterative algorithm to find Nash equilibrium strategies and analyze the scalability of the algorithm. Finally, we validate our approach and present numerical results based on simulations, demonstrating that our game model successfully enhances network security. Additionally, we have proposed additional enhancements to improve the scalability of the proposed approach.

Keywords: Dynamic Games · Game Theory · Cyber Deception

Distribution Statement A: Approved for public release. Distribution is unlimited. Research was sponsored by the DEVCOM Army Research Laboratory and was accomplished under Cooperative Agreement Numbers W911NF-23-2-0012 and W911NF-13-2-0045 (ARL Cyber Security CRA). The views and conclusions contained in this document are those of the authors and should not be interpreted as representing the official policies, either expressed or implied, of the Army Research Laboratory or the U.S. Government. The U.S. Government is authorized to reproduce and distribute reprints for Government purposes notwithstanding any copyright notation herein.

J. Fu et al. (Eds.): GameSec 2023, LNCS 14167, pp. 195–214, 2023.
https://doi.org/10.1007/978-3-031-50670-3_10

1 Introduction

The cybersecurity domain encounters numerous complex issues due to the dynamic nature of threats and the intricate decision-making processes involved. One of the most powerful threats in cybersecurity is the Advanced Persistent Threat (APT) attack where attackers carry out highly targeted, long-term, stealthy attacks against government, military, and corporate organizations [1]. In many instances, APTs manage to establish a persistent and concealed presence within a targeted network for extended periods, sometimes lasting months or even years, without being detected.

Additional challenges include protecting dynamic and diverse mobile networks from intense, short attacks such as denial of service (DoS), especially in the context of the Internet of Battlefield Things (IoBT) [2] and tactical dynamic networks [3]. The attackers rely on lateral movement to utilize the network resources in reaching their targets. To counter this, defenders can employ appropriate actions to effectively detect and mitigate lateral movement. In this context, we consider cyber deception via honeypots to proactively mislead attackers.

Computer networks face several challenges that can impact their performance, security, and reliability. The rapid expansion of wireless networking has introduced numerous challenges, including network scalability, resource allocation, interference mitigation, and security. Software-Defined Networking (SDN) encounters new challenges and opportunities in networks, specifically regarding the functionality, performance, and scalability of SDN in cloud computing, IT organizations, and networking enterprises [4].

Mobility is a significant characteristic of tactical networks, which introduces distinct challenges such as intermittent network connectivity, temporary power loss, and communication issues. These challenges can be particularly problematic when multiple autonomous computers communicate through a network and interact with each other [5]. As a result, fixed deception policies are suboptimal since one needs to consider the connectivity of the computer network. In our work, we primarily focus on modeling cyber deception in dynamic tactical networks.

Cyber deception represents an advanced proactive technology in the field of cyber defense. Its purpose is to provide attackers with credible yet misleading information, effectively leading them astray. While deception techniques have traditionally been employed in the physical domain as a tactic of traditional warfare, their application has extended to the realm of cyberspace, serving as a means of intrusion detection and defense. In many ways, cyber deception shares similarities with non-cyber deception, encompassing comparable philosophical and psychological characteristics. Proactive measures can be employed with the objective of capturing the attackers and closely monitoring their actions. Honeypots play a vital role in this process, acting as simulated entities within the system or network to deceive the attacker. By studying the attacker's strategies and intentions through the use of honeypots, defenders can enhance their comprehension of the attack and subsequently develop more effective deception schemes [6].

Honeypots play a crucial role in the realm of cyber deception by serving as effective tools to mislead and divert attackers while consuming their valuable resources. These deceptive elements can be categorized into two types: low-interaction honeypots and high-interaction honeypots. Low-interaction honeypots simulate specific services and are typically implemented in a virtualized environment, offering a relatively simpler setup and operational process compared to high-interaction honeypots. However, it is important to note that low-interaction honeypots are more prone to detection by adversaries, making them easier to identify and bypass [7].

A key challenge in securing tactical networks lies in their mobile nature, rendering the defender's base policy ineffective and sub-optimal over time. For instance, defender honeypot allocation based on the initial network is not useful as network connectivity changes over time as well as not optimal over whole state space. Despite the increasing attention given to cyber deception in the past decade, there remains a gap in the literature regarding its incorporation of mobility features and anticipation of the future evolution of tactical networks. In this paper, we utilize dynamic attack graphs and game theory to model mobility in tactical networks. Specifically, when network mobility is present, the connectivity of the corresponding attack graph undergoes changes in specific edges, thereby redefining potential attack paths and possibly rendering some defender strategies ineffective. To the best of our knowledge, this framework represents a novel approach for proactive defense in the presence of network mobility.

This paper presents a novel approach for dynamic cyber deception via strategic honeypot allocation given a limited deception budget. By leveraging a game theoretic framework, our objective is to devise an effective honeypot allocation policy throughout the network attack graph that takes into account future changes in network connectivity. We model this problem as a two-player Markov game. In our analysis, the defender anticipates future network mobility. We assume a well-known attacker performed reconnaissance before launching this attack. The proposed model takes into account different node values that reflect the significance of each node in the network.

We design the state space according to potential changes in network connectivity assuming that a mobile node may lose communications with its neighbors inducing a transition to a new state. As shown in the results sections, it is beneficial for the defender to allocate honeypots according to the current network topology while taking into account the potential transitions to new topologies as well to reduce the cost of reconfiguration in the future. This results in a Markov game model that can be solved via standard Q-minimax algorithm [8]. We validate the efficiency of the proposed algorithm that showed a substantial improvement in mitigating attacker impact via deception using strategic allocation for honeypots. We balance the need for future look-ahead transitions and our numerical results show a faster convergence rate with a reasonable amount of iterations. We compare our defensive deception strategies to other allocation policies. Moreover, we demonstrate that our approach exhibits greater improvement against a less informed attacker that fails to anticipate future transitions.

This finding underscores the significance of cyber deception in enhancing network security.

We summarize our main contribution below:

- We design a dynamic game between defender and attacker, to generate a cyber deception strategy against lateral move attacks leveraging attack graphs under network mobility. The game is played on attack graphs that capture vulnerabilities, node importance, and network topology.
- We design a realistic set of future states considering the possibility of different node losing communications.
- We model our predictive model in the transition matrix of the Markov game model and solve for the stationary Nash equilibrium strategy at different states.
- Finally, we present numerical results that show the effectiveness of cyber deception as well as the fast convergence of the game solver with the presence of network mobility. We evaluated our approach under symmetric and asymmetric information between both players and analyzed the scalability of our approach under different assumptions.

The rest of the paper is organized as follows. We describe related work in Sect. 2. In Sect. 3, we discuss the system model, define the game model, and propose our deception approach. In Sect. 4 we present the methodology of network mobility-assisted cyber deception. Our numerical results are presented in Sect. 5 and in Sect. 6 we conclude our work and discuss the potential future extension of our research.

2   Related Work

Our research builds upon existing work on cyber deception and games on attack graphs to model lateral movement attacks and characterizes game-theoretic deception strategies with the presence of network mobility.

2.1   Attack Graph

Attack modeling techniques, such as attack graphs (AGs), provide a graph-based approach to representing and visualizing cyber-attacks on computer networks [9]. However, the scalability of generating attack graphs poses a significant challenge, with existing works struggling to handle large enterprise networks [10]. In this study, we focus on a simplified attack graph where nodes represent vulnerable hosts and edges represent specific exploits for attacker reachability. While this model may not capture every vulnerability, it effectively demonstrates potential attack paths that adversaries can exploit, which is crucial for generating optimal honeypot allocation policies. It is important to note that attack graphs are limited in their ability to directly model mobility, but effectively modifying attack graphs can be used to model mobility in tactical networks.

2.2   Game Theoretic Deception

In cybersecurity research, game theoretic defensive deception has been extensively addressed. Schlenker et al. [11] propose a deception game for defender who decides on deception in response to the attacker's observation while the attacker is either uninformed of the deceit or aware of it. The comprehensive game model of hypergame theory [12] has been used to simulate the many subjective viewpoints of participants in uncertain situations. Wan et al. [13] discuss hypergame-based deception against advanced persistent threat attacks performing multiple attacks performed in the stages of cyber kill chain. Sayed et al. [14] propose a game theoretic approach for zero-day vulnerability analysis and deceptive mitigation against zero-day vulnerability. Zhu et al. [15] discuss the synergies between game theory and machine learning [16, 17] to formulate defensive deception. In this paper, we extend cyber deception under network mobility.

2.3   Network Deception

Computer network deception research focuses on developing techniques, strategies, and technologies to enhance the effectiveness of deception as a proactive cyber defense. Lu et al. [18] describe the fabrication or manipulation of network-level information such as network topology, host information, tarpits, and traffic information. Chiang et al. [19] discuss the use of defensive cyber deception to enhance the security, dependability of network systems, and focus on the application of Software-Defined Networking (SDN). Urias et al. [20] discuss the use of computer network deception as a means to gather threat intelligence.

2.4   Mobility in Tactical Network

In tactical networks, mobility refers to the ability of devices or agents to move within the network while maintaining connectivity and resource access. Mobility involves features like protocol support, seamless roaming, handover management, and location tracking. However, it presents challenges such as intermittent connectivity, location management, handover & roaming efficiency, quality of service, security & privacy, and scalability. Overcoming these challenges is essential to achieve uninterrupted connectivity and adaptability in various environments [5]. Mobility also does not follow the same pattern as traffic expansion [21].

The characteristics of mobility in tactical networks include various aspects related to the movement and connection of users or nodes within network. Pirozmand et al. [22] examined human mobility in terms of its geographical, temporal, and connectivity properties. They explore mobility models, traces, and forecasting methods to give a thorough picture of how nodes move within networks. Abdulla et al. [23] analyzed the mobility characteristics of commonly used models, focusing on inter-contact times and the approximation of exponential distributions in opportunistic network scenarios.

The impact of node mobility in tactical networks is a crucial area of research, focusing on how the movement of nodes within a network affects various network characteristics and performance. Fu et al. [24] investigated the impact of node mobility on cascading failures in spatial networks. This includes studying the influence of node mobility on network load redistribution, the cascading process, and the robustness of network configurations against cascading failures. Xia et al. [25] proposed a cluster-based routing protocol called FASTR to mitigate the impact of node mobility in networks with high node mobility and low group mobility. This protocol utilizes a mobile backbone to address the challenges associated with node mobility.

The mobility model and its parameters significantly impact network communication in wireless mobile opportunistic networks. Various mobility models are proposed to describe random movement patterns of nodes in ad hoc networks, emphasizing the importance of considering node mobility in network design and analysis [26]. Pala et al. [27] investigate how node mobility influences energy consumption and network lifetime. Results show that mobility can improve energy balancing up to a certain level, but excessive mobility may degrade energy balancing in wireless networks.

Urias et al. [28] highlighted the limited number of deception platforms that have been successfully shown to enable strategic deception in computer network operations environments. This indicates that the development of specific tools and techniques for combining network mobility and cyber deception may still be an area of ongoing exploration. Therefore, network mobility can be incorporated in designing deception techniques such as dynamic movement and placement of deceptive elements within the network.

In our work, we develop deception techniques against lateral movement attacks considering network mobility. This is the first model that explicitly considers the impact of network mobility in designing proactive game-theoretic policies for optimizing deception resources. We present our system model and game formulation in the following sections.

3   System Model

3.1   Attack Graph Model

We consider a targeted attack that follows a thorough reconnaissance phase, during which the adversary gathers all the necessary information about the network structure, node properties, and existing vulnerabilities. To represent these features, we adopt a modified version of the attack graph model [29] denoted as $G_1(\mathcal{N}, \mathcal{E}, \theta, \mathcal{V})$ where

- $\mathcal{N}$ represents the set of nodes
- $\mathcal{E}$ represents the set of edges
- θ represents the set of node types. We assume that each non-leaf[1] node can have two types such as $\wedge$ (AND), $\vee$ (OR).
- $\mathcal{V}$ represents the value associate with each node.

---

[1] Non-leaf nodes can be predecessor of at least one node.

The set of nodes is interconnected through the set of edges, which depict their accessibility and network connectivity. The defender classifies the nodes based on their importance, functionality, and role through a course of an attack action. Within this classification, there are two distinct subsets of nodes, the set of entry nodes E and the set of target nodes T. The remaining nodes are intermediate nodes that an attacker must compromise while progressing from an entry node (attack start node $\in E$) toward a target node $\in T$. The defender decides what nodes are most valuable and are more likely to be targeted and hence labels them as targets either based on previous attack reports or according to expert decisions.

In this graph, each node represents a host that has one or more vulnerabilities that can be exploited to reach a neighboring node. The edge represents the connection that can be utilized by malicious users to reach the next targeted node. A legitimate user at node v possesses the appropriate credentials to access node u. However, an adversary can only reach node u by exploiting a vulnerability. At the same time, there must exist an exploitable vulnerability at u, an open port at v and node v is reachable via a communication link from node u. Such exploitation possibility is represented by $e_{u,v} \in \mathcal{E}$. Each node $i \in \mathcal{N}$ is assigned a value $\mathcal{V}(i)$ which denotes node importance. Therefore, $G_1(\mathcal{N}, \mathcal{E}, \theta, \mathcal{V})$ represents the attack graph, which is assumed to be known to both the defender and the attacker.

The attack graph model also considers node types θ. The types of nodes, denoted by $\wedge$ (AND) or $\vee$ (OR), determine the conditions under which a node can be controlled by an adversary. If a node is marked with $\wedge$ (AND), it means that all of its predecessor nodes must be controlled by the adversary for the node itself to come under adversary control. On the other hand, if a node is marked with $\vee$ (OR), it means that only one of its predecessor nodes needs to be controlled by the adversary for the node to come under adversary control.

In the case of computer network attacks, each adversary operates independently, and exploits a set of nodes to reach a specific target. Therefore, all the nodes within the attack graph are designated with the $\vee$ (OR) node type.

Node mobility denotes node removal on the computer network due to multiple factors including hardware failure, network maintenance, network redesign, security concern, decommissioning, network upgrade, and network optimization. In a tactical network, if all nodes are moving in the same direction and speed which allows them to maintain communications the attack remains static. However, due to specific tactical requirements, one or more nodes may be assigned to change their course and go in other directions resulting in a new attack graph. Removing a node eliminates all exploitable vulnerabilities of that node. In other words, it removes all edges connected to it. We consider a complete information structure where the defender and attacker can observe node mobility in the network. Hence, both players can update the attack graph of the game.

Figure 1 represents a 7-node tree attack graph consisting of one entry node (1), four intermediate nodes (2, 3, 4, 6), and two target nodes (5, 7). In this network, there is one available path for reaching target node (7), while there

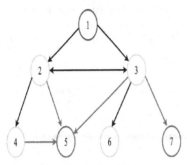

(a) Initial network with 7 nodes.

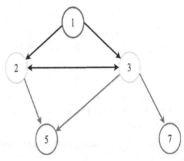

(b) Network after mobility with 5 nodes.

Fig. 1. 7-node tree network topology with a single entry node and two target nodes (5, 7) and because of node mobility, node 4 and node 6 will likely abandon the group in the future.

are three paths for reaching target node (5). Due to node mobility, nodes 4 and 6 are likely to lose communications in the future, leaving only two available attack paths to reach target node (5). Future mobility information should impact the initial honeypot allocation strategy deployed by the defender from the beginning. Our model quantifies and captures the advantages of considering the network's future evolution. In this example, we consider nodes leaving the network, however, the proposed model is general to adapt any future topologies including adding or removing new connections, or new nodes.

3.2 Defender Model

At a given state, the defender strategically places a set of honeypots along the network edges among the set of edges leading to the set of target nodes T to deceive the attacker. The honeypot budget is denoted as H. Hence, the defender's action space, denoted as $\mathcal{A}_d$, consists of possible allocation vector $\mathbf{e}$ in which $\mathcal{A}_d = \{\mathbf{e} \in 2^{\mathcal{E}} \mid \mathbf{e}^T 1 \leq H\}$. Where, $\mathbf{e}$ is a binary vector of length $|\mathcal{E}|$, where each entry $\mathbf{e}(i)$ equals 1 if a honeypot is allocated along the ith edge, and is set to zero otherwise. To balance the defender strategies, the defender pays a cost, C_d, per each installed honeypot in the network, otherwise, the defender will always try to maximize the number of allocated honeypots. The total cost can be expressed as $C_d \times |a_d|_1$, where $|a_d|_1$ is the number of honeypots associated with the action a_d. Finally, assuming both players are rational, the defender aims to reduce the attacker's reward by placing honeypots on edges that are attractive to the attacker, while minimizing the total cost of the played deception strategy.

3.3 Attacker Model

The defender considers a practical scenario where the attacker had gathered valuable reconnaissance information about the network topology before launching this attack. Hence, the attacker is launching a targeted attack to compromise a specific subset of nodes, T. Therefore, she selects one of the possible attack paths to reach a target node to maximize its expected reward. Thus, the attacker's action space, denoted as $\mathcal{A}_a$, consists of all possible attack paths starting from an entry node $u \in E$ to a target node $v \in T$. The attacker incurs an attack cost that depends on the selected attack path. We consider a cost due to traversing a node in the attack graph denoted by C_a. The attacker faces a tradeoff between traversing important nodes while reducing his overall attack cost.

3.4 Reward Function

The reward function is formulated to capture the tradeoff that faces each player. For each action profile played $(a_d, a_a) \in \mathcal{A}_d \times \mathcal{A}_a$, the defender receives a reward $R_d(a_d, a_a)$ and the attacker reward is R_a. We consider a zero-sum game where $R_a + R_d = 0$. Recall that each node $i \in \mathcal{N}$ is assigned a value $v(i) \in \mathcal{V}$ that reflects its importance, the defender gains more by protecting high-valued nodes via correct placement of honeypots. On the other hand, the attacker reward increases when attacking nodes of high values along the selected attack path while evading honeypots.

The defender reward is expressed as:

$$R_d(a_d, a_a) = \sum_{i \in a_a} \left[Cap \cdot v(i) \cdot \mathbf{1}_{\{i \in a_d\}} - Esc \cdot v(i) \cdot \mathbf{1}_{\{i \notin a_d\}} \right]$$

$$- C_d \cdot \|a_d\|_1 + C_a(a_a) \qquad (1)$$

Here, Cap represents the capture reward received by the defender when the attacker encounters a honeypot along the selected attack path a_a. On the other hand, Esc denotes the gain for the attacker upon a successful attack from one node to another while progressing toward the target node.

Finally, C_d and $C_a(a_a)$ are the cost per honeypot, and attack cost, respectively. The attack cost is proportional to the length of the attack path as the attacker could become less stealthy due to numerous moves.

Now we define a two-player zero-sum game for a particular state, s, $\Gamma(s)(\mathcal{P}, \mathcal{A}, \mathcal{R})$, where $\mathcal{P}$ is the set of the two players (i.e., defender and attacker). The game action space $\mathcal{A} = \mathcal{A}_d \times \mathcal{A}_a$ as defined above, and the reward function $\mathcal{R} = (R_d, R_a)$.

The finite game developed above admits at least one NE in mixed strategies [30]. Let $\mathbf{x}$ and $\mathbf{y}$ denote the mixed strategies of defender, and attacker when the game is played on graph, G. The defender expected reward of the game can be expressed as:

$$U_d(G) = \mathbf{x}^T R_d(G) \mathbf{y} \qquad (2)$$

where $R_d(G)$ is the matrix of the game played on G and the attacker expected reward $U_a(G) = -U_d(G)$. Both defender and attacker can obtain their NE mixed strategies $\mathbf{x}^*$ and $\mathbf{y}^*$ via a linear program (LP) as follows,

$$\text{maximize} \atop \mathbf{x} \qquad\qquad U_d$$

$$\text{subject to} \quad \sum_{a_d \in \mathcal{A}_d} R_d(a_d, a_a) x_{a_d} \geq U_d, \qquad \forall a_a \in \mathcal{A}_a. \tag{3}$$

$$\sum_{a_d \in \mathcal{A}_d} x_{a_d} = 1, \quad x_{a_d} \geq 0,$$

where x_{a_d} is the probability of taking action $a_d \in \mathcal{A}_d$.

Similarly, the attacker's mixed strategy can be obtained through a minimizer LP under $\mathbf{y}$ of U_d.

4   Dynamic Game Model

In the previous section, we show the formulation of one stage game. In this section, we extend the formulation for a dynamic muti-stage game (Markov game) between the defender and the attacker due to network mobility.

In a dynamic environment, the game is played under varying circumstances each time, encompassing different network connectivity configurations, changes in connectivity, and as well as patching existing vulnerabilities. In our work, we primarily focus on the mobility of the network over time. To comprehensively analyze the progression and evolution of this game, we employ a Markov game framework where the state of the game captures all information needed to generate a honeypot allocation strategy. We assume that the defender changes the allocations based on the new topology. Players reward is the total reward over all future states.

Let s denote the state of the game defined as the attack graph associated with the network topology at state s. A dynamic game Γ is defined as the tuple $(\mathcal{K}, \mathcal{A}, \mathcal{S}, \mathcal{P}, \mathcal{R})$, where $\mathcal{K}$ is a set of two players, $\mathcal{S}$ is a finite set of states. We consider an uncontrolled dynamic game where $\mathcal{P} : \mathcal{S} \times \mathcal{S}' \to [0, 1]$ is a transition probability function between states such as $P(s, s')$ denotes the probability of transitioning from state s to the future state s'. The action space $\mathcal{A} = \Pi_{s \in \mathcal{S}} \mathcal{A}(s)$ and reward function $\mathcal{R}$. Each player aims to maximize his long-term expected payoff. Where $R(s')$ is the immediate reward as defined in Sect. 3 for any state s'. A terminal state $s'' \in \mathcal{S}$ is a state, where no transition future transitions can be reached from s''. In other words, at any terminal state, players receive immediate rewards onward.

4.1   State Space and Game Transitions

Given an initial attack graph (full topology), network mobility may induce new connections, and/or result in removing nodes from the network topology. As we discussed in the Sect. 1, node mobility in tactical networks renders the defender's base strategy ineffective, and requires reconfigurations to the initial honeypot allocation strategies as well as other security resources in the network.

For practical constraints, it is difficult for the defender to anticipate new connections to be added to the initial attack graph due to mobility from the initial topology. Therefore, and without loss of generality, our model does not consider transitioning to such states. Additionally, we focus on removing connections due to losing communications between mobile nodes/agents. The defender builds this model using information regarding node movement patterns in the future. For simplicity, we consider one node change at a time. In other words, $\mathcal{N}(s) - \mathcal{N}(s') = u$, where u is a node moving away from the tactical network set of nodes/agents. To formally define our Markov game, the defender needs to compute the transition probability matrix, $\mathcal{P}$. When node u moves away, it is removed from the attack graph state, and hence we transition to a new state s'. The transition probability, denoted as $P(s, s')$, is defined as $1 - (\text{value proportion} \times \text{degree proportion})$

$$p(s, s') = 1 - \frac{\nu(u)}{\nu_{\max}} \times \frac{\delta(u)}{\delta_{\max}}, \tag{4}$$

where $0 < \nu(u) < \nu_{\max}$ is the value assigned to node u, $\delta(u)$ is the degree of node u where $\delta_{\max}$ is the max node degree in the network. The formulation in (4) follows a practical assumption that high-valued nodes and central nodes in the network are less likely to abandon the tactical network. However, a node with less connectivity and leaf nodes will have a higher probability of being disconnected. Additionally, we assign a non-zero probability for no state change (i.e., self-transition). Hence, $p(s, s) = \mu$, and $\sum_{s' \neq s} p(s, s') = 1 - \mu$, $\forall s \in \mathcal{S}$, such that μ is the chance of experiencing no mobility. This fully defines the dynamic game model.

4.2   Nash Equilibrium Analysis

Let $x^i(s)$; $i = 1, \ldots, |\mathcal{A}_d|(s)$, and $y^j(s)$; $j = 1, \ldots, |\mathcal{A}_a|(s)$, denote the probability that the defender and attacker play the ith and j^{th} pure actions at state s from their corresponding available actions spaces, $\mathcal{A}_d(s)$ and $\mathcal{A}_a(s)$, respectively. A stochastic stationary policy is readily defined over all states as $\pi_d = \{\mathbf{x}(s^1), \ldots, \mathbf{x}(s^n)\}$ for the defender, and $\pi_a = \{\mathbf{y}(s^1), \ldots, \mathbf{y}(s^n)\}$ for the attacker, where $n = |\mathcal{S}|$ is the total number of states.

Each player can maximize their expected reward by greedily maximizing the $Q(s)$-function at each state which is defined below in Eq. (10). The main goal of the defender is to maximize the expected discounted rewards. Under some stationary defense and attack policies, π_d and π_a respectively, the expected sum of discounted rewards starting from some initial state $s \in \mathcal{S}$ at time $t = 0$ is given by:

$$V(s, \pi_d, \pi_a) = \mathbb{E}\left[\sum_{t=0}^{\infty} \gamma^t R_d\left(s_t, a_d, a_a, s_{t+1}\right) \Big| s_0 = s, \pi_d, \pi_a\right], \tag{5}$$

It is worth noting that, the immediate reward $R_d(.)$ depends not only on the current state s but on the future state s' as well. The expectation in (5) is taken over the players' stationary policies (noting that π_d and π_a are randomized policies) and the state evolution, denoted as $\mathcal{P}(.)$. The subscript t represents the t-th stage, and $0 < \gamma < 1$ is a discount factor. Based on the findings in Sect. 3, this finite game achieves a value $V(s)$ at each state s. Moreover, there exists a mixed strategy Nash equilibrium (NE) where $V^{(}s)$ denotes the value under the equilibrium mixed strategies $\pi_d^*(s)$ and $\pi_a^*(s)$ at this state. To determine the optimal stationary policies for both players (i.e., NE), can be learned using value iteration over the value function at each state which is equivalent to finding the value of the game which is defined as:

$$V^*(s) := V(s, \mathbf{x}^*(s)^*, \mathbf{y}^*(s)^*) = \max_{\mathbf{x}(s)} \min_{\mathbf{y}(s)} V(s, \mathbf{x}(s), \mathbf{y}(s)); \qquad \forall s \in \mathcal{S} \qquad (6)$$

The optimal randomized stationary policies $\mathbf{x}^*(s)$ and $\mathbf{y}^*(s)$ for state s are the solutions to the following equation:

$$V^*(s) = \max_{\mathbf{x}(s)} \min_{\mathbf{y}(s)} \mathbb{E}\left[R(s, a^{(d)}, a^{(a)}, s') + \gamma V^*(s') \Big| \mathbf{x}(s), \mathbf{y}(s) \right], \qquad (7)$$

where the immediate reward term is given by

$$\mathbb{E}\left[R(s, a_d, a_a, s') \Big| \mathbf{x}(s), \mathbf{y}(s) \right] = \sum_{s' \in \mathcal{S}} \sum_{a_d \in \mathcal{A}_d} \sum_{a_a \in \mathcal{A}_a} R(s, a_d, a_a, s') x(s) y(s) p(s', s) \qquad (8)$$

Thus, the optimal stationary policies are $\pi_d^* = \{\mathbf{x}^*(s^1), \dots, \mathbf{x}^*(s^n)\}$, $\pi_a^* = \{\mathbf{y}^*(s^1), \dots, \mathbf{y}^*(s^n)\}$.

A Dynamic game can be solved using value iteration following Markov Decision Process (MDP) intuition [8]. In this context, the value of state s by solving:

$$V(s) = \max_{\pi_d \in \Delta(\mathcal{A}_d)} \min_{a_a \in \mathcal{A}_a} Q(s, a_d, a_a), \qquad (9)$$

where $Q(., a_d, a_a)$ denotes the quality of the state-action pair defined as the total expected discounted reward achieved by following a non-stationary policy that takes action a_d and then continues with the optimal policy thereafter. For a dynamic game, the state-action quality function is defined as:

$$Q(s, a_d, a_a) = \mathbb{E}\left[R(s, a_d, a_a, s') + \gamma V^*(s') \Big| a_d, a_a \right] \qquad (10)$$

We solve (7) to find the optimal policy, by iterating over the value function following the Q-minimax algorithm introduced in [8].

$$V^*(s) = \max_{\mathbf{x}(s) \in \Delta(\mathcal{A}_d)} \min_{a_a \in \mathcal{A}_a} \sum_{a_d \in \mathcal{A}_d} Q(s, a_d, a_a) x^{a_d}(s), \qquad (11)$$

The tabular nature of the Q-minimax algorithm evidently faces the curse of dimensionality due to the size of the state-action space. To enhance its scalability, we experiment with various techniques, such as limiting the state space to include future states that impact the attack paths leading to target nodes. In the following section, we present our numerical results and compare the performance of the learned policies derived from our game model with other deceptive policies.

Algorithm 1. Predictive Model (Proposed Algorithm)

 1: **procedure** INPUT(Topology, H, Esc, Cap, C_d, C_a, $\mathcal{V}$)
 2:     Initialize: $\mathcal{S}$, s0, entry node, E, T
 3:     $h = 1$
 4:     **while** $h < \ell$ **do**
 5:         Generate all new nodes at depth h
 6:         Define and solve all static game at depth h
 7:         $h + +$
 8:     **end while**
 9:     $h = l - 1$
10:     **while** $h > 0$ **do**
11:         Calculate $(\mathbf{x}^*(s^h), \mathbf{y}^*(s^h))$
12:         $h - -$
13:     **end while**
14:     **Return** (π_d^*, π_a^*)
15: **end procedure**

---

5   Numerical Results

In this section, we analyze and validate our game-theoretic model by examining the obtained numerical results. Specifically, we evaluate the convergence, effectiveness, and scalability of our approach. Firstly, we ensure and demonstrate the convergence of the extended Q-Learning algorithm to optimal (Nash equilibrium) strategies as well as the convergence of both the state value function as well as the rate of convergence at different networks. Secondly, we evaluate the performance of the developed approach by comparing the attacker's reward against various deception policies, including random, myopic (which ignores future transitions), and our policy based on the proposed predictive model. We consider formulation including full state space and compact state space. Lastly, we assess the scalability of our algorithm by comparing its performance on both full state and compact state space formulations.

We analyze the potential impact of network mobility by generating attack graph by NetworkX library and the attack graph also follows the definition in Sect. 3.1. We identify the subsets of entry and target nodes. Each intermediate node is assigned a value generated randomly between 10 and 50. Our 20-node network topology has 3 entry nodes (in blue) and 3 target nodes (in red) as shown in Fig. 2. For this 20-node network, the defender has 10 actions for honeypot allocations including (6, 12), (5, 11), (16, 19), (11, 15), (0, 5), (16, 20), (12, 16),

Fig. 2. Network topology consists of 20 nodes, with entry nodes represented in blue, target nodes in red, and intermediate nodes in yellow. (Color figure online)

(0, 6), (15, 19), (15, 18), while the attacker selects between 4 attack paths: path1 = [0, 5, 11, 15, 18], path2 = [0, 5, 11, 15, 19], path3 = [0, 6, 12, 16, 19], path4 = [0, 6, 12, 16, 20].

To incorporate network mobility, we remove nodes from the attack graph, leading to transitioning to a new state and having a modified attack graph. We then explore how to update the defender's base policy by considering both future rewards and transitions. To address the dimensionality of the Q-minimax algorithm, we adopt a formulation with a two-step look-ahead. Additionally, we explore two different state-space representations. The first is a full state space that encompasses all possible transitions, where any node in the intermediate subset can leave the network, resulting in a new state transition. The second is a compact state space that includes only future states associated with nodes belonging to attack paths. The compact state representation is based on the intuition that the mobility of nodes that do not belong to any attack path will have no impact on the optimality of the defender's strategies. For the 20-node network, the full state space consists of 272 states, while the compact state space has 19 states.

Convergence: In Fig. 3, we illustrate the convergence of the value function for a sample state S_0 in both the full and compact state formulation. The value function reaches convergence in less than 15 iterations. In each iteration, $Q(s, a_d, a_a)$ is updated, and the value of the state updates based on that. The convergence value of the state S_0 is different for full and compact state space as they have different numbers of states, but both signify that incorporating mobility info in player strategies is always beneficial in tactical networks. This is associated with the convergence of the corresponding defense and attack strategies, as shown in Fig. 4a and 4b.

Defender's strategy reaches convergence to the Nash Equilibrium (NE) policy depicted in Fig. 4a, where three actions have non-zero probability values while seven actions have zero probability values. Defender mixes between these 3 locations to deploy honeypot based on node significance and potential future rewards afterward. Simultaneously, the attacker's strategy converges to a NE

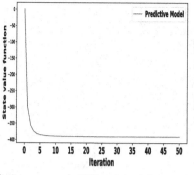

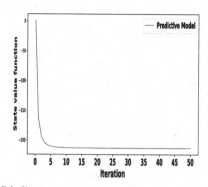

(a) Convergence of the state value function over full state space.

(b) Convergence of the state value function over compact state space.

Fig. 3. Convergence of the state value function under various state spaces over network mobility.

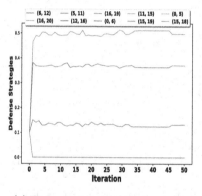

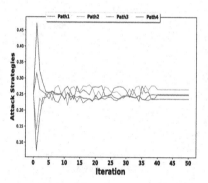

(a) Defender strategy convergences.

(b) Attacker strategy convergences.

Fig. 4. Defender and attacker strategy at a sample state converges to a mixed NE strategy at full state space.

policy as shown in Fig. 4b. Attacker selects (mixing randomly) among paths 2,3,4 with the presence of mobility as selecting between these paths maximizes the attacker expected reward as well as assists the attacker in successfully conducting lateral movement attacks and reaching the target, while playing path 1 with zero probability.

Performance: In Fig. 5, we analyze the attacker's reward under different defender policies, considering random, myopic, and our predictive model policies, for both the full state and compact state formulations. Both figures (a, b) demonstrate that the predictive model policy outperforms both other policies, weak deception policies result in increasing the attacker reward. The variations in the attacker's reward across different entry nodes can be attributed to changes in the attacker and defender action spaces, the availability of new attack paths, as

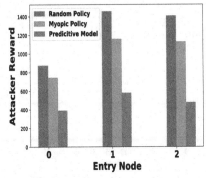
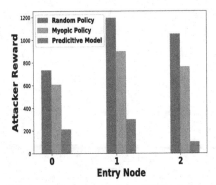

(a) Attacker reward over various defender policy in full state space.

(b) Attacker reward over different defender policy in compact state space.

Fig. 5. Attacker reward for different defender policies over entry nodes under various state spaces.

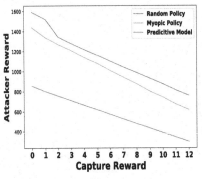
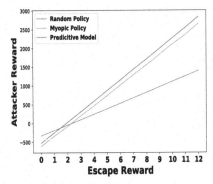

(a) Attacker reward for different defender policy over capture values.

(b) Attacker reward for various defender policy over escape values.

Fig. 6. Attacker reward at a sample state for different capture and escape values.

well as the intermediate node spaces showing that entry node 1 is more impactful when compromised.

Figure 6a demonstrates when the capture reward increases, the attacker's overall reward decreases across various defender policies. It is worth noting here that the attacker has no option to completely back off assuming a persistent attacker. On the other hand, Fig. 6b shows that as the attacker's escape reward increases, the attacker's reward continuously increases across different defender policies. It is important to note that the negative values of the escape rewards (0–2) do not contradict the results, as they signify a decrease in the attacker's reward. Overall, it shows again that the myopic policy outperforms the random policy while adhering to the predictive model policy results in the most significant reduction in the attacker's reward.

Figure 7 illustrates the attacker reward for different points of time at different deception policies for a 50-node network. For the node at S_2 (terminal state), the attacker reward remains the same for both the myopic and predictive model policies, as there are no future states reward to be considered onward from that state. At S_1, the attacker reward is slightly higher for the defender's myopic policy compared to the predictive model policy. However, the improvement between the two policies becomes more significant at S_0, highlighting the importance of accounting for future evolution due to mobility instead of responding to sudden changes in network connectivity in a reactive fashion. Consequently, this demonstrates that proactive deception provides an advantage to the defender, highlighting the potential impact of implementing a moving target defense strategy alongside deception. Such an approach can disrupt the reconnaissance information that an adversary may gather regarding future transitions in the network.

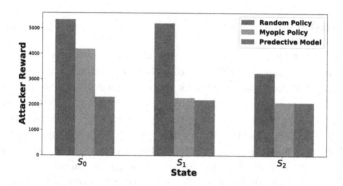

Fig. 7. Attacker reward over various depth nodes in 50 nodes network.

Scalability: We generate different Watts-Strogatz graphs by NetworkX library and demonstrate the overall complexity of different formulations under various parameters in Fig. 8. In this context, the variable H represents the number of honeypots, and K represents the average number of nearest neighbors to each node. In Fig. 8 the running time increases exponentially for the full state-space consideration due to the involvement of the intermediate node space in mobility. In addition, increasing the honeypot budget increases, which enlarges the defender's action space, and also increases the runtime. However, considering the compact state-space formulation results in 44% reduction in runtime compared to full state space for a network of 100 nodes, and $H = 2$.

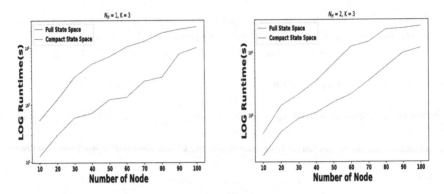

Fig. 8. Scalability in the number of nodes in the network under full and compact state spaces.

6   Conclusion and Future Work

In this paper, we present a dynamic game model involving a defender and an attacker to analyze the effectiveness of cyber deception in mitigating lateral move attacks in the presence of network mobility. Our proposed approach incorporates a multistage node removal technique and a predictive model to determine stationary mixed strategies by solving the dynamic game. We evaluate the effectiveness of the deception method under different network settings. Our numerical results and simulations it is evidence that cyber deception strategies were able to mitigate the attack impact. Finally, we showcase the scalability of our approach in terms of network size under mobility and provide a compact state space.

There are several potential extensions to this work. One avenue for further exploration is optimizing the node removal process through parallel computation, which can significantly improve speed. However, addressing the inter-dependency between states in parallel calculations requires further investigation. Additionally, network mobility can be modeled as a moving target defense, involving the implementation of various strategies and techniques to make the network more dynamic and unpredictable for potential attackers. This can be achieved through careful planning and coordination. We also would like to consider the erroneous topology case, where the defender can obtain a noisy version of the topology. Quantifying the noise and leveraging stochastic attack graph models can help address this case which is part of our ongoing research. Another obvious extension is using function approximation such as deep Q-learning to scale to much larger/more complex games.

References

1. Mandiant Intelligence Center. Apt1: Exposing one of China's cyber espionage units. Mandian.com (2013)
2. Abuzainab, N., Saad, W.: Dynamic connectivity game for adversarial internet of battlefield things systems. IEEE Internet Things J. **5**(1), 378–390 (2017)

3. Burbank, J.L., Chimento, P.F., Haberman, B.K., Kasch, W.T.: Key challenges of military tactical networking and the elusive promise of manet technology. IEEE Commun. Mag. **44**(11), 39–45 (2006)
4. Jammal, M., Singh, T., Shami, A., Asal, R., Li, Y.: Software defined networking: state of the art and research challenges. Comput. Netw. **72**, 74–98 (2014)
5. National Science Foundation. Advances in computer mobility, connectivity and networks. https://new.nsf.gov/news/advances-computer-mobility-connectivity-networks. Accessed Jan 2023
6. Wang, C., Zhuo, L.: Cyber deception: overview and the road ahead. IEEE Secur. Priv. **16**(2), 80–85 (2018)
7. Mokube, I., Adams, M.: Honeypots: concepts, approaches, and challenges. In: Proceedings of the 45th Annual Southeast Regional Conference, pp. 321–326 (2007)
8. Littman, M.L.: Markov games as a framework for multi-agent reinforcement learning. In: Machine Learning Proceedings 1994, pp. 157–163. Elsevier (1994)
9. Lallie, H.S., Debattista, K., Bal, J.: A review of attack graph and attack tree visual syntax in cyber security. Comput. Sci. Rev. **35**, 100219 (2020)
10. Ou, X., Boyer, W.F., McQueen, M.A.: A scalable approach to attack graph generation. In: Proceedings of the 13th ACM Conference on Computer and Communications Security, pp. 336–345 (2006)
11. Schlenker, A., Thakoor, O., Xu, H., Fang, F., Tambe, M., Vayanos, P.: Game theoretic cyber deception to foil adversarial network reconnaissance. In: Jajodia, S., Cybenko, G., Subrahmanian, V.S., Swarup, V., Wang, C., Wellman, M. (eds.) Adaptive Autonomous Secure Cyber Systems, pp. 183–204. Springer, Cham (2020). https://doi.org/10.1007/978-3-030-33432-1_9
12. Fraser, N.M., Hipel, K.W.: Conflict Analysis: Models and Resolutions. North-Holland (1984)
13. Wan, Z., Cho, J.-H., Zhu, M., Anwar, A.H., Kamhoua, C., Singh, M.P.: Four-eye: defensive deception against advanced persistent threats via hypergame theory. IEEE Trans. Netw. Serv. Manag. **19**(1), 112–129 (2021)
14. Sayed, M.A., Anwar, A.H., Kiekintveld, C., Bosansky, B., Kamhoua, C.: Cyber deception against zero-day attacks: a game theoretic approach. In: Fang, F., Xu, H., Hayel, Y. (eds.) GameSec 2022. LNCS, vol. 13727, pp. 44–63. Springer, Cham (2022). https://doi.org/10.1007/978-3-031-26369-9_3
15. Zhu, M., Anwar, A.H., Wan, Z., Cho, J.-H., Kamhoua, C.A., Singh, M.P.: A survey of defensive deception: approaches using game theory and machine learning. IEEE Commun. Surv. Tutor. **23**(4), 2460–2493 (2021)
16. Mahmud, S., et al.: Machine learning approaches for predicting suicidal behaviors among university students in Bangladesh during the COVID-19 pandemic: a cross-sectional study. Medicine **102**(28), e34285 (2023)
17. Raju, M.A., Mia, M.S., Sayed, M.A., Uddin, M.R.: Predicting the outcome of English premier league matches using machine learning. In: 2020 2nd International Conference on Sustainable Technologies for Industry 4.0 (STI), pp. 1–6. IEEE (2020)
18. Lu, Z., Wang, C., Zhao, S.: Cyber deception for computer and network security: survey and challenges. arXiv preprint arXiv:2007.14497 (2020)
19. Chiang, C.-Y.J., et al.: On defensive cyber deception: a case study using SDN. In: MILCOM 2018–2018 IEEE Military Communications Conference (MILCOM), pp. 110–115. IEEE (2018)
20. Urias, V.E., Stout, W.M.S., Lin, H.W.: Gathering threat intelligence through computer network deception. In: 2016 IEEE Symposium on Technologies for Homeland Security (HST), pp. 1–6. IEEE (2016)

21. Sayed, M.A., Rahman, M.M., Zaber, M.I., Ali, A.A.: Understanding Dhaka city traffic intensity and traffic expansion using gravity model. In: 2017 20th International Conference of Computer and Information Technology (ICCIT), pp. 1–6. IEEE (2017)
22. Pirozmand, P., Guowei, W., Jedari, B., Xia, F.: Human mobility in opportunistic networks: characteristics, models and prediction methods. J. Netw. Comput. Appl. **42**, 45–58 (2014)
23. Abdulla, M., Simon, R.: Characteristics of common mobility models for opportunistic networks. In: Proceedings of the 2nd ACM Workshop on Performance Monitoring and Measurement of Heterogeneous Wireless and Wired Networks, pp. 105–109 (2007)
24. Xiuwen, F., Li, W., Yang, Y.: Exploring the impact of node mobility on cascading failures in spatial networks. Inf. Sci. **576**, 140–156 (2021)
25. Xia, Y., Yeo, C.K.: Mitigating the impact of node mobility using mobile backbone for heterogeneous MANETs. Comput. Commun. **35**(10), 1217–1230 (2012)
26. Lin, Y., Wang, X., Zhang, L., Li, P., Zhang, D., Liu, S.: The impact of node velocity diversity on mobile opportunistic network performance. J. Netw. Comput. Appl. **55**, 47–58 (2015)
27. Pala, Z., Bicakci, K., Turk, M.: Effects of node mobility on energy balancing in wireless networks. Comput. Electr. Eng. **41**, 314–324 (2015)
28. Urias, V.E., Stout, W.M.S., Luc-Watson, J., Grim, C., Liebrock, L., Merza, M.: Technologies to enable cyber deception. In: 2017 International Carnahan Conference on Security Technology (ICCST), pp. 1–6. IEEE (2017)
29. Miehling, E., Rasouli, M., Teneketzis, D.: Optimal defense policies for partially observable spreading processes on Bayesian attack graphs. In: Proceedings of the Second ACM Workshop on Moving Target Defense, pp. 67–76 (2015)
30. Başar, T., Olsder, G.J.: Dynamic Noncooperative Game Theory. SIAM (1998)

Optimal Resource Allocation for Proactive Defense with Deception in Probabilistic Attack Graphs

Haoxiang Ma[1]($\boxtimes$) ![ORCID], Shuo Han[2] ![ORCID], Charles Kamhoua[3] ![ORCID], and Jie Fu[4] ![ORCID]

[1] University of Florida, Gainesville, FL 32611, USA
hma2@ufl.edu
[2] University of Illinois Chicago, Chicago, IL 60607, USA
hanshuo@uic.edu
[3] DEVCOM Army Research Laboratory, Adelphi, MD 20783, USA
charles.a.kamhoua.civ@mail.mil
[4] University of Florida, Gainesville, FL 32611, USA
fujie@ufl.edu

Abstract. This paper investigates the problem of synthesizing proactive defense systems with deception. We model the interaction between the attacker and the system using a formal security model: a probabilistic attack graph. By allocating fake targets/decoys, the defender aims to distract the attacker from compromising true targets. By increasing the cost of some attack actions, the defender aims to discourage the attacker from committing to certain policies. To optimally deploy limited decoy resources and modify attack action costs with operational constraints, we formulate the synthesis problem as a bi-level optimization problem, while the defender designs the system, in anticipation of the attacker's best response given that the attacker has disinformation about the system due to the use of decoys. We investigate the bi-level optimization formulation against both rational and bounded rational attackers. We show the problem against a rational attacker can be formulated as a bi-level linear program. For attackers with bounded rationality, we show that under certain assumptions, the problem can be transformed into a constrained optimization problem. We proposed an algorithm to approximately solve this constrained optimization problem using a novel projected gradient ascent based on the idea of incentive-design. We demonstrate the effectiveness of the proposed methods using experiments and provide our insights in defense design against rational and bounded rational attackers.

Keywords: Deception · Attack Graph · Bi-Level Optimization · Markov Decision Process

This work was sponsored in part by the Army Research Office and was accomplished under Grant Number W911NF-22-1-0034 and W911NF2210166 and in part by NSF under grant No. 2144113.
DISTRIBUTION A: Approved for Public Release. Distribution is Unlimited.

J. Fu et al. (Eds.): GameSec 2023, LNCS 14167, pp. 215–233, 2023.
https://doi.org/10.1007/978-3-031-50670-3_11

1 Introduction

Proactive defense refers to a class of defense mechanisms for the defender to detect any ongoing attacks, distract the attacker with deception, or use randomization to increase the difficulty of an attack to the system. In this paper, we propose a mathematical framework and solution approach for synthesizing a proactive defense system with deception.

We start by formulating the attack planning problem using a probabilistic attack graph, which can be viewed as a Markov decision process (MDP) with a set of attack target states. Attack graphs (AGs) [9] can be used in modeling computer networks. They are widely used in network security to identify the minimal subset of vulnerability/sensors to be used in order to prevent all known attacks [16,19]. Probabilistic attack graphs introduce uncertain outcomes of attack actions that account for action failures in a stochastic environment. For example, in [7,8], probabilistic transitions in attack graphs capture uncertainties originating from network-based randomization. Under the probabilistic attack graph modeling framework, we investigate how to allocate decoy resources as fake targets to distract the attacker into attacking the fake targets and how to modify the attack action costs to discourage the attacker from reaching the true targets.

The joint design of decoy resource allocation and action cost modification can be cast as a bi-level optimization problem, where the defender (at the upper level) designs the system, in anticipation of the attacker's (at the lower level) best response, given that the attacker has disinformation about the system due to allocated decoys. However, bi-level optimization problems are generally NP-hard [4]. We investigate two possible types of attackers: A rational attacker who maximizes the total reward and a bounded rational attacker whose action choices are computed using quantal response [3,12], where the probability of an action is proportional to the exponential of the total (discounted) return of that action.

For the rational attacker, we show that the bi-level optimization problem can be converted into a single-level optimization problem using KarushKuhnTucker (KKT) conditions of the lower-level optimization problem. For the bounded rational attacker, we formulated a constrained optimization problem and developed a new projected gradient ascent method to solve a (local) optimal policy. We build two important relations: First, we show that the projection step of a defender's desired attack policy to the set of realizable attack policy space can be performed using Inverse Reinforcement Learning (IRL) [23]. Essentially, IRL shapes the attacker's *perceived reward* so that the rational attacker will mimic a strategy chosen by the defender. Second, the gradient ascent step can be performed using policy improvement, which is a subroutine in policy iteration with respect to maximizing the defender's total reward. The projected gradient ascent is ensured to converge to a (local) optimal solution to this nonconvex-constrained optimization problem.

Related Work. The proactive defense design problem is closely related to the Stackelberg security game (SSG) (surveyed in [21]). In an SSG, the defender is to protect a set of targets with limited resources, while the attacker selects the optimal attack strategy given the knowledge of the defender's strategy. In [15], the authors study security countermeasure-allocation and use attack graphs to evaluate the network's security given the allocated resources. However, traditionally SSG does not account for the use of deception.

Deceptions create incorrect/incomplete information for the attacker. In [22], the authors formulate a security game to allocate limited decoy resources to mask a network configuration from the cyber attacker. The decoy-based deception manipulates the adversary's perception of the payoff matrix. In [2], the authors study honeypot allocation in deterministic attack graphs and determine the optimal allocation strategy using the minimax theorem. In [13], the authors study directed acyclic attack graphs that can be modified by the defender using deceptive and protective resources. They propose a mixed-integer linear program (MILP)-based algorithm to determine the allocation of deceptive and protective resources in the graph. In [5], they harden the network by using honeypots so that the attacker can not discriminate between a true target and a fake target. In [13], the authors assign fake edges in the attack graph to interdict the attacker and employ MILP to find the optimal solution.

Compared to existing work, our work makes the following contributions: First, we do not assume any graph structure in the attack graph and consider probabilistic attack graphs instead of deterministic ones. As the attacker can take a randomized strategy in the probabilistic attack graph, it is impossible to construct a payoff matrix and apply the minimax theorem for decoy resource allocation. Second, we consider simultaneously allocating limited decoy resources and modifying the cost of attack actions, and analyzing the best response of the attacker given the disinformation caused by deception. Third, we propose tractable solutions for dealing with different types of attackers: rational and bounded rational. We show that by modifying the action reward and decoy resource allocation properly, it is possible to shape the attacker's behavior so that the misperceived attacker is incentivized to commit an attack strategy that maximizes the defender's reward. Finally, we evaluate our solution under different attacker types and test the scalability of our method on different problem sizes.

2 Preliminaries and Problem Formulation

Notations. Let $\mathbf{R}$ denote the set of real numbers and $\mathbf{R}^n$ the set of real n-vectors. Let $\mathbf{R}_{>0}^n$ (resp. $\mathbf{R}_{<0}^n$) be the set of positive (resp. negative) real n-vectors. We use $\mathbf{1}$ to represent the vector of all ones. Given a vector $z \in \mathbf{R}^n$, let z_i be the i-th component. Given a finite set Z, the set of probability distributions over Z is represented as $\mathrm{Dist}(Z)$. Given $d \in \mathrm{Dist}(Z)$, the support of d is denoted as $\mathrm{Supp}(d) = \{z \in Z \mid d(z) > 0\}$. Let I_B be the indicator function, *i.e.*, $I_B(x) = 1$ if $x \in B$, and $I_B(x) = 0$ otherwise.

We consider the adversarial interaction between a defender (player 1, pronoun she/her) and an attacker (player 2, pronoun he/him/his) in a system equipped with proactive defense (formally defined later). We first introduce a formal model, called probabilistic attack graph, to capture how the attacker plans to achieve the attack objective. Then, we introduce proactive defense countermeasures with deception.

Attack Planning Problem. The attack planning problem is modeled as a probabilistic attack graph,

$$M = (S, A, P, \nu, \gamma, F, R_2),$$

where S is a set of states (nodes in the attack graph), A is a set of attack actions, $P : S \times A \rightarrow \text{Dist}(S)$ is a probabilistic transition function such that $P(s'|s, a)$ is the probability of reaching state s' given action a being taken at state s, $\nu \in \text{Dist}(S)$ is the initial state distribution, $\gamma \in (0, 1]$ is a discount factor. The attacker's objective is described by a set F of *target states* and a *target reward* function $R_2 : F \times A \rightarrow \mathbf{R}_{\geq 0}$, which assigns each state-action pair (s, a) where $s \in F$ and $a \in A$ to a nonnegative value of reaching that target for the attacker. The reward function can be extended to the entire state space by defining $R_2(s, a) = 0$ for any $s \in S \setminus F, a \in A$. To capture the termination of attacks, we introduce a unique sink state $s_{\text{sink}} \in S \setminus F$ such that $P(s_{\text{sink}}|s_{\text{sink}}, a) = 1$ for all $a \in A$ and $P(s_{\text{sink}}|s, a) = 1$ for any target $s \in F$ and $a \in A$.

The probabilistic attack graph characterizes goal-directed attacks encountered in cyber security [10, 17], in which by reaching a target state, the attacker compromises certain critical network hosts. Probabilistic attack graphs [13, 20] capture the uncertain outcomes of the attack actions using the probabilistic transition function and generalize deterministic attack graphs [9].

The attacker is to maximize his discounted total reward, starting from the initial state $S_0 \sim \nu$. A randomized, finite-memory attack policy is a function $\pi: S^* \rightarrow \text{Dist}(A)$, which maps a finite run $\rho \in S^*$ into a distribution $\pi(\rho)$ over actions. A policy is called Markovian if it only depends on the most recent state, i.e., $\pi: S \rightarrow \text{Dist}(A)$. We only consider Markovian policies because it suffices to search within Markovian policies for an optimal attack policy.

Let $(\Omega, \mathcal{F})$ be the canonical sample space for $(S_0, A_0, (S_t, A_t)_{t>1})$ with the Borel σ-algebra $\mathcal{F} = \mathcal{B}(\Omega)$ and $\Omega = S \times A \times \prod_{t=1}^{\infty}(S \times A)$. The probability measure Pr^π on $(\Omega, \mathcal{F})$ induced by a Markov policy π satisfies: $\text{Pr}^\pi(S_0 = s) = \mu_0(s)$, $\text{Pr}^\pi(A_0 = a \mid S_0 = s) = \pi(s, a)$, and $\text{Pr}^\pi(S_t = s \mid (S_k, A_k)_{k<t}) = P(s \mid S_k, A_k)$, and $\text{Pr}^\pi(A_t = a \mid (S_k, A_k)_{k<t}, S_t) = \pi(S_t, a)$.

Given a Markovian policy $\pi: S \rightarrow \text{Dist}(A)$, we define the attacker's value function $V_2^\pi : S \rightarrow \mathbf{R}$ as $V_2^\pi(s) = \mathbf{E}_\pi[\sum_{k=0}^{\infty} \gamma^k R_2(S_k, A_k)|S_0 = s]$, where $\mathbf{E}_\pi$ is the expectation given the probability measure Pr^π.

Proactive Defense with Deception. We assume that the defender knows the attacker's objective given by the tuple $\langle F, R_2 \rangle$, i.e., the target states and target reward function. The defender's proactive defense mechanisms are the following:

- Defend by deception: The defender employs a deception method called "revealing the fake". Specifically, the defender has a set $D \subset S \setminus F$ of states in the Markov decision process (MDP) M that can be set to be *fake target states* with fake target rewards $y \in \mathbf{R}^{|D|}$. The attacker cannot distinguish the real targets F from fake targets D.
- Defend by state-action reward modification: The defender has a set $W \subset (S \setminus (F \cup D)) \times A$ of state action pairs in the MDP M whose reward can be modified. Once the reward of the state action pair (s, a) is modified, the attacker's perceived reward $R_2(s, a) < 0$, i.e., the cost of attack action a at state s is $-R_2(s, a)$.

The defender can determine how to allocate her decoy resource and limited state-action reward modification ability.

Definition 1 (Decoy allocation under constraints). *The defender's decoy allocation design is a nonnegative real-valued vector* $y \in \mathbf{R}_{\geq 0}^{|S|}$ *satisfying* $y(s) = 0$ *for any* $s \in S \setminus D$ *and constrained by* $\mathbf{1}^\mathsf{T} y \leq h$ *for some* $h \geq 0$. *Given a decoy allocation* y, *the attacker's perceptual reward function is defined by*

$$R_2^y(s, a) = \begin{cases} y(s) & \textit{if } y(s) > 0, \\ R_2(s, a) & \textit{if } y(s) = 0. \end{cases}$$

Definition 2 (Action reward modification). *Given a set* $W \subset (S \setminus (F \cup D)) \times A$, *the defender's action reward modification is a nonpositive reward-valued vector* $x \in \mathbf{R}_{\leq 0}^{|S \times A|}$ *satisfying* $x(s, a) = 0$ *for any* $(s, a) \notin W$ *and* $-\mathbf{1}^\mathsf{T} x \leq k$ *for some* $k \geq 0$. *Given an action reward modification* x, *the attacker's perceptual reward function is defined by*

$$R_2^x(s, a) = \begin{cases} x(s, a) & \textit{if } x(s, a) < 0, \\ R_2(s, a) & \textit{if } x(s, a) = 0. \end{cases}$$

The defender does not consider modifying the state-action reward for (fake or real) target states $F \cup D$ because once a state in $F \cup D$ is reached, the attack is terminated.

Definition 3. *The defender's proactive defense strategy is a tuple* (x, y) *including an action reward modification* x *and a decoy allocation design* y.

Because the action reward modification is independent of the decoy allocation design, the reward function given a defender's strategy (x, y) is the composition of R_2^x and R_2^y and thus omitted.

Assumption 1. *The attack process terminates under two cases: Either the attack succeeds, in which the attacker reaches a target* $s \in F$, *or the attack is interdicted, in which the attacker reaches a state allocated with a decoy.*

Our problem can be informally stated as follows.

Problem 1. In the attack planning scenario we mentioned above, determine the defender's strategy to allocate decoy resources and modify action rewards so as to maximize the probability that the attacker reaches a fake target given the best response of the attacker.

3 Main Results

In this section, we first define the attacker's perceptual planning problem for a fixed action reward modification and decoy resource allocation (x, y). Then we show that the design of the proactive defense can be formulated as a bi-level optimization problem. We investigate the special property of the formulated bi-level optimization problem to develop an optimization-based approach for synthesizing the proactive defense strategy.

3.1   A Bi-level Optimization Formulation

The defender's strategy changes how the attacker perceives the attack planning problem as follows:

Definition 4 (Perceptual attack planning problem with modified reward and decoys). *Let the action reward modification be x and decoy allocation be y, and the attacker's original planning problem $M = (S, A, P, \nu, \gamma, F, R_2)$, the perceptual planning problem of the attacker is defined by the following MDP with terminating states:*

$$M(x, y) = (S, A, P^y, \nu, \gamma, F \cup D^y, R_2^{x,y}),$$

where S, A, ν, γ are the same as those in M, $D^y = \{s \in D \mid y(s) \neq 0\}$ are decoy target states and absorbing. The transition function P^y is obtained from the original transition function P by only making all states in D^y absorbing. The reward $R_2^{x,y}$ is defined based on Definition 1 and Definition 2.

The perceptual value for the attacker is

$$V_2^\pi(\nu; x, y) = \mathbf{E}_\pi \left[\sum_{k=0}^{\infty} \gamma^k R_2^{x,y}(S_k, A_k) \mid S_0 \sim \nu \right],$$

where $\mathbf{E}_\pi$ is the expectation given the probability measure Pr^π induced by π from the MDP $M(x, y)$.

The defender's deception objective is given by a reward function $R_1^y : S \to \mathbf{R}$, defined by

$$R_1^y(s) = \begin{cases} 1 & \text{if } s \in D^y, \\ 0 & \text{otherwise.} \end{cases} \tag{1}$$

Given the probability measure Pr^π, we denote the defender's value by

$$V_1^\pi(\nu; y) = \mathbf{E}_\pi \left[\sum_{k=0}^{\infty} \gamma^k R_1(S_k) \mid S_0 \sim \nu \right].$$

With this reward definition, the value $V_1^\pi(\nu; y)$ is the probability of the attacker reaching a fake target in D^y.

Then the problem of synthesizing an optimal proactive defense strategy (x, y) can be mathematically formulated as

Problem 2.

$$\max_{x \in X, y \in Y} \quad V_1^{\pi^*}(\nu; y)$$

$$\text{s.t.} \qquad \pi^* \in \operatorname*{argmax}_\pi V_2^\pi(\nu; x, y).$$

where $X = \{x \in \mathbf{R}_{\leq 0}^{|W|} \mid -\mathbf{1}^\mathsf{T} x \leq k\}$ and $Y = \{y \mid \forall s \in S \setminus D, y(s) = 0 \text{ and } \mathbf{1}^\mathsf{T} y \leq h\}$ are the ranges for variables x and y correspondingly.

In words, the defender decides (x, y) so that the attacker's best response in his perceptual attack planning problem turns out to be an attack policy most preferred by the defender, as it maximizes the defender's value.

3.2 Synthesizing Proactive Defense Against a Rational Attacker

The bi-level optimization problem is known to be strongly NP-hard [6]. In this section, we show that when the attacker is rational, then the lower-level problem can be formulated as a LP. Thus, the original bi-level optimization is a special case–bi-level LP. Using the KKT condition of the lower-level problem, the bi-level LP reduces to a single-level optimization with special ordered set (SOS) constraints. We formulate the lower-level LP using occupancy measures [1]. For a given defense strategy $(\boldsymbol{x}, \boldsymbol{y})$, the optimal policy perceived by the attacker can be solved using the following LP:

$$\max_{m} \quad \sum_{s \in S, a \in A} R_2^{\boldsymbol{x}, \boldsymbol{y}}(s, a) m(s, a).$$

$$\text{s.t.} \quad \sum_{a \in A} m(s, a) = \gamma \sum_{s' \in S, a' \in A} P(s|s', a') m(s', a') + \nu(s), \forall s \in S, \qquad (2)$$

$$m(s, a) \geq 0, \forall s \in S, a \in A. \qquad (3)$$

where $m(s, a)$ is the (discounted) occupancy measure that represents the frequency a state s is visited and a is taken. Using the solution of the LP, the optimal attacker policy π is recovered via: $\pi(s, a) = \frac{m(s,a)}{\sum_{a' \in A} m(s, a')}$.

The original bi-level optimization reduces to

$$\max_{\boldsymbol{x} \in X, \boldsymbol{y} \in Y} \quad \sum_{s \in S, a \in A} R_1(s, a) m(s, a)$$

$$\text{s.t.} \quad \max_{m} \quad \sum_{s \in S, a \in A} R_2^{\boldsymbol{x}, \boldsymbol{y}}(s, a) m(s, a), \quad \text{s.t. (2), (3).}$$

By rewriting the lower-level LP using its KKT conditions, we convert the bi-level optimization problem into a single-level optimization problem with SOS1 constraints. First, we have the lower-level problem:

$$\max_{m} \quad \sum_{s \in S, a \in A} R_2^{\boldsymbol{x}, \boldsymbol{y}}(s, a) m(s, a).$$

$$\text{s.t.} \quad \sum_{a \in A} m(s, a) = \gamma \sum_{s' \in S, a' \in A} P(s|s', a') m(s', a') + \nu, \forall s \in S, \qquad (4)$$

$$m(s, a) \geq 0, \forall s \in S, a \in A. \qquad (5)$$

where we have $R_2^{\boldsymbol{x}, \boldsymbol{y}}(s, a) = R_2(s, a) + \boldsymbol{x}(s, a) + \boldsymbol{y}(s), \forall s \in S, a \in A$. Thus we can use KKT condition to form the lower-level problem to a Lagrangian function. We first rewrite

$$\sum_{a \in A} m(s, a) = \gamma \sum_{s' \in S, a' \in A} P(s|s', a') m(s', a') + \nu(s), \forall s \in S. \qquad (6)$$

to the matrix form, which is equivalent to

$$\mathcal{C}m - \gamma\mathcal{D}m - \nu = 0.$$

where $\mathcal{C}, \mathcal{D}$ corresponds to the parameters in Eq. 6. And $m \in \mathbf{R}_{\geq 0}^{|S \times A|}$ denotes the vector of state-action visiting frequency.

Thus the Lagrangian function can be written as

$$\mathcal{L}(m, \mu, \lambda) = (R_2 + x + y)^T m(s, a) + \mu^T m + \lambda^T (\mathcal{C}m - \gamma\mathcal{D}m - \nu). \quad (7)$$

where y is extended to $S \times A$ domain by defining $y(s, a) = y(s)$

The necessary conditions are listed as follows:

$$-(R_2 + x + y) + \mu + (\mathcal{C} - \gamma\mathcal{D})^T \lambda = 0,$$
$$\mathcal{C}m - \gamma\mathcal{D}m - \nu = 0,$$
$$-m \leq 0,$$
$$\mu \geq 0,$$
$$\mu(i)m(i) = 0, i = 1, 2, ..., |S \times A|. \quad (8)$$

And the Eq. 8 can be written in the form of special order set (SOS). We then combine these necessary conditions with the upper-level problem, the bi-level problem can be rewritten as:

$$\max_{x \in X, y \in Y, m} \sum_{s \in S, a \in A} R_1(s, a)m(s, a)$$

$$\text{s.t.} \quad \mathbf{1}^T y \leq h,$$
$$-\mathbf{1}^T x \leq k,$$
$$y \geq 0,$$
$$x \leq 0,$$
$$-(R_2 + x + y) + \mu + (\mathcal{C} - \gamma\mathcal{D})^T \lambda = 0,$$
$$\mathcal{C}m - \gamma\mathcal{D}m - \nu = 0,$$
$$-m \leq 0,$$
$$\mu \geq 0,$$
$$\mu(i)m(i) = 0, i = 1, 2, ..., |S \times A|. \quad (9)$$

where (9) are special ordered sets of type 1 (SOS1) constraints. This optimization problem can be solved using the Gurobi Optimization toolbox.

3.3 Synthesizing Proactive Defense Against a Bounded Rational Attacker

The defense against a rational agent can be sensitive to potential mismatches on the rationality assumption: Consider the defender aims to protect two targets $\{1, 2\}$. Both targets have similar values but target 1's value is slightly higher than that of target 2.

Knowing a rational agent will aim at target 1, the defender will enforce all resources to guard target 1 and may leave target 2 unprotected. However, a bounded rational attacker, based on the quantal response [3, 12], will compromise either target with almost equal probabilities. We investigate how to design a defense strategy against attackers with bounded rationality.

Transforming into a Constrained Optimization Problem. Based on the quantal response model, an attacker with bounded rationality aims to compute a quantal response policy π^* in the perceived MDP $M(x, y)$ by solving the following entropy-regularized Bellman equation [14]:

$$V_2^*(s; x, y) = \tau \log \sum_a \exp\{(R_2(s; x, y) + \gamma V_2^*(s; x, y))/\tau\},$$

where $\tau > 0$ is the temperature parameter that controls the degree of entropy regularization, if τ approaches 0, the Bellman equation recovers the optimal Bellman equation under a rational attacker. However, due to the bounded rationality assumption, the original bi-level optimization cannot be reduced into a bi-level LP as the objective function using occupancy measures includes an additional nonlinear term which is the weighted entropy of the policy.

Next, we propose a gradient-based method to solve Problem 2 assuming the attacker is bounded rational. First, we show the original problem can be formulated as a constrained optimization problem. Let $\Pi(x, y)$ be the set of quantal response policies in the attacker's perceived planning problem with respect to a choice of variables x and y. The bi-level optimization problem is then equivalently written as the following constrained optimization problem:

$$\max_{\pi^*, x \in X, y \in Y} \quad V_1^{\pi^*}(\nu; y)$$

$$\text{s.t.} \quad \pi^* \in \Pi(x, y). \tag{10}$$

This, in turn, is equivalent to

$$\max_{\pi^*} \quad V_1^{\pi^*}(\nu; y)$$

$$\text{s.t.} \quad \pi^* \in \bigcup_{x \in X, y \in Y} \Pi(x, y). \tag{11}$$

Here, the constraint means the attacker's response π^* can be selected from the collection of optimal attack policies given all possible values for x, y.

By the definition of the defender's value function, it is noted that $V_1^\pi(\nu; y)$ does not depend on the exact value of y but only depends on whether $y(s) > 0$ for each state $s \in D$. Formally,

Lemma 1. *For any* $y_1, y_2 \in Y$, *if* $y_1(s) = 0 \implies y_2(s) = 0$ *and vice versa, then* $V_1^\pi(\nu; y_1) = V_1^\pi(\nu; y_2)$.

Proof. Given two different vectors y_1 and y_2, we can construct two MDPs: $M_1 := M(x, y_1) = (S, A, P^{y_1}, \nu, \gamma, F, R_1)$ and $M_2 := M(x, y_2) = (S, A, P^{y_2}, \nu, \gamma, F, R_1)$, respectively.

If $y_1(s) = 0$ if and only if $y_2(s) = 0$, then the transition functions P^{y_1} of M_1 and P^{y_2} of M_2 are the same (see Definition 4).

Further, the defender's reward function $R_1^{y_1}$ also equals to $R_1^{y_2}$ (see (1)), given both the transition dynamics and reward are the same, we have $V_1^\pi(\nu; y_1) = V_1^\pi(\nu; y_2)$.

Lemma 1 proves given an attacker's policy π, the defender's value only relates to where the decoys are located. Next, to remove the dependency of $V_1^\pi(\nu; y)$ on y, we make the following assumption:

Assumption 2. *The set $D^y = \{s \in D \mid y(s) \neq 0\}$ of states where decoys are allocated is given.*

Under this assumption, we simply assume all states in the given set D have to be assigned with nonzero decoy resources. That is $D^y = D$.

This assumption further reduces the defender's synthesis problem into a constrained optimization problem.

$$\max_{\pi^*}. \quad V_1^{\pi^*}(\nu)$$
$$\text{s.t.} \quad \pi^* \in \overline{\Pi} \triangleq \bigcup_{y \in Y, x \in X} \Pi(x, y),$$
$$y(s) > 0, \forall s \in D. \tag{12}$$

Because the above problem is a standard-constrained optimization problem, one can obtain a locally optimal solution using the projected gradient method:

$$\pi^{k+1} = \text{proj}_{\overline{\Pi}}(\pi^k + \eta \nabla V_1^{\pi^k}(\nu)).$$

where $\text{proj}_{\overline{\Pi}}(\pi)$ denotes projecting policy π onto the policy space $\overline{\Pi}$ and η is the step size.

Connecting Inverse-Reinforcement Learning with Projected Gradient Ascent. A key step in performing Projected Gradient Ascent (PGA) is to evaluate, for any policy $\hat{\pi}$, the projection $\text{proj}_{\overline{\Pi}}(\hat{\pi})$. However, this is nontrivial because the set $\overline{\Pi}$ includes a set of attack policies, each of which corresponds to a choice of vectors (x, y). As a result, $\overline{\Pi}$ does not have a compact representation. Next, we propose a novel algorithm that computes the projection.

First, it is noted that this projection step is equivalent to solving the following optimization problem:

$$\min_{\pi}. \quad \mathbf{D}(\hat{\pi}, \pi)$$
$$\text{s.t.} \quad \pi \in \overline{\Pi},$$
$$y(s) > 0; \forall s \in D. \tag{13}$$

where $\mathbf{D}(\hat{\pi}, \pi)$ is the distance between the two policies $\hat{\pi}, \pi$.

The distance function $\mathbf{D}$ can be chosen to be the Kullback-Leibler (KL)-divergence between policy-induced Markov chains. Specifically, the KL divergence in (13) can be expressed as

$$
\begin{aligned}
\mathbf{D}_{\mathrm{KL}}\left(M_{\hat{\pi}}(\boldsymbol{x}, \boldsymbol{y}) \| M_{\pi}(\boldsymbol{x}, \boldsymbol{y})\right) &= \sum_{\rho} \widehat{\Pr}(\rho) \log \frac{\widehat{\Pr}(\rho)}{\Pr(\rho | \boldsymbol{x}, \boldsymbol{y})} \\
&= \sum_{\rho} \widehat{\Pr}(\rho) \log \widehat{\Pr}(\rho) - \sum_{\rho} \widehat{\Pr}(\rho) \log \Pr(\rho | \boldsymbol{x}, \boldsymbol{y}), \quad (14)
\end{aligned}
$$

where $\widehat{\Pr}(\rho)$ is the probability of path ρ in the Markov chain $M_{\hat{\pi}}(\boldsymbol{x}, \boldsymbol{y})$, and $\Pr(\rho | \boldsymbol{y})$ is the probability of path ρ in the Markov chain $M_{\pi}(\boldsymbol{x}, \boldsymbol{y})$ induced by a policy π.

Because the first term in the sum in (14) is a constant for $\hat{\pi}$ is fixed, the KL divergence minimization problem is equivalent to the following maximization problem:

$$
\max_{\boldsymbol{x} \in X, \boldsymbol{y} \in Y} \sum_{\rho} \widehat{\Pr}(\rho) \log \Pr(\rho | \boldsymbol{x}, \boldsymbol{y}) \tag{15}
$$

Problem (15) can be solved by an extension of the Maximum Entropy (MAXENT) IRL algorithm [23], which was originally developed in the absence of constraints on the reward parameters. It is well-known that IRL is to infer, from the expert demonstrations, a reward function for which the policy generating the demonstrations is optimal.

The use of IRL to perform the projection is intuitively understood as follows: The goal is to compute a pair of vectors $(\boldsymbol{x}, \boldsymbol{y})$ that alters the attacker's perceived reward function so that the bounded rational attacker's optimal policy given $(\boldsymbol{x}, \boldsymbol{y})$ is closed to the "expert policy" $\hat{\pi}$, under the constraints of $\boldsymbol{x}, \boldsymbol{y}$. Importantly, we used the MAXENT IRL because it assumes the expect policy is entropy-regulated, and thus is consistent with the assumption of the quantal response of a bounded rational attacker.

To enforce the constraints $\boldsymbol{x} \in X, \boldsymbol{y} \in Y$, we approximate the constraint using a logarithmic barrier function and compute the optimal solution $(\boldsymbol{x}^*, \boldsymbol{y}^*)$ using gradient-based numerical optimization Considering the constraint $\mathbf{1}^{\top} \boldsymbol{y} \leq h$, we implement the barrier function to approximate the inequality constraints and rewrite the optimization problem as:

$$
\max_{\boldsymbol{x}, \boldsymbol{y}} \sum_{\rho} \widehat{\Pr}(\rho) \log \Pr(\rho | \boldsymbol{x}, \boldsymbol{y}) + \frac{1}{t} \log(h - \mathbf{1}^{\top} \boldsymbol{y}) + \frac{1}{t} \log(k + \mathbf{1}^{\top} \boldsymbol{x})
$$

$$
\text{s.t.} \quad \boldsymbol{y}(s) = 0, \quad \forall s \in S \setminus D,
$$

$$
\boldsymbol{x}(s, a) = 0, \forall (s, a) \in S \times A \setminus W.
$$

where t is the weighting parameter of the logarithmic barrier function. In our experiment, t is fixed to be 1000.

Let $L(\boldsymbol{x}, \boldsymbol{y})$ be the objective function. Specifically, $\boldsymbol{x}$ and $\boldsymbol{y}$ can be updated via $\boldsymbol{x}^{k+1} = \mathrm{proj}_{\mathbf{X}}(\boldsymbol{x}^k + \eta_x \nabla L(\boldsymbol{x}, \boldsymbol{y})), \boldsymbol{y}^{k+1} = \mathrm{proj}_{\mathbf{Y}}(\boldsymbol{y}^k + \eta_y \nabla L(\boldsymbol{x}, \boldsymbol{y}))$.

Policy Improvement for Gradient Ascent Step. After the projection step to obtain a policy π^k and the corresponding vector $(\boldsymbol{x}, \boldsymbol{y})$, we aim to compute a one-step gradient ascent to improve the objective function's value

$$V_1^{k+1}(\nu) = V_1^k(\nu) + \nabla V_1^k(\nu),$$

where $V_1^k(\nu)$ is the defender's value evaluated given the attack policy π^k at the k-th iteration.

For this step, we perform a policy improvement step with respect to the defender's reward function R_1^y. It is shown in [11,18] that policy improvement is a one-step Newton update of optimizing the value function.

Specifically, the policy improvement is to compute

$$\tilde{\pi}^{k+1}(s, a) = \frac{\exp\left((R_1(s, a) + \gamma V_1^k(s'))/\tau\right)}{\sum_{a \in A} \exp\left((R_1(s, a) + \gamma V_1^k(s'))/\tau\right)},$$

The policy at iteration $k + 1$ is obtained by performing the projection step (13) in which $\hat{\pi} \triangleq \tilde{\pi}_{k+1}$.

The iteration stops when $|V_1^{k+1}(\nu) - V_1^k(\nu)| \leq \epsilon$ where ϵ is a manually defined threshold. The output yields a tuple $(\boldsymbol{x}^*, \boldsymbol{y}^*)$ which is the (local) optimal proactive defense strategy. We can only obtain a local optimal proactive defense strategy here due to the transferred constrained optimization problem having a nonconvex constraint set. However, we can start from different initial policies and select the best one.

To summarize, the proposed algorithm starts with an initial policy $\tilde{\pi}^0$, and use the IRL to find the projection π^0 as well as the corresponding vectors $(\boldsymbol{x}^0, \boldsymbol{y}^0)$ that shape the attacker's perceptual reward function for which π^0 is optimal. Then a policy improvement is performed to update π^0 to $\tilde{\pi}^1$. By alternating the projection and policy improvement, the process terminates until the stopping criteria is satisfied.

Remark 1. In our problem, we assume the set D is given. If the set D is not given but to be determined from a candidate set of states. Then the bi-level optimization is combinatorial and NP-hard. A naive approach is to enumerate all possible combinations and evaluate the defender's value for every subset and select the one that yields the highest defender's value.

4 Experiment

We illustrate the proposed methods with two sets of examples, one is a probabilistic attack graph and another is an attack planning problem formulated in a stochastic grid-world. For all case studies, the workstation used is powered by Intel i7-11700K and 32 GB RAM.

Figure 1 shows a probabilistic attack graph with the targets $F = \{10\}$. The attacker has four actions $\{a, b, c, d\}$. For clarity, the graph only shows the transition given action a where a thick (resp. thin) arrow represents a high (resp. low) transition probability. For example, $P(0, a) = \{1 : 0.7, 2 : 0.1, 3 : 0.1, 4 : 0.1\}^1$. The defender can allocate

---

[1] The exact transition function is provided: https://www.dropbox.com/s/nyycf57vdry139j/MDPTransition.pdf?dl=0.

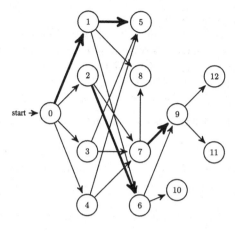

Fig. 1. A probabilistic attack graph.

decoy resources at a set $D = \{11, 12\}$ of decoy states and receive a reward of 1 if the attacker reaches the decoy instead of the true targets. If no decoy resource is allocated, the attacker receives a reward $R_2(s, a) = 1$ for any $s \in F$ and the optimal attack policy has probability 60.33% of reaching the target set F from the initial state 0. In the meantime, the defender's expected value is 0.149. That is, with probability 14.9%, the attacker will reach decoy set D and the attack is terminated.

Consider a defender who has a limited decoy resource constrained by $\mathbf{1}^{\mathsf{T}} \boldsymbol{y} \leq 3$ and cannot modify the state-action reward. First, we consider the decoy allocation against a rational attacker, from the bi-level LP solution, the decoy resource allocation is $\boldsymbol{y}_1(11) = 1.218, \boldsymbol{y}_1(12) = 0$. The defender's value is 0.654 given the best response of a rational attacker in $M(\boldsymbol{y}_1)$. Then, the same problem is solved for defending against a bounded rational attacker. The decoy resource allocation based on the PGA method yields $\boldsymbol{y}_2(11) = \boldsymbol{y}_2(12) = 1.313$. Based on the given decoy resource allocation, the attacker has an 8.63% probability of reaching the target set F and the defender's expected value is 0.653 at initial state 0. In these two cases, we observed that the defender's values are similar: By assigning resources to decoys to attract the attacker, the defender reduces the attacker's probability of reaching the target state significantly (85% reduction) and improves the defender's value by 3.38 times.

A key observation is that the decoy allocation against rational attacker $\boldsymbol{y}_1$ places resources only at one decoy state. This is because, when $\boldsymbol{y}_1(11) = 1.218$, the rational attacker selects the optimal action to reach state 9 and then 11 from state 6 instead of the true target 10. If the attacker is bounded rational, then at state 6, he will choose the action leading to either 9 or 10 with nearly equal probabilities. Thus, the design $\boldsymbol{y}_1$ against a rational attacker can be sensitive to possible mismatches in the rationality assumption. To see this, we perform the following comparison: We use the design $\boldsymbol{y}_1$ against a rational attacker to construct the attack planning MDP and then solve the optimal attack policy of a bounded rational attacker in this MDP. The defender's value is obtained by evaluating the bounded rational attacker policy in $M(\boldsymbol{y}_1)$ with the defender's reward. In this example, we observe that the defender's value is 0.444, which indicates that the defender would have a performance drop of 33% if the rationality assumption is violated. On the other hand, when we solve a rational attack policy in the MDP $M(\boldsymbol{y}_2)$, whose defense is optimized against the bounded rational attacker, we observe the defender's value is 0.654, which is similar to the case against a bounded rational attacker. The result is shown in Table 1.

Table 1. Defender's values in the probabilistic attack graph.

Defense Strategies	Types of Attackers	
	Rational	Bounded Rational
$\boldsymbol{y}_1$ optimized for rational attackers	0.654	0.444
$\boldsymbol{y}_2$ optimized for bounded rational attackers	0.654	0.653

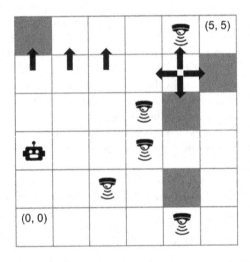

Fig. 2. A 6 × 6 gridworld.

Next, we consider a robot motion planning problem in attack graphs modeled by stochastic gridworlds. The purpose of choosing such an environment is to make the results more interpretable. Consider first a small 6 by 6 gridworld in Fig. 2. The attacker/robot aims to reach a set of goal states while avoiding detection from the defender. The attacker can move in four compass directions. Given an action, say, "N", the attacker enters the intended cell with $1 - 2\alpha$ probability and enters the neighboring cells, which are west and east cells with α probability. In our experiments, α is selected to be 0.1. A state (i, j) means the cell at row i and column j.

The defender has deployed sensors shown in Fig. 2 to detect an attack. Once the attacker enters a sensor state, his task fails. The decoy set D is given as blue cells and

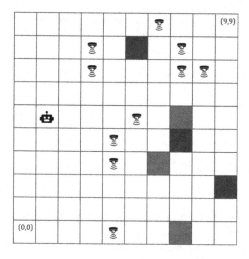

Fig. 3. A 10×10 gridworld.

the target set F is given as green cells. The robot icon represents the robot's initial state. If no decoy resource is allocated, the attacker's policy has a probability of 98.98% of reaching the target set from the initial state. In the meantime, the defender's expected value is 3.56×10^{-6}, which means the attacker's probability of reaching decoys is close to 0.

We employ the bi-level LP to solve decoy allocation against a rational attacker and the result is $y_1((1,4)) = 1.946, y_2((4,5)) = 1.774$, the defender's value is 0.433. Then the same problem is solved for defending against a bounded rational attacker. The PGA method yields $y_2((1,4)) = 2.016, y_2((4,5)) = 1.826$. Based on the given decoy resource allocation, the attacker has a 9.9% probability of reaching the target set F, and the defender's expected value at the initial state is 0.388.

To see how sensitive y_1 is to the rationality assumption of the attacker, we evaluate the defense strategy y_1, y_2 against these two types of attackers: rational and bounded rational attackers. We observe a 26% decrease of defender's value when using y_1, optimized against rational attacker, to defend against a bounded rational attacker. When the optimal defense y_2 against a bounded rational attacker is used against a rational attacker, the performance loss for the defender is negligible. The result is shown in Table 2.

The Effects of Allowing Action-Reward Modification and Different Choices of Decoy States. We study how much the defense can be improved by allowing additional state-action reward modification. The actions the defender can modify are marked as arrows in Fig. 2. The *PGA* method yields $x_2((4,0), \text{'N'}) = -1, x_2((4,1), \text{'N'}) = -0.94, x_2((4,2), \text{'N'}) = -0.904, x_2((4,4), \text{'N'}) = x_2((4,4), \text{'W'}) = x_2((4,4), \text{'S'}) = -1, x_2((4,4), \text{'E'}) = 0, y_2((1,4)) = 1.938, y_2((4,5)) = 1.734$. The defender's value is 0.394 given the joint decoy allocation and action reward modification, and the attacker has a probability of 8.6% to reach the true goal, which is 13.13% reduction compared to that when only the decoy resource allocation is allowed. The result is shown in Table 3.

Table 2. Defender's values in 6×6 gridworld with only decoy allocation.

Defense Strategies	Types of Attackers	
	Rational	Bounded Rational
y_1 optimized for rational attackers	0.433	0.321
y_2 optimized for bounded rational attackers	0.431	0.388

In order to test how the decoy set D influences the result. We re-allocate the position of decoys to $\{(0,2),(5,3)\}$. The result is shown in Table 4. If we do not allocate decoy resources, the attacker reaches the target set with 98.97% probability, and the defender's value is 7.61×10^{-8} at the initial state. If the defender can allocate resources to the decoys, PGA method yields $y_2((0,2)) = 1.141$ and $y_2((5,3)) = 1.0$. The attacker's probability of reaching the target set is 3.99% and the defender's expected value is 0.699. If the defender is allowed to modify the same set of state-action rewards as she is in the previous example, PGA method yields $x_2((4,0), \text{'N'}) = -1, x_2((4,1), \text{'N'}) = -0.85, x_2((4,2), \text{'N'}) = -0.081, x_2((4,4), \text{'N'}) = x_2((4,4), \text{'W'}) = x_2((4,4), \text{'S'}) = -1, x_2((4,4), \text{'E'}) = 0, y_2((0,2)) = 0.985$ and $y_2((5,3)) = 1.068$. Under this configuration, the attacker's probability of reaching the target set is 0.3% (93% reduction compared to only allocating decoy resources) and the defender's expected value is 0.730 (4.4% increase compared to only allocate decoy resources). Clearly, the choice of decoy states D influences the attacker's probability of reaching the target set and the defender's expected value: the second set $D' = \{(0,2),(5,3)\}$ appears to outperform the first set $D = \{(1,4),(4,5)\}$. The defender's value is 0.73 given decoy set D', compared to 0.39 given decoy set D.

Table 3. Experiment result in 6×6 gridworld given $D = \{(1,4),(4,5)\}$.

	No decoy	Decoy only	Decoy and action reward
Attacker's value	0.99	0.099	0.086
Defender's value	3.56×10^{-6}	0.388	0.394

4.1 Scalability

We increase the gridworld size to 10×10 as shown in Fig. 3. The sensors, decoy set, and target set are represented using the same notations as the 6×6 gridworld. The results obtained from bi-level LP and PGA are shown in Table 5.

Table 4. Experiment result in 6×6 gridworld given $D = \{(0, 2), (5, 3)\}$.

	No decoy	Decoy only	Decoy and action reward
Attacker's value	0.99	0.04	0.003
Defender's value	7.61×10^{-8}	0.699	0.730

Table 5. Defender's values in 10×10 gridworld.

Defense Strategies	Types of Attackers	
	Rational	Bounded Rational
y_1 optimized for rational attackers	0.476	0.469
y_2 optimized for bounded rational attackers	0.476	0.472

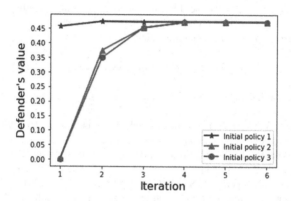

Fig. 4. The convergence of PGA for computing an optimal defense strategy in 10×10 gridworld given different initializations.

We also test the convergence of the PGA method using different initial policies as shown in Fig. 4. From Fig. 4, we observe that different initial policies result in a similar converged value for the objective function. However, the rate of convergence depends on the initialization of the PGA. The PGA method solved the 10×10 gridworld using 2112.25 s and the 6×6 example using 537.58 s. The bi-level LP solution running time increases from 0.17 s to 0.89 s when we increase the gridworld size from 6×6 to 10×10. The running time shows both methods can be extended to moderate problem sizes.

5 Conclusion and Future Work

We present a mathematical framework and algorithms for decoy allocation and reward modification in a proactive defense system against rational and bounded rational attackers. The formulation and solutions can be extended to a broad set of adversarial interactions in which proactive defense with deception can be deployed. In the future, it would be interesting to consider more complex attack and defense objectives and investigate the decoy allocation given the uncertainty in the attacker's goal or capability. Apart from "revealing the fake" studied herein, another direction is to explore how to "conceal the truth" by manipulating the attacker's perceptual reward of compromising true targets.

References

1. Altman, E.: Constrained Markov Decision Processes: Stochastic Modeling, 1st edn. Routledge, Boca Raton (2021)
2. Anwar, A.H., Kamhoua, C., Leslie, N.: Honeypot allocation over attack graphs in cyber deception games. In: 2020 International Conference on Computing, Networking and Communications (ICNC), pp. 502–506 (2020)
3. Chen, H.C., Friedman, J.W., Thisse, J.F.: Boundedly rational nash equilibrium: a probabilistic choice approach. Games Econom. Behav. **18**(1), 32–54 (1997)
4. Dempe, S., Zemkoho, A.: Bilevel Optimization. Springer, Cham (2020)
5. Durkota, K., Lisỳ, V., Bošanskỳ, B., Kiekintveld, C.: Optimal network security hardening using attack graph games. In: Twenty-Fourth International Joint Conference on Artificial Intelligence (2015)
6. Hansen, P., Jaumard, B., Savard, G.: New branch-and-bound rules for linear bilevel programming. SIAM J. Sci. Stat. Comput. **13**(5), 1194–1217 (1992)
7. Hong, J., Kim, D.S.: HARMs: hierarchical attack representation models for network security analysis. In: Australian Information Security Management Conference, p. 9. SRI Security Research Institute, Edith Cowan University, Perth, Western Australia (2012)
8. Hong, J.B., Kim, D.S.: Assessing the effectiveness of moving target defenses using security models. IEEE Trans. Dependable Secure Comput. **13**(2), 163–177 (2016)
9. Jha, S., Sheyner, O., Wing, J.: Two formal analyses of attack graphs. In: Proceedings 15th IEEE Computer Security Foundations Workshop, CSFW-15, pp. 49–63 (2002)
10. Lallie, H.S., Debattista, K., Bal, J.: A review of attack graph and attack tree visual syntax in cyber security. Comput. Sci. Rev. **35**, 100219 (2020)
11. Madani, O.: On policy iteration as a newton's method and polynomial policy iteration algorithms. In: Eighteenth National Conference on Artificial Intelligence, pp. 273–278. American Association for Artificial Intelligence, USA (2002)
12. Mattsson, L.G., Weibull, J.W.: Probabilistic choice and procedurally bounded rationality. Games Econom. Behav. **41**(1), 61–78 (2002)
13. Milani, S., et al.: Harnessing the power of deception in attack graph-based security games. In: Zhu, Q., Baras, J.S., Poovendran, R., Chen, J. (eds.) GameSec 2020. LNCS, vol. 12513, pp. 147–167. Springer, Cham (2020). https://doi.org/10.1007/978-3-030-64793-3_8
14. Nachum, O., Norouzi, M., Xu, K., Schuurmans, D.: Bridging the gap between value and policy based reinforcement learning. In: Advances in Neural Information Processing Systems, vol. 30. Curran Associates, Inc. (2017)
15. Nguyen, T.H., Wright, M., Wellman, M.P., Singh, S.: Multistage attack graph security games: heuristic strategies, with empirical game-theoretic analysis. Secur. Commun. Netw. **2018**, 1–28 (2018)
16. Noel, S., Jajodia, S.: Optimal ids sensor placement and alert prioritization using attack graphs. J. Netw. Syst. Manage. **16**(3), 259–275 (2008)
17. Noel, S., Jajodia, S., Wang, L., Singhal, A.: Measuring security risk of networks using attack graphs. Int. J. Next-Gener. Comput. **1**(1), 135–147 (2010)

18. Puterman, M.L.: Markov Decision Processes: Discrete Stochastic Dynamic Programming. Wiley, Hoboken (2014)

19. Sheyner, O., Haines, J., Jha, S., Lippmann, R., Wing, J.M.: Automated generation and analysis of attack graphs. In: Proceedings 2002 IEEE Symposium on Security and Privacy, pp. 273–284. IEEE (2002)

20. Singhal, A., Ou, X.: Security risk analysis of enterprise networks using probabilistic attack graphs. In: Wang, L., Jajodia, S., Singhal, A. (eds.) Network Security Metrics, pp. 53–73. Springer, Cham (2017). https://doi.org/10.1007/978-3-319-66505-4_3

21. Sinha, A., Fang, F., An, B., Kiekintveld, C., Tambe, M.: Stackelberg security games: looking beyond a decade of success. In: Proceedings of the Twenty-Seventh International Joint Conference on Artificial Intelligence (IJCAI 2018), Stockholm, Sweden, 13–19 July, pp. 5494–5501 (2018)

22. Thakoor, O., Tambe, M., Vayanos, P., Xu, H., Kiekintveld, C., Fang, F.: Cyber camouflage games for strategic deception. In: Alpcan, T., Vorobeychik, Y., Baras, J.S., Dán, G. (eds.) Decision and Game Theory for Security. LNCS, vol. 11836, pp. 525–541. Springer (2019). https://doi.org/10.1007/978-3-030-32430-8_31

23. Ziebart, B.D., Maas, A.L., Bagnell, J.A., Dey, A.K., et al.: Maximum entropy inverse reinforcement learning. In: AAAI, Chicago, IL, USA, vol. 8, pp. 1433–1438 (2008)

The Credential is Not Enough: Deception with Honeypots and Fake Credentials

Sonia Cromp[1]([✉])[ID], Mark Bilinski[2][ID], Ryan Gabrys[2][ID], and Frederic Sala[1][ID]

[1] University of Wisconsin-Madison, Madison, WI 53706, USA
cromp@wisc.edu, fredsala@cs.wisc.edu
[2] Naval Information Warfare Center Pacific, San Diego, CA, USA
{mark.bilinski.civ,ryan.c.gabrys.civ}@us.navy.mil

Abstract. Honeypots are a classic cyber-deceptive technique that allows a defender to add false information into the system in an effort to deter/delay/distract potential attackers. However, the effectiveness of honeypots is dependent on their design along with the environment into which they are deployed. In this work, we consider the scenario where there is a collection of honeypots along with a set of fake credentials. In the first part of the paper, we uncover fundamental bounds that relate to how long these deceptive elements remain effective. In the second part of the paper, we take our results one step further and analyze a two-person game where the attacker attempts to access desired resources within a system according to a preference model and the defender attempts to design honeypots that slow attacker progress. While prior work has demonstrated the defender's ability to learn attacker preferences by observing the attacker's actions, we enrich both parties' action spaces by allowing the attacker to query whether a server is real or honeypot and by allowing the defender to choose between honeypots that better reveal attacker behavior, or honeypots that exploit current knowledge of attacker behavior. In this setting, we provide and analyze optimal strategies for the attacker, along with a learning bound for and simulation of defender strategies.

Keywords: Adversarial game · Cyber-deception · Active learning

1 Introduction

Cybersecurity is an area of great importance for any organization, whether in industry, government, military, or other settings [4,13]. Despite increased focus, systems meant to provide security face two challenges. First, many techniques offer a plausible approach to defense, but lack provable security guarantees, or offer them in highly narrow settings. Second, the space is dynamic, with frequent appearances of new cyberattacks and defenses, as well as combinations of extant techniques. These obstacles must be overcome for organizations to have confidence in their cybersecurity. As a result, we are interested in studying settings that have rich attack models and defense strategies with provable guarantees.

J. Fu et al. (Eds.): GameSec 2023, LNCS 14167, pp. 234–254, 2023.
https://doi.org/10.1007/978-3-031-50670-3_12

Among the most important such settings involve the use of *deception* for providing means of defense [1]. For defenders, such deception can be expressed through *honeypots*—false information or devices that are added within an ecosystem to slow down or block attackers [3,6]. Honeypot-based systems naturally admit a game-theoretical formulation [12], but there is a wide variety of such settings. Many of the most realistic settings have not yet been addressed.

We focus on cyberattack settings where the attacker's interests can be described via a preference model, as in [6,7]. In contrast to earlier work, the attacker may choose between two attack vectors. In one approach, the attacker attempts to use accessible credentials to gain access to a system, allowing the attacker to access resources within the system of the most interest to the attacker. In the other, the attacker performs random attacks, which may be faster than relying on credentials but is less targeted towards the specific resources which the attacker would like to access. To prevent these attacks, the defender has the ability to use *deception*—setting up honeypot systems and creating false sets of credentials in order to slow down or prevent the attacker from breaking in. This work studies the fundamentals of such multiple-attack scenarios.

2   Related Work

A rich line of literature has studied deception in the context of cybersecurity. In such work, a typical scenario involves a two-player game between an *attacker* and a *defender*. The goal of the attacker is to access some system resources. The defender can prevent this from happening (or slow it down) by presenting honeypots—fake resources—to the user. Such games have been extensively studied [2,5,11], usually in the form of zero-sum games.

A closely related line of work involves learning from preferences. For example, attackers may have particular interests in accessing certain resources. Defenders therefore seek to learn these preferences. Doing so enables them to potentially deploy honeypots and other means of deception. Such work, including [6], obtain learning bounds on the number of *interactions* required for defenders to learn a sufficiently accurate estimate of the attacker model.

This work studies richer scenarios with multiple attack vectors. The first of these is inspired by [15]; here the attacker seeks to obtain credentials via querying servers, but must deal with honeypot servers that do not tell the truth (like the *spies* in [15]). The second involves a preferential model as in [6]. In contrast to this work, we tackle two additional factors. The first is that defenders must handle the two attack factors. The second is that the environment is changed by deployment of honeypots—complicating learning attacker preferences.

3   Setup and Structure

In this work, we consider a system of s servers, of which ℓ are honeypots and μ are real, and c credentials, of which ρ are fake. Let $\mathcal{S}$ denote the set of indices of all servers, $\mathcal{S}_h$ the set of honeypots and $\mathcal{S}_r$ the set of real servers. While the defender knows the identities of all servers and credentials, the attacker discovers them over the course of the game. Instead, the attacker only knows that there are *at most* t_H honeypot servers and t_F false credentials.

The i-th server is described by a feature vector $x_i \in \mathbb{R}_+^d$, which intuitively may be thought of as the embedding of various features which describe the server, such as name and location. The attacker has a vector of preferences within the same embedding space, denoted $w \in \mathbb{R}_+^d$. For instance, the attacker may be interested in servers located in a particular region. Both attacker and defender observe x_i for each server i, while only the attacker knows their own preference vector w. We say that the attacker's relative "interest" in a server i is proportional to $w^T x_i$. We refer to the α real servers with highest attacker interest as the attacker's *desired servers* $\mathcal{S}_d$. The game ends when the attacker performs β accesses to each of the α desired servers.

The attacker may choose one of two strategies: performing queries to learn the identities of each server and credential, then accessing the desired servers over the following $\alpha\beta$ timesteps, or performing random attacks. If the attacker elects to perform identity queries, the attacker selects a server $i \in [s]$ and credential $j \in [c]$, then poses a question of the form "Server i, is credential j real (R) or fake (F)?" in each timestep until learning all identities. If instead they perform random attacks, they access the i-th server with probability

$$p_i = \frac{\exp(w^T x_i)}{\sum_{j \in \mathcal{S}} \exp(w^T x_j)}.$$

One attack is carried out in each timestep until all $\alpha\beta$ goal accesses are performed. When attacking server i, the attacker gains access to a portion of its private data if i is real; otherwise, the attacker discovers that i is a honeypot.

The attacker gains 1 point each time they complete one of the $\alpha\beta$ desired accesses and loses 1 point each time they attack a honeypot – upon accessing or querying server i for the j-th time in timestep t, the attacker reward is

$$R^t(i,j) = \begin{cases} -1 & \text{if attack and } i \in \mathcal{S}_h \\ 1 & \text{if attack, } i \in \mathcal{S}_d \text{ and } j < \beta \\ 0 & \text{otherwise.} \end{cases} \tag{1}$$

Rewards are also multiplied by a discount factor Δ^t in timestep t, for $0 < \Delta \leq 1$. While the identity query strategy avoids the random access strategy's risk of penalization from attacking honeypots, this strategy's accesses may be performed later than random strategy accesses, and thus encounter lower rewards due to the discount Δ.

Meanwhile, the defender chooses the x-vectors of their ℓ honeypots, selecting between honeypot placements that allow the defender to learn a better estimate $\tilde{W}$ of w and placements that maximize honeypot attack probability. The defender receives reward $-R^t(i,j)$ in timestep t, forming a zero-sum game.

The remainder of this work is structured as follows. First, we consider the attacker's two actions in Sect. 4. Sections 4.1 and 4.2 discuss the amount of queries needed for the attacker to learn servers' and credentials' identities prior to performing the $\alpha\beta$ desired accesses, while Sect. 4.3 analyzes the random attack strategy, determining the expected number of random attacks needed to perform the $\alpha\beta$ desired accesses. We then discuss the game from the defender's point of view in Sect. 5. This section compares honeypot placement strategies, establishing a learning bound on the defender's ability to learn w (and thereby more effectively target honeypots that lure the attacker) and demonstrating the defender's strategies in a simulated game environment.

4 Attacker Strategy

In this section, the defender is fixed such that the x-vectors of honeypots are held constant. We first study the attacker's identity query strategy, where the attacker asks a query of the form, "Server i, is credential j real (R) or fake (F)?" in each timestep until learning all identities and performing the desired accesses.

We assume that our ℓ honeypots are low-interaction, which implies that they will always respond with the answer F, whereas the remaining μ real servers will respond truthfully with either R or F, depending on whether the credential is real or fake, respectively. As such, a response of R only occurs when i and j are both real; otherwise the response is F. Only once that the attacker has learned the identities of all s servers and c credentials can the attacker perform their desired $\alpha\beta$ accesses. Under this setup, Sect. 4.1 determines the worst-case maximum number of identity queries until the attacker can perform their desired accesses, while Sect. 4.2 finds the average case number of queries. A greater number of timesteps prior to the desired accesses will result in a greater time penalty on the attacker's positive rewards during the desired accesses in (1).

Lastly, Sect. 4.3 considers the attacker's random attack strategy.

4.1 Determining Server and Credential Identities - Worst Case

We refer to the property of a credential being real or fake as the "type" of the credential. Analogously, we refer to the property of a server being a real server or a honeypot as the identity of the server. We will study the following problems:

1. How many questions are necessary and sufficient to determine the type of each of the credentials?
2. How many questions are necessary and sufficient to determine the identity of each of the servers?

We note that as a result of the symmetry of the game setup, the solutions to both of these problems is the same, and consequently we will focus on the first problem. For shorthand, we will refer to the solution to 1) above as $Q^*(s, c, t_H, t_F)$ so that after $Q^*(s, c, t_H, t_F)$ questions, the attacker will always be able to determine the type of each of the c credentials. For notational convenience, when the parameters s, c, t_H, t_F are understood, we will abbreviate $Q^*(s, c, t_H, t_F)$ as Q^*.

Our main result is to show that, for the case where $t_H \geq t_F - 1$, at most $Q^* = t_H + t_F - 1 + c$ questions (or queries) are necessary and sufficient. This implies that, under the scenario where there are roughly as many fake credentials as honeypots, both types of deception appear to impact the attacker nearly equally. However, when $t_H << t_F - 1$, this trend does not hold. We show in Sect. 4.1 that at most only $c + \mathcal{O}(\sqrt{t_F})$ queries are needed for the case where t_H is a constant. From a defender point of view, this implies that increasing the number of fake credentials (typically easier) has a similar effect as increasing the number of honeypots, provided they are roughly comparable in number. In this setting, introducing either one additional fake honeypot or one additional fake credential requires the attacker ask one additional query. When $t_H << t_F - 1$, introducing a honeypot appears to be significantly more impactful than a fake credential. For this setting, introducing one honeypot requires the attacker ask at most $\sqrt{t_F}$ additional queries whereas increasing the number of fake credentials in certain cases only increases the overall number of queries by at most a constant.

Upper Bound on Q^*. In the following, we show that $Q^* \leq t_H + t_F - 1 + c$. This result is stated more formally in Lemma 1. Afterwards, for the setting where $t_H < \sqrt{t_F}$, we show that this quantity is at most only $\sqrt{t_F}(2t_H + 1) + 1 + c$. We begin with the following observation, which we state as a claim for clarity.

Claim 1. *If server i responds R when queried about credential j, then credential j is real and server i is a real machine.*

The basic idea behind our first approach, which shows $Q^* \leq t_H + t_F - 1 + c$, is to ask as few questions as possible in order to produce an answer of R to one of our questions. Afterwards, we will query this server about the identity of each of the other $c - 1$ credentials. The output of the following procedure will be the set $\mathcal{C}_R \subseteq [c]$, which we will later show, contains the identity of the real credentials.
Initialize $\mathcal{C}_R = \emptyset$. We proceed as follows:

- Step 1: Generate $t_H + t_F + 1$ pairs of elements say $(i_1, j_1), (i_2, j_2), \ldots, (i_{t_H+t_F+1}, j_{t_H+t_F+1})$ where $|\{i_1, \ldots, i_{t_H+t_F+1}\}| = |\{j_1, \ldots, j_{t_H+t_F+1}\}| = t_H + t_F + 1$. (i_k, j_k) represents the question: "Server i_k, is credential j_k R or F?"
- Step 2: Starting with question (i_1, j_1), the attacker asks each of the questions in the list generated at step 1. Suppose that k^* is the first question that generates the response R. Claim 1 implies that server i_{k^*} is a real machine and also that credential j_{k^*} is a real credential. Add j_{k^*} to the set $\mathcal{C}_R$.
- Step 3: If $k^* = t_H + t_R + 1$, then add $[c] \setminus [k^*]$ to $\mathcal{C}_R$. Otherwise, ask server i_{k^*} about the credentials $\{j_{k^*+1}, \ldots, j_c\}$. For any $k \in [c] \setminus [k^*]$, if server i_{k^*} responds R, then add j_k to the set $\mathcal{C}_R$.
- Step 4: For $k \in \{1, 2, \ldots, k^* - 1\}$ ask server i_{k^*} about credential j_k. For any $k \in [k^* - 1]$, if server i_{k^*} responds R, then add j_k to the set $\mathcal{C}_R$.

We begin with the following observation.

Claim 2. *In step 2, $k^* \leq t_H + t_F + 1$. Furthermore, if $k^* = t_H + t_F + 1$, then the credentials $\{j_{t_H+t_F+1}, j_{t_H+t_F+2}, \ldots, j_c\}$ are real.*

Note that according to Claim 1, server i_k^* has correctly identified $c - k^* + 1$ of the m credentials by the end of step 3, which implies that we have not asked server i_k^* about the identity of $k^* - 1$ credentials and in particular about the credentials $\{1, 2, \ldots, k^* - 1\}$. We now arrive at the main result of this section.

Lemma 1. *For any $j \in [c]$, $j \in \mathcal{C}_R$ if and only if credential j is real. The number of questions asked in steps 1–4 is at most $t_H + t_F - 1 + c$ provided $c, s \geq t_H + t_F + 2$.*

Proof. The fact that the set $\mathcal{C}_R$ contains the identities of each of the real credentials follows immediately from the previous discussion. The number of questions asked at steps 1) and 4) are k^* and $k^* - 1$, respectively. Letting q_3 denote the number of questions asked at step 3, the total number of questions is:

$$2k^* - 1 + q_3. \tag{2}$$

Here, there are two cases to consider. If $k^* < t_H + t_F + 1$, then $q_3 \leq c - k^*$ and (2) is at most $c + t_H + t_F - 1$ as desired. Otherwise, if $k^* = t_H + t_F + 1$, then $q_3 = 0$ and (2) is $2(t_H + t_F + 1) - 1$.

Although the previous approach has the advantage of working for a wide range of parameter choices for t_H, t_F, it is far from optimal in many cases. In particular, for the setting where t_H is a constant with respect to t_F, it turns out that a better strategy exists which requires $c + \mathcal{O}(\sqrt{t_F})$.

For simplicity, we assume that t_F is a square, although it is straightforward to extend to a more general setting. The attacker first chooses a set of t_F credentials, denoted $j_1, \ldots, j_{t_F}$ and partitions this set of credentials into $\sqrt{t_F}$ groups denoted:

$$\mathcal{J}_1 = \{j_1, \ldots, j_{\sqrt{t_F}}\},$$
$$\mathcal{J}_2 = \{j_{\sqrt{t_F}+1}, \ldots, j_{2\sqrt{t_F}}\},$$
$$\vdots$$
$$\mathcal{J}_{\sqrt{t_F}} = \{j_{t_F - \sqrt{t_F}+1}, \ldots, j_{t_F}\}.$$

Initialize $\mathcal{C}_R = \emptyset$. We proceed as follows.

- Step 1: Generate t_F pairs of questions (i_1, j_1), $(i_1, j_2), \ldots, (i_1, j_{\sqrt{t_F}})$, $(i_2, j_{\sqrt{t_F}+1})$, $(i_2, j_{\sqrt{t_F}+2}), \ldots, (i_2, j_{2\sqrt{t_F}}), \ldots, (i_{\sqrt{t_F}}, j_{t_F})$ where $i_1, \ldots, i_{\sqrt{t_F}}$ are $\sqrt{t_F}$ distinct hosts. Starting with (i_1, j_1) ask each of these t_F queries.
- Step 2: Generate an additional (at most) $t_H \sqrt{t_F} + 1$ queries of the form (i, j) such that for each such query the following holds: (i) Host i has not been queried previously and (ii) Credential j has not appeared in any previous queries. If any point we receive the response T, we proceed to Step 3).
- Step 3: At this point, we have received the response T. Suppose the query which receives this response is (i_k, j_k). Insert j_k into $\mathcal{C}_R$. We next ask the following $\sqrt{t_F}$ questions: $(i_1, j_k), (i_2, j_k), \ldots, (i_{\sqrt{t_F}}, j_k)$. Let $\mathcal{I}_F$ denote the set of servers whose response is F. Go to Step 4).

- Step 4: For each $v \in [\sqrt{t_F}]$, if $i_v \in \mathcal{I}_F$, then for each $j \in \mathcal{J}_v$, we perform the query (i_k, j) and if the response is T, then we add credential j to $\mathcal{C}_R$.
- Step 5: For each credential j outside the set $j_1, j_2, \ldots, j_{t_F}$, we perform the query (i_k, j) and if the response if T, we add j to the set $\mathcal{C}_R$.

Lemma 2 states that the maximum number of queries necessary to determine the type of each of the c credentials. First, we present an illustrative example.

Example 1. Suppose $t_H = 1$, and $t_F = 16$. We assume in the following that i_1 is a honeypot and $j_5, j_6, \ldots, j_{16}, j_{17}, j_{18}, j_{19}$ are fake credentials. According to the previous procedure, in step 1 suppose we formulate $t = 16$ queries:

$$
\begin{bmatrix}
(i_1, j_1) & (i_2, j_5) & (i_3, j_9) & (i_4, j_{13}) \\
(i_1, j_2) & (i_2, j_6) & (i_3, j_{10}) & (i_4, j_{14}) \\
(i_1, j_3) & (i_2, j_7) & (i_3, j_{11}) & (i_4, j_{15}) \\
(i_1, j_4) & (i_2, j_8) & (i_3, j_{12}) & (i_4, j_{16})
\end{bmatrix}.
\tag{3}
$$

More specifically the attacker will first ask the query (i_1, j_1) followed by (i_1, j_2) and so on until we have asked all 16 queries. Since i_1 is a honeypot and $j_5, \ldots, j_{20}$ are fake, it follows that the response to each of these queries is F.

For step 2, assume the next 5 queries are $(i_5, j_{17}), (i_6, j_{18}), (i_7, j_{19}), (i_8, j_{20}),$ (i_9, j_{21}). We will receive the response T on the second to last query since i_8 is not a honeypot and j_{20} is a real credential. At this point we add j_{20} to our list of real credentials and after the query (i_8, j_{20}) we will proceed to the third step.

At step 3), we ask $(i_1, j_{20}), (i_2, j_{20}), (i_3, j_{20}), (i_4, j_{20})$. (i_1, j_{20}) returns F and the others return T. Because of the T responses, each of the credentials in the last 3 columns of (3) are of type fake. Next we proceed to step 4).

At step 4), in order to determine the identity of the credentials in the set $j_1, \ldots, j_{20}$ it suffices to query the host i_8 (which we know is not a honeypot) about each of the credentials in the first column of (3). Since each of these credentials are by assumption real, it follows that $j_1, \ldots, j_4$ will be added to $\mathcal{C}_R$.

Finally, in step 5) we add each credential outside $\{j_5, j_6, \ldots, j_{19}\}$ to $\mathcal{C}_R$. Note that this step requires $c - 16$ additional queries to i_8. In all, for each subsequent step we have performed respectively 16, 4, 4, 4, and $c - 16$ queries. In total $c + 12$ queries which, for this choice of parameters, is less than or equal to $c + \sqrt{t_F}(2t_H + 1) + 1 = c + 4 \cdot (2 + 1) + 1 = c + 13$ as claimed.

Lemma 2. *For the setup where $t_H < \sqrt{t_F}$ and where $c, s > t_H + t_F$, the number of queries to determine the type of each credential is at most $Q^* \leq \sqrt{t_F}(2t_H + 1) + 1 + c$.*

Lower Bound on Q^*. We next turn to the question of optimality and we will show that for the case where $t_H \geq t_F - 1$, at least $t_H + t_F - 1 + c$ questions are also necessary. We can consider our setup as a game, that is being played between an attacker and Mother Nature (MN) where the attacker is allowed to ask any questions of the same form as described earlier and Mother Nature is allowed to fix the identities and types of each of the servers and credentials.

The main challenge, which we focus on now, is to establish the result for the case where $t_H = t_F - 1$. Our key technical result is described in the next lemma.

Lemma 3. *Suppose the attacker asks $t_H + t_F - 1$ queries and, among these queries, there are exactly c_0 credentials contained across the $t_H + t_F - 1$ queries. Then, in order to determine the identity of these c_0 credentials, there exists an assignment of identities to credentials and servers by MN such that c_0 additional queries are necessary.*

Under our setup, we assume that MN always assigns at most t_H honeypots and at $t_F - 1$ fake credentials to ensure that the first $t_H + t_F - 1$ queries receive the response F where during these first $t_H + t_F - 1$ queries at least $t_H + 1$ servers are queried and at least $t_H + 1$ credentials are also queried. Note that this scenario is always indeed possible since it can be the case that the first t_H hosts queried are honeypots and the following $t_F - 1 = t_H$ credentials queried are of type fake. Using the result stated in the previous lemma, we will show in Theorem 1 that an additional c_0 queries are necessary to determine the first c_0 credentials that were queried along with an additional $c - c_0$ queries (which each pertain to credentials outside the first c_0 queried), implying a total of $t_H + t_F - 1 + c_0 + (c - c_0) = t_H + t_F - 1 + c$ queries are necessary.

In order to tackle this problem, we will visualize the first $t_H + t_F - 1$ queries by means of edges in a bi-partite graph where the vertices on the left side of this graph, which we denote as V_S, represent each of the servers queried in the first $t_H + t_F - 1$ queries and the vertices on the right hand side of the graph, which we denote as V_C, represent the credentials queried in the first $t_H + t_F - 1$ queries. There exists an edge between vertex i on the left side of the graph and vertex j on the right hand side of the graph if the attacker asks the question (i, j). We illustrate this setup by means of the next example. For shorthand, we refer to this graph as the **question graph** $\mathcal{G}$ for the game.

Example 2. Suppose the attacker asks $(i_1, j_1), (i_2, j_2), (i_1, j_3), (i_3, j_2)$. Then, the question graph $\mathcal{G}$ that represents this sequence of questions is shown below:

For our analysis, we assume that the first $t_H + t_F - 1$ queries, which by assumption all have received the response F, are fixed before the start of the game. We say that the question sequence $\mathcal{Q}$ *belongs to* $\mathcal{G}$ if for every query in $\mathcal{Q}$ either the server queried or the credential queried about (or both) are contained in $\mathcal{G}$ and we represent this as $\mathcal{Q} \in \mathcal{G}$. As will be discussed in Claim 6, we assume that when a query contains either a host or credential *not* represented in $\mathcal{G}$, then their identity is not labeled F. Conceptually, the questions in $\mathcal{Q}$ are questions that are asked by an attacker (after the initial $t_H + t_F - 1$ queries) that can be used to recover the identity of each credential in $\mathcal{G}$.

The graph $\mathcal{G}$ will always have $t_H + t_F - 1$ edges. Given the graph $\mathcal{G}$, we can recast our problem as a labeling game for MN where she can label at most t_H vertices in V_S to be F (which means they are honeypots) and at most t_H vertices in V_C to be F (which means the corresponding credential is of type fake). In order to make this a binary labeling, we will assume the other vertices that are not labeled F are labeled R. The goal will be to show that for any given $\mathcal{G}$ and $\mathcal{Q}$, there exists a *labeling procedure*, denoted by the function L, which takes as input $\mathcal{G}$ and $\mathcal{Q}$ and outputs a labeling $L(\mathcal{G}, \mathcal{Q})$ such that:

1. The labeling $L(\mathcal{G}, \mathcal{Q})$ is **consistent** - This means that for any edge in the question graph $\mathcal{G}$ at least one vertex in that edge is labeled F under $L(\mathcal{G}, \mathcal{Q})$.
2. The labeling procedure $L(\mathcal{G}, \mathcal{Q})$ is **robust** - If $|\mathcal{Q}| < |V_C|$ it is not possible for the attacker to ascertain the identity of each credential in $\mathcal{G}$ by asking the queries in $\mathcal{Q}$ and $\mathcal{G}$.

Note that in order to satisfy the consistency constraint, for any edge $(i, j) \in E_{\mathcal{G}}$ (where $E_{\mathcal{G}}$ represents the edge set for the question graph $\mathcal{G}$), either i is labeled F or j is labeled F or both. Note also that if i is labeled R and $(i, j) \in E_{\mathcal{G}}$, then it follows under our setup that j must be labeled F and vice versa.

Next, we introduce notation addressing robustness. Let $\mathcal{D}$ be a decoding rule such that given $\mathcal{Q}$ along with a sequence of responses F_R to each of the queries in $\mathcal{Q}$, the output of $\mathcal{D}$ is the set of credentials whose identities are known. Given an assignment of identities to the vertices in $\mathcal{G}$, the response from each of the servers is deterministic. We capture this relationship by letting F_R be a function which takes as input the assignment of identities to servers and credentials. The robustness property of L requires that for any sequence of queries $\mathcal{Q} \in \mathcal{G}$ of cardinality less than $|V_C|$, there exists a labeling $L(\mathcal{G}, \mathcal{Q})$ such that

$$|\mathcal{D}(\mathcal{Q}, F_R(L(G, \mathcal{Q})))| < |V_C|. \tag{4}$$

Thus, the goal will be to show that there exists a labeling procedure L, which is consistent and robust. With an abuse of notation, we will also say that a labeling for a particular graph $\mathcal{G}$ and a particular set of queries $\mathcal{Q}$ is consistent with respect to $\mathcal{G}$ if each edge in $\mathcal{G}$ has a vertex labeled F. Furthermore, for a specific question sequence $\mathcal{Q}$, we will say that the labeling is robust with respect to $\mathcal{G}, \mathcal{Q}$ if (4) holds provided $|\mathcal{Q}| < |V_C|$.

The next three claims, whose proofs are deferred for the extended version of the paper, will be useful in our subsequent derivations and in particular will be invoked in the proof of Lemma 4. Let $L_{t_H, t_F - 1}(\mathcal{G}, \mathcal{Q})$ be a labeling procedure that assigns at most t_H F labels to vertices in V_S and $t_F - 1$ F labels to vertices to vertices in V_C. When it is clear from the context, the parameters $t_H, t_F - 1$ may be omitted from the notation for the labeling procedure L.

Claim 3. *Let $\mathcal{G}'$ be a question graph and $\mathcal{Q} \in \mathcal{G}'$ be a question sequence where $\mathcal{G}'$ has vertex set $V_S \cup V_C$ and $\mathcal{G}'$ has edge set $E_{\mathcal{G}'}$. Let $\mathcal{G} = \mathcal{G}' + e_1, e_2$ where $e_1 = (i_1, j_1), e_2 = (i_2, j_2)$ and where the degree of any vertex in $\mathcal{G}'$ is at most t_H and $j_1 \neq j_2$. If, for any sequence $\mathcal{Q}$ there exists a labeling $L_{t_H - 1, t_F - 2}(\mathcal{G}', \mathcal{Q})$, which is consistent and robust with respect to $\mathcal{G}', \mathcal{Q}$, then there exists a labeling $L_{t_H, t_F - 1}(\mathcal{G}, \mathcal{Q})$ that is consistent and robust with respect to $\mathcal{G}, \mathcal{Q}$.*

Claim 4. *Suppose $t_H = t_F - 1$ and $\mathcal{G}$ is a question graph after $t_H + t_F - 1$ queries by the attacker where $|V_C| \geq t_H + 1$, $|V_S| \geq t_H + 1$, and at most one* vertex in V_C has degree at least 2 and the remaining vertices in V_C have degree one. For any question sequence $Q \in \mathcal{G}$, there exists a labeling that is consistent and robust with respect to $\mathcal{G}, Q$.

Claim 5. *Let $\mathcal{G}$ be a question graph where there exists $v^* \in V_S$ with degree t_H and where each neighbor of v^* has degree exactly one. For any question sequence $Q \in \mathcal{G}$, there exists a labeling that is consistent and robust with respect to $\mathcal{G}, Q$.*

We now aim to prove Lemma 3 by induction on $t_H = t_F - 1$ and the next claim considers the base case. Recall that for now, we assume the degree of each vertex in V_C is less than $t_H + 1$ after the initial $t_H + t_F - 1$ queries. We will show later that when this restriction is removed the result still holds afterwards.

Claim 6. *Suppose $t_H = t_F - 1 = 1$, $\mathcal{G}$ is the question graph after $t_H + t_F - 1 = 2$ queries by the attacker where $|V_C| \geq t_H + 1 = 2$ and $|V_S| \geq t_H + 1 = 2$. Then, there exists a labeling procedure that is consistent and robust.*

Using the previous claim, we have the following lemma.

Lemma 4. *Suppose $t_H = t_F - 1 > 1$ and $\mathcal{G}$ is a question graph after $t_H + t_F - 1$ queries by the attacker where $|V_C| \geq t_H + 1$, $|V_S| \geq t_H + 1$, and the degree of any vertex in $\mathcal{G}$ is at most t_H. Then, for any question sequence Q, there exists a labeling procedure that is consistent and robust.*

Proof. The proof will be by induction on t_H (and $t_F - 1$) where the base case was proven in Claim 6. Suppose the result holds for all $t_H, t_F - 1 \leq L$ and consider the case where $t_H = t_F - 1 = L + 1$. Let $\mathcal{G}'$ denote the question graph if we remove two edges (or queries) from $\mathcal{G}$ where $j_1 \neq j_2$. By the induction hypothesis, $\mathcal{G}'$ has a labeling procedure that is consistent and robust. If $\mathcal{G}'$ has any unconnected vertices, we remove those from the graph as well. For the case where there exists a vertex $v \in V_C$ or $v \in V_S$ with degree t_H then one of the edges removed from $\mathcal{G}$ must be adjacent to v. Because $|V_C|, |V_S| \geq t_H + 1$, there can be at most one vertex in V_C with a degree t_H and at most one vertex in V_S with degree t_H. Let $\mathcal{E} = \{(i_{r_1}, j_{r_1}), (i_{r_2}, j_{r_2})\}$ denote the set of two vertices that were removed from $\mathcal{G}$ to obtain $\mathcal{G}'$ where we require that $j_{r_1} \neq j_{r_2}$.

Next we consider the choice of the two edges in $\mathcal{E}$. If there is a choice of edges such that no vertices are isolated by their removal, then the vertex sets of $\mathcal{G}$ and $\mathcal{G}'$ are the same and the result follows from Claim 3. Next, we consider the case where at least one vertex in V_C appears in $\mathcal{G}$ but not $\mathcal{G}'$. Note that if this scenario occurs, then one of the following holds:

1) All the vertices in V_C have degree one,
2) There is exactly one vertex in V_C that has degree at least two and the remaining have degree one, or
3) $\mathcal{G}$ contains a vertex $v \in V_S$ that has degree t_H and each neighbor of v has degree exactly one.

1) and 2) fall under the conditions of Claim 4. 3) is handled by Claim 5.

Next, we consider scenarios where there appears at least one vertex from V_S that appears in $\mathcal{G}$ but not $\mathcal{G}'$ as a result of removing edges $(i_{r_1}, j_{r_1}), (i_{j_2}, j_{r_2})$ where $j_{r_1} \neq j_{r_2}$. This result can be proven using similar logic to Claim 3. Suppose that $\mathcal{Q} \in \mathcal{G}$ is any valid question sequence $\mathcal{Q} \in \mathcal{G}$. Let $\mathcal{Q}' \subseteq \mathcal{Q}$ be such that $\mathcal{Q}' \in \mathcal{G}'$. Note that $\mathcal{Q}'$ is simply the result of removing at most two queries that involve either i_{r_1}, i_{r_2} and some credential outside $\mathcal{G}$. By the inductive assumption, there exists a labeling which is consistent and robust with respect to $\mathcal{G}', \mathcal{Q}'$. Suppose $v \in \mathcal{G}'$ ($v \in \mathcal{G}$ as well) represents a credential which is unknown given the queries $\mathcal{G}', \mathcal{Q}'$. If v is not adjacent to i_{r_1}, i_{r_2} and it is not equal to j_1, j_2, then setting i_{r_1}, j_{r_2} to be F results in a labeling which is robust and consistent with respect to $\mathcal{G}, \mathcal{Q}$. If v is adjacent to i_{r_1}, then setting i_{r_1} to be F and j_{r_2} to be F results in a robust and consistent labeling. Otherwise, if v is adjacent to i_{r_2} setting i_{r_2} to be F and j_{r_1} to be F results in a robust and consistent labeling.

Theorem 1. *In order to identify the identity of all c credentials, there exists a strategy for MN that always requires the attacker to ask at least $t_H + t_F - 1 + c$ questions when $t_H = t_F - 1$.*

Proof. Suppose first that there exists a vertex $v \in V_S$ that is queried $t_H + 1$ times. Then in this case, we can assume MN labels v to be F. Furthermore, if MN labels the next $t_H - 1$ servers to be F, then it follows that at least $t_H + 1 + (t_H - 1) + c = c + t_H + t_F - 1$ queries are necessary. Similarly, if there exists a vertex $v \in V_C$ that is queried $t_H + 1$ times then we can also assume v is labeled F and so given $t_H + 1$ queries the attacker will have identified exactly one credential. We can assume that MN labels the next t_H honeypots queried to be F, which implies in this case that an additional t_H queries are required. Finally, since at this point, the attacker has recovered the identity of only a single credential, the attacker needs to produce an additional $c - 1$ queries implying a total of $t_H + 1 + t_H + (c - 1) = c + t_H + t_F - 1$ queries are necessary in this case as well.

As a result of the logic in the previous paragraph, we can assume that credential is queried at most t_H times and each server is also queried at most t_H times, which means we can invoke Lemma 3. Suppose that given this setup, the first $t_H + t_F - 1$ queries each receive F from the attacker and the following query receives T. Then according to Lemmas 3 and 4, in order to determine the set of c_0 credentials asked about during the first $t_H + t_F - 1$ queries at least another c_0 queries are necessary. Since among these c_0 credentials there are at most $t_F - 1$ fake credentials, the attacker must also query each of the remaining $c - 1 - c_0$ credentials to determine their identity implying that a total of $t_H + t_F - 1 + 1 + c_0 + (c - 1 - c_0) = c + t_H + t_F - 1$ queries are necessary.

The next result follows by induction on t_H with base case in Theorem 1.

Corollary 1. *For $t_H \geq t_F - 1$, there exists a strategy for MN that always requires the attacker to ask at least $t_H + t_F - 1 + c$ questions.*

4.2   Determining Server and Credential Identities - Average Case

In this section, we derive an explicit expression for the expected number of queries that are sufficient to determine the identity of each of the fake credentials provided the strategy outlined in Lemma 1. Recall we have s servers, of which ℓ are honeypots along with c credentials among which there are ρ that are fake.

First, we compute the probability that we can use exactly $k+1$ questions to obtain the first T response. This means that the first k questions in our strategy either have a fake credential, a honeypot, or both. Suppose that of these, j of the k questions involve a fake credential, and the remaining $k - j$ involve a true credential. This constrains these last $k - j$ to use a honeypot, while the j questions involving a fake credential can have a true or honeypot server.

Next, we count the ways we can obtain the credentials. This is just $\binom{\rho}{j}\binom{c-\rho}{k-j}$, where the two coefficients select from the false and then true credentials. Next, we must allocate the servers. Recalling our constraint, the $k - j$ questions with a true credential must be allocated to $k - j$ of ℓ honeypots, while the remaining j servers can be either real or honeypots. Suppose u of these j servers are chosen as honeypots. This gives $\binom{\ell}{k-j+u}\binom{s-\ell}{j-u}$. Further, there are $\binom{j}{u}$ ways of ordering the two types of servers paired with fake credentials relative to each other.

Our focus thus far has been aimed at getting an F response for the first k questions. We need to now obtain T for the $k + 1$st question. This means using remaining true credentials and true servers, of which we now have $(c - \rho - (k - j)) \times (s - \ell - (j - u))$. Next we must sum over the possibilities j and u, so that our overall number of ways to select the questions is given by $B_k =$

$$\sum_{j=0}^{k}\sum_{u=0}^{j}\binom{\rho}{j}\binom{c-\rho}{k-j}\binom{\ell}{k-j+u}\binom{s-\ell}{j-u}\binom{j}{u}(c-\rho-(k-j))\times(s-\ell-(j-u)),$$

noting, of course, that there are cases where these coefficients reduce to zero simply because there are insufficient credentials or questions to allocate.

The probability that we obtain the first T response on the $(k+1)$-th question is simply the number of possible sequences of k F responses followed by one T response divided by the number of sequences of F responses of any length followed by one T response, i.e. $P_k = \sum_{i=0}^{t+\ell}\frac{B_k}{B_i}$.

Further, after the first "true" answer at the $(k+1)$-th query, we must perform $c - 1$ more queries to identify the remaining credentials. As such, $c + k$ questions are required in total which yields an expected number of questions

$$\mathbb{E}[Q] = \sum_{k=0}^{\rho+\ell}(c + k)P_k. \tag{5}$$

4.3   Attacker Random Access Strategy

We next analyze the game scenario in which the attacker repeatedly performs random accesses. Holding all honeypots constant, we bound the expected number of timesteps for the attacker to complete their $\alpha\beta$ desired accesses. Let $T_{\alpha,\beta}$

denote this quantity of timesteps. Then, the attacker can select between pursuing this all-access strategy (incurring $\mathbb{E}[T_{\alpha,\beta}]$ accesses on average) or pursuing Sect. 4.1's all-credential querying strategy (incurring $\mathbb{E}[Q]$ as defined in Eq. (5), plus $\alpha\beta$). Below, we provide bounds on $\mathbb{E}[T_{\alpha,\beta}]$ (Fig. 1).

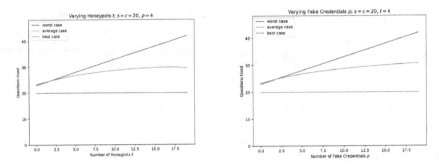

Fig. 1. # of questions used to learn identities of all credentials given average, worst, or best case, varying quantity of honeypots or fake credentials respectively.

Let p_i be the probability the real server with the i-th highest value of wx_i is accessed. Further, let p_0 equal the probability a honeypot or real server outside the top α is accessed. Clearly, $\sum_{i=0}^{\alpha} p_i = 1$, while the probability of a desired $\alpha\beta$ access at the first timestep is no less than αp_α and no greater than αp_1.

Theorem 2 (Necessary and sufficient total number of accesses). *Let* $h(\alpha, \beta) = \log \alpha + (\beta - 1) \log \log \alpha - \log \log (\beta - 1)! + C$. *Then, for a constant C,*

$$\frac{1}{p_1} h(\alpha, \beta) \leq \mathbb{E}[T_{\alpha,\beta}] \leq \frac{1}{p_\alpha} h(\alpha, \beta).$$

Proof. Let $\nu_{\alpha,\beta}$ be the total number of accesses to the α desired servers in order for each server to have β accesses, and let $P(p_0 = \eta - \pi, \nu_{\alpha,\beta} = \pi)$ be the probability that out of η accesses, $\eta - \pi$ are to p_0 and the remaining π are enough to complete the desired accesses. Where line 2 follows by the binomial theorem and using p_1 as an upper bound for the probability that any one desired server is accessed (i.e. $p_1 = \max_{i \in [\alpha]} p_i$), we have that $P(T_{\alpha,\beta} = \eta) =$

$$\sum_{\pi=\alpha\beta}^{\eta} P(p_0 = \eta - \pi, \nu_{\alpha,\beta} = \pi) \leq \sum_{\pi=\alpha\beta}^{\eta} \binom{\eta-1}{\eta-\pi}(1 - \alpha p_1)^{\eta-\pi}(\alpha p_1)^\pi P(\nu_{\alpha,\beta} = \pi)$$

$$= \sum_{\pi=\alpha\beta}^{\eta} \binom{\eta-1}{\eta-\pi}(1 - \alpha p_1)^{\eta-\pi}(\alpha p_1)^\pi \times$$

$$\left[\exp\left(-\frac{e^{-(\pi-r_{\alpha,\beta})/\alpha}}{\beta!}\right) - \exp\left(-\frac{e^{-(\pi-r_{\alpha,\beta}-1)/\alpha}}{\beta!}\right)\right],$$

for $r_{\alpha,\beta} = \alpha \log \alpha + \alpha\beta \log \log \alpha$. Line 3 follows by [9], who also show that $\mathbb{E}[\nu_{\alpha,\beta}] = \alpha \log \alpha + \alpha(\beta - 1) \log \log \alpha - \alpha \log \log (\beta - 1)! + \alpha C$. Therefore, $\mathbb{E}[T_{\alpha,\beta}] \leq \frac{1}{\alpha p_1}(\alpha \log \alpha + \alpha(\beta - 1) \log \log \alpha - \alpha \log \log (\beta - 1)! + \alpha C)$.

$$\mathbb{E}[T_{\alpha,\beta}] \leq \frac{1}{\alpha p_1}(\alpha \log \alpha + \alpha(\beta - 1) \log \log \alpha - \alpha \log \log (\beta - 1)! + \alpha C)$$
$$= \frac{1}{p_1}(\log \alpha + (\beta - 1) \log \log \alpha - \log \log (\beta - 1)! + C) = \frac{1}{p_1}h(\alpha, \beta).$$

The same process, with p_α to lower bound any one desired server's access probability, gives that $P(T_{\alpha,\beta} = \eta) \geq \sum_{\pi=\alpha\beta}^{\eta} \binom{\eta-1}{\eta-\pi}(1 - \alpha p_\alpha)^{\eta-\pi}(\alpha p_\alpha)^\pi *$ $\left[\exp\left(-\frac{e^{-(\pi-r_{\alpha,\beta})/\alpha}}{\beta!}\right) - \exp\left(-\frac{e^{-(\pi-r_{\alpha,\beta}-1)/\alpha}}{\beta!}\right)\right]$, so $\mathbb{E}[T_{\alpha,\beta}] \geq \frac{1}{p_\alpha}h(\alpha, \beta)$.

5 Defender Strategy

We next analyze the game from the defender's perspective. While real servers are held constant, the defender will design honeypots to "mimic" the real servers: dynamically setting $x_i = x_j$ for honeypot i and real server j to confuse and distract the attacker. For simplicity, the attacker is fixed to perform random accesses; we save the attacker's identity query strategy for future work.

We will demonstrate that specific honeypot placements are most effective for exploiting knowledge of the attacker's preferences, while other honeypot placements are most effective for gaining knowledge of the attacker's preferences. Specifically, setting honeypot server i to mimic real server j with maximum attack probability increases the chance of the honeypot being attacked. This is an "exploit" action. However, the defender must form an estimate $\tilde{W}$ of the attacker's preferences w to determine which server is max. As we shall see, mimicking servers with low attack probabilities enables faster rates of learning. This is an "explore" action, where the reward is not maximized in the short term.

We begin by providing theoretical results on the defender's ability to learn the attacker preferences w in Sect. 5.1. Then, Sect. 5.2 validates our theoretical results using a simulation, demonstrating that the defender stalls the attacker from finishing their desired accesses by an average of 5.8% timesteps and scores an average of 32% points more than a defender baseline with constant honeypots.

5.1 Theoretical Results

We bound the expected preference estimation error $\mathbb{E}[||\tilde{W} - w||]$ in terms of parameters such as the number of timesteps and servers. For notational simplicity, we shall make the following assumption: the defender may change one honeypot's x-vector every τ interactions between the attacker and defender. Let T denote the total number of periods with constant honeypot values. Though the final time period may be shorter than τ timesteps if the attacker completes their $\alpha\beta$ desired accesses prior to the period's τ-th timestep, we suppose for simplicity that all periods contain τ steps. However, all results are easily modified to accommodate a shorter final time period.

Estimating Attacker Preferences. First, we outline a procedure for the defender to form their estimate $\tilde{W}$. Concretely, suppose that each honeypot takes on the x-value of a real server. While there are consequences on the reward when the attacker accesses real server i versus a honeypot server with vector x_i (i.e., if the honeypot is sampled by the attacker, the defender has a positive reward), there is *no difference* from the point of view of learning w. For this reason, we can restrict the learning problem to operate on $x_1, \ldots, x_\mu$, where $\mu = |\mathcal{S}_r|$, the number of real servers. Let b_i^k be the total number of servers, real or honeypot, that have value x_i in time period $1 \leq k \leq T$, so that $\sum_{j \in [\mu]} b_j^k = \mu + \ell = s$ and that $1 \leq b_j^k \leq 1 + \ell$ for all j. Then, the distribution p^k in time period k is

$$p_i^k = \frac{b_i^k \exp(w^T x_i)}{\sum_{j \in \mathcal{S}} b_j^k \exp(w^T x_j)}. \tag{6}$$

The defender will run the following algorithm: for the k-th time period, let a_i^k be the number of observed attacks on any of the b_i^k servers with x-vector equal to that of the i-th real server. The defender will estimate the attack distribution as $\tilde{p}_i^k = a_i^k/\tau$ for all $1 \leq i \leq \mu$, then apply smoothing with a small constant ω so that $\tilde{p}_i^k > 0$. Smoothing avoids dividing by 0 in the learning process. The defender will then form and solve a system as in [8], i.e., $A\tilde{w}^k = \tilde{Y}^k$ for

$$A = \begin{bmatrix} x_1 - x_2 \\ x_2 - x_3 \\ \cdots \\ x_{\mu-1} - x_\mu \end{bmatrix} \text{ and } \tilde{Y}^k = \begin{bmatrix} \log(\tilde{p}_1^k/\tilde{p}_2^k) \\ \log(\tilde{p}_2^k/\tilde{p}_3^k) \\ \cdots \\ \log(\tilde{p}_{\mu-1}^k/\tilde{p}_\mu^k) \end{bmatrix} - \begin{bmatrix} \log(b_1^k/b_2^k) \\ \log(b_2^k/b_3^k) \\ \cdots \\ \log(b_{\mu-1}^k/b_\mu^k) \end{bmatrix}.$$

In order to perform linear least squares, we assume $\mu - 1 \geq d$. This will produce an estimate $\tilde{w}^k$ for each period. The final estimate is then just $\tilde{W} = 1/T \sum_{k=1}^T \tilde{w}^k$.

Preference Learning Bound. At first glance, the learning bound in [8] appears to have a similar flavor, where we could use the τT observed interactions to obtain a bound on $\|\tilde{W} - w\|$. Critically, this result does not apply to our setting, because the distributions of our samples are different in each of the T periods due to the varying b^k. Instead, we find

Theorem 3. *Let $B = (A^T A)^{-1} A^T$. Further, let $g(p^k, \delta) = c_1^2 \|B\|^2 \log^2\left(\frac{2T\mu}{\delta}\right)$ $\sum_{j=1}^\mu \frac{1}{(p_j^k)^4}$ for constant c_1 and $k_{\max} = \arg\max_k g(p^k, \delta)$. Then, the defender can learn an estimate $\tilde{W}$ that with probability at least $1 - \delta$ satisfies $\mathbb{E}[\|\tilde{W} - w\|] \leq$*

$$\frac{1}{\tau T} \sqrt{\log(d+1) \sum_{k=1}^T g(p^k, \delta)} + \frac{2\log(d+1)}{3\tau T} \sqrt{\frac{1}{8} g(p^{k_{\max}}, \delta)} + \frac{1}{\tau T} \sum_{k=1}^T \sqrt{\frac{1}{8} g(p^k, \delta)}$$

Interpreting the Bound. Before tackling the proof, we make some remarks. First, there are three summands in the bound. The scaling with respect to game length for the first two summands is given by $O(\frac{1}{\tau\sqrt{T}})$, for the second by $O(\frac{1}{\tau T})$ and for the third by $O(1/\tau)$. To see this, note that we are summing over T terms in the first and third summand. In the first, this is inside the square root, while in the third, there is no square root, canceling the $1/T$ in front. Therefore, the third term is dominant. However, when $\tau > T$, we have that $\frac{1}{\tau} < \frac{1}{\sqrt{\tau T}}$ so that we obtain the same overall learning rate as if all the distributions were identical.

Next, consider the term $g(p^k, \delta)$. We have that $\mathbb{E}[\|\tilde{W} - w\|]$ scales with μT (the product of the number of periods with the number of genuine servers), though the factor is only squared-logarithmic. A more interesting term is $\sum_{j=1}^{\mu} \frac{1}{(p_j^k)^4}$. The learning rate is worse when particular probabilities p_j^k are small. In fact, to obtain the best learning rate, *the defender would want a uniform distribution.* To this end, the defender may design their honeypots so as to cause p^k to most closely resemble the uniform distribution.

The last observation translates into a simple "explore" strategy for the defender. Given ℓ total honeypots, and that $\sum_j b_j^k = \mu + \ell$, the defender should allocate b_i^k's so the resulting model in (6) is as close to uniform as possible.

We now prove the result. The following lemma will prove useful.

Lemma 5. *For any k, with probability at least $1 - \delta$, it holds that*

$$\|\mathbb{E}[\tilde{w}^k - w]\| \le \mathbb{E}[\|\tilde{w}^k - w\|] \le \|B\| \frac{c_1}{\tau} \log\left(\frac{2\mu T}{\delta}\right) \sqrt{\frac{1}{8} \sum_{j=1}^{\mu} \frac{1}{(p_j^k)^4}}.$$

Proof (Proof of Lemma 5). Observe that $\tilde{w}^k = B\tilde{Y}^k$ and $w = BY^k$, where Y^k is analogous to $\tilde{Y}^k$ for p^k. Let $e_i^k = \tilde{p}_i^k - p_i^k$. Then,

$$\tilde{w}^k - w = B \begin{bmatrix} \log(\frac{\tilde{p}_1^k}{\tilde{p}_2^k}) \\ \dots \\ \log(\frac{\tilde{p}_{\mu-1}^k}{\tilde{p}_\mu^k}) \end{bmatrix} - B \begin{bmatrix} \log(\frac{p_1^k}{p_2^k}) \\ \dots \\ \log(\frac{p_{\mu-1}^k}{p_\mu^k}) \end{bmatrix} = B \begin{bmatrix} \log(1 + \frac{e_1^k}{p_1^k}) - \log(1 + \frac{e_2^k}{p_2^k}) \\ \dots \\ \log(1 + \frac{e_{\mu-1}^k}{p_{\mu-1}^k}) - \log(1 + \frac{e_\mu^k}{p_\mu^k}) \end{bmatrix}.$$

So,
$$\frac{\mathbb{E}[\|\tilde{w}^k - w\|]}{\|B\|} \le \mathbb{E}\left[\left\| \begin{bmatrix} \log(1 + \frac{e_1^k}{p_1^k}) - \log(1 + \frac{e_2^k}{p_2^k}) \\ \dots \\ \log(1 + \frac{e_{\mu-1}^k}{p_{\mu-1}^k}) - \log(1 + \frac{e_\mu^k}{p_\mu^k}) \end{bmatrix} \right\| \right]$$

$$= \mathbb{E}\left[\sqrt{\sum_{j=1}^{\mu-1} \left(\log\left(1 + \frac{e_j^k}{p_j^k}\right) - \log\left(1 + \frac{e_{j+1}^k}{p_{j+1}^k}\right)\right)^2}\right]$$

$$\le \mathbb{E}\left[\sqrt{\sum_{j=1}^{\mu-1} \log^2\left(1 + \frac{e_j^k}{p_j^k}\right) + \log^2\left(1 + \frac{e_{j+1}^k}{p_{j+1}^k}\right)}\right] \le \mathbb{E}\left[\sqrt{2\sum_{j=1}^{\mu} \log^2\left(1 + \frac{e_j^k}{p_j^k}\right)}\right]$$

and by Jensen's inequality, since $\mathbb{E}[\cdot^{1/2}] \leq \mathbb{E}[\cdot]^{1/2}$,

$$\mathbb{E}[\|\tilde{w}^k - w\|] \leq \|B\| \mathbb{E}\left[2\sum_{j=1}^{\mu} \log^2\left(1 + \frac{e_j^k}{p_j^k}\right)\right]^{1/2}. \tag{7}$$

We will now derive a bound on $\log^2\left(1 + \frac{e_j^k}{p_j^k}\right)$. From Hoeffding's inequality [10], we have $P(|e_j^k| \geq \epsilon) = P(|\tilde{p}_j^k - p_j^k| \geq \epsilon) \leq 2\exp(-2\tau\epsilon^2)$. Suppose we want $P(|e_j^k| \leq \epsilon)$ with probability $1 - \delta$, then $\delta = 2\exp(-2\tau\epsilon^2)$ so that $\epsilon = \sqrt{\frac{1}{2\tau}\log\frac{2}{\delta}}$. We next apply union bound to simultaneously control the deviations for all μT probabilities p_j^k. With probability at least $1 - \delta$, we have for all $1 \leq j \leq \mu$ and for all $1 \leq k \leq T$ that $|e_j^k| \leq \sqrt{\frac{1}{2\tau}\log\frac{2\mu T}{\delta}}$.

Note that $\mathbb{E}[|e_j|] = 0$, so by the Taylor expansion and for some constant c_1,

$$\mathbb{E}\left[\log\left(1 + \frac{e_j^k}{p_j^k}\right)\right] = \mathbb{E}[\sum_{i=1}^{\infty}(-1)^{i+1}\frac{1}{i}\frac{(e_j^k)^i}{(p_j^k)^i}] = \sum_{i=2}^{\infty}(-1)^{i+1}\frac{1}{i}\frac{\mathbb{E}[(e_j^k)^i]}{(p_j^k)^i}$$

$$\leq \sum_{i=2}^{\infty}(-1)^i\frac{1}{i}\frac{\mathbb{E}[(e_j^k)^i]}{(p_j^k)^i} = \frac{1}{2(p_j^k)^2}\mathbb{E}[|e_j|]^2 + \sum_{i=3}^{\infty}(-1)^i\frac{1}{i}\frac{\mathbb{E}[(e_j^k)^i]}{(p_j^k)^i}$$

$$\leq \frac{c_1}{2(p_j^k)^2}\sqrt{\frac{1}{2\tau}\log\frac{2\mu T}{\delta}}^2 = \frac{c_1}{4\tau(p_j^k)^2}\log\frac{2\mu T}{\delta}.$$

Since $\mathbb{E}[\log^2(\cdot)] = \mathbb{E}[|\log(\cdot)|]^2 = \mathbb{E}[\log(\cdot)]^2$, from (7) and linearity,

$$\mathbb{E}[\|\tilde{w}^k - w\|] \leq \|B\|\left[2\sum_{j=1}^{\mu}\frac{c_1^2}{16\tau^2(p_j^k)^4}\log^2\frac{2\mu T}{\delta}\right]^{1/2}$$

$$= \|B\|\frac{c_1}{\tau}\log\left(\frac{2\mu T}{\delta}\right)\sqrt{\frac{1}{8}\sum_{j=1}^{\mu}\frac{1}{(p_j^k)^4}}$$

Lastly, $\|\mathbb{E}[\tilde{w}^k - w]\| \leq \mathbb{E}[\|\tilde{w}^k - w\|]$ by Jensen's inequality.

Proof (Proof of Theorem 3). We will bound $\mathbb{E}[\|\tilde{W} - w\|]$ using the matrix Bernstein inequality [14]. We first define and bound $S^k = (\tilde{w}^k - w) - \mathbb{E}[\tilde{w}^k - w]$. This is a centered version of the error from estimating $\tilde{w}^k$ in one period k. $\mathbb{E}[S^k] = 0$ and $\mathbb{E}[\|S^k\|] \leq \mathbb{E}[\|\tilde{w}^k - w\|] + \|\mathbb{E}[\tilde{w}^k - w]\| \leq 2\mathbb{E}[\|\tilde{w}^k - w\|]$. By Lemma 5,

$$\mathbb{E}[\|S^k\|] \leq 2\|B\|\frac{c_1}{\tau}\log\left(\frac{2\mu T}{\delta}\right)\sqrt{\frac{1}{8}\sum_{j=1}^{\mu}\frac{1}{(p_j^k)^4}} := L_k.$$

Let $k_{\max} = \arg\max_k L_k$. Note that $\mathbb{E}[\|S^k\|^2] = \mathbb{E}[\|S^k\|]^2$. Next, define $Z = \sum_{k=1}^{T}\frac{1}{T}S^k$, so that $\mathbb{E}\left[\|Z\|^2\right] = \mathbb{E}\left[\left\|\sum_{k=1}^{T}\frac{1}{T}S^k\right\|^2\right] = \sum_{k=1}^{T}\frac{1}{T^2}\mathbb{E}\left[\|S^k\|^2\right]$. This follows since the cross terms are products of uncorrelated terms with zero mean.

By the matrix Bernstein inequality [14] applied to a d-element vector, $\mathbb{E}[\|Z\|] \leq \sqrt{2\mathbb{E}[\|Z\|^2]\log(d+1)} + \frac{L_{k_{\max}}}{3T}\log(d+1)$, we obtain

$$\mathbb{E}[\|Z\|] \leq \sqrt{2\log(d+1)\sum_{k=1}^{T}\frac{1}{T^2}\mathbb{E}[\|S^k\|^2]}$$

$$+ \frac{2}{3T}\log(d+1)\|B\|\frac{c_1}{\tau}\log\left(\frac{2\mu T}{\delta}\right)\sqrt{\frac{1}{8}\sum_{j=1}^{\mu}\frac{1}{(p_j^{k_{\max}})^4}}$$

$$\leq \frac{c_1}{\tau T}\|B\|\log\left(\frac{2\mu T}{\delta}\right)\sqrt{\log(d+1)\sum_{k=1}^{T}\sum_{j=1}^{\mu}\frac{1}{(p_j^k)^4}}$$

$$+ \frac{2}{3T}\log(d+1)\|B\|\frac{c_1}{\tau}\log\left(\frac{2\mu T}{\delta}\right)\sqrt{\frac{1}{8}\sum_{j=1}^{\mu}\frac{1}{(p_j^{k_{\max}})^4}}.$$

Ultimately, $\mathbb{E}[\|\tilde{W} - w\|] =$

$$\frac{1}{T}\mathbb{E}\left[\left\|\sum_{k=1}^{T}(\tilde{w}^k - w)\right\|\right] = \frac{1}{T}\mathbb{E}\left[\left\|\sum_{k=1}^{T}(\tilde{w}^k - w - \mathbb{E}[\tilde{w}^k - w] + \mathbb{E}[\tilde{w}^k - w])\right\|\right]$$

$$= \frac{1}{T}\mathbb{E}\left[\left\|\sum_{k=1}^{T}(S_k + \mathbb{E}[\tilde{w}^k - w])\right\|\right] \leq \frac{1}{T}\mathbb{E}\left[\left\|\sum_{k=1}^{T}S_k\right\| + \left\|\sum_{k=1}^{T}\mathbb{E}[\tilde{w}^k - w]\right\|\right]$$

$$= \mathbb{E}[\|Z\|] + \frac{1}{T}\left\|\sum_{k=1}^{T}\mathbb{E}[\tilde{w}^k - w]\right\| \leq \mathbb{E}[\|Z\|] + \frac{1}{T}\sum_{k=1}^{T}\|\mathbb{E}[\tilde{w}^k - w]\|.$$

Substituting for $\mathbb{E}[\|Z\|]$ and $\|\mathbb{E}[\tilde{w}^k - w]\|$ (from Lemma 5) gives the result.

5.2   Simulation

We implement the defender strategy with a simple thresholding heuristic: the defender begins by exploring in each time period, then switches to exploiting after the first time period k for which $\|\tilde{w}^k - \tilde{w}^{k-1}\|$ is less than a hyperparameter ϵ. We use hyperparameters $s = 4, \ell = 1, d = 2, \tau = 100, \epsilon = 0.1, \Delta = 1, \alpha = 2$ and $\beta = 4000$. Further, we use a simplified reward scheme where the defender loses no points when the attacker completes a desired access. We compare our strategy, "mimic explore/exploit" with a constant strategy where the honeypot is set to mimic a random real server at the beginning of the game, as well as a "mimic explore" strategy where the defender never exploits. See Table 1 for a summary; results are averaged across 100 runs.

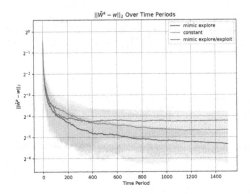

Fig. 2. Preference estimation error $\|\tilde{W}^k - w\|$ across 1500 time periods ($\tau = 100$). We find that the explore strategy achieves lowest error, while explore/exploit achieves highest and the constant strategy serves as a middle ground.

For ease of comparison, we first fix each run to last $T = 1500$ time periods. Figure 2 depicts $\|\tilde{W}^k - w\|$, the error in estimating attacker preferences, across time periods. As expected, the mimic explore strategy consistently achieves the smallest preference estimation error. Mimic explore/exploit begins with comparable performance to mimic explore, but it soon plateaus as it switches to exploiting at time period 741 on average ($\sigma = 446$). Despite that, mimic explore/exploit ultimately does not estimate preferences as well as the constant method, explore/exploit method achieves the highest average score as shown by Fig. 3b. Figure 3a demonstrates that, as mimic explore/exploit switches to exploit, it soon overtakes both mimic explore and constant strategies in encouraging the attacker to access the honeypot. Explore/exploit is able to effectively leverage the knowledge gained during explore phase – applying it during exploit phase and scoring an average of 32% more points than constant defender.

We lastly examine game length, an alternative metric for measuring the effectiveness of honeypot placements in slowing the attacker's progress. Mimic explore/exploit strategy prolongs the attacker from achieving their goal the longest, requiring an average of 5.8% more time periods than the constant method.

Table 1. Standard deviation in parenthesis

	Periods to complete desired accesses	Final preference estimation error	Final score
Mimic explore/exploit	1932.81 (16.18)	0.054 (0.019)	43613.80 (1426.84)
Mimic explore	1756.01 (6.97)	0.025 (0.012)	33038.49 (176.22)
Constant	1826.59 (90.52)	0.040 (0.029)	38015.75 (5544.89)

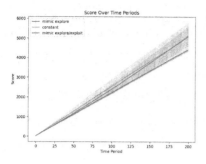

(a) During first 200 time periods.

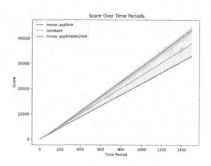

(b) During 1500 time periods.

Fig. 3. Defender reward during first 200 or 1500 periods. While explore/exploit performance initially matches the lowest-scoring explore strategy, it surpasses the constant strategy as it switches to exploit, with widening performance gap.

References

1. Aggarwal, P., Gonzalez, C., Dutt, V.: Cyber-security: role of deception in cyber-attack detection. In: Nicholson, D. (ed.) Advances in Human Factors in Cybersecurity, pp. 85–96. Springer, Cham (2016). https://doi.org/10.1007/978-3-319-41932-9_8
2. Zhang, J., et al.: Modeling multi-target defender-attacker games with quantal response attack strategies. Reliab. Eng. Syst. Saf. **205**, 107165 (2021)
3. Campbell, R.M., et al.: A survey of honeypot research: Trends and opportunities. In: ICITST, pp. 208–212 (2015)
4. Wang, Y., et al.: A survey of game theoretic methods for cyber security. In: IEEE International Conference on Data Science in Cyberspace, pp. 631–636 (2016)
5. Pawlick, J., et al.: A game-theoretic taxonomy and survey of defensive deception for cybersecurity and privacy. ACM Comput. Surv. **52**(4), 1–28 (2019)
6. Bilinski, M., Gabrys, R., Mauger, J.: Optimal placement of honeypots for network defense. In: Bushnell, L., Poovendran, R., Başar, T. (eds.) GameSec 2018. LNCS, vol. 11199, pp. 115–126. Springer, Cham (2018). https://doi.org/10.1007/978-3-030-01554-1_7
7. Bilinski, M., diVita, J., Ferguson-Walter, K., Fugate, S., Gabrys, R., Mauger, J., Souza, B.: Lie another day: demonstrating bias in a multi-round cyber deception game of questionable veracity. In: Zhu, Q., Baras, J.S., Poovendran, R., Chen, J. (eds.) GameSec 2020. LNCS, vol. 12513, pp. 80–100. Springer, Cham (2020). https://doi.org/10.1007/978-3-030-64793-3_5
8. Bilinski, M., et al.: No time to lie: bounds on the learning rate of a defender for inferring attacker target preferences. In: Bošanský, B., Gonzalez, C., Rass, S., Sinha, A. (eds.) GameSec 2021. LNCS, vol. 13061, pp. 138–157. Springer, Cham (2021). https://doi.org/10.1007/978-3-030-90370-1_8
9. Erdős, P., Rényi, A.: On a classical problem of probability theory. Magyar Tud. Akad. Mat. Kutató Int. Közl **6**, 215–220 (1961)
10. Hoeffding, W.: Probability inequalities for sums of bounded random variables. In: Fisher, N.I., Sen, P.K. (eds.) The Collected Works of Wassily Hoeffding, pp. 409–426. Springer, New York (1994). https://doi.org/10.1007/978-1-4612-0865-5_26

11. Nguyen, T., et al.: Deception in finitely repeated security games. In: AAAI (2019)
12. Schlenker, A., et al.: Deceiving cyber adversaries: a game theoretic approach. In: IFAAMAS, pp. 892–900 (2018)
13. Sun, N., et al.: Data-driven cybersecurity incident prediction: a survey. IEEE Commun. Surv. Tutor. **21**(2), 1744–1772 (2019)
14. Tropp, J.A., et al.: An introduction to matrix concentration inequalities. Found. Trends® Mach. Learn. **8**, 1–230 (2015)
15. Wildon, M.: Knights, spies, games and ballot sequences. Discrete Math. **310**(21), 2974–2983 (2010)

Economics of Security

Playing Repeated Coopetitive Polymatrix Games with Small Manipulation Cost

Shivakumar Mahesh[1], Nicholas Bishop[2], Le Cong Dinh[3],
and Long Tran-Thanh[1(✉)]

[1] University of Warwick, Coventry, UK
`long.tran-thanh@warwick.ac.uk`
[2] University of Oxford, Oxford, UK
`nicholas.bishop@cs.ox.ac.uk`
[3] University of Southampton, Southampton, UK
`lcd1u18@soton.ac.uk`

Abstract. Repeated coopetitive games capture the situation when one must efficiently balance between cooperation and competition with the other agents over time in order to win the game (e.g., to become the player with highest total utility). Achieving this balance is typically very challenging or even impossible when explicit communication is not feasible (e.g., negotiation or bargaining are not allowed). In this paper we investigate how an agent can achieve this balance to win in repeated coopetitive polymatrix games, without explicit communication. In particular, we consider a 3-player repeated game setting in which our agent is allowed to (slightly) manipulate the underlying game matrices of the other agents for which she pays a manipulation cost, while the other agents satisfy weak behavioural assumptions. We first propose a payoff matrix manipulation scheme and sequence of strategies for our agent that provably guarantees that the utility of any opponent would converge to a value we desire. We then use this scheme to design winning policies for our agent. We also prove that these winning policies can be found in polynomial running time. We then turn to demonstrate the efficiency of our framework in several concrete coopetitive polymatrix games, and prove that the manipulation costs needed to win are bounded above by small budgets. For instance, in the social distancing game, a polymatrix version of the lemonade stand coopetitive game, we showcase a policy with an infinitesimally small manipulation cost per round, along with a provable guarantee that, using this policy leads our agent to win in the long-run. Note that our findings can be trivially extended to n-player game settings as well (with $n > 3$).

1 Introduction

Repeated coopetitive games play a central role in multi-agent learning [3,11,18, 23], as well as in many other areas of multi-agent systems (MAS) [14,16,24][?]. They capture the situation in which a number of competing agents repeatedly playing an underlying multi-player game. The goal of each agent is not just

J. Fu et al. (Eds.): GameSec 2023, LNCS 14167, pp. 257–276, 2023.
https://doi.org/10.1007/978-3-031-50670-3_13

simply maximizing their total payoff, but also to have the highest one (a.k.a. to win the game). The agents, however, cannot achieve this by just solely focusing on their own policies, but they need to coordinate with some of their competitors to play against the rest (hence the term coopetition, which is a portmanteau of the words cooperation and competition). When communication between agents is explicitly feasible, many MAS based approaches can be used to initiate and maintain these cooperation, ranging from negotiation and bargaining theory, to coalitional game theory and coordination [14,22].

However, when explicit communication is not feasible, achieving those necessary cooperative behaviours becomes a significantly more difficult situation. Recently, there has been a line of research investigating whether such cooperative behaviours can emerge by just observing and reacting to the played strategies of the opponents [4,6,16]. A key challenge here is not just to identify the appropriate opponents to cooperate, but to know when to switch sides as well. For example, in the lemonade stand game [25], three players simultaneously place their stands on one of the twelve positions uniformly distributed on the shore of a circle-shaped island. The payoff of each player is the sum of the distances between their stand and that of their opponents (a more detailed description of its polymatrix game version, called social distancing Game, can be found in Sect. 7). The goal of each agent is then to win the game, that is, to be the one with the highest total payoff over a finite period of time. Now, in order to achieve this, the agent must pick one of the two opponents and start cooperating (e.g., by placing their stands at the opposite positions of the circle). By doing so, one can easily prove that the average payoff of the two cooperating players will be significantly higher than that of the third one. However, this cooperation alone would not provide a guaranteed win (as the cooperating partner can still get higher payoffs). Thus, a key step in this game is to know the right time to switch the team and start cooperating with the third player (by doing so, one might be able to become the one with the highest payoff in the long run).

Note that although the LSG has rather a simplistic setting, it captures the essence of many real-world applications, ranging from technological battles (e.g., the high-definition optical disc format war between Blu-ray and DVD) and R&D alliances [2], to environmental politics [5], and multiplayer video gaming [19], where strategically switching side and its timing are critical.

This paper seeks to address this problem in the following way: we relax the original setting by considering the case when one of the players is keen to sacrifice a (small) portion of their received payoff to modify the others' payoff value (e.g., the player donates some of their payoffs to the opponents, or makes some costly effort to reduce the others' payoff). We refer to this type of actions as payoff manipulation, the corresponding cost as manipulation cost, and the player who performs this as the manipulator (or as player 1 in the technical sections, we will make this clear later in the paper). We also assume that the opponents of the manipulator satisfy a series of stronger and stronger assumptions for which we present different policies for the manipulator that exploit these behavioural assumptions. The weakest of which is learning to play a strictly dominant action over time, and the strongest of which is being no-regret (for a more detailed discussion of the behaviour of the opponents, see Sect. 3). Note that even the strongest assumption we make is mild and widely used in the game theory and online learning/optimization communities. To focus on the essence of the problem, we only deal with the 3-player setting in this paper. Note that our findings can be extended to the generic n-player setting. In addition, we assume that the game is a polymatrix game. Against this background, our contributions are as follows:

- First we propose a number of winning policies for the manipulator. In particular, we show that there exist a set of dominance solvable policies that can guarantee the win for the manipulator (Theorem 1) and they can be calculated in polynomial running time (Theorem 2).
- We then further improve these results by proposing another novel class of methods called batch coordination policies that can provably guarantee low manipulation cost (Theorem 3), which can also be calculated in polynomial time (Theorem 4).
- We also investigate a number of additional objectives, apart from just aiming to win the game (e.g., winning with the largest possible margin, or achieving socially good outcome, etc.,).
- Finally we further refine our findings to a number of concrete polymatrix games. In particular, we show that for these games, the total manipulation cost the manipulator needs to spend is very small. For example, in the Social Distancing Game, the manipulator can already achieve guaranteed win by just using an infinitesimally small amount of manipulation (Sect. 7).

Note that due to page limitations, we have deferred all the proofs, example game analyses, and numerical results to the online ArXiv version of this paper (under the same title).

1.1 Related Work

From the manipulating agent's perspective, our setting can be viewed as a mechanism design (MD) problem [9,13]. In particular, we can consider the game matrix chosen by the manipulator (i.e., the designer) as the mechanism, and the actions chosen by each participant as the information they choose to report. In this domain, perhaps the most similar to our problem setting is the online MD framework [7,15], in which a central mechanism must make decisions over time as different agents arrive and depart at different time steps. However, our setting deals with agents which do not depart or arrive, but rather gain knowledge about the central mechanism as time moves on. Secondly, the goal of the designer is distinct from typical MD settings. Rather than standard solution concepts such as incentive compatibility or social welfare, we aim for the goal of guiding players into playing specific strategies. Such solution concepts are common amongst the online learning community in which the problem of playing a repeated game against another agent is explored under various conditions.

The problem of constructing zero-sum games with a pre-specified (strictly) dominant strategy is similar to designing games with unique minimax equilibrium [1,8,20][?] (for a more detailed description of this topic, we refer the reader to Appendix ??).

While the work above only focuses on the existence of unique equilibria, methods for constructing games with unique equilibria were also developed in tandem. Following the aforementioned work of [20], a parameterized construction for bimatrix games was proposed by [17], which subsumes an earlier construction proposed by [10]. It is worth noting that the closest to our setting is the work from [4], which also considers the problem of payoff matrix manipulation so that the unique Nash equilibrium of the new game is a predefined strategy profile. To the best of our knowledge, neither this work nor the other above-mentioned settings have considered manipulation cost (as we do in our paper), and therefore might not be able to find winning policies with small manipulation costs in our setting.

2   Preliminaries

To begin, we introduce some basic definitions from game theory through which our problem setting will be formally described. We define a finite normal form three-player general-sum game, Γ, as a tuple $(\mathcal{N}, \mathcal{A}, u)$. We denote the set of players by $\mathcal{N} = \{1, 2, 3\}$. Each player $i \in \mathcal{N}$ must simultaneously select an action from a finite set $\mathcal{A}_i$. For the sake of brevity, we use n, m and l to denote the cardinalities of $\mathcal{A}_1$, $\mathcal{A}_2$ and $\mathcal{A}_3$ respectively. We denote by $\mathcal{A} = \mathcal{A}_1 \times \mathcal{A}_2 \times \mathcal{A}_3$ the set of all possible combinations of actions that may be chosen by the players.

Furthermore, each player is allowed to randomize their choice of action. In other words, player i can select any probability distribution $s \in \Delta(\mathcal{A}_i)$ over her action set. An action is then selected by randomly sampling according to this distribution. We refer to this set of probability distributions as the set of strategies available to the player. We say that a strategy is pure if it corresponds to the deterministic choice a single action, otherwise we say that a strategy is mixed. Hereafter we refer to the manipulating agent as player 1. We denote the strategy chosen by player 1 by the vector $\mathbf{x}$, where $\mathbf{x}(i)$ indicates the probability that player 1 selects action i. Similarly, we use $\mathbf{y}$ and $\mathbf{z}$ to denote the strategies chosen by players 2 and 3 respectively.

After strategies have been selected, player i receives a reward given by her utility function $u_i : \mathcal{A} \to \mathbb{R}$, which we consider to be a random variable under the probability space $(\mathcal{A}, \mathcal{F}, \mathbb{P})$ where we define the event space $\mathcal{F}$ to be the power set of $\mathcal{A}$ along with the probability measure $\mathbb{P}$ to be the real-valued function $\mathbb{P} : \mathcal{F} \to [0, 1]$ such that for any $a_1 \in \mathcal{A}_1$, $a_2 \in \mathcal{A}_2$ and $a_3 \in \mathcal{A}_3$, $\mathbb{P}(\{(a_1, a_2, a_3)\}) = \mathbf{x}(a_1) \cdot \mathbf{y}(a_2) \cdot \mathbf{z}(a_3)$.

In this paper, we restrict our focus to polymatrix games. That is we assume that the utility function for each agent is of the form $u_i = \sum_{i \neq j} u_{ij}$, where $u_{ij} : \mathcal{A}_i \times \mathcal{A}_j \to \mathbb{R}$ describes the payoff player i receives from its interaction with player j. Observe that any three-player polymatrix game can be succinctly represented by six payoff matrices $A^{(i,j)}$, which each correspond to a function u_{ij}. Additionally, we let $\|A\|_\infty := \max_{k,l} |A(k,l)|$ denote the infinity norm of a given payoff matrix.

In what follows, we consider a direct extension of the three-player polymatrix setting, in which player 1 takes the role of a manipulator, and is allowed to alter the payoff matrices $A^{(2,1)}$ and $A^{(3,1)}$. In other words, we assume that player 1 has control over the payoffs other players receive when interacting with her. Thus, in addition to selecting a strategy, player 1 is also tasked with specifying the payoff matrices $A^{(2,1)}$ and $A^{(3,1)}$. We refer to the joint submission of a strategy and payoff matrices as player 1's complete strategy. We denote player 1's complete strategy by the tuple $(\mathbf{x}, (A^{(i,j)})_{(i,j)\in P})$, where P is the index set $\{(2,1),(3,1)\}$.

We use A_0 to denote the original payoff matrices of the game before they are altered by player 1. One can interpret A_0 as a description of the dynamics of interaction between players, before the manipulator has implemented rules and restrictions. In a realistic setting, player 1 should not be able to modify the original game wherever there is interaction between player 2 and 3 alone. We clearly capture this notion in polymatrix games by specifying that player 1 cannot modify the matrices $A_0^{(2,3)}$ and $A_0^{(3,2)}$.

We assume that there is an associated cost for modifying the payoff matrices, which takes the form $\sum_{(i,j)\in P} \|A^{(i,j)} - A_0^{(i,j)}\|_\infty$. This cost has a natural interpretation when the manipulator uses monetary incentives in attempt to alter the behaviour of fellow players. More specifically, the cost corresponds to the sum of the maximum monetary payments (or fines) each player can receive, and thus represents, in the worst case, how much the manipulator may need to pay (or charge) in order to implement an altered version of the game.

With this cost in mind, observe that the expected payoff (or utility) of player 1 is given by the expected payoff it receives when participating in the altered polymatrix game, minus the cost it incurs for altering payoff matrices:

$$\mathbf{x}^T A^{(1,2)}\mathbf{y} + \mathbf{x}^T A^{(1,3)}\mathbf{z} - \sum_{(i,j)\in P} \left\|A^{(i,j)} - A_0^{(i,j)}\right\|_\infty.$$

In contrast, the expected utility of player 2 is simply given by the expected payoff it receives from participating in the altered game: $\mathbf{x}^T A^{(2,1)}\mathbf{y} + \mathbf{y}^T A^{(2,3)}\mathbf{z}$. Similarly, the expected payoff of player 3 is given by $\mathbf{x}^T A^{(3,1)}\mathbf{z} + \mathbf{y}^T A^{(3,2)}\mathbf{z}$.

Note that since all three players are employing mixed strategies, the payoff observed by each player may not be the same as the expected payoff. For example, if the players sample actions (a_1, a_2, a_3) from the distributions $(\mathbf{x}, \mathbf{y}$ and $\mathbf{z})$, then the utility player 1 observes is

$$u_1(\mathbf{x},\mathbf{y},\mathbf{z}) = A^{(1,2)}(a_1, a_2) + A^{(1,3)}(a_1, a_3) - \sum_{(i,j)\in P} \left\|A^{(i,j)} - A_0^{(i,j)}\right\|_\infty$$

Similarly, the utility for player 2 is $u_2(\mathbf{x},\mathbf{y},\mathbf{z}) = A^{(2,1)}(a_1, a_2) + A^{(2,3)}(a_2, a_3)$ and the observed utility for player 3 follows in a analogous manner. When the strategies used are clear from context we will drop them from notation and use

u_1, u_2, u_3. We say player 1 has won the game if her utility is higher than the utilities of other players.

3   Problem Setting

In many cases, a manipulator will engage repeatedly with the same system participants. Additionally, aside from the manipulator, players are often unaware of their own, and others, utility functions and must learn them over time. With these concerns in mind, we consider a repeated version of the setting described above. More specifically, we consider a setting in which players engage in the aforementioned polymatrix game repeatedly for T time steps. At each time step t, each player is required to commit to a strategy, $\mathbf{x}_t$, $\mathbf{y}_t$ and $\mathbf{z}_t$. In addition, player 1, in her role as manipulator, must select the set of payoff matrices $A_t^{(i,j)}$, for $(i,j) \in P$, at each time step. We assume that players 2 and 3 have no initial knowledge of A_0, but receive feedback, at the end of every time step detailing the payoff they received. More precisely, player 2 receives feedback $u_{2,t} = u_2(\mathbf{x}_t, \mathbf{y}_t, \mathbf{z}_t)$, at the end of time step t. Player 3 receives feedback in a similar fashion. Therefore, when selecting their strategy in round $t + 1$, players 2 and 3 have access to a history of feedback (and a history of their own strategy choices) up to time step t to inform their decision. In contrast, whilst also receiving feedback at the end of each time step, we assume that player 1 has full knowledge of A_0 prior to the start of play.

We use $H_t = (u_{1,t'}, \mathbf{x}_{t'})_{t'=1}^t$ to denote the history observed by player 1 up to time step t. We use the notation $\mathcal{H}_t$ to denote the set of all observable histories of length t. Given a time horizon T, we define a policy $\rho = (\rho_t)_{t=1}^T$ as a sequence of, potentially randomized, mappings $\rho_t : \mathcal{H}_t \to \Delta(\mathcal{A}_1) \times \mathbb{R}^{n \times m} \times \mathbb{R}^{n \times l}$ from feedback histories to complete strategies. In other words, a policy ρ is a specification of which complete strategy to choose given the feedback observed so far.

Generalizing from the single-shot setting, we define the utility of each player in the repeated setting as the time average of their respective utilities in each round. That is: $U_i(\mathbf{x}_t, \mathbf{y}_t, \mathbf{z}_t)_{t=1}^T := \frac{1}{T} \sum_{t=1}^T u_i(\mathbf{x}_t, \mathbf{y}_t, \mathbf{z}_t)$. As before, when the sequence of strategies used by each player is clear from context, we write U_1, U_2 and U_3 for the sake of brevity. We say that player 1 has won the game, if her utility is the highest. We assume that player 1 participates in the game with the aim of winning. On the other hand, we assume that players 2 and 3 are 'consistent' agents.

Definition 1. *(Consistent Agent) Suppose that for an agent there exists an action a^* that is the unique best response for her for every round of the game. Suppose that within T rounds of the game, the number of rounds the agent plays action a^* is T^*. If $\mathbb{P}\left(\lim_{T \to \infty} \frac{T^*}{T} = 1 \right) = 1$ then the agent is 'consistent'.*

In other words, if an agent has a single action that performs the best in all rounds, and the proportion of time she plays that action converges to 1 almost surely, then we say she is consistent. If a consistent agent does not have an action that always performs the best, we make no assumption on the behaviour of the player.

Unless stated otherwise, we restrict our focus to players who are consistent, no matter the strategies submitted by the other players. This assumption is much weaker that the standard assumption of rationality in full information mechanism design settings. In the sections that follow, we will develop a number of policies which guarantee player 1 a winning outcome with high probability under this assumption.

4 Winning Policies

In this section, we present a number of policies which guarantee player 1 a winning outcome with high probability. Before describing these policies in detail, we first present a brief conceptual argument showcasing the underlying idea behind all the policies we present.

Consider the policy where player 1 plays the same action i^* in every round. Assume that player 2 and player 3 each have strictly dominant actions j^* and k^* respectively against, the action i^* of player 1. That is, $u_2(\mathbf{e}_{i^*}, \mathbf{e}_{j^*}, \mathbf{e}_k) > u_2(\mathbf{e}_{i^*}, \mathbf{e}_j, \mathbf{e}_k)$ for all $j \neq j^*$ and k and $u_3(\mathbf{e}_{i^*}, \mathbf{e}_j, \mathbf{e}_{k^*}) > u_3(\mathbf{e}_{i^*}, \mathbf{e}_j, \mathbf{e}_k)$ for all j and $k \neq k^*$. Since both players are consistent, the proportion of time each of them plays their strictly dominant action converges to 1 almost surely. Therefore, if $u_1(\mathbf{e}_{i^*}, \mathbf{e}_{j^*}, \mathbf{e}_{k^*}) \geq \max\{u_2(\mathbf{e}_{i^*}, \mathbf{e}_{j^*}, \mathbf{e}_{k^*}), u_3(\mathbf{e}_{i^*}, \mathbf{e}_{j^*}, \mathbf{e}_{k^*})\}$, then intuitively, player 1 will eventually win if T is large enough. Unfortunately such an action i^*, which satisfies the above assumptions, may not exist in the original game. However, player 1 can always guarantee the existence of such an action by altering payoff matrices. If player 1 can find a low cost alteration, then she can win the game with high probability.

We then present another policy of a similar flavor where player 1 plays the same action i^* in every round. We assume that player 2 has a strictly dominant action j^* against the action i^* of player 1, but player 3 only has a strictly dominant action k^* against the action i^* of player 1 and the action j^* of player 2. Therefore if player 3, is an agent who is willing to wait for some action to eventually become her unique best response, then the manipulator can modify the payoff matrices appropriately to ensure that she wins if T is large enough. Therefore in order for such a policy to work successfully, we must make a slightly stronger behavioural assumption on player 3, which leads us to the definition of a 'persistent' agent.

All of the policies we present here combine games constructed to satisfy assumptions similar to those above, with a simple time-dependent deterministic policy. First in Sect. 4.1 we show how to construct payoff matrices such that actions j^* and k^* are strictly dominant for players 2 and 3, under the assumption that player 1 uses action i^*. In Sect. 4.2, we present the class of dominance solvable policies, which consist of stationary policies leveraging the methodologies developed in the previous section. Lastly, we present the class of batch coordination policies, which spend half the time horizon cooperating with one player, and half of the time horizon cooperating with the other.

4.1 Designing Dominance Solvable Games

Here, we describe several constructions of three player games which will be used extensively in our definitions for different kinds of policies. In particular, we show how to find a matrix $A^{(2,1)}$ (or $A^{(3,1)}$) such that a particular action for player 2 (or 3) is strictly dominant against all actions of player 3 (or 2) and a particular action of the manipulator. We also show how to find a matrix $A^{(3,1)}$ (or $A^{(2,1)}$) such that a particular action for player 3 (or 2) is strictly dominant against a particular action of player 2 (or 3) and a particular action of the player 1. For the sake of brevity we refer to players 1, 2 and 3 by P1, P2 and P3 respectively.

Let $\mathbf{x}$ be the fixed strategy of the manipulator. To ensure that P2 has a strictly dominant strategy $\mathbf{e}_{j^*}$ against $\mathbf{x}$ and all actions of P3, For some $v_2 \in \mathbb{R}^l$ we must choose a matrix $A^{(2,1)}$ that satisfies the system

$$
\begin{aligned}
[\mathbf{x}^T A^{(2,1)} \mathbf{e}_j + \mathbf{e}_j^T A^{(2,3)} \mathbf{e}_k] &= v_{2,k} \ \ \forall k \in [l] \text{ and } j = j^* \\
[\mathbf{x}^T A^{(2,1)} \mathbf{e}_j + \mathbf{e}_j^T A^{(2,3)} \mathbf{e}_k] &< v_{2,k} \ \ \forall k \in [l] \text{ and } j \neq j^*
\end{aligned}
\tag{1}
$$

By symmetry, to ensure that P3 has a strictly dominant strategy $\mathbf{e}_{k^*}$ against $\mathbf{x}$ and all actions of P2, for some $v_3 \in \mathbb{R}^m$ we must choose a matrix $A^{(3,1)}$ that satisfies the system

$$
\begin{aligned}
[\mathbf{x}^T A^{(3,1)} \mathbf{e}_k + \mathbf{e}_j^T A^{(3,2)} \mathbf{e}_k] &= v_{3,j} \ \ \forall j \in [m] \text{ and } k = k^* \\
[\mathbf{x}^T A^{(3,1)} \mathbf{e}_k + \mathbf{e}_j^T A^{(3,2)} \mathbf{e}_k] &< v_{3,j} \ \ \forall j \in [m] \text{ and } k \neq k^*
\end{aligned}
\tag{2}
$$

Now further suppose that P2 plays the fixed strategy $\mathbf{y}$. In order to make $\mathbf{e}_{k^*}$ the dominant strategy against the strategies $\mathbf{x}$ and $\mathbf{y}$ of P1 and P2 respectively, for some $v_0 \in \mathbb{R}$ we must choose a matrix $A^{(2,1)}$ that satisfies the system

$$
\begin{aligned}
[\mathbf{x}^T A^{(3,1)} \mathbf{e}_k + \mathbf{y}^T A^{(3,2)} \mathbf{e}_k] &= v_0 \ \ k = k^* \\
[\mathbf{x}^T A^{(3,1)} \mathbf{e}_k + \mathbf{y}^T A^{(3,2)} \mathbf{e}_k] &< v_0 \ \ k \neq k^*
\end{aligned}
\tag{3}
$$

With the following lemma, we show that strategy profiles satisfying systems (1) and (2) always exist.

Proposition 1. *Fix $i^* \in [n]$, $j^* \in [m]$ and $k^* \in [l]$ with $\mathbf{x} = \mathbf{e}_{i^*}$. Matrices $A^{(2,1)}$ and $A^{(3,1)}$ that satisfy the systems (1) and (2) exist.*

Proof. Set the entries of $A^{(2,1)}$ to

$$
\begin{aligned}
A^{(2,1)}(i^*, j) &:= 2\|A_0^{(2,3)}\|_\infty + 1 \quad \text{for } j = j^* \\
A^{(2,1)}(i^*, j) &:= 0 \quad \text{for } j \neq j^*
\end{aligned}
$$

and the entries of $A^{(3,1)}$ to

$$
\begin{aligned}
A^{(3,1)}(i^*, k) &:= 2\|A_0^{(3,2)}\|_\infty + 1 \quad \text{for } k = k^* \\
A^{(3,1)}(i^*, k) &:= 0 \quad \text{for } k \neq k^*
\end{aligned}
$$

now both of these matrices together satisfy systems (1) and (2).

In addition, this result clearly extends to system (3), as any matrix satisfying system (2) satisfies system (3).

Corollary 11. *Fix $i^* \in [n]$, $j^* \in [m]$ and $k^* \in [l]$ with $\mathbf{x} = \mathbf{e}_{i^*}$ and $\mathbf{y} = \mathbf{e}_{j^*}$. Matrices $A^{(2,1)}$ and $A^{(3,1)}$ that satisfy the systems (1) and (3) exist.*

Proof. The same as the proof of Proposition 1. If system (2) is satisfied, so is system (3).

In what follows, we will develop policies based on payoff matrices which satisfy systems (1), (2) and (3).

4.2   Dominance Solvable Policies

In this section, we introduce the class of dominance solvable policies. In short, dominance solvable policies consist of player 1 playing a constant complete strategy which satisfies a number of the linear systems. We first introduce type-I dominance solvable policies.

Definition 2. *(Dominance Solvable Type-I Policy)*
Let $\left(A^{(2,1)}, A^{(3,1)} \right)$ satisfy systems (1) and (2) for some $i^* \in [n]$, $j^* \in [m]$, $k^* \in [l]$. Then, the policy $\rho_t(H_t) = \left(\mathbf{e}_{i^*}, A^{(2,1)}, A^{(3,1)} \right)$ for $t \in \mathbb{N}$ is a dominance solvable type-I policy.

In words, a dominance solvable type-I policy is one in which player 1 plays a constant complete strategy which satisfies systems (1) and (2). Similarly, we define dominance solvable type-II policies as those in which player 1 plays a constant complete strategy which satisfies systems (1) and (3).

Definition 3. *(Dominance Solvable Type-II Policy)*
Let $\left(A^{(2,1)}, A^{(3,1)} \right)$ satisfy systems (1) and (3) for some $i^* \in [n]$, $j^* \in [m]$, $k^* \in [l]$. Then, the policy $\rho_t(H_t) = \left(\mathbf{e}_{i^*}, A^{(2,1)}, A^{(3,1)} \right)$ for $t \in \mathbb{N}$ is a dominance solvable type-II policy.

If one uses iterated elimination of strictly dominated strategies and there is only one strategy left for each player, the game is called dominance solvable [12]. We name the policies described above dominance solvable since the underlying single-shot game that results from these policies is almost dominance solvable. In the game that results from these policies, if we eliminate all the actions of player 1 except i^* and then implement iterated elimination of strictly dominated strategies, there will be only one strategy left for each player.

We say that a dominance solvable policy is winning if player 1 wins the corresponding single-shot game when $(\mathbf{e}_{i^*}, \mathbf{e}_{j^*}, \mathbf{e}_{k^*})$ is played:

$$u_1(\mathbf{e}_{i^*}, \mathbf{e}_{j^*}, \mathbf{e}_{k^*}) \geq u_2(\mathbf{e}_{i^*}, \mathbf{e}_{j^*}, \mathbf{e}_{k^*}) \quad \text{and} \quad u_1(\mathbf{e}_{i^*}, \mathbf{e}_{j^*}, \mathbf{e}_{k^*}) \geq u_3(\mathbf{e}_{i^*}, \mathbf{e}_{j^*}, \mathbf{e}_{k^*}) \tag{4}$$

Winning dominance solvable type-I policies are highly attractive as they allow the manipulator to win in the long-run against consistent agents. This claim is formalized in the following theorem.

Theorem 1. *If the manipulator uses a winning dominance solvable type-I policy against consistent agents in an infinitely repeated game then,*

$$\mathbb{P}\Big(U_1(\boldsymbol{x}_t, \boldsymbol{y}_t, \boldsymbol{z}_t)_{t=1}^{\infty} \geq U_2(\boldsymbol{x}_t, \boldsymbol{y}_t, \boldsymbol{z}_t)_{t=1}^{\infty} \text{ and } U_1(\boldsymbol{x}_t, \boldsymbol{y}_t, \boldsymbol{z}_t)_{t=1}^{\infty} \geq U_3(\boldsymbol{x}_t, \boldsymbol{y}_t, \boldsymbol{z}_t)_{t=1}^{\infty}\Big) = 1$$

At times, for the sake of brevity, we use U_1^{∞}, U_2^{∞} and U_3^{∞} to denote the long-run utilities $U_1(\mathbf{x}_t, \mathbf{y}_t, \mathbf{z}_t)_{t=1}^{\infty}$, $U_2(\mathbf{x}_t, \mathbf{y}_t, \mathbf{z}_t)_{t=1}^{\infty}$ and $U_3(\mathbf{x}_t, \mathbf{y}_t, \mathbf{z}_t)_{t=1}^{\infty}$ respectively.

For the analogous guarantee on type-II policies we assume a slightly stronger behavioural assumption than being 'consistent' on one of the agents. We assume that player 3 is 'persistent', i.e. if there is some finite-time cutoff point after which there exists an action that always remains the unique best-response in hindsight then she will play that action a large fraction of time.

Definition 4. *(Persistent Agent) Suppose that the action k^* is the best action in hindsight for player 3 eventually, with probability 1. That is,*

$$\mathbb{P}\Big(e_{k^*} = \arg\max_{z \in \Delta_l} U_3(\boldsymbol{x}_t, \boldsymbol{y}_t, z)_{t=1}^{T} \text{ eventually}\Big) = 1$$

Let T^* denote the number of rounds within T rounds, that player 3 plays action k^*. If $\mathbb{P}\Big(\lim_{T \to \infty} \frac{T^*}{T} = 1\Big) = 1$ then player 3 is 'persistent'.

Note that every persistent agent is consistent. We prove this in Proposition 2. The guarantee of winning when using type-II policies is exactly the same as type-I policies except that we assume one of the players is persistent.

Theorem 2. *If the manipulator uses a winning dominance solvable type-II policy against a consistent player 2 and a persistent player 3 in an infinitely repeated game then,*

$$\mathbb{P}\Big(U_1(\boldsymbol{x}_t, \boldsymbol{y}_t, \boldsymbol{z}_t)_{t=1}^{\infty} \geq U_2(\boldsymbol{x}_t, \boldsymbol{y}_t, \boldsymbol{z}_t)_{t=1}^{\infty} \text{ and } U_1(\boldsymbol{x}_t, \boldsymbol{y}_t, \boldsymbol{z}_t)_{t=1}^{\infty} \geq U_3(\boldsymbol{x}_t, \boldsymbol{y}_t, \boldsymbol{z}_t)_{t=1}^{\infty}\Big) = 1$$

Observe that any constant complete strategy is dominance solvable as long as it satisfies the linear systems (1) and (2) (or (3)) for a given triple of actions (i^*, j^*, k^*). Furthermore, a dominance solvable policy is winning if and only if it satisfies the pair of linear inequalities in system (4). As a result, winning dominance solvable policies, if they exist, can be found in polynomial time by solving a sequence of linear feasibility problems, where each linear feasibility problem corresponds to a different triple of actions.

Theorem 3. *If winning dominance solvable policies exist, then there exists an algorithm that can find such policies with running time that is polynomial in the number of actions of the players.*

If player 1 uses a type-I policy, she can make a very weak behavioural assumption on the other players to guarantee winning in the long run. On the other hand, type-II policies are guaranteed to be at least as cost-effective as type-I policies, as all type-I policies are also type-II policies.

4.3   Batch Coordination Policies

Note that, even if a winning dominance solvable policy exists, it may be very costly to alter the payoff matrix. However, the manipulator may be able to beat one player through very cheap alterations whilst losing to the other, and vice versa. In this case it makes sense for player 1 to divide the time horizon, spending half the horizon winning over one player, and spending the other half winning over the other, using cheap alterations to the original payoff matrices in the process. This is the central idea behind batch coordination policies. The following definition makes this idea rigorous.

Definition 5. *(Winning Batch Coordination policy) Suppose the matrices $\hat{A}^{(2,1)}$ and $\hat{A}^{(3,1)}$ satisfy systems (1) and (2) for some $i_2 \in [n]$, $j_2 \in [m]$, $k_2 \in [l]$ and that the matrices $\tilde{A}^{(2,1)}$ and $\tilde{A}^{(3,1)}$ satisfy systems (1) and (2) for some $i_3 \in [n]$, $j_3 \in [m]$, $k_3 \in [l]$ such that for $i \neq 1$*

$$\mathbb{E}[u_1(e_{i_2}, e_{j_2}, e_{k_2})] + \mathbb{E}[u_1(e_{i_3}, e_{j_3}, e_{k_3})] > \mathbb{E}[u_i(e_{i_3}, e_{j_3}, e_{k_3})] + \mathbb{E}[u_i(e_{i_3}, e_{j_3}, e_{k_3})]$$

then the policy

$$\rho_t = \begin{cases} (e_{i_1}, \hat{A}^{(2,1)}, \hat{A}^{(3,1)}) & \text{if } 1 \leq t \leq T/2 \\ (e_{i_2}, \tilde{A}^{(2,1)}, \tilde{A}^{(3,1)}) & \text{if } T/2 < t \leq T \end{cases}$$

is called a winning batch coordination policy.

Winning batch coordination policies can be interpreted as following different dominance solvable policies for each half of the game. Therefore, winning batch coordination policies are more general than winning dominance solvable policies. Note that the dominance solvable polices played in each half of the time horizon may not be winning by themselves. However, when combined, these subpolicies must form a winning policy for the overall batch coordination policy to be winning.

Before we present the guarantee for player 1 when using winning batch coordination policies, we make a slightly stronger behavioural assumption on both players than the assumption of being 'persistent'. We now assume that both players aim to maximize their expected utility. We use the well-established notion of regret as a metric for measuring the performance of players 2 and 3 with respect to the payoffs they accumulate over time.

Definition 6. *The regret of any sequence of strategies $(y_1, ..., y_T)$ chosen by player 2 with respect to a fixed strategy y is given by*

$$\mathcal{R}_{T,y} = \sum_{t=1}^{T} x_t^T A_t^{(2,1)} y_t + y_t^T A_0^{(2,3)} z_t - \sum_{t=1}^{T} x_t^T A_t^{(2,1)} y + y^T A_0^{(2,3)} z_t$$

That is, the regret is the difference between the payoff accumulated by the sequence $(y_1, ..., y_T)$ and the payoff accumulated by the sequence where a given fixed mixed strategy y is chosen at each time step. A similar notion of regret is defined for the player 3. We say that a player is 'no-regret' if her regret with respect to the sequence of strategies chosen by the other two players is sublinear in T: $\lim_{T\to\infty} \max_{\mathbf{y}\in\Delta_m} \frac{\mathcal{R}_{T,\mathbf{y}}}{T} = 0$.

Note that every no-regret player is persistent. We prove this in Proposition 2. If the manipulator uses a winning batch coordination policy against no-regret players, then the probability that there exists some finite number of rounds in which she wins is 1. This result is formalized in the following theorem.

Theorem 4. *If the manipulator uses a winning batch coordination policy against no-regret players then*

$$\mathbb{P}\Big(U_1(\mathbf{x}_t, \mathbf{y}_t, \mathbf{z}_t)_{t=1}^T \geq U_2(\mathbf{x}_t, \mathbf{y}_t, \mathbf{z}_t)_{t=1}^T \text{ and } U_1(\mathbf{x}_t, \mathbf{y}_t, \mathbf{z}_t)_{t=1}^T \geq U_3(\mathbf{x}_t, \mathbf{y}_t, \mathbf{z}_t)_{t=1}^T \text{ eventually}\Big) = 1$$

It is worth noting that this guarantee on the convergence of utilities is stronger than the one given for winning dominance solvable policies in Theorem 1. This is because of the strict inequality on the utilities of the players in Definition 5. By presenting this guarantee instead of a guarantee on the infinite horizon utilities, we are ensured that the guarantee of winning in a finite number of rounds with probability 1 implies that the manipulator can use one set of game matrices for half the rounds and another set for the second half.

Similarly to winning dominance solvable policies, winning batch coordination policies can be found in polynomial time by solving a number of linear feasibility problems.

Theorem 5. *If winning batch coordination policies exist, then there exists an algorithm that can find such policies with running time that is polynomial in the number of actions of the players.*

We present the following proposition that states all persistent players are consistent, and that all no-regret players are persistent.

Proposition 2. *All persistent players are consistent. Further, all no-regret players are persistent.*

That is, each assumption on the behaviour of the agents is successively stronger. To emphasize this, we prove that there exists a type of player who is persistent but not no-regret.

Proposition 3. *If an agent uses the Follow the Leader algorithm, then she is persistent but not no-regret.*

For the remainder of the paper we use the weakest assumption, that players are consistent but not necessarily persistent.

5   Additional Objectives

The manipulator may have additional goals and objectives aside from simply winning the game. For example, the manipulator may want to win by a large margin, or win by making the smallest alterations to the payoff matrices possible, or even have a goal completely different to winning, such as maximizing the egalitarian social welfare. For each of the policy classes from Sect. 4, the manipulator can solve a sequence of linear feasibility problems in order to find a winning policy if one exists. As long as the linear constraints of one of these problems are satisfied, the manipulator is guaranteed to win (i.e. she has found a winning policy). Therefore, the manipulator can specify any additional objectives she may have as a linear function to optimize with respect to the linear constraints imposed by the policy class. In other words, the manipulator may choose a linear objective function which captures her additional goals, and solve a sequence of linear programs (LPs), instead of a sequence of linear feasibility problems. For example let d_2 and d_3 be the cost of altering matrices $A_0^{(2,1)}$ and $A_0^{(3,1)}$ respectively. If we consider a minimization problem with objective $d_2 + d_3$, then this amounts to finding a winning policy which makes the least cost modification possible. Similarly, let v_2 be the payoff for player 2 and v_3 be the payoff for player 3 in the strategy profile of consideration. Setting v_2 as a maximization objective amounts to winning whilst ensuring player 2 does as well as possible. We could also act adversarially against player 2, by instead minimizing v_2. Meanwhile, setting $v_2 + v_3$ as a maximization objective corresponds to winning whilst maximizing the utilitarian welfare of the other players.

In what follows, we investigate additional objectives and goals of wider interest. In Sect. 5.1 we investigate how player 1 can maximize her margin of victory, in Sect. 5.2 we investigate how the manipulator may win in the most cost efficient way possible. Meanwhile, in Sect. 5.3 we investigate how the manipulator may maximizing the egalitarian social welfare.

5.1 Winning by the Largest Margin

In strictly competitive settings, it is often desirable for players to win, whilst ensuring that their long run utility is much higher than the other players. This motivates the following definition:

Definition 7. *The margin of a policy $\rho_t(H_t) = (\mathbf{x}_t, (A_t^{(i,j)})_{(i,j) \in P})$ for $t \in \mathbb{N}$ when playing against player 2 and player 3's no-regret sequence of strategies $(\mathbf{y}_t)_{t=1}^{\infty}$ and $(\mathbf{z}_t)_{t=1}^{\infty}$ is defined to be*

$$\min \left\{ \mathbb{E}\left[U_1(\mathbf{x}_t, \mathbf{y}_t, \mathbf{z}_t)_{t=1}^{\infty} - U_2(\mathbf{x}_t, \mathbf{y}_t, \mathbf{z}_t)_{t=1}^{\infty}\right], \mathbb{E}\left[U_1(\mathbf{x}_t, \mathbf{y}_t, \mathbf{z}_t)_{t=1}^{\infty} - U_3(\mathbf{x}_t, \mathbf{y}_t, \mathbf{z}_t)_{t=1}^{\infty}\right] \right\}$$

That is, the margin is the minimum difference between the long run expected utility of player 1 and another player. Any winning dominance solvable policy will have a margin of at least zero. Additionally, for any of the policy classes discussed above, if a winning policy exists, then a winning policy with the largest margin can be found efficiently via the addition of a linear objective and a small number of linear constraints and variables.

Theorem 6. *If winning dominance solvable policies exist, then there exists an algorithm that can find the largest margin dominance solvable policy, with running time that is polynomial in the number of actions of the players.*

5.2   Winning with the Lowest Inefficiency Ratio

In many scenarios, it is only sensible to make changes to payoff matrices if one would see a large relative improvement compared to the cost of alteration. We characterize the notion of relative improvement using the following definition.

Definition 8. *The Inefficiency Ratio of a policy $\rho_t(H_t) = (\mathbf{x}_t, (A_t^{(i,j)})_{(i,j) \in P})$ for $t \in \mathbb{N}$ when playing against player 2 and player 3's no-regret sequence of strategies $(\mathbf{y}_t)_{t=1}^{\infty}$ and $(\mathbf{z}_t)_{t=1}^{\infty}$ is defined to be*

$$\frac{\lim_{T \to \infty} \frac{1}{T} \sum_{t=1}^{T} \sum_{(i,j) \in P} \|A_t^{(i,j)} - A_0^{(i,j)}\|_{\infty}}{\mathbb{E}\left[\lim_{T \to \infty} \frac{1}{T} \sum_{t=1}^{T} \left(\mathbf{x}_t^T A_t^{(1,2)} \mathbf{y}_t + \mathbf{x}_t^T A_t^{(1,3)} \mathbf{z}_t \right) \right] - K}$$

where $K = \min_{i,j,k} \left(A^{(1,2)}(i,j) + A^{(1,3)}(j,k) \right)$ is the minimum revenue for player 1.

In other words, the inefficiency ratio is the ratio between the cost for modifying the payoff matrices and the expected increase in long run payoffs from the worst case payoff. Note that this fraction must converge for the definition to be meaningful. In a similar fashion to maximizing the margin of victory, policies which minimize the inefficiency ratio can be found in polynomial time.

Theorem 7. *If winning dominance solvable policies exist, then there exists an algorithm that can find the winning dominance solvable policy with the lowest inefficiency ratio, with running time that is polynomial in the number of actions of the players.*

5.3   Maximizing the Egalitarian Social Welfare

We now consider an altruistic goal for the manipulator that is different from the original goal of winning. Here, we relax the original goal of winning and develop a policy that ensures the utility of all players are as large as possible. To further this notion, we define the quantity we call the egalitarian social welfare, which we aim to maximize.

Definition 9. *The Egalitarian Social Welfare of a strategy profile $(\mathbf{x}, \mathbf{y}, \mathbf{z})$ is defined to be*

$$S(\mathbf{x}, \mathbf{y}, \mathbf{z}) := \min \left\{ U_1(\mathbf{x}, \mathbf{y}, \mathbf{z}), U_2(\mathbf{x}, \mathbf{y}, \mathbf{z}), U_3(\mathbf{x}, \mathbf{y}, \mathbf{z}) \right\}$$

We can find the dominance solvable policy that maximizes egalitarian social welfare in polynomial running time. Note that such a policy will always exist.

Theorem 8. *There exists an algorithm that can find the dominance solvable policy that maximizes egalitarian social welfare with running time that is polynomial in the number of actions of the players.*

Now, we present a number of examples of the theory we have developed. Each example highlights a different aspect of the theory.

6   Three-Player Iterated Prisoner's Dilemma

The first example we consider is a three-player version of the iterated prisoner's dilemma. As in the two-player version, each player must choose from a set of two actions $\mathcal{A} = \{C, D\}$ which stand for cooperate and defect respectively. The payoff matrices for each player are defined as follows:

$$A_0^{(i,j)} = \begin{bmatrix} 3 & 0 \\ 5 & 1 \end{bmatrix} \text{ if } i < j \text{ and } A_0^{(i,j)} = \begin{bmatrix} 3 & 5 \\ 0 & 1 \end{bmatrix} \text{ if } i > j$$

6.1   Winning Strategy for a Manipulator

Note that defection is a strictly dominant strategy for each player. Moreover, the payoff awarded to each player is the same when everyone defects. As a result, by Theorem 1, player 1 can win the game with high probability by repeatedly defecting, and never altering payoff matrices. Note that this policy is zero cost in the sense that the manipulator never needs to alter any payoff matrices. However, the margin is also zero. We now illustrate how alterations to the payoff matrices can result in a winning policy for the manipulator, which has positive margin, and encourages cooperation between players. In particular, we outline a policy which the manipulator may use to converge to the strategy profile (D, C, C). For $0 \leq \epsilon \leq 7/6$ set

$$\hat{A} = \begin{bmatrix} 3 & 5 \\ 3/2 + \epsilon & -1/2 \end{bmatrix}.$$

Let player 1 adopt the policy $\rho_t = \left(\mathbf{e}_2, \hat{A}, \hat{A}\right)$. Note that the mixed strategy of any player is characterized by the probability that they cooperate. If player 3 cooperates with probability λ then the expected utility player 2 receives from cooperating is $3/2 + \epsilon + 3\lambda$. Meanwhile, the expected utility player 2 receives by defecting is $1/2 + 4\lambda$. Since, $\lambda \in [0, 1]$, this implies that cooperation is a strictly dominant strategy for player 2. By symmetry, cooperation is also a strictly dominant strategy for player 3.

The single shot utility under the profile (D, C, C) for player 1 is $7 - 2\epsilon$. Meanwhile the utilities of players 2 and 3 are both $4.5 + \epsilon$. By Theorem 4.2, this implies

$$\mathbb{P}\left(U_1(\mathbf{x}_t, \mathbf{y}_t, \mathbf{z}_t)_{t=1}^\infty \geq U_2(\mathbf{x}_t, \mathbf{y}_t, \mathbf{z}_t)_{t=1}^\infty \text{ and } U_1(\mathbf{x}_t, \mathbf{y}_t, \mathbf{z}_t)_{t=1}^\infty \geq U_3(\mathbf{x}_t, \mathbf{y}_t, \mathbf{z}_t)_{t=1}^\infty\right) = 1$$

since $\epsilon \leq 7/6$.

Observe that the policy ρ has a much improved margin relative to the trivial policy of repeated defection we first considered. In fact, the margin of policy ρ is $2.5 - \epsilon$, which is the maximum margin achievable by a dominance solvable policy as $\epsilon \to 0$.

7   Social Distancing Game

Next, we consider a more practical application of the theory above. More precisely, we consider the social distancing game which is a small variation of the lemonade stand game introduced by [25]: It is summer on a remote island, and you need to survive. You decide to set up camp on the beach (which you may shift anywhere around the island), as do two others. There are twelve places to set up around the island like the numbers on a clock. The game is repeated. Every night, everyone moves under cover of darkness (simultaneously). There is no cost to move. The pandemic is eternal, so the game is infinitely repeated. The utility of the repeated game is the time-averaged utility of the single-shot games. The only person that survives is the one with the highest total utility at the end of the game (Figs. 1 and 2).

Fig. 1. Example Social Distancing Game

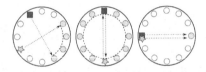

Fig. 2. Best-responses for different opponent configurations: The dashed and shaded segment indicates the third player's best-response actions, and arrows point to the action opposite each opponent. (Figures reworked from [21])

The utility of a player in a single round of the social distancing game is the sum of its distances from the other two players. The distance between two players is the length of the shortest path between them along the circumference of the clock. More formally, the distance between two positions is defined as follows:

$$d(i,j) = \begin{cases} |i - j| & |i - j| \le 6 \\ 12 - |i - j| & otherwise \end{cases}$$

For example, if Alice sets up at the 3 o'clock location, Bob sets up at 10 o'clock, and Candy sets up at 6 o'clock, then the utility of Alice is $d(3, 10) + d(3, 6) = 5 + 3 = 8$, the utility of Bob is $d(10, 3) + d(10, 6) = 5 + 4 = 9$, and the utility of Candy is $d(6, 3) + d(6, 10) = 3 + 4 = 7$. If all the camps are set up in the same spot, everyone gets 0. If exactly two camps are located at the same spot, the two collocated camps get the distance to the non-collated camp as their utility and the non-collated camp gets twice the same distance as her utility. In contrast to the lemonade stand game, the social distancing game is not constant-sum. However, it is a polymatrix game, and thus the techniques developed above can be applied. In what follows, we consider a three-player, infinitely repeated version of the social distancing game. Each player i has 12 actions, $\mathcal{A}_i = \{1, \ldots, 12\}$, each corresponding to a number on the clock. The payoff matrix for each pair of players (i, j) is derived directly from the distance function d. That is, $A_0^{(i,j)}(k, l) = d(k, l)$ for all $k, l \in \mathcal{A}_i$.

7.1   Winning Strategy for a Manipulator

We now present a winning dominance solvable type-I policy for the social distancing game. By definition, for any pair of positions (k, l) on the clock, $d(k, l) \leq 6$. This implies that the maximum utility achievable by any player is 12. In addition, a player i only achieves their maximum payoff when both remaining players place themselves directly opposite of player i. Thus, there are only 12 combinations of pure strategies which maximize the utility of player 1, each corresponding to a single number on the clock. In particular, we choose to work with one such strategy profile, $(\mathbf{e}_{12}, \mathbf{e}_6, \mathbf{e}_6)$. Consider the following dominance solvable policy. Set

$$\hat{A}(k, l) = \begin{cases} d(k, l) - \epsilon & \text{if } d(k, l) < 6 \\ d(k, l) + \epsilon & \text{if } d(k, l) = 6 \end{cases}$$

and let player 1 adopt the policy $\rho_t = \left(\mathbf{e}_{12}, \hat{A}, \hat{A}\right)$. First, observe that, under policy ρ, $\mathbf{e}_6$ is a dominant strategy for player 2 against the fixed strategy $\mathbf{e}_{12}$ of player 1. Additionally, by symmetry, $\mathbf{e}_6$ is also a dominant strategy for player 3 against the fixed strategy of player 1. Moreover, note that player 1's utility under the strategy profile $(\mathbf{e}_{12}, \mathbf{e}_6, \mathbf{e}_6)$ is $12 - 2\epsilon$. Meanwhile, the utilities of both players 2 and 3 is $6 + \epsilon$. Thus, by Theorem 1, for sufficiently small ϵ we have

$$\mathbb{P}\left(U_1(\mathbf{x}_t, \mathbf{y}_t, \mathbf{z}_t)_{t=1}^{\infty} \geq U_2(\mathbf{x}_t, \mathbf{y}_t, \mathbf{z}_t)_{t=1}^{\infty} \text{ and } U_1(\mathbf{x}_t, \mathbf{y}_t, \mathbf{z}_t)_{t=1}^{\infty} \geq U_3(\mathbf{x}_t, \mathbf{y}_t, \mathbf{z}_t)_{t=1}^{\infty}\right) = 1$$

Note that such a result implies that player 1 can guarantee her maximum payoff in the long run by only making an infinitesimal change to the payoff matrices!

7.2   Maximizing Egalitarian Social Welfare

We now present a socially good solution a manipulator can guide the players to converge to by using a winning dominance solvable policy. In the standard version of the game without a manipulator, one of the "socially optimal" strategy profiles is $(\mathbf{e}_{12}, \mathbf{e}_4, \mathbf{e}_8)$, since in this profile, all the players are spread out evenly around the clock. It is possible for a manipulator to guide the players to an approximately optimal solution, in the sense that she can enable convergence to the strategy profile $(\mathbf{e}_{12}, \mathbf{e}_5, \mathbf{e}_7)$.

Consider the following dominance solvable policy. Set

$$\hat{A}(k,l) = \begin{cases} d(k,l) & \text{if } k \neq 12 \\ d(k,l) - 1 - 2\epsilon & \text{if } k = 12 \text{ and } l \neq 5 \\ d(k,l) + 1 - \epsilon & \text{if } k = 12 \text{ and } l = 5 \end{cases}$$

and

$$\tilde{A}(k,l) = \begin{cases} d(k,l) & \text{if } k \neq 12 \\ d(k,l) - 1 + \epsilon & \text{if } k = 12 \text{ and } l \neq 7 \\ d(k,l) + 1 - \epsilon & \text{if } k = 12 \text{ and } l = 7 \end{cases}$$

and let player 1 adopt the policy $\rho_t = \left(\mathbf{e}_{12}, \hat{A}, \tilde{A}\right)$. First, observe that, under policy ρ, $\mathbf{e}_5$ is a dominant strategy for player 2 against the fixed strategy $\mathbf{e}_{12}$ of player 1. Additionally, $\mathbf{e}_7$ is a dominant strategy for player 3 against the fixed strategy of player 1. Moreover, note that player 1's utility under the strategy profile $(\mathbf{e}_{12}, \mathbf{e}_5, \mathbf{e}_6)$ is $10 - (2 + \epsilon) = 8 - \epsilon$. Meanwhile, the utilities of both players 2 and 3 is also $8 - \epsilon$. Thus, by Theorem 1, for sufficiently small $\epsilon > 0$ we have

$$\mathbb{P}\left(U_1(\mathbf{x}_t, \mathbf{y}_t, \mathbf{z}_t)_{t=1}^{\infty} \geq U_2(\mathbf{x}_t, \mathbf{y}_t, \mathbf{z}_t)_{t=1}^{\infty} \text{ and } U_1(\mathbf{x}_t, \mathbf{y}_t, \mathbf{z}_t)_{t=1}^{\infty} \geq U_3(\mathbf{x}_t, \mathbf{y}_t, \mathbf{z}_t)_{t=1}^{\infty}\right) = 1$$

Note that such a result implies that player 1 can guarantee that the game converges to an approximately socially optimal solution whilst ensuring that she still wins the game!

8   Conclusions

In this paper, we considered a 3-player repeated polymatrix game setting in which our agent is allowed to (slightly) manipulate the underlying game matrices of the other agents for which she pays a manipulation cost, while the other agents are 'consistent'. In our framework, two examples of consistent agents are those that use follow-the-leader or any no-regret algorithm to play the game. We first proposed a payoff matrix manipulation scheme and sequence of strategies for our agent that provably guarantees that the utility of any consistent opponent would converge to a value we desire. Using this theory we developed winning dominance solvable policies and winning batch coordination policies, both of which have strong theoretical guarantees such as tractability and the ability to win in a finite number of rounds almost surely. In addition, we showed that these policies can be found efficiently by solving a sequence of linear feasibility problems. We then considered additional objectives the manipulator may have, such as winning by the largest margin or whilst seeing a large improvement relative to the cost of modifying the payoff matrices. We then considered a socially good objective different from winning, namely maximization of the egalitarian social welfare. We showed that our framework could be extended to capture such objectives via linear objective functions. After this, we considered a social distancing game and showed that, by making only infinitesimal changes to the payoff matrices, the manipulator can maximize her payoff i.e. maximize her distance from the other players. The manipulator can also guide the utilities of all players to converge to a socially optimal solution. Note that due to page limitations, we have deferred all the proofs, example game analyses, and numerical results to the online ArXiv version of this paper (under the same title). Therefore we refer readers interested in more detailed discussions to that longer version of our paper.

References

1. Appa, G.: On the uniqueness of solutions to linear programs. J. Oper. Res. Soc. **53**(10), 1127–1132 (2002)
2. Baglieri, D., Carfì, D., Dagnino, G.B.: Asymmetric R&D alliances and coopetitive games. In: Greco, S., Bouchon-Meunier, B., Coletti, G., Fedrizzi, M., Matarazzo, B., Yager, R.R. (eds.) IPMU 2012. CCIS, vol. 300, pp. 607–621. Springer, Heidelberg (2012). https://doi.org/10.1007/978-3-642-31724-8_64
3. Bansal, T., Pachocki, J., Sidor, S., Sutskever, I., Mordatch, I.: Emergent complexity via multi-agent competition. In: International Conference on Learning Representations (2018)
4. Bishop, N., Dinh, L.C., Tran-Thanh, L.: How to guide a non-cooperative learner to cooperate: Exploiting no-regret algorithms in system design. In: Proceedings of the 20th International Conference on Autonomous Agents and MultiAgent Systems (2021)
5. Carfì, D., Schilirò, D.: Global green economy and environmental sustainability: a coopetitive model. In: Greco, S., Bouchon-Meunier, B., Coletti, G., Fedrizzi, M., Matarazzo, B., Yager, R.R. (eds.) IPMU 2012. CCIS, vol. 300, pp. 593–606. Springer, Heidelberg (2012). https://doi.org/10.1007/978-3-642-31724-8_63
6. Dinh, L.C., Nguyen, T.D., Zemhoho, A.B., Tran-Thanh, L., et al.: Last round convergence and no-dynamic regret in asymmetric repeated games. In: Algorithmic Learning Theory, pp. 553–577. PMLR (2021)
7. Gerding, E.H., Robu, V., Stein, S., Parkes, D.C., Rogers, A., Jennings, N.R.: Online mechanism design for electric vehicle charging. In: AAMAS, pp. 811–818 (2011)
8. Goldman, A., Tucker, A.: Theory in linear programming. In: Kuhn, H., Tucker, A. (eds.) Linear Inequalities and Related Systems, pp. 53–97. Princeton University Press, Princeton (1956)
9. Grzeundefined, M.: Reward shaping in episodic reinforcement learning. In: Proceedings of the 16th Conference on Autonomous Agents and MultiAgent Systems, AAMAS 2017, pp. 565–573. International Foundation for Autonomous Agents and Multiagent Systems, Richland, SC (2017)
10. Heuer, G.A.: Uniqueness of equilibrium points in bimatrix games. Int. J. Game Theory **8**(1), 13–25 (1979). https://doi.org/10.1007/BF01763049
11. Lowe, R., et al.: Multi-agent actor-critic for mixed cooperative-competitive environments. In: Advances in Neural Information Processing Systems, vol. 30, pp. 6379–6390 (2017)
12. Myerson, R.B.: Game Theory: Analysis of Conflict. Harvard University Press, Cambridge (1991). http://www.jstor.org/stable/j.ctvjsf522
13. Nisan, N.: Introduction to mechanism design (for computer scientists). In: Nisan, N., Roughgarden, T., Tardos, E., Vazirani, V.V. (eds.) Algorithmic Game Theory, chap. 9, pp. 209–242. Cambridge University Press, Cambridge (2007)

14. Panait, L., Luke, S.: Cooperative multi-agent learning: the state of the art. Auton. Agent. Multi-Agent Syst. **11**(3), 387–434 (2005)

15. Parkes, D.C.: Online mechanisms. In: Nisan, N., Roughgarden, T., Tardos, E., Vazirani, V.V. (eds.) Algorithmic Game Theory, chap. 16, pp. 411–442. Cambridge University Press, Cambridge (2007)

16. Phan, T., et al.: Learning and testing resilience in cooperative multi-agent systems. In: Proceedings of the 19th International Conference on Autonomous Agents and MultiAgent Systems, pp. 1055–1063 (2020)

17. Quintas, L.G.: Uniqueness of nash equilibrium points in bimatrix games. Econ. Lett. **27**(2), 123–127 (1988). https://doi.org/10.1016/0165-1765(88)90083-3. http://www.sciencedirect.com/science/article/pii/0165176588900833

18. Ryu, H., Shin, H., Park, J.: Cooperative and competitive biases for multi-agent reinforcement learning. In: Proceedings of the 20th International Conference on Autonomous Agents and MultiAgent Systems, pp. 1091–1099 (2021)

19. Samvelyan, M., et al.: The starcraft multi-agent challenge. In: AAMAS (2019)

20. Shapley, L., Karlin, S., Bohnenblust, H.: Solutions of discrete, two-person games. Contrib. Theory Games **1**, 51–72 (1950)

21. Sykulski, A., Chapman, A., Munoz de Cote, E., Jennings, N.: Ea^2: the winning strategy for the inaugural lemonade stand game tournament. Front. Artif. Intell. Appl. **215** (2010). https://doi.org/10.3233/978-1-60750-606-5-209

22. Tan, M.: Multi-agent reinforcement learning: independent vs. cooperative agents. In: Proceedings of the tenth International Conference on Machine Learning, pp. 330–337 (1993)

23. Wen, C., et al.: A cooperative-competitive multi-agent framework for auto-bidding in online advertising. arXiv e-prints pp. arXiv-2106 (2021)

24. Yuan, Q., Li, S., Wang, C., Xie, G.: Cooperative-competitive game based approach to the local path planning problem of distributed multi-agent systems. In: 2020 European Control Conference (ECC), pp. 680–685. IEEE (2020)

25. Zinkevich, M.A., Bowling, M., Wunder, M.: The lemonade stand game competition: solving unsolvable games. ACM SIGecom Exchanges **10**(1), 35–38 (2011)

Rational Broadcast Protocols Against Timid Adversaries

Keigo Yamashita and Kenji Yasunaga[✉]

Tokyo Institute of Technology, Tokyo, Japan
yasunaga@c.titech.ac.jp

Abstract. We present a constant-round deterministic broadcast protocol against *timid* adversaries in the synchronous authenticated setting. A timid adversary is a game-theoretically rational adversary who tries to attack the protocol but prefers the actions to be undetected. Our protocol is secure against such an adversary corrupting t out of n parties for any $t < n$. The round complexity is 5 for timid adversaries and is at most $t + 5$ for general malicious adversaries. Our results demonstrate that game-theoretic rationality enables us to circumvent the impossibility of constructing constant-round deterministic broadcast protocols for $t = \omega(1)$.

Keywords: Broadcast protocol · Game theory · Timid adversary

1 Introduction

Byzantine broadcast is a fundamental protocol in distributed computing used to construct fault-tolerant distributed systems and cryptographic protocols, including multiparty computation [28,43,44] and blockchains [27,35,41]. The Byzantine broadcast problem is that a specific party called the sender distributes a message among n parties in the presence of a malicious adversary who corrupts at most t parties. The difficulty is in a requirement that all non-corrupted parties should output the same value even if the sender is corrupted.

In synchronous networks with pairwise authenticated channels, the classical results [40,42] show that broadcast is possible if and only if $t < n/3$. By assuming the setup of digital signatures, which is referred to as the *authenticated* setting, Dolev and Strong [17] presented a deterministic protocol with round complexity $t + 1$ for any $t < n$. They also showed the round complexity lower bound of $t + 1$ for deterministic protocols in the authenticated setting. Since then, many studies have been devoted to constructing randomized protocols with expected constant-round complexity [1,12,18,24,36,47,48].

In this work, we demonstrate that game-theoretic *rationality* can be used to circumvent the impossibility result of [17]. Specifically, we consider rational adversaries who prefer to violate the requirements of the broadcast protocol but do not prefer their actions to be detected. Namely, such adversaries prefer to attack the protocol stealthily. We call them *timid* adversaries.

J. Fu et al. (Eds.): GameSec 2023, LNCS 14167, pp. 277–293, 2023.
https://doi.org/10.1007/978-3-031-50670-3_14

Table 1. Previous and Our Results on Authenticated Broadcast Protocols

References	Resilience	Round Complexity	Adversary Model	Results
[17]	$t < n$	$t + 1$	Malicious	∃determ. protocol
[17]	$t < n$	t	Malicious	No determ. protocol
[20]	$t < n$	$t + 3$	Malicious	∃detectable protocol
[36]	$t < n/2$	57	Malicious	∃rand. protocol
[24]	$t < n/2 + k$	$O(k^2)$	Malicious	∃rand. protocol
[24]	$t < n$	$o(2n/(n - t))$	Malicious	No rand. protocol
[21]	$t < n/2 + k$	$O(k)$	Malicious	∃rand. protocol
[1]	$t < n/2$	10	Malicious	∃rand. protocol
[12]	$t < n$	$O(n/(n - t))$	Malicious	∃rand. protocol
This work	$t < n$	5	Rational	∃determ. protocol

A timid adversary is an adversary model that lies between semi-honest and malicious adversaries. A semi-honest adversary only tries to extract secret information by honestly performing the protocol. The model seems artificial and cannot be applied to protocols without secrecy requirements, such as broadcast. A malicious adversary does anything to attack the protocol and is a good model for studying the worst-case scenarios. However, the worst-case model restricts the usability of protocols and may not reflect real-life situations. A timid adversary attacks the protocol carefully so that his behavior will not be detected. Since the actions of a timid adversary vary depending on the detection mechanism of the protocol, we model it as a rational player in game theory who behaves to maximize his utility. A timid adversary can behave maliciously if the protocol does not employ any detection system. The adversary may behave like a semi-honest adversary if the protocol checks the validity of each computation.

Our Contributions. We introduce a game-theoretic security notion for broadcast protocols that takes into account adversaries' rational behavior. In our model, a single rational adversary corrupts a subset of participants of the broadcast protocol. The non-corrupted participants honestly follow the protocol. The adversary has a preference for the outcome of the protocol execution. We say a protocol is secure if (1) it satisfies the requirements for the broadcast protocol for a "harmless" adversary and (2) no timid adversary obtains higher utility than the harmless adversary. In other words, the protocol is secure in the sense that the best strategy for timid adversaries is doing nothing.

We construct a constant-round deterministic broadcast protocol against timid adversaries in the authenticated setting. The round complexity is 5 for timid adversaries and is at most $t + 5$ for any malicious adversaries. The communication complexity of our protocol against timid adversaries is $O(\kappa n^2)$, where κ is a security parameter of the signature scheme. We summarize the previous and our results on authenticated broadcast protocols in Table 1.

The basic idea of our protocol is to use digital signatures as proofs/certificates. Consider a countersignature $\pi = (m, \sigma_B(\sigma_A(m)))$, where $\sigma_i(x)$ is a signature of player i for x. If player C has π, it means that C knows that player B has a proof that A has message m. Suppose that all players are prescribed to send the received countersignature to everyone by appending their own signature. If some player got the same countersignature as π from $t + 1$ different players, it means that everyone knows that B has a proof that A has m. This is because there are at most t corrupted parties, and thus at least one honest party sent π to everyone. We use and generalize this idea to construct a constant-round protocol for timid adversaries.

Related Security Notions for Broadcast. We compare our security notion of rational broadcast against timid adversaries with the related notions in the literature.

In [19,20], Fitzi et al. showed that *detectable broadcast* could be achieved for any $t < n$. In detectable broadcast, all honest parties either accept or reject the execution. A malicious adversary can cause an honest party to abort the protocol, but in that case, all the honest parties noticed the fact. Since a malicious action can be detected, any detectable broadcast protocol can be used as a rational protocol against timid adversaries. As far as we know, no constant-round detectable broadcast protocol exists.

Goldwasser and Lindell [29] presented a simple two-round protocol for *broadcast with abort* for any $t < n$. A requirement is relaxed such that any honest party needs to output either some same value or $\bot$. Since a broadcast protocol with abort may not have a mechanism for detecting malicious behaviors, the notion of broadcast with abort is incompatible with our security notion.

Aumann and Lindell [9] introduced the notion of *covert security*, where any deviation from the protocol can be detected with some probability ϵ. Although existing studies [8,15,30,39] for covert security have been aimed at constructing general multiparty computation protocols, the security notion can be adopted to broadcast. If the probability ϵ is high enough, a protocol with covert security can be used as a broadcast protocol for timid adversaries. As observed in [45], the standard definition of covert security is not necessarily weaker than standard security against malicious adversaries. Since a secure Byzantine broadcast protocol is also secure for timid adversaries, the notion of covert security is strictly stronger than ours.

Our results of constructing a protocol that takes 5 rounds for rational adversaries and $t + 5$ rounds for malicious adversaries are similar to the notion of *early stopping* [16], where the protocol may halt early if the actual number of corrupted parties is less than its maximum t. More specifically, Albouy et al. [5] studied the problem of constructing Byzantine broadcast protocols with good-case latency; they gave a deterministic broadcast protocol in the authenticated setting such that the round complexity may be a constant if the actual number of honest parties is sufficiently large. However, it is difficult to employ their protocol in our setting because it has no mechanism for detecting cheaters. Namely, a rational adversary may have no incentive to refrain from attacking the protocol.

Related Work. A game-theoretic analysis of players in cryptographic protocols was initiated by Halpern and Teague [33] for secret sharing. The problem is achieving fair secret reconstruction among rational parties, which has been extensively studied in the literature. See [2,7,22,37,38] and the references therein. Fairness among rational parties has been studied for other problems such as multiparty computation [6,31], leader election [3,4,13,49], consensus [34], and coin toss [14].

There have been studies on protocols against rational adversaries to circumvent the known impossibility results. Groce et al. [32] studied the possibility of constructing a Byzantine agreement tolerating t corruptions for $t \geq n/2$, which is impossible in the traditional setting. Garay et al. [25] introduced a framework of rational protocol design to capture incentive-driven adversaries within the simulation-based paradigm. Their framework was used to relax fairness in multiparty computation [26] and analyze Bitcoin [10]. The notion of timid adversaries was introduced by Fujita et al. [23] as a game-theoretically relaxed model of a malicious adversary. They presented perfectly secure message transmission protocols that circumvent the known impossibility results.

2   Preliminaries

We briefly describe our network model, the setup assumptions, and the definition of Byzantine broadcast.

There are n parties on the network. A protocol is said to be t-*resilient* if it works correctly, even if at most t parties are corrupted and controlled by an adversary. We assume the synchronous communication model. Namely, the protocol proceeds in rounds, and each party can send messages to other parties in each round. The messages of non-corrupted (honest) parties can be correctly delivered at the beginning of the next round.

We assume a public-key infrastructure (PKI) and digital signature schemes. Each party can generate a signature using his secret key, and the validity can be checked with the corresponding public key. It is called an *authenticated* setting.

A signature scheme consists of three algorithms (Gen, Sign, Ver). A key-generation algorithm Gen, on input security parameter n, outputs a pair of keys (pk, sk). The security parameter is usually represented by the string $1 \cdots 1$ of length n, denoted by 1^n. A signing algorithm Sign, on input secret key sk and message m, outputs a signature σ. A verification algorithm Ver, on input public key pk and pair (m, σ), checks if σ is a valid signature of m. Here, we give a formal definition of the standard security notion of signature schemes.

Definition 1 (Security of Signature Scheme). *A signature scheme* (Gen, Sign, Ver) *is existentially unforgeable against chosen-message attack (EUF-CMA) or simply secure if for every polynomial-time adversary A,*

$$\Pr\left[(pk, sk) \leftarrow \mathsf{Gen}(1^n); (m, \sigma) \leftarrow A^{\mathsf{Sign}_{sk}(\cdot)}(vk) : m \notin Q \wedge \mathsf{Ver}_{pk}(m, \sigma) = 1\right]$$

is negligible in n, where $Q = \{m_i\}_i$ is the set of queries m_i made by A to oracle $\mathsf{Sign}_{sk}(\cdot)$*, for which A received σ_i generated by $\mathsf{Sign}_{sk}(m_i)$ as a response.*

In the above definition, an adversary A can use the signing oracle $\mathsf{Sign}_{sk}(\cdot)$ as many times as A wants to obtain valid pairs $\{(m_i, \sigma_i)\}_i$ of message m_i and signature σ_i, where each m_i was chosen by A. Finally, A outputs a pair (m, σ). The winning condition that $m \notin Q \wedge \mathsf{Ver}_{pk}(m, \sigma) = 1$ means that the submitted message m should differ from the messages queried to the signing oracle, and the pair should be a valid message-signature pair. Thus, the above security guarantees that no adversary can generate a valid signature-message pair except those generated by a valid signing algorithm.

As a correctness property, we require that for any (pk, sk) generated by $\mathsf{Gen}(1^n)$ and message m, it holds that $\mathsf{Ver}_{vk}(m, \mathsf{Sign}_{sk}(m)) = 1$. For simplicity, we assume an ideal signature scheme where the above probability is equal to zero.

The following is a traditional definition of Byzantine broadcast.

Definition 2 (Byzantine Broadcast). *A protocol Π for n parties is said to be a t-resilient Byzantine broadcast protocol if the following conditions hold for any adversary controlling at most t parties:*

1. *Validity: If the sender is honest and holds an initial input m, then all honest parties output m.*
2. *Agreement: All honest parties output the same value.*

Dolev and Strong [17] presented a polynomial-time authenticated broadcast protocol with round complexity $t + 1$ for any $t < n$. Also, they showed that as long as protocols are deterministic, the round complexity must be at least $t + 1$, even in the authenticated setting.

3   Rational Broadcast Protocols

We define a game-theoretically rational adversary model. First, we define a game played by a rational player/adversary. The outcome of the game consists of the information that represents whether the adversary successfully violates the security requirements. Since timid adversaries care whether their actions were detected, the outcome also includes such information. After that, we define a security notion of rational broadcast protocols, which roughly says that the best strategy for rational adversaries is doing nothing on the protocol.

Broadcast Game. We define the *broadcast game*. First, set parameters incorrect = disagree = undetect = 0. Given the protocol Π, an adversary A chooses the sender $s \in [n]$, the message m, and the set of parties $C \subseteq [n]$ with $|C| \leq t$. The protocol is executed by specifying s as the sender with initial message m, where the parties in C are controlled by A, and the other parties honestly follow the protocol description of Π. After running the protocol, each party $i \in [n]$ outputs val_i. Let $H = [n] \setminus C$. If $s \in H$ and there exists $i \in H$ such that $\mathsf{val}_i \notin \{m, \perp\}$, set incorrect = 1. If there exist $i, j \in H$ such that $\mathsf{val}_i \neq \mathsf{val}_j$, set disagree = 1. In executing the protocol, every player may send a message "DETECT i" indicating that the player detected that player i cheating. If no player sent messages "DETECT i" during the protocol for $i \in C$, set undetect = 1. The outcome of the game against adversary A is $\mathsf{out}_A = (\mathsf{incorrect}, \mathsf{disagree}, \mathsf{undetect})$.

In the above definition of incorrect, the case that $\mathsf{val}_i = \perp$ for $i \in H$ is not considered a successful attack by adversaries. One reason is that if $\mathsf{val}_i = \perp$ for some honest party i, i may propose to execute the protocol again. If so, we cannot say that the adversary attacked successfully. Another reason is that the output value $\perp$ usually implies that some attack was detected. Hence, timid adversaries naturally consider that outcome a failure.

Utility. The utility $u(A)$ of the adversary A is the expected value $\mathbb{E}[U(\mathsf{out}_A)]$, where U is a function that maps the outcome out_A of the game to real values.

Definition 3 (Security of Rational Broadcast). *A broadcast protocol Π is said to be* secure against rational t-adversaries with utility function U *if there exists a "harmless" adversary B controlling at most t parties such that*

1. *Security: Π satisfies validity and agreement for B;*
2. *Nash equilibrium: For any adversary A controlling at most t parties, $u(A) \leq u(B)$.*

The above notion captures game-theoretic security; if protocol Π satisfies the above, a strategy of harmless adversary B is the best response since every other strategy (following adversary A) cannot increase the expected utility. Thus, every adversary rationally behaves harmlessly in protocol Π.

Timid Adversaries. We consider a *timid* adversary who tries to violate the security requirements of protocols but does not prefer the attacks to be detected. Specifically, we consider the set of utility functions that satisfy the following conditions:

1. $U(\mathsf{out}) > U(\mathsf{out}')$ if incorrect > incorrect', disagree = disagree', and undetect = undetect';
2. $U(\mathsf{out}) > U(\mathsf{out}')$ if incorrect = incorrect', disagree > disagree', and undetect = undetect';
3. $U(\mathsf{out}) > U(\mathsf{out}')$ if incorrect = incorrect', disagree = disagree', and undetect > undetect',

where out $=$ (incorrect, disagree, undetect) and out$'$ $=$ (incorrect$'$, disagree$'$, undetect$'$) are two outcomes of the broadcast game. We denote by U_{timid} the set of utility functions satisfying the above conditions.

By definition, for any $U \in U_{\text{timid}}$, it holds that

$$U(1,1,1) > \max\{U(0,1,1), U(1,0,1)\}$$
$$\geq \min\{U(0,1,1), U(1,0,1)\} > U(0,0,1) > U(0,0,0).$$

We use the above relation in the analysis.

Note that if protocol Π satisfies t-resilient Byzantine broadcast of Definition 2, any adversary controlling at most t parties achieves either $U(0,0,0)$ or $U(0,0,1)$. Since a harmless adversary will achieve $U(0,0,1)$, Π is also secure against rational t-adversaries. Namely, Definition 3 for timid adversaries is a relaxation of Definition 2.

4   Our Protocol

We assume that a PKI is established on the network. Let (Gen, Sign, Ver) be a signature scheme. We assume that each party $i \in [n]$ has a pair (pk_i, sk_i) of keys generated by Gen(1^n) and all parties know $\{pk_i\}_{i \in [n]}$. With the secret key sk_i, party i can generate a signature $\sigma_i(m)$ of message m by Sign$_{sk_i}(m)$. The validity of a pair (m, σ_i) can be verified with the public key pk_i by Ver$_{pk_i}(m, \sigma_i)$.

First, we recall the Dolev-Strong authenticated broadcast protocol [17]. The protocol uses a *signature chain*. A signature chain for value v of length ℓ is defined as (1) $(v, \sigma_i(v))$ for some $i \in [n]$ if $\ell = 1$; (2) $(c, \sigma_i(c))$ for some $i \in [n]$ for $\ell > 1$, where c is a signature chain for v of length $\ell - 1$ that consists of signatures with $\ell - 1$ distinct signers other than i. A signature chain is valid if it satisfies the above conditions and all signatures are valid.

Dolev-Strong Protocol

1. The sender s with input m sends $(m, \sigma_s(m))$ to all parties.
2. For round $r = 2, \ldots, t + 1$, each party i does the following:
   - If i received a valid signature chain c for value v of length $r - 1$ where no signature of i is included, then i signs it and sends $(c, \sigma_i(c))$ to all parties. (Party i does this procedure once for each value v. Namely, if i appended a signature for value v and sent to all parties, i does nothing for value v henceforth.)
   - At the end of round $t + 1$, let V be the set of values of valid signature chains of length $t + 1$ that i received. If $|V| = 0$ or $|V| > 1$, i outputs $\bot$. Otherwise, i output the value in V.

Before presenting the formal description, we give an overview of our protocol. In the following, we introduce three notions: proof of dissemination (PoD), proof of agreement (PoA), and proof of termination (PoT). They help us understand our protocol and make the security proof easy to follow.

Protocol Overview

1. The sender sends the initial input m and its signature to all parties.
2. Each party generates a countersignature from the received message and sends it to all parties.
3. Each party collects countersignatures. A set of $t+1$ valid countersignatures functions as a "proof of dissemination" of message m. It means that a non-corrupted party has sent a countersignature of m to all parties. Party i sends the local proof PoD_m^i for message m to all parties. If i found valid countersignatures for different values, i does nothing.

$$\mathsf{PoD}_m^i = \text{"Party } i \text{ knows that everyone got the proof that } s \text{ sent } m \text{."}$$

Note that, even if party i has PoD_m^i, there may be the case that s sent $m' \neq m$ to some party.

4. Each party collects proofs of dissemination $\{\mathsf{PoD}_m^j\}$. A set of $t+1$ valid proofs for consistent m is a "proof of agreement," implying that a non-corrupted party has found no inconsistency and sent a proof of dissemination to all parties. If party i gets a proof of agreement $\mathsf{PoA}_m^i = \{\mathsf{PoD}_m^j\}_j$, i sends the local proof PoA_m^i to all parties via the Dolev-Strong protocol. Otherwise, party i does nothing.

$$\mathsf{PoA}_m^i = \begin{array}{c} \text{"Party } i \text{ knows that everyone knows that} \\ \text{everyone got the proof that } s \text{ sent } m \text{."} \end{array}$$

Even if party i has PoA_m^i, there may be the case that another party j does not have PoA_m^j. Namely, j got the proof that s sent m, but j does not know everyone knows this fact.

5. A set of $t+1$ valid proofs $\{\mathsf{PoA}_m^j\}$ works as a "proof of termination" since it implies that a valid proof of agreement has been sent to all parties. If party i gets a proof of termination $\mathsf{PoT} = \{\mathsf{PoA}_m^j\}_j$, i outputs the value m. If another party j has not obtained a proof of termination, j continues to run the Dolev-Strong protocol, in which party i also needs to participate. At the end of the Dolev-Strong protocol, if party i found a valid PoA_m^j, i outputs m. Otherwise, i outputs $\perp$ and sends a message "DETECT s," meaning that the sender s has cheated.

$$\mathsf{PoT} = \begin{array}{c} \text{"Everyone knows that everyone knows that} \\ \text{everyone got the proof that } s \text{ sent } m \text{."} \end{array}$$

We give a formal description of our protocol. Since we define several *validity* notions, we summarize them in Table 2.

Our Protocol Π_{rbc}

Note that, in each round, if party i received a message containing $(x, \sigma_j(x))$ from party j such that $\sigma_j(x)$ is not a valid signature, then i considers j has sent i nothing.

Table 2. Validity Notions

Objects	Validity Conditions
Signature $\sigma_i(m)$	$\mathsf{Ver}_{vk_i}(m, \sigma_i(m)) = 1$
Countersignature $\sigma_i(\sigma_s(m))$	$\mathsf{Ver}_{vk_i}(\sigma_s(m), \sigma_i(\sigma_s(m))) = 1$ $\wedge\ \mathsf{Ver}_{vk_s}(m, \sigma_s(m)) = 1$
Countersignature set $\mathsf{CSigSet}^i_m = \{\sigma_j(\sigma_s(m))\}_j$	$\forall j,\ \sigma_j(\sigma_s(m))$ is valid $\wedge$ each j in $\mathsf{CSigSet}^i_m$ is distinct $\wedge\ |\mathsf{CSigSet}^i_m| \geq t+1$
Proof of dissemination $\mathsf{PoD}^i_m = (m, \mathsf{CSigSet}^i_m, \sigma^i_m)$	$\mathsf{Ver}_{vk_i}((m, \mathsf{CSigSet}^i_m), \sigma^i_m) = 1$ $\wedge\ \ \mathsf{CSigSet}^i_m$ is valid
(Signed) proof of agreement $\mathsf{PoA}^i_m = (\mathsf{PoA}_m, \sigma^i_m)$, where $\mathsf{PoA}_m = (m, \{(\mathsf{CSigSet}^j_m, \sigma^j_m)\}_j)$	$\mathsf{Ver}_{sk_i}(\mathsf{PoA}_m, \sigma^i_m) = 1$ $\wedge\ \forall j,\ \big(\mathsf{Ver}_{vk_j}(\mathsf{CSigSet}^j_m, \sigma^j_m) = 1$ $\wedge\ \mathsf{CSigSet}^j_m$ is valid $\big)$ $\wedge$ each j of $\mathsf{CSigSet}^j_m$ is distinct $\wedge\ |\{(\mathsf{CSigSet}^j_m, \sigma^j_m)\}_j| \geq t+1$
Signature chain $C^j = (\mathsf{PoA}^j_m, \sigma^j_m)$ of length k	$\sigma^j_m = \sigma_{i_k}(\sigma_{i_{k-1}}(\cdots(\sigma_{i_1}(\mathsf{PoA}^j_m))\cdots))$ $\wedge\ \mathsf{PoA}^j_m$ is valid $\wedge\ \forall \ell \in [k], \sigma_{i_\ell}(\cdots)$ is valid $\wedge$ each i_ℓ in σ^j_m is distinct $\wedge$ received in round $4+k$

1. The sender s with input m sends $(m, \sigma_s(m))$ to all parties.
2. For each party i, if i received a valid signature $(m, \sigma_s(m))$ from s and received no valid signature for other value $m' \neq m$, then i signs it and sends the countersignature $(m, \sigma_i(\sigma_s(m)))$ to all parties. Otherwise, i sends nothing.
3. For each party i, if i received at least $t+1$ valid countersignatures of distinct signers for the same value m and did not see any valid countersignature for other value $m' \neq m$, then i sends a proof of dissemination

$$\mathsf{PoD}^i_m = (m, \mathsf{CSigSet}^i_m, \sigma_i(\mathsf{CSigSet}^i_m))$$

to all parties, where

$$\mathsf{CSigSet}^i_m = \{\sigma_j(\sigma_s(m))\}_j$$

is the set of valid countersignatures of distinct signers for m that i received and $|\mathsf{CSigSet}^i_m| \geq t+1$.

Otherwise, i sends nothing.
4. For each party i, if i received at least $t+1$ valid proofs of dissemination $\{\mathsf{PoD}^j_m\}$ of distinct j for the same value m and did not see any valid proof for other value $m' \neq m$, then i sends a signed proof of agreement $\mathsf{PoA}^i_m =$

$(\mathsf{PoA}_m, \sigma_i(\mathsf{PoA}_m))$ to all parties, where

$$\mathsf{PoA}_m = (m, \{(\mathsf{CSigSet}_m^j, \sigma_j(\mathsf{CSigSet}_m^j))\}_j)$$

is generated from a set of valid proofs of dissemination of distinct j for m that i received and $|\{(\mathsf{CSigSet}_m^j, \sigma_m^j)\}_j| \geq t+1$.
Otherwise, i sends nothing.

5. For round $r = 4 + k$ with $k = 1, \ldots, t+1$, each party i does the following:
   (a) In each round, if i received from j a valid signature chain $C^j = (\mathsf{PoA}_m^j, \sigma_m^j)$ containing no signature of i and did not see any valid chain for other value $m' \neq m$, i sends $(\mathsf{PoA}_m^j, \sigma_i(\sigma_m^j))$ to all parties. (Note that i does this procedure once for each value PoA_m^j.)

   If i obtained at least $t+1$ signed proofs of agreement $\{(\mathsf{PoA}_m^j, \sigma_\ell(\sigma_m^j))\}_\ell$ (including i's one) with valid signatures of distinct ℓ for the same value m and did not see any valid proof for other value $m' \neq m$, i outputs m and halts.

   Otherwise, i sends nothing.
   (b) At the end of round $t + 5$, if party i received a valid signature chain of length $t + 1$ containing valid PoA_m^j and did not see any valid proof for other value $m' \neq m$, i outputs m and halts.

   Otherwise, i sends "DETECT s" to all parties, outputs $\perp$, and halts.

4.1   Security Proofs

We give a security proof of our protocol. Before proving the main theorem (Theorem 1), we give a technical lemma used in the proof.

Lemma 1. *In every broadcast game of Π_{rbc} in the presence of rational t-adversary with utility function $U \in U_{\mathsf{timid}}$ for $t < n$, it holds that (1) if $i \in H$ outputs $m \neq \perp$, then i have obtained a valid PoA_m^j for some $j \in [n]$; (2) if $i \in H$ outputs $\perp$, every $\ell \in H$ have failed to generate a signed proof of agreement $(\mathsf{PoA}_m^j, \sigma_\ell(\mathsf{PoA}_m^j))$ for a valid PoA_m^j for some $j \in [n]$ in round 4.*

Proof. Since every $i \in H$ follows the prescribed protocol, we can see that i outputs $m \neq \perp$ in round 5 or $t+5$. For the former case, i obtained at least $t+1$ signed proofs of agreement $\{(\mathsf{PoA}_m^j, \sigma_\ell(\sigma_m^j))\}_\ell$; for the latter case, i received a valid signature chain containing valid PoA_m^j. Thus, in both cases, $i \in H$ have obtained a valid PoA_m^j, implying (1).

Similarly, $i \in H$ outputs $\perp$ only when i failed to obtain a valid signature chain of length $t+1$ in round $t+5$. This event happens only when every honest party ℓ failed to obtain a valid PoA_m^j in round 4; this is because if $\ell \in H$ obtained a valid PoA_m^j, ℓ performs the Dolev-Strong protocol as a sender to broadcast $(\mathsf{PoA}_m^j, \sigma_\ell(\mathsf{PoA}_m^j))$ to all parties. By the agreement property of the Dolev-Strong protocol, honest party i would obtain a valid PoA_m^j, a contradiction. Hence, (2) follows. $\square$

Theorem 1. *The broadcast protocol Π_{rbc} is secure against rational t-adversaries with utility function $U \in U_{\text{timid}}$ for any $t < n$. The round complexity is 5 for a harmless adversary and is at most $t + 5$ for any adversary controlling t parties.*

Proof. We consider a harmless adversary B that chooses a random sender $s \in [n]$, a random message m, and $C = \emptyset$. Namely, B does not make any attacks on the protocol. It is not difficult to see that the protocol satisfies validity and agreement against B. In the presence of B, each party i receives n valid proofs of agreement in round 5. Thus, the round complexity for a harmless adversary is 5.

We show the Nash equilibrium property. Since $u(B) = U(0,0,1)$, we need to show that for any adversary A, $u(A) \le U(0,0,1)$. To achieve a higher utility, an adversary needs outcomes of incorrect $= 1$ or disagree $= 1$.

Consider the case that incorrect $= 1$. By definition, when incorrect $= 1$, the sender must not be corrupted. Since no party other than s can generate $\sigma_s(m')$ for $m' \ne m$, parties will not output messages other than m or $\perp$. Namely, as long as the signature scheme is unforgeable, it is not possible to be the case that incorrect $= 1$.

Next, consider the case that disagree $= 1$. Suppose for contradiction that two parties $i, j \in H$ output $\text{val}_i = m$, $\text{val}_j = m' \ne m$, respectively.

First, we consider the case that $\perp \notin \{m, m'\}$. By (1) of Lemma 1, i and j have obtained valid PoA_m and $\text{PoA}_{m'}$, respectively. A valid PoA_m contains a set $\{\text{CSigSet}_m^\ell\}_\ell$ of size at least $t + 1$ for distinct ℓ, where each CSigSet_m^ℓ is valid. Since there are at most t corrupted parties, the existence of valid PoA_m implies that some non-corrupted party ℓ sent CSigSet_m^ℓ to all parties in round 3. Since each CSigSet_m^ℓ consists of at least $t + 1$ valid countersignatures for m, some non-corrupted party ℓ' sent $(m, \sigma_{\ell'}(\sigma_s(m)))$ to all parties in round 2. Similarly, one can deduce that the existence of valid $\text{PoA}_{m'}$ implies that some party ℓ'' sent $(m', \sigma_{\ell''}(\sigma_s(m')))$ to all parties in round 2. Thus, all parties must have received valid countersignatures for distinct m and m'. In that case, all non-corrupted parties would have sent nothing in round 3, a contradiction.

Next, we consider the case that $m \ne \perp$ and $m' = \perp$. Since $\text{val}_j = \perp$, (2) of Lemma 1 implies that every $\ell \in H$ has failed to generate a signed proof of agreement. In that case, since there are at most t corrupted parties, no party can receive at least $t + 1$ valid proofs of agreement $\{\text{PoA}^j\}$ of distinct j in round 5. Thus, it must be the case that party i output m after performing the Dolev-Strong protocol. By the agreement property of the Dolev-Strong protocol, party $j \in H$ would output m, contradicting the fact that $\text{val}_j = \perp$. Thus, it is impossible to achieve disagree $= 1$.

By the above analysis, for any adversary A, the utility $u(A)$ is either $U(0,0,1)$ or $U(0,0,0)$. Note that $u(A) = U(0,0,0)$ when A corrupts the sender s, the protocol halts in round $t + 5$, and the cheating of s is detected. Since $u(A) \le U(0,0,1) = u(B)$, the protocol satisfies a Nash equilibrium.

To prove the worst-case round complexity, consider the case that some party i sent a valid signature chain $C^i = (\text{PoA}_m^i, \sigma_m^i)$ of length k to some honest party j in round $4 + k$ for some $k = 1, \ldots, t + 1$. In that case, by the property of the

Dolev-Strong protocol, every honest party can obtain a valid signature chain of length $t + 1$ in round $t + 5$. Otherwise, no honest party will receive a valid signature chain of length $t + 1$ in round $t + 5$, and thus all honest parties output $\perp$ by sending "DETECT s". In either case, the worst-case round complexity is $t + 5$.   □

Communication Complexity. The communication complexity of the above protocol against a harmless adversary is $O(\kappa n^3)$, where κ is a security parameter of the signature scheme, and we assume that each signature is of length $O(\kappa)$. We can employ *non-interactive threshold signatures* [11,46] to reduce the communication complexity. In a non-interactive threshold signature scheme, each party can generate a signature share of message x, and there is an algorithm that converts k valid shares to a signature of x. No set of less than k parties can forge a valid signature. In our protocol, a set $\mathsf{CSigSet}_m^j$ of countersignatures can be replaced with a threshold signature. Namely, in round 2, each party sends a signature share of $(m, \sigma_s(m))$ to all parties, and in round 3, each party generates a valid threshold signature of $(m, \sigma_s(m))$ instead of $\mathsf{CSigSet}_m^i$. Since the size of PoD_m^i can be reduced from $O(\kappa n)$ to $O(\kappa)$, the total communication complexity of the resulting protocol is $O(\kappa n^2)$.

4.2 Detecting Cheaters

In our protocol, the sender is the only player who can be detected as a cheater. Regarding this point, we can show that as long as $t \leq \lfloor (n-1)/2 \rfloor$, the sender s can be declared a cheater only when s is corrupted.

Proposition 1. *In every broadcast game of Π_{rbc} in the presence of rational t-adversary A with utility function $U \in U_{\mathsf{timid}}$ for $t \leq \lfloor (n-1)/2 \rfloor$, if $i \in H$ outputs $\perp$, then A chose the sender $s \in [n]$ and $C \subseteq [n]$ such that $s \in C$.*

Proof. Suppose for contradiction that A chose the sender $s \in [n]$ and C such that $s \notin C$. Since $s \in H$, every player receives a valid signature $\sigma_s(m)$ in round 2. Then, every player $i \in H$ sends a valid countersignature $\sigma_i(\sigma_s(m))$ to all players. Since the number of honest players satisfies

$$|H| = n - t \geq n - \left\lfloor \frac{n-1}{2} \right\rfloor \geq \left\lfloor \frac{2n - (n-1)}{2} \right\rfloor = \left\lfloor \frac{n-1}{2} + 1 \right\rfloor \geq t + 1,$$

every player $i \in H$ obtains at least $t + 1$ valid countersignatures in round 3. By a similar argument, every player $i \in H$ obtains at least $t + 1$ valid proofs of dissemination in round 4 and obtains at least $t + 1$ valid signed proofs of agreement in round 5. Hence, every player $i \in H$ outputs m in round 5 and halts, which contradicts the assumption that some honest player outputs $\perp$. Therefore, the statement follows.   □

Proposition 1 guarantees a sort of soundness of the detection mechanism in our protocol. However, we can see that the guaranteed bound $t \leq \lfloor (n-1)/2 \rfloor$

is optimal and cannot be extended to $t > \lfloor (n-1)/2 \rfloor$. Specifically, there is a t-adversary A with $t = \lfloor (n-1)/2 \rfloor + 1$ such that A chooses the sender s and C with $s \notin C$, but every $i \in H$ outputs $\bot$. The strategy of A is fairly simple; every party $i \in C$ does nothing in the protocol. For such A, the number of honest players satisfies

$$|H| = n - t = n - \left(\left\lfloor \frac{n-1}{2} \right\rfloor + 1 \right) \leq t.$$

Since only at most t players are active, every honest player cannot generate any valid countersignature set, for which at least $t+1$ valid countersignatures are needed. Thus, honest players will output $\bot$ in the game against A.

The above weakness of our protocol does not contradict the game-theoretic security of Definition 3. Since every honest player outputs $\bot$, the outcome of the game is $\mathsf{out}_A = (\mathsf{incorrect}, \mathsf{disagree}, \mathsf{undetect}) = (0, 0, 1)$, where $s \in H$ is wrongly detected as a cheater, but no player $i \in C$ is detected. The above strategy of A achieves the same utility as a harmless one and does not violate a Nash equilibrium.

5   Discussion

In this work, we introduce a game-theoretic security notion for broadcast protocols, which can be used in various cryptographic protocols such as multiparty computation and blockchains. We have developed a constant-round broadcast protocol against adversaries corrupting t out of n players for any $t < n$. Since constructing constant-round protocols is impossible for malicious adversaries, our protocol heavily relies on the rationality of timid adversaries who prefer their actions to be undetected in protocol executions.

There are several interesting open problems. First, as discussed in Sect. 4.2, our protocol may wrongly detect an honest player as a cheater for $t \geq \lfloor (n-1)/2 \rfloor + 1$. Possible future work is constructing a protocol without such weakness or proving it is impossible. Another one is improving our protocol with respect to round complexity and communication complexity. The worst-case round complexity of our protocol is $t + 5$, which depends on the number of corrupted players. It may be interesting to incorporate randomized protocols [1,12,47,48] instead of the Dolev-Strong protocol [17] for constructing protocols with expected constant-round protocols for (worst-case) malicious adversaries.

Acknowledgments. This study was supported in part by JSPS KAKENHI Grant Numbers 23H00468 and 23K17455. The second author would like to thank Toshihiko Ishihara for the discussion at an early stage of this work.

References

1. Abraham, I., Devadas, S., Dolev, D., Nayak, K., Ren, L.: Synchronous Byzantine agreement with expected $O(1)$ rounds, expected $O(n^2)$ communication, and optimal resilience. In: Goldberg, I., Moore, T. (eds.) FC 2019. LNCS, vol. 11598, pp. 320–334. Springer, Cham (2019). https://doi.org/10.1007/978-3-030-32101-7_20

2. Abraham, I., Dolev, D., Gonen, R., Halpern, J.Y.: Distributed computing meets game theory: robust mechanisms for rational secret sharing and multiparty computation. In: Ruppert, E., Malkhi, D. (eds.) Proceedings of the Twenty-Fifth Annual ACM Symposium on Principles of Distributed Computing, PODC 2006, Denver, CO, USA, 23–26 July 2006, pp. 53–62. ACM (2006)

3. Abraham, I., Dolev, D., Halpern, J.Y.: Distributed protocols for leader election: a game-theoretic perspective. ACM Trans. Econ. Comput. **7**(1), 4:1-4:26 (2019)

4. Afek, Y., Ginzberg, Y., Feibish, S.L., Sulamy, M.: Distributed computing building blocks for rational agents. In: Halldórsson, M.M., Dolev, S. (eds.) ACM Symposium on Principles of Distributed Computing, PODC 2014, Paris, France, 15–18 July 2014, pp. 406–415. ACM (2014)

5. Albouy, T., Frey, D., Raynal, M., Taïani, F.: Good-case early-stopping latency of synchronous Byzantine reliable broadcast: the deterministic case. In: Scheideler, C. (ed.) 36th International Symposium on Distributed Computing, DISC 2022, Volume 246 of LIPIcs, Augusta, Georgia, USA, 25–27 October 2022, pp. 4:1-4:22. Schloss Dagstuhl - Leibniz-Zentrum für Informatik (2022)

6. Asharov, G., Canetti, R., Hazay, C.: Toward a game theoretic view of secure computation. J. Cryptol. **29**(4), 879–926 (2016). https://doi.org/10.1007/s00145-015-9212-6

7. Asharov, G., Lindell, Y.: Utility dependence in correct and fair rational secret sharing. J. Cryptol. **24**(1), 157–202 (2011). https://doi.org/10.1007/s00145-010-9064-z

8. Asharov, G., Orlandi, C.: Calling out cheaters: covert security with public verifiability. In: Wang, X., Sako, K. (eds.) ASIACRYPT 2012. LNCS, vol. 7658, pp. 681–698. Springer, Heidelberg (2012). https://doi.org/10.1007/978-3-642-34961-4_41

9. Aumann, Y., Lindell, Y.: Security against covert adversaries: efficient protocols for realistic adversaries. J. Cryptol. **23**(2), 281–343 (2010). https://doi.org/10.1007/s00145-009-9040-7

10. Badertscher, C., Garay, J., Maurer, U., Tschudi, D., Zikas, V.: But why does it work? A rational protocol design treatment of bitcoin. In: Nielsen, J.B., Rijmen, V. (eds.) EUROCRYPT 2018. LNCS, vol. 10821, pp. 34–65. Springer, Cham (2018). https://doi.org/10.1007/978-3-319-78375-8_2

11. Cachin, C., Kursawe, K., Shoup, V.: Random oracles in constantipole: practical asynchronous Byzantine agreement using cryptography (extended abstract). In: Neiger, G. (ed.) Proceedings of the Nineteenth Annual ACM Symposium on Principles of Distributed Computing, Portland, Oregon, USA, 16–19 July 2000, pp. 123–132. ACM (2000)

12. Chan, T.-H.H., Pass, R., Shi, E.: Sublinear-round Byzantine agreement under corrupt majority. In: Kiayias, A., Kohlweiss, M., Wallden, P., Zikas, V. (eds.) PKC 2020. LNCS, vol. 12111, pp. 246–265. Springer, Cham (2020). https://doi.org/10.1007/978-3-030-45388-6_9

13. Chung, K.-M., Chan, T.-H.H., Wen, T., Shi, E.: Game-theoretic fairness meets multi-party protocols: the case of leader election. In: Malkin, T., Peikert, C. (eds.) CRYPTO 2021. LNCS, vol. 12826, pp. 3–32. Springer, Cham (2021). https://doi.org/10.1007/978-3-030-84245-1_1

14. Chung, K.-M., Guo, Y., Lin, W.-K., Pass, R., Shi, E.: Game theoretic notions of fairness in multi-party coin toss. In: Beimel, A., Dziembowski, S. (eds.) TCC 2018. LNCS, vol. 11239, pp. 563–596. Springer, Cham (2018). https://doi.org/10.1007/978-3-030-03807-6_21

15. Damgård, I., Orlandi, C., Simkin, M.: Black-box transformations from passive to covert security with public verifiability. In: Micciancio, D., Ristenpart, T. (eds.) CRYPTO 2020. LNCS, vol. 12171, pp. 647–676. Springer, Cham (2020). https://doi.org/10.1007/978-3-030-56880-1_23

16. Dolev, D., Reischuk, R., Strong, H.R.: Early stopping in Byzantine agreement. J. ACM **37**(4), 720–741 (1990)

17. Dolev, D., Strong, H.R.: Authenticated algorithms for Byzantine agreement. SIAM J. Comput. **12**(4), 656–666 (1983)

18. Feldman, P., Micali, S.: An optimal probabilistic protocol for synchronous Byzantine agreement. SIAM J. Comput. **26**(4), 873–933 (1997)

19. Fitzi, M., Gisin, N., Maurer, U., von Rotz, O.: Unconditional Byzantine agreement and multi-party computation secure against dishonest minorities from scratch. In: Knudsen, L.R. (ed.) EUROCRYPT 2002. LNCS, vol. 2332, pp. 482–501. Springer, Heidelberg (2002). https://doi.org/10.1007/3-540-46035-7_32

20. Fitzi, M., Gottesman, D., Hirt, M., Holenstein, T., Smith, A.D.: Detectable Byzantine agreement secure against faulty majorities. In: Ricciardi, A. (ed.) Proceedings of the Twenty-First Annual ACM Symposium on Principles of Distributed Computing, PODC 2002, Monterey, California, USA, 21–24 July 2002, pp. 118–126. ACM (2002)

21. Fitzi, M., Nielsen, J.B.: On the number of synchronous rounds sufficient for authenticated Byzantine agreement. In: Keidar, I. (ed.) DISC 2009. LNCS, vol. 5805, pp. 449–463. Springer, Heidelberg (2009). https://doi.org/10.1007/978-3-642-04355-0_46

22. Fuchsbauer, G., Katz, J., Naccache, D.: Efficient rational secret sharing in standard communication networks. In: Micciancio, D. (ed.) TCC 2010. LNCS, vol. 5978, pp. 419–436. Springer, Heidelberg (2010). https://doi.org/10.1007/978-3-642-11799-2_25

23. Fujita, M., Koshiba, T., Yasunaga, K.: Perfectly secure message transmission against rational adversaries. IEEE J. Sel. Areas Inf. Theory **3**(2), 390–404 (2022)

24. Garay, J.A., Katz, J., Koo, C., Ostrovsky, R.: Round complexity of authenticated broadcast with a dishonest majority. In: 48th Annual IEEE Symposium on Foundations of Computer Science (FOCS 2007), Providence, RI, USA, 20–23 October 2007, Proceedings, pp. 658–668. IEEE Computer Society (2007)

25. Garay, J.A., Katz, J., Maurer, U., Tackmann, B., Zikas, V.: Rational protocol design: cryptography against incentive-driven adversaries. In: 54th Annual IEEE Symposium on Foundations of Computer Science, FOCS 2013, Berkeley, CA, USA, 26–29 October 2013, pp. 648–657. IEEE Computer Society (2013)

26. Garay, J.A., Katz, J., Tackmann, B., Zikas, V.: How fair is your protocol?: A utility-based approach to protocol optimality. In: Georgiou, C., Spirakis, P.G. (eds.) Proceedings of the 2015 ACM Symposium on Principles of Distributed Computing, PODC 2015, Donostia-San Sebastián, Spain, 21–23 July 2015, pp. 281–290. ACM (2015)

27. Gilad, Y., Hemo, R., Micali, S., Vlachos, G., Zeldovich, N.: Algorand: scaling Byzantine agreements for cryptocurrencies. In: Proceedings of the 26th Symposium on Operating Systems Principles, Shanghai, China, 28–31 October 2017, pp. 51–68. ACM (2017)

28. Goldreich, O., Micali, S., Wigderson, A.: How to play any mental game or a completeness theorem for protocols with honest majority. In: Aho, A.V. (ed.) Proceedings of the 19th Annual ACM Symposium on Theory of Computing, New York, New York, USA, pp. 218–229. ACM (1987)

29. Goldwasser, S., Lindell, Y.: Secure multi-party computation without agreement. J. Cryptol. **18**(3), 247–287 (2005). https://doi.org/10.1007/s00145-005-0319-z

30. Goyal, V., Mohassel, P., Smith, A.: Efficient two party and multi party computation against covert adversaries. In: Smart, N. (ed.) EUROCRYPT 2008. LNCS, vol. 4965, pp. 289–306. Springer, Heidelberg (2008). https://doi.org/10.1007/978-3-540-78967-3_17

31. Groce, A., Katz, J.: Fair computation with rational players. In: Pointcheval, D., Johansson, T. (eds.) EUROCRYPT 2012. LNCS, vol. 7237, pp. 81–98. Springer, Heidelberg (2012). https://doi.org/10.1007/978-3-642-29011-4_7

32. Groce, A., Katz, J., Thiruvengadam, A., Zikas, V.: Byzantine agreement with a rational adversary. In: Czumaj, A., Mehlhorn, K., Pitts, A., Wattenhofer, R. (eds.) ICALP 2012. LNCS, vol. 7392, pp. 561–572. Springer, Heidelberg (2012). https://doi.org/10.1007/978-3-642-31585-5_50

33. Halpern, J.Y., Teague, V.: Rational secret sharing and multiparty computation: extended abstract. In: Babai, L. (ed.) Proceedings of the 36th Annual ACM Symposium on Theory of Computing, Chicago, IL, USA, 13–16 June 2004, pp. 623–632. ACM (2004)

34. Halpern, J.Y., Vilaça, X.: Rational consensus: extended abstract. In: Giakkoupis, G. (ed.) Proceedings of the 2016 ACM Symposium on Principles of Distributed Computing, PODC 2016, Chicago, IL, USA, 25–28 July 2016, pp. 137–146. ACM (2016)

35. Hou, R., Yu, H., Saxena, P.: Using throughput-centric Byzantine broadcast to tolerate malicious majority in blockchains. In: 43rd IEEE Symposium on Security and Privacy, SP 2022, San Francisco, CA, USA, 22–26 May 2022, pp. 1263–1280. IEEE (2022)

36. Katz, J., Koo, C.: On expected constant-round protocols for Byzantine agreement. J. Comput. Syst. Sci. **75**(2), 91–112 (2009)

37. Kawachi, A., Okamoto, Y., Tanaka, K., Yasunaga, K.: General constructions of rational secret sharing with expected constant-round reconstruction. Comput. J. **60**(5), 711–728 (2017)

38. Kol, G., Naor, M.: Games for exchanging information. In: Dwork, C. (ed.) Proceedings of the 40th Annual ACM Symposium on Theory of Computing, Victoria, British Columbia, Canada, 17–20 May 2008, pp. 423–432. ACM (2008)

39. Kolesnikov, V., Malozemoff, A.J.: Public verifiability in the covert model (almost) for free. In: Iwata, T., Cheon, J.H. (eds.) ASIACRYPT 2015. LNCS, vol. 9453, pp. 210–235. Springer, Heidelberg (2015). https://doi.org/10.1007/978-3-662-48800-3_9

40. Lamport, L., Shostak, R.E., Pease, M.C.: The Byzantine generals problem. ACM Trans. Program. Lang. Syst. **4**(3), 382–401 (1982)

41. Pass, R., Shi, E.: Thunderella: blockchains with optimistic instant confirmation. In: Nielsen, J.B., Rijmen, V. (eds.) EUROCRYPT 2018. LNCS, vol. 10821, pp. 3–33. Springer, Cham (2018). https://doi.org/10.1007/978-3-319-78375-8_1

42. Pease, M.C., Shostak, R.E., Lamport, L.: Reaching agreement in the presence of faults. J. ACM **27**(2), 228–234 (1980)

43. Rabin, T.: Robust sharing of secrets when the dealer is honest or cheating. J. ACM **41**(6), 1089–1109 (1994)

44. Rabin, T., Ben-Or, M.: Verifiable secret sharing and multiparty protocols with honest majority (extended abstract). In: Johnson, D.S. (ed.) Proceedings of the 21st Annual ACM Symposium on Theory of Computing, Seattle, Washigton, USA, 14–17 May 1989, pp. 73–85. ACM (1989)

45. Scholl, P., Simkin, M., Siniscalchi, L.: Multiparty computation with covert security and public verifiability. IACR Cryptology ePrint Archive 2021/366 (2021)

46. Shoup, V.: Practical threshold signatures. In: Preneel, B. (ed.) EUROCRYPT 2000. LNCS, vol. 1807, pp. 207–220. Springer, Heidelberg (2000). https://doi.org/10.1007/3-540-45539-6_15

47. Wan, J., Xiao, H., Devadas, S., Shi, E.: Round-efficient Byzantine broadcast under strongly adaptive and majority corruptions. In: Pass, R., Pietrzak, K. (eds.) TCC 2020. LNCS, vol. 12550, pp. 412–456. Springer, Cham (2020). https://doi.org/10.1007/978-3-030-64375-1_15

48. Wan, J., Xiao, H., Shi, E., Devadas, S.: Expected constant round Byzantine broadcast under dishonest majority. In: Pass, R., Pietrzak, K. (eds.) TCC 2020. LNCS, vol. 12550, pp. 381–411. Springer, Cham (2020). https://doi.org/10.1007/978-3-030-64375-1_14

49. Yifrach, A., Mansour, Y.: Fair leader election for rational agents in asynchronous rings and networks. In: Newport, C., Keidar, I. (eds.) Proceedings of the 2018 ACM Symposium on Principles of Distributed Computing, PODC 2018, Egham, United Kingdom, 23–27 July 2018, pp. 217–226. ACM (2018)

FlipPath Game to Counter Stealthy Attacks in SDN-Based Tactical Networks

Fabrice Mvah[1(✉)] , Vianney Kengne Tchendji[1] ,
Clémentin Djamegni Tayou[1] , Ahmed H. Anwar[2] , Deepak K. Tosh[3] ,
and Charles Kamhoua[2]

[1] Department of Mathematics and Computer Science, University of Dschang,
Dschang, Cameroon
fabricemvah@gmail.com
[2] DEVCOM Army Research Laboratory, Adelphi, USA
[3] Department of Computer Science, University of Texas at El Paso, El Paso, USA

Abstract. Software-Defined Networking (SDN) is an evolving network paradigm that separates the control and forwarding functions of network devices. Its application in tactical networks can help to automate Virtual Private Networks (VPN) establishments, Unit Task Reorganization (UTRs), security certificate management, and security solution automation. Despite these advantages, tactical networks continue to face new threats. In this paper, we introduce a new stealthy packet-dropping scenario that can appear during data forwarding in tactical networks. To overcome this attack scenario, we propose a new game-theoretic approach called FlipPath to provide an optimal data forwarding strategy that prevents packet-dropping on a network path. The forwarding path is considered a shared resource, and each player wants to control it for a long period while minimizing the related costs. We use periodic strategies to characterize the Nash equilibria that identify the defender's optimal data-forwarding strategies. Our computational results have shown that the defender who adopts the proposed methodology can mitigate the attacker's stealthy packet-dropping.

Keywords: Stealthy Attack · FlipIt Game · Software-Defined Network · Tactical Network · Nash Equilibrium

1 Introduction

Software-Defined Networking (SDN) is a flexible architecture model in which network functions are automatically programmed by a central controller according to evolving requirements [1]. This architecture enables the implementation of new services without knowing the specific technologies of the underlying infrastructure. The level of programmability of SDN can enable rapid deployment of services, easier reconfiguration, and interoperability between different networks.

© The Author(s), under exclusive license to Springer Nature Switzerland AG 2023
J. Fu et al. (Eds.): GameSec 2023, LNCS 14167, pp. 294–308, 2023.
https://doi.org/10.1007/978-3-031-50670-3_15

The application of SDN in a tactical network can help to avoid time-consuming by automating Virtual Private Network (VPN) establishments, security certificate management, security solution automation, and Unit Task Reorganizations (UTRs) that are frequent in army's tactical networks [2]. Despite these advantages, tactical networks continue to face sophisticated threats such as stealthy attacks.

In general, stealthy attacks are highly sophisticated and can remain undetected for long periods. Some notorious cyber attacks have gone undetected for months or even longer [3]. The first widely reported stealthy attack (Operation Aurora) was made public by Google in January 2010, and its malicious activity was suspected to have begun six months earlier. This cyber attack was very large in scale and reportedly targeted 34 organizations, including Yahoo, Symantec, and Google itself [4]. Another example is the notorious Stuxnet virus that reportedly damaged nearly a thousand uranium hexafluoride centrifuges in Iran's Natanz facility [5]. Stealthy attacks are preferred by attackers because their signatures are not necessarily known by the defender. As technology grows, attackers are developing new threats to evade current intrusion detection systems. In [6], Khalil and Bagchi introduced four modes of stealthy packet-dropping attacks and provided countermeasures. These modes include misrouting, power control attacks, controlled-jamming attacks, and identity delegation attacks.

In this paper, we introduce a new stealthy packet-dropping scenario that can appear during data forwarding in tactical networks. In this scenario, the attacker is one of the intermediate nodes of the forwarding path and has a packet-dropping function that can be enabled or disabled. The attacker drops packets when its dropping function is enabled and forwards data when this function is disabled. We assume that the network includes an intrusion detection system that detects an attacker when its dropping function remains enabled for a long period. Thus, a stealthy attacker will drop packets at relatively short time intervals to remain undetectable. In a tactical network, this stealthy behavior can lead to traffic degradation between tactical force units, and negatively impact operational processes and situational awareness. As tactical force units are deployed for a specific mission, a lack of situational awareness can lead to mission failure. The FlipIt game model can be used to overcome this problem. However, existing FlipIt game approaches [7–9] cannot work because they do not consider some features such as the probability of taking control and the case in which the attacker and the defender may have more than one action, as in the new stealthy attack scenario. To overcome this problem, we propose a novel game-theoretic approach called FlipPath to model the strategic interaction between the source node (defender) and the malicious node (attacker) on the forwarding path. We consider a forwarding path as a shared resource, where at any time, either the defender or the attacker can move (flip) to try to take over the path. At any time t, the path is under the control of one player, who is not necessarily the player who makes the last move before t. To capture players' stealthy behavior, we assume that neither the defender nor the attacker has any real-time feedback about the other side. The goal of each player is to control the path for a long time while minimizing the related costs. There is a random starting phase (the first move is selected uniformly at random from a given interval) and a fixed inter-arrival time between two consecutive moves. Thus, we consider a periodic strategy for each player. As proven in [7], when there is no real-time feedback, periodic defense is optimal against periodic attacks, and vice versa. We characterized the Nash equilibrium of the game where the defender first determines and declares its strategy and the attacker answers accordingly. Our contribution can be summarized as follows:

- Introducing a new attacker's stealthy packet-dropping scenario in a tactical network. In this scenario, the attacker attempts to drop packets for a long period while remaining undetectable;
- Propose a novel game-theoretic model called FlipPath to prevent the attacker's stealthy packet-dropping in a tactical network path. In this game, players compete to control the forwarding path, and a player can take over the path according to a probability distribution. We use periodic strategies to characterize the Nash equilibria that identify the defender's optimal data-sending strategies.

The rest of this paper is organized as follows: Sect. 2 presents the related work. Section 3 describes the network architecture. In Sect. 4, we describe a new attacker's stealthy packet-dropping scenario. In Sect. 5, the proposed game-theoretic approach is presented. Section 6 validates the proposed game model through computational simulation. Section 7 concludes this paper and presents future directions.

2   Related Work

As mentioned earlier, cyber-attacks are becoming more and more sophisticated to evade current intrusion detection systems. These attacks consist in compromising a system while remaining undetectable. In general, several methodologies have been proposed in wireless networks to deal with cyber-attacks. One of these methodologies is local monitoring. The local monitoring in a node's neighborhood consists of listening to nearby traffic and exchanging information within a node's transmission range to detect malicious nodes. The idea of monitoring traffic in the neighborhood makes it possible to establish trust relationships between nodes, detect and mitigate certain types of attacks, or discover routes in the network [10]. In local monitoring, nodes supervise a portion of their neighbors' incoming and outgoing traffic, and each node performs a local check on the observed traffic to determine malicious behavior. Several protocols rely on local monitoring for intrusion detection [11,12]. These protocols build trust and reputation between nodes to protect the network against attacks. In [13], Buchegger et al. proposed an approach based on overhearing packets transmitted by neighbors and establishing reputation scores. This solution is ineffective because adversary nodes obtain high reputation scores, and malicious actions cannot be detected [6]. Awerbuch et al. [14] proposed an approach for detecting malicious behavior involving selective packet dropping. This method can detect stealthy packets dropping at the destination node. However, it involves a significant communication overhead and requires other techniques to identify and isolate malicious nodes. In [6], Khalil and Bagchi introduced four ways of achieving stealthy packet dropping including misrouting, power control attack, controlled-jamming attack, and identity delegation attack. They provide a protocol to remedy each of these attacks. Overall, local monitoring can work when a node has several neighbors. It may be unable to work when there is only one possible forwarding path including an attacker as an intermediate node.

The above drawback can be addressed by using a FlipIt game methodology [7]. However, existing FlipIt game approaches [7–9,15–18] cannot work because they do not consider some features such as the probability of taking control and the case where the attacker and defender each have more than one action. To remedy these shortcomings, we propose a novel game-theoretic approach called FlipPath to model the strategic interaction between the source node (defender) and the malicious node (attacker) on the forwarding path. In Sect. 3 below, we describe the network architecture.

3   Network Architecture and Operation

The network architecture includes the infrastructure layer, control layer, and application layer as shown in Fig. 1. This architecture is inspired by those proposed in [19,20]. The infrastructure layer includes mobile nodes organized in clusters, and each cluster has a local controller that acts as a cluster head. The latter manages the cluster and establishes connections between nodes through flow rules. Some nodes have Wi-Fi and LTE interfaces, while others support only the Wi-Fi connection. The LTE is used to connect the node to the central SDN controller, while the Wi-Fi connection is used for the connection between nodes. The cluster head is mobile and changeable and can be changed depending on its remaining energy, location, and moving speed. Only nodes with Wi-Fi and LTE interfaces can work as a cluster head. If no node has the LTE connection in a group of nodes, this group is controlled by the neighboring cluster head through a multi-hop connection. Each cluster head contains a database to record information such as nodes, remaining node energy, and the connection between nodes. Once the information is collected, the cluster head sends it to the central SDN controller.

To manage the network, we provide three main components: Route Building Agent, Lifetime Prediction Agent, and Data Collector Agent. Each cluster head includes these components to manage its cluster. The Route Building Agent (RBA) is used for route discovery in a cluster or in a whole network. This agent aims to find a possible forwarding path between the source and the destination nodes. Figure 2 shows two cases in which the route discovery has been performed. This figure shows that for route discovery, the source node sends a Route Request (RReQ) packet to the controller. The controller receives the request, computes the path, and returns a Route Reply (RReP) packet. After replying, the controller installs forwarding rules in all the intermediate nodes to inform them

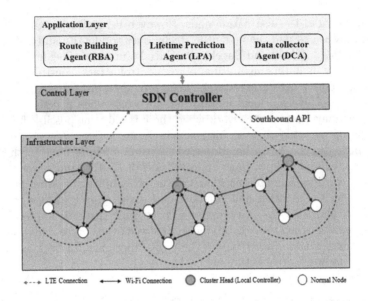

Fig. 1. Network architecture.

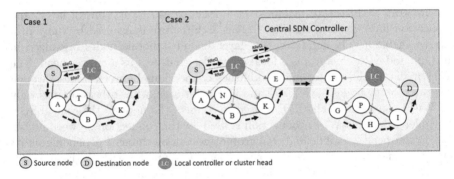

Fig. 2. Forwarding path in different cases.

about the flow identifier and how to manage it. If the source and destination nodes are in the same cluster, as shown in Fig. 2 (case 1), the RReQ is sent to the cluster head. Otherwise, the cluster head forwards the RReQ to the central SDN controller, as shown in Fig. 2 (case 2). After establishing the forwarding path, the Lifetime Prediction Agent (LPA) computes the lifetime of the path to prevent data loss due to nodes' mobility. This lifetime represents the time to use the forwarding path. Finally, the Data Collector Agent (DCA) collects data within a cluster or across the entire network. When receiving data from nodes or cluster heads, the DCA saves them into a database implemented at the control plane. The controller uses this database to manage the network. In Sect. 4, we formulate the problem we address in this paper.

4   Problem Formulation

As nodes are mobile in a tactical environment, the network may be in a situation where there is only one path from the source node to the destination. We consider such a situation with an attacker as an intermediate node in the forwarding path as shown in Fig. 3. This figure shows the two cases in which the attacker can be on the forwarding path. In the first case, the forwarding path is within a cluster, while in case 2, the forwarding path involves two clusters. In both cases, the attacker and the source nodes are on the same path and the source node is aware of the malicious node's presence on the path.   The attacker

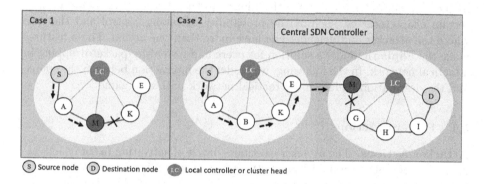

Fig. 3. Different attack scenarios.

has a packet-dropping function that can be enabled or disabled. It drops packets when its dropping function is enabled and forwards data when this function is disabled. We assume that the network includes an intrusion detection system that detects an attacker when its dropping function remains enabled for a long period. Thus, a stealthy attacker will drop packets at relatively short time intervals and remains undetectable. In a tactical network, this stealthy behavior can lead to traffic degradation between tactical force units, and negatively impact operational processes and situational awareness. As the attacker cannot be detected by the intrusion detection system, the source node must find the best time interval to successfully send the data to the recipient. In Sect. 5, we describe the proposed game model to address this problem.

5   Proposed FlipPath Game Model

FlipPath is a game in which players compete to control a forwarding path for a long period while minimizing the related costs. The forwarding path is considered a shared resource between the source node (defender) and the malicious node (attacker). A player gets a reward of δ when controlling the path and a cost of C when not controlling it. When a player moves (flips), it can take control according to a probability P. Thus, at a given time t, a player who controls the path is not necessarily the one who makes the last move. A flip is costly for a player, and it corresponds to the action taken to try to take control. Only one player can control the path at a given time. When both players move at the same time, only one player keeps control based on the resulting action profile. A player's flip is considered unnecessary when the player who was controlling the path keeps control after the flip. When moving, a player pays a certain move cost of K. The player's benefit is defined as the fraction of time the latter controls the resource minus the average move cost. The best strategy for a given player is the one that gives it control of the resource a large fraction of the time with few moves. Since a player must pay a move cost, the latter will be disincentivized to move too frequently. FlipPath differs from the FlipIt model in that it takes into account certain characteristics, such as the probability of taking control and the case where the attacker and defender can have more than one action. These features make the FlipPath model a solution for overcoming stealthy packet-dropping in a tactical network. In the following, we model the interaction between the source and the destination nodes on the tactical network path as a game.

5.1 Players' Actions

Attacker Actions. The attacker's actions consist of activating (a) or deactivating (d) its packet-dropping function. When this function is enabled or activated, the attacker drops packets transmitted in the path. Similarly, when the dropping function is deactivated, the attacker just forwards data to the next node on the forwarding path. As explained before, the attacker activates its dropping function to try to get control, and it deactivates the function to avoid detection. We consider $A_a = \{a, d\}$ as the set of attacker actions where a and d are respectively for the activation of deactivation.

Defender Actions. The defender's actions consist of sending (s) data or waiting (w) a certain amount of time before sending data on the forwarding path. The defender waits a certain amount of time before sending data to avoid the attacker or the time interval in which the attacker can be activated. We consider $A_d = \{s, w\}$ as the set of defender actions where s and w are respectively for sending data and waiting a certain amount of time before sending data.

5.2 Players' Strategies

We consider periodic strategies with a random phase (in such a strategy, moves are spaced at equal intervals, with the exception of the first randomly selected move called the phase). A periodic strategy with a random phase is characterized by a fixed interval π between consecutive moves. π can be calculated using the rate of play of the player, as follows: $\pi = \frac{1}{\sigma}$. We consider π_a and π_d respectively the attacker and the defender strategy. Figure 4 shows how the game is played between attacker and defender using periodic strategies. The defender strategy

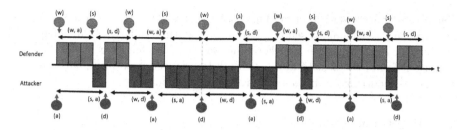

Fig. 4. Example of players' interaction on the path.

$\pi_d = 3$ s, and the attacker's $\pi_a = 4$ s. As shown in Fig. 4, each player moves by choosing an action at the end of its period. Given A_a and A_d, there are four possible action profiles that can appear: *(s, a), (s, d), (w, a), and (w, d).* Each player has action profiles for which it controls the path. Thus, a player takes control if its action profile appears after a strategy choice.

5.3   Game Formulation

We formulate the game by describing the different cases in which each player controls the forwarding path (Fig. 5). As in Fig. 5, if the defender is sending data

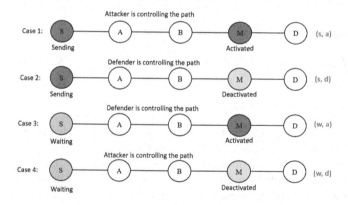

Fig. 5. Different cases in which each player controls the path.

while the attacker is activated, the attacker takes control. In this case, all data going from the source node to the destination will be dropped by the attacker. Similarly, if the attacker is deactivated while the defender is waiting for a certain amount of time, the attacker takes control. We assume that the attacker controls the path because it has found the best time interval to remain deactivated without incurring an unnecessary risk of detection. On the other hand, if data are successfully going from the source node to the destination, we consider that the defender is controlling the path. This case appears when the attacker is deactivated while the defender is sending data on the path. Similarly, if the defender is not sending data while the attacker is activated, the defender controls the path because it found the best time to not send data on the forwarding path and the attacker is incurring an unnecessary risk of detection.

5.4 Payoff Functions

In a periodic game, the benefit of a player depends of players' rate of play. Let σ_a and σ_d be respectively the rate of play of the attacker and that of the defender. We denote the benefit of player i by $U_i(\sigma_a, \sigma_d)$. Let's consider two players i and j. In [7], it has been proven that in the interval $[0, 1]$, if player i is moving no faster than player j, the time in which it will control the shared resource is expressed as follows: $\frac{\sigma_i}{2\sigma_j}$. Thus, the time in which player i will not control the path is $1 - \frac{\sigma_i}{2\sigma_j}$. The average flip cost is given by $k_i\sigma_i$. Thus, we design the payoff functions as follows:

Case 1 : $\sigma_a \leq \sigma_d$

$$U_a(\sigma_a, \sigma_d) = P_a * (\frac{\sigma_a}{2\sigma_d})\delta_a - (1 - P_a) * (1 - \frac{\sigma_a}{2\sigma_d})C_a - k_a\sigma_a \tag{1}$$

$$U_d(\sigma_a, \sigma_d) = P_d * (1 - \frac{\sigma_a}{2\sigma_d})\delta_d - (1 - P_d) * (\frac{\sigma_a}{2\sigma_d})C_d - k_d\sigma_d \tag{2}$$

Case 2 : $\sigma_a \geq \sigma_d$

$$U_a(\sigma_a, \sigma_d) = P_a * (1 - \frac{\sigma_d}{2\sigma_a})\delta_a - (1 - P_a) * (\frac{\sigma_d}{2\sigma_a})C_a - k_a\sigma_a \tag{3}$$

$$U_d(\sigma_a, \sigma_d) = P_d * (\frac{\sigma_d}{2\sigma_a})\delta_d - (1 - P_d) * (1 - \frac{\sigma_d}{2\sigma_a})C_d - k_d\sigma_d \tag{4}$$

Equations 1 and Eq. 2 present the attacker and the defender payoff functions when the attacker is moving no faster than the defender. Equation 3 and Eq. 4 show the attacker and defender payoff functions when the attacker is moving faster than the defender. In these equations, δ_a is the attacker's reward for controlling the path. This reward represents the fraction of packets dropped or the time the attacker loses to the defender before sending packets. C_a is the cost to the attacker of not controlling the path. This cost represents the fraction of packets successfully transmitted or the energy expended by the attacker to monitor the traffic to be able to drop the packets. Similarly, δ_d is the defender's reward for controlling the path, and C_d is the defender's cost of not controlling the path. After formulating the payoff functions, we analyze the Nash equilibrium in Sect. 5.5 below.

5.5   Nash Equilibrium Analysis

The Nash equilibrium is a strategy profile for which no player can get a better payoff by changing its strategy. In the proposed game model, the Nash equilibrium identifies the optimal rate of play for both players. To compute the Nash equilibrium, we consider the case in which the attacker is moving no faster ($\sigma_a \leq \sigma_d$) than the defender, and that the attacker is moving faster ($\sigma_a \geq \sigma_d$) than the defender.

Case 1: ($\sigma_a \leq \sigma_d$) Taking the partial derivative of $U_a(\sigma_a, \sigma_d)$, we obtain:

$$\frac{\partial U_a(\sigma_a, \sigma_d)}{\partial \sigma_a} = \frac{\partial (P_a * (\frac{\sigma_a}{2\sigma_d})\delta_a - (1 - P_a) * (1 - \frac{\sigma_a}{2\sigma_d})C_a - k_a\sigma_a)}{\partial \sigma_a}$$

$$= \frac{P * \delta_a + (1 - P_a) * C_a}{2\sigma_d} - k_a$$

It follows that $U_a(., \sigma_d)$ is increasing if $\sigma_d < \frac{P_a * \delta_a + (1 - P_a) * C_a}{2k_a}$, and decreasing if $\sigma_d > \frac{P_a * \delta_a + (1 - P_a) * C_a}{2k_a}$.

Case 2: ($\sigma_a \geq \sigma_d$) In this case, the attacker is moving faster than the defender. As in case 1, taking the partial derivative of $U_a(\sigma_a, \sigma_d)$, we obtain:

$$\frac{\partial U_a(\sigma_a, \sigma_d)}{\partial \sigma_a} = \frac{\partial (P_a * (1 - \frac{\sigma_d}{2\sigma_a})\delta_a - (1 - P_a) * (\frac{\sigma_d}{2\sigma_a})C_a - k_a\sigma_a)}{\partial \sigma_a}$$

$$= \frac{P_a\sigma_d}{2\sigma_a^2}\delta_a + \frac{(1 - P_a)\sigma_d}{2\sigma_a^2}C_a - k_a$$

It follows that, $U_a(., \sigma_d)$ is increasing on $[0, \sqrt{\frac{\sigma_d(P_a\delta_a + C(1 - P_a)_a)}{2k_a}}]$, decreasing on $[\sqrt{\frac{\sigma_d(P_a\delta_a + (1 - P_a)C_a)}{2k_a}}, \infty]$ and thus has a maximum at

$\sigma_a = max\{\sigma_d, \sqrt{\frac{\sigma_d(P_a\delta_a + (1 - P_a)C_a)}{2k_a}}\}$.

Let's σ_a^* and σ_d^* be respectively the attacker and defender rate of play at the Nash equilibrium. We need to consider the constraints of cases 1 and 2 to calculate the values of σ_a^* and σ_d^*. Based on these constraints over σ_d, we perform the following analysis.

If $\sigma_d < \frac{P_a * \delta_a + (1 - P_a) * C_a}{2k_a}$, then $\sqrt{\frac{\sigma_d(P_a\delta_a + (1 - P_a)C_a)}{2k_a}} > \sigma_d$. Thus, the optimal benefit of the attacker is achieved at rate $\sigma_a = \sqrt{\frac{\sigma_d(P_a\delta_a + (1 - P_a)C_a)}{2k_a}}$.

If $\sigma_d = \frac{P_a * \delta_a + (1 - P_a) * C_a}{2k_a}$, then $U_a(\sigma_a, \sigma_d) = \frac{P_a\sigma_a k_a\delta_a}{P_a\delta_a + (1 - P_a)C_a} - (1 - P_a)(1 - \frac{P_a\sigma_a k_a\delta_a}{P\delta_a + (1 - P_a)C_a})C_a - k_a\sigma_a)$, for all $\sigma_a \in [0, \frac{P_a * \delta_a + (1 - P_a) * C_a}{2k_a}]$.

For $\sigma_a \geq \sigma_d$, we have: $\sigma_a \geq \sqrt{\frac{\sigma_a(P_a * \delta_a + (1 - P_a) * C_a)}{2k_a}} \geq \sqrt{\frac{\sigma_d(P * \delta_a + (1 - P) * C_a^h)}{2k_a}} \Rightarrow$

$\sigma_a \in [\sqrt{\frac{\sigma_d(P_a*\delta_a+(1-P_a)*C_a)}{2k_a}}, \infty]$. Based on the first case we considered, the benefit $U_a(\sigma_a, \sigma_d)$ decreases in σ_a. In this case, the maximum value of $U_a(\sigma_a, \sigma_d)$ is achieved for any σ_a in $[0, \sqrt{\frac{\sigma_d(P_a\delta_a+(1-P_a)C_a)}{2k_a}}]$.

If $\sigma_d > \frac{P_a*\delta_a+(1-P_a)*C_a}{2k_a}$, we obtain, $\frac{1}{2\sigma_d} < \frac{2k_a}{P*\delta_a+(1-P_a)*C_a} \Rightarrow P_a*(\frac{\sigma_a}{2\sigma_d})\delta_a + (1 - P_a)*(1-\frac{\sigma_a}{2\sigma_d})C_a - k_a\sigma_a < 0 \Rightarrow U_a(\sigma_a, \sigma_d) < 0$. it follows from both cases that the attacker's benefit is always non-positive and as such the attacker's optimal strategy is not playing at all.

Let $\Phi_a(\sigma_d)$ be the set of values σ_a that optimize the attacker's benefit for a fixed rate of play σ_d. $\Phi_d(\sigma_a)$, the set of values σ_d that optimize the defender's benefit for a fixed rate of play σ_a. Let consider $\mu = \frac{P_a\delta_a+(1-P_a)C_a}{2k_a}$ and $\rho = \frac{P_d\delta_d+(1-P_d)C_d}{2k_d}$. Φ_a is given by Eq. 5.

$$\Phi_a(\sigma_d) = \begin{cases} \sqrt{\frac{\sigma_d(P_a\delta_a+(1-P_a)C_a)}{2k_a}} & \text{if } \sigma_d \leq \mu \\ 0 \text{ if } \sigma_d > \mu \end{cases} \tag{5}$$

As we did to obtain Φ_a, the same process can lead to obtaining Φ_d. The value of Φ_d is given by Eq. 6.

$$\Phi_d(\sigma_a) = \begin{cases} \sqrt{\frac{\sigma_a(P_d\delta_d+(1-P_d)C_d)}{2k_d}} & \text{if } \sigma_a \leq \rho \\ 0 \text{ if } \sigma_a > \rho \end{cases} \tag{6}$$

Equation 5 and Eq. 6 show that it is better for a player to not play at all when the rate of play of the other player is greater than a certain threshold. μ can be seen as a threshold for the attacker and ρ is the threshold for the defender. Thus, the attacker will decide to not play at all if $\sigma_d > \mu$. Likewise, the defender will decide to not play at all ($\sigma_d = 0$) if $\sigma_a > \rho$. The Nash equilibrium is the intersection between Φ_a and Φ_d. We use the same computation as in [7] to compute the values of σ_a^* and σ_d^*.

– **Case 1:** If $k_a < k_d$. The Nash equilibrium is obtained for rates:

$$\sigma_a^* = \frac{P_d\delta_d + (1 - P_d)C_d}{2k_d} \quad ; \quad \sigma_d^* = \frac{1}{2}(\frac{K_a}{\delta_a + C_a})(\frac{\delta_d + C_d}{K_d})^2$$

– **Case 2:** If $k_a > k_d$. The Nash equilibrium is obtained for rates:

$$\sigma_a^* = \frac{1}{2}(\frac{K_d}{\delta_d + C_d})(\frac{\delta_a + C_a}{\delta_d + C_d}) \quad ; \quad \sigma_d^* = \frac{P_a\delta_a + (1 - P_a)C_d)}{2k_a}$$

– **Case 3:** If $k_a = k_d$. We obtain the following Nash equilibrium:

$$\sigma_a^* = \frac{P_d\delta_d + (1 - P)C_d}{2k_d} \quad ; \quad \sigma_d^* = \frac{P_a\delta_a + (1 - P_a)C_a)}{2k_a}$$

In the following, we have performed some evaluations to validate the proposed methodology. Section 6 presents computational simulation

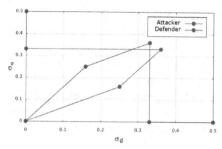

(a) Nash equilibrium using the same flip cost: $K_a = K_d = 0.5$, $P_a = P_d = 0.5$, $\delta_a = \delta_d = 0.6$, $C_a = C_d = 0.2$.

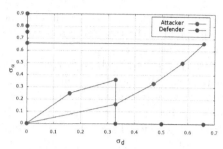

(b) Nash equilibrium using different flip-cost: $K_a = 0.3$ $K_d = 0.5$, $P_a = P_d = 0.5$, $\delta_a = \delta_d = 0.6$, $C_a = C_d = 0.2$.

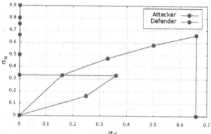

(c) Nash equilibrium using different flip-cost: $K_a = 0.5$ $K_d = 0.3$, $P_a = P_d = 0.5$, $\delta_a = \delta_d = 0.6$, $C_a = C_d = 0.2$.

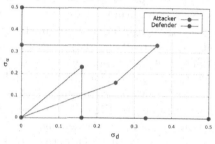

(d) Nash equilibrium using different probabilities: $K_a = 0.5$ $K_d = 0.5$, $P_a = 0.3$, $P_d = 0.5$, $\delta_a = \delta_d = 0.6$, $C_a = C_d = 0.2$.

Fig. 6. Nash equilibrium considering different parameters.

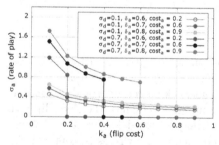

(a) Attacker's rate of play over the flip cost with different values of δ_d and $cost_d$. $P_d = 0.5$

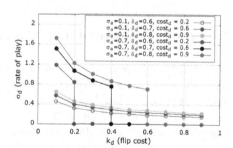

(b) Defender's rate of play over the flip cost with different values of δ_d and $cost_d$. $P_d = 0.5$.

Fig. 7. Players' rate of plays.

6   Computational Simulation

As shown earlier, the Nash equilibrium depends on several parameters, which are: the probability of taking control, the reward of controlling the path, the cost of not controlling the path, and the flip cost. As explained above, the Nash equilibrium is the intersection between Φ_a and Φ_d, where $\Phi_a(\sigma_d)$ represents the set of values σ_a that optimize the attacker's benefit for a fixed rate of play σ_d. $\Phi_d(\sigma_a)$ is the set of values σ_d that optimize the attacker's benefit for a fixed rate of play σ_a. We plotted Φ_a and Φ_d functions considering different values of k_a and k_d. Figure 6 shows the obtained results. This figure shows Nash equilibria as a function of different parameters. Indeed, when the values of payoffs, costs, and probabilities change, the Nash equilibrium changes. In Fig. 6a, we have three points of intersection, while in Fig. 6b, Fig. 6c, and Fig. 6d, there is only one point of intersection. This result is related to the values of parameters. As in Fig. 6b and Fig. 6c, when the flip cost changes, the Nash equilibrium also changes. Let $(r1, r2)$ be a pair that respectively represents the defender's gain when it plays the Nash equilibrium strategy and when it does not. For cases (a), (b), (c), and (d), we have respectively obtained the following gains: (0.8, 0.3), (0.7, −0.2), (0.6, 0.1), and (0.5, −0.4). These results show that the defender who employs Nash's strategy obtains a better gain. This gain is an indicator of how many packets the source node can successfully transmit to the destination.

We also evaluate the impact of reward and cost on the rate of play with different flip costs. Figure 7a presents the results obtained from this evaluation. This figure shows that when the reward to control the path and the cost of not controlling the path increase, the attacker's rate of play also increases. This result shows that when the cost of not controlling the path is high, the attacker will move quickly to try to get control. As the players' rate of play is symmetrical, the defender will also try to get control as shown in Fig. 7b. When moving, the player should carefully look at the other player's strategy to avoid being forced to not play at all.

7   Conclusion and Future Work

The aim of this paper was to propose a solution against stealthy attacks in SDN-based tactical networks. We introduced a new stealthy packet-dropping scenario that can appear during data forwarding in a network path and provide a countermeasure. The proposed approach is a novel game-theoretic model called FlipPath that provides an optimal data-forwarding strategy for the defender. The forwarding path is considered a shared resource, and each player wishes to control it for a long period while minimizing the related costs. We used periodic strategies to characterize Nash equilibria. The results showed that the defender who adopts the proposed methodology will obtain a better result. In future work, as the players' rate of play is symmetrical, we will investigate how this symmetrical nature can impact the defender's reward. In addition, we will perform simulations in the Mininet simulator.

Acknowledgements. Research was sponsored by the Army Research Office and was accomplished under Grant Number W911NF-21-1-0326. The views and conclusions contained in this document are those of the authors and should not be interpreted as representing the official policies, either expressed or implied, of the Army Research Office or the U.S. Government. The U.S. Government is authorized to reproduce and distribute reprints for Government purposes notwithstanding any copyright notation herein.

References

1. Agile communication systems for the armed forces. https://csiac.org/articles/software-defined-networking-for-armys-tactical-network-promises-challenges-and-an-architectural-approach. Accessed 05 June 2023
2. Doshi, B., Cansever, D.: Software defined networking for army's tactical network: Promises, challenges, and an architectural approach. Cybersecurity & Information systems, Information Analysis Center (2018). Accessed 05 June 2023
3. Bencsáth, B., Pék, G., Buttyán, L., Félegyházi, M.: The cousins of stuxnet: duqu, flame, and gauss. Future Internet 4(4), 971–1003 (2012)
4. Tankard, C.: Advanced persistent threats and how to monitor and deter them. Netw. Secur. 2011(8), 16–19 (2011)
5. Kushner, D.: The real story of Stuxnet. IEEE Spectr. 50(3), 48–53 (2013)
6. Khalil, I., Bagchi, S.: MISPAR: mitigating stealthy packet dropping in locally-monitored multi-hop wireless ad hoc networks. In: 4th International ICST Conference on Security and Privacy in Communication Networks, SECURECOMM 2008, Istanbul, Turkey, 22–25 September 2008, p. 28. ACM (2008)
7. van Dijk, M., Juels, A., Oprea, A., Rivest, R.L.: FLIPIT: the game of "stealthy takeover". J. Cryptol. 26(4), 655–713 (2013)
8. Feng, X., Zheng, Z., Hu, P., Cansever, D., Mohapatra, P.: Stealthy attacks meets insider threats: a three-player game model. In: 34th IEEE Military Communications Conference, MILCOM 2015, Tampa, FL, USA, 26–28 October 2015, pp. 25–30. IEEE (2015)
9. Feng, X., Zheng, Z., Cansever, D., Swami, A., Mohapatra, P.: Stealthy attacks with insider information: a game theoretic model with asymmetric feedback. In: 2016 IEEE Military Communications Conference, MILCOM 2016, Baltimore, MD, USA, 1–3 November 2016, pp. 277–282. IEEE (2016)
10. Huang, Y.A., Lee, W.: A cooperative intrusion detection system for ad hoc networks. In: Proceedings of the 1st ACM Workshop on Security of ad hoc and Sensor Networks, SASN 2003, Fairfax, Virginia, USA, 2003, pp. 135–147. ACM (2003)
11. Khalil, I., Bagchi, S., Shroff, N.B.: LITEWORP: a lightweight countermeasure for the wormhole attack in multihop wireless networks. In: Proceedings of 2005 International Conference on Dependable Systems and Networks (DSN 2005), 28 June–1 July 2005, Yokohama, Japan, pp. 612–621. IEEE Computer Society (2005)
12. Solomon, A.: A Novel Cooperative Intrusion Detection System for Mobile Ad Hoc Networks. PhD thesis, Nova Southeastern University, Fort Lauderdale, Florida, USA (2018)
13. Sonja, B.U.C.H.E.G.G.E.R.: A robust reputation system for P2P and mobile ad-hoc networks. P2PEcon, 2004 (2004)
14. Awerbuch, B., Curtmola, R., Holmer, D., Nita-Rotaru, C., Rubens, H.: ODSBR: an on-demand secure byzantine resilient routing protocol for wireless ad hoc networks. ACM Trans. Inf. Syst. Secur. 10(4), 6:1–6:35 (2008)
15. Hu, P., Li, H., Fu, H., Cansever, D., Mohapatra, P.: Dynamic defense strategy against advanced persistent threat with insiders. In: 2015 IEEE Conference on

Computer Communications, INFOCOM 2015, Kowloon, Hong Kong, 26 April–1 May 2015, pp. 747–755. IEEE (2015)

16. Pawlick, J., Farhang, S., Zhu, Q.: Flip the cloud: cyber-physical signaling games in the presence of advanced persistent threats. In: Khouzani, M.H.R., Panaousis, E., Theodorakopoulos, G. (eds.) GameSec 2015. LNCS, vol. 9406, pp. 289–308. Springer, Cham (2015). https://doi.org/10.1007/978-3-319-25594-1_16

17. Oakley, L., Oprea, A.: QFlip: an adaptive reinforcement learning strategy for the FlipIt security game. In: Alpcan, T., Vorobeychik, Y., Baras, J.S., Dán, G. (eds.) GameSec 2019. LNCS, vol. 11836, pp. 364–384. Springer, Cham (2019). https://doi.org/10.1007/978-3-030-32430-8_22

18. Greige, L., Chin, P.: Deep reinforcement learning for Flipit security game. In: Benito, R.M., Cherifi, C., Cherifi, H., Moro, E., Rocha, L.M., Sales-Pardo, M. (eds.) Complex Networks & Their Applications X. COMPLEX NETWORKS 2021. Studies in Computational Intelligence, vol. 1072, pp. 831–843. Springer, Cham (2021). https://doi.org/10.1007/978-3-030-93409-5_68

19. Kadhim, A., Hosseini Seno, S.A., Shihab, R.A.: Routing protocol for SDN-cluster based manet. J. Theor. Appl. Inf. Technol. **96** (2018)

20. Naser, J.I., Kadhim, A.J.: Multicast routing strategy for SDN-cluster based manet. Int. J. Electr. Comput. Eng. (2088–8708) **10**(5) (2020)

Information and Privacy

Double-Sided Information Asymmetry in Double Extortion Ransomware

Tom Meurs[1]([⊠])[iD], Edward Cartwright[2][iD], and Anna Cartwright[3][iD]

[1] University of Twente: Enschede, Enschede, The Netherlands
t.w.a.meurs@utwente.nl
[2] De Montfort University: Leicester, Leicestershire, UK
edward.cartwright@dmu.ac.uk
[3] Oxford Brookes University: Oxford, Oxfordshire, UK
a.cartwright@brookes.ac.uk

Abstract. Double extortion ransomware attacks consist of an attack where victims files are both encrypted and exfiltrated for extortion purposes. There is empirical evidence this leads to an increased willingness to pay a ransom, and higher ransoms, compared to encryption-only attacks, depending on the value of the exfiltrated files. However, there seem to be two complications: First, victims are uncertain whether data is exfiltrated, due to for example misconfigured monitoring systems. Second, it is hard for attackers to estimate the value of compromised files. Thus, victims have an incentive to hide what they know and attackers an incentive to find out information. The goal of this study is to use game theory to explore the payoff consequences for attackers of victims having private information. We analyse a signaling game with double-sided information asymmetry: (1) attackers know whether data is exfiltrated and victims do not, and (2) victims know the value of data if it is exfiltrated, but the attackers do not. Our analysis of the game indicates that private information substantially lowers the return to attackers. These results imply that victims should be careful to not reveal the value of files during negotiations.

Keywords: Ransomware · Data exfiltration · Information asymmetry

1 Introduction

The last decade has seen a rapid rise in crypto-ransomware attacks [7,8,10,19,20, 23]. Crypto-ransomware, or ransomware for short, is broadly defined as the use of crypto-techniques to encrypt the files of a victim, after which the attackers ask for a ransom to decrypt the files [29]. Ransomware has proved highly profitable for criminal gangs, primarily because many victims pay the ransom in order to receive the decryption keys [21]. Since roughly 2019, ransomware groups have been experimenting with double extortion [6,13]. In this case the attackers not only encrypt files, but also exfiltrate data with the purpose to sell or publish the data if the victim does not pay [16,17,20]. Double extortion has increased the ransom requested and probability of victims paying [19].

© The Author(s), under exclusive license to Springer Nature Switzerland AG 2023
J. Fu et al. (Eds.): GameSec 2023, LNCS 14167, pp. 311–328, 2023.
https://doi.org/10.1007/978-3-031-50670-3_16

One important issue for victims of a ransomware attack is determining whether data was exfiltrated. Due to the deletion of log files by attackers, or misconfigured monitoring systems, victims often do not know whether data was exfiltrated [25, 26]. This means that an attacker who has not exfiltrated data can still threaten the publication of data, to get a larger ransom paid. On the flip side, the claims of an attacker that has exfiltrated data may be viewed as less-credible, empty threats, by the victim. Attackers are, thus, increasingly trying to send credible signals that data was exfiltrated. For instance, to back up their claim, some attackers send evidence of exfiltration by means of a file tree of the exfiltrated data or a couple of files. Such signals could, however, still be sent, even if at a higher cost, by attackers who have not exfiltrated data.

Another limitation of sending 'evidence' of data exfiltration is that it might give the victim the opportunity to determine the value of the exfiltrated data. In practice, it is hard for attackers to determine the value of the files to the victim. The filenames and files which contain text are often in a foreign language, and the sensitivity of data is difficult to judge without insider understanding. Furthermore, it takes effort to estimate the importance of, potentially, millions of files. Attackers are, therefore, likely to be imperfectly informed of the value of files, even if data is exfiltrated. Combined, therefore, we have two information asymmetries in double extortion ransomware attacks. First, the victim does not know whether data was exfiltrated or not, but the attacker does. Second, the victim can assess whether potentially exfiltrated data is valuable or not, but the attacker cannot. Here, we define valuable data for the victim, as data with large reputation costs if it gets accessible for the general public, competitors or similar.

To our knowledge, no previous studies have modelled this two-sided information asymmetry of data exfiltration, and analysed how it effects the profitability of attacks. Most empirical [19] and game-theoretical modeling [16, 17] of double extortion ransomware has focused on the extra profits for attackers by conducting data exfiltration and encryption, compared to only data encryption. We address the relationship between the uncertainty of data exfiltration and profitability by analysing a signaling game. Signaling games provide a way to model a strategic game with incomplete information and sequential choice [1, 11, 14, 18, 22]. The basic premise is that a player holding extra information could try to influence the other players by sending a credible signal of their information. Signalling games provide a natural framework with which to explore double extortion and the payoff consequences of assymetric information. For a more detailed explanation of signaling games we refer to [22].

Our work provides the following key contributions: First, we provide a game-theoretical framework to analyse the double-sided information asymmetry in double extortion ransomware attacks. The framework consists of a signaling game, wherein the attacker can send a costly signal of data exfiltration that can inform the victim's beliefs and payment decision. Second, we identify four separating and four pooling equilibria of the game and their underlying conditions. The type of equilibria that exists in the game will depend on the parameters of the game, particularly the cost of signaling data exfiltration, the cost to recover files without decryption, the reputation loss from data leakage, and the probability the victim's files contain valuable data. We identify the factors determining how much surplus the attacker can extract from the victim. Third, we analyse the impact that private information of the victim has on the profitability of the attacked. Through examples, we show that the payoff loss to the criminal from now knowing the value of files can range from zero to over 20%. Private information can, therefore, potentially disrupt the business model of ransomware games by reducing the profits they can make.

We remark that our paper adds to a growing literature using game theory to analyse the ransomware decision process [4,5,12]. Prior game-theoretical studies have focused on the interaction of ransomware and victim's decision to invest in security measures like backups or insurance [2,24,28,29]. For instance, Laszka, Farhang and Grossklags [15] focused on modeling the ransomware ecosystem as a whole and how backup decisions affect the ransomware ecosystem. Vakilinia et al. [27] take a different approach in exploring how a double sided auction can facilitate the negotiation between attacker and victim to achieve a 'fair' ransom. Galinkin [12] analyses measures that an attacker can disrupt the business model of the attackers by lowering the profitability of ransomware attacks. The main intervention suggested is that of back-ups. We note, however, that in a setting with double extortion, back-ups are not enough to combat the ransomware threat. We must also consider the reputational costs from the publication of exfiltrated data.

We proceed as follows. In Sect. 2 we introduce the signalling game. In Sect. 3 we provide our main results. In Sect. 4 we conclude.

2 Signaling Game

We consider a game between a criminal, henceforth called the attacker, and a victim. We take as given that the victim has been subject to a ransomware attack and their data has been encrypted. The attacker is demanding a ransom for the decryption key. If the victim does not pay the ransom then it will cost V_P to recover normal operations. If the victim does pay the ransom then we assume the attackers will provide the decryption key and it will cost V_{NP} to recover normal operations. From a game theoretic point of view, the predictions of our model depend solely on the difference in recovery cost from paying versus not paying $V_P - V_{NP}$. Thus, to simplify the model, and without loss of generality, we set $V_{NP} = 0$ and $V_P = V$. We assume that $V > 0$ and so access to the decryption key reduces recovery costs.

We take it as given that, as well as encrypting files, the attacker attempted to exfiltrate data from the victim. This attempt may or may not have been 'successful'. In either case, the attacker can threaten to publish exfiltrated data unless the ransom is paid. We model two forms of incomplete information:

1. The attacker knows if data is exfiltrated but the victim does not know. Let α denote the probability that data was exfiltrated. The value of α is common knowledge to attacker and victim. We use the term NDE and DE to

distinguish the type of attacker as no data exfiltration and data exfiltration, respectively.

2. The victim knows the reputational damage that would result from data exfiltration but the attacker does not know. We assume that there are two types of victim: those with sensitive data, called high type, and those without, called low type. If exfiltrated data were to be leaked then the victim would incur reputation costs T_1 or $T_0 < T_1$ depending on whether they are high or low type, respectively. If the data is not leaked then we assume there is no reputation cost. The probability the victim is high type is β. The value of β is common knowledge to attacker and victim.

The game has three stages. Following the approach of Harnsanyi [9], Nature determines the the type of the victim (high or low type) and the type of the criminal (data exfiltrated or no data exfiltrated) in Stage 1 of the game. The victim learns their type (with probability β they are high type), and the attacker learns whether data was exfiltrated (with probability α it is exfiltrated).

In stage 2 the attacker chooses (a) whether or not to send a signal that data has been exfiltrated, and (b) a ransom demand. The signal can, for instance, consist of a picture of the file tree of the exfiltrated data, or a sample of exfiltrated data. The cost to the attacker of sending a signal when data is exfiltrated is k_D, whereas if data is not exfiltrated it is k_N. We assume that it is harder to send a credible signal if no data is exfiltrated, so $k_D < k_N$. The attacker can choose any ransom demand. To simplify notation we denote by R^S the ransom demand of the attacker if they send a signal and R^{NS} the demand if no signal is sent.[1]

In stage 3 the victim observes whether or not a signal was sent, and learns the ransom demand. The victim then chooses whether to pay the ransom or not. To simplify the analysis we assume an ultimatum bargaining game in which their is no opportunity for negotiation, and the choice to pay or not ends the game.

The variables of the game are summarized in Table 1. One additional variable we introduce is $L \geq 0$ which captures the legal fees and costs (including psychologically and moral) of paying a ransom. We also introduce variable μ to represent the beliefs of the victim on the likelihood that data has been exfiltrated. Finally, we use variable ϵ to represent the smallest unit of currency. This will allow us to characterise the optimal ransom in a more succinct way. We exclude from the analysis any fixed costs incurred by the attacker and victim that are not dependent on the strategic elements of the game. For instance we do not include the cost to the attacker of implementing the attack. We can

---

[1] The attacker could choose any ransom above 0 for any combination of both own type and signal. So, suppose, more generally, we denote by $R^S_{DE}, R^S_{NDE}, R^{NS}_{DE}$ and R^{NS}_{NDE} the ransom of a type DE or NDE if they signal or do not signal. There cannot be an equilibrium in which an attacker of type DE and NDE signal and $R^S_{NDE} \neq R^S_{DE}$; this would reveal the attacker if type NDE and, thus, make their signal ineffective. Similarly, there cannot be an equilibrium in which an attacker of type DE and NDE would not signal and $R^{NS}_{NDE} \neq R^{NS}_{DE}$; this would again reveal the attacker if type NDE and lower the ransom the victim would rationally pay.

Table 1. Variables used in the data exfiltration signaling game

	Variable	Description
Attacker	R^S	Ransom when signaling
	R^{NS}	Ransom when not signaling
	k_D	Cost of signal with data exfiltration
	k_N	Cost of signal without data exfiltration
	β	Probability of data being valuable
Victim	T_1	Reputation cost for valuable data
	T_0	Reputation cost for non-valuable data
	V	Recovery cost without decryption key
	L	Legal fees of paying ransom
	α	Probability of data exfiltration
	μ	Belief on probability of data exfiltration
	ϵ	The smallest unit of currency

exclude such costs, without loss of generality, because they will not influence the equilibrium outcomes of the game. We depict the game in Fig. 1.

3   Results

In the following we solve for Bayesian equilibria of the game that satisfy the D1 Criterion [11]. Informally, a Bayesian equilibrium has the property that both attacker and victim: (1) maximise their expected payoffs given the strategy of the other and their beliefs, (2) update their beliefs using Bayes rule. Thus, in equilibrium, players appropriately interpret information, and have no incentive to change their actions given their beliefs and the actions of the other player. The D1 Criterion is used to place 'common sense' restrictions on beliefs. Specifically, a Bayesian equilibrium may not tie down beliefs off the equilibrium path, because play could reach nodes that have zero probability and so Bayes rule is indeterminate. The D1 Criterion imposes extra conditions on beliefs by saying that any deviation from the equilibrium path is assumed to be done by the type with the most incentive to deviate [3].

The D1 Criterion is useful to rule out equilibria sustained by 'non-intuitive beliefs' [14]. For instance, consider a candidate equilibria in which the attacker chooses to not signal if they are type DE or NDE. On the equilibrium path the attacker should not signal. Thus, Bayes rule does not impose any restrictions on beliefs were the attacker to signal. Yet, informally, a type DE has the most incentive to deviate and signal. The D1 Criterion would, thus, require the victim to believe the deviation was by a type DE. This rules out 'non-intuitive' equilibria that are only sustained by the victim believing a signal would be from the type NDE.

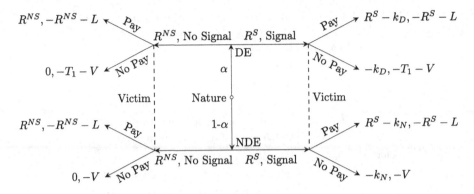

Case T_1 (Prob. β): Important files exfiltrated.

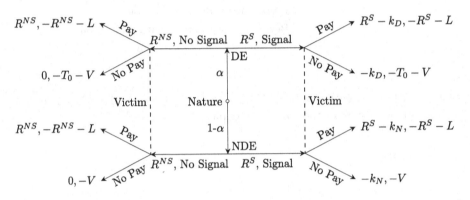

Case T_0 (Prob. 1-β): No important files exfiltrated.

Fig. 1. Description of the game.

To focus the analysis on what we believe are the most realistic cases, we distinguish and characterize two broad types of equilibrium: (a) separating equilibria in which the type DE signals data is exfiltrated and the type NDE does not, and a (b) pooling equilibria in which both the type DE and NDE signal that data is exfiltrated. We exclude from analysis pooling equilibria in which both the type DE and NDE do not signal that data is exfiltrated, as well as hybrid equilibria in which the attacker randomises their actions. In the following we discuss separating and pooling equilibria in turn before analysing the impact of private information. Throughout, we assume that if the victim is indifferent between paying and not paying then they will not pay.

3.1 Separating Equilibrium

A separating equilibrium has the basic characteristic that the attacker signals data exfiltration if they are of type DE (i.e. data was exfiltrated) and does not signal if they are of type NDE (i.e. data was not exfiltrated). The existence of a separating equilibrium and the exact form of any equilibrium will depend on the parameters of the game. Specifically, we identified four types of separating equilibria, which we will label A1-A4. These are summarised in Table 2. As you can see the equilibria differ by whether or not the victim pays the ransom. For example, in equilibrium A3 the victim pays the ransom if the attacker signals but does not pay the ransom if the attacker does not signal. In equilibrium A4 the victim only pays if they are a high type and the attacker signals.

Table 2. Equilibria satisfying the D1 criterion in the signaling game.

Equilibrium	Attacker		Victim			
	DE	NDE	T_1		T_0	
			Signal	No signal	Signal	No signal
A1	Signal	No signal	Pay	Pay	Pay	Pay
A2	Signal	No signal	Pay	Pay	No pay	Pay
A3	Signal	No signal	Pay	No Pay	Pay	No Pay
A4	Signal	No Signal	Pay	No Pay	No pay	No pay
B1	Signal	Signal	Pay	Pay	Pay	Pay
B2	Signal	Signal	Pay	Pay	No pay	Pay
B3	Signal	Signal	Pay	No pay	Pay	No pay
B4	Signal	Signal	Pay	No pay	No pay	No pay

In all four equilibria A1-A4 the high type victim pays if they receive a signal of data exfiltration. The equilibria differ in whether a low type victim pays if they receive a signal of data exfiltration and/or whether the victim pays if they receive no signal. To provide some intuition for the four equilibria we introduce three ransom demands that prove particularly relevant: (1) $R_{S0}^* = T_0 + V - L - \epsilon$, (2) $R_{S1}^* = T_1 + V - L - \epsilon$, and (3) $R_{NS}^* = \max\{V - L - \epsilon, 0\}$. Informally, see the proof of Theorem 1 for the full details, R_{S0}^* and R_{S1}^* are the maximum ransom the low type and high type, respectively, are willing to pay if they believe data has been exfiltrated. While, R_{NS}^* is the maximum ransom the attacker can ask if the victim believes data is not exfiltrated. We readily see that if $V < L$ the victim would not pay any positive ransom demand if they know data has not been exfiltrated.

If data exfiltration is believed to have taken place then the high type is willing to pay a larger ransom than the low type, $R_{S1}^* > R_{S0}^*$. This provides a strategic trade-off for the attacker: (a) if they ask for a high ransom, R_{S1}^*, then they extract maximum surplus from the high type victim, but the low type will not pay the ransom. (b) If they ask for a low ransom, R_{S0}^*, then both the low and high type victim will pay the ransom but they do not fully extract surplus from the high type. This trade-off is captured by the following term:

$$\Phi_S = \beta(R_{S1}^* - R_{S0}^*) - (1 - \beta)R_{S0}^* = \beta(T_1 - T_0) - (1 - \beta)(T_0 + V - L - \epsilon). \quad (1)$$

The first term in Φ_S is the expected gain for the attacker from extracting maximum surplus from the high type, while the second term is the expected loss from charging a ransom the low type is not willing to pay.

We are now in a position to state our first main result. As the preceding discussion preempts we need to consider combinations of $V \gtrless L$ and $\Phi \gtrless 0$ giving rise to the four different cases and equilibria.

Theorem 1. *There exists a separating equilibrium satisfying the D1 criterion if and only if the following conditions hold:*

(A1) If $L < V$ and $\Phi_S < 0$ then $k_D < T_0 < k_N$.
(A2) If $L < V$ and $\Phi_S > 0$ then $k_D < \beta T_1 - (1 - \beta)(V - L) < k_N$.
(A3) If $L > V$ and $\Phi_S < 0$ then $k_D < T_0 + V - L < k_N$.
(A4) If $L > V$ and $\Phi_S > 0$ then $k_D < \beta(T_1 + V - L) < k_N$.

Proof. We first consider the strategy of the victim. Suppose the attacker sends a signal and ransom demand R_S. Suppose the victim infers the attacker is type DE. In other words, $\mu = 1$. If the victim is low type and pays the ransom their expected payoff is $-R_S - L$. Their expected payoff if they do not pay is $-T_0 - V$. It follows the low type victim will optimally pay the ransom if and only if $-R_S - L > -T_0 - V$ or equivalently $R_S < T_0 + V - L$. They would, therefore, pay ransom R_{S0}^*. If the victim is high type and pays the ransom their expected payoff is $-R_S - L$. Their expected payoff if they do not pay is $-T_1 - V$. It follows the high type victim will optimally pay the ransom if and only if $R_S < T_1 + V - L$. They would, therefore, pay ransom R_{S1}^*. Given that $T_1 > T_0$ we also have that the high type would pay ransom R_{S0}^*.

Now suppose the attacker does not send a signal and sets ransom demand R_{NS}. Suppose the victim infers the attacker is type NDE. In other words, $\mu = 0$. If the victim is low type and pays the ransom their expected payoff is $-R_{NS} - L$. Their expected payoff if they do not pay is $-V$. It follows the low type victim will optimally pay the ransom if and only if $-R_S - L > -V$ or equivalently $R_S < V - L$. They would, therefore, pay ransom R_{NS}^* if $V > L$ and not pay if $V < L$. The same logic holds if the victim is high type.

We now consider the incentives of the attacker. Suppose the attacker is type DE. Also suppose that on the equilibrium path they signal and set ransom R_{S0}^*. Their expected payoff in equilibrium is $\pi(S, R_{S0}^*) = T_0 + V - L - \epsilon - k_D$. In exploring incentives to deviate from the equilibrium path, we first consider the possibility the attacker signals but sets a different ransom demand $R_S \neq R_S^*$. If $R_S < R_{S0}^*$ then the expected payoff of the attacker is $\pi(S, R_S) = R_S - k_D < \pi(S, R_{S0}^*)$ and so the attacker receives a lower payoff than on the equilibrium path. If $R_{S1}^* > R_S > R_{S0}^*$ (and $\mu = 1$) then the high type victim would pay the ransom but the low type victim would not. The expected payoff of the attacker is, therefore, $\pi(S, R_S) = \beta R_S - k_D \leq \beta R_{S1}^* - k_D$. It follows the attacker prefers the equilibrium path if and only if $\beta(T_1 + V - L - \epsilon) \leq T_0 + V - L - \epsilon$. Rearranging gives the condition on $\Phi_S < 0$. Reversing this argument we can say it is on the equilibrium path for the attacker of type DE to signal and set ransom R_{S1}^* if and only if $\Phi_S > 0$.

We next consider the possibility that an attacker of type DE chooses to not signal. Suppose they set ransom demand R_{NS} (and are inferred to be type NDE). Their expected payoff is at most $\pi(NS, R_{NS}) = R_{NS}^*$. We then have four different cases to consider. (a) Suppose $V > L$ and $R_S^* = R_{S0}^*$. It follows the attacker prefers the equilibrium path if and only if $V - L - \epsilon < T_0 + V - L - \epsilon - k_D$ or, equivalently, $k_D < T_0$. (b) Suppose $V > L$ and $R_S^* = R_{S1}^*$. It follows the attacker prefers the equilibrium path if and only if $V - L - \epsilon < \beta(T_1 + V - L - \epsilon) - k_D$ or, equivalently, $k_D + (1 - \beta)(V - L - \epsilon) < \beta T_1$. (c) Suppose $V < L$ and $R_S^* = R_{S0}^*$. It follows the attacker prefers the equilibrium path if and only if $0 < T_0 + V - L - \epsilon - k_D$ or, equivalently, $k_D < T_0 + V - L$. (d) Suppose $V < L$ and $R_S^* = R_{S1}^*$. It follows the attacker prefers the equilibrium path if and only if $0 < \beta(T_1 + V - L - \epsilon) - k_D$ or, equivalently, $k_D < \beta(T_1 + V - L - \epsilon)$.

Next suppose the attacker is type NDE. Extending the logic of the preceding discussion there is no incentive for the attacker to choose a ransom other than R_{NS}^*. We focus, therefore, on the incentive to signal and choose ransom demand R_S^*. We again have four different cases to consider. (a) Suppose $V > L$ and $R_S^* = R_{S0}^*$. On the equilibrium path the attacker has expected payoff $\pi(NS, R_{NS}^*) = V - L - \epsilon$. It follows the attacker prefers the equilibrium path if and only if $V - L - \epsilon > T_0 + V - L - \epsilon - k_N$ or, equivalently, $k_N > T_0$. (b) Suppose $V > L$ and $R_S^* = R_{S1}^*$. It follows the attacker prefers the equilibrium path if and only if $V - L - \epsilon > \beta(T_1 + V - L - \epsilon) - k_N$ or, equivalently, $k_N + (1 - \beta)(V - L - \epsilon) > \beta T_1$. (c) Suppose $V < L$ and $R_S^* = R_{S0}^*$. It follows the attacker prefers the equilibrium path if and only if $0 > T_0 + V - L - \epsilon - k_N$ or, equivalently, $k_N > T_0 + V - L$. (d) Suppose $V < L$ and $R_S^* = R_{S1}^*$. It follows the attacker prefers the equilibrium path if and only if $0 > \beta(T_1 + V - L - \epsilon) - k_N$ or, equivalently, $k_N > \beta(T_1 + V - L - \epsilon)$.

It remains to check the D1 criterion is satisfied. The only game path we need to consider in any detail is that where the attacker does not signal and sets ransom $R_{NS} \neq R_{NS}^*$. We have assumed the victim will infer the attacker is type NDE. Given that $K_N > k_D$, the attacker has most incentive to not signal when of type NDE. This assumption, therefore, naturally satisfies the D1 criterion. □

In interpretation of Theorem 1 we can see that there exists a separating equilibrium if and only if k_D is sufficiently small and k_D is sufficiently large. In other words, a separating equilibrium exists if it is 'cheap' for the attacker to signal when they have exfiltrated data and 'expensive' for the attacker to signal if they have not exfiltrated data. This would imply, for instance, that if victims have invested in good monitoring systems to identify data exfiltration, they could make it harder for the attacker of type NDE to send a credible signal; then, k_N would increase and we would expect the improved monitoring to result in a separating equilibrium.

3.2 Pooling Equilibrium

We turn our attention now to pooling equilibria. We focus on pooling equilibrium in which the attacker signals. That is, the attacker signals that data is exfiltrated whether they are type NDE or DE. Consequently a signal does not convey any useful information to the victim on whether or not data has been exfiltrated. We identify four types of pooling equilibria, which we will label B1-B4. These are summarised in Table 2. Two ransom demands that prove particularly relevant in this case are: (4) $R^*_{P0} = \alpha T_0 + V - L - \epsilon$, and (5) $R^*_{P1} = \alpha T_1 + V - L - \epsilon$. Informally, R^*_{P0} and R^*_{P1} are the maximum ransom the low and high type, respectively, are willing to pay if they believe the attacker has exfiltrated data with probability α.

As with the separating equilibrium, the optimal ransom demand of the attacker involves a trade-off between setting a high ransom R^*_{P1} that only the high type will pay and a low ransom R^*_{P0} that both the high and low type will pay. This trade-off is captured by the term:

$$\Phi_P = \beta\alpha(T_1 - T_0) - (1 - \beta)(\alpha T_0 + V - L - \epsilon). \tag{2}$$

We can now state our second result.

Theorem 2. *There exists a pooling equilibrium in which the attacker signals, satisfying the D1 criterion, if and only if the following conditions hold:*

(B1) If $L < V$ and $\Phi_P < 0$ then $k_N < \alpha T_0$.
(B2) If $L < V$ and $\Phi_P > 0$ then $k_N < \beta\alpha T_1 - (1 - \beta)(V - L)$.
(B3) If $L > V$ and $\Phi_P < 0$ then $k_N < \alpha T_0 + V - L$.
(B4) If $L > V$ and $\Phi_P > 0$ then $k_N < \beta(\alpha T_1 + V - L)$.

Proof. Consider the strategy of the victim. Suppose the attacker sends a signal and ransom demand R_S. Suppose the victim infers the attacker is type DE with probability $\mu = \alpha$. If the victim is low type and pays the ransom their expected payoff is $-R_S - L$. Their expected payoff if they do not pay is $-\alpha T_0 - V$. It follows the low type victim will optimally pay the ransom if and only if $-R_S - L > -\alpha T_0 - V$ or equivalently $R_S < \alpha T_0 + V - L$. They would, therefore, pay ransom R^*_{P0}. If the victim is high type and pays the ransom their expected payoff is $-R_S - L$. Their expected payoff if they do not pay is $-\alpha T_1 - V$. It follows the high type victim will optimally pay the ransom if and only if $R_S < \alpha T_1 + V - L$. They would, therefore, pay ransom R^*_{P1}. Given that $T_1 > T_0$ we also have that the high type would pay ransom R^*_{P0}.

Now suppose the attacker does not send a signal and sets ransom demand R_{NS}. Suppose the victim infers the attacker is type NDE. In other words, $\mu = 0$. If the victim is low type and pays the ransom their expected payoff is $-R_{NS} - L$. Their expected payoff if they do not pay is $-V$. It follows the low type victim will optimally pay the ransom if and only if $-R_S - L > -V$ or equivalently $R_S < V - L$. They would, therefore, pay ransom R^*_{NS} if $V > L$ and not pay if $V < L$. The same logic holds if the victim is high type.

Next consider the incentives of the attacker. Suppose the attacker is type DE. Also suppose that on the equilibrium path they signal and set ransom R^*_{P0}. Their expected payoff in equilibrium is $\pi(S, R^*_{P0}) = \alpha T_0 + V - L - \epsilon - k_D$. Suppose the attacker signals but sets a different ransom demand $R_S \neq R^*_S$. If

$R_S < R_{S0}^*$ then the expected payoff of the attacker is $\pi(S, R_S) = R_S - k_D < \pi(S, R_{P0}^*)$ and so the attacker receives a lower payoff than on the equilibrium path. If $R_{P1}^* > R_S > R_{P0}^*$ (and $\mu = \beta$) then the high type victim would pay the ransom but the low type victim would not. The expected payoff of the attacker is, therefore, $\pi(S, R_S) = \beta R_S - k_D \leq \beta R_{P1}^* - k_D$. It follows the attacker prefers the equilibrium path if and only if $\beta(\alpha T_1 + V - L - \epsilon) \leq \alpha T_0 + V - L - \epsilon$. Rearranging gives $\Phi_P < 0$. Reversing this argument we can say it is on the equilibrium path for the attacker of type DE to signal and set ransom R_{P1}^* if and only if $\Phi_P > 0$.

Now consider the possibility that an attacker of type NDE chooses to not signal. Suppose they set ransom demand R_{NS} (and are inferred to be type NDE). Their expected payoff is at most $\pi(NS, R_{NS}) = R_{NS}^*$. We then have four different cases to consider. (a) Suppose $V > L$ and $R_S^* = R_{P0}^*$. It follows the attacker prefers the equilibrium path if and only if $V - L - \epsilon < \alpha T_0 + V - L - \epsilon - k_N$ or, equivalently, $k_N < \alpha T_0$. (b) Suppose $V > L$ and $R_S^* = R_{P1}^*$. It follows the attacker prefers the equilibrium path if and only if $V - L - \epsilon < \beta(\alpha T_1 + V - L - \epsilon) - k_N$ or, equivalently, $k_N + (1 - \beta)(V - L - \epsilon) < \beta \alpha T_1$. (c) Suppose $V < L$ and $R_S^* = R_{P0}^*$. It follows the attacker prefers the equilibrium path if and only if $0 < \alpha T_0 + V - L - \epsilon - k_N$ or, equivalently, $k_N < \alpha T_0 + V - L$. (d) Suppose $V < L$ and $R_S^* = R_{P1}^*$. It follows the attacker prefers the equilibrium path if and only if $0 < \beta(\alpha T_1 + V - L - \epsilon) - k_N$ or, equivalently, $k_N < \beta(\alpha T_1 + V - L - \epsilon)$. One can show, using $k_D < k_N$, that the analogous conditions for a type DE to prefer signalling to not signalling are less binding.

It remains to check the D1 criterion is satisfied. The only game path we need to consider in any detail is that where the attacker does not signal and sets ransom $R_{NS} \neq R_{NS}^*$. We have assumed the victim will infer the attacker is type NDE. Given that $K_N > k_D$, the attacker has most incentive to not signal when of type NDE. This assumption, therefore, naturally satisfies the D1 criterion. $\square$

In interpretation of Theorem 2 there exists a pooling equilibrium if and only if k_N is sufficiently small. In other words, there exists a pooling equilibrium if and only if it is cheap for the attacker to signal even if data has not been exfiltrated. In practical terms this would suggest the victim does not have any monitoring technology to identify or evaluate a data breach. It would also suggest the criminals could easily extract some information, e.g. file tree or sample file, that would allow them to signal data exfiltration even though data was not exfiltrated.

Depending on the parameters of the game there may exist a separating equilibrium, a pooling equilibrium, or neither. To illustrate, consider the parameters $L = 0, V = 5, \alpha = 0.9, \beta = 0.5, T_0 = 1$ and $T_1 = 5$. Then $\Phi_S < 0$ and so there exists a separating equilibrium if and only if $k_D < 1 < k_N$. Also $\Phi_P < 0$ and so there exists a pooling equilibrium if $k_N < 0.9$. Thus, for $k_N < 0.9$ there is a pooling equilibrium, for $0.9 < k_N < 1$ there is neither a separating nor pooling equilibrium, and for $1 < k_N$ there is a separating equilibrium. The relative size of the cost for the attacker to signal data exifiltration when they have not exfiltrated data is, thus, crucial to determining the equilibrium outcome.

3.3   The Value of Private Information

A key objective of our work is to analyse the payoff consequences, for both victim and attacker, of private information on the side of the victim. In Table 3 we detail the expected payoff of the attacker and victim in equilibria A1-A4 and B1-B4. These are ex-ante expected payoffs before own type is known. For instance, in equilibrium A1 there is probability α the attacker is type DE and obtains payoff $R_{S0}^* - k_D$ and probability $1 - \alpha$ the attacker is type NDE and obtains payoff R_{NS}^*. The expected payoff is, therefore, $\alpha(R_{S0}^* - k_D) + (1-\alpha)R_{NS}^*$ Given that ϵ can be arbitrarily small we have omitted it from calculations of expected payoff.

Table 3. Expected payoff of attacker and victim in equilibrium.

Equilibrium	attacker	Victim
A1	$\alpha T_0 + V - L - \alpha k_D$	$-\alpha T_0 - V$
A2	$\alpha(\beta(T_1 + V - L) - k_D) + (1 - \alpha)(V - L)$	$-\alpha(\beta T_1 + (1 - \beta)T_0) - V$
A3	$\alpha(T_0 + V - L - k_D)$	$-\alpha T_0 - V$
A4	$\alpha(\beta(T_1 + V - L) - k_D)$	$-\alpha(\beta T_1 + (1 - \beta)T_0) - V$
B1 & B3	$\alpha T_0 + V - L - \alpha k_D - (1 - \alpha)k_N$	$-\alpha T_0 - V$
B2 & B4	$\beta(\alpha T_1 + V - L) - \alpha k_D - (1 - \alpha)k_N$	$-\beta \alpha T_1 - (1 - \beta)\alpha T_0 - V$

To analyse the consequences of private information we need to consider an alternative game in which the attacker knows the type of the victim and so knows if the reputational damage that would result from data publication is T_0 or T_1. We can apply Theorems 1 and 2 to distinguish the conditions under which there exist separating and pooling equilibirum in this revised game. Specifically, by setting $\beta = 0$ or 1 we derive the following corollaries.

Corollary 1. *If the victim is known to be type $i = \{0, 1\}$ there exists a separating equilibrium satisfying the D1 criterion if and only if the following conditions hold:*

A1A2. If $L < V$, then $k_D < T_i < k_N$.
A3A4. If $L > V$, then $k_D < T_i + V - L < k_N$.

Proof. Suppose $\beta = 0$. Then $\Phi_S < 0$. Applying Theorem 1 we obtain conditions: (A1) $L < V$ and $k_D < T_0 < k_N$, and (A3) $L > V$ and $k_D < T_0 + V - L < k_N$. Suppose $\beta = 1$. Then $\Phi_S > 0$. Applying Theorem 1 we obtain conditions: (A2) $L < V$ and $k_D < T_1 < k_N$, and (A4) $L > V$ and $k_D < T_1 + V - L < k_N$. □

Corollary 2. *If the victim is known to be type $i = \{0, 1\}$ there exists a pooling equilibrium with a signal satisfying the D1 criterion if and only if the following conditions hold:*

B1B2. If $L < V$ then $k_N < \alpha T_i$.
B3B4. If $L > V$ then $k_N < \alpha T_i + V - L$.

Proof. Suppose $\beta = 0$. Then $\Phi_P < 0$. Applying Theorem 2 we obtain conditions: (B1) $L < V$ and $k_N < \alpha T_0$, and (B3) $L > V$ and $k_N < \alpha T_0 + V - L$. Suppose $\beta = 1$. Then $\Phi_P > 0$. Applying Theorem 2 we obtain conditions: (B2) $L < V$ and $k_N < \alpha T_1$, and (B4) $L > V$ and $k_N < \alpha T_1 + V - L$. $\square$

With these two corollaries we can derive the expected payoff of the attacker and victim in a game where the victim's type is known. The lower half of Table 4 details the payoffs from equilibria of the game in which the victims type is known. For instance, the expected payoff of the attacker under equilibrium A3A4 if the victim is type 0 is $\alpha(T_0+V-L-k_D)$ and the expected payoff of the attacker under equilibrium A3A4 if the victim is type 1 is $\alpha(T_1+V-L-k_D)$. Some care is needed in deriving ex-ante expected payoffs because the existence of equilibrium A3A4 for the low type does not guarantee existence of equilibrium A3A4 for the high type, and vice-versa. Even so, by calculating which equilibrium emerges for each type we can determine an ex-ante expected payoff. For instance, if equilibrium A3A4 does exist for both the low type and high type then the attackers ex-ante expected payoff (before victim type is known) is $\alpha(\beta T_1+(1-\beta)T_0+V-L-k_D)$.

Table 4. Expected payoff of attacker and victim in equilibrium when type is known.

Equilibrium	attacker	Victim
A1A2 ($i = \{0,1\}$)	$\alpha T_i + V - L - \alpha k_D$	$-\alpha T_i - V$
A3A4 ($i = \{0,1\}$)	$\alpha(T_i + V - L - k_D)$	$-\alpha T_i - V$
B1-B4 ($i = \{0,1\}$)	$\alpha T_i + V - L - \alpha k_D - (1-\alpha)k_N$	$-\alpha T_i - V$

We are now in a position to quantify the payoff consequences of private information for the victim. For any set of parameters $L, V, T_0, T_1, k_D, k_N, \alpha$ and β we can determine which, if any equilibrium will hold in a game with incomplete information on victim's type, and the games where victim's type is known to be high or low. We can then calculate expected payoffs of the attacker and victim with and without incomplete information on victim's type. We provide two examples.

In Fig. 2 we plot expected payoffs as a function of β when $L = 1, V = 3, \alpha = 0.5, T_0 = 2, T_1 = 4, k_D = 0.1$ and $k_N = 6$. This is a case with a separating equilibrium. You can see that the payoff of the attacker is substantially lower when the type of the victim is not known. The loss reaches a maximum at the point of transition between equilibria A1 and A2 given by $T_0 = \beta T_1 - (1-\beta)(V - L)$ or equivalently

$$\beta = \frac{T_0 + V - L}{T_1 + V - L}. \tag{3}$$

For the parameters in our example this gives $\beta = 2/3$. If the type of the victim is unknown the expected payoff of the attacker is 2.95. If the type of the victim is known the ex-ante expected payoff of the attacker is 3.62. So, the attacker's payoff is 18.43% lower if it does not know the type of the victim.

We can see the victim's payoff is higher if the attacker does not know their type and $\beta < 2/3$. The intuition being that the attacker sets the ransom as if the victim is low type (equilibrium A1) and, thus, the high type is not exploited as much as they would have been if type was known. If $\beta > 2/3$ we see that the payoff of the victim is the same whether or not the attacker knows their type. In this case the attacker sets the ransom as if the victim is high type (equilibrium A2). This means the high type is maximally exploited by the attacker, while the low type does not pay the ransom and, therefore, suffers recovery and reputational losses. The net effect for the victim is the same as if the attacker knew their type and they were maximally exploited. We remind that the attacker's payoff is lower if the victim's type is not known. This is because they also lose when the ransom is set at a level the low type will not pay.

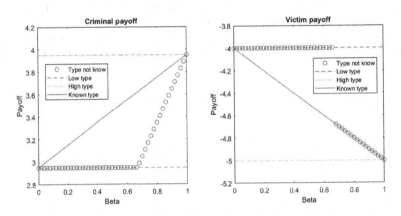

Fig. 2. Expected payoff of the attacker and victim when $L = 1, V = 3, \alpha = 0.5, T_0 = 2, T_1 = 4, k_N = 6, k_D = 0.1$. An example of a separating equilibrium.

In Fig. 3 we plot the corresponding payoffs when, everything else the same, $k_N = 0.9$. This is a case with a pooling equilibrium. Again, we see that the attacker loses payoff from not knowing the type of the victim. This loss is maximal at the transition from equilibrium B1 to B2, given by $\alpha T_0 = \beta \alpha T_1 - (1 - \beta)(V - L)$ or equivalently

$$\beta = \frac{\alpha T_0 + V - L}{\alpha T_1 + V - L}. \tag{4}$$

For the parameters in our example this gives $\beta = 3/4$. If the type of the victim is unknown the expected payoff of the attacker is 2.5. If the type of the victim is known the ex-ante expected payoff of the attacker is 3.25. So, the attacker's payoff is 23.08% lower because it does not know the type of the victim.

The relative trade-offs for the victim are similar in the pooling example as the separating example. In particular, if the attacker sets the ransom for a victim of low type (equilibrium B1) then the victim gains from their type being private

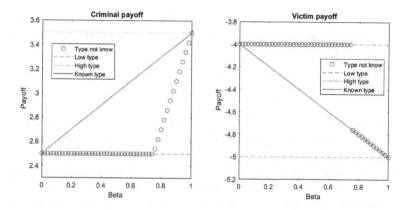

Fig. 3. Expected payoff of the attacker and victim when $L = 1, V = 3, \alpha = 0.5, T_0 = 2, T_1 = 4, k_N = 0.9, k_D = 0.1$. An example of a separating equilibrium.

if they are high type. If, however, the attacker sets the ransom for a victim of high type (equilibrium B2) then the victim does not gain from their type being unknown. In summary, the attacker loses payoff from not knowing the victim's type. The victim gains from their type being unknown in the case of equilibrium A1, B1 and also A3 and B3. The victim does not gain from the type being unknown in the case of equilibrium A2, A4, B2 and B4.

It is interesting to compare payoffs when $k_N = 0.9$ with those when $k_N = 6$ (for, say, $\beta = 2/3$). You can see that the attackers expected payoff is higher when $k_N = 6$. This may seem counter-intuitive given that a high k_N means a higher cost from signalling. Note, however, that a high k_N results in a separating equilibrium that allows the type DE attacker to extract a high ransom because their signal of data exfiltration is credible. Specifically, when $k_N = 6$ the type DE sets ransom $R^*_{S0} = T_0 + V - L = 4$, while a type NDE sets ransom $R^*_{NS} = V - L = 2$. The expected payoff of the attacker is, therefore, $\alpha(R^*_{S0} - k_D) + (1 - \alpha)R^*_{NS} = 3.9\alpha + 2(1 - \alpha) = 2.95$.

By contrast, when $k_N = 0.9$ we obtain a pooling equilibrium in which the attacker's signal of data exfiltration is not sufficiently credible. This lowers the ransom the attacker can demand to $R^*_{P0} = \alpha T_0 + V - L = 3$. Consequently the type DE gets a lower payoff with the lower k_N (2.9 compared to 3.9). The type NDE, by contrast, has a higher payoff (2.1 compared to 2) because they are also able to demand ransom R^*_{P0}, although they incur cost k_N. The expected payoff of the attacker is $R^*_{P0} - 0.1\alpha - 0.9(1 - \alpha) = 2.5$. Overall, therefore, the attacker has a lower expected payoff when $k_N = 0.9$ compared to $k_N = 6$ (2.5 compared to 2.95). This trade-off is apparent from the payoffs in Table 3, comparing A1 and B1.

You can also see in Table 3 that the payoff of the victim is not impacted by k_N. This is because the criminal is able to extract the same surplus from the victim in equilibria A1, A3, B1 and B3. Generally, speaking, as would be expected, the loss to the victim is reduced by lowering T_0, T_1, V and β. The victim's payoff is also reduced by lowering α. Thus, reduced the losses from data exfiltration as well as reducing the probability of data exfiltration reduce the losses to the victim.

4 Conclusion

This paper provides a game-theoretic analysis of the double-sided information asymmetry in double extortion ransomware attacks. We recognised that victims are typically unable to verify if data was exfiltrated or not, while attackers typically do not know the value of any data exfiltrated. We modeled the ransomware attack as a signaling game, where attackers could signal if data is exfiltrated and victims pay based on the ransom, signal and the value of information. Our key contribution is that, depending on the parameters of the game, private information of the victim (about the value of exfiltrated data) significantly lowers the profitability of the attack for the criminal. It is, therefore, in the interests of potential victims, businesses, organisations, and/or individuals, to retain and amplify the extent of their private information.

According to our model, the most effective way to disrupt the attackers profitability is to: lower the probability of 'successful' data exfiltration, lower the probability the victim has files of high reputational cost, and lower the recovery cost from an attack. This would involve a mix of prevention (to lower the probability of data exfiltration and loss of sensitive data) as well as improved recovery options, such as back-ups. Crucially there is an externality effect: the more victims safeguard their sensitive data the more that benefits other businesses, including those with vulnerable sensitive data. This is because it would revise downwards the beliefs of attackers about the ransoms they can reasonably expect victims to pay. This externality effect should be acknowledged by policy makers. In particular, it means businesses will under-invest in cyber security prevention and recovery compared to the social optimum. This can justify government support for cyber security investment.

References

1. Akerlof, G.A.: The market for "lemons": quality uncertainty and the market mechanism. Q. J. Econ. **84**(3), 488–500 (1970)
2. Baksi, R.P., Upadhyaya, S.J.: Game theoretic analysis of ransomware: a preliminary study. In: ICISSP, pp. 242–251 (2022)
3. Banks, J.S., Sobel, J.: Equilibrium selection in signaling games. Econometrica: J. Econometric Soc. 647–661 (1987)
4. Cartwright, A., et al.: How cyber insurance influences the ransomware payment decision: theory and evidence. Geneva Papers Risk Insur. Issues Pract. **48**(2), 300–331 (2023)
5. Cartwright, E., Hernandez Castro, J., Cartwright, A.: To pay or not: game theoretic models of ransomware. J. Cybersecur. **5**(1), tyz009 (2019)
6. Cong, L.W., Harvey, C.R., Rabetti, D., Wu, Z.Y.: An anatomy of crypto-enabled cybercrimes. National Bureau of Economic Research (2023)

7. Connolly, L.Y., Wall, D.S.: The rise of crypto-ransomware in a changing cybercrime landscape: taxonomising countermeasures. Comput. Secur. **87**, 101568 (2019)
8. Connolly, Y.L., Wall, D.S., Lang, M., Oddson, B.: An empirical study of ransomware attacks on organizations: an assessment of severity and salient factors affecting vulnerability. J. Cybersecur. **6**(1), tyaa023 (2020)
9. Harsanyi, J.C.: Games with incomplete information played by "Bayesian" players, I-III part I. The basic model. Manag. Sci. **14**(3), 159–182 (1967)
10. Humayun, M., Jhanjhi, N.Z., Alsayat, A., Ponnusamy, V.: Internet of things and ransomware: evolution, mitigation and prevention. Egypt. Inform. J. **22**(1), 105–117 (2021)
11. Fudenberg, D., Tirole, J.: Game Theory. MIT press, Cambridge (1991)
12. Galinkin, E.: Winning the ransomware lottery. In: Bošanský, B., Gonzalez, C., Rass, S., Sinha, A. (eds.) GameSec 2021. LNCS, vol. 13061, pp. 195–207. Springer, Cham (2021). https://doi.org/10.1007/978-3-030-90370-1_11
13. Kerns, Q., Payne, B., Abegaz, T.: Double-extortion ransomware: a technical analysis of maze ransomware. In: Arai, K. (ed.) FTC 2021. LNNS, vol. 360, pp. 82–94. Springer, Cham (2022). https://doi.org/10.1007/978-3-030-89912-7_7
14. Kreps, D.M., Sobel, J.: Signalling. Handb. Game Theory Econ. Appl. **2**, 849–867 (1994)
15. Laszka, A., Farhang, S., Grossklags, J.: On the economics of ransomware. In: Rass, S., An, B., Kiekintveld, C., Fang, F., Schauer, S. (eds.) GameSec 2017. LNCS, vol. 10575, pp. 397–417. Springer, Cham (2017). https://doi.org/10.1007/978-3-319-68711-7_21
16. Li, Z., Liao, Q.: Preventive portfolio against data-selling ransomware-A game theory of encryption and deception. Comput. Secur. **116**, 102644 (2022)
17. Li, Z., Liao, Q.: Game theory of data-selling ransomware. J. Cyber Secur. Mobil. 65–96 (2021)
18. Maschler, M., Zamir, S., Solan, E.: Game Theory. Cambridge University Press, Cambridge (2020)
19. Meurs, T., Junger, M., Tews, E., Abhishta, A.: Ransomware: How attacker's effort, victim characteristics and context influence ransom requested, payment and financial loss. In: Symposium on Electronic Crime Research, eCrime (2022)
20. Mott, G., et al.: Between a rock and a hard (ening) place: cyber insurance in the ransomware era. Comput. Secur. **128**, 103162 (2023)
21. Oosthoek, K., Cable, J., Smaragdakis, G.: A Tale of Two Markets: investigating the ransomware payments economy. arXiv preprint arXiv:2205.05028 (2022)
22. Osborne, M.J.: An Introduction to Game Theory, 3rd edn. Oxford University Press, New York (2004)
23. Oz, H., Aris, A., Levi, A., Uluagac, A.S.: A survey on ransomware: evolution, taxonomy, and defense solutions. ACM Comput. Surv. (CSUR) **54**(11s), 1–37 (2022)
24. Ryan, P., Fokker, J., Healy, S., Amann, A.: Dynamics of targeted ransomware negotiation. IEEE Access **10**, 32836–32844 (2022)
25. Sabir, B., Ullah, F., Babar, M.A., Gaire, R.: Machine learning for detecting data exfiltration: a review. ACM Comput. Surv. (CSUR) **54**(3), 1–47 (2021)
26. Ullah, F., Edwards, M., Ramdhany, R., Chitchyan, R., Babar, M.A., Rashid, A.: Data exfiltration: a review of external attack vectors and countermeasures. J. Netw. Comput. Appl. **101**, 18–54 (2018)
27. Vakilinia, I., Khalili, M.M., Li, M.: A mechanism design approach to solve ransomware dilemmas. In: Bošanský, B., Gonzalez, C., Rass, S., Sinha, A. (eds.) GameSec 2021. LNCS, vol. 13061, pp. 181–194. Springer, Cham (2021). https://doi.org/10.1007/978-3-030-90370-1_10

328 T. Meurs et al.

28. Yin, T., Sarabi, A., Liu, M.: Deterrence, backup, or insurance: game-theoretic modeling of ransomware. Games **14**(2), 20 (2023)
29. Zhao, Y., Ge, Y., Zhu, Q.: Combating ransomware in internet of things: a games-in-games approach for cross-layer cyber defense and security investment. In: Bošanský, B., Gonzalez, C., Rass, S., Sinha, A. (eds.) GameSec 2021. LNCS, vol. 13061, pp. 208–228. Springer, Cham (2021). https://doi.org/10.1007/978-3-030-90370-1_12

Opacity-Enforcing Active Perception and Control Against Eavesdropping Attacks

Sumukha Udupa[✉][iD], Hazhar Rahmani[iD], and Jie Fu[iD]

University of Florida, Gainesville, FL 32611, USA
{sudupa,h.rahmani,fujie}@ufl.edu

Abstract. In this paper, we consider *opacity-enforcing* planning with temporally-extended goals in partially observable stochastic environment. We consider a probabilistic environment modeled as partially observable Markov decision process (POMDP) in which the observation function is actively controlled as the agent decides which sensors to query at each decision step. The agent's objective is to achieve a temporal objective, expressed using linear temporal logic for finite traces (LTL_f), while making achieving its goal *opaque* to a passive observer who can access the sensor readings of a subset of sensors that are unsecured. Opacity, as a security property, means that when from the observer's perspective, the execution that satisfied the temporal goal is observational-equivalent to an execution that does not satisfy the temporal goal. When both secured and unsecured sensors are available upon query, the agent must be selective in its sensor query to prevent information leaking to the observer and to ensure task completion. We propose an algorithm that synthesizes a strategy that decides jointly the control actions and sensor queries to guarantee that the temporal goal is achieved and made opaque with probability 1. Our approach is based on planning with augmented belief state space. Further, we show how to employ properties in the temporal logic formula to reduce the size of the planning state space and improve scalability. We show the applicability of our algorithm on a case study with robotic planning in a stochastic gridworld with partial observations.

Keywords: Game theory · Opacity · Markov decision processes · Eavesdropping Attacks

1 Introduction

Opacity is a security property, specified for a system interacting with a passive observer (also called an attacker). By enforcing opacity, the goal is to make the attacker, who knows the system model and observes the system execution, confused about if a secret state has been reached or a secret behavior has been realized. The notion of opacity was first introduced by Mazaré [13] for cryptographic

This work was supported in part by ARL W911NF-22-2-0233, ARO W911NF-22-1-0034, and NSF #2144113.

protocols. Since then, variants of opacity have been studied for different classes of systems including Petri nets [4], labeled transitions systems [3], finite state automata [15], probabilistic finite automata [18], hidden Markov models [10], and Markov decision processes (MDPs) [1]. Depending on the nature of the secret to be made opaque, there are different variants of opacity, including *state-based*, which requires the secret behavior of the system (i.e., the membership of its current state to the set) to remain opaque (uncertain) until the system enters a non-secret state; *language-based*, which aims to hide a set of secret executions; and *"model-based"*, which wants to prevents the observer to find out the true model of the system among several potential models known to the observer.

In this work, we investigate language-based opacity in stochastic systems with asymmetric, incomplete information to the planning agent and the eavesdropping attacker. To motivate the problem formulation, consider a scenario where an autonomous robot, denoted Player 1 (P1), is entrusted with the confidential task of delivering vital medical supplies to remote camp sites. The robot must retrieve these supplies from a base station and navigate through a probabilistic environment characterized by slippery conditions and the absence of GPS signals. P1 employs a sensor network to monitor its own location. However, this sensor network includes certain vulnerable sensors that leak information to an adversarial observer. The planning question is how can the robot ensure the success of its mission, while ensuring its opacity to the observer? That is, the observer cannot tell if the task is achieved or not from the observations. This problem is interesting because instead of considering a passive observer/attacker has a stationary observation function, the robot can strategically select sensor queries and thus control the amount of information leaked to the attacker with access to only unsecured sensors.

Our Approach and Contributions: We propose to investigate a *joint active perception and control* framework for the planning agent (P1) to decide if the opacity and mission success can be both achieved given different initial states of the stochastic system and initial observations for both P1 and the passive observer (P2). Our contributions involve incorporating 2-beliefs system to capture P1's knowledge about the current state and P1's knowledge about P2's knowledge about the current state. Reasoning with this 2-beliefs system, we develop an algorithm that computes a strategy for P1 that actively selects which sensor to query and which control action to exercise to ensure satisfaction of the mission objective and opacity constraint simultaneously. However, maintaining and updating the 2-belief system requires exponential memory due to the subset construction. To address the issue of scalability, we introduce a method to determine when to stop tracking P2's belief, while ensuring the correctness in the computed strategy. Finally, we demonstrate the correctness of our method on robot motion planning in a stochastic gridworld environment with partial observations provided by range sensors and location sensors.

Related Work: Opacity-enforcing control has been extensively studied in the context of discrete event systems (DESs). Previous work in the supervisory control framework focuses on enforcing opacity in deterministic systems by modeling the control system as a deterministic finite state automaton in the presence of a passive observer [14,15,23]. Different approaches have been proposed to synthesize opacity [5,21,22] or to verify if a system is opaque [11,16,20]. To synthesize opacity in deterministic systems, Saboori et al. [17] synthesizes supervisor that restricts certain system behaviors to ensure opacity. Cassez et al. [5] propose the use of dynamic masks that filter out unobservable events and verify the opaqueness of a secret by reducing the opacity enforcement problem to a 2-player safety game. Xie et al. [22] design non-deterministic supervisors (controller) so that the observer, knowing the nondeterministic supervisor, cannot determine if a secret is satisfied or not. Besides masking and nondeterministic control design, [9,21] investigate how to edit the observations to ensure opacity using a non-deterministic edit function.

Game-theoretic approach for opacity enforcement has also been proposed. Maubert et al. [12] introduce the game with opacity condition, in which one player with perfect observation aims to enforce current-state opacity against another player with imperfect observation during their two-player interactions. They reduce the opacity-guarantee game to a safety game and the opacity-violating game to a reachability game, for which existing solution can be used to solve players' strategies. Hélouët et al.[8] present a framework for enforcing opacity against different types of attackers with different information about the input and the observations. The existing approaches for opacity-enforcement in deterministic systems or games are not applicable for stochastic systems with partial observations to both the system and the observer.

For opacity in stochastic DESs, Saboori and Hadjicostis [18] propose three probabilistic variants of current state opacity and develop opacity verification algorithms for systems modeled as probabilistic finite automata. Keroglou and Hadjicostis [10] investigate model-based opacity where the user wants to conceal a true system modeled by a hidden Markov model among several potential hidden Markov models from an intruder. Bérard et al. [1] extend language-based opacity for ω-regular properties on MDPs. They assume a static observation function and present several decidability results. In contrast, we focus on synthesizing an opacity-enforcing strategy for an agent operating in a stochastic environment and utilizing active sensor queries of secured and unsecured sensors.

2   Preliminaries and Problem Formulation

Notations. Given a finite set X, $\mathcal{D}(X)$ denotes the set of all probability distributions over X. For a probability distribution $d \in \mathcal{D}(X)$, $\mathsf{Supp}(d)$, the support of d, is the set of elements in X with non-zero probabilities under d.

We model the interaction between an agent, Player 1/P1, and the environment as a Partially Observable Markov Decision Process (POMDP). The agent actively queries sensors in the environment to obtain task-relevant information.

Definition 1 (POMDP with active perception). *The* stochastic system with partial observations *is a tuple*

$$M = (S, A, \mathbf{P}, \Omega, \Gamma = \Gamma_1 \cup \Gamma_2, O, s_0, \omega_0, \omega_0^+, AP, L)$$

in which (1) S is a finite set of states; (2) A is the set of P1's control actions that change the state in S; (3) $\mathbf{P}: S \times A \to \mathcal{D}(S)$ *is a* probability transition function *such that for each* $s, s' \in S$ *and* $a \in A$, $\mathbf{P}(s, a, s')$ *is the probability of reaching* s' *given action a taken at state s; (4)* $\Omega \subseteq 2^S$ *is the set of all observations; (5)* $\Gamma = \{\gamma_0, \gamma_1, \cdots, \gamma_N\}$ *is a set of* indexed sensors, *partitioned into secured sensors* Γ_1 *and unsecured sensors* Γ_2; *(6)* $O: S \times 2^\Gamma \to \Omega$ *is the* observation function *such that for a state* $s \in S$ *and a sensor subset* $X \subseteq \Gamma$, $O(s, X) \in \Omega$ *is the set of states whose sensor readings for sensor set X are the same as the readings given state s (we call* $O(s, X)$ *the set of observation-equivalent states to s based on sensor information in X); (7)* $s_0 \in S$ *is the initial state; (8)* ω_0 *and* ω_0^+ *are respectively the initial observations of P1 and P2, where* $s_0 \in \omega_0 \cap \omega_0^+$ *and* $\omega_0 \subseteq \omega_0^+$; *(9) AP is a set of atomic propositions; and (10)* $L: S \to 2^{AP}$ *is the labeling function that maps a state* $s \in S$ *to a set* $L(s)$ *of atomic propositions evaluated to true at s.*

The following regularity assumption is made on the observation function.

Assumption 1. *Let* $X_1, X_2 \subseteq \Gamma$ *be two sets of sensors. If* $X_1 \subseteq X_2$, *then for any state* $s \in S$, $O(s, X_2) \subseteq O(s, X_1)$.

That is, the more sensor readings the less uncertainty about the current state. A *perception action* is a subset of sensors being queried. A *joint control and perception action* of P1, or a *control-perception action* for short, is a tuple (a, X) including a control action $a \in A$ and a perception action $X \subseteq \Gamma$. In the following, by a P1's action, we mean a control-perception action, from $\mathcal{A}_1 = A \times 2^\Gamma$.

We consider an eavesdropping attacker, Player 2/P2, who accesses the information from the *unsecured* sensors queried by P1.

Definition 2 (Observations of an eavesdropping attacker P2). *For any state* $s \in S$, *for any perception action* $X \subseteq \Gamma$ *performed by P1 when the system entered s, P2's observation is* $O(s, X \cap \Gamma_2)$ *where* $X \cap \Gamma_2$ *is the subset of unsecured sensors in the queried sensor set X. In addition, P2 does not observe the control actions taken by P1.*

Remark 1. We assume that a sensor will emit signal only if it is queried by P1 and P2 can only obtain information from the *unsecured* sensors queried by P1. However, this assumption can be easily lifted for the case where there is a subset $\mathcal{Z}$ of sensors that always emit signals and P2 can access the subset of unsecured sensors in $\mathcal{Z}$ at all times. In this case, we only need to include these sensors $\mathcal{Z}$ into each perception action of P1.

Game Play. The game play in M is constructed as follows. The game starts from the initial state s_0, P1 gets the observation ω_0, and P2 receives observation ω_0^+. Based on ω_0, P1 takes an action $(a_0, X_0) \in \mathcal{A}_1$. The system then moves to a state s_1, drawn randomly based on $\mathbf{P}(s_0, a_0, \cdot)$. P1 receives observation $O(s_1, X_0)$ and P2 receives observation $O(s_1, X_0 \cap \Gamma_2)$. At each step, P1 can either decide to terminate the game play or take a control-perception action and move to the next state. Assuming that the game play will be eventually terminated, the resulting play is a finite sequence of state-action pairs $\rho = s_0(a_0, X_0)s_1(a_1, X_1)s_2 \ldots s_n$ such that $\mathbf{P}(s_i, a_i, s_{i+1}) > 0$ for all integers $0 \le i < n$. The labeling of this play is $L(\rho) = L(s_0)L(s_1) \ldots L(s_n)$. The set of finite plays in M is denoted by $\mathsf{Plays}(M)$.

The finite play generates a sequence of observations for both players. For P1, given that P1 knows his own action decisions, we have

$$O_1(\rho) = \omega_0(a_0, X_0)\omega_1(a_1, X_1) \ldots \omega_n,$$

where ω_0 is the initial observation and for $i \ge 1$, ω_i is the observation of state s_i given the sensor query X_{i-1}, i.e., $\omega_i = O(s_i, X_{i-1})$. For P2, as P1's control actions are invisible,

$$O_2(\rho) = \omega_0^+(X_0 \cap \Gamma_2)\omega_1^+(X_1 \cap \Gamma_2) \ldots (X_{n-1} \cap \Gamma_2)\omega_n^+,$$

where ω_0^+ is the initial P2's observation and for $i \ge 1$, ω_i^+ is P2's observation of state s_i given the sensor query $X_{i-1} \cap \Gamma_2$, i.e., $\omega_i^+ = O(s_i, X_{i-1} \cap \Gamma_2)$. Two plays $\rho_1, \rho_2 \in \mathsf{Plays}(M)$ are observation-equivalent to player i iff $O_i(\rho_1) = O_i(\rho_2)$. Given a play $\rho \in \mathsf{Plays}(M)$, we denote by $[\rho]_1$ (resp. $[\rho]_2$) the set of plays that are observation-equivalent to ρ from P1's perception (resp. P2's perception). The set of all sequences of observations P1 (resp. P2) can observe for the plays of M is denoted $\mathsf{Obs}_1(M)$ ($\mathsf{Obs}_2(M)$). The inverse of observation function for player i is the function $O_i^{-1} : \mathsf{Obs}_i(M) \to 2^{\mathsf{Plays}(M)}$ such that for each $\eta \in \mathsf{Obs}_i(M)$, $O_i^{-1}(\eta) = \{\rho \in \mathsf{Plays}(M) \mid O_i(\rho) = \eta\}$. The following property is easy to prove:

Proposition 1. *For every play $\rho \in \mathsf{Plays}(M)$ and for each player i, $\rho \in O_i^{-1}(O_i(\rho))$.*

Objective in Temporal Logic: P1 has a temporal objective φ specified in Linear Temporal Logic over Finite Traces (LTL$_f$). The syntax of LTL$_f$ formulas is given as follows.

Definition 3 (LTL$_f$ [7]). *Let AP be a set of atomic propositions. An (LTL$_f$) formula over AP is defined inductively as follows:*

$$\varphi := p \mid \neg\varphi \mid \varphi_1 \wedge \varphi_2 \mid \varphi_1 \wedge \varphi_2 \mid \bigcirc\varphi \mid \varphi_1 \cup \varphi_2 \mid \Diamond\varphi \mid \Box\varphi,$$

*where $p \in AP$; $\neg$, $\wedge$ and $\wedge$ are the Boolean operators negation, conjunction and disjunction, respectively; and $\bigcirc$, $\cup$, $\Diamond$ and $\Box$ denote the temporal modal operators for **next**, **until**, **eventually** and **always** respectively.*

The operator $\bigcirc\varphi$ specifies that formula φ holds at the next time instant, while the operator $\varphi_1 \cup \varphi_2$ denotes that there exists a future time instant at which φ_2 holds, and that φ_1 holds at all time instants up to and including that future instant. That is, the system must satisfy φ_1 continuously until a time instant in future at which φ_2 holds. The temporal operator $\Diamond\varphi$ specifies that φ holds at some instant in the future and the operator $\Box\varphi$ specifies that φ holds at all time instants from the current instant.

For any LTL$_f$ formula φ over AP, a set of words $\mathsf{Words}(\varphi) \subseteq (2^{AP})^*$ that satisfy the formula is associated. A finite word $w \in (2^{AP})^*$ satisfies φ, denoted by $w \models \varphi$, iff w belongs to $\mathsf{Words}(\varphi)$. See [7] for detailed semantics of LTL$_f$.

To illustrate our definitions, we introduce a running example.

Example 1. (Part I) Consider the POMDP in Fig. 1. To reduce visual clutter, only the transitions with non-zero probabilities are drawn and the exact probabilities of those transitions are omitted. The POMDP has 5 states, s_1 through s_5, and the sensor set Γ consists of sensors, A,B,C and D, which cover $\{s_2, s_3\}$, $\{s_3\}$, $\{s_4, s_5\}$ and $\{s_2, s_3, s_4\}$, respectively (shown by the dotted shapes in the figure). All the sensors are Boolean sensors. A Boolean sensor returns True when the current state is covered by the sensor and False otherwise. This sensor set is divided into the secured sensors $\Gamma_1 = \{B\}$ and the unsecured sensors $\Gamma_2 = \{A, C, D\}$. P1's task is to eventually reach state s_5, which is expressed using the LTL$_f$ formula $\varphi = \Diamond s_5$. An example of the observations obtained by P1 and P2 is as follows. P1 starts from state s_1 and takes a control-perception action $(a, \{A, B\})$, and reaches state s_2 probabilistically. P1 obtains the observations based on both the sensors and thus $O_1(s_2, \{A, B\}) = \{s_2\}$, while P2 obtains the observations only based on the unsecured sensors $O_2(s_2, \{A, B\} \cap \Gamma_2) = O_2(s_2, \{A\}) = \{s_2, s_3\}$.

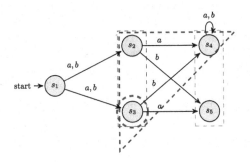

Fig. 1. An illustrative running example, POMDP with active perception M. The dashed region represents the sensors: red (A), blue (B), green (C) and violet (D). (Color figure online)

P1's Strategy. In the POMDP with active perception M, P1 has to simultaneously either determine a control-perception action or terminate the game. A finite-memory, randomised strategy for P1 is a function π:Plays$(M) \rightarrow \mathcal{D}(\mathcal{A}_1 \cup \{\varkappa\})$ where $\varkappa$ means P1 terminates the play. Because P1 has partial observations, P1 can only use observation-based strategy $\pi : \text{Obs}_1(M) \rightarrow \mathcal{D}(\mathcal{A}_1 \cup \{\varkappa\})$ that maps an observation of a play to an action. P1 maintains for each time step k, the observation sequence $\eta_k = w_0(a_0, X_0)w_1 \ldots w_k$ it has perceived up to time step k, and then, it feeds η_k to π to choose an action. A policy π induces a probability distribution Pr^π over Plays(M). Let Π be the set of all finite-memory, randomized, observation-based strategies for P1.

Definition 4 (Qualitative opacity). *An LTL$_f$ formula φ is opaque to P2 with respect to a play $\rho \in$ Plays(M) if and only if 1. $L(\rho) \models \varphi$; and 2. there exists at least one observation-equivalent play $\rho' \in [\rho]_2$ such that $L(\rho') \not\models \varphi$.*

In words, P2 cannot tell from its observation if the formula is satisfied or not.

Definition 5 (Opacity-enforcing winning play). *Given a secret φ, a play $\rho \in$ Plays(M) is winning if $L(\rho) \models \varphi$. The set of winning plays is denoted* WPlays.

A winning play ρ is opaque-enforcing winning *if φ is opaque to P2 with respect to ρ. The set of opacity-enforcing winning plays is denoted* OWPlays.

Definition 6 (Opacity-enforcing winning strategy). *Given a prefix $\rho \in$* Plays(M), *a strategy $\pi \in \Pi$ is said to be a* winning strategy *for P1 if P1 can ensure to satisfy φ with probability one, that is, $\Pr^{\pi}(\{\rho'|\rho \cdot \rho' \in$ WPlays$)\} = 1$. A strategy π is said to be* opacity-enforcing winning strategy *for P1 if P1 can enforce an opacity-enforcing winning play starting from ρ with probability one, that is, $\Pr^{\pi}(\{\rho'|\rho \cdot \rho' \in$ OWPlays$\}) = 1$.*

Problem 1. Given a POMDP with active perception M in Definition 1 and P1's specification φ, given that P2 receives all sensor readings from unsecured sensors, compute, if exists, an opacity-enforcing winning strategy for P1.

3   Main Result: Opacity-Enforcing Winning with 2-Beliefs

In this section, we present a solution to Problem 1. We first make use of the fact that an LTL$_f$ formula can be represented as a deterministic finite automaton to construct a product POMDP that augments the original POMDP states with task-relevant information. We use this product POMDP to formulate the opacity-enforcing planning problem and present solutions to compute P1's opacity-enforcing winning strategy using joint active perception and control.

As a first step, we encode the LTL$_f$ formula into a finite-state automaton.

Definition 7 (Deterministic Finite Automaton (DFA)). *A DFA is a tuple $\mathbf{A} = (Q, \Sigma, \delta, \iota, F)$ with a finite set of states Q, a finite alphabet Σ, a transition function $\delta : Q \times \Sigma \to Q$, an initial state ι, and a set of accepting states $F \subseteq Q$.*

We assume the transition function is complete. That is, for any $(q, \sigma) \in Q \times \Sigma$, $\delta(q, \sigma)$ is defined.[1] The extended transition function $\delta : Q \times \Sigma^* \to Q$ is defined in the usual manner, i.e. , for each state $q \in Q$ and word $w_0 w_1 \ldots w_n \in \Sigma^*$, $\delta(q, w_0 w_1 \ldots w_n) = \delta(\delta(q, w_0), w_1 \ldots w_n)$. Word $w = w_0 w_1 \ldots w_n \in \Sigma^*$ is accepted by $\mathbf{A}$ if and only if $\delta(\iota, w) \in F$. The language of $\mathbf{A}$, denoted $L(\mathbf{A})$, consists of all those words accepted by $\mathbf{A}$, i.e. , $L(\mathbf{A}) = \{w \in \Sigma^* \mid \delta(\iota, w) \in F\}$.

The algorithm uses the idea of De Giacomo and Vardi [7] to convert the LTL$_f$ formula φ into a DFA $\mathbf{A}$ with $\Sigma = 2^{AP}$ such that Words$(\varphi) = L(\mathbf{A})$. From now on, we assume $\Sigma = 2^{AP}$. In the next step, we construct a product POMDP from the POMDP M and the DFA $\mathbf{A}$ to determine whether P1 can enforce an opacity-enforcing winning play from the initial state s_0.

Definition 8 (Product POMDP). *The product POMDP between the POMDP with active perception $M = (S, A, \mathbf{P}, \Omega, \Gamma = \Gamma_1 \cup \Gamma_2, O, s_0, \omega_1^0, AP, L)$ and the DFA $\mathbf{A} = (Q, \Sigma, \delta, \iota, F)$ is a tuple*

$$\mathcal{M} = (S \times Q, A, \Gamma, T, (s_0, q_0), Z, \mathcal{O}, B_1^0, B_2^0, S \times F)$$

---

[1] Any incomplete transition function can be made complete by adding a sink state and redirecting all the missing transitions to it.

*in which (1) $S \times Q$ is the set of states; (2) A is the set of control actions; (3) Γ
is the set of sensors; (4) $T : (S \times Q) \times A \to \mathcal{D}(S \times Q)$ is the transition function
s.t. for states (s, q) and (s', q') and action a, $T((s, q), a, (s', q')) = \boldsymbol{P}(s, a, s')$ if
$\delta(q, L(s')) = q'$. Otherwise, $T((s, q), a, (s', q')) = 0$; (5) (s_0, q_0) is the initial state
where $q_0 = \delta(\iota, L(s_0))$; (6) $Z \subseteq 2^{(S \times Q)}$ is the set of observations; (7) $\mathcal{O} : (S \times Q) \times$
$2^{\Gamma} \to Z$ is the observation function s.t. for a state $(s, q) \in S \times Q$ and sensor subset
$X \subseteq \Gamma$, $\mathcal{O}((s, q), X) = O(s, X) \times Q$; (8) $B_1^0 = \{(s, q) \mid s \in \omega_0, q = \delta(q_0, L(s))\}$ is the
initial observation for P1; (9) $B_2^0 = \{(s, q) \mid s \in \omega_0^+, q = \delta(q_0, L(s))\}$ is the initial
observation for P2; and (10) $S \times F$ is the set of goal states.*

A finite play $\gamma = (s_0, q_0)(a_0, X_0)(s_1, q_1)(a_1, X_1) \ldots (s_n, q_n)$ in $\mathcal{M}$, by the construction of the product POMDP, can be projected into a single finite play
$\rho = s_0(a_0, X_0)s_1(a_1, X_1) \ldots s_n$ in M. The projection of plays in $\mathcal{M}$ to plays in M
is a bijection due to the deterministic transitions in the DFA.

By construction, the play ρ satisfies the specification φ iff there exists an
integer $0 \leq i \leq n$ such that $(s_i, q_i) \in S \times F$.

The observation function in this product game is used to update both P1's
belief and P2's belief. Let X be a sensor query performed by P1 and $(s, q) \in S \times Q$
be the state the product game $\mathcal{M}$ enters. P1's belief about the current state is
updated using $\mathcal{O}((s, q), X)$ and P2's belief is updated using $\mathcal{O}((s, q), X \cap \Gamma_2)$. For
this product game, function $\mathsf{Post}_{\mathcal{M}} : (S \times Q) \times A \to 2^{S \times Q}$ maps a state $(s, q) \in S \times Q$
and an action $a \in A$ to the set of possible reachable states as $\mathsf{Post}_{\mathcal{M}}((s, q), a) =$
$\{(s', q') \in S \times Q \mid T((s, q), a, (s', q')) > 0\}$. We extend this function for domains
$2^{(S \times Q)} \times A$ and $2^{(S \times Q)} \times 2^A$ such that for each $B \subseteq S \times Q$, $a \in A$, and $Y \subseteq A$,
$\mathsf{Post}_{\mathcal{M}}(B, a) = \bigcup_{(s,q) \in B} \mathsf{Post}_{\mathcal{M}}((s, q), a)$ and $\mathsf{Post}_{\mathcal{M}}(B, Y) = \bigcup_{a \in Y} \mathsf{Post}_{\mathcal{M}}(B, a)$. Given
a state $(s, q) \in S \times Q$, we use $\mathcal{M}[(s, q)]$ to denote a product POMDP obtained
from $\mathcal{M}$ by letting (s, q) to be the initial state.

3.1   Computing an Opacity-Enforcing Strategy

From the product POMDP $\mathcal{M}$, we formulate a one-player stochastic game to
model the interaction of P1 and the environment, along with P2's observation.

Definition 9 (POMDP augmented with 2-beliefs). *Given the product
POMDP $\mathcal{M}=(S \times Q, A, \Gamma, T, (s_0, q_0), Z, \mathcal{O}, B_1^0, B_2^0, S \times F)$, the POMDP augmented
with 2-beliefs is a tuple*

$$\mathcal{G} = \langle V, \mathcal{A}_1, v_0, V_F, \Delta \rangle,$$

*where (1) $V = \{((s, q), B_1, B_2) \mid s \in S, q \in Q, B_1 \subseteq (S \times Q), B_2 \subseteq (S \times Q)\}$ is the set of
states, where B_1 and B_2 are beliefs of P1 and P2, respectively; (2) $\mathcal{A}_1 = A \times 2^{\Gamma}$
is the set of control-perception actions that can be taken by P1, as given in $\mathcal{M}$;
(3) $v_0 = ((s_0, q_0), B_1^0, B_2^0)$ is the initial state; (4) $V_F = \{((s_F, q_F), B_1^F, B_2^F) \in V \mid$
$(s_F, q_F) \in (S \times F), B_1^F \subseteq (S \times F), B_2^F \cap (S \times F) \neq \varnothing, B_2^F \cap S \times (Q \setminus F) \neq \varnothing\}$ are
the set of goal states (P1 aims to reach one of such a goal state); and (5)
$\Delta : V \times \mathcal{A}_1 \to \mathcal{D}(V)$ is the probabilistic transition function such that all states in
V_F are sink states, and for each state $v = ((s, q), B_1, B_2) \in V_F$, action $(a, X) \in$*

$\mathcal{A}_1$, and state $v' = ((s',q'), B'_1, B'_2)) \in V$, $\Delta(v, (a, X), v') = T((s,q), a, (s',q'))$ if $B'_1 = \mathsf{Post}_{\mathcal{M}}(B_1, a) \cap \mathcal{O}((s',q'), X)$, $B'_2 = \mathsf{Post}_{\mathcal{M}}(B_2, A) \cap \mathcal{O}((s',q'), X \cap \Gamma_2)$, and $q' = \delta(q, L(s'))$, and otherwise, $\Delta(v, (a, X), v') = 0$.

Each state $((s,q), B_1, B_2)$ of this product game indicates a situation where the true state of the system is (s,q), P1's belief about the current state is B_1, and P2's belief about the current state is B_2. Each transition $((s,q), B_1, B_2) \xrightarrow{(a,X)} ((s',q'), B'_1, B'_2)$ corresponds to a situation where P1 selects an action $(a, X) \in \mathcal{A}_1$, after which, the game stochastically transitions from the true state (s,q) to the new true state (s',q'). Then, with the sensor query, P1 observes $\mathcal{O}((s',q'), X)$ and thus updates its belief from B_1 to B'_1 by considering the possible states in which it can be given the taken action a and eliminating the states that are inconsistent with the observation. Likewise, P2 observes $\mathcal{O}((s',q'), X \cap \Gamma_2)$ and updates P2's belief from B_2 to B'_2 based on the information from unsecured sensors. If a state in V_F is reached, P1 chooses to terminate the play.

The following example shows the construction as described in Definition 9.

Example 2. (Part II)   In Example 1, the secret task for P1 is $\varphi = \Diamond s_5$. The DFA corresponding to φ is shown in the Fig. 2a. Figure 2b shows the product POMDP of this DFA and the POMDP in Example 1. From this product POMDP, the POMDP augmented with 2-beliefs $\mathcal{G}$ is constructed. Figure 2c shows a partial construction of $\mathcal{G}$. In this figure, $B_1^0 = \{(s_1, 0)\}$, $B_2^0 = \{(s_1, 0), (s_2, 0), (s_3, 0), (s_4, 0), (s_5, 1)\}$, $B_1^4 = \{(s_5, 1)\}$ and $B_2^4 = \{(s_4, 0), (s_5, 1)\}$. To see how the belief is updated, consider state $((s_3, 0), \{(s_3, 0)\}, \{(s_2, 0), (s_3, 0)\})$, at which P1 knows the exact current state and P2 is uncertain if the current state is s_2 or s_3. If P1 takes action a and query sensor set $\{C, D\}$, state $(s_5, 1)$ is reached with probability one. The sensor C returns 1 and sensor D returns 0. In this case, P2, who has access to both C and D, will know that $(s_5, 1)$ is reached. On the other hand, if P1 takes action a and queries B and C, at state s_5, B outputs 0 and C outputs 1. P1 will know that s_5 is reached. P2, with only sensor C's information, cannot distinguish if state $(s_5, 1)$ or $(s_4, 0)$ is reached. The opacity is enforced and the play is winning for P1. The goal state in this figure has a self-loop for all actions. This is because all states in V_F are absorbing.

The opacity-enforcing winning strategy computation relies on the proof that in the presence of the eavesdropping attacker and partial observations, either player is sure that one of the states in its belief is the true state.

We now also show that the belief of P2 always includes the belief of P1.

Lemma 1. *For any state* $((s,q), B_1, B_2) \in V$ *reachable from the initial state* v_0, $B_1 \subseteq B_2$.

Proof. By induction on the lengths of the plays in the product game. For the initial state $v_0 = ((s_0, q_0), B_1^0, B_2^0)$, by the construction of B_1^0 and B_2^0 in Definition 8 and the assumption that $w_0 \subseteq w_0^+$ in Definition 1, we have $B_1^0 \subseteq B_2^0$.

Consider a play with length k in $\mathcal{G}$ such that $v_k = ((s_k, q_k), B_1^k, B_2^k)$ is the last state of the play. By induction hypothesis, $B_1^k \subseteq B_2^k$. For any state

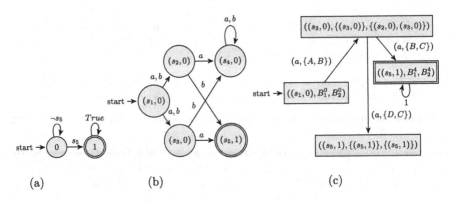

Fig. 2. (a) DFA for the temporal goal $\varphi = \Diamond s_5$. (b) Product POMDP $\mathcal{M}$. (c) A fragment of POMDP with 2-beliefs $\mathcal{G}$, constructed from $\mathcal{M}$.

$v_{k+1} = ((s_{k+1}, q_{k+1}), B_1^{k+1}, B_2^{k+1})$ reached by an action $(a, X) \in \mathcal{A}_1$ from v_k, it holds that $B_1^{k+1} = \mathsf{Post}_{\mathcal{M}}(B_1^k, a) \cap \mathcal{O}((s_{k+1}, q_{k+1}), X)$ and $B_2^{k+1} = \mathsf{Post}_{\mathcal{M}}(B_2^k, A) \cap \mathcal{O}((s_{k+1}, q_{k+1}), X \cap \Gamma_s)$. Since $B_1^k \subseteq B_2^k$ and $a \subseteq A$, $\mathsf{Post}_{\mathcal{M}}(B_1^k, a) \subseteq \mathsf{Post}_{\mathcal{M}}(B_2^k, A)$. Also, given $(X \cap \Gamma_2) \subseteq X$, it holds that $\mathcal{O}((s_{k+1}, q_{k+1}), X) \subseteq \mathcal{O}((s_{k+1}, q_{k+1}), X \cap \Gamma_2)$. Hence, $B_1^{k+1} \subseteq B_2^{k+1}$. $\qquad\square$

Lemma 2. *For any state $((s, q), B_1, B_2) \in V$ that is reachable from the initial state v_0, it holds that $(s, q) \in B_1$ and $(s, q) \in B_2$.*

Proof. We first show that $(s, q) \in B_1$ using induction on the lengths of the plays of $\mathcal{G}$. For the initial state $v_0 = ((s_0, q_0), B_1^0, B_2^0)$, by construction of belief from the initial observation, $(s_0, q_0) \in B_1^0$. Consider a play with length k in $\mathcal{G}$ such that $v_k = ((s_k, q_k), B_1^k, B_2^k)$ is the k-th state reached by a sequence of P1's actions. Assume $(s_k, q_k) \in B_1^k$. For any state $v_{k+1} = ((s_{k+1}, q_{k+1}), B_1^{k+1}, B_2^{k+1})$ reached from v_k by an action $(a, X) \in \mathcal{A}_1$, taken by P1, it holds that $T((s_k, q_k), a, (s_{k+1}, q_{k+1})) > 0$, $B_1^{k+1} = \mathsf{Post}_{\mathcal{M}}(B_1^k, a) \cap \mathcal{O}((s_{k+1}, q_{k+1}), X)$. Because $(s_k, q_k) \in B_1^k$, by construction we have $(s_{k+1}, q_{k+1}) \in \mathsf{Post}_{\mathcal{M}}(B_1^k, a)$. Also, because $s_{k+1} \in O(s_{k+1}, X)$, $(s_{k+1}, q_{k+1}) \in \mathcal{O}((s_{k+1}, q_{k+1}), X)$. Thus, $(s_{k+1}, q_{k+1}) \in B_1^{k+1}$.

This proof combined with the result of Lemma 1 proves $(s, q) \in B_2$. $\qquad\square$

Lemma 3. *Let $\rho_{\mathcal{G}} = ((s_0, q_0), B_1^0, B_2^0)(a_0, X_0)((s_1, q_1), B_1^1, B_2^1) \ldots ((s_n, q_n), B_1^n, B_2^n)$ be a play of $\mathcal{G}$. For each $(s_n', q_n') \in B_2^n$, there exists a play $\rho_{\mathcal{M}} = (s_0', q_0')(a_0', X_0')(s_1', q_1')(a_1', X_1') \ldots (s_n', q_n')$ of $\mathcal{M}$ such that for each $0 \leq i < n$, $(s_i', q_i') \in B_2^i$ and $X_i' = X_i \cap \Gamma_2$.*

Proof. Proof by induction on $k = n, n-1, \ldots, 0$. For $k = n$, $\rho_{\mathcal{G}}^n = ((s_n, q_n), B_1^n, B_2^n)$. By the statement assumption, $(s_n', q_n') \in B_2^n$, and clearly $\rho_{\mathcal{M}}^n = (s_n', q_n')$ is a play of $\mathcal{M}[(s_n', q_n')]$. Therefore, the statement holds for the induction's base case.

For the induction hypothesis, assume given the play

$$\rho_{\mathcal{G}}^k = ((s_k, q_k), B_1^k, B_2^k)(a_k, X_k)((s_{k+1}, q_{k+1}), B_1^{k+1}, B_2^{k+1}) \ldots ((s_n, q_n), B_1^n, B_2^n)$$

of $\mathcal{G}$, there exists a sequence

$$\rho_{\mathcal{M}}^k = (s'_k, q'_k)(a'_k, X_k \cap \Gamma_2)(s'_{k+1}, q'_{k+1})(a'_{k+1}, X_{k+1} \cap \Gamma_2) \ldots ((s'_n, q'_n))$$

where $(s'_i, q'_i) \in B_2^i$ for each $k \leq i \leq n$, is a play of $\mathcal{M}$. Now, consider the play

$$\rho_{\mathcal{G}}^{k-1} = ((s_{k-1}, q_{k-1}), B_1^{k-1}, B_2^{k-1})(a_{k-1}, X_{k-1}) \ldots ((s_n, q_n), B_1^n, B_2^n)$$

of $\mathcal{G}$. Given $\rho_{\mathcal{G}}^{k-1}$ is a play in $\mathcal{G}$, $\mathcal{G}$ has a transition from $((s_{k-1}, q_{k-1}), B_1^{k-1}, B_2^{k-1})$ to $((s_k, q_k), B_1^k, B_2^k)$ with action (a_{k-1}, X_{k-1}). By the construction of $\mathcal{G}$'s transition function, this implies that $B_2^k = \mathsf{Post}_{\mathcal{M}}(B_2^{k-1}, A) \cap \mathcal{O}((s_k, q_k), X_{k-1} \cap \Gamma_2)$, which means (1) $B_2^k \subseteq \mathsf{Post}_{\mathcal{M}}(B_2^{k-1}, A)$, and (2) $B_2^k \subseteq \mathcal{O}((s_k, q_k), X_{k-1} \cap \Gamma_2)$. Given (1) and that $(s'_k, q'_k) \in B_2^k$, it holds that there exists $(s'_{k-1}, q'_{k-1}) \in B_2^{k-1}$ and $a'_{k-1} \in A$ such that $(s'_k, q'_k) \in \mathsf{Post}_{\mathcal{M}}((s'_{k-1}, q'_{k-1}), a'_{k-1})$, which implies that in $\mathcal{M}$, there exists a transition with action a'_{k-1} from state (s'_{k-1}, q'_{k-1}) to state (s'_k, q'_k), and by (2), it holds that $(s'_k, q'_k) \in \mathcal{O}((s_k, q_k), X_{k-1} \cap \Gamma_2)$. These two combined imply that $\rho_{\mathcal{M}}^{k-1} = (s'_{k-1}, q'_{k-1})(a'_{k-1}, X_{k-1} \cap \Gamma_2)(s'_k, q'_k)(a'_k, X_k \cap \Gamma_2) \ldots ((s'_n, q'_n))$ is a play of $\mathcal{M}$ and for each $k \leq i \leq n$, $(s'_k, q'_k) \in B_2^k$. $\square$

The above properties are important to construct an opacity-enforcing strategy to satisfy the given specification. Even in situations where P1 may only have a belief such that it is a subset of $(S \times F)$ and P1 does not perfectly know the current true state, P1 knows that the specification has been satisfied from Lemma 2. Also, with Lemma 1, we know that for P1 to enforce opacity, it is not sufficient to reach a state such that only P1's belief is a subset of $(S \times F)$ as it means that P2's belief always encompasses P1's belief and hence, P1 must ensure that P2's belief has at least one additional state that is not in $(S \times F)$.

In the above constructed *POMDP augmented with 2-beliefs*, P1 is tasked with reaching the goal states in V_F with probability one. We show that reaching these goal states with probability one would ensure that P1 would satisfy the given specification while ensuring opacity in the POMDP M.

Definition 10 (Belief-Based Winning Strategy/Region).
A strategy $\pi : V \to \mathcal{D}(\mathcal{A}_1)$ in the POMDP with 2-beliefs $\mathcal{G}$ is winning at state v_0 for P1 if by starting from v_0 and following π, P1 ensures to reach a state $((s, q), B_1, B_2)$ where $B_1 \subseteq S \times F$ with probability 1. Strategy π is opacity-enforcing winning at a state v_0 if by starting from v_0 and following π, P1 guarantees to reach a goal state V_F with probability 1. It is well known that belief-based strategies are sufficient to win almost-surely the reachability game for P1 [2] and thus, a strategy $\pi : V \to \mathcal{D}(\mathcal{A}_1)$ is belief-based if for every pair of states $((s, q), B_1, B_2), ((s', q'), B_1, B_2) \in V$, it holds $\pi((s, q), B_1, B_2) = \pi((s', q'), B_1, B_2)$. A set of states from which P1 has a belief-based winning strategy is called P1's winning region, denoted as $\mathsf{Win}(\mathcal{G})$. P1's opacity-enforcing winning region, denoted $\mathsf{OWin}(\mathcal{G})$, consists of those states from which P1 has an opacity-enforcing winning strategy.

Theorem 1. *A belief-based winning strategy π in the POMDP augmented with 2-beliefs $\mathcal{G}$ is also winning in the POMDP with active perception M and enforces opacity and winning with respect to its temporal objective φ.*

Proof. Let $\rho_o = ((s_0, q_0), B_1^0, B_2^0)(a_0, X_0)((s_1, q_1), B_1^1, B_2^1) \ldots ((s_n, q_n), B_1^n, B_2^n)$ be a play generated by π over $\mathcal{G}$. This play is projected onto play $\rho_M = s_0(a_0, X_0)s_1 \ldots s_n$ on M. Because π is a winning strategy, $((s_n, q_n), B_1^n, B_2^n) \in V_F$, implying $q_n \in F$ and $B_1^n \subseteq (S \times F)$. This means that $L(s_0 s_1 \cdots s_n) \models \varphi$, which means that $\rho_M \models \varphi$ and the play ρ_M is winning for P1. Because this ρ_o is selected arbitrarily, then this means π is a winning strategy for M. Also, given that $B_1^n \subseteq (S \times F)$, P1 knows that being in any one of the states in its belief, it satisfies the specification.

For P2's belief, it holds that $B_2^n \cap (S \times (Q \setminus F)) \neq \varnothing$. That is, there exists a state $(s', q') \in B_2^n$ such that $q' \neq F$. For each such a state (s', q'), by Lemma 3, there exists a play $\rho_\mathcal{M}' = (s_0', q_0')(a_0', X_0')(s_1', q_1') \ldots (s_n', q_n')$ of $\mathcal{M}$ where $X_i' = X_i \cap \Gamma_2$ for all $0 \leq i < n$. This implies that $\sigma_M^- = s_0' s_1' \ldots s_n'$ is a run of M and $L(\sigma_M^-) \not\models \varphi$. Given Proposition 1, P2 believes that run $\sigma_M^+ = s_0 s_1 \ldots s_n$ has a non-zero probability to have been executed. Therefore, because P2 believes any of the two runs $\sigma_M^+ = s_0 s_1 \ldots s_n$ and σ_M^- of M where $L(\sigma_M^+) \models \varphi$ and $L(\sigma_M^-) \not\models \varphi$ could have been executed, π is opacity-enforcing. $\square$

We introduce Algorithm 1 to compute a belief-based winning strategy for P1. The algorithm initializes a set $Y_0 = V$ and iteratively computes Y_{k+1} from Y_k for $k \geq 0$. At each iteration k, Algorithm 1 computes the set of states from which it can reach a state in V_F with a positive probability while ensuring to stay within the set Y_k with probability 1. The algorithm uses the following function

$$\mathsf{Allow}(v, Y) = \{(a, X) \in \mathcal{A}_1 \mid \mathsf{Post}_\mathcal{G}(v, (a, X)) \subseteq Y\}, \forall v \in V, Y \subseteq V$$

where $\mathsf{Post}_\mathcal{G}(v, (a, X)) = \{v' \in V \mid \Delta(v, (a, X), v') > 0\}$ is the set of states reachable from state v by playing action (a, X). By definition, by playing an action from the allowed set $\mathsf{Allow}(v, Y)$, P1 can be sure to stay within state set Y. Let for a state $v = ((s, q), B_1, B_2) \in V$, $[v]_\sim$ denote the set of belief-equivalent states with v such that $[v]_\sim = \{((s'q'), B_1', B_2') \in V \mid B_1' = B_1, B_2' = B_2\}$. Then, let

$$\mathsf{Allow}([v]_\sim, Y) = \bigcap_{v' \in [v]_\sim} \mathsf{Allow}(v', Y).$$

Thus, we have that an action is allowed for P1 to play at a state v if and only if that action is allowed for P1 at all of its belief-equivalent states v'.

Next, we define the following progress function given a set of states $Y \subseteq V$ and a set $R \subseteq Y$,

$$\mathsf{Prog}(R, Y) = \{v \in Y \mid \exists (a, X) \in \mathsf{Allow}([v]_\sim, Y), \mathsf{Post}_\mathcal{G}(v, (a, X)) \cap R \neq \varnothing\}.$$

The progress function yields a set of states from which P1 has at least one allowed action to reach R in the next state.

In the inner loop of Algorithm 1 (Lines 4–7), we fix the Y_k and iteratively update R_i until a fixed point is reached. Intuitively, the fixed point is a set of states from which P1 can ensure to reach V_F with probability ≥ 0 and stay within Y_k with probability 1. Then, we set this fixed point in the inner loop as Y_{k+1} and continue with the computation until the fixed point is reached at the outer loop $Y_{n+1} = Y_n$ for some $n \geq 0$. The belief-based winning region for P1 is $\mathsf{OWin}(\mathcal{G}) = Y_n$.

We next show that $\mathsf{OWin}(\mathcal{G})$ obtained using Algorithm 1 is, in fact, the opacity-enforcing almost-sure winning region for P1 and at every state in $\mathsf{OWin}(\mathcal{G})$, P1 has an opacity-enforcing strategy to reach R with probability one.

Algorithm 1. Belief-Based Opacity-Enforcing ASW Region

Inputs: POMDP augmented with 2-belief $\mathcal{G}$.
Outputs: P1's opacity-enforcing ASW region, $\mathsf{OWin}(\mathcal{G})$.
1: $k \leftarrow 0$; $Y_k \leftarrow V$
2: **repeat**
3:     $i \leftarrow 0$; $R_i \leftarrow V_F$
4:     **repeat**
5:         $R_{i+1} \leftarrow R_i \cup \mathsf{Prog}(R_i, Y_k)$
6:         $i \leftarrow i + 1$
7:     **until** $R_{i+1} = R_i$
8:     $Y_{k+1} \leftarrow R_i$; $k \leftarrow k + 1$
9: **until** $Y_{k+1} = Y_k$
10: **return** $\mathsf{OWin}(\mathcal{G}) \leftarrow Y_k$.

Lemma 4. $\mathsf{OWin}(\mathcal{G})$ *computed by Algorithm 1 is opacity-enforcing winning for P1.*

Proof is in the appendix. From the obtained $\mathsf{OWin}(\mathcal{G})$, P1's opacity-enforcing belief-based strategy can be defined as function $\pi_1^* : \mathsf{OWin}(\mathcal{G}) \to 2^{\mathcal{A}_1}$ such that

$$\pi_1^*(v) = \{(a, X) \in \mathcal{A}_1 \mid (a, X) \in \mathsf{Allow}([v]_\sim, \mathsf{OWin}(\mathcal{G}))\}. \tag{1}$$

Thus, at each state $v \in \mathsf{OWin}(\mathcal{G})$, P1 has to play an action in $\pi_1^*(v)$. Also, by the construction of $\mathsf{Allow}(\cdot)$, for every states $v = ((s, q), B_1, B_2)$ and $v' = ((s', q'), B_1', B_2')$, if $B_1 = B_1'$ and $B_2 = B_2'$, then $\pi_1^*(v) = \pi_1^*(v')$.

Theorem 2. *By playing the strategy π_1^* defined in Eq. 1, P1 ensures that the game eventually reaches V_F.*

The proof for the theorem is provided in the appendix.

Complexity Analysis: The algorithm first encodes the secret goal φ into a DFA. This step takes a doubly-exponential time in the size of φ in the worst case [6,19]. However, for commonly seen LTL$_f$ formulas in robotic planning and AI applications, this translation is tractable. The POMDP augmented with 2-beliefs has $O(|S||Q|2^{|S||Q|}2^{|S||Q|})$ reachable states in the worst case. Each non-goal state $v = ((s, q), B_1, B_2)$ has $O(|S|)$ transitions with non-zero probabilities for each action $(a, X) \in A \times 2^\Gamma$ in the worst case. Accordingly, using appropriate data structures, mainly hash tables, it takes $O(|A||S||Q|2^{2|S||Q|+|S|})$ to construct the POMDP augmented with 2-beliefs. Computing an opacity-enforcing winning strategy for $\mathcal{G}$ takes a quadratic time to the size of $\mathcal{G}$ in the worst case. Therefore, the final running time of our algorithm is $O(|A|^2|S|^2|Q|^2 2^{(4|S||Q|+2|S|)})$.

Example 3. (Part III) We show how to use Algorithm 1 to obtain the opacity-enforcing winning region for the fragment of the opacity-enforcing game in Fig. 2c. From Fig. 2c, we have, $v_1 = \{((s_1, 0), B_1^0, B_2^0)\}$, $v_2 =$

$\{((s_3,0),\{(s_3,0)\},\{(s_2,0),(s_3,0)\})\}$, $v_3 = \{((s_5,1),\{(s_5,1)\},\{(s_5,1)\})\}$ and $v_4 = \{((s_5,1),\{(s_5,1)\},\{(s_4,0),(s_5,1)\})\}$.

We start with $Y_0 = \{v_1, v_2, v_3, v_4\}$ where v_1 is the initial state in Fig. 2c, and v_4 is the final state.

Moving on to the inner loop, we initialize the set R_0 as $\{v_4\}$ since it is the only final state in the fragment under consideration. Next, we compute $\mathsf{Prog}(R_0, Y_0)$, which yields $\{v_2, v_4\}$. Subsequently, R_1 is updated as $\{v_2, v_4\}$, and we compute $\mathsf{Prog}(R_1, Y_0)$, resulting in $\{v_1, v_2, v_4\}$. This set represents the fixed point for this iteration. Consequently, we update Y_1 as $\{v_1, v_2, v_4\}$, which is the fixed point for the outer loop and the opacity-enforcing winning region.

3.2 When to Stop Tracking P2's Beliefs?

In the construction of the POMDP augmented with 2-beliefs presented in Definition 9, we face the issue of exponential growth of the state space. To mitigate the issue, we use the minimal DFA accepting φ. This reduces the state space of $\mathcal{M}$ and $\mathcal{G}$. Additionally, in certain situations, we can stop tracking P2's belief by leveraging certain properties in the specification automaton and P1's winning region computed from the product POMDP without opacity constraints.

First, we introduce some notions.

Given a DFA $\mathcal{I}$, we define the subautomata for each state $q \in Q$ as follows:

Definition 11. *Given a DFA* $\mathcal{I} = (Q, \Sigma, \delta, \iota, F)$, *for any* $q \in Q$,

- *good suffixes* $\mathcal{L}_q$ *is the language of the DFA* $\mathcal{I}_q = (Q, \Sigma, \delta, q, F)$.
- *bad suffixes* $\overline{\mathcal{L}}_q$ *is the language of the DFA* $\overline{\mathcal{I}}_q = (Q, \Sigma, \delta, q, Q \setminus F)$.

Given two languages $\mathcal{L}_1$ and $\mathcal{L}_2$, represented by DFAs $\mathcal{I}_1 = (Q_1, \Sigma, \delta_1, \iota_1, F_1)$ and $\mathcal{I}_2 = (Q_2, \Sigma, \delta_2, \iota_2, F_2)$, checking if $\mathcal{L}_1 \subseteq \mathcal{L}_2$ is equivalent to see whether $\mathcal{L}_1 \cap \overline{\mathcal{L}}_2 = \varnothing$, which can be achieved by checking whether the language of the product DFA $\mathcal{I}_1 \times \mathcal{I}_2 = (Q_1 \times Q_2, \Sigma, \delta, (\iota_1, \iota_2), F_1 \times (Q \setminus F_2))$ where $\delta((q_1, q_2), \sigma) = (\delta_1(q_1, \sigma), \delta_2(q_2, \sigma))$ for each $(q_1, q_2) \in Q_1 \times Q_2$ and $\sigma \in \Sigma$, is empty or not.

Next, we solve P1's belief-based winning strategy without enforcing opacity to the observer. In this case, we need not to keep track of P2's belief.

Definition 12 (Product POMDP augmented with P1's belief). *Given the product POMDP* $\mathcal{M} = (S \times Q, A, \Gamma, T, (s_0, q_0), Z, \mathcal{O}, B_1^0, B_2^0, S \times F)$, *the product POMDP augmented with P1's belief is a tuple*

$$\mathcal{H} = \langle H, \mathcal{A}_1, H_F, \mathcal{T}, h_0 \rangle$$

in which 1. $H = \{((s, q), B_1) \mid s \in S, q \in Q, B_1 \subseteq (S \times Q)\}$ *is the set of states, where* B_1 *is P1's belief; 2.* $\mathcal{A}_1$ *is the set of control-perception actions that can be taken by P1, as given in* $\mathcal{M}$; *3.* $h_0 = ((s_0, q_0), B_1^0)$ *is the initial state, where* B_1^0 *is the initial belief as in* $\mathcal{M}$; *4.* $H_F = \{((s_F, q_F), B_1^F) \mid (s_F, q_F) \in (S \times F), B_1^F \subseteq (S \times F)\}$ *is the set of final states, which ensure P1 satisfies the objective* φ; *and 5.* $\mathcal{T} : H \times \mathcal{A}_1 \to \mathcal{D}(H)$ *is the probabilistic transition function. First, all states in* H_F *are sink states. For a state* $h \in H \setminus H_F$, *for each action* $(a, X) \in \mathcal{A}_1$ *and state* $h' = ((s', q'), B_1') \in H$, $\mathcal{T}(h, (a, X), h') = \mathcal{T}((s, q), a, (s', q'))$ *if* $B_1' = \mathsf{Post}_{\mathcal{M}}(B_1, a) \cap \mathcal{O}((s', q'), X)$, *and otherwise,* $\mathcal{T}(h, (a, X), h') = 0$.

P1's belief-based winning strategy in $\mathcal{H}$ can be solved using a slight modification of Algorithm 1: Let

$$\mathsf{Allow}(h, Y) = \{(a, X) \in \mathcal{A}_1 \mid \mathsf{Post}_{\mathcal{H}}(h, (a, X)) \subseteq Y\}, \forall h \in H, Y \subseteq H.$$

and $\mathsf{Allow}([h]_\sim, Y) = \bigcap_{h' \in [h]_\sim} \mathsf{Allow}(h', Y).$ where $[((s, q), B_1))]_\sim = \{((s'q'), B_1') \in H \mid$
$B_1' = B_1\}$.

The progress function is defined as

$$\mathsf{Prog}(R, Y) = \{h \in Y \mid \exists (a, X) \in \mathsf{Allow}([h]_\sim, Y), \mathsf{Post}_{\mathcal{H}}(h, (a, X)) \cap R \neq \varnothing\}.$$

We have that Y_k is initialized to H and R_i is initialized to H_F. Intuitively, these modification allows P1 to compute belief-based winning strategy only considering his own belief.

Thus, without constructing the POMDP with two-beliefs $\mathcal{G}$, we can obtain $\mathsf{Win}(\mathcal{G}) = \{((s, q), B_1, B_2) \in V \mid ((s, q), B_1) \in \mathsf{Win}(\mathcal{H})\}$ that includes a set of states P1 can enforce a winning play (with/without opacity to P2).

Remark 2. $\mathsf{OWin}(\mathcal{G}) \subseteq \mathsf{Win}(\mathcal{G}).$

The following Lemma is crucial: It enables us to determine if an opacity-enforcing winning strategy exists without enumerating all beliefs that can be reached in the POMDP augmented with 2-beliefs $\mathcal{G}$.

Lemma 5. *For any state $v = ((s, q), B_1, B_2) \in V$ where $v \in \mathsf{Win}(\mathcal{G})$, if there exists $p \in Q$ s.t. $(s, p) \in B_2$ and $\mathcal{L}_q \subseteq \overline{\mathcal{L}}_p$, then $v \in \mathsf{OWin}(\mathcal{G})$.*

Proof. Given that $v \in \mathsf{Win}(\mathcal{G})$, P1 can enforce a play $\rho = s_0(a_0, X_0)s_1(a_1, X_1) \ldots s_n$ where $s_0 = s$ such that $\delta(q, L(\rho)) \in F$. As a result, $L(\rho) \in \mathcal{L}_q$ is a good suffix for the language $\mathcal{L}(\mathbf{A})$ given the state q.

Given that $\mathcal{L}_q \subseteq \overline{\mathcal{L}}_p$, $L(\rho) \in \overline{\mathcal{L}}_p$. Let $\mathsf{p} = ((s_0, q_0), B_1^0, B_2^0)(a_0, X_0) \ldots ((s_n, q_n),$ $B_1^n, B_2^n)$ be in $\mathcal{G}$, the play corresponding to the play ρ. That is, the projection of p onto S is ρ. Let $p_n = \delta(\mathsf{p}, L(\rho))$. It holds that $(s_n, p_n) \in B_2^n$ by the construction of P2's belief. Because $L(\rho) \subseteq \overline{\mathcal{L}}_p$, then $p_n \in Q \smallsetminus F$. Further since $B_1^n \subseteq B_2^n$ and $B_1^n \subseteq S \times F$, then $B_2^n \cap (S \times (Q \smallsetminus F)) \neq \varnothing$ and $B_2^n \cap S \times F \neq \varnothing$. The play ρ is opaque and winning for P1. $\square$

Definition 13 (Augmented POMDPs with Trimmed 2-Beliefs). *Given the product POMDP $\mathcal{M}$ and the winning region of P1 without opacity constraint $\mathsf{Win}(\mathcal{G})$, the Augmented POMDPs with Trimmed 2-Beliefs is a tuple*

$$\mathcal{G}' = \langle W : = \mathsf{Win}(\mathcal{G}) \cup \mathsf{Win}(\mathcal{H}), \mathcal{A}_1, W_F : = V_F \cup \mathsf{Win}(\mathcal{H}), \Delta', v_0\rangle$$

where W is the set of states; $\mathcal{A}_1$ and v_0 are from Definition 9; W_F is the set of goals states and is the union of V_F (the goal states of $\mathcal{G}$, as in Definition 9) and $\mathsf{Win}(\mathcal{H})$; and Δ' is the probabilistic transition function s.t. all the goal states in W_F are sink states, and for each non-goal state $w = ((s, q), B_1, B_2) \in \mathsf{Win}(\mathcal{G}) \smallsetminus W_F$,

- *if there exists $(s,p) \in B_2$ such that $\mathcal{L}_q \subseteq \overline{\mathcal{L}_p}$, $\Delta'(w,((s,q),B_1)) = 1$. That is, with probability one, P1 reaches a state in $\mathrm{Win}(\mathcal{H})$ and stop tracking P2's belief.*
- *otherwise, for each action $(a,X) \in \mathcal{A}_1$, $\Delta'(w,(a,X),((s',q'),B'_1,B'_2)) = T((s,q),a,(s',q'))$, where $B'_1 = \mathrm{Post}_\mathcal{M}(B_1,a) \cap \mathcal{O}((s',q'),X)$ and $B'_2 = \mathrm{Post}_\mathcal{M}(B_2,A) \cap \mathcal{O}((s',q'),X \cap \Gamma_2)$.*

We now solve the above augmented POMDPs with trimmed 2-beliefs using Algorithm 1. P1 follows the policy computed from $\mathcal{G}'$ until a state $((s,q),B_1) \in \mathrm{Win}(\mathcal{H})$ or a goal state V_F is reached. If a state $((s,q),B_1) \in \mathrm{Win}(\mathcal{H})$ is reached, then P1 transitions to the winning policy of the game $\mathcal{H}$ and adhere to it.

4   Experimental Validation

In this section, we demonstrate the use of the developed opacity-enforcing planning for P1, an autonomous robot tasked with delivering medicine in a GPS denied environment. Figure 3a shows the environment setup. The robot is tasked with first reaching the base station, A in the gridworld, to pick up essential supplies and then delivering the critical supplies to one of the critical zones B and C. This task is specified by the LTL$_f$ formula $\varphi = \neg(B \wedge C) \cup (A \wedge \Diamond(B \wedge C))$. The robot is expected to keep this task opaque from the adversarial observer.

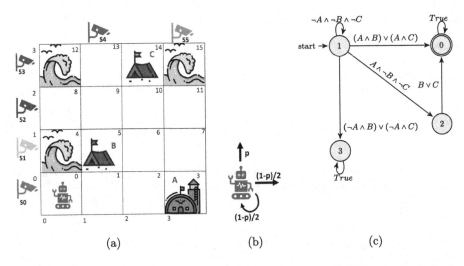

(a)   (b)   (c)

Fig. 3. (a) Autonomous robot in an adversarial environment. (b) The stochasticity in the environment when robot chooses to traverse N. (c) Specification DFA for $\varphi = \neg(B \wedge C) \cup (A \wedge (B \wedge C))$.

The environment is monitored by the sensors $\{S_0, S_1, S_2, S_3, S_2, S_5\}$ as shown in the Fig. 3a. The sensors S_0, S_1, S_2 and S_3 respectively cover the rows 0, 1, 2 and 3, and the sensors S_4 and S_5 cover the columns 1 and 3 respectively. Only

S_4 is a secured sensor. Sensors S_0 and S_2 are precision range sensors and each returns the exact position of the robot if the robot is in a cell in the range of the sensor and returns FALSE otherwise. The other sensors are Boolean range sensors and each returns TRUE if the robot is in a cell that is covered by the sensor and returns FALSE if not. The robot has partial observations of its position, obtained from the deployed sensor network. The eavesdropping adversary has partial observation of the robot's position from unsecured sensors. Due to limited communication constraint, for any belief B and any control action in A, the set of perception actions for the robot to select along with the control action includes querying any two sensors that cover at least one of the possible next states, i.e. , states in $\mathsf{Post}_{\mathcal{M}}(B, A)$. The robot traverses through the environment with four possible actions $\{\mathsf{N}, \mathsf{S}, \mathsf{E}, \mathsf{W}\}$. When the robot performs an action, its actuators guarantee that it reaches the *intended* cell with a probability p, make the robot to *stay* in the same cell with a probability $(1-p)/2$, and transit the robot to the cell that is 90 degrees (clockwise) apart from the intended cell with a probability $(1-p)/2$ as shown in the Fig. 3b. The gridworld environment is surrounded by bouncy walls. If the agent takes an action and hits a wall, it remains in the original cell. The cells 4, 12, and 15 are the unsafe zones for the robot. In a unsafe zone is reached, the robot gets stuck.

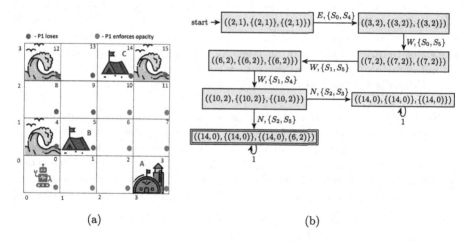

(a)   (b)

Fig. 4. (a) The results of experimentation for every initial state in the gridworld. (b) Fragment of opacity-enforcing and not enforcing run starting from cell 2.

Figure 3c shows the DFA encoding the temporal formula φ. This DFA has a non-accepting sink state state 3, and an accepting goal state 0. Figure 4 shows results obtained from solving the opacity-enforcing winning strategy for the robot. Each green dot represents an initial state from which the robot has a opacity-enforcing winning strategy. Each red dot represent a state that has no winning strategy.

We discuss our results for the case where P1's initial position is cell 0 and both P1 and P2 are aware of this. Figure 4b shows a fragment of a run in the modified opacity-enforcing game for the above example. In the shown fragment, we have an opacity-enforcing winning run and a run that does not enforce opacity when the robot starts from the cell 0 and has reached the cell 2. Here, we encode a state as $((s, q), B_1, B_2)$ where (s, q) represents the robot's true state with s being the cell number and q the automata state, B_1 is the robot's belief of its position and B_2 is the observer's belief of the robots position. From Fig. 4b, we observe that the sensor query of the robot affects the enforcement of opacity at state $((10, 2), \{(10, 2)\}, \{(10, 2)\})$. From state $((10, 2), \{(10, 2)\}, \{(10, 2)\})$, for the robot to reach the critical zone C it can take action N along with one perception action, i.e. , a query of a pair of sensors selected from $\{S_2, S_5\}$, $\{S_2, S_3\}$, $\{S_2, S_4\}$ or $\{S_2, S_1\}$ since any of these possible perception actions will enable the robot know it's true next state. Querying $\{S_2, S_3\}$ or $\{S_2, S_1\}$ does not enforce opacity as they provide the observer with enough information to ensure that the robot is precisely in the critical zone C.

To assess the effectiveness of the opacity-enforcing policy, we conducted empirical evaluations through statistical analysis. We performed $50,000$ iterations of the simulation in the gridworld setup, starting from the initial state $((0, 1), \{(0, 1)\}, \{(0, 1)\})$, for which the robot has an opacity-enforcing winning strategy. We let the robot to randomly select actions from the winning strategy computed from $\mathsf{Win}(\mathcal{H})$. We observed the robot achieved task satisfaction in all iterations while enforcing opacity in 47.07% of the iterations. In the remaining 52.93% of iterations, the robot successfully satisfied the task specification but did not enforce opacity. If the robot uses the strategy computed from $\mathsf{Win}(\mathcal{G})$, with probability 1, the robot not only satisfies the task specification but also enforces opacity.

Next, we see how the trimming technique reduces computation. The construction of $\mathcal{G}$ resulted in a total of $135,334$ states, and with the use of the modified construction of the game, i.e. on constructing the game $\mathcal{G}'$ with the trimming of the beliefs results in a total of $51,763$. This significant reduction of the state space aids in faster computation of the almost-sure winning region/strategy.

The experiments were executed on an Intel (R) Core (TM) i7 CPU @ 3.2 GHz.

5   Conclusion and Future Work

In this work, we formulated and solved the problem of synthesizing a joint control and active perception for an agent in a stochastic environment to satisfy a secret temporal goal while enforcing opacity against a passive observer with partial observations. Building on the modeling and solution approaches, several future directions can be considered: First, a quantitative variant of opacity-enforcing planning remains to be investigated. For example, from the set of states at which P1 does not have a winning and opacity-enforcing strategy, is it possible to compute a strategy that ensures winning with probability $\geq p$ and opacity with probability $\geq \epsilon$? This would enable a more nuanced understanding of opacity enforcement and the development of strategies that account for varying degrees of opacity and task performance. Second, opacity-enforcement can be considered for the agent and the observer with different capabilities in control and perception. In this work, the information to the observer is a subset of the agent's information. This assumption is no longer valid if the observer has a different information channel that is uncontrollable and inaccessible by the agent. It would be interesting to know which subsets of opacity-enforcing games are decidable.

A   Proof for Lemma 4

Proof. Let N be the index where $Y_N = Y_{N+1}$. To prove $Y_N = \mathsf{OWin}(\mathcal{G})$, we prove the following: 1. $\mathsf{OWin}(\mathcal{G}) \subseteq Y_j$ for all $0 < j \le N$, using induction. Since $Y_0 = V$, we have that $\mathsf{OWin}(\mathcal{G}) \subseteq Y_0$. Assume that $\mathsf{OWin}(\mathcal{G}) \subseteq Y_i$ for some $i > 0$. Then, Y_{i+1} includes any state that has a strategy to reach V_F with positive probability while staying within Y_i. Thus, for any state in $Y_i \setminus Y_{i+1}$, P1 cannot stay within Y_i with probability one. However, P1 has a strategy to ensure that the game stays within $\mathsf{OWin}(\mathcal{G})$ and thereby Y_i, given $\mathsf{OWin}(\mathcal{G}) \subseteq Y_i$. As Y_{i+1} only removes the states that cannot ensure to stay within $\mathsf{OWin}(\mathcal{G})$, we have that $\mathsf{OWin}(\mathcal{G}) \subseteq Y_{i+1}$.

2. $Y_N \setminus \mathsf{OWin}(\mathcal{G}) = \varnothing$, by contradiction. Assume that there exists a state $v \in Y_N \setminus \mathsf{OWin}(\mathcal{G})$. Then, by construction, for any $v \in R_k \cup \mathsf{Prog}(R_k, Y_N)$, P1 has a strategy to reach V_F with positive probability in finitely many steps. Let E_T be the event that "starting from a state in Y_N, a run reaches a state in V_F within T steps" and let $\gamma > 0$ be the minimal probability for an event E_T to occur for any state $v \in Y_N$. Then, the probability of not reaching a state in V_F in infinitely many steps can be upper bounded by $\lim_{k \to \infty} (1-\gamma)^k = 0$. Therefore, for any $v \in Y_N$, P1 has a strategy to ensure a state in V_F is reached with probability one. This contradicts the assumption $v \notin \mathsf{OWin}(\mathcal{G})$. Thus, $Y_N = \mathsf{OWin}(\mathcal{G})$. □

B   Proof for Theorem 2

Proof. Consider the level sets $R_0, \dots, R_N$ obtained using Algorithm 1 with input $\mathsf{OWin}(\mathcal{G})$. Let $0 < k \le K$ be a level and $v \in R_k$ be a state. Suppose there exists an action $(a, X) \in \pi_1^*(v)$ s.t. $\mathsf{Post}_{\mathcal{G}}(v, (a, X)) \in R_{k-1}$. Since the probability of taking action (a, X) is non-zero, the level strictly decreases with a positive probability. Moreover, for any action in $\pi_1^*(v)$ and its probabilistic outcomes, the game remains within $\mathsf{OWin}(\mathcal{G})$ with probability 1. Let E_n denote the event of "Reaching R_{k-1} from a state in R_k in n steps". It follows $\lim_{n \to \infty} P(E_n) = 1$. By repeating for levels $k = K, \dots, 1$, we conclude $R_0 = V_F$ is reached with probability 1. □

References

1. Bérard, B., Chatterjee, K., Sznajder, N.: Probabilistic opacity for Markov decision processes. Inf. Process. Lett. **115**(1), 52–59 (2015)

2. Bertrand, N., Genest, B., Gimbert, H.: Qualitative determinacy and decidability of stochastic games with signals. J. ACM (JACM) **64**(5), 1–48 (2017)
3. Bryans, J.W., Koutny, M., Mazaré, L., Ryan, P.Y.: Opacity generalised to transition systems. Int. J. Inf. Secur. **7**, 421–435 (2008)
4. Bryans, J.W., Koutny, M., Ryan, P.Y.: Modelling opacity using Petri nets. Electron. Notes Theor. Comput. Sci. **121**, 101–115 (2005)
5. Cassez, F., Dubreil, J., Marchand, H.: Synthesis of opaque systems with static and dynamic masks. Formal Methods Syst. Des. **40**, 88–115 (2012)
6. De Giacomo, G., Favorito, M.: Compositional approach to translate LTLf/LDLf into deterministic finite automata. In: Proceedings of the International Conference on Automated Planning and Scheduling, vol. 31, pp. 122–130 (2021)
7. De Giacomo, G., Vardi, M.Y.: Linear temporal logic and linear dynamic logic on finite traces. In: Proceedings of the Twenty-Third International Joint Conference on Artificial Intelligence, pp. 854–860. ACM (2013)
8. Hélouët, L., Marchand, H., Ricker, L.: Opacity with powerful attackers. IFAC-PapersOnLine **51**(7), 464–471 (2018)
9. Ji, Y., Yin, X., Lafortune, S.: Opacity enforcement using nondeterministic publicly known edit functions. IEEE Trans. Autom. Control **64**(10), 4369–4376 (2019)
10. Keroglou, C., Hadjicostis, C.N.: Probabilistic system opacity in discrete event systems. Discret. Event Dyn. Syst. **28**, 289–314 (2018)
11. Lin, F.: Opacity of discrete event systems and its applications. Automatica **47**(3), 496–503 (2011)
12. Maubert, B., Pinchinat, S., Bozzelli, L.: Opacity issues in games with imperfect information. arXiv preprint arXiv:1106.1233 (2011)
13. Mazaré, L.: Using unification for opacity properties. In: Proceedings of the 4th IFIP WG1, vol. 7, pp. 165–176 (2004)
14. Saboori, A.: Verification and enforcement of state-based notions of opacity in discrete event systems. University of Illinois at Urbana-Champaign (2010)
15. Saboori, A., Hadjicostis, C.N.: Notions of security and opacity in discrete event systems. In: IEEE Conference on Decision and Control, pp. 5056–5061 (2007)
16. Saboori, A., Hadjicostis, C.N.: Verification of initial-state opacity in security applications of des. In: 9th International Workshop on Discrete Event Systems, pp. 328–333. IEEE (2008)
17. Saboori, A., Hadjicostis, C.N.: Opacity-enforcing supervisory strategies via state estimator constructions. IEEE Trans. Autom. Control **57**(5), 1155–1165 (2012)
18. Saboori, A., Hadjicostis, C.N.: Current-state opacity formulations in probabilistic finite automata. IEEE Trans. Autom. Control **59**(1), 120–133 (2014)
19. Wolper, P.: Constructing automata from temporal logic formulas: a tutorial. In: Brinksma, E., Hermanns, H., Katoen, J.-P. (eds.) EEF School 2000. LNCS, vol. 2090, pp. 261–277. Springer, Heidelberg (2001). https://doi.org/10.1007/3-540-44667-2_7
20. Wu, Y.-C., Lafortune, S.: Comparative analysis of related notions of opacity in centralized and coordinated architectures. Discret. Event Dyn. Syst. **23**(3), 307–339 (2013)
21. Wu, Y.-C., Lafortune, S.: Synthesis of insertion functions for enforcement of opacity security properties. Automatica **50**(5), 1336–1348 (2014)
22. Xie, Y., Yin, X., Li, S.: Opacity enforcing supervisory control using nondeterministic supervisors. IEEE Trans. Autom. Control **67**(12), 6567–6582 (2021)
23. Zhou, Y., Chen, Z., Liu, Z.: Verification and enforcement of current-state opacity based on a state space approach. Eur. J. Control **71**, 100795 (2023)

A Game-Theoretic Analysis of Auditing Differentially Private Algorithms with Epistemically Disparate Herd

Ya-Ting Yang[✉], Tao Zhang, and Quanyan Zhu

New York University, Brooklyn, NY, USA
{yy4348,tz636,qz494}@nyu.edu

Abstract. Privacy-preserving AI algorithms are widely adopted in various domains, but the lack of transparency might pose accountability issues. While auditing algorithms can address this issue, machine-based audit approaches are often costly and time-consuming. Herd audit, on the other hand, offers an alternative solution by harnessing collective intelligence. Nevertheless, the presence of epistemic disparity among auditors, resulting in varying levels of expertise and access to knowledge, may impact audit performance. An effective herd audit will establish a credible accountability threat for algorithm developers, incentivizing them to uphold their claims. In this study, our objective is to develop a systematic framework that examines the impact of herd audit on algorithm developers using the Stackelberg game approach. The optimal strategy for auditors emphasizes the importance of easy access to relevant information, as it increases the auditors' confidence in the audit process. Similarly, the optimal choice for developers suggests that herd audit is viable when auditors face lower costs in acquiring knowledge. By enhancing transparency and accountability, herd audit contributes to the responsible development of privacy-preserving algorithms.

1 Introduction

AI and algorithmic decision-making have become pervasive in both business and society. However, the lack of transparency in algorithms poses significant challenges when it comes to accountability and responsibility. When algorithms are treated as "black boxes" and their inner workings remain undisclosed, it becomes difficult to ensure that they perform as intended and adhering to necessary standards [19]. One specific category of algorithms that exemplifies this challenge is privacy-preserving algorithms [10]. These algorithms have been widely embraced by product developers to safeguard the privacy of consumer users. For instance, prominent platforms like Facebook Ad Recommendation Systems, Google SQL, and Safari to have integrated differential privacy into their products to provide enhanced privacy protection. Nevertheless, verifying such claims can be arduous and intricate, for example see [4,9,20].

The adoption of privacy-preserving algorithms is a positive step toward addressing privacy concerns in AI applications. However, the lack of transparency

© The Author(s), under exclusive license to Springer Nature Switzerland AG 2023
J. Fu et al. (Eds.): GameSec 2023, LNCS 14167, pp. 349–368, 2023.
https://doi.org/10.1007/978-3-031-50670-3_18

and the inability to scrutinize these algorithms can cast doubt on the effectiveness of the privacy measures. Greater efforts need to be made to establish independent auditing mechanisms or standardized practices that allow for the verification and validation of privacy claims made by algorithmic systems. By promoting transparency and accountability, we ensure that privacy-preserving algorithms genuinely deliver on their promises and provide the necessary protection for users' privacy.

Herd Audit: Auditing algorithms [3,29] play a crucial role in tackling this challenge. However, traditional machine-based audit methods like direct scraping, sock puppet, and carrier puppet often necessitate the development of custom computer programs to gather data. Not only can these approaches be expensive, but they also consume a significant amount of time. A cost-effective alternative approach to auditing involves leveraging citizen science and the principles of crowd-sourcing to establish a democratic audit process that engages a diverse population of end users. This concept gives rise to *herd-audit* (or group-audit) approaches, which incentivize end users to contribute collectively to the auditing process.

By harnessing the power of collective intelligence [26], herd-audit approaches tap into the knowledge, experiences, and perspectives of a wide range of individuals. This distributed effort can result in a more comprehensive and diverse audit of algorithms. Implementing herd-audit approaches not only addresses the limitations of traditional methods but also promotes transparency and inclusivity. It allows a broader segment of the population to actively participate in holding algorithmic systems accountable. By empowering end users as auditors, we can foster a more democratic and participatory approach to algorithmic auditing while minimizing costs and time investments (Fig. 1).

Fig. 1. A herd of diverse end-users act as auditors to inspect the AI algorithm used in the developed product.

Epistemic Disparity: One significant challenge in implementing herd-audit approaches is the presence of epistemic disparity [13,17]. Not all users possess the same level of expertise or knowledge required to conduct comprehensive audits of algorithms. There is a wide distribution of knowledge and variations in users' access to relevant information. These variations stem from differences in cognitive and reasoning capabilities among users. A user-auditor who approaches the task with meticulous scrutiny is more likely to arrive at accurate outcomes during the evaluation process. Conversely, a user-auditor with limited cognitive resources may inadvertently provide opportunities for algorithm developers to evade their responsibility. To some extent, the incorporation of audit into the algorithm design process itself establishes a reliable accountability mechanism for algorithm developers. When algorithms are transparent and capable of herd-audit, any deviations from the claimed performance are readily evident. For example, in relation to privacy protection, if an algorithm designer asserts the inclusion of differential privacy and the algorithm undergoes herd-audit, any inconsistencies between the claimed privacy assurances and the actual performance will be revealed. This accountability mechanism acts as an incentive for algorithm developers to uphold their claims and create responsible algorithms.

Game-Theoretic Framework: To design an effective herd-audit mechanism, this work aims to develop a comprehensive system framework that investigates the influence of herd-audit on algorithm developers. One of the primary aims of this framework is to gain insights into the behavior and motivations of developers when subjected to herd-audit. To accomplish the goal, the system framework adopts a Stackelberg game approach [12,27]. In this approach, the developer assumes the role of the leader and determines the desired level of performance for differential privacy. The followers, comprising idiosyncratic end-users or auditors, are selected from a user population characterized by varying levels of epistemic capabilities. The proposed framework assumes that algorithms and their associated guarantees are clearly communicated to the end-users through a privacy protection agreement. This leader-and-follower structure allows us to analyze the optimal strategies employed by both the developer and the auditors, providing insights into the potential noncompliant behaviors of developers in worst-case scenarios. Furthermore, it helps in understanding how to incentivize developers to create responsible algorithms and explore the accountability mechanisms that emerge in situations of transparency.

In order to capture the magnitude of epistemic disparity experienced by end-users (auditors), this work employs a rational inattention model [5,28], which takes into account the costs associated with accessing information during the decision-making process. It acknowledges that end-users have limited cognitive resources and are unable to fully attend to or process all available information. One notable advantage of this model is its incorporation of the concept of mental effort, which provides a high-level abstraction of cognitive processes. This abstraction facilitates the characterization of cognitive processes at a population level by aggregating diverse behaviors. The rational inattention model has played an important role recently in explaining various economic phenomena involving individuals with cognitive constraints, such as consumer behavior, investment decisions, and financial markets.

We analyze the concept of epistemic disparity among auditors, characterized by the epistemic factor, which measures the difficulty of accessing information. We find that auditors with lower epistemic factors exhibit higher audit confidence, indicating a better audit performance. Furthermore, our investigation reveals that herd audit is a viable approach when auditors face lower costs in accessing information. In such circumstances, the algorithm developer is less likely to deviate significantly from their claims. Our findings highlight the importance of reducing epistemic injustice as well as lowering information costs in order to enhance the effectiveness of herd audit. By doing so, we can foster a more reliable and accountable environment for the development and evaluation of algorithms.

Paper Organization: The rest of this paper is organized as follows. Section 2 provides an overview of recent research on algorithm auditing and explores related game-theoretic approaches. Section 3 introduces the rational inattention model, which captures the reasoning process of herd auditors with varying levels of epistemic disparity. In Sect. 4, a Stackelberg herd audit game is proposed for a specific class of privacy-preserving algorithms. Section 5 discusses the equilibrium solutions that characterize the behaviors of both auditors and developers. Finally, Sect. 6 concludes the paper, summarizing the key findings and implications.

2   Related Work

Algorithm auditing refers to the process of evaluating and assessing the algorithms used in various systems or applications to ensure they are fair, transparent, unbiased, and comply with ethical standards [3]. In the context of differential privacy, several machine-based verification methods have been proposed for privacy-preserving algorithms [4,9,20]. These machine auditors are capable of acquiring a large number of samples and utilizing the law of large numbers to estimate the probability of outcomes and verify the algorithms. While there has been a rich literature on citizen science and its applications in crowdsensing [34], crowdsourcing [40], and crowd defense [32], herd-audit is a concept in its infancy. It not only reduces auditing costs but also poses a reputational threat to product developers, as public perception [14], and consequently market value, can be directly influenced by the results of the audit.

The disparity in the capability of herd behaviors has been extensively studied in collective intelligence [8,11,26,37]. The literature has examined the performance [30], reliability [25], and trustworthiness [36] of participants engaged in outsourced tasks. In order to address this variability, researchers have employed processes such as risk and reputation management [1,38] to understand the differences among participants. Notably, many studies have placed emphasis on the careful selection of participants to effectively achieve the goals of the task at hand. This body of work primarily focuses on understanding the impact of cognitive variabilities in herd audits, as participants exhibit diverse cognitive abilities and processes in assessing whether algorithms perform as claimed.

Numerous studies have focused on the modeling and understanding of cognitive behaviors in humans. One prominent example is cognitive-behavioral theory [15,16,24], which integrates cognitive and behavioral perspectives to elucidate how thoughts, beliefs, and cognitive processes shape behavior. This theory underscores the significance of cognitive processes in interpreting and responding to environmental stimuli, while highlighting the potential for modifying these processes to achieve desired behavioral outcomes. More recently, efforts have been directed toward developing the theory of mind [2], which involves attributing mental states such as beliefs, desires, intentions, and emotions to comprehend and predict individuals' behavior. In our work, we adopt a higher-level approach by employing the concept of rational inattention. Rational inattention establishes a connection between mental effort and information gathering and processing, examining the influence of effort on individuals' decision-making processes. This approach, as studied in [35], provides an economics and mathematical framework that formally analyzes how decision-makers acquire and process information while considering associated costs. Utilizing this framework offers several advantages, including a high-level abstraction of mental effort, which encompasses attention, perception, memory, and problem-solving in cognitive functioning. Additionally, it facilitates the exploration of the interplay between cognition and decision-making processes, enabling a focused investigation into the cognitive impact on audit decisions.

A game-theoretic approach is commonly employed to capture the threat posed by followers in dynamic games, such as ultimatum games [33], Stackelberg games [6], bargaining games [18], as well as in mechanism design problems involving contract designs [7,39] and incentive mechanisms [23,41]. In this study, we adopt a Stackelberg game framework to evaluate the dependability of herd auditors, who are modeled as randomly sampled idiosyncratic individuals, and to assess the opportunities available to the product designer to evade compliance. Recently, there has been increased interest in the investigation of evasion behaviors within the context of detection and machine problems. This includes studying evasion behaviors, exploiting evasion-aware detection methods to counter intelligent and strategic adversaries [22], as well as developing evaders for subsequent test of collaborative cognition-assisted detector [31]. Additionally, the literature on cyber deception has explored evasion strategies to gain a better understanding of attackers' stealthiness [21].

3 Herd Auditors with Epistemic Disparity

In the context of herd-auditing an algorithm, the auditor is uncertain about the true state $\omega \in \Omega = \{g, b\}$, where g indicates the null hypothesis, implying that the algorithm is consistent with the claim, while b is for the alternative hypothesis, meaning that the algorithm does not comply. The prior belief of state ω can be denoted as $\mu(\omega)$, implying the auditor's uncertainty in the algorithm's compliance.

In order to reduce the uncertainty, the auditor can obtain information s about the state according to the information obtaining strategy $d(s|\omega)$. More specifically, s can be viewed as the outcome of the algorithm, and $d(s|\omega)$ indicates how the auditor accesses (obtains) it. The information s together with the obtaining strategy leads to a posterior belief of the state $\mu(\omega|s) = \frac{\mu(\omega)d(s|\omega)}{\sum_{\omega} \mu(\omega)d(s|\omega)}$.

Based on the information s (correspondingly, the posterior belief $\mu(\omega|s)$), the auditor can select an element from a finite action set $a \in \mathcal{A} = \{T, F\}$, where T means reporting algorithm compliance, while F indicates reporting non-compliance. The decision rule $\delta : \mathcal{S} \mapsto \mathcal{A}$ aims to maximize the expected utility of $u(\omega, a)$, where $u : \Omega \times \mathcal{A} \mapsto \mathbb{R}$ is the utility of choosing action a when the state is ω (Fig. 2).

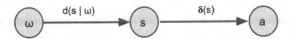

Fig. 2. An illustration of how the auditor performs audit. The auditor acquires information s about the unknown state ω using strategy d and then makes a decision a using strategy δ.

However, the acquisition of information can incur costs, which can be viewed as the discrepancy between the prior belief $\mu(\omega)$ and the posterior belief $\mu(\omega|s)$ regarding the state ω. In conventional rational inattention research, a common method to model the cost is through the lens of Shannon mutual information. Furthermore, due to variations in epistemic disparities, the cost incurred for accessing information (i.e., reduction in uncertainty) differs among auditors. To account for this, we introduce the concept of an *epistemic factor* for each auditor, denoted as λ, which quantifies the differences in the cost experienced by different auditors when reducing the same amount of uncertainty. The larger value of λ implies harder access to relevant information, as the cost for the same amount of uncertainty reduction becomes higher.

To this end, the auditor's objective becomes

$$\max_{d,\delta} \mathbb{E}[u(\omega, a)] - \lambda I(\omega; s), \tag{1}$$

where the expected utility is given by

$$\mathbb{E}[u(\omega, a)] = \sum_{\omega} \sum_{a} \mu(\omega) u(\omega, a) \sum_{s:\delta(s)=a} d(s|\omega) \tag{2}$$

represents the expected utility in correct audit, and

$$I(\omega; s) = \sum_{\omega} \sum_{s} d(s|\omega) \mu(\omega) \ln \frac{d(s|\omega)}{\sum_{\omega} d(s|\omega) \mu(\omega)} \tag{3}$$

stands for the information cost.

3.1 Bayes Hypothesis Testing as the Auditor's Decision Rule

Conventionally, Bayes hypothesis testing deals with the optimization problem

$$\max_{\delta} \mathbb{E}[u(\omega, a)] = \sum_{\omega} \sum_{a} \mu(\omega) u(\omega, a) \sum_{\delta(s)=a} d(s|\omega) \tag{4}$$

with given distributions for both hypotheses $d(s|g)$ and $d(s|b)$ during decision-making, which coincides with the first term in the auditor's objective (1). For null hypothesis $d(s|g)$ and alternative hypothesis $d(s|b)$, the expected utility can be reformulated as

$$\mathbb{E}[u(\omega, a)] = \sum_{\omega}\sum_{a} \mu(\omega)u(\omega, a) \sum_{\delta(s)=a} d(s|\omega)$$

$$= \mu(g)u(g, F) + \mu(b)u(b, F)$$

$$+ \sum_{\delta(s)=T} \mu(g)\big[u(g, T) - u(g, F)\big]d(s|g) - \mu(b)\big[u(b, F) - u(b, T)\big]d(s|b).$$

$$(5)$$

Therefore, the auditor should decide $\delta(s) = T$ if $\mu(g)\big[u(g, T) - u(g, F)\big]d(s|g) > \mu(b)\big[u(b, F) - u(b, T)\big]d(s|b)$. More formally, the optimal decision rule can be written as

$$\delta^*(s) = \begin{cases} T, & \frac{\mu(b)d(s|b)}{\mu(g)d(s|g)} < \frac{u(g,T)-u(g,F)}{u(b,F)-u(b,T)}, \\ F, & \frac{\mu(b)d(s|b)}{\mu(g)d(s|g)} > \frac{u(g,T)-u(g,F)}{u(b,F)-u(b,T)}, \\ \{T, F\}, & \frac{\mu(b)d(s|b)}{\mu(g)d(s|g)} = \frac{u(g,T)-u(g,F)}{u(b,F)-u(b,T)}, \end{cases} \quad (6)$$

which leads us to a threshold decision rule and can be viewed as making a decision based on the posteriors. We then represent the optimal decision rule corresponding to given $d(s|g)$ and $d(s|b)$ as $\delta_d^*(s)$. We denote the signal set partitioned by $\delta_d^*(s)$ as

$$\begin{cases} S_{d,T} = \{s : \delta_d^*(s) = T\}, \\ S_{d,F} = \{s : \delta_d^*(s) = F\}. \end{cases} \quad (7)$$

3.2   Auditor's Choice of the Information Strategy

With the optimal decision rule δ_d^*, the auditor's objective becomes

$$\max_{d,\delta} \mathbb{E}[u(\omega, a)] - \lambda I(\omega; s), \text{ with } \delta = \delta_d^*, \quad (8)$$

which leads to the constrained optimization problem

$$\max_{d} \sum_{\omega}\sum_{a} \mu(\omega)u(\omega, a) \sum_{s:\delta_d^*(s)=a} d(s|\omega)$$

$$- \lambda \sum_{\omega}\sum_{s} d(s|\omega)\mu(\omega) \ln \frac{d(s|\omega)}{\sum_{\omega} d(s|\omega)\mu(\omega)}, \quad (9)$$

$$\text{s.t. } \sum_{s} d(s|\omega) = 1, d(s|\omega) \geq 0, \forall s \in \mathcal{S}, \forall \omega \in \Omega.$$

To analyze the problem, we use the method of Lagrange multipliers and denote

$$J(d, y) = \sum_{\omega}\sum_{a} \mu(\omega)u(\omega, a) \sum_{s:\delta_d^*(s)=a} d(s|\omega)$$

$$- \lambda \sum_{\omega}\sum_{s} d(s|\omega)\mu(\omega) \ln \frac{d(s|\omega)}{\sum_{\omega} d(s|\omega)\mu(\omega)} - \sum_{\omega} y(\omega)d(s|\omega),$$

with the last term corresponding to the constraint that $d(s|\omega)$ should be a conditional probability mass function.

Then, for $d(s|g)$ with $s \in S_{d,T}$, according to the first-order and the second-order condition,

$$\frac{\partial J(d,y)}{\partial d(s|g)} = \mu(g)u(g,T) - \lambda\mu(g)\log(\frac{d(s|g)}{v(s)}) - y(g) = 0,$$

$$\frac{\partial^2 J(d,y)}{\partial d(s|g)^2} = -\lambda\mu(g)\frac{\mu(b)d(s|b)}{d(s|g)v(s)} \leq 0,$$

where $v(s) = \sum_\omega d(s|\omega)\mu(\omega)$. Letting $\log(y'(g)) = \frac{y(g)}{\lambda\mu(g)}$ leads to the following $d(s|g)$ that maximizes (9).

$$\lambda\mu(g)\left[\frac{u(g,T)}{\lambda} - \log(\frac{d(s|g)}{v(s)}) - \log y'(g)\right] = 0,$$

$$d(s|g) = \frac{v(s)\exp(\frac{u(g,T)}{\lambda})}{y'(g)}.$$

Similarly, for $d(s|g)$ with $s \in S_{d,F}$ and $d(s|b)$, we arrive at

$$d(s|g) = \begin{cases} \frac{v(s)\exp(\frac{u(g,T)}{\lambda})}{\sum_{S_{d,T}} v(s)\exp(\frac{u(g,T)}{\lambda})+\sum_{S_{d,F}} v(s)\exp(\frac{u(g,F)}{\lambda})}, & s \in S_{d,T}, \\ \frac{v(s)\exp(\frac{u(g,F)}{\lambda})}{\sum_{S_{d,T}} v(s)\exp(\frac{u(g,T)}{\lambda})+\sum_{S_{d,F}} v(s)\exp(\frac{u(g,F)}{\lambda})}, & s \in S_{d,F}, \end{cases} \tag{10}$$

$$d(s|b) = \begin{cases} \frac{v(s)\exp(\frac{u(b,T)}{\lambda})}{\sum_{S_{d,T}} v(s)\exp(\frac{u(b,T)}{\lambda})+\sum_{S_{d,F}} v(s)\exp(\frac{u(b,F)}{\lambda})}, & s \in S_{d,T}, \\ \frac{v(s)\exp(\frac{u(b,F)}{\lambda})}{\sum_{S_{d,T}} v(s)\exp(\frac{u(b,T)}{\lambda})+\sum_{S_{d,F}} v(s)\exp(\frac{u(b,F)}{\lambda})}, & s \in S_{d,F}. \end{cases} \tag{11}$$

The corresponding posterior belief $\mu(g|s) = \frac{\mu(g)d(s|g)}{\sum_\omega \mu(\omega)d(s|\omega)} = \frac{\mu(g)d(s|g)}{v(s)}$ can then be written as

$$\mu(g|s) = \begin{cases} \frac{\mu(g)\exp(\frac{u(g,T)}{\lambda})}{\sum_{S_{d,T}} v(s)\exp(\frac{u(g,T)}{\lambda})+\sum_{S_{d,F}} v(s)\exp(\frac{u(g,F)}{\lambda})}, & s \in S_{d,T}, \quad (12a) \\ \frac{\mu(g)\exp(\frac{u(g,F)}{\lambda})}{\sum_{S_{d,T}} v(s)\exp(\frac{u(g,T)}{\lambda})+\sum_{S_{d,F}} v(s)\exp(\frac{u(g,F)}{\lambda})}, & s \in S_{d,F}, \quad (12b) \end{cases}$$

Note that (12a) can be viewed as the posterior belief $\mu(g|s)$ given s that results in an action $a = T$ (i.e., $\mu(g|s) = \mu(g|T)$, $s \in S_{d,T}$), while (12b) can be viewed as the posterior belief $\mu(g|s)$ given s that results in an action $a = F$ (i.e., $\mu(g|s) = \mu(g|F)$, $s \in S_{d,F}$). A similar expression can be found for $\mu(b|s)$.

$$\mu(b|s) = \begin{cases} \frac{\mu(b)\exp(\frac{u(b,T)}{\lambda})}{\sum_{S_{d,T}} v(s)\exp(\frac{u(b,T)}{\lambda})+\sum_{S_{d,F}} v(s)\exp(\frac{u(b,F)}{\lambda})}, & s \in S_{d,T}, \quad (13a) \\ \frac{\mu(b)\exp(\frac{u(b,F)}{\lambda})}{\sum_{S_{d,T}} v(s)\exp(\frac{u(b,T)}{\lambda})+\sum_{S_{d,F}} v(s)\exp(\frac{u(b,F)}{\lambda})}, & s \in S_{d,F}. \quad (13b) \end{cases}$$

Remark 1. For an auditor with epistemic factor λ, the information obtaining strategy represented by the conditional probability $d(s|\omega)$ is chosen if its resulting posterior belief $\mu(\omega|s)$ maximizes the value of $\mathbb{E}[u(\omega, a)] - \lambda I(\omega; s)$, where $u(\omega, a)$ is the utility and $I(\omega; s)$ is the mutual information between ω and s that measures the expected reduction of uncertainty from the prior belief to the posterior belief caused by $d(s|\omega)$.

The $\mu(g|s), \forall s \in S_{d,T}$, can also be interpreted as the *audit confidence* for making the decision $a = T$ when observing the information s. Since $u(g, T) > u(g, F)$, it is evident that auditors with a smaller epistemic factor λ have higher confidence in the audit process. This implies that auditors who can easily access relative information are more likely to perform better in the audit.

4   Stackelberg Herd Audit Game

To examine the impact of herd-audit on the algorithm developer's incentive to create irresponsible algorithms, we formulate the interplay between the herd-auditor (she) and the algorithm developer (he) as a Stackelberg herd audit game in a specific context of privacy-preserving algorithms.

4.1   Connection to Differential Privacy

To begin with, we first give the definition of ϵ-differential privacy.

Definition 1 (ϵ-DP). *A (randomized) mechanism $M : \mathcal{D} \mapsto \mathcal{B}$ is ϵ-differentially private (ϵ-DP) if for every pair of neighboring inputs $D_1, D_2 \in \mathcal{D}$, and for every (measurable) output set $B \in \mathcal{B}$, the probabilities of events $M(D_1; F, \epsilon) \in B$ and $M(D_2; F, \epsilon) \in B$ are closer than a factor of $\exp(\epsilon)$:*

$$Pr(M(D_1; F, \epsilon) \in B) \le \exp(\epsilon) \cdot Pr(M(D_2; F, \epsilon) \in B). \qquad (14)$$

In the context of differential privacy, consider a scenario in which there is a public-known privacy protection agreement that requires ϵ' privacy budget. However, since more privacy budget (which means decreasing the privacy protection and making the results more distinguishable) often leads to better algorithm accuracy, the algorithm developer has the incentive to use some $\epsilon > \epsilon'$ when performing the algorithm, which creates irresponsibility. Hence, we consider the state $\omega = g$ means $\epsilon = \epsilon'$ and the state $\omega = b$ means $\epsilon > \epsilon'$. Since privacy protection is often achieved by adding noise, it is assumed that for a given algorithm M with input dataset D, the privacy budget ϵ results in an output distribution $p(M(D)|\epsilon)$ for later usage.

4.2   Problem Setting for the Developer

Considering that there are two types of algorithm developers g and b, and they play a mixed strategy for executing ϵ, which are $q(\epsilon|g)$ and $q(\epsilon|b)$, respectively (for discrete choices of ϵ, $\epsilon \in \mathcal{E}$). Each ϵ results in an algorithm accuracy $A(\epsilon)$, where $A : \mathcal{E} \mapsto \mathbb{R}$, under the assumption that a larger ϵ leads to better accuracy.

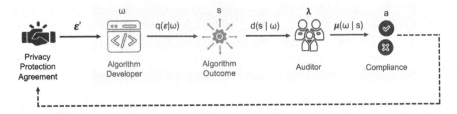

Fig. 3. The Stackelberg herd audit game involves a privacy protection agreement that specifies a privacy budget ϵ'. In this game, the algorithm developer takes the first step by selecting a strategy $q(\epsilon|\omega)$, determining the value of ϵ to be executed. Subsequently, the auditor, characterized by an epistemic factor λ, decides how to acquire information that influences her audit confidence (μ in the figure and r in the context.)

Assumption 1. *Given an algorithm M with input dataset D, a privacy budget ϵ results in an unique output distribution $p(M(D)|\epsilon)$.*

Assumption 2. *For a given algorithm, the algorithmic accuracy under the privacy budget $\epsilon \in \mathcal{E} \subseteq \mathbb{R}$ is governed by $A : \mathcal{E} \mapsto \mathbb{R}$, and it is increasing in $\epsilon \in \mathcal{E}$.*

In this context, the developer's choice of strategy $q(\epsilon|\omega)$ given his own type ω will lead to the distributions for the two hypotheses

$$Q_g(s) = \sum_\epsilon p(s|\epsilon)q(\epsilon|g), \tag{15}$$

$$Q_b(s) = \sum_\epsilon p(s|\epsilon)q(\epsilon|b), \tag{16}$$

where $p(s|\epsilon)$ is the output distribution $p(M(D)|\epsilon)$ in Assumption 1.

Responsible Developer. For a responsible algorithm developer, the mixed strategy $q(\epsilon|g)$ should have mass 0 for $\epsilon > \epsilon'$, which means that he always provides privacy protection at least comply with the agreement. Moreover, in order to maximize $A(\epsilon)$, a responsible algorithm developer tends to put all the mass on $\epsilon = \epsilon'$ since $A(\epsilon) < A(\epsilon'), \forall \epsilon < \epsilon'$.

Proposition 1 (Responsible Developer's Strategy). *A responsible developer's mixed strategy reduces to a pure strategy by letting all the mass on $\epsilon = \epsilon'$. Hence, $Q_g(s) = \sum_\epsilon p(s|\epsilon)q(\epsilon|g) = p(s|\epsilon')$.*

Irresponsible Developer. However, it is important to consider various scenarios involving an irresponsible algorithm developer who prioritizes algorithm performance and disregards compliance with the agreement. If there is no auditor or no penalty imposed when the developer fails to pass the audit (i.e., when the auditor determines that $a = F$), the irresponsible developer can choose an extremely large value for ϵ. Consequently, it is reasonable to assume that a penalty will be enforced if the irresponsible developer is detected. In such a situation, the irresponsible developer may attempt to maximize the probability of avoiding penalties, which corresponds to the probability of the auditor deciding $a = T$.

Assumption 3. *The irresponsible algorithm developer's mixed strategy will not put any mass on $\epsilon = \epsilon'$. That is, $q(\epsilon'|b) = 0$.*

4.3 Revisiting the Auditor's Problem

Considering that the penalty term for the irresponsible developer is influenced by the actions of the auditor, particularly in terms of whether the irresponsible developer is caught or not, it is necessary to reexamine the problem from the auditor's perspective when the developer is also a strategic player aiming to evade the audit.

First, we reformulate the auditor's problem by setting $u(g, T) = u(b, F) = 0$ and setting the penalty terms $u(b, T)$ and $u(g, F)$ with negative values. However, within the context of DP, it is important to note that the auditor does not possess the discretion in determining the distributions for both hypotheses. In particular, the distributions for these hypotheses are predefined by the output distribution $p(s|\epsilon)$ and the developer's mixed strategy. What the auditor can decide is the probability of establishing her audit confidence r. In other words, the auditor determines the audit confidence $r(g|s)$ and $r(b|s)$, which favors the null and the alternative hypothesis, respectively, given the observed signal s. These audit confidences are analogous to those provided in (12) and (13).

Assumption 4. *Assume that $u(b, T) < 0$ and $u(g, F) < 0$ are the negative utilities for making wrong audit decision.*

Given the distributions for the two hypotheses $Q_g(s)$ and $Q_b(s)$, the auditor aims to achieve the following:

$$\max_r \ u(g, F) \underbrace{\sum_s Q_g(s)r(b|s)}_{\text{false positive error}} + u(b, T) \underbrace{\sum_s Q_b(s)r(g|s)}_{\text{false negative error}}$$

$$- \lambda \, \mathbb{E}_s \left[D_{KL}(r(\omega|s)\|\mu(\omega)) \right],$$

(17)

where the first two terms put negative weights on the audit error, and the last term quantifies the expected reduction in uncertainty for the state ω, measured in terms of the Kullback-Leibler (KL) divergence:

$$\lambda \sum_s \left[\sum_\epsilon p(s|\epsilon)q(\epsilon|g) + \sum_\epsilon p(s|\epsilon)q(\epsilon|b) \right] \sum_\omega r(\omega|s) \log \frac{r(\omega|s)}{\mu(\omega)}.$$

This term encapsulates the epistemic disparity and its influence on the informational cost by the parameter λ.

Note that the decision of $r(g|s)$ and $r(b|s)$ already incorporate the information obtaining strategy $d(s|\omega)$ for the auditor since $r(\omega|s) = \frac{\mu(\omega)d(s|\omega)}{\sum_\omega \mu(\omega)d(s|\omega)}$. (The observation follows from Remark 1 in Sect. 3.2.)

Remark 2. It is important to distinguish between the probability distributions of an output sample s under both hypotheses, $Q_g(s), Q_b(s)$, and the information obtaining strategy for the auditor, $d(s|g), d(s|b)$. Note that $Q_g(s), Q_b(s)$ are given by the output distribution based on Assumption 1 and the developer's mixed strategy $q(\epsilon|g), q(\epsilon|b)$, and that the information obtaining strategy on how to observe output sample $d(s|g), d(s|b)$ mainly comes from the auditor's preference over utility $u(\omega, a)$ and the epistemic factor λ, which leads to the audit confidence (posterior belief of the state) $r(g|s)$ and $r(b|s)$.

4.4   Revisit the Irresponsible Developer's Problem

Until now, the irresponsible developer's objective has become the following.

$$\max_{q(\cdot|b)} \sum_\epsilon q(\epsilon|b)A(\epsilon) + \beta \sum_s \left[\sum_\epsilon p(s|\epsilon)q(\epsilon|b)\right] r(g|s), \tag{18}$$

with $r(g|s)$ comes from the auditor's problem. The former term is the expected algorithm accuracy, and the latter term corresponds to the false negative rate of the auditor's decision, which is the rate of the irresponsible developer successfully passing the audit (and thus, the irresponsible developer seeks to maximize it). Note that $\beta > 0$ indicates the irresponsible developer's preference on the two goals (the successful passing rate and the expected accuracy). The interaction between two players is illustrated in Fig. 3.

5   Equilibrium Analysis

For simplicity, we initially consider a scenario where the cardinality of the set $\mathcal{E}$ is three; i.e., $|\mathcal{E}| = 3$ with $\mathcal{E} = \{\epsilon_l, \epsilon_m, \epsilon_h\}$, where $\epsilon_l < \epsilon_m < \epsilon_h$ and it's assumed that the claimed differential privacy budget is $\epsilon' = \epsilon_l$. A more general case will be presented in Sect. 5.3. Furthermore, we assume that the distinguishability— quantified by distance or discrepancy measures such as the Kullback-Leibler divergence—between the output distributions $p(\cdot|\epsilon)$ and $p(\cdot|\epsilon')$ increases when the difference between ϵ and ϵ' expands. Then, $Q_g(s) = \sum_\epsilon p(s|\epsilon)q(\epsilon|g) = p(s|\epsilon') = p(s|\epsilon_l)$ and $Q_b(s) = \sum_\epsilon p(s|\epsilon)q(\epsilon|b) = p(s|\epsilon_m)q(\epsilon_m|b) + p(s|\epsilon_h)q(\epsilon_h|b)$.

5.1   The Auditor's Optimal Strategy

The decision-making process of the auditor is captured by the following optimization problem:

$$\max_r \; u(g, F) \sum_s \left[\sum_\epsilon p(s|\epsilon)q(\epsilon|g)\right] r(b|s) + u(b, T) \sum_s \left[\sum_\epsilon p(s|\epsilon)q(\epsilon|b)\right] r(g|s)$$
$$- \lambda \, \mathbb{E}_s \left[D_{kL}(r(\omega|s)\|\mu(\omega))\right],$$
$$\text{s.t.} \sum_\omega r(\omega|s) = 1, r(w|s) \geq 0, \forall w \in \{g, b\}, \forall s \in \mathcal{S}.$$

$$\tag{19}$$

In (19), the KL divergence term with a negative sign is concave with respect to the decision variables $r(\cdot)$ given fixed priors $\mu(\cdot)$. Therefore, the combination of the terms in the objective function forms a weighted sum of concave functions. This makes the overall objective function concave. Given the linear constraints, the feasibility set is convex. Hence, the optimization problem (19) is a concave maximization over a convex set.

The Lagrangian corresponding to (19) is then given by

$$
\begin{aligned}
J(r, y, z) = {} & u(g, F) \sum_s \left[\sum_\epsilon p(s|\epsilon) q(\epsilon|g) \right] r(b|s) \\
& + u(b, T) \sum_s \left[\sum_\epsilon p(s|\epsilon) q(\epsilon|b) \right] r(g|s) - \lambda \sum_s \left[\sum_\epsilon p(s|\epsilon) q(\epsilon|g) \right. \\
& \left. + \sum_\epsilon p(s|\epsilon) q(\epsilon|b) \right] \sum_\omega r(\omega|s) \log \frac{r(\omega|s)}{\mu(\omega)} - y r(g|s) - z r(b|s),
\end{aligned} \tag{20}
$$

where $y \in \mathbb{R}$ and $z \in \mathbb{R}$ are the associated Lagrange multipliers. Then, the first-order condition concerning $r(g|s)$ implies

$$
\begin{aligned}
\frac{\partial J(r)}{\partial r(g|s)} = {} & u(b, T) \Big[p(s|\epsilon_m) q(\epsilon_m|b) + p(s|\epsilon_h) q(\epsilon_h|b) \Big] \\
& - \lambda \Big[p(s|\epsilon_l) + p(s|\epsilon_m) q(\epsilon_m|b) + p(s|\epsilon_h) q(\epsilon_h|b) \Big] \left(\log \frac{r(g|s)}{\mu(g)} + 1 \right) - y \\
= {} & 0.
\end{aligned}
$$

Hence, we obtain

$$
u(b, T) Q_b(s) - \lambda v(s) \left(\log \frac{r(g|s)}{\mu(g)} + 1 \right) - y = 0,
$$

$$
\frac{u(b, T) Q_b(s)}{\lambda v(s)} - \left(\frac{y}{\lambda v(s)} + 1 \right) = \log \frac{r(g|s)}{\mu(g)}.
$$

By letting $\log y'(s) = \left(\frac{y}{\lambda v(s)} + 1 \right)$, $r(g|s)$ can be written as,

$$
r(g|s) = \frac{\mu(g) \exp\left(\frac{u(b,T) Q_b(s)}{\lambda v(s)} \right)}{\mu(g) \exp\left(\frac{u(b,T) Q_b(s)}{\lambda v(s)} \right) + \mu(b) \exp\left(\frac{u(g,F) Q_g(s)}{\lambda v(s)} \right)}, \tag{21}
$$

Following the similar procedure for $r(b|s)$ yields

$$
r(b|s) = \frac{\mu(b) \exp\left(\frac{u(g,F) Q_g(s)}{\lambda v(s)} \right)}{\mu(g) \exp\left(\frac{u(b,T) Q_b(s)}{\lambda v(s)} \right) + \mu(b) \exp\left(\frac{u(g,F) Q_g(s)}{\lambda v(s)} \right)}. \tag{22}
$$

Proposition 2. *The strategy specified by (21) and (22) is optimal for the auditor with epistemic factor λ.*

Remark 3. The results coincide with the intuition. We first take a look at $r(g|s)$. Recall that $\frac{u(b,T)}{\lambda}$ is negative. Consider the case where the penalty term $u(b,T)$ is the same across all the auditors, we can see that the auditor with a larger epistemic factor (harder to access to information) λ achieves $r(g|s)$ that is closer to $\mu(g)$. Combining with the auditor's objective in the maximization problem (19), it means that the larger-λ auditor might have a larger false negative error. Similarly, for $r(b|s)$, the larger-λ auditor might have a larger false positive error.

5.2   The Irresponsible Developer's Optimal Strategy

The irresponsible developer endeavors to enhance algorithmic accuracy while concurrently maximizing the probability of evading detection by the auditor, thereby increasing the likelihood of being perceived as a responsible developer. Hence, the irresponsible developer's decision-making can be described by the following optimization problem:

$$\max_{q(\cdot|b)} \left[q(\epsilon_m|b)A(\epsilon_m) + q(\epsilon_h|b)A(\epsilon_h) \right]$$
$$+ \beta \sum_s \left[p(s|\epsilon_m)q(\epsilon_m|b) + p(s|\epsilon_h)q(\epsilon_h|b) \right] r(g|s). \tag{23}$$

By leveraging $q(\epsilon_m|b) = 1 - q(\epsilon_h|b)$, we rewrite the problem (23) as follows:

$$\max_{q(\epsilon_l|b)} \quad A(\epsilon_h) + \beta \sum_s r(g|s)p(s|\epsilon_h),$$
$$+ \left\{ \left[A(\epsilon_m) - A(\epsilon_h) \right] + \beta \sum_s r(g|s) \left[p(s|\epsilon_m) - p(s|\epsilon_h) \right] \right\} q(\epsilon_m|b). \tag{24}$$

Since the first two terms $A(\epsilon_h) + \beta \sum_s r(g|s)p(s|\epsilon_h)$ are independent of $q(\cdot|b)$, (24) suggests the following strategy for the irresponsible developer:

$$\begin{cases} q(\epsilon_m|b) = 1, & \text{if } A(\epsilon_m) - A(\epsilon_h) + \beta \sum_s r(g|s) \left[p(s|\epsilon_m) - p(s|\epsilon_h) \right] > 0 \\ q(\epsilon_h|b) = 1, & \text{otherwise.} \end{cases}$$

That is, the irresponsible developer has a pure strategy by choosing either $q(\epsilon_m|b) = 1$ or $q(\epsilon_h|b) = 1$.

Proposition 3. *If $A(\epsilon)$ is increasing in ϵ, the irresponsible developer always chooses the largest ϵ (namely, ϵ_h in the case) if $r(g|s) = r(g|s'), \forall s, s' \in \mathcal{S}$.*

Proof. We sketch the proof for $|\mathcal{S}| = 2$ with $\mathcal{S} = \{s_1, s_2\}$. In this example, $p(s_1|\epsilon_m) + p(s_2|\epsilon_m) = 1$ and $p(s_1|\epsilon_h) + p(s_2|\epsilon_h) = 1$, then $r(g|s_1)[p(s_1|\epsilon_m) - p(s_1|\epsilon_h)] + r(g|s_2)[p(s_2|\epsilon_m) - p(s_2|\epsilon_h)] = 1 - 1 = 0$ if $r(g|s_1) = r(g|s_2)$. Hence, $A(\epsilon_m) - A(\epsilon_h) + \sum_s r(g|s)[p(s|\epsilon_m) - p(s|\epsilon_h)] < 0$ in the case where $A(\epsilon_m) < A(\epsilon_h)$, which leads to $q(\epsilon_m|b) = 0$ and $q(\epsilon_h|b) = 1$.

That is, in the case where $\lambda = \infty$, $r(g|s) = \mu(g), \forall s \in \mathcal{S}$, the irresponsible developer's best response is $q(\epsilon_h|b) = 1$ (regardless of how much $A(\epsilon_h)$ is greater than $A(\epsilon_m)$ and the value of β). It implies that when the auditor's epistemic factor λ is extremely large, indicating a lack of information acquisition, the auditor may refrain from obtaining crucial information. Consequently, the irresponsible developer is likely to consistently maximize their violations of the claim.

Remark 4. The irresponsible developer always violates as much as possible when the epistemic factor for the auditor $\lambda = \infty$.

Remark 5. When the auditor's epistemic factor λ is small, indicating easy access to relevant information, an irresponsible developer is more likely to exhibit a lower tendency to violate.

Remark 6. If the auditor's epistemic factor λ is large, it is likely that an irresponsible developer with a larger β (placing more value on the success rate of passing audits) will also exhibit a tendency to violate the claim more severely.

5.3   Multiple Choices of Privacy Budgets

In the case when there are more than three choices of privacy budgets; i.e., $\mathcal{E} = \{\epsilon_0, \cdots \epsilon_i, \cdots, \epsilon_{|\mathcal{E}|-1}\}$. We assume that the claimed privacy budget is $\epsilon' = \epsilon_0$. The characterizations of the auditor's optimal strategy hold for this general case. That is, the auditor's strategy is given by

$$r(g|s) = \frac{\mu(g) \exp\left(\frac{u(b,T)Q_b(s)}{\lambda v(s)}\right)}{\mu(g) \exp\left(\frac{u(b,T)Q_b(s)}{\lambda v(s)}\right) + \mu(b) \exp\left(\frac{u(g,F)Q_g(s)}{\lambda v(s)}\right)}, \tag{25}$$

$$r(b|s) = \frac{\mu(b) \exp\left(\frac{u(g,F)Q_g(s)}{\lambda v(s)}\right)}{\mu(g) \exp\left(\frac{u(b,T)Q_b(s)}{\lambda v(s)}\right) + \mu(b) \exp\left(\frac{u(g,F)Q_g(s)}{\lambda v(s)}\right)}, \tag{26}$$

where $Q_b(s) = \sum_{\mathcal{E}\backslash\epsilon_0} p(s|\epsilon)q(\epsilon|b)$ and $v(s) = p(s|\epsilon_0) + \sum_{\mathcal{E}\backslash\epsilon_0} p(s|\epsilon)q(\epsilon|b)$. The irresponsible developer's problem (23) is generalized to

$$\sum_\epsilon q(\epsilon|b)A(\epsilon) + \beta \sum_s \left[\sum_\epsilon p(s|\epsilon)q(\epsilon|b)\right] r(g|s)$$

$$= \sum_{\epsilon_i \in \mathcal{E}} q(\epsilon_i|b)\left[A(\epsilon_i) + \beta \sum_s r(g|s)p(s|\epsilon_i)\right]. \tag{27}$$

The irresponsible developer determines his optimal pure strategy ϵ to maximize (27). Specifically, the irresponsible developer assigns $q(\epsilon|b) = 1$ to the ϵ that achieves the largest $\left[A(\epsilon) + \beta \sum_s r(g|s)p(s|\epsilon)\right]$.

Proposition 4. *The irresponsible developer's optimal strategy is choosing the ϵ that maximizes* $\left[A(\epsilon) + \beta \sum_s r(g|s)p(s|\epsilon)\right]$.

Auditor's Audit Confidence and Epistemic Factor. With respect to Fig. 4, the optimal solution to the auditor's problem given by (21) and (22) establishes a relationship between the epistemic factor λ and the auditor's confidence $r(\cdot|s)$ under fixed utilities $u(\omega, a)$.

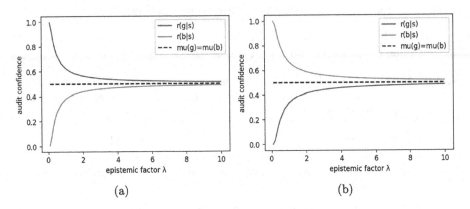

Fig. 4. The trend between the auditor's audit confidence (posterior belief) and the auditor's epistemic factor. Left: the case where $\left(u(g, F)\frac{Q_g(s)}{v(s)} - u(b, T)\frac{Q_b(s)}{v(s)} \right) < 0.$ $(\mu(g) = \mu(b) = 0.5, u(b, T) = u(g, F) = -1, Q_b(s)/v(s) = 0.25)$ Right: the case where $\left(u(b, T)\frac{Q_b(s)}{v(s)} - u(g, F)\frac{Q_g(s)}{v(s)} \right) < 0.$ $(\mu(g) = \mu(b) = 0.5, u(b, T) = u(g, F) = -1, Q_b(s)/v(s) = 0.85)$

Taking the partial derivative of $r(g|s)$ with respect to λ yields

$$\frac{\partial r(g|s)}{\partial \lambda} = \frac{\mu(g)\mu(b)\left(u(g, F)\frac{Q_g(s)}{v(s)} - u(b, T)\frac{Q_b(s)}{v(s)} \right) \exp\left(\frac{u(g,F)\frac{Q_g(s)}{v(s)} + u(b,T)\frac{Q_b(s)}{v(s)}}{\lambda} \right)}{\lambda^2 y'(s)^2}.$$

(28)

Here, if the developer is irresponsible, then he never chooses a privacy budget ϵ that is equal to the claimed budget ϵ_0. Hence, $\left(u(g, F)\frac{Q_g(s)}{v(s)} - u(b, T)\frac{Q_b(s)}{v(s)} \right) \neq 0.$ The term $\frac{\partial r(g|s)}{\partial \lambda}$ is (strictly) positive if $\left(u(g, F)\frac{Q_g(s)}{v(s)} - u(b, T)\frac{Q_b(s)}{v(s)} \right) > 0$ and (strictly) negative otherwise. When $\left(u(g, F)\frac{Q_g(s)}{v(s)} - u(b, T)\frac{Q_b(s)}{v(s)} \right) < 0$, $r(g|s)$ is close to 1 when λ goes close to 0. Furthermore, the audit confidences for g and b become closer to 0.5 when λ increases, which coincides with the setting that higher λ leads to a weaker incentive to acquire more accurate information, thereby inducing lower audit confidences. Similarly,

$$\frac{\partial r(b|s)}{\partial \lambda} = \frac{\mu(g)\mu(b)\left(u(b, T)\frac{Q_b(s)}{v(s)} - u(g, F)\frac{Q_g(s)}{v(s)} \right) \exp\left(\frac{u(g,F)\frac{Q_g(s)}{v(s)} + u(b,T)\frac{Q_b(s)}{v(s)}}{\lambda} \right)}{\lambda^2 y'(s)^2}.$$

(29)

The term $\frac{\partial r(b|s)}{\partial \lambda}$ is positive if $\left(u(b,T)\frac{Q_b(s)}{v(s)} - u(g,F)\frac{Q_g(s)}{v(s)} \right) > 0$ and negative otherwise. When $\left(u(b,T)\frac{Q_b(s)}{v(s)} - u(g,F)\frac{Q_g(s)}{v(s)} \right) < 0$, $r(b|s)$ is close to 1 when λ goes close to 0. Furthermore, the audit confidences for g and b become closer to 0.5 when λ increases, which coincides with the setting that higher λ leads to a weaker incentive to acquire more accurate information, thereby inducing lower audit confidences. Note that audit confidence is determined by optimizing the objective, which consists of penalties for audit errors and costs associated with information acquisition. In this context, it is important to carefully select reasonable intervals for $u(\omega, a)$ and λ. In practice, as auditors are end-users for the algorithm, and given the disparities in end-users across different algorithms, the range for the epistemic factor needs to be contingent upon the ease with which corresponding end-users of the algorithm can access relevant information.

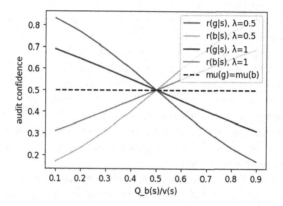

Fig. 5. The trend between the auditor's audit confidence (posterior belief) and the irresponsible developer's choice that leads to $\frac{Q_b(s)}{v(s)}$. Here, $\mu(g) = \mu(b) = 0.5, u(b,T) = u(g,F) = -1, \lambda = 1$.

Irresponsible Developer's Choice and Auditor's Audit Confidence. According to (15) and (16), the irresponsible developer's budget choice determines $Q_b(\cdot)$ given $p(\cdot)$. Hence, (21) and (22) (shown in Fig. 5) also establish a relationship between the irresponsible developer's choice and the auditor's audit confidence.

By taking partial derivative of $r(g|s)$ with respect to $\frac{Q_b(s)}{v(s)}$, we obtain

$$\frac{\partial r(g|s)}{\partial \frac{Q_b(s)}{v(s)}} = \frac{\mu(g)\mu(b)\frac{u(g,F)+u(b,T)}{\lambda} \exp\left(\frac{u(g,F)\frac{Q_g(s)}{v(s)}+u(b,T)\frac{Q_b(s)}{v(s)}}{\lambda} \right)}{\left(\mu(g)\exp\left(\frac{u(b,T)Q_b(s)}{\lambda v(s)}\right) + \mu(b)\exp\left(\frac{u(g,F)Q_g(s)}{\lambda v(s)}\right) \right)^2}, \tag{30}$$

which is negative since $u(g, F) + u(b, T) < 0$. Additionally, as the value of λ increases (when auditors incur higher costs for information acquisition), the magnitude of $\partial r(g|s)/\partial(\frac{Q_b(s)}{v(s)})$ decreases, implying relatively less influence on audit confidence. This trend is evident in Fig. 5, where a greater λ corresponds to a flatter curve for $r(g|s)$.

6   Discussion and Conclusions

Herd audit is a collective mechanism that empowers users to hold algorithm developers accountable, fostering the development of compliant and responsible digital products for the betterment of society. In this study, we examine herd audit through a game-theoretic lens, capturing the interactions between an idiosyncratic user and a privacy-preserving algorithm developer. Our framework adopts a Stackelberg game approach, enabling us to assess the impact of herd audit on responsible algorithm design and understand selfish and irresponsible strategies in worst-case scenarios.

We have specifically explored the presence of auditors with varying cognitive and reasoning capabilities, capturing epistemic disparities. Within our game-theoretic framework, we have consolidated the concept of rational inattention. The optimal strategy for auditors underscores the importance of easy access to relevant information, which enhances their confidence in the herd-audit process. Similarly, the optimal decision for algorithm developers has revealed that herd audit is a viable approach when auditors face lower costs in accessing knowledge, as denoted by smaller epistemic factors.

Based on our findings, we conclude that herd audit poses a credit threat to developers and plays a vital role in promoting the responsible development of privacy-preserving algorithms. As future work, we aim to enrich the game-theoretic framework by incorporating end-users' incentives. This extension allows us to design an incentive mechanism that encourages participation in herd audit. Additionally, we plan to explore the fusion and aggregation of distributed audits alongside a central audit center. Leveraging tools from decentralized hypothesis testing, game theory, information theory, and differential privacy, this research direction holds promise for advancing the field further.

References

1. Allahbakhsh, M., Ignjatovic, A., Benatallah, B., Bertino, E., Foo, N., et al.: Reputation management in crowdsourcing systems. In: 8th International Conference on Collaborative Computing: Networking, Applications and Worksharing (CollaborateCom), pp. 664–671. IEEE (2012)
2. Anderson, J.R., Bothell, D., Byrne, M.D., Douglass, S., Lebiere, C., Qin, Y.: An integrated theory of the mind. Psychol. Rev. **111**(4), 1036 (2004)
3. Bandy, J.: Problematic machine behavior: a systematic literature review of algorithm audits. Proc. ACM Hum.-Comput. Interact. **5**(CSCW1), 1–34 (2021)

4. Bichsel, B., Gehr, T., Drachsler-Cohen, D., Tsankov, P., Vechev, M.: DP-finder: finding differential privacy violations by sampling and optimization. In: Proceedings of the 2018 ACM SIGSAC Conference on Computer and Communications Security, CCS 2018, pp. 508–524. Association for Computing Machinery, New York (2018). https://doi.org/10.1145/3243734.3243863

5. Caplin, A., Dean, M.: Revealed preference, rational inattention, and costly information acquisition. Am. Econ. Rev. **105**(7), 2183–2203 (2015). https://doi.org/10.1257/aer.20140117

6. Casorrán, C., Fortz, B., Labbé, M., Ordóñez, F.: A study of general and security stackelberg game formulations. Eur. J. Oper. Res. **278**(3), 855–868 (2019)

7. Chen, J., Zhu, Q.: Optimal contract design under asymmetric information for cloud-enabled internet of controlled things. In: Zhu, Q., Alpcan, T., Panaousis, E., Tambe, M., Casey, W. (eds.) GameSec 2016. LNCS, vol. 9996, pp. 329–348. Springer, Cham (2016). https://doi.org/10.1007/978-3-319-47413-7_19

8. Comeig, I., Mesa-Vázquez, E., Sendra-Pons, P., Urbano, A.: Rational herding in reward-based crowdfunding: An mturk experiment. Sustainability **12**(23), 9827 (2020)

9. Ding, Z., Wang, Y., Wang, G., Zhang, D., Kifer, D.: Detecting violations of differential privacy. In: Proceedings of the 2018 ACM SIGSAC Conference on Computer and Communications Security, pp. 475–489 (2018)

10. Dwork, C.: Differential privacy: a survey of results. In: Agrawal, M., Du, D., Duan, Z., Li, A. (eds.) TAMC 2008. LNCS, vol. 4978, pp. 1–19. Springer, Heidelberg (2008). https://doi.org/10.1007/978-3-540-79228-4_1

11. Eickhoff, C.: Cognitive biases in crowdsourcing. In: Proceedings of the Eleventh ACM International Conference on Web Search and Data Mining, pp. 162–170 (2018)

12. Fang, F., Liu, S., Basak, A., Zhu, Q., Kiekintveld, C.D., Kamhoua, C.A.: Introduction to game theory. In: Game Theory and Machine Learning for Cyber Security, pp. 21–46 (2021)

13. Fricker, M.: Epistemic Injustice: Power and the Ethics of Knowing. Oxford University Press, Oxford (2007)

14. Frye, H.: The technology of public shaming. Soc. Philos. Policy **38**(2), 128–145 (2021)

15. Fum, D., Del Missier, F., Stocco, A., et al.: The cognitive modeling of human behavior: why a model is (sometimes) better than 10,000 words. Cogn. Syst. Res. **8**(3), 135–142 (2007)

16. González-Prendes, A.A., Resko, S.M.: Cognitive-behavioral theory (2012)

17. Grasswick, H.: Epistemic injustice in science. In: The Routledge Handbook of Epistemic Injustice, pp. 313–323. Routledge (2017)

18. Guerrero, D., Carsteanu, A.A., Clempner, J.B.: Solving stackelberg security Markov games employing the bargaining nash approach: convergence analysis. Comput. Secur. **74**, 240–257 (2018)

19. Guszcza, J., Rahwan, I., Bible, W., Cebrian, M., Katyal, V.: Why we need to audit algorithms (2018). https://hdl.handle.net/21.11116/0000-0003-1C9E-D

20. Han, Y., Martínez, S.: A numerical verification framework for differential privacy in estimation. IEEE Control Syst. Lett. **6**, 1712–1717 (2021)

21. Horák, K., Zhu, Q., Bošanský, B.: Manipulating adversary's belief: a dynamic game approach to deception by design for proactive network security. In: Rass, S., An, B., Kiekintveld, C., Fang, F., Schauer, S. (eds.) GameSec 2017. LNCS, vol. 10575, pp. 273–294. Springer, Cham (2017). https://doi.org/10.1007/978-3-319-68711-7_15

22. Hu, Y., Zhu, Q.: Evasion-aware Neyman-Pearson detectors: a game-theoretic approach. In: 2022 IEEE 61st Conference on Decision and Control (CDC), pp. 6111–6117 (2022). https://doi.org/10.1109/CDC51059.2022.9993423

23. Huang, L., Zhu, Q.: Duplicity games for deception design with an application to insider threat mitigation. IEEE Trans. Inf. Forensics Secur. 16, 4843–4856 (2021)

24. Huang, L., Zhu, Q.: Cognitive Security: A System-Scientific Approach. Springer, Cham (2023). https://doi.org/10.1007/978-3-031-30709-6

25. Karger, D.R., Oh, S., Shah, D.: Budget-optimal task allocation for reliable crowdsourcing systems. Oper. Res. 62(1), 1–24 (2014)

26. Leimeister, J.M.: Collective intelligence. Bus. Inf. Syst. Eng. 2, 245–248 (2010)

27. Manshaei, M.H., Zhu, Q., Alpcan, T., Bacşar, T., Hubaux, J.P.: Game theory meets network security and privacy. ACM Comput. Surv. (CSUR) 45(3), 1–39 (2013)

28. Matějka, F., McKay, A.: Rational inattention to discrete choices: a new foundation for the multinomial logit model. Am. Econ. Rev. 105(1), 272–298 (2015)

29. Mittelstadt, B.: Automation, algorithms, and politics| auditing for transparency in content personalization systems. Int. J. Commun. 10, 12 (2016)

30. Morris, R.R., Dontcheva, M., Gerber, E.M.: Priming for better performance in microtask crowdsourcing environments. IEEE Internet Comput. 16(5), 13–19 (2012)

31. Narayanan, S.N., Ganesan, A., Joshi, K., Oates, T., Joshi, A., Finin, T.: Early detection of cybersecurity threats using collaborative cognition. In: 2018 IEEE 4th International Conference on Collaboration and Internet Computing (CIC), pp. 354–363 (2018). https://doi.org/10.1109/CIC.2018.00054

32. Pawlick, J., Zhu, Q.: Active crowd defense. In: Game Theory for Cyber Deception: From Theory to Applications, pp. 147–167 (2021)

33. Rajtmajer, S., Squicciarini, A., Such, J.M., Semonsen, J., Belmonte, A.: An ultimatum game model for the evolution of privacy in jointly managed content. In: Rass, S., An, B., Kiekintveld, C., Fang, F., Schauer, S. (eds.) GameSec 2017. LNCS, vol. 10575, pp. 112–130. Springer, Cham (2017). https://doi.org/10.1007/978-3-319-68711-7_7

34. Restuccia, F., Ghosh, N., Bhattacharjee, S., Das, S.K., Melodia, T.: Quality of information in mobile crowdsensing: survey and research challenges. ACM Trans. Sensor Netw. (TOSN) 13(4), 1–43 (2017)

35. Sims, C.A.: Implications of rational inattention. J. Monet. Econ. 50(3), 665–690 (2003)

36. Wang, K., Qi, X., Shu, L., Deng, D.J., Rodrigues, J.J.: Toward trustworthy crowdsourcing in the social internet of things. IEEE Wirel. Commun. 23(5), 30–36 (2016)

37. Yu, H., et al.: Mitigating herding in hierarchical crowdsourcing networks. Sci. Rep. 6(1), 4 (2016)

38. Yu, Y., Liu, S., Guo, L., Yeoh, P.L., Vucetic, B., Li, Y.: CrowdR-FBC: a distributed fog-blockchains for mobile crowdsourcing reputation management. IEEE Internet Things J. 7(9), 8722–8735 (2020)

39. Zhang, R., Zhu, Q.: FlipIn: a game-theoretic cyber insurance framework for incentive-compatible cyber risk management of internet of things. IEEE Trans. Inf. Forensics Secur. 15, 2026–2041 (2019)

40. Zhao, Y., Zhu, Q.: Evaluation on crowdsourcing research: current status and future direction. Inf. Syst. Front. 16, 417–434 (2014)

41. Zhu, Q., Fung, C., Boutaba, R., Basar, T.: GUIDEX: a game-theoretic incentive-based mechanism for intrusion detection networks. IEEE J. Sel. Areas Commun. 30(11), 2220–2230 (2012)

Modeling and Analysis of a Nonlinear Security Game with Mixed Armament

Jean Le Hénaff[1]([⊠]) and Hélène Le Cadre[2]

[1] CEA/DAM/Direction de l'Analyse Stratégique, 91297 Arpajon, France
jean.le-henaff@ponts.org
[2] Inria, CNRS, Univ. of Lille, Centrale Lille, UMR 9189 - CRIStAL, 59000 Lille, France
helene.le-cadre@inria.fr

Abstract. We formulate a security game in a context of mixed armament acquisition, involving a finite set of Nations in strategic relationship, with utility functions which are nonlinear and non-differentiable on the boundary of their sets of definition. Since we want to study the long-term effect of the Nations' investment in nuclear weapons, we focus on the steady-state analysis of the game. This requires us to extend the classical results from Rosen on compact-concave games, to unbounded concave games, relying on the coercivity property of the Nations' utility functions. In addition, we prove the existence and uniqueness, under mild assumptions, of an interior point Nash Equilibrium solution of the game. Simulations are performed in case of a duopoly, highlighting the efficiency loss reduction and stabilizing effect of nuclear armaments by comparison with the conventional-only setting.

Keywords: Security Game · Nash Equilibrium · Uniform Coercivity · Strategic Stability

1 Introduction

The primary goal of Nations is to maximize their perceived security, which requires each Nation to develop an effective deterrence strategy [15]. In classical game theoretic models, deterrence as a military strategy is based upon a standard, iterated two-player prisoner's dilemma model by which cooperation can be assured if a rational player understands the punishment or cost of defection [3,14,26]. Models in this area are often inspired by the USA and USSR-allied, or at least Western vs Eastern blocs, nuclear arms race, and formulate the security dilemma in arms procurement as a two-player noncooperative game in normal form [23,29]. However, many of the actions taken by Nations in pursuit of the maximization of their perceived security – such as arms procurement and the development of new military technologies – might, in turn, lead to a decrease rather than an increase in their perceived security. This dilemma is explained by the fact that the increase in military capability of one Nation might be interpreted as a risk that the arming Nation will use it to perform an attack in

J. Fu et al. (Eds.): GameSec 2023, LNCS 14167, pp. 369–388, 2023.
https://doi.org/10.1007/978-3-031-50670-3_19

the future. In this context, in order to re-establish the balance of power, the other Nations could either increase their own military capabilities or initiate a preemptive strike. Choosing the first option may result in a security spiral, in which several Nations are tied in an arms race, responding to increases in arms procurement and defense expenditure by others by arming themselves more and more heavily, and may lead to war in the long run. Such a situation is known as the security dilemma [11,12], and is one possible outcome of arms race models.

Standard literature dealing with arms race models [24,30] focuses on the dynamic process of the arms race over the time or on fitting real data collected over the years using this model. In this setting, game theory is a useful tool to model interactions between Nations with conflicting interests. The classical literature dealing with nuclear strategy using game theory focuses mainly on discrete decision space repeated games [22] and differential games. Within repeated games, iterated prisoners' dilemmas between two Nations [17,18] have been extensively studied. At each iteration, each Nation has a choice between a high or low level of arms. In the static version, each Nation's dominant strategy is to choose a high level of arms. The Nash Equilibrium outcome of the static prisoner dilemma model for arms race is therefore that both Nations choose high. As a result, the static game outcome is worse for both Nations than if both had chosen a low level of arms. However, in reality, the game is not played once and for all, but is an ongoing series of decisions, i.e., the prisoner dilemma is played repeatedly by the two Nations. This opens the possibility for cooperation to emerge through rewards and punishment strategies, e.g., tit-for-tat [10].

A somewhat equivalent framework stems from Richardson-type models of arms race [16,27], which provide parametrized systems of differential equations to represent the evolution of the weapons stockpile. These equations can be derived as closed-loop Nash Equilibria of linear-quadratic differential games that implement an interpretable reasoning of players [19,20,27,28]. However, military strategies that hinge on nuclear weapons imply that Nations' evaluation of the effect of each other's actions should be nonlinear, and Richardson-type's models fail to represent accurately the specific nature of nuclear armaments [6,8]. Indeed, contrary to conventional war, nuclear warfare allows for significant preemptive and retaliatory strikes whose magnitude depend nonlinearly on the initial stockpiles. A two-stage game model may show that a second-strike capability decreases as the exponential of the ratio of the initial stockpiles [5].

If the goal of game-theoretic models is to quantify the outcomes of situations of conflict between armed Nations, non-proliferation policies and containment treaties are often designed with the goal to stabilize the rivalry between Nations and reduce strategic risks. For example, during the Cold War, several agreements between the USA and the USSR, such as the intermediate-range nuclear forces (INF) treaty, helped balance nuclear-able weapons so that each side could survive a preemptive nuclear attack with a sufficiently large stockpile of ballistic missiles to launch a retaliatory strike, in the context of nuclear strategies heavily influenced by the concept of MAD (mutually assured destruction). Nowadays, 9 countries are thought to possess nuclear weapons. Within them, only 5 – the

USA, Russia, China, France and the United Kingdom – have signed the treaty on the non-proliferation of nuclear weapons (NPT), the second most widely ratified treaty after the United Nations charter. Under the NPT, each of the 191 parties 'undertakes to pursue negotiations in good faith on effective measures relating to the cessation of the nuclear arms race at an early date and to nuclear disarmament, and on a treaty on general and complete disarmament under strict and effective international control' [1]. The security architecture is completed by the comprehensive nuclear-test-ban treaty (CTBT) with 177 parties, which prohibits nuclear tests and as such limits the possibility to develop nuclear weapons[1].

1.1   Problem Statement

We model the interactions among Nations possessing both conventional and nuclear weapons, i.e., mixed armament, using noncooperative game theory. Contrary to most papers which focus on the dynamics of arms procurement, we focus on the steady-state analysis of the game, which captures the long-term solution of the dynamical model, and is formulated as a one-shot (static) game. On the quantitative side, a first difficulty appears in modeling the Nations' utility functions such that they reflect the security perceived at a Nation-wide level – thus, depending on the Nation's armament strategy and on that of its rivals. This leads us to define utility functions which are nonlinear and non-differentiable on the boundary of their sets of definition. A second difficulty arises from this modeling choice and requires that we extend classical results from noncooperative game theory, to characterize the game equilibria. On the qualitative side, we aim to assess the effects of long-term investments in nuclear weapons on the efficiency and strategic stability of the Nations' international system.

1.2   Main Contributions

We propose a multipolar security model which addresses the specific logic of nuclear strategies in a context involving mixed armament, i.e., both conventional and nuclear weapons. The model is formulated in a dynamic setting, but since we want to study the stabilizing and security dilemma reduction potential of mixed armament, we focus on the one-shot game steady-state formulation, which captures the long-term effects of the competition among Nations. This paper provides three important contributions to the state of the art. First, considering a new way to model the security perceived at the Nation-wide level, that takes inspiration from [5], we extend the classical results from Rosen [25] on compact-convex games to unbounded convex games relying on the coercivity property of the Nations' utility functions. This allows us, in a second step, to prove the existence of an interior point Nash Equilibrium solution of the one-shot game. The proof of uniqueness of the interior point Nash Equilibrium follows, under mild assumption on the game parameters. In a last step, our model is used to

---

[1] Currently, while it is already enforced by parties, the CTBT has not yet entered into force because 8 out of 44 Annex 2 Nations have not ratified it.

determine numerically that nuclear weapons have a stabilizing effect and can potentially reduce the efficiency loss by comparison with a conventional-only setting, therefore providing possible guidelines for current treaties refinements.

Paper Organisation

This paper is organized as follows. In Sect. 1, we provide an overview of the game theoretic approaches for arms procurement competition modeling and how their outcomes can be used to design containment treaties with stabilizing effects. We also introduce the problem statement, and main contributions. In Sect. 2, the arms building model is formulated as a one-shot noncooperative game. Conditions for the existence and uniqueness of an interior point Nash Equilibrium solution of this game are studied in Sect. 3. Analytical results and numerical illustrations in case of a duopoly are discussed in Sect. 4. We conclude in Sect. 5.

2   The Mixed Armament Competition Model

The international system is first and foremost made up of Nations, that we will indifferently call players. In international relations [2], an organization is said to be unitary if and only if its decisions contain all the information useful for its interaction with the international system. Moreover, an organization is said to be rational if its decision-making process consists in maximizing its (well-ordered) preferences through its actions, given the information available to it and its anticipation of what other organizations might do. Hence, in our work, Nations can be represented as rational unitary players. Note that no hypothesis is made a priori on the order of the preferences.

We aim to study the strategies of Nations to invest in nuclear and conventional weapons in order to maximize their security while minimizing their storage and R&D costs. We start by placing ourselves in a framework of discrete time evolution. Nations seek to ensure their own security within a certain time horizon (finite or infinite), and in anticipation of a crisis. They can acquire conventional and nuclear weapons to maximize their security, while bearing storage and R&D costs. We choose a realistic framework [31], and assume that Nations are primarily defensive and secondarily aggressive. This means that they seek through conventional and nuclear armaments to ensure their own security, and that their marginal gain from arming themselves increases with the levels of adversary armaments.

2.1   Dynamics of Arms Building

Let $\mathcal{N}$ be a finite set of N Nations, and T be the horizon of the game (possibly infinite). We propose a model with continuous decision spaces, i.e., the Nations (as players) do not decide whether to attack or not, but they decide on the power drawn from their investment in nuclear and conventional weapons. Models with continuous decision spaces prove themselves more realistic [4,15,27,28]. We might assume that the power drawn for each category of armament depends linearly on the Nation's arms production and that the coefficients relating the arms production to the power drawn out of it differ between the categories of weapons. In absence of numerical values for these coefficients, we will not consider this level of details in the present work. In what follows, $\tau = \{nuc\}$ or $\{conv\}$ and denotes nuclear or conventional.

Let $u_n^\tau(t)$ be the power drawn from the quantity of weapons of class τ produced by Nation $n \in \mathcal{N}$ and $x_n^\tau(t)$ be the power drawn from its stockpile of weapons of class τ at time period t. We define $u_n(t) \stackrel{\text{def}}{=} \left(u_n^\tau(t)\right)_\tau$, the column vector which contains the power drawn from the production of Nation n for each class of weapons, $u(t) \stackrel{\text{def}}{=} \text{col}((u_n(t))_n)$ be the stack of the power drawn from the weapons production by the N Nations. Similarly, $x_n(t) \stackrel{\text{def}}{=} \left(x_n^\tau(t)\right)_\tau$ is the column vector which contains the power drawn from stockpile of Nation n for each class of weapons, and $x(t) \stackrel{\text{def}}{=} \text{col}((x_n(t))_n)$ be the stack of the power drawn from the stockpiles of the N Nations. Furthermore, we define the following sequences: $x \stackrel{\text{def}}{=} (x(t))_t$ and $u_n \stackrel{\text{def}}{=} (u_n(t))_t$. The dynamics of Nation n's power drawn from stockpile of class τ weapons is defined as follows:

$$\forall n \in \mathcal{N}, \quad x_n^\tau(t+1) = x_n^\tau(t) + u_n^\tau(t) - \nu x_n^\tau(t), \tag{1}$$

with an obsolescence rate $\nu \geq 0$. The players' utility at time period t writes:

$$J_n\left(u_n(t), x(t)\right) = f_n\left(x(t)\right) - c_n^S\left(x_n(t)\right) - c_n^D\left(u_n(t)\right), \tag{2}$$

where $f_n(\cdot)$ is the security function of player n, $c_n^S(\cdot)$ its storage (operational) cost and $c_n^D(\cdot)$ its development (R&D) cost. The players may have local constraints, e.g., finite budget, maximum capacity of production, etc., which may evolve dynamically. We denote $\mathcal{U}_n(t) \subset \mathbb{R}_+^2$ the set of $u_n(t)$ that preserve these constraints, i.e., the feasibility set of player n. Each player $n \in \mathcal{N}$ maximizes the sum $J_n(\cdot)$ over time of its future utility, with discounting rate $\rho_n \in]0;1[$, $n \in \mathcal{N}$:

$$V_n(x) = \max_{u_n(t) \in \mathcal{U}_n(t), \forall t} \bar{J}_n\left(u_n, x\right),$$

$$\text{where} \quad \bar{J}_n(u_n, x) \stackrel{\text{def}}{=} \sum_{t=0}^{T} \rho_n^t J_n\left(u_n(t), x(t)\right). \tag{3}$$

We aim to study this model in the long run, with $\nu = 0$. In what follows, we denote $x_n \stackrel{\text{def}}{=} \lim_{t \to +\infty} x_n(t)$ player n's steady state, with $\lim_{t \to +\infty} u(t) = 0$. Using a slight abuse of notation, the static model is given by:

$$V_n(x) = \max_{x_n \in \mathbb{R}_+^2} \bar{J}_n(x) \quad \text{where} \quad \bar{J}_n(x) \stackrel{\text{def}}{=} J_n(0, x). \tag{4}$$

with the decision variable now being Nation n's power drawn from its stockpiles, $x_n \in \mathcal{U}_n$. Let $x_{-n} \stackrel{\text{def}}{=} \text{col}((x_m)_{m \neq n}), \forall n$ be the vector that contains the stack of the power drawn from the stockpiles of weapons of all Nations in $\mathcal{N}$ except n.

2.2   Strategic Relationship

For each Nation, the international system is divided into opponents, neutrals and allies (commercial or military). A commercial alliance is a binding agreement allowing transfer of military capacities between parties. A military alliance is a binding agreement establishing a coalition of military interests and capacities between parties. To simplify the setting, we will not consider alliances in the following. In what follows, we make the assumption that the decisions of Nations are not affected by those of neutrals.

We now want to structure the set of Nations, by taking into account how their decisions impact those of the others. For each Nation $n \in \mathcal{N}$, the set of opponents $\sigma(n) \subset \mathcal{N}$ is defined by a binary relation of hostility, represented by the hostility function $\sigma(\cdot)$. It is reasonable to assume that a Nation is never its own opponent and that any opponent of a Nation must treat the considered Nation as an opponent in return. Therefore, we assume that the relation of hostility is irreflexive and symmetric, i.e.:

$$\forall n \in \mathcal{N}, \qquad\qquad\qquad n \notin \sigma(n),$$
$$\forall n, m \in \mathcal{N}, \qquad m \in \sigma(n) \Longleftrightarrow n \in \sigma(m).$$

We introduce the strategic relation as the reflexive-transitive closure of the hostility relation:

Definition 1 (Strategic relation). *We say that two Nations n and m are in strategic relationship and write $n \sim m$ if a (possibly degenerate) sequence of hostility relations connects n to m, i.e., if there exists $k \in \mathbb{N}$ such that $m \in \sigma^k(n)$.*

Lemma 1. *The strategic relation is an equivalence relation.*

Proof. By definition, the strategic relation is symmetric. It is transitive because $\forall n, m, l \in \mathcal{N}$ such that $n \neq m, m \neq l, n \neq l$, $n \sim m$ and $m \sim l$ mean that there exist $k, k' \in \mathbb{N}$ such that $m \in \sigma^k(n)$ and $l \in \sigma^{k'}(m)$. Then, by composition of the strategic relation, we get that $l \in \sigma^{k+k'}(n)$. Therefore, the strategic relation is transitive. Now, $\forall n \in \mathcal{N}, \sigma^0(n) = \{n\}$, thus the strategic relation is an equivalence relation. $\square$

Lemma 1 implies that the decisions of Nations belonging to the same equivalence class are independent of the decisions of the Nations out of it. Hence, we can split the set of players into a finite number of equivalence classes. This allows to decompose the main noncooperative game into the same number of noncooperative games, that can be solved independently. In what follows, we assume this procedure has already been done, and focus on a game in which the N Nations share strategic relations:

Assumption 1. *All Nations in $\mathcal{N}$ are in strategic relationship.*

In particular, if the game is nontrivial and consists of at least two players, then every Nation has an opponent.

2.3 Target Value

For Nation $n \in \mathcal{N}$, the target value of adverse armament of class τ is denoted by $x^\tau_{\sigma(n)}$, which is a function of x^τ_{-n}. Later, we will call it Nation n target value. This value represents the level of threat caused by the set of opponents. Several modeling choices are possible. For instance, Nations preparing for a one-off crisis will evaluate the target value as the maximum level of armaments of class τ of the set of opponents. In any case, it must satisfy the following assumption:

Assumption 2. *There exist* $\kappa^-, \kappa^+ > 0$ *input coefficients that do not depend on the power drawn from the weapon stockpiles, such that:*

$$\kappa^- \max_{m \in \sigma(n)} x^\tau_m \leq x^\tau_{\sigma(n)} \leq \kappa^+ \max_{m \neq n} x^\tau_m.$$

Remark 1. Target values defined as the maximum, the sum or the mean over $\sigma(n)$ of the power drawn from the weapon stockpiles satisfy Assumption 2:

$$\max_{m \in \sigma(n)} x^\tau_m \leq \max_{m \in \sigma(n)} x^\tau_m \leq \max_{m \neq n} x^\tau_m,$$

$$\max_{m \in \sigma(n)} x^\tau_m \leq \sum_{m \in \sigma(n)} x^\tau_m \leq N \max_{m \neq n} x^\tau_m,$$

$$\frac{1}{N} \max_{m \in \sigma(n)} x^\tau_m \leq \frac{\sum_{m \in \sigma(n)} x^\tau_m}{|\sigma(n)|} \leq \max_{m \neq n} x^\tau_m.$$

Let us discuss briefly the interpretation of Assumption 2. The right hand side of the inequality ensures that Nations use armaments levels of others to compute the level of threat they face, while the left hand side ensures that Nations do not ignore the greatest opponent in the computation of the threat they face.

2.4 Security Functions

The perceived security of a Nation $n \in \mathcal{N}$ is a function of the power drawn from its own weapon stockpile x_n and of its target value $x_{\sigma(n)}$, where $x_{\sigma(n)}$ is the column vector which contains the target value of Nation n in each weapon class. As Nations seek to maximize their perceived security, it increases with their effective weapon stockpile and decreases with the opponents' effective weapon stockpiles. Using deterrence terminology, the effective stockpile value can be defined as the maximum available quantity of armaments, a Nation is both credible, and capable to use in a potential conflict. We shall assume that Nations have a credible threat in using the military capacities we consider. However, the capability of the weapon stockpiles may depend on the quality and type of armaments as well as on the military doctrine of each Nation. We distinguish between two classes of armaments: nuclear (strategic) weapons allowing for preemptive strikes, and conventional (tactical) weapons which can be used on the battlefield. Therefore, Nation n's security function can be decomposed as follows:

$$f_n(x_n, x_{-n}) = \sum_\tau \alpha^\tau f^\tau_n(x_n, x_{-n}), \quad \text{where} \sum_\tau \alpha^\tau = 1, \alpha^\tau \geq 0, \forall \tau. \quad (5)$$

Extrinsic and Intrinsic Perceived Security. For each class τ of armaments, we decompose f_n^τ into two parts: the extrinsic part, which represents the loss of perceived security due to the environment, and the intrinsic part, which represents the gain of perceived security due to the possession of armaments of class τ. The extrinsic perceived security of Nation n brought by class τ armaments coincides with its opponents' effective stockpile of class τ. Now, as Nations are primarily defensive and secondarily aggressive, the intrinsic perceived security of Nation n brought by class τ armaments is modeled as a linear function of Nation n's effective stockpile value of armaments of class τ. Its slope is a concave function $\phi(\cdot)$ of the weapons they are supposed to deter. Nuclear strategies are generally dual-purpose, contrary to conventional strategies. Thus, the slope is $\phi\left(\frac{x_{\sigma(n)}^{conv}+x_{\sigma(n)}^{nuc}}{\xi_n}\right)$ for nuclear, and $\phi\left(\frac{x_{\sigma(n)}^{conv}}{\xi_n}\right)$ for conventional, where $\xi_n > 0$ is a threshold which captures Nation n's peacefulness. To go further we need to evaluate the effective stockpile value for nuclear and conventional armaments.

Effective Stockpiles. Consider first conventional weapons. It is reasonable to assume that Nations are able to use at some point in a potential conflict all of the conventional weapons they possess. Therefore, Nation n's power drawn from effective stockpile of conventional weapons is equal to the power drawn from its actual stockpile of conventional weapons x_n^{conv}.

Now, consider nuclear weapons. Depending on multiple factors, Nations can be cautious and prepare for an adversarial first strike by seeking a second-strike capability, or they can hinge on their preemptive first-strike capability to deter their counterparts. Therefore, stochastic multi-stage games can be used to model the succession of strikes [5]. We use this setting to derive the closed form expression of the expected number of remaining weapons in case of a conflict between two armed Nations, after a single preemptive strike.

Following [5], we consider two Nations called n and $m \in \mathcal{N}, n \neq m$. Nation n holds $W_n \in \mathbb{N}$ weapons. It is attacking Nation m, which holds $W_m \in \mathbb{N}^*$ weapons. Nation n aims to destroy with a preemptive strike as much as possible of Nation m's weapons. Assume that Nation n's weapons have an accuracy $\lambda_n > 0$, i.e., each weapon has a probability $p_n = 1 - e^{-\lambda_n}$ of destroying its target. Assume that both weapons and targets are indistinguishable. Let W_m^r be the random variable that gives the number of remaining weapons for Nation m after a single preemptive strike of Nation n. Let $K \stackrel{\text{def}}{=} \lfloor \frac{W_n}{W_m} \rfloor$ and $w \stackrel{\text{def}}{=} W_n - KW_m$.

Proposition 1. *After an optimal single preemptive strike by Nation n, the expected number of remaining weapons for Nation m is:*

$$\mathbb{E}[W_m^r] = (W_m - w)\exp(-K\lambda_n) + w\exp\left(-(K+1)\lambda_n\right),$$

$$= W_m \exp\left(-\lambda_n \frac{W_n}{W_m}\right), \qquad \text{if } K \in \mathbb{N}.$$

Proof. Let $\mathcal{W}_n = [\![1, W_n]\!]$ and $\mathcal{W}_m = [\![1, W_m]\!]$. For all $k \in \mathcal{W}_m$, let $g(k) \in \mathcal{W}_n$ be the number of weapons assigned by Nation n to target k. We order the targets such that $g(\cdot)$ is decreasing. Notice that W_m^r is a function of $g(\cdot)$, but to simplify the notation we omit this dependence. Nation n has to solve the following optimization problem:

$$\min_{g(\cdot)} \; \mathbb{E}\left[W_m^r\right], \qquad \text{s.t.} \quad \sum_{k \in W_m} g(k) = W_n, \tag{6}$$

which consists in finding a minimizer of a function over a non-empty finite set, whence the minimizer exists. We argue that the (unique) minimizer is given by

$$g(k) = \begin{cases} K+1 & \text{if } 1 \leq k \leq W_n - KW_m, \\ K & \text{else.} \end{cases} \tag{7}$$

First, consider a strike on a single target $k \in W_m$. Up to a reordering, let $(X_l)_{l \in [\![1, g(k)]\!]}$ be a collection of Bernoulli independent and identically distributed random variables with parameter p_n. $X_l = 1$ means that weapon l destroys its target k, with probability $p_n = 1 - e^{-\lambda_n}$. Let $Y_k = \sum_{l=1}^{g(k)} X_l$. Target k remains intact if and only if $Y_k = 0$, with probability $\mathbb{P}\left(Y_k = 0\right) = e^{-g(k)\lambda_n}$. Nation m has $W_m^r = \sum_{k \in W_m} \mathbf{1}_{\{Y_k = 0\}}$ remaining weapons. Therefore:

$$\mathbb{E}\left[W_m^r\right] = \sum_{k \in W_m} \mathbb{E}\left[\mathbf{1}_{\{Y_k=0\}}\right] = \sum_{k \in W_m} \mathbb{P}\left(Y_k = 0\right) = \sum_{k \in W_m} e^{-g(k)\lambda_n}.$$

Let $g(\cdot)$ be a minimizer of problem (6). Let us show that $g(0) \leq g(W_m)+1$ using on a proof by contradiction. Assume the converse: $g(0) \geq g(W_m) + 2$. As $g(\cdot)$ is decreasing, there exists l, l' such that $g(0) = g(l) > g(l+1) \geq g(l') = g(W_m)$ and l' is minimal. Define $g^\sharp(\cdot)$ by

$$g^\sharp(l) = g(l) - 1, \quad g^\sharp(l') = g(l+1), \quad g^\sharp(k) = g(k), \; \forall k \in W_m \setminus \{l, l'\},$$

$g^\sharp$ is decreasing and sums to W_n. Note that $g(l')+1 = g(W_m)+1 < g(0) = g(l)$. Whence, one can compute:

$$\mathbb{E}\left[W_m^r\right]\big|_{g^\sharp} - \mathbb{E}\left[W_m^r\right]\big|_g = (e^{\lambda_n} - 1)\left(e^{-\lambda_n g(l)} - e^{-\lambda_n (g(l')+1)}\right) < 0,$$

which contradicts that g be minimal. Whence, the minimizer g is decreasing and satisfies $g(0) \leq g(W_m) + 1$, i.e., it is given by (7). In turn, the minimum is:

$$\mathbb{E}\left[W_m^r\right] = (W_m - w)\exp\left(-K\lambda_n\right) + w\exp\left(-(K+1)\lambda_n\right).$$

Now, if $W_n = KW_m$, i.e., $w = 0$, then $\mathbb{E}\left[W_m^r\right] = W_m \exp\left(-K\lambda_n\right)$. $\square$

Nation n's opponents have $x_{\sigma(n)}^\tau$ weapons of class τ. Thus Proposition 1 shows that the effective power drawn from stockpile value of class τ weapons, after a single preemptive strike by Nation n with nuclear weapons, is given by $x_{\sigma(n)}^\tau \exp\left(-\lambda_n \frac{x_n^{\text{conv}}}{x_{\sigma(n)}^\tau}\right)$.

Generic Security Function. Combining all of the above, we can define a generic security function for both conventional and nuclear armaments. Let $a, b \in \{0, 1\}$. Define Nation n's security function for conventional armaments as:

$$f_n^{\text{conv}}(x_n, x_{-n}) = x_n^{\text{conv}} \exp\left(-\lambda_{\sigma(n)} \frac{x_{\sigma(n)}^{\text{nuc}}}{x_n^{\text{conv}}}\right)^a \phi\left(\frac{x_{\sigma(n)}^{\text{conv}}}{\xi_n}\right) - x_{\sigma(n)}^{\text{conv}} \exp\left(-\lambda_n \frac{x_n^{\text{nuc}}}{x_{\sigma(n)}^{\text{conv}}}\right)^b, \tag{8}$$

and Nation n's security function for nuclear armaments as

$$
\begin{aligned}
f_n^{\mathrm{nuc}}(x_n, x_{-n}) = & \ x_n^{\mathrm{nuc}} \exp\left(-\lambda_{\sigma(n)} \frac{x_{\sigma(n)}^{\mathrm{nuc}}}{x_n^{\mathrm{nuc}}}\right)^a \phi\left(\frac{x_{\sigma(n)}^{\mathrm{conv}} + x_{\sigma(n)}^{\mathrm{nuc}}}{\xi_n}\right) \\
& - x_{\sigma(n)}^{\mathrm{nuc}} \exp\left(-\lambda_n \frac{x_n^{\mathrm{nuc}}}{x_{\sigma(n)}^{\mathrm{nuc}}}\right)^b ,
\end{aligned}
\tag{9}
$$

where $\lambda_{\sigma(n)}$ is a measure of the accuracy of the nuclear weapons of Nation n's opponents. In general, Nations might choose among four doctrine choices, shaping their security functions. Indeed, each Nation will choose whether it relies on its vulnerable second-strike capacity ($a = 1$) or not ($a = 0$); and whether it relies on its preemptive first strike capacity ($b = 1$) or not ($b = 0$). We focus on the case $(a, b) = (0, 1)$, more representative of modern nuclear military capabilities. Therefore, applying (5), the security function of Nation $n \in \mathcal{N}$ will be given by:

$$
\begin{aligned}
f_n(x_n, x_{-n}) = & \ \alpha^{\mathrm{nuc}}\left[x_n^{\mathrm{nuc}}\phi\left((x_{\sigma(n)}^{\mathrm{conv}} + x_{\sigma(n)}^{\mathrm{nuc}})/\xi_n\right) - x_{\sigma(n)}^{\mathrm{nuc}} \exp\left(-\lambda_n x_n^{\mathrm{nuc}}/x_{\sigma(n)}^{\mathrm{nuc}}\right)\right] \\
& + \alpha^{\mathrm{conv}}\left[x_n^{\mathrm{conv}}\phi\left(x_{\sigma(n)}^{\mathrm{conv}}/\xi_n\right) - x_{\sigma(n)}^{\mathrm{conv}} \exp\left(-\lambda_n x_n^{\mathrm{nuc}}/x_{\sigma(n)}^{\mathrm{conv}}\right)\right] ,
\end{aligned}
\tag{10}
$$

with $\alpha^{\mathrm{nuc}} + \alpha^{\mathrm{conv}} = 1$, $\alpha^{\mathrm{nuc}}, \alpha^{\mathrm{conv}} \geq 0$, λ_n is Nation n's nuclear armaments accuracy, and $\xi_n > 0$ is a Nation-specific constant which models Nation n's peacefulness. Remind that $\phi(\cdot)$ is a concave, strictly increasing function. We also assume $\phi(0) = 0$, $\phi'(0) = 1$, $\phi^{(3)}(0) > 0$ and that $\phi(x) = o(x)$ at infinity.

Remark 2. In what follows, we will choose $\phi : s \mapsto \ln(1 + s)$ in numerical computations. Furthermore, for technical purposes, let $k > 0$, $\phi^k : s \mapsto \min\{\phi(s), \phi(k)\}$ and denote $\bar{J}_n^k(.)$ the utility function defined as $\bar{J}_n(.)$ by replacing $\phi(.)$ by $\phi^k(.)$. Let $\nabla_n \cdot \bar{J}_n(x) \stackrel{\mathrm{def}}{=} \frac{\langle \nabla_{x_n} \bar{J}_n(x), x_n \rangle}{\|x_n\|}$ be the directional derivative of $\bar{J}_n(\cdot)$ along x_n. Also, observe that under Assumption 2, the following inequality holds:

$$
\nabla_n \cdot \bar{J}_n(x_n, x_{-n}) \leq \widehat{\lambda} + \phi\left(\sqrt{2}\frac{\kappa_+}{\widehat{\xi}}\|\widehat{x}\|\right) - \check{C}\|x_n\|, \quad \forall n \in \mathcal{N}
\tag{11}
$$

where $\widehat{x} = (\widehat{x}_\tau)_\tau$ with $\widehat{x}^\tau = \max_{m \in \mathcal{N}} x_m^\tau$, $\check{C} = \min_{m \in \mathcal{N}, \tau} \check{C}_m^\tau$, $\widehat{\lambda} = \max_{m \in \mathcal{N}} \lambda_m$, and $\widehat{\xi} = \max_{m \in \mathcal{N}} \xi_m$. An analogous inequality holds for $\left(\bar{J}_n^k(\cdot), \phi^k(\cdot)\right)$.

We observe that $f(\cdot, x_{-n})$ is a $\mathcal{C}^\infty$ function on $\left(\mathbb{R}_+^*\right)^2$. It is also well-defined on $\partial(\mathbb{R}_+^*)^2 \setminus \{0\}$. Moreover, around this set, it is continuous and bounded thus one can extend it by continuity at 0 by the value 0. However, it is not differentiable on $\partial(\mathbb{R}_+^*)^2$. Therefore, we cannot directly apply standard results from game theory, which require that the players' utility functions be defined on a closed-convex domain and be differentiable. The analysis of the one-shot game will therefore require to deal, first, with the degenerate case of the boundary and, second, to develop theoretical tools to study objective functions defined on open unbounded domains.

3   Analysis of the One-Shot Game

Let $\mathcal{U} \stackrel{\text{def}}{=} \prod_n \mathcal{U}_n$. We define $\mathcal{G} \stackrel{\text{def}}{=} \left(\mathcal{N}, \mathcal{U}, (\bar{J}_n)_n\right)$ as the one-shot (static) game involving a set $\mathcal{N}$ of N armed Nations. For all $n \in \mathcal{N}$, Nation n's utility function is derived from (4), with target value satisfying Assumption 2. The security functions are defined in (5), and we assume quadratic cost functions, $c_n^S(\cdot)$, $\forall n$:

$$c_n^S(x_n) = \frac{1}{2} C_n^{\text{conv}} \left(x_n^{\text{conv}}\right)^2 + \frac{1}{2} C_n^{\text{nuc}} \left(x_n^{\text{nuc}}\right)^2,$$

where $C_n^{\text{conv}}, C_n^{\text{nuc}} > 0$ are storage marginal costs for conventional and nuclear weapons respectively, assuming $c_n^D(0) = 0$. Nation n's utility function takes the form: $\bar{J}_n(x_n, x_{-n}) = f_n(x) - c_n^S(x_n)$. We will analyze the outcome of the noncooperative game $\mathcal{G}$ relying on the classical Nash Equilibrium, as solution concept.

Definition 2 (Nash Equilibrium). *A Nash Equilibrium $x^* = (x_n^*)_n$ of $\mathcal{G}$ is a vector of power drawn from the stockpiles of weapons, such that $\bar{J}_n(x^*) \geq \bar{J}_n(x_n, x_{-n}^*), \forall x_n \in \mathcal{U}_n, \forall n \in \mathcal{N}$.*

We recall below the definition of a concave game.

Definition 3 (Concave N-player game). *Let $E \stackrel{def}{=} \prod_{n=1}^N E_n$ be a product of Euclidean spaces $(E_n)_n$. Let $\mathcal{U} \subset E$ be a convex subset of E and for all $n \in \mathcal{N}$ assume the utility functions $\bar{J}_n : \mathcal{U} \to \mathbb{R}$ are continuous. The game $\mathcal{G}$, where each player $n \in \mathcal{N}$ solves the parametrized optimization problem:*

$$\max_{x_n \in E_n} \bar{J}_n(x_n, x_{-n}) \quad s.t. \ x \in \mathcal{U}, \quad \forall n \in \mathcal{N},$$

is called a concave game if for all $n \in \mathcal{N}$, $x_n \mapsto \bar{J}_n(x_n, x_{-n})$ is a concave function for each fixed value of x_{-n} such that $x \in \mathcal{U}$. If $\mathcal{U}$ is compact, then it is called a compact-concave game.

A classical result [25, Theorem 1] ensures the existence of Nash Equilibria for concave N-player games whose joint strategy set is a compact convex. In the follow up, we extend this result to the case where: (i) the joint strategy set is a closed convex; and, (ii) the players' utility functions satisfy a coercivity property. Finally, we prove the existence of an interior point Nash Equilibrium for the N-player static game $\mathcal{G}$.

Remark 3. Note that contrary to the finite-horizon game involving a finite number of time steps in the dynamic game, decision variables cannot be normalized in the one-shot game. Indeed, as we study the equilibria in the long-run, i.e., steady states, without requiring *a priori* budget constraints, there is no reason that Nash Equilibria take bounded values when time goes to infinity, e.g., in the case of a security spiral.

The following proposition deals with the *degenerate cases* where, at a Nash Equilibrium, a Nation would disarm and give up a weapons class. We show that this kind of solution requires all Nations to disarm for the same weapons class.

Proposition 2 (Disarmament). *Let x be a Nash Equilibrium. Let $\tau \in \{nuc, conv\}$ and $n \in \mathcal{N}$. The following statements hold true:*

1. *If $x^\tau_{\sigma(n)} = 0$, then for all $m \in \sigma(n)$, $x^\tau_m = 0$;*
2. *If $x^\tau_n = 0$, then for all $m \in \mathcal{N}$, $x^\tau_m = 0$.*

Proof. To prove the first statement, let $x^\tau_{\sigma(n)} = 0$. Then, for all $m \in \sigma(n)$,

$$0 \leq x^\tau_m \leq \max_{\ell \in \sigma(n)} x^\tau_\ell \leq \frac{x^\tau_{\sigma(n)}}{\kappa^-} = 0, \text{ by Assumption 2.}$$

Therefore, $\forall m \in \sigma(n)$, $x^\tau_m = 0$. Now, we want to prove the second statement. First, let us show that if $x^\tau_n = 0$, then $\forall m \in \sigma(n)$, $x^\tau_m = 0$ by contraposition. Assume that there exists $m \in \sigma(n)$ such that $x^\tau_m > 0$, which implies $x^\tau_{\sigma(n)} > 0$ using the first statement. Now, as $x^\tau_{\sigma(n)} > 0$, a direct computation yields a lower bound on the gradient of the security function at $(x^{\text{nuc}}_n, x^{\text{conv}}_n) \in (\mathbb{R}_+)^2$:
$\frac{\partial f_n}{\partial x^\tau_n}(x_n, x_{-n}) \geq \alpha^\tau \phi\left(\frac{x^\tau_{\sigma(n)}}{\xi_n}\right) > 0$, because $\phi(\cdot)$ is strictly increasing and $\phi(0) = 0$.
Note that, at $x^\tau_n = 0$, $\frac{\partial c^S_n}{\partial x^\tau_n}(x_n) = C^\tau_n x^\tau_n = 0$. Therefore,

$$\frac{\partial \bar{J}_n}{\partial x^\tau_n}(x_n, x_{-n}) = \frac{\partial f_n}{\partial x^\tau_n}(x_n, x_{-n}) - \frac{\partial c^S_n}{\partial x^\tau_n}(x_n) = \frac{\partial f_n}{\partial x^\tau_n}(x_n, x_{-n}) > 0.$$

Hence, all strategies with $x^\tau_n = 0$ are dominated, i.e., if x is a Nash Equilibrium, we have that $x^\tau_n > 0$. Therefore, if $x^\tau_n = 0$, then $\forall m \in \sigma(n)$, $x^\tau_m = 0$. Now, assume that $x^\tau_n = 0$. Then, by induction, $\forall k \in \mathbb{N}$, $\forall m \in \sigma^k(n)$, $x^\tau_m = 0$. As $\mathcal{N}$ is a strategic relationship class, $\mathcal{N} = \sigma^{|\mathcal{N}|}(n)$. Therefore, $x^\tau_m = 0$. □

Let $\mathcal{U}^\dagger \overset{\text{def}}{=} \mathcal{U} \cap (\mathbb{R}^*_+)^{2N}$ and $\mathcal{U}^\dagger_n \overset{\text{def}}{=} \mathcal{U}_n \cap (\mathbb{R}^*_+)^2$. As a consequence of Proposition 2, there exists a trivial Nash Equilibrium which coincides with a "general and complete disarmament" strategy ($x = 0$). In the following sections, we prove the existence and uniqueness of interior points Nash Equilibria $x^* \in \mathcal{U}^\dagger$. An interior point Nash Equilibrium does not lie on the boundary of $(\mathbb{R}^*_+)^2$.

3.1   Existence of a Nash Equilibrium

It is well-known that every compact-concave game admits a Nash Equilibrium. As the utility functions of the game $\mathcal{G}$ are concave in their own strategy space, we can build a compact concave game $\mathcal{G}'$ by imposing constraints to $\mathcal{G}$, ensuring the existence of a Nash Equilibrium for $\mathcal{G}'$. Let $\mathcal{U}' \subset \mathcal{U}$ be a compact convex.

Lemma 2. *Assume that a Nash Equilibrium is reached at an interior point of $\mathcal{U}'$. Then, since the players' utility functions are concave in their own strategy space, it is also a Nash Equilibrium for the game with strategy space $\mathcal{U}$.*

Proof. The proof relies directly on the concavity of the objective functions.

Using this property, we can show under further assumptions on the asymptotic behavior of the utility functions that the boundedness of $\mathcal{U}$ is not required.

Definition 4. *Let $\Psi : \mathcal{U} \subset E \to \mathbb{R}$ be a continuous function. We say that $\Psi(\cdot)$ is uniformly coercive in x_n over E_n if and only if there exists $r_n > 0$ and $g : E_n \to \mathbb{R}$ such that:*

$$\forall x \in \mathcal{U}, \qquad \nabla_n \cdot \Psi(x) \geq g(x_n),$$
$$\forall y \in E_n, \qquad \|y\| \geq r_n \implies g(y) > 0.$$

where $\nabla_n \cdot \Psi(x) = \frac{\langle \nabla_{x_n} \Psi(x), x_n \rangle}{\|x_n\|}$ is the directional derivative of $\Psi(\cdot)$ along x_n.

Using (11) and that $\phi_k(\cdot)$ are bounded, we check that the opposite of objective functions $-\bar{J}_n^k(\cdot), \forall n$ are uniformly coercive over their own strategy space.

Proposition 3. *Let $\widetilde{\mathcal{G}} = (\mathcal{N}, \mathcal{U}, (\Psi_n)_n)$ be a concave game. Assume $\mathcal{U} \subset E$ is closed and $-\Psi_n(\cdot)$ is uniformly coercive over its own strategy space $\mathcal{U}_n, \forall n$. Then, $\widetilde{\mathcal{G}}$ admits a Nash Equilibrium.*

Proof. Let $\mathcal{B}_n(r)$ be the closed ball of radius $r > 0$ in E_n. Let $\mathcal{B}(r) \overset{\text{def}}{=} \prod_{n=1}^{N} \mathcal{B}_n(r)$. Hence, $\Gamma(r) \overset{\text{def}}{=} \mathcal{B}(0, r) \cap \mathcal{U} \subset \mathcal{U}$ is the intersection of two closed convex sets and is bounded, thus it is a compact convex. Then, $\widetilde{\mathcal{G}}$ is a compact concave game over $\Gamma(r)$ and admits a Nash Equilibrium, denoted by x^*. Now, for all $n \in \mathcal{N}$, $-\Psi_n(\cdot)$ is uniformly coercive over E_n. Hence, there exists $r_n > 0$ and $g_n(\cdot)$ such that

$$\forall x \in \mathcal{U}, \qquad -\nabla_n \cdot \Psi_n(x) \geq g(x_n),$$
$$\forall y \in E_n, \qquad \|y\| \geq r_n \implies g(y) > 0.$$

Set $r > \max_{n}\{r_n\}$. If there existed $n \in \mathcal{N}$ such that $x_n \in \partial\mathcal{B}_n(r)$, then the optimality conditions would write:

$$\nabla_n \cdot \Psi_n(x) \geq 0 \quad \text{with } \|x_n\| = r,$$

Now, $\|x_n\| = r \geq r_n$ thus $\frac{\partial \Psi}{\partial n}(x) \leq -g_n(x_n) < 0$, which is a contradiction. Therefore, for $r > 0$ large enough, Nash Equilibria of $\widetilde{\mathcal{G}}$ are either interior points of $\Gamma(r) \subset \mathcal{U}$ or boundary points of $\mathcal{U}$. Notice that in the former case, by Lemma 2, they are also interior points Nash Equilibria for the game with strategy space $\mathcal{U}$. Therefore, the game $\widetilde{\mathcal{G}}$ admits a Nash Equilibrium. $\qquad\square$

Proposition 4. *There exists a Nash Equilibrium solution of $\mathcal{G}$*

Proof. From Proposition 3 that for all $k > 0$, the game $\mathcal{G}^k \overset{\text{def}}{=} \left(\mathcal{N}, \mathcal{U}, (\bar{J}_n^k)_n\right)$ admits a Nash Equilibrium x^{*k}. Thus, the directional derivative of $\bar{J}_n^k(.)$ at x^{*k}

must be non-negative. For all $\zeta > 0$, let $F(\zeta) = \hat{\lambda} + \phi\left(\sqrt{2}\frac{\kappa_+}{\check{C}\check{\xi}}\zeta\right)$. From (11), we infer that $z \leq F(z)$ where $z = \check{C}\left\|\widehat{x^{*k}}\right\|$. As $\phi(.)$ is strictly increasing, for all $p \in \mathbb{N}$, $z \leq F^p(z)$. Now, the assumptions on ϕ imply that F has a unique fixed point z_0 over $\mathbb{R}_+^*$ that depends only on ϕ, $\hat{\lambda}$, $\frac{\kappa_+}{\check{C}\check{\xi}}$ and that $F^p(z)$ converges to z_0. Therefore, $z \leq z_0$. Let $r > z_0/\check{C}$ and $k > \sqrt{2}\frac{\kappa_+}{\check{\xi}}r$. Hence, one can check that the games $\tilde{\mathcal{G}}^k = \left(\mathcal{N}, \mathcal{U} \cap B(r), (\bar{J}_n^k)_n\right)$ and $\tilde{\mathcal{G}} = \left(\mathcal{N}, \mathcal{U} \cap B(r), (\bar{J}_n)_n\right)$ are identical. Now, let x^* a Nash Equilibrium of $\tilde{\mathcal{G}}$. As $\|x^*\| \leq z/\check{C} \leq z_0/\check{C} < r$, x^* does not lie on $\partial B(r)$ thus it is a Nash Equilibrium of $\mathcal{G}$. $\qquad \square$

Theorem 1. *The game $\mathcal{G}$ admits an interior point Nash Equilibrium $x^* \in \mathcal{U}^\dagger$ under the sufficient conditions:*

$$C_n^{nuc}\xi_n < 2\kappa^-\alpha_n^{nuc}, \quad C_n^{conv}\xi_n < \kappa^-\alpha_n^{conv}.$$

Proof. Let $\varepsilon > 0$ and $\Gamma_\varepsilon = \bigcap_{n,\tau}\{x_n^\tau > \varepsilon\} \subset \mathcal{U}^\dagger$. From Proposition 3, as Γ_ε is a closed convex set, the game $\mathcal{G}^\sharp \overset{def}{=} (\mathcal{N}, \Gamma_\varepsilon, (\bar{J}_n)_n)$ admits a Nash equilibrium x^*. Reasoning by contradiction, suppose that $x^* \in \partial\Gamma_\varepsilon$. This means that there exists $n \in \mathcal{N}$ and $\tau \in \{nuc, conv\}$ such that $x_n^{*\tau} = \varepsilon$. Hence, using first order Taylor-Lagrange expansion, at least one of the following inequalities holds true:

$$\frac{\partial \bar{J}_n}{\partial x_n^{conv}}(x^*) \geq \left(\kappa^-\alpha^{conv} - C_n^{conv}\xi_n\right)\frac{\varepsilon}{\xi_n} + o(\varepsilon),$$

$$\frac{\partial \bar{J}_n}{\partial x_n^{nuc}}(x^*) \geq \left(2\kappa^-\alpha^{nuc} - C_n^{nuc}\xi_n\right)\frac{\varepsilon}{\xi_n} + o(\varepsilon).$$

If $\mathcal{G}$ parameters are chosen such that $\kappa^-\alpha^{conv} > C_n^{conv}\xi_n$, $2\kappa^-\alpha^{nuc} > C_n^{nuc}\xi_n$, for ε small enough, $\frac{\partial \bar{J}_n}{\partial x_n^\tau}(x^*) > 0$. It contradicts the necessary optimality condition $\frac{\partial}{\partial x_n^\tau}\bar{J}_n(x^*) \leq 0$ thus $x^* \in \mathcal{U}^\dagger$. Hence, $\mathcal{G}^\dagger \overset{def}{=} (\mathcal{N}, \mathcal{U}^\dagger, (\bar{J}_n)_n)$ admits the same Nash Equilibrium x^*, which is also an interior point Nash Equilibrium of $\mathcal{G}$. $\qquad \square$

3.2   Uniqueness of the Interior Point Nash Equilibrium

Assumption 3. $\forall n \in \mathcal{N}, 1 - \frac{1}{x_{\sigma(n)}^{nuc}}\sum_{m\neq n}\frac{\partial x_{\sigma(n)}^{nuc}}{\partial x_m^{nuc}} \geq 0$ and $C_n^{nuc} - \frac{\alpha^{nuc}}{\xi_n}\sum_{m\neq n}\frac{\partial x_{\sigma(n)}^{nuc}}{\partial x_m^{nuc}}$ ≥ 0.

In the rest of the paper, we assume that Assumption 3 holds.

Proposition 5. *The game $\mathcal{G}^\dagger$ is strongly monotone.*

Proof. Let $F_n \stackrel{\text{def}}{=} \left[\frac{\partial \bar{J}_n(x)}{\partial x_n^{\text{nuc}}} \frac{\partial \bar{J}_n(x)}{\partial x_n^{\text{conv}}} \right]^T$ be the gradient of player n's utility with respect to its own actions. We get: $\forall x_n \in \mathcal{U}$, $\frac{\partial \bar{J}_n(x)}{\partial x_n^{\text{conv}}} = \alpha^{\text{conv}} \phi(x_{\sigma(n)}^{\text{conv}}/\xi_n) - C_n^{\text{conv}} x_n^{\text{conv}}$, which implies that $\bar{J}_n(\cdot)$ reaches its maximum in the variable x_n^{conv} at $(x_n^{\text{conv}})^* = \frac{\alpha^{\text{conv}}}{C_n^{\text{conv}}} \phi\left(\frac{x_{\sigma(n)}^{\text{conv}}}{\xi_n} \right)$, if $(x_n^{\text{conv}})^*$ is admissible, or, else, at the border of the interval of definition of x_n^{conv}. Similarly, for Nation n's other decision variable, we get: $\frac{\partial \bar{J}_n(x)}{\partial x_n^{\text{nuc}}} = \alpha^{\text{nuc}} \phi\left(\frac{x_{\sigma(n)}^{\text{conv}} + x_{\sigma(n)}^{\text{nuc}}}{\xi_n} \right) + \lambda_n \sum_\tau \alpha^\tau \exp\left(-\lambda_n \frac{x_n^{\text{nuc}}}{x_{\sigma(n)}^\tau} \right) - C_n^{\text{nuc}} x_n^{\text{nuc}}$.

Consider the pseudo-Hessian matrix H^{nuc} of the players' utilities considering only nuclear weapons where each nth row and m^{th} column component is given as $H_{n,m}^{\text{nuc}} = \frac{\partial F_n^{\text{nuc}}}{\partial x_m^{\text{nuc}}}, n, m \in \mathcal{N}$, i.e., in details:

$$H_{n,m}^{\text{nuc}} = \begin{cases} -\lambda_n^2 \sum_\tau \frac{\alpha^\tau}{x_{\sigma(n)}^\tau} \exp\left(-\lambda_n \frac{x_n^{\text{nuc}}}{x_{\sigma(n)}^\tau} \right) - C_n^{\text{nuc}} & \text{if } m = n, \\ \left(\left(\frac{\alpha^{\text{nuc}}}{\xi_n} \phi'\left(\frac{x_{\sigma(n)}^{\text{conv}} + x_{\sigma(n)}^{\text{nuc}}}{\xi_n} \right) + \lambda_n^2 \frac{\alpha^{\text{nuc}} x_n^{\text{nuc}}}{(x_{\sigma(n)}^{\text{nuc}})^2} \exp\left(-\lambda_n \frac{x_n^{\text{nuc}}}{x_{\sigma(n)}^{\text{nuc}}} \right) \right) \right) \frac{\partial x_{\sigma(n)}^{\text{nuc}}}{\partial x_m^{\text{nuc}}} & \text{if } m \neq n. \end{cases}$$

Thus $-H^{\text{nuc}}$ is a Z-matrix as its-off diagonal entries are negative. Under Assumption 3, we observe that $-H^{\text{nuc}}$ is strictly diagonally dominant thus $-H^{\text{nuc}}$ is an M-matrix, i.e., a Z-matrix with eigenvalues whose real parts are nonnegative [32]. Thus, H^{nuc} is negative definite. Furthermore, letting $F \stackrel{\text{def}}{=} \text{col}((F_n)_n)$, as $\frac{\partial F_n}{\partial x_n^{\text{conv}}}$ is constant for all $n \in \mathcal{N}$, the inequality $(y-x)^T \left[F(y) - F(x) \right] < 0, \forall x \neq y$ follows from [25, Theorem 6] and the game $\mathcal{G}^\dagger$ is strongly monotone.   □

Theorem 2. *The game $\mathcal{G}$ has a unique interior point Nash Equilibrium $x^* \in \mathcal{U}^\dagger$.*

Proof. Let us consider that there exists two Nash Equilibria x^* and x^{**} solutions of the game $\mathcal{G}^\dagger$. As both x^* and x^{**} are Nash Equilibria they must satisfy the stationarity condition. Mutliplying the first order condition with $(y - x^*)$ at point x^* and $(y - x^{**})$ at point x^{**}, we get:

$$(y - x^*)^T F(x^*) = 0, \quad \forall y \in \mathcal{U}^\dagger, \tag{12a}$$

$$(y - x^{**})^T F(x^{**}) = 0, \quad \forall y \in \mathcal{U}^\dagger. \tag{12b}$$

Taking (12a) in $y = x^*$ and (12b) in $y = x^{**}$ and summing the two above equations, we get: $(x^{**} - x^*)^T (F(x^{**}) - F(x^*)) = 0$, which contradicts the fact that the game $\mathcal{G}^\dagger$ is strongly monotone from Proposition 5. Therefore, the game $\mathcal{G}^\dagger$ admits a unique Nash Equilibrium.   □

3.3   Distributed Nash Equilibrium Seeking

When more than two Nations are involved, algorithmic methods need to be developed to compute Nash Equilibria.

Proposition 6. *The pseudo-gradient $F(x)$ of the game $\mathcal{G}$ is Lipschitz continuous in $x \in \mathcal{U}^\dagger$.*

Proof. The proof relies on the Triangle Inequality and Mean Value Theorem. Due to space limit, it is omitted.   □

We assume that the Nations are in a full information feedback setting.

Assumption 4. *Each player $n \in \mathcal{N}$ can get the decisions of all its opponents* $x_{-n} \in \prod_{m \neq n} \mathcal{U}_m$.

Under Propositions 5 and 6, and Assumption 4, various gradient-based algorithms can be proposed to compute the interior point Nash Equilibrium solution of $\mathcal{G}$ and are proved to converge [9]. We will implement a regularization algorithm for monotone game, called proximal point method (PPM). PPM is an alternative method to distributed gradient descent schemes, whose interest lies in the fact that it avoids having to coordinate the players in their steplength choice. At iteration l, x^l is the solution of a Variational Inequality (VI) of the type: $(y - x)^T F^l(x) \leq 0, \quad \forall y \in \mathcal{U}$, with $F^l(x) = F(x) - \theta(x - x^l)$, and $\theta > 0$ is a regularization parameter which implicitly determines iteration bounds to reach a prescribed error level [21]. In this setting, the regularization parameters are required to be the same for all the players. Extensions of iterative proximal point method for monotone games where each player can independently select and adapt its algorithm parameter after each iteration [13] exist, but will not be considered in the current version of the work. In practice, the PPM algorithm can be implemented by solving at each iteration l:

$$x_n^{l+1} = \arg\max_{u \in \mathcal{U}_n} \left(\bar{J}_n(u, x_{-n}^l) - \theta \|u - x_n^l\|^2 \right), \quad \forall n \in \mathcal{N}.$$

4   Analysis and Simulations in Case of a Duopoly

4.1   Analytical Analysis

In the case of a duopoly ($N = 2$), we provide an analytical characterization of the interior point Nash Equilibrium of $\mathcal{G}$. We define $\widetilde{\mathcal{N}} \stackrel{\text{def}}{=} \{(n, m) \in \mathcal{N}^2 \mid n \neq m\}$. For all $(n, m) \in \widetilde{\mathcal{N}}$, we let x_m denote x_{-n} and $\sigma(n) \stackrel{\text{def}}{=} \{m\}$. Then, the interior point Nash Equilibrium of $\mathcal{G}$ is obtained by solving the following system:

$$\max_{x \in (\mathbb{R}_+^*)^2} \bar{J}_n(x_n, x_m), \quad \forall (n, m) \in \widetilde{\mathcal{N}},$$

leading to the following first order (necessary) optimality conditions:

$$\frac{\partial \bar{J}_n}{\partial x_n^{\text{conv}}}(x_n, x_m) = 0, \quad \frac{\partial \bar{J}_n}{\partial x_n^{\text{nuc}}}(x_n, x_m) = 0, \quad \forall (n, m) \in \widetilde{\mathcal{N}},$$

which can be written explicitly as the following system of equations:

$$\forall (n, m) \in \widetilde{\mathcal{N}}, \qquad C_n^{\text{conv}} x_n^{\text{conv}} - \alpha^{\text{conv}} \phi\left(\frac{x_m^{\text{conv}}}{\xi_n}\right) = 0, \tag{13a}$$

$$C_n^{\text{nuc}} x_n^{\text{nuc}} - \lambda_n \sum_\tau \exp\left(-\frac{\lambda_n x_n^{\text{nuc}}}{x_m^\tau}\right) - \alpha^{\text{nuc}} \phi\left(\frac{x_m^{\text{nuc}} + x_m^{\text{conv}}}{\xi_n}\right) = 0. \tag{13b}$$

Let $(n,m) \in \tilde{\mathcal{N}}$. Define $\mathcal{R}_n^{\text{conv}} : x \mapsto \frac{\alpha^{\text{conv}}}{C_n^{\text{conv}}} \phi\left(\frac{x}{\xi_n}\right)$. Then one can rewrite (13a) as $x_n^{\text{conv}} = \mathcal{R}_n^{\text{conv}}(x_m^{\text{conv}})$. Hence, when dealing with two players, the Nash Equilibrium components $(x_n^{\text{conv}})_n$ are found at the intersection (χ_2, χ_1) of curves $(u, \mathcal{R}_1^{\text{conv}}(u))_{u>0}$ and $(\mathcal{R}_2^{\text{conv}}(v), v)_{v>0}$. Consider the following functional equations with unknowns $\mathcal{R}_n^{\text{nuc}} : x \mapsto y$:

$$C_n^{\text{nuc}} y - \lambda_n \left(\exp\left(-\frac{\lambda_n y}{x}\right) + \exp\left(-\frac{\lambda_n y}{\chi_n}\right) \right) - \alpha^{\text{nuc}} \phi\left(\frac{x + \chi_n}{\xi_n}\right) = 0, \quad \forall n \in \mathcal{N}. \quad (14)$$

Then (13b) is equivalent to $\mathcal{R}_n^{\text{nuc}}(x_m^{\text{nuc}}) = x_n^{\text{nuc}}$ by setting $x = x_m^{\text{nuc}}$ and $y = x_n^{\text{nuc}}$. Let $\mu_n = \frac{\chi_n}{\xi_n}$, $\rho_n = C_n^{\text{nuc}} \xi_n$ and the change of variables $(X, Y) = \left(\frac{x^{\text{nuc}}}{\xi_n}, C_n^{\text{nuc}} y^{\text{nuc}}\right)$, then (14) recasts as:

$$Y - \lambda_n \left(\exp\left(-\frac{\lambda_n}{\rho_n} \frac{Y}{X}\right) + \exp\left(-\frac{\lambda_n}{\rho_n} \frac{Y}{\mu_n}\right) \right) - \alpha^{\text{nuc}} \phi(X + \mu_n) = 0, \quad \forall n \in \mathcal{N}. \quad (15)$$

Proposition 7. *Equation (15) has a unique solution.*

Proof. Let $\rho, \mu, \lambda > 0$ and $\alpha \in (0, 1)$. For all $X, Y \geq 0$, define

$$h(X, Y) = \begin{cases} Y - \lambda \exp\left(-\frac{\lambda}{\rho} \frac{Y}{X}\right) - \lambda \exp\left(-\frac{\lambda}{\rho} \frac{Y}{\mu}\right) - \alpha \phi(X + \mu) & \text{if } X \neq 0, \\ Y - \lambda \exp\left(-\frac{\lambda}{\rho} \frac{Y}{\mu}\right) - \alpha \phi(\mu) & \text{else.} \end{cases}$$

For all $X \geq 0$, $Y \mapsto h(X, Y)$ is continuous and strictly increasing over $\mathbb{R}_+$. As $h(X, 0) \leq -\lambda < 0$ and $\lim_{Y \to +\infty} h(X, Y) = +\infty$, it is one-to-one from $\mathbb{R}_+$ to a set containing 0. Thus it has a unique zero on $\mathbb{R}_+$ and (15) has a unique solution. $\square$

Due to limited space and for the sake of simplicity, we assume in what follows that $\lambda_n \exp\left(-\frac{\lambda_n}{\rho_n} \frac{Y}{\mu_n}\right)$ is negligible, i.e., we assume that preemptive nuclear strikes onto conventional targets achieve little security gain when compared to nuclear targets. Setting it to 0 yields the following equation:

$$Y - \lambda_n \exp\left(-\frac{\lambda_n}{\rho_n} \frac{Y}{X}\right) - \alpha^{\text{nuc}} \phi(X + \mu_n) = 0, \quad \forall n \in \mathcal{N}. \quad (16)$$

In the following, we provide a closed-form expression of the solution of (16), which relies on the special function $\mathcal{W}(\cdot)$, defined as the principal branch of the Lambert $\mathcal{W}$-function [7] , solution to $we^w = r$, $r \geq 0$. $\mathcal{W}(\cdot)$ cannot be expressed in terms of elementary functions, although some approximations, bounds, and integral representations, e.g., $\mathcal{W}(x) = \frac{1}{\pi} \int_0^\pi \ln\left(1 + x \frac{\sin t}{t} e^{t \cot t}\right) dt$ are well-known. For all $X, \rho, \lambda, \mu > 0$, let

$$G(X; \rho, \lambda, \mu) \stackrel{\text{def}}{=} \frac{\alpha^{\text{nuc}}}{\rho} \phi(X + \mu) + \frac{1}{\lambda} X \mathcal{W}\left(\lambda \exp\left(-\alpha^{\text{nuc}} \frac{\lambda}{\rho} \frac{\phi(X + \mu)}{X}\right)\right).$$

Proposition 8. *The functional equation (16) with unknown $X \mapsto Y(X)$ admits a unique solution on $\mathcal{C}^\infty(\mathbb{R}_+^*)$ which satisfies :*

$$Y = \rho_n G(X; \rho_n, \lambda_n, \mu_n). \tag{17}$$

Proof. Let $n \in \mathcal{N}$. For all $X, Y > 0$, define $w = \frac{\lambda_n}{\rho_n X}(Y - \alpha^{\mathrm{nuc}}\phi(X + \mu_n))$ and $r = \lambda_n \exp\left(-\alpha^{\mathrm{nuc}}\frac{\lambda_n}{\rho_n}\frac{\phi(X+\mu_n)}{X}\right)$. One has the expression

$$w - r\exp(-w) = \frac{\lambda_n}{\rho_n X}\left(Y - \lambda_n \exp\left(-\frac{\lambda_n}{\rho_n}\frac{Y}{X}\right) - \alpha^{\mathrm{nuc}}\phi(X + \mu_n)\right).$$

Consequently, $(X, Y) \in (\mathbb{R}_+^*)^2$ satisfies (16) if and only if $we^w = r$, i.e., if and only if $w = \mathcal{W}(r)$, which writes as (17). □

From Proposition 8, we infer the closed-form expressions of the best-replies:

$$x_n^{\mathrm{nuc}} = \mathcal{R}_n^{\mathrm{nuc}}(x_m^{\mathrm{nuc}}) = \xi_n G\left(\frac{x_m^{\mathrm{nuc}}}{\xi_m}; C_n^{\mathrm{nuc}}\xi_n, \frac{\lambda_n}{C_n^{\mathrm{nuc}}\xi_n}\right), \quad \forall (n, m) \in \widetilde{\mathcal{N}}. \tag{18}$$

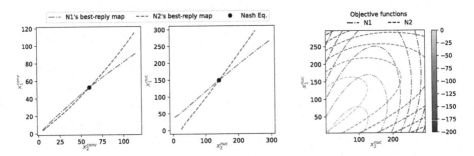

Fig. 1. In the special case of the duopoly, the interior point Nash Equilibrium is found graphically at the intersection point of the best-reply maps $(\mathcal{R}_n^{\mathrm{nuc}})_{n=\mathrm{N1,N2}}$ of each Nation as defined in (18). The model's parameters are given in Table 1.

4.2   Numerical Results and Discussions

As shown in Fig. 1, Nash Equilibria can be numerically obtained when computing the intersection points of the curves drawn by the best-reply maps $\mathcal{R}_n^{\mathrm{nuc}}$ computed as with (18) and $\alpha^{\mathrm{conv}} = \alpha^{\mathrm{nuc}} = \frac{1}{2}$. Note that the security and the utility of both Nations with mixed armaments in a mutual deterrence relationship are greater than with only conventional weapons. Indeed, from Table 1 we can compute the efficiency gap between the social optimum of disarmament and the interior point Nash Equilibrium. With only conventional armaments the efficiency gap is of 108 whereas with mixed armaments it drops to 74, representing an inefficiency reduction of 31%. This can be interpreted as a stabilizing effect of nuclear armaments.

Depending on the observed efficiency loss, it might be interesting, in an extension of our work, to provide a method for specifying a Pareto dominating solution that depends on the Nations' threshold thresholds.

Table 1. Utility (bold-red) and security (italic-black) functions at Nash Equilibrium. Parameters: $\xi_{N1} = 200$, $\xi_{N2} = 150$, $C_n^{conv} = C_n^{nuc} = 5 \times 10^{-3}$, $\lambda_n = 0.7$, $\forall n \in \{N1, N2\}$.

	Nash Equilibrium Strategy (x_n^{conv}, x_n^{nuc})	Conventional-only		Mixed armaments	
		Utility	Security	Utility	Security
Nation 1	$(52, 149)$	-53	6	-45	14
Nation 2	$(60, 141)$	-55	7	-29	33

5   Conclusion

We formulate a security game in a context of mixed armament acquisition, involving a finite set of Nations in strategic relationship. Our model incorporates key elements such as resource allocation to R&D and storage, defense capabilities, and geopolitical considerations, to provide a realistic representation of the arms procurement process. To analyze the long-term solution of the dynamical model, we study the steady states of the dynamical game by solving the associated one-shot game. On the theoretical side, we provide two important contributions to the state of the art. First, we extend classical results about compact-convex games to unbounded convex games relying on the coercivity property of the utility functions. Second, our results showcase the stabilizing effect of nuclear armaments and provide possible guidelines for current treaties refinements or for the understanding of various arms competition scenarios, including multilateral arms competitions and asymmetric weaponry.

Future research could focus on studying other identified factors such as alliances and the role of emerging technologies. Additionally, empirical studies and use case analyses would be valuable to validate the model outcomes and assess its real-world applicability. Finally, we anticipate that our contributions will serve as a valuable tool for policymakers, analysts, and researchers, assisting in the development of effective arms control measures and promoting stability in international relations.

References

1. Treaty on the Non-Proliferation of Nuclear Weapons, Article VI, 5 March 1970
2. Achen, C.H.: A state with bureaucratic politics is representable as a unitary rational actor. In: Annual meeting of the American Political Science Association, Washington, DC, vol. 31 (1988)
3. Axelrod, R.: The Evolution of Cooperation. ISBN (1984)
4. Basar, T., Olsder, G.J.: Dynamic Noncooperative Game Theory. SIAM (1999)
5. Bracken, J.: Multipolar nuclear stability: incentives to strike and incentives to preempt. Mil. Oper. Res. 3(1), 5–21 (1997)
6. Deger, S., Sen, S.: Optimal control and differential game models of military expenditure in less developed countries. J. Econ. Dyn. Control 7(2), 153–169 (1984)
7. NIST Digital Library of Mathematical Functions. Release 1.1.9 of 15 March 2023. https://dlmf.nist.gov/4.13

8. Dunne, J.P., Smith, R.P.: The econometrics of military arms races. In: Handbook of Defense Economics, vol. 2, pp. 913–940. Elsevier (2007)

9. Facchinei, F., Pang, J.S.: Finite-Dimensional Variational Inequalities and Complementarity Problems. Springer, New York (2003). https://doi.org/10.1007/b97543

10. Fudenberg, D., Levine, D.K.: The Theory of Learning in Games. The MIT Press, Cambridge (1998)

11. Herz, J.H.: Idealist internationalism and the security dilemma. World Polit. 2(2), 171–201 (1950)

12. Jervis, R.: Cooperation under the security dilemma. World Polit. 30(2), 167–214 (1978)

13. Kannan, A., Shanbhag, U.V.: Distributed computation of equilibria in monotone nash games via iterative regularization techniques. SIAM J. Optim. 22(4), 1177–1205 (2012)

14. Kennan, G.F.: Containment, then and now. Foreign Aff. 65(4), 885–890 (1987)

15. Koepsell, D., Stankova, K.: Non-proliferation regimes, immoral and risky: a game-theoretic approach. Int. J. World Peace 27(2), 63–83 (2012)

16. Lichbach, M.I.: Stability in Richardson's arms races and cooperation in prisoner's dilemma arms rivalries. Am. J. Polit. Sci. 33(4), 1016 (1989)

17. Lichbach, M.I.: When is an arms rivalry a prisoner's dilemma?: Richardson's models and 2 × 2 games. J. Conflict Resolut. 34(1), 29–56 (1990)

18. Majeski, S.J.: Arms races as iterated prisoner's dilemma games. Math. Soc. Sci. 7(3), 253–266 (1984)

19. Melese, F., Michel, P.: Reversing the arms race: a differential game model. South. Econ. J. 57(4), 1133 (1991)

20. Moriarty, G.: Differential game theory applied to a model of the arms race. IEEE Technol. Soc. Mag. 3(3), 10–17 (1984)

21. Nesterov, Y.: Dual extrapolation and its applications to solving variational inequalities and related problems. Math. Program. 109(2–3), 319–344 (2006). https://doi.org/10.1007/s10107-006-0034-z

22. O'Neill, B.: Game theory models of peace and war. In: Handbook of Game Theory with Economic Applications, vol. 2(Chap. 29), pp. 995–1053 (1994)

23. Plous, S.: The nuclear arms race: prisoner's dilemma or perceptual dilemma? J. Peace Res. 30(2), 163–179 (1993)

24. Richardson, L.F.: Arms and Insecurity, p. 200. Qaudrangle Press, Chicago (1960)

25. Rosen, J.B.: Existence and uniqueness of equilibrium points for concave N-person games. Econometrica 33(3), 520 (1965)

26. Schlosser, J., Wendroff, B.: Iterated games and arms race models. Math. Comput. Model. 15(9), 39–45 (1991)

27. Simaan, M., Cruz, J.B.: Formulation of Richardson's model of arms race from a differential game viewpoint. Rev. Econ. Stud. 42(1), 67 (1975)

28. Simaan, M., Cruz, J.B.: Nash equilibrium strategies for the problem of armament race and control. Manage. Sci. 22(1), 67 (1975)

29. Snyder, G.H.: Prisoner's dilemma and chicken models in international politics. Int. Stud. Quart. 15(1), 66 (1971)

30. Wallace, M.D., Wilson, J.M.: Non-linear arms race models. J. Peace Res. 15(2), 175–192 (1978)

31. Waltz, K.N.: Theory of International Politics. Waveland Press, Long Grove (2010)

32. Young, D.M.: Iterative solution of large linear systems. Computer Science and Applied Mathematics. Academic Press, San Diego (1971)

Author Index

J. Fu et al. (Eds.): GameSec 2023, LNCS 14167, pp. 389–390, 2023.
https://doi.org/10.1007/978-3-031-50670-3

Printed in the United States
by Baker & Taylor Publisher Services